POWER

...the most successful

introductory Mass Media

text in years, now updated

to reflect the latest

changes in the media!

.... USING

.... MULTIMEDIA

.... TO

.... TEACH

.... THE

.... MEDIA

JOHN VIVIAN's
THE MEDIA OF MASS COMMUNICATION
THIRD EDITION

No other textbook uses the power of the media to help you teach your students about the media. That's why Vivian remains the leader in the field. And with this new edition, Vivian's package is breaking new ground, creating the most lively and inviting atmosphere for learning yet.

CAPTURE THE POWER OF VIVIAN AGAIN.

USING MULTIMEDIA TO TEACH THE MEDIA

New chapter on the mass media of tomorrow!

TURN ON THE TEACHING POWER!

This new edition of Vivian helps you welcome the mass media revolution and provides the most up-to-date material on the role new technology is playing in the media of tomorrow. Not only does this third edition devote an entire chapter to the subject of multimedia but it provides new opportunities for you and your students to actually USE multimedia products to LEARN about multimedia!

NEW CHAPTER ON MEDIA TECHNOLOGY

CHAPTER 9 "Mass Media Tomorrow" invites your students into the new world created by the mass media revolution. The chapter explores new frontiers created by the ability to compress messages for storage and transmission — CD-ROM, online, and fiber-optic. Highly current coverage also includes...

■ **The Information Highway** — covering the Internet, commercial online services, and the information superhighway of tomorrow that could displace today's mass media. Vivian even has a special AMERICA ONLINE offer for you and your students! (Find out more in the following pages.)

■ **Financing the New Media** — with material on restructuring media economics and advertising and digital media

■ **Public Policy and New Media**

■ **Electronic Magazines and Books**

■ **The Future of the Newspaper**

A CONTEMPORARY APPROACH

Vivian's design is unparalleled in the market!

ENGAGES YOUR STUDENTS FROM THE VERY BEGINNING!

Students are immediately drawn to Vivian's current coverage, dramatic magazine style design, and lively writing. Vivian builds upon what students already know from their daily exposure to the media, and moves beyond it, to explain in clear, approachable narrative the ramifications, implications, and inner workings of each of the media industries. Nearly 200 up-to-date photographs add to the interest in this new edition, as well as extensive coverage of media effects and media and culture.

■ **All new media examples** — including Macintosh Newton, Benetton's outrageous advertising, coverage of the O.J. Simpson case, and the sale of Paramount.

■ **Historical perspectives** — in every chapter, concisely recounted key events in media history give students the perspective they need to understand media today.

■ **Solid coverage of media effects** — two full chapters (14 & 15) on the subject as well as discussions at appropriate points throughout. Most chapters discuss societal/individual effects.

DESIGNED FOR EFFICIENT STUDY

TURN ON THE LEARNING POWER!

Media events, people, technology — all brought to life in Vivian's attention grabbing boxed features. Providing additional depth and interest, these learning aids offer students exciting coverage of media industries, individuals, and issues. All material has been updated to reflect the most current statistics..

■ **MEDIA ABROAD**
boxes discuss international issues

■ **MEDIA DATABANK**
boxes summarize media statistics

■ **MEDIA: PEOPLE**
boxes profile today's leaders in key media industries

■ **MEDIA AND YOU**
boxes probe students' own responses and relationships to media

Compelling boxed features help students stay involved!

Reader's Digest in Russian

One hundred thousand people in the Ukrainian city of Kharkov opened their mail in August 1991 to find a four-page flier announcing that "the world's most popular journal" soon would be available. The flier marked the entry of *Reader's Digest*, that homey embodiment of conservative, middle-class American values, into areas that were once part of the closed Soviet empire. A few days later, 50,000 copies of the 160-page debut issue were delivered to newsracks in Kharkov, Kiev, St. Petersburg and Moscow, and they sold out. The people liked the mix of brief articles on international life, health and psychology. The press run soon was increased to 100,000.

Although the Russian-language *Reader's Digest* sells for the ruble equivalent of $1.50, twice as much as most Russian magazines, the Reader's Digest Association of Pleasantville, New York, was not seeking early profits. Start-up and distribution costs were high, and the inaugural issue carried a mere five pages of advertising—from Coca-Cola, Colgate toothpaste, Pepsi-Cola, Smirnoff vodka and Toshiba televisions.

The marketing-savvy *Reader's Digest* organization viewed the Russian-language edition as an investment. The company wanted to learn how to reach mass audiences in the former Soviet Union with the goal eventually of selling not only magazines but also books, music and other products.

Mass mailing, a key to the success of *Reader's Digest* elsewhere, is a special challenge in the former Soviet republics. Not only are the mails slow and unreliable, but the remnants of the notorious Soviet black market system include the postal structure, which swallows

A key to the Reader's Digest Association's marketing

Jann Wenner

Jann Wenner was a student at the University of California's Berkeley campus as the hippie movement of the mid-1960s was flowering across the bay in San Francisco. Wenner dabbled in the loose, bohemian Haight-Ashbury life-style himself, including the drugs, but it was the music of the new generation that intrigued him the most—and he wanted to write about it.

In his second year at Berkeley, Wenner persuaded the editors of the campus newspaper, the *Daily Californian*, to give him a music column. In many ways, the column was a preview of Wenner's yet-to-come *Rolling Stone* magazine. Amid obscure egocentric references, Wenner reported music news seriously with a focus on his favorites: Bob Dylan, Mick Jagger, the Beatles. There were literary allusions, particularly to F. Scott Fitzgerald, and he found ways to tie the emerging psychedelic drug culture into politics. "One of these days," he wrote, "Lyndon Johnson is going to find out why the 'leaders of tomorrow' are hung up on LSD instead of LBJ."

Wenner gave up the column when he dropped out of college, but he tried to continue writing. The problem was that nobody would print his work. *Stereo Review* turned him down. So did the San Francisco dailies. Wenner went to London to propose covering the San Francisco music scene for *Melody Maker*, but that editor too said no.

Wenner decided to start his own magazine.

From friends, Wenner picked up venture capital totaling $6,500, and when his father gave him $1,000 in stock for his 21st birthday, he sold it to help fund the magazine. It was enough for Wenner, age 21, to launch *Rolling Stone*. That was in 1967. Within two years, *Rolling Stone* was widely regarded as the most authoritative rock 'n' roll magazine. It also became the voice for a new generation—not just the flower children of Haight-Ashbury but young people disenchanted with President Lyndon Johnson, the Vietnam war and the Establishment in general, and later with Richard Nixon and Watergate.

There were other magazines aimed at young people, but only Wenner realized that music was what bound the new generation together. Always at *Rolling Stone's* core, amid the fiction and political coverage, was rock 'n' roll.

The magazine became home for great writers of the new generation. Gonzo journalist Hunter Thompson

Jann Wenner

was an early *Rolling Stone* regular, and later there were Truman Capote, Tom Wolfe and P. J. O'Rourke. Wenner encouraged writers to uninhibited truth-seeking and truth-telling. In his history of the magazine, Robert Draper wrote: "Wenner urged his writers to scrape away the bullshit. If the President lies, call him a liar; if Dylan is a poet, call him one."

By its sixth year, 1973, *Rolling Stone* turned profitable. No longer just "a little rock 'n' roll newspaper in San Francisco," as Wenner fondly referred to it in the early days, *Rolling Stone* has grown to maturity along with its original 1960s generation readership. The focus remains rock 'n' roll but without the beads and other symbols of the psychedelic era. In middle age, *Rolling Stone* now is edited in New York. The instinctive seat-of-the-pants approach to editing that marked the early San Francisco days now is tempered by audience analysis from people who are comfortable in pin-stripe suits. The magazine's new mainstream respectability was cemented in 1985 when David Black won a National Magazine Award for a pioneering and explosive series on AIDS.

Today, circulation is 1.2 million. Wenner's company, Straight Arrow Publishers, is worth $250 million—more than 30,000 times the initial 1967 capitalization. Wenner himself is worth an estimated $100 million, not bad for a college dropout who started out with only $7,500 and a vision.

INNOVATIVE PEDAGOGY FOR YOUR STUDENTS

The gee-whiz, sometimes offbeat style endeared the *Daily News* to readers, at least until recent years. Today, there are doubts whether the *Daily News* can survive.

Despite its circulation, the New York *Daily News* never was a great newspaper, at least not in the sense of the serious, somber New York Times, and in the late 1960s circulation dropped precipitously. So did advertising and profits. As many *Daily News* readers moved upscale, with more education and more income, the *Daily News* no longer was their kind of newspaper. There were fewer Sweeneys in New York.

The Tribune Company in Chicago, which still owned the *Daily News*, put the paper up for sale in the 1980s, but there were no takers. Labor turmoil further weakened the paper, and many readers, sympathetic to the unions, boycotted the paper. At one low point, circulation reportedly slipped to 350,000. With losses mounting at $700,000 a day, the Tribune Company announced that it would shut down the paper.

Three days before the scheduled shutdown, British press tycoon Robert Maxwell agreed to buy the newspaper. But when he died a few weeks later, it was learned he was a world-class crook who had been raiding his employees' pension funds and committing other financial shenanigans. The *Daily News* went to Maxwell's creditors.

Although the future of the *Daily News* is unclear, the story of its rise and decline illustrates several fundamental realities of today's newspaper business. One is that many people love hyped news. In this sense, the *Daily News* could be considered the U.S. progenitor of today's supermarket tabloids. At the same time, people generally are more educated and sophisticated today than when the *Daily News* peaked. This has reduced markets for local gee-whiz scandal sheets. Also, television has cut into newspaper readership and led to a shakeout in the newspaper industry. Only the strongest newspapers survive.

The most fundamental lesson from the saga of the New York *Daily News* is that newspapers prosper when they attract a large audience that advertisers want to reach. When the audience diminishes or becomes an audience that advertisers aren't interested in, a newspaper is in trouble. If advertisers perceive that a newspaper doesn't reach the "right readers," they go elsewhere. So do the profits.

IMPORTANCE OF NEWSPAPERS

STUDY PREVIEW Newspapers are the primary mass medium from which people receive news. In most cities, no other news source comes close to the local newspaper's range and depth of coverage. This contributes to the popularity and influence of newspapers.

NEWSPAPER INDUSTRY DIMENSIONS

The newspaper industry dwarfs other news media by almost every measure. Nearly one out of two people in the United States reads a newspaper every day, far more than tune in the network news on television in the evening. The data are staggering:

- About 1,570 daily newspapers put out 60 million copies a day, more on Sundays. Because each copy is passed along to an average of 2.2 people, daily newspapers reach 132 million people a day.
- Weekly newspapers put out 50 million copies. With their pass-along circulation of four people a copy, these newspapers reach somewhere around 200 million people a week.

Can newspapers survive? Even if people were to stop buying newspapers tomorrow, newspaper organizations would survive because they have an asset that competing media lack: the largest, most skilled newsroom staffs in their communities. The presses and the ink-on-newsprint medium for carrying the message may not have a long future, but newspapers' news-gathering capability will endure. Already newspapers have experimented with facsimile and television text delivery, gaining familiarity with alternate technology for disseminating their main product, which is news, not newsprint.

Besides the daily national, metro and hometown newspapers, the United States has thousands of weekly community newspapers and special-interest papers. By focusing on audiences with special interests, many of these newspapers are attracting more advertisers and either solidifying their existing financial base or building strong new foundations for the future.

QUESTIONS FOR REVIEW

1. Describe how newspapers are important in the lives of most Americans.
2. Explain the rise of newspaper chains. Have they been good for readers?
3. Why is the United States a nation mostly of provincial newspapers?
4. Many metropolitan daily newspapers have lost circulation and some have shut down. Why?

5. What challenges to their dominance as a news and advertising medium do newspapers face?
6. Community newspapers, especially suburban weeklies, are booming. Why?
7. What kinds of newspapers aimed at narrow audience segments are prospering?

QUESTIONS FOR CRITICAL THINKING

1. The United States is called a nation of provincial newspapers. Is the label correct? Do the *Wall Street Journal*, *USA Today* and the *Christian Science Monitor* fit the provincial characterization?
2. How can you explain the declining number of U.S. newspapers and their losses in market penetration in view of the newspaper industry's profitability?
3. How have newspapers met challenges to their advertising revenue from radio, television, direct mail and shoppers?
4. Can you explain why a greater percentage of American newspapers are published for morning reading, not afternoon?

5. Identify advantages and disadvantages in the consolidation of U.S. newspapers, daily and weekly, into chains and cross-media conglomerates.
6. Can you identify how *USA Today* has changed American newspapers by comparing your hometown paper today with an issue from the 1970s?
7. How have improvements in American newspapers led to fewer households taking more than a single newspaper?
8. Considering the business orientation that makes newspaper chains so profitable, does it seem unusual that someone like Al Neuharth, whose background was in journalism rather than business, led Gannett through its incredible and profitable growth?

FOR FURTHER LEARNING

Bill Bishop. "A Warning from Smithville: Owning Your Own Weekly," *Washington Journalism Review* 10 (May 1988):4, 25–32. Bishop offers a first-person case study on how chains are consolidating the weekly newspaper industry. He deals with the pleasure and pain of publishing an independent rural weekly.

Leo Bogart. *Preserving the Press: How Daily Newspapers Mobilized to Keep Their Readers* (Columbia University Press, 1991). Bogart, a newspaper industry analyst, describes the strengths and weaknesses of newspapers in times of changing technology, reader life-style changes and preferences, and new options for advertisers through other media.

TURN UP *THE LEARNING POWER!*

From initial chapter objectives to end-of-chapter questions, Vivian offers something for every student's learning style.

- **Chapter Opening Objectives** alert students to what they will be learning

- **Chapter Opening Vignettes** of current or historical figures engage students' interest

- **Study Preview** sections throughout each chapter guide learning

- **Chapter Wrap-Ups** summarize what's been covered

- **CNN Video Case Studies** provide a brief story about a media person, institution, or event profiled on the CNN video

- **Questions for Review** offer students an opportunity to evaluate their understanding of important chapter material

- **For Further Learning** direct students to additional information

CNN NEWS VIDEOS

ON VIDEOTAPE AND NEW LASERDISC FORMAT!

We've redefined the boundaries of learning. Our multimedia teaching aids help your students see, hear, and EXPERIENCE the impact of media! 46 specially edited video segments from CNN's news reports on the media are presented on a 2-hour videotape and through a NEW laserdisc for this third edition — FREE to adopters!

What better way for students who grew up with TV to understand the impact of the media than through the use of carefully integrated video you can use in your classroom! Vivian's third edition continues and expands upon the unique integration of CNN video with the text. Every chapter cites newsworthy CNN video news and feature segments, collected on an ancillary videotape and new laserdisc format for classroom instruction.

■ **EASY TO USE** — the Instructor's Annotated Edition references each videotape and laserdisc segment with a CNN logo positioned next to the appropriate text material. When you see the CNN icon, you'll know exactly what segment to play for a lively supplement to the textbook material.

■ Covers contemporary topics, including HOWARD STERN, THE DATA HIGHWAY, TOBACCO ADVERTISING

CNN video case study

HOWARD STERN AND THE FEDERAL COMMUNICATIONS COMMISSION

Howard Stern regularly tweaks the federal agency that regulates broadcasting. The syndicated New York shock jock's antics continually raise fundamental questions about whether the government should be in the business of regulating broadcasting. Whether by intention or otherwise, Stern raises these issues:

■ Should the Federal Communications Commission be permitted to muzzle a broadcast performer because he or she is suggestive and lewd on the air?

■ Should the FCC be able to deny people access to a broadcast performer because of the content of the show?

■ Should the FCC be able to punish stations that carry popular programming that some people find objectionable?

■ Should the FCC be able to bar a company from purchasing a station because its other stations carry objectionable programming?

These are First Amendment questions that have been shrugged off by the government and also most broadcasters for 70 years, but Stern is bringing them to the fore. This is the heart of the issue:

■ **First Amendment.** The First Amendment to the U.S. Constitution, which dates to 1791, guarantees free expression. This includes freedom of speech and freedom of the press, which everyone agrees applies to radio and television even though the authors of the amendment thought only in terms of the print media.

■ **1927 Federal Radio Act.** Congress put the government into the business of regulating broadcasting in 1927 when it created an agency that eventually became the FCC. The agency decides who can own a station and go on the air by licensing companies with the best potential to contribute to the "public interest." Some companies are denied a

license because the FCC sees less potential in them to serve this public interest.

The conflict between the First Amendment and the 1927 Radio Act sneaked up on many people. In 1927, the U.S. radio industry was a mess. There was room for only 568 stations on the air, but many more stations were broadcasting. Stations, none of them regulated, could broadcast at whatever signal strength they wanted. Signals overlapped. When a station was squeezed off a certain frequency by more powerful signals, it moved to another frequency. The radio industry tried to sort out the problem, but could not, so it turned to Congress for government regulation.

Through the 1927 Federal Radio Act, Congress created the Federal Radio Commission. The agency's duties included assigning frequencies to stations that would broadcast in "the public interest, convenience and necessity." There needed to be some standard to decide who could be on the air and who could not, and public service seemed a good one.

The inherent First Amendment conflict emerged soon thereafter. The FRC refused to renew the license of a Los Angeles church station that aired a hate-mongering preacher. The commission also refused renewal to a station owned by a quack medicine man in Kansas who hawked his cures over the air. Both stations argued that the FRC was taking away their electronic megaphones because of what they put on the air, which, they said, was censorship.

The issue was difficult. On the one hand, regulation was needed if radio was to be a useful medium. Otherwise, cacophony and confusion would rule the airwaves. On the other hand, government licensing meant some people got licenses and some people did not. With content a factor in deciding who was licensed, and with government issuing the licenses, government was in a position to decide what it liked and did not like on the

184

A SPECIAL COMPANION READER

BY EXCLUSIVE ARRANGEMENT! ALLYN & BACON BRINGS YOU THE THIRD EDITION OF A HIGHLY SUCCESSFUL ANTHOLOGY OF ARTICLES ON MEDIA!

from the Washington Post Writers Group

MESSAGES 3: The Washington Post Media Companion

Prepared from the columns of one of the nation's most distinguished newspapers, this companion to Vivian's third edition takes students right to the action — where the daily experience of media affects us all. Ninety-three articles provide up-to-the minute coverage of media industries and issues with a critical perspective on media economics, media effects, and media practices.

■ **Organized in chapters that parallel Vivian's third edition**

■ **Includes top journalists writing on media today** — including Jonathan Yardley on books, Martha Sherrill on magazines, and Tom Shales on television

MORE POWER TO THE TEACHING PACKAGE...

Pages from the IAE with helpful blue annotations in the margins.

FULL SUPPORT EVERY STEP OF THE WAY!

Vivian offers everything you need to teach the concepts of mass communication to your students. From a highly useful Instructor's Annotated Edition to easy-to-use testing programs, our teaching ancillaries will reward both you and your students.

THE INSTRUCTOR'S ANNOTATED EDITION (IAE)

The IAE is designed to ease the time-consuming demands of instructional preparation. It contains margin annotations to refer you to the Instructor's Resource Manual, a separate guide, where you'll find activities and demonstrations to complement the material in the text. Some find the IAE a great help in preparing lectures, others find it helpful in making the transition from one text to the next.

Instructor's Resource Manual (IRM)

Prepared to accompany the IAE, this comprehensive guide for classroom preparation contains a variety of notes and helpful features for each chapter, including...

- ■ **CHAPTER SYNOPSIS**
- ■ **CHAPTER OUTLINE**

KEY PERSON
John Russworm and Samuel Cornish.

KEY PERSON
Frederick Douglass.

KEY PERSON
W.E.B. DuBois.

KEY PERSON
Malcolm X.

CNN Afro-American Newspapers
The people who own and run the Baltimore Afro-American discuss the importance of black newspapers in the United States. The occasion for this report, by CNN's Kathleen Koch, was Afro-American's 100th anniversary. Despite the continuing contribution and importance of black dailies, Koch points out that their "peak" has long past peaked. This segment aired August 8, 1992.

black dailies today, the Atlanta *Daily World*, Chicago *Daily Defender* and New York *Daily Challenge*, together have a circulation of 106,000, almost all local.

Black newspapers have been important in the U.S. civil rights movement, beginning in 1827 with *John Russworm* and *Samuel Cornish*'s *Freedom's Journal*, the first black newspaper. *Frederick Douglass*'s *North Star*, founded in 1847, was a strident abolitionist sheet before the Civil War, and *W. E. B. Du Bois*'s *Crisis*, founded in 1910, was a militant voice for black advancement. Today, some black newspapers, like *A. M. Journal*, founded by American Muslim *Malcolm X* in 1961, crusade for causes in the tradition of their early predecessors. In the early 1990s, the Chicago *Defender* was alone among U.S. news media in covering the Haitian refugee situation until others picked up the issue and forced public attention on it. In general, though, black newspapers focus on neighborhood social, church and sports events, and the tone is moderate.

Prospects for black newspapers generally do not appear strong. Only 15 percent of the advertising placed in black media, including television, radio and magazines, goes to newspapers. Media scholar James Tinney found that middle-income blacks look to establishment rather than black newspapers for information, even while relying on other black institutions, like the church and universities, for intellectual stimulation.

FOREIGN-LANGUAGE NEWSPAPERS

Through every wave of immigration, newspapers in foreign languages have sprouted to serve newcomers to the United States in their native tongue. In 1914, there were 140 foreign-language dailies published in the United States. About one-third were German, led by New York *Vorwarts* with a circulation of 175,000. The U.S. German-language press withered during World War I when its loyalty was challenged, but, like other foreign-language newspapers, it undoubtedly would have eventually disappeared anyway as the immigrants assimilated into the mainstream culture.

Today, the fast-growing Hispanic minority represents about 1 of every 15 Americans, and although most are bilingual, 6 daily newspapers and about 150 weeklies are published in Spanish. In general, these newspapers are thriving. The Knight-Ridder newspaper chain publishes *El Herald* as a daily Spanish-language companion to its Miami *Herald* and sells 67,000 copies a day. In New York, the Gannett chain operates the 63,000-circulation daily *El Diario-La Prensa*. Most Spanish-language newspapers are owned by Hispanics, but the presence of the gigantic, profitable Knight-Ridder and Gannett chains bespeaks the commercial viability of these papers.

The profitability of Spanish-language newspapers is fueled partly by the desire of many national advertisers to tap into the large Hispanic market. The newspapers' penetration, however, is not especially high. In heavily Hispanic Los Angeles, *La Opinion* has a circulation of only 55,000 a day. In Miami the competing *El Herald* and *Diario Las Americas* together sell only 130,000 copies a day. In New York *El Diario-La Prensa* and *Noticias del Mundo* together have a circulation of less than 130,000 in a metropolitan area with 2.5 million Hispanic people.

Whether Spanish-language newspapers will disappear as did earlier foreign-language newspapers is uncertain. While assimilation is occurring, many Hispanics are intent on maintaining their distinctive cultural identity and resist adopting English. Also, there is more sympathy for multiculturalism in the society than in the past. For the foreseeable future, Spanish-language newspapers will have a strong following among the continuing influx of people from Latin America and

---

- ■ **TEACHING OBJECTIVES** keyed to the learning objectives in the student text

- ■ **TEACHING OBJECTIVES** keyed to CNN "Connections" Video segments and *MESSAGES 3*

- ■ **LECTURE RESOURCE** suggestions for guest lecturers, class exercises, and videotapes

- ■ **KEY TERMS, CONCEPTS, PERSONALITIES, AND INSTITUTIONS**

- ■ **BOXES** which summarize these learning aids

Steven Spielberg

Steven Spielberg. Perhaps no other moviemaker can project stories so compellingly across such a diverse range as Steven Spielberg. His *Jurassic Park*, which raised questions about DNA preservation of extinct life forms, became the most profitable movie in history, surpassing *E.T.* by over $165 million. *Schindler's List*, which depicts one aspect of the World War II Holocaust, etched powerful, not-to-be-forgotten images into viewers' consciousness.

CNN *Schindler's List*
Even anti-Semites and bigots were deeply moved by Steven Spielberg's movie *Schindler's List*. CNN reporter Jeanne Moos tells about early screenings and special showings that were intended to ease hatred and bigotry. A question raised by the segment is whether the media can be effective in undermining aberrant human attitudes. This segment aired February 28, 1994.

Steven Spielberg's work embodies a whole range of qualities that tell us a lot about Hollywood and the role of movies in our culture. He is a wonderful, audience-oriented storyteller: "I want people to love my movies, and I'll be a whore to get them into theaters," he once said.

Spielberg's films also represent the glitz and glamour of Hollywood. Most are spectacularly filmed with dazzling special effects. And their box-office success has helped fuel the extravagances that are part of the image Hollywood cultivates for itself.

But Spielberg is deeper than that. He entwines observations from his personal life into film commentary on fundamental human issues. The fantasy *E.T.* centers on a boy growing up alienated in a broken home who identifies with the alien E.T. Movie analysts see the boy as a metaphorical stand-in for Spielberg, who was taunted as a Jew when he transferred into a new high school and found himself alienated for something over which he had no control.

Moviegoers entranced by Spielberg's adventure stories sometimes forget his serious works. His 1985 *The Color Purple*, adapted from Alice Walker's Pulitzer Prize–winning book, was a painful, insightful account of a southern African-American family during the first half of the century. *Schindler's List*, his acclaimed 1993 account of the Holocaust, flows from his own heritage. These movies, some say Spielberg's best, represent the potential of the medium to help us individually and collectively to sort through the

---

Edison movies were viewed by looking into a box. In France, brothers *Auguste* and *Louis Lumière* brought projection to motion pictures. By running the film in front of a specially aimed powerful lightbulb, the Lumières projected movie images on a wall. In 1895 they opened an exhibition hall in Paris—the first movie house. Edison recognized the commercial advantage of projection, and himself patented the *Vitascope* projector, which he put on the market in 1896.

KEY PEOPLE
Auguste and Louis Lumière projected movie images on wall.

KEY PEOPLE
Thomas Edison perfected projector. See Index.

ADDING SOUND TO PICTURES

Dickson at Edison's lab came up with a sound system for movies in 1889. In the first successful commercial application, Fox used sound in its 1922 Movietone newsreels. But it was four upstart moviemakers, the brothers *Albert, Harry, Jack* and *Sam Warner*, who revolutionized movies with sound. In 1927 the Warners released *The Jazz Singer* starring Al Jolson. There was sound for only two segments, but it caught the public's fancy. By 1930, 9,000 movie houses around the country were equipped for sound.

KEY PEOPLE
Albert, Harry, Jack and Sam Warner developed "talkies."

THREE CRISES THAT RESHAPED HOLLYWOOD

STUDY PREVIEW In quick succession, Hollywood took three body blows in the late 1940s. Right-wing political leaders sent some directors and screenwriters to jail in 1947 and intimidated moviemakers into creative cowardice. In 1948 the U.S. Supreme Court broke up the economic structure of the movie industry. Then television stole people from the box office.

THE HOLLYWOOD 10

Hollywood had a creative crisis in 1947 when Congressman *Parnell Thomas*, chair of the House Un-American Activities Subcommittee, began hearings on communists in Hollywood. Thomas summoned 47 screenwriters, directors and actors and demanded answers to accusations about leftist influences in Hollywood and the Screen Writers Guild. Ten witnesses who refused to answer insulting accusations went to jail for contempt of Congress. It was one of the most highly visible manifestations of *McCarthyism*, a post–World War II overreaction to Soviet communism as a national threat.

The Thomas hearings had longer deleterious effects. Movie producers, afraid the smear would extend to them, declined to hire the *Hollywood 10*. Other careers were also ruined. One expert identified 11 directors, 36 actors, 106 writers and 61 others who suddenly were unwelcome in their old circles and could not find work.

Among the Hollywood 10 was screenwriter *Dalton Trumbo*. His powerful pacifist novel *Johnny Got His Gun* made Trumbo an obvious target for the jingoist Thomas committee. After Trumbo refused to answer committee questions, he was jailed. On his release, Trumbo could not find anybody who would accept his screenplays, so he resorted to writing under the pseudonym Robert Rich. The best he could earn was $15,000 per script, one-fifth his former rate. When his screenplay for *The Brave One* won an Academy Award in 1957, Robert Rich did not dare show up to accept it.

In a courageous act, *Kirk Douglas* hired Trumbo in 1959 to write *Spartacus*. Then *Otto Preminger* did the same with *Exodus*. Besides Trumbo, only screenwriter *Ring Lardner Jr.* rose from the 1947 ashes. In 1970, after two decades on the blacklist, Lardner won an Academy Award for *M*A*S*H*.

TEACHING OBJECTIVE 6-3
Political and economic crises reshaped movie industry in 1940s.

KEY PERSON
Parnell Thomas led hunt for Hollywood communists.

KEY PERSON
Dalton Trumbo blacklisted as screenwriter.

KEY PERSON
Screenwriter Ring Lardner Jr. overcame 1947 blacklist.

NOW YOU CAN REALLY USE MULTIMEDIA TO LEARN ABOUT THE MEDIA...

WITH AMERICA ONLINE!
CONNECT TO A WHOLE NEW WORLD OF TEACHING AND LEARNING ABOUT THE MEDIA!

If you adopt Vivian, 3/e we'll waive the AMERICA ONLINE membership fee for the first two months!

Use this introductory membership to access a wide range of interactive services and educational information including a fast and easy gateway to the Internet. AMERICA ONLINE's award-winning interface makes navigating easy. Just point and click to...

■ download any of thousands of programs...

■ keep in touch through electronic mail

■ get the latest news and information from leading magazines, broadcast and cable, and news wires.

All you need is a computer and a modem. We'll make it easy for your students to get started too! What's more, Simon & Schuster Higher Education Group has developed **COLLEGE ONLINE** ™, an online service specifically for college and university faculty and student use!

Ask your local representative for more details. Or, if you have already selected this new edition for your course adoption, please give us a call at 1-800-827-6364, extension 4314, and we'll send you your FREE America Online Faculty Starter Kit right away!

THE MEDIA OF

MASS COMMUNICATION

THE MEDIA OF

MASS COMMUNICATION

THIRD EDITION

JOHN VIVIAN
WINONA STATE UNIVERSITY

ALLYN AND BACON BOSTON LONDON TORONTO SYDNEY TOKYO SINGAPORE

Editor-in-Chief, Humanities: Joseph Opiela
Series Editor: Steve Hull
Marketing Manager: Karon Bowers
Production Coordinator: Karen Mason
Chapter Openers: Gayle A. Robertson
Electronic Page Make-up: DeNee Reiton Skipper
Cover Administrator: Linda Knowles
Cover Designer: Susan Paradise
Composition Buyer: Linda Cox
Manufacturing Buyer: Megan Cochran

ISBN 0-205-16452-8

Printed in the United States of America
10 9 8 7 6 5 4 3 2 1   99 98 97 96 95

Photo and Text Credits
(Listed on page 495, which constitutes a continuation of this copyright page)

To Harold Vivian, my father,
who sparked my curiosity about the mass
media at age five by asking what was black and
white and read all over.

And to Elaine Vivian, my mother,
who nurtured this curiosity by keeping the
house stocked with books, magazines and
reading material of every sort.

CONTENTS-AT-A-GLANCE

CONTENTS

chapter 2

BOOKS: FIRST OF THE MASS MEDIA 30

chapter 3

MAGAZINES: AN INNOVATIVE MASS MEDIUM 54

chapter 4

chapter 5

SOUND RECORDINGS: SPINNING THE MUSIC   110

chapter 6
MOVIES: A GLAMOUR MEDIUM   136

chapter 7

RADIO: A MEDIUM OF INSTANT COMMUNICATION 160

chapter 8

TELEVISION: ELECTRONIC MOVING PICTURES 186

chapter 9

MASS MEDIA TOMORROW 212

chapter 10

JOURNALISM: GATHERING AND TELLING NEWS   238

chapter 11

PUBLIC RELATIONS: WINNING HEARTS AND MINDS   272

chapter 12

ADVERTISING: SELLING GOODS AND SERVICES   298

chapter 13

MEDIA RESEARCH: THE QUEST FOR USEFUL DATA   328

chapter 14

MASS MEDIA: EFFECTS ON INDIVIDUALS 352

chapter 15
MASS MEDIA AND SOCIETY 380

chapter 16

MASS MEDIA IN A POLITICAL ENVIRONMENT 402

chapter 17

ETHICS AND THE MASS MEDIA   **426**

chapter 18

MASS MEDIA LAW   448

PREFACE

How did you keep up to date on the O. J. Simpson drama? On the U.S. military intervention in Haiti? Why did you choose one brand of athletic shoes over another? Do you trust Bill Clinton? Bob Dole? Saddam Hussein? David Letterman? If you saw the movie *The Lion King* but not *The Color of Night*, why? How did you learn about the existence of the latest CD or tape you purchased? Would you agree if your local library removed *Playboy* magazine from the shelves? Should *In the Night Kitchen* be banned? *Grapes of Wrath*? *Huckleberry Finn*? Who decides what music gets played on the radio? Who chooses the news stories? Can you trust *The New York Times*? *The National Enquirer*? CNN? *Rolling Stone*? Should you worry about little children imitating Rambo? Barbie? Butt-head? Is there too much sex on television?

Everybody faces these kinds of questions in this age of mass communication. The media are everywhere, and they affect almost every aspect of our lives, including our knowledge of the world around us, the decisions we make as consumers and the values we embrace. The third edition of *The Media of Mass Communication* is designed to help you become more informed and discerning as a user of the mass media. It is also designed to provide a comprehensive foundation for students majoring in mass communication.

New in this edition is a chapter on the emerging new media. You will learn what is at stake on the information superhighway everyone is talking about. You also will get a peek at the forms the media will take in the future. For example, the next generation of college students probably won't be learning from a textbook like this one. What will replace it? Read on.

How This Book Is Organized

OVERVIEW. Chapter 1 orients you to the mass media and the process of mass communication. You will learn some of the themes that come up in later chapters.

THE MEDIA. Separate chapters deal with each major mass medium in the sequence they developed: books, magazines, newspapers, sound recordings, movies, radio and television.

NEW MEDIA. Chapter 9, "Mass Media Tomorrow," is new in this edition. You will learn about the emerging technology that is transforming the mass media.

MEDIA ISSUES.   The remaining nine chapters focus on media research, theories, effects, law and ethics.

QUESTIONS FOR REVIEW.   These questions are keyed to the major topics and themes in the chapter. Use them for a quick assessment of whether you caught the major points.

QUESTIONS FOR CRITICAL THINKING.   These questions ask you both to recall specific information and to use your imagination and critical thinking abilities to restructure the material.

FOR FURTHER LEARNING.   If you have a special interest in the material introduced in a chapter, you can use the end-of-chapter bibliographies to identify more detailed examinations in other sources. The notes can help orient you to the perspective of the authors of these sources, as well as to the level at which they are written. The sources range from easily digested articles in popular magazines to scholarly works that press the boundaries of human knowledge and understanding.

FOR KEEPING UP TO DATE.   These sections list professional and trade journals, magazines, newspapers and other periodical references to help you keep current on media developments and issues. Most of these periodicals are available in college libraries.

BOXES.   Throughout the book, you will find four kinds of boxes that illustrate significant points. *Media People* boxes introduce personalities who have had a major impact on the media or whose story illustrates a major point of media history. *Media Abroad* boxes tell about practices in other countries to help you assess our own media's performance. The *Media Databank* boxes contain tables to help you see certain facts about the mass media at a glance. In the *Media and You* boxes, you will be challenged to bring your experience as a media consumer to major issues and come to your own conclusions.

USING THIS BOOK

The Media of Mass Communication, third edition, contains many tools to help you master the material:

INTRODUCTORY VIGNETTES.   Chapters open with colorful descriptions of major mass media traditions or issues. These are stories about people who contributed significantly to the mass media or who exemplify important aspects of media operations.

LEARNING GOALS.   Chapters begin with learning goals to help guide your thoughts as you read through the chapters.

STUDY PREVIEWS.   Chapters include frequent summaries of the material in subsequent paragraphs. These study previews can help prepare you for the material ahead.

ACKNOWLEDGEMENTS

This book represents many new approaches for introducing students to the media of mass communication. The imaginative and far-sighted team at Allyn and Bacon deserves much of the credit for these innovations. When Bill Barke was vice president and editorial director, he chose to make this the most colorful and visually oriented text available for mass communication survey courses. Communications editor Steve Hull, who has a passion for the mass media, especially movies, and who shared Bill's commitment to make this book as colorful and interesting as the media themselves, organized the people and resources to see the project to completion.

The innovations would have been for naught had not Lou Kennedy brought her promotional genius to the project. Lou has created a series of attention-grabbing campaigns that put the book on the agenda of masscom professors throughout the country. The book has been adopted at more than 300 colleges and universities.

By every measure, my students during 23 years of teaching mass media survey courses have been the most influential factor in the creation of this third edition of *The Media of Mass Communication*. In responding to their curiosity and questions, I have developed a storehouse of ideas on how the story of mass media and their role in our lives should be told. To these students, at Marquette University, the University of Wisconsin—Waukesha County, UW—Washington County, New Mexico State University, University of North Dakota and Winona State University, I am deeply grateful.

I also appreciate the thoughtful suggestions of colleagues who reviewed the manuscript in whole or in part, at various stages in the first or subsequent editions:

Edward Adams, Angelo State University;
Ralph D. Barney, Brigham Young University;
Thomas Beell, Iowa State University;
Robert Bellamy, Duquesne University;
ElDean Bennett, Arizona State University;
Lori Bergen, Wichita State University;
Bob Bode, Western Washington University;
Kevin Boneske, Stephen F. Austin State University;
Michael L. Carlebach, University of Miami;
Meta Carstarphen, University of North Texas;

Debbie Chasteen, Mercer University;
Danae Clark, University of Pittsburgh;
Jeremy Cohen, Stanford University;
Thomas R. Donohue, Virginia Commonwealth University;
Tom DuVal, University of North Dakota;
Kathleen A. Endres, University of Akron;
Donald Fishman, Boston College;
Mary Lou Galician, Arizona State University;
Ronald Garay, Louisiana State University;
Bill Holden, University of North Dakota;
Peggy Holecek, Northern Illinois University;
Anita Howard, Austin Community College;
William Knowles, University of Montana;
Chuck Lewis, Mankato State University;
Larry Lorenz, Loyola University;
Maclyn McClary, Humbolt State University;
Gaylon Murray, Grambling State University;
Richard Alan Nelson, Kansas State University;
Tina Pieraccini, SUNY—Oswego;
Thom Prentice, Southwest Texas State University;
Benjamin H. Resnick, Glassboro State College;
Marshel Rossow, Mankato State University;
Quentin Schultz, Calvin College;
Todd Simon, Michigan State University;
Penelope Summers, Northern Kentucky University;
Edgar D. Trotter, California State University—Fullerton;
Helen Varner, Hawaii Pacific University;
Donald K. Wright, University of South Alabama;
Alan Zaremba, Northeastern University;
Eugenia Zerbinos, University of Maryland;
Julie Zuehlke, University of Wisconsin—La Crosse.

At Winona State University in Minnesota, where I teach, I am deeply appreciative of Paula Wiczek. As mass communication department secretary, she has found ways to weave my needs as an author into the flow of other activities in a very busy office.

The dazzling cover and other design revisions reflect the talent of Linda Knowles, Gayle Robertson and DeNee Reiton Skipper, who built on the eye-catching yet functional interior design that Cynthia Newby created for the last edition, which has been retained.

Appreciation goes also to Suzi Howard, whose zest and energy as a photo researcher have contributed to this book becoming a leader among mass communication textbooks in showing, not just telling, the story of the mass media. I am also indebted to copy editor Karen Stone, whose eagle eyes headed off a great many gremlins that inevitably creep into a manuscript. To Karen Mason, DeNee Reiton Skipper, Phyllis Coyne et al. and Michele Locatelli who put the package together, my thanks too.

While a tremendous amount of talent has gone into *The Media of Mass Communication*, third edition, a book like this is never finished. The media are rapidly changing,and the next edition will reflect that. You as a student using this textbook can be the most significant contributor the next time. Please let me know how this book has helped you through your course and, also, how I can improve the next edition. My address is Box 160, Fountain City, WI 54629-0160. You can also call me at (507) 457-5231 or fax me at (608) 687-3104. On e-mail, I'm at

jvivian@vax2.msus.winona.edu

May your experience with *The Media of Mass Communication*, third edition, be a good one.

John Vivian
Fountain City, Wisconsin

THE MEDIA OF
MASS COMMUNICATION

THE MASS MEDIA ARE PERVASIVE IN OUR EVERYDAY LIVES

THE PRIMARY MASS MEDIA ARE BUILT ON PRINT, ELECTRONIC AND PHOTOGRAPHIC TECHNOLOGIES

SCHOLARS HAVE DEVISED MODELS THAT HELP EXPLAIN THE MASS MEDIA

MOST MASS MEDIA ORGANIZATIONS MUST BE PROFITABLE TO STAY IN BUSINESS

THE MASS MEDIA ARE UNDERGOING CHANGE, INCLUDING GLOBAL CONSOLIDATION

MASS COMMUNICATORS CREATE MASS MESSAGES THAT ARE SENT THROUGH MASS COMMUNICATION VIA MASS MEDIA TO MASS AUDIENCES

SCHOLARS HAVE DEVISED MODELS TO EXPLAIN THE MYSTERIOUS PROCESS OF MASS COMMUNICATION

chapter 1

THE MEDIA OF MASS COMMUNICATION

Presbyterian social reformers founded the St. Louis Observer as a reform newspaper in 1833. They asked *Elijah Lovejoy* to be the editor. It made sense. Lovejoy was a minister sympathetic to reform, including abolition of slavery, and he was an experienced journalist. He accepted. Over the next three years, Lovejoy became increasingly opposed to slavery—a controversial position in Missouri before the Civil War. The fervor of his editorials grew.

Although Lovejoy's followers were abolitionists, most St. Louis people either favored slavery or hated seeing the issue split their city. Hostile public meetings were called to protest Lovejoy's abolitionist crusade. At one meeting it was decided that the free press provision of the U.S. Constitution should be ignored if the peace of the community was threatened. The resolution was aimed at Lovejoy.

At first Lovejoy refused to yield. However, after his printshop was vandalized and he heard that a mob was intent on beating him up or killing him, he decided to move the *Observer* a few miles up the Mississippi River to Alton, Illinois. While the steamboat carrying his press sat on the Alton dock, a new mob showed up with sledgehammers and crowbars, uncrated the press and dumped it in the river.

Elijah Lovejoy

Mob Attacks the Press. Elijah Lovejoy's' persistent anti-slavery articles in his Alton, Illinois, *Observer* led to riot after riot in which his presses were destroyed. Finally, in 1837, the mob shot the abolitionist editor dead.

KEY PERSON
Elijah Lovejoy died a martyr for using the media for a righteous cause.

Undeterred, Lovejoy appealed to abolitionists nationally for money for a new press. Three weeks later, with a new press, he published the first Alton *Observer*. Still undeterred in his crusade, Lovejoy called on readers to help create a state abolitionist society. Within a few days, the mob responded by destroying Lovejoy's new press. Again, with financial support from the national abolitionist movement, Lovejoy ordered another press. On arrival, it was locked up in a warehouse, but the mob broke in and dumped it in the river. At a public meeting, Lovejoy declared he would not give in to any mob, and he ordered yet another press. The mob destroyed this fourth press too, and this time they shot and killed Elijah Lovejoy.

Elijah Lovejoy stands today as testimony to the importance of the mass media as a way for people of strong opinions to persuade others to their point of view. While Lovejoy did not prevail against the mob, his murder made him a martyr. Other abolitionist editors invoked his memory as a battle cry, and eventually their view became public policy. Black slavery was over.

IMPORTANCE OF MASS MEDIA

STUDY PREVIEW   Mass media usually are thought of as sources of news and entertainment. They also carry messages of persuasion. Important, though often overlooked, is how mass messages bind people into communities, even into nations.

PERVASIVENESS

TEACHING OBJECTIVE 1-1
Mass media are vehicles of information, entertainment, persuasion and social cohesion.

Mass media are pervasive in modern life. Every morning millions of Americans wake up to clock radios. Political candidates spend most of their campaign dollars on television to woo voters. The U.S. consumer economy is dependent on advertising to create mass markets. American children see 30,000 to 40,000 commercial messages a year. With mass media so influential, we need to know as much as we can about how they work. Consider:

- Through the mass media, we learn almost everything we know about the world beyond our immediate environs. What would you know about the Whitewater deal or Tonya Harding or the Super Bowl if it were not for newspapers, television and other mass media?
- An informed and involved citizenry is possible in modern democracy only when the mass media work well.
- People need the mass media to express their ideas widely. Without mass media, your expression would be limited to people within earshot and to whom you write letters.
- Powerful forces use the mass media to influence us with their ideologies and for their commercial purposes. The mass media are the main tools of propagandists, advertisers and other persuaders.

INFORMATION SOURCE

The most listened-for item in morning newscasts is the weather forecast. People want to know how to prepare for the day. The quality of their lives is at stake. Not carrying an umbrella to work if rain is expected can mean getting wet on the way home, perhaps catching pneumonia, at worst dying. There used to be a joke that the most important thing the mass media did was to tell us whether a tornado was coming or whether the Russians were coming.

The heart of the media's informing function lies in messages called *news*. Journalists themselves are hard pressed to agree on a definition of news. One useful

Media in Revolution. Control of the mass media is a high priority for both the government and insurgents during a revolution. In 1989, in a revolution that ousted Romanian strongman Nicolae Ceausescu, the fiercest fighting was at the government-controlled Bucharest television headquarters.

definition is that news is reports on things that people want or need to know. In the United States, reporters usually tell the news without taking sides.

Advertising also is part of the mass media's information function. The media, especially newspapers, are bulletin boards for trade and commerce. People look to grocery advertisements for specials. Classified advertisements provide useful information.

ENTERTAINMENT SOURCE

The mass media can be wonderful entertainers, bringing together huge audiences not otherwise possible. No matter how many people saw Charlie Chaplin on the vaudeville stage, more people saw him in movie houses. Even more have been entertained by his impersonator in the IBM personal computer advertisements on television and in magazines and newspapers.

Almost all mass media have an entertainment component. The thrust of the American movie industry is almost wholly entertainment, although there can be a strong informational and persuasive element. Even the most serious newspaper has an occasional humor column. Most mass media are a mix of information and entertainment—and also persuasion.

PERSUASION FORUM

People form opinions from the information and interpretations to which they are exposed, which means that even news coverage has an element of persuasion. The media's attempts to persuade, however, are usually in editorials and commentaries whose purposes are obvious. Most news media separate material designed to persuade from news. Newspapers package their opinion articles in an editorial section. Commentary on television is introduced as opinion.

The most obvious of the media messages designed to persuade is *advertising*. Ads exhort the audience to action—to go out and buy toothpaste, cornflakes and automobiles. *Public relations* is subtler, seeking to persuade but usually not to induce

Mass Media and National Development

The British Broadcasting Corporation and the United Nations periodically gather data on the number of television and radio sets around the globe. The data underscore the importance of an advanced mass media system with national development.

	Radios per 1,000 People	Televisons per 1,000 People		Radios per 1,000 People	Televisions per 1,000 People
Western Democracies			*Developing Countries*		
United States	2,043	612	Yemen	20	3
Canada	n/a	458	Ethiopia	89	40
Australia	1,301	395	India	55	4
United Kingdom	993	359	Bangladesh	8	1
Japan	713	250	Burkina Faso	19	5

immediate action. Public relations tries to shape attitudes, usually by persuading mass media audiences to see an institution or activity in a particular light.

BINDING INFLUENCE

The mass media bind communities together by giving messages that become a shared experience. In the United States, a rural newspaper editor scrambling to get out an issue may not be thinking how her work creates a common identity among readers, but it does. The town newspaper is something everyone in town has in common. In the same way, what subway riders in Philadelphia read on their way to work in the morning gives them something in common. A shared knowledge and a shared experience are created by mass media, and thus they create a base for community.

The same phenomenon occurs on a national level. Stories on the 1986 Challenger space shuttle disaster bound Americans in a nationwide grieving process. Coverage of the Iran-Contra scandal prompted a nationwide dialogue on what *our* foreign policy should be. Stories on the Whitewater scandal help us figure out what we as a society regard as right and wrong. The importance of mass media in binding people into nationhood is clear in every revolution and coup d'état: the leaders try to take over the national media system right away.

PRIMARY MASS MEDIA

STUDY PREVIEW The mass media fall into three categories based on the technology by which they are produced—print, electronic and photographic. The primary print media are books, magazines and newspapers. The primary electronic media are television, radio and sound recordings. The one primarily photographic medium is movies.

PRINT MEDIA

Books, magazines and newspapers can generally be distinguished in the following four categories: binding, regularity, content and timeliness:

	Books	Magazines	Newspapers
Binding	Stitched or glued	Stapled	Unbound
Regularity	Single issue	At least quarterly	At least weekly
Content	Single topic	Diverse topics	Diverse topics
Timeliness	Generally not timely	Timeliness not an issue	Timeliness important

TEACHING OBJECTIVE 1-2
There are seven primary mass media.

LECTURE RESOURCE 1-C
Slides: *Mass Media in Color.*

LECTURE RESOURCE 1-D
Bill Moyers, *Illusions of News.*

Although these distinctions are helpful, they cannot be applied rigidly. For example, timeliness is critical to *Time* and *Newsweek*. Sunday newspaper magazines like *Parade* are not bound. Over the past 20 years, book publishers have found ways to produce "instant books" on major news events within a couple weeks so that their topics can be timely.

The definition problem was illustrated when comedian Carol Burnett sued the *National Enquirer* for reporting falsely that she had been tipsy at a restaurant. The case was tried in California, where state law was more tolerant of slanderous stories in newspapers than those in magazines. Defending itself, the *National Enquirer* tried to convince the judge that it was a newspaper. The judge did not buy the argument, and the *National Enquirer* was tried under the magazine rules and lost. But it was not an easy call. The *National Enquirer* has characteristics of both a newspaper and a magazine.

The technological basis of books, magazines and newspapers, as well as that of lesser print media such as brochures, pamphlets and billboards, is the printing press, which for practical purposes dates back to the 1440s. Print media messages are in tangible form. They can be picked up physically and laid down, stacked, and filed and stored for later reference. Even though newspapers may be used to wrap up the leftovers from dinner for tomorrow's garbage, there also is a permanency about the print media.

ELECTRONIC MEDIA

Television, radio and sound recordings flash their messages electronically. Pioneer work on electronic media began in the late 1800s, but they are mostly a 20th-century development. Unlike print messages, television and radio messages disappear as soon as they are transmitted. Messages can be stored on tape and other means, but usually they reach listeners and viewers in a nonconcrete form. Television is especially distinctive because it engages several senses at once with sound, sight and movement.

PHOTOGRAPHIC MEDIA

The technology of movies is based on the chemistry of photography. Movies, however, may not be with us much longer as a chemical medium. While Hollywood still makes movies on film that is pulled "through the soup," a lot of video production, including some prime-time television, is shot on tape and stored digitally. Photography itself is moving from chemistry to digital technology, which means production and editing occurs at computer screens rather than in darkrooms. An end may be coming for darkrooms, hypo and fixer.

Digital Photography. Today, images can be captured, stored, manipulated and reproduced digitally, without using chemicals. Kodak has a system that stores images on CD-ROM, which allows them to be viewed on a computer and television screens. And with a computer, images can be easily enhanced and changed in ways a photographer in a darkroom could never have done. Because this digital technology is easy to use and study too, it is rapidly displacing the chemistry that had been the sole basis of photograph.

MASS MEDIA MODELS

STUDY PREVIEW   Scholars have devised numerous ways to dissect and categorize the mass media. These include the hot-cool, entertain-inform and elitist-populist models. Each offers insights, but all of them have short-comings in explaining the mass media.

HOT AND COOL

Theorist *Marshall McLuhan* developed an innovative model to help explain the mass media. To McLuhan's thinking, books, magazines and newspapers were *hot media* because they require a high degree of thinking to use. To read a book, for example, you must immerse yourself to derive anything from it. The relationship between medium and user is intimate. The same is true with magazines and newspapers. McLuhan also considered movies a hot medium because they involve viewers so completely. Huge screens command the viewers' full attention, and sealed, darkened viewing rooms shut out distractions.

In contrast, McLuhan classified electronic media, especially television, as cool because they can be used with less intellectual involvement and hardly any effort. Although television has many of the sensory appeals of movies, including sight, motion and sound, it does not overwhelm viewers to the point that all else is pushed out of their immediate consciousness. When radio is heard merely as background noise, it does not require any listener involvement at all, and McLuhan would call it a *cool medium*. Radio is warmer, however, when it engages listeners' imaginations, as with radio drama.

KEY PERSON
Marshall McLuhan explained human involvement with mass media by placing it on a hot-cool continuum.

TEACHING OBJECTIVE 1-3
Models help us understand the mass media.

Marshall McLuhan

Hot and Cool. Scholar Marshall McLuhan developed the idea of *hot* and *cool* media. The more that the audience is immersed in the message, the warmer McLuhan considered the medium. He saw movies as very warm because they can engage so many human senses simultaneously with a darkened environment and huge screen edging out competing stimuli.

McLuhan's point is underscored by research that has found people remember much more from reading a newspaper or magazine than from watching television or listening to the radio. The harder you work to receive a message from the media, the more you remember.

ENTERTAINMENT AND INFORMATION

Many people find it helpful to define media by whether the thrust of their content is entertainment or information. By this definition, newspapers almost always are considered an information medium, and audio recording and movies are considered entertainment. As a medium, books both inform and entertain. So do television and radio, although some networks, stations and programs do more of one than the other. The same is true with magazines, with some titles geared more for informing, some for entertaining.

Although widely used, the entertainment-information dichotomy has limitations. Nothing inherent in newspapers, for example, precludes them from being entertaining. Consider the *National Enquirer* and other supermarket tabloids, which are newspapers but which hardly anybody takes seriously as an information source. The neatness of the entertainment-information dichotomy doesn't work well with mainstream newspapers either. Most daily newspapers have dozens of items intended to entertain. Open a paper and start counting with Calvin and Hobbs, Garfield and the astrology column.

The entertainment-information dichotomy has other weaknesses. It misses the potential of all mass media to do more than entertain and inform. The dichotomy misses the persuasion function, which you read about earlier in this chapter. People may consider most movies as entertainment, but there is no question that Steven Spielberg has broad social messages even in his most rollicking adventure sagas. In the same sense, just about every television sitcom is a morality tale wrapped up in an entertaining package. The persuasion may be soft-peddled, but it's everywhere.

Dividing mass media into entertainment and information categories is becoming increasingly difficult as newspapers, usually considered the leading information medium, back off from hard-hitting content to woo readers with softer, entertaining stuff. For better or worse, this same shift is taking place also at *Time* and *Newsweek*. This melding even has a name that's come into fashion: *infotainment*.

While the entertainment-information model will continue to be widely used, generally it is better to think in terms of four media functions—to entertain, to inform, to persuade, and to bind communities—and to recognize that all media do all of these things to a greater or lesser degree.

ELITIST VERSUS POPULIST

An ongoing tension in the mass media exists between advancing social and cultural interests and giving broad segments of the population what they want. This tension, between extremes on a continuum, takes many forms:

- Classical music versus pop music.
- Nudes in art books versus nudes in *Playboy* magazine.
- The *New York Times* versus the *National Enquirer.*
- A Salman Rushdie novel versus pulp romances.
- Ted Koppel's "Nightline" versus "Oprah Winfrey."
- A Public Broadcasting Service documentary on crime versus Fox Television's "Ten Most Wanted" re-creations.

At one end of the continuum is serious media content that appeals to people who can be called *elitists* because they feel the mass media have a responsibility to contribute to a better society and a refinement of the culture, regardless of whether the media attract large audiences. At the other end of the continuum are *populists*, who are entirely oriented to the marketplace. Populists feel the mass media are at their best when they give people what they want.

The mass media have been significant historically in shaping social and cultural values. Media committed to promoting these values generally forsake the largest possible audiences. In New York City, the serious-minded *Times*, which carries no comics, has generally lagged in circulation behind the *Daily News*, a screaming tabloid that emphasizes crime and disaster coverage, loves scandals and sex, and carries popular comics. The *Times* can be accused of *elitism*, gearing its coverage to a high level for an audience that appreciates thorough news coverage and serious commentary. The *Daily News*, on the other hand, can be charged with catering to a low level of audience and providing hardly any social or cultural leadership. The *Daily News* is in the populist tradition.

A lot of media criticism can be understood in the context of this *elitist-populist* continuum. People who see a responsibility for the mass media to provide cultural and intellectual leadership fall at one extreme. At the other extreme are people who trust the general population to determine media content through marketplace dynamics. Certainly there are economic incentives for the media to cater to mass tastes.

Most mass media in the United States are somewhere in the middle of the elitist-populist continuum. Fox Television offers some serious fare, not only hyped crime re-creations, and the *New York Times* has a sense of humor that shows itself in the wit of its columnists and in other ways.

CNN Paramount Finale

The ownership of the mass media is becoming more concentrated. CNN reporter Stuart Varney makes this point in discussing why Sumner Redstone's Viacom needed to buy Paramount. Otherwise, it could not complete with giants like Time Warner. In fact, Viacom itself had to buy another media company, Blockbuster Entertainment, and enter a deal with the NYNEX telephone giant to finance the Paramount acquisition. This report, which aired February 15, 1994, mentions Barry Diller of QVC, who has emerged as a major media player and is profiled at the opening of Chapter 8 on television. He too had wanted Paramount but lost to Viacom in the bidding. Since this report, the merger of Bell Atlantic and TCI, which is mentioned, fell apart.

ECONOMICS OF MASS MEDIA

STUDY PREVIEW   With few exceptions, the U.S. mass media are privately owned and must turn profits to stay in business. Except for books, sound recordings and movies, most media income is from advertising, with lesser amounts directly from media consumers. These economic realities are potent shapers of media content.

ECONOMIC FOUNDATION

The mass media are expensive to set up and operate. The equipment and facilities require major investment. Meeting the payroll requires a bankroll. Print media must buy paper by the ton. Broadcasters have gigantic electricity bills to pump their messages through the ether.

To meet their expenses, the mass media sell their product in two ways. Either they derive their income from selling a product directly to mass audiences, as do the movie, record and book industries, or they derive their income from advertisers who pay for the access to mass audiences that the media provide, as do newspapers, magazines, radio and television. In short, the mass media operate in a capitalistic environment, and, with few exceptions, they are in business to make money.

ADVERTISING REVENUE.   Advertisers pay the mass media for access to potential customers. From print media, advertisers buy space. From broadcasters, they buy time.

The more potential customers a media company can deliver to advertisers, the more advertisers are charged for time or space. NBC had 40 million viewers for the

TEACHING OBJECTIVE 1-4
Mass media rely on advertiser and audience support to profit.

CNN Newspaper Merger
Mergers and acquisitions are continuing to concentrate ownership in fewer companies. In one of the latest newspaper deals, the *New York Times* purchased the Boston *Globe*. This report, by CNN reporter Steve Young, emphasizes the economic issues that figure into every media deal. This underscores an essential reality that the mass media are economic entities. This report aired June 10, 1993.

Tune In. The mass media put great effort into amassing large audiences. Those numbers translate into advertising revenue because advertisers continually look for the most cost-effective way to reach potential customers. In general, the large a media audience, the more that an advertiser is charged for time or space to get a message to that audience.

1994 Super Bowl, and it charged $900,000 for a 30-second commercial. A spot on a daytime program, with a fraction of the Super Bowl audience, typically goes for $85,000. *Time* magazine, claiming a 4.6 million circulation, charges $138,200 for a full-page advertisement. If *Time*'s circulation were to plummet, so would its advertising rates. Although there are exceptions, newspapers, magazines, television and radio support themselves with advertising revenues.

Book publishers once relied solely on readers for revenue, but that has changed. Today, book publishers charge for film rights whenever Hollywood turns a book into a movie or a television program. The result is that publishing houses now profit indirectly from the advertising revenue that television networks pull in from broadcasting movies.

Movies too have come to benefit from advertising. Until the 1950s, movies relied entirely on box-office receipts for profits, but moviemakers now calculate what profits they can realize not only from movie house traffic but also from recycling their movies through advertising-supported television and home videos. The home video aftermarket, in fact, now accounts for the lion's share of movie studio income. Today, moviemakers even pick up advertising directly by charging commercial companies to include their products in the scenes they shoot.

CIRCULATION REVENUE.   While some advertising-supported mass media, such as network television, do not charge their audiences, others do. *Wall Street Journal* readers pay 50 cents a copy at the newsrack. *Rolling Stone* costs $1.95. Little if any of the newsrack charge or even subscription revenue ends up with the *Wall Street Journal* or *Rolling Stone*. Distribution is costly, and distributors all along the way take their cut. For some publications, however, subscription income makes the difference between profit and loss.

Direct audience payments have emerged in recent years in broadcasting. Cable subscribers pay a monthly fee. Audience support is the basis of subscription television like commercial-free HBO. Noncommercial broadcasting, including the Public Broadcasting Service and National Public Radio, relies heavily on viewer and listener contributions. Record makers, moviemakers and book publishers depend on direct sales to the consumer.

PRIVATELY SUPPORTED MEDIA.   The *Christian Science Monitor*, which maintains an expensive staff of foreign correspondents, has lost money for 25 years. Neither advertising nor subscription income is sufficient to meet expenses. In

MEDIA DATABANK

Buying Space and Time

Here is a sampler of rates for time and space in major U.S. media for one-time placements. Major advertisers pay less because they are given discounts as repeat customers.

New York Times	Sunday full page	$ 53,000
Los Angeles Times	Sunday full page	52,900
Wall Street Journal	Full page	99,400
Time	Full page	138,200
Newsweek	Full page	111,100
NBC, "Cheers"	30-second spot	400,000
NBC, Super Bowl	30-second spot	900,000

recent years, the *Monitor* has been in the red $12 million to $16 million a year. The losses were made up as always by the Church of Christ, Scientist, which sees part of its mission as providing quality news coverage of world affairs. Similarly, the Unification Church of the Reverend Sun Myung Moon underwrites the money-losing Washington *Times*.

Private support, largely from philanthropic organizations, helps keep the Public Broadcasting Service and National Public Radio on the air. The Federal Communications Commission does not allow PBS, NPR or their affiliate stations to accept advertising.

Many limited-circulation publications are supported by organizations that seek to influence limited audiences. Corporations like Exxon produce classy magazines geared for opinion leaders—state legislators, municipal officials and college professors. Special-interest groups such as the trucking industry, religious denominations and professional groups produce ad-free publications and video productions to promote their views.

GOVERNMENT SUBSIDIES. The idea of government support for the mass media might seem contrary to the democratic ideal of a press that is fiercely independent of government, if not adversarial. The fact, however, is that Congress has provided as much as $90 million a year in tax-generated dollars for a quasi-government agency, the Corporation for Public Broadcasting, to funnel to the nation's noncommercial television and radio system. Buffers are built in to the structure to prevent governmental interference in programming. The buffers seem generally to have worked. Some states, including Minnesota, New Mexico and Wisconsin, provide tax dollars for noncommercial broadcasting.

Government dollars also constitute a small portion of mass media advertising revenue. State legislatures appropriate money to buy television and broadcast time, as well as newspaper and magazine space, to promote tourism and to attract new industry. The Defense Department buys space in publications for recruiting troops. The U.S. Postal Service promotes its services through advertising. Newspapers and magazines benefit from discount postal rates, a kind of government subsidy.

Some states require regulated industries, such as insurance companies, to buy space in the state's newspapers to publicize their financial reports. Although these reports, called *legal advertisements* or *legals*, are in tiny agate type, the same size as classified ads, the fees from them are important income for many publications. Some publications also have an indirect subsidy from school boards and other government units that are required by law to publish their minutes and sometimes budgets and other documents. These too are called *legals*.

ECONOMIC IMPERATIVE

Economics figures into which messages make it to print or the airwaves. To realize their profit potential, the media that seek large audiences choose to deal with subjects of wide appeal and to present them in ways that attract great numbers of people. A subject interesting only to small numbers of people does not make it into *Time* magazine. ABC drops programs that do not do well in the television ratings. This is a function of economics for those media that depend on advertising revenue to stay in business. The larger the audience, the more advertisers are willing to pay for time and space to pitch their goods and services.

Even media that seek narrow segments of the population need to reach as many people within their segments as possible to attract advertisers. A jazz radio

CNN Media Subsidies

A controversial government subsidy of the U.S. advertising industry is state money given to trade associations for promoting sales abroad. CNN reporter Anthony Collings reports $200 million in federal money goes to agricultural trade associations and companies. In his report, which aired January 20, 1992, he identifies major beneficiaries of these subsidies as the Cotton Council International, $18 million; American Soybean Association, $16 million; and the Wine Institute, $15 million. He focuses on a California Raisin Advisory Board campaign in Japan that cost $2 million.

station that attracts 90 percent of the jazz fans in a city will be more successful with advertisers than a competing jazz station that attracts only 10 percent.

Media that do not depend on advertising also are geared to finding large audiences. For example, a novel that flops does not go into a second printing. Only successful movies generate sequels.

UPSIDE AND DOWNSIDE

The drive to attract advertising can affect media messages in sinister ways. For example, the television station that overplays the ribbon-cutting ceremony at a new store usually is motivated more by pleasing an advertiser than by telling news. The economic dependence of the mass media on advertising income gives considerable clout to advertisers who threaten to yank advertising out of a publication if a certain negative story appears. Such threats occur, although not frequently.

At a subtler level, lack of advertiser support can work against certain messages. During the 1950s, as racial injustice was emerging as an issue that would rip apart the nation a decade later, American television avoided documentaries on the subject. No advertisers were interested.

The quest for audience also affects how messages are put together. The effect is relatively benign, although real, when a television preacher like Oral Roberts avoids mentioning that he is a Methodist so as not to lose listeners of other faiths. Leaving things unsaid can be serious. For years, many high school science textbooks have danced gingerly around the subject of evolution rather than become embroiled with creationists and lose sales.

MASS MEDIA TRENDS

STUDY PREVIEW   Giant corporations with diverse interests have purchased most U.S. mass media, and this trend toward conglomeration is accelerating on a global scale. Two other trends, contradictory in some ways, are the moves to seek both ever larger and narrower audiences. Meanwhile, technological advances, mostly electronic, are blurring old distinctions among media.

CONGLOMERATION

TEACHING OBJECTIVE 1-5
Mass media undergoing fundamental changes: conglomeration, globalization, demassification, melding.

The trend toward *conglomeration* involves a process of mergers, acquisitions and buyouts that consolidates the ownership of the media into fewer and fewer companies. The deep pockets of a wealthy corporate parent can see a financially troubled media unit, such as a radio station, through a rough period, but there is a price. In time, the corporate parent wants a financial return on its investment, and pressure builds on the station to generate more and more profit. This would not be so bad if the people running the radio station loved radio and had a sense of public service, but the process of conglomeration often doesn't work out that way. Parent corporations tend to replace media people with career-climbing, bottom-line managers whose motivation is looking good to their superiors in faraway cities who are under serious pressure to increase profits. Management experts, not radio people, end up running the station, and the quality of media content suffers.

A myopic profit orientation is not surprising, considering that the executives of parent corporations are responsible to their shareholders to return the most profit possible from their diverse holdings. When a conglomerate's interests include enterprises as diverse as soccer teams, airlines, newspapers and timberland, as did the business empire of the late Robert Maxwell, it is easy to understand how the focus is more on the bottom line than on the product. The essence of this phe-

Beavis and Butt-head Everywhere. The unlikely MTV characters Beavis and Butt-head became big-time profit makers for Viacom, which owns MTV, through promotion in other media. With Viacom's 1994 acquisition of Paramount and Simon and Schuster, the company has in-house movie, book, television and other outlets for synergetic promotions of its products. Critics of conglomeration fret that the concentration of corporate attention on high-visibility products reduce diversity.

nomenon was captured by *Esquire* magazine when it put this title on an article about the hotel magnate and financier who took over CBS in 1986 and, some say, hastened its decline: "Larry Tisch, Who Mistook His Network for a Spreadsheet."

How extensive is conglomeration? Media critic *Ben Bagdikian*, speaking at the Madison Institute in 1989, offered these statistics, which remain true today:

- Six publishing houses have most of the nation's book sales.
- Six companies have most of the magazine revenues.
- Twelve companies have more than half the daily newspaper circulation.
- Three companies have most of the national television audience and revenues.
- Three major studios have most of the movie business.

Critics like Bagdikian say conglomeration affects the diversity of messages offered by the mass media. At the Madison Institute, Bagdikian portrayed conglomeration in bleak terms: "They are trying to buy control or market domination not just in one medium but in all the media. The aim is to control the entire process from an original manuscript or new series to its use in as many forms as possible. A magazine article owned by *the company* becomes a book owned by *the company*. That becomes a television program owned by *the company*, which then becomes a movie owned by *the company*. It is shown in theaters owned by *the company*, and the movie sound track is issued on a record label owned by *the company*, featuring the vocalist on the cover of one of *the company* magazines. It does not take an angel from heaven to tell us that *the company* will be less enthusiastic about outside ideas and production that it does not own, and more and more we will be dealing with closed circuits to control access to most of the public."

As an example, Viacom, the conglomerate that owned MTV, lost no time in exploiting Beavis and Butt-head's notoriety when they reached icon status. Viacom's copyright became a book, a movie and a videogame, and hundreds of other applications were licensed. That began before 1994, when Viacom subsumed the already-gigantic Paramount Communications. Imagine the new vehicles available for exploiting the next Beavis and Butt-head phenomenon now that Viacom is a

KEY PERSON
Ben Bagdikian is leading critic of media conglomeration.

LECTURE RESOURCE 1-E
Video: Ben Bagdikian, *Ownership and Stewardship in American News*.

LECTURE RESOURCE 1-F
Video: *The Knight-Ridder Promise*.

LECTURE RESOURCE 1-G
Class Exercise: Annual report to shareholders by media conglomerates.

$26 billion empire that includes Blockbuster Video, Paramount Pictures, Paramount Television, Nickelodeon television, and the world's largest commercial book publisher, Simon and Schuster.

GLOBALIZATION

One of the largest book publishers in the United States is a 150-year-old German company whose name most Americans do not even recognize: Bertelsmann. The Bertelsmann presence in the United States typifies the globalization of the mass media, a trend that is changing the structure of the mass media worldwide.

Bertelsmann illustrates the pervasiveness of media globalization. Bertelsmann owns 200 book companies, magazines and other operating units with 44,000 employees in 25 countries. These units generate almost $7 billion in sales a year, 30 percent of it from the United States. In the United States, Bertelsmann owns book companies with such familiar names as Bantam, Doubleday and Dell. It also owns RCA and Arista records. It publishes *YM* and *Parents* magazines, and it owns Brown Publishing, one of the largest printing companies in the United States, which prints *Time, Sports Illustrated, Working Woman* and countless catalogs. Worldwide, Bertelsmann dwarfs such better known media companies as CBS, Hearst and Murdoch.

Bertelsmann is one of many international media companies that, often quietly and behind the scenes, are changing the structure of media ownership. The French company Hachette has significant U.S. magazine holdings. PolyGram, of Britain, is aggressively positioning itself in the U.S. movie, television and pop music fields, including the 1993 acquisition of Motown Records and earlier Island, A&M and Mercury records. The Australia-based companies of Rupert Murdoch have major interests in U.S. magazines, television and newspapers. The biggest players in the magazine acquisition business in the United States in recent years have been Bertelsmann, Hachette and Murdoch, none of which is American owned.

In 1991 Time Warner, the result of the merger of Time-Life and Warner Communications, both old American media names, became 17.5 percent Japanese owned. Japanese companies also have heavy stakes in the U.S. entertainment industry, including Columbia Pictures, CBS Records and MCA, whose full name, ironically, was once "Music Corporation of America."

Globalization is not only a matter of foreign ownership of U.S. media. American companies have extensive operations abroad, and in recent years the U.S. entertainment media industry has been a continuing bright spot in the nation's balance of trade. Far more is exported than imported.

Experts disagree about the effect of globalization. Some critics, including Ben Bagdikian, fret that "anonymous superpowers" like Bertelsmann are a potential threat to American cultural autonomy and the free flow of information and ideas. In his book *The Media Monopoly*, Bagdikian said: "The highest levels of world finance have become intertwined with the highest levels of mass media ownership, with the result of tighter control over the systems on which most of the public depends for its news and information." Other observers, such as Toni Heinzl and Robert Stevenson at the University of North Carolina, note that many global media companies, including Bertelsmann, have learned to let their local operating companies adapt to local cultures: "Following a global strategy, it is the company's policy to respect the national characteristics and cultural traditions in each of the more than two dozen countries in which it operates. It is impossible to detect even hints of German culture from the product lineup of Bertelsmann's companies abroad. Targeting specific preference of a national public or audience, the company has custom-tailored its products for each country: French culture in France, Spanish culture in Spain, American culture in the United States, and so on."

By and large, the agenda of media conglomerates is profits and nothing more. They do not promote ideology. American moviegoers have not seen Japanese overtones in Columbia movies or CBS records since the Sony takeover, nor with MCA products after the Matsushita takeover. At the same time, it cannot be ignored that Bertelsmann tried to transplant its successful German geographic magazine *Geo* in the United States in 1979, only to give it up two years and $50 million later when it realized that *National Geographic*'s following was unshakable. Similarly, the French company Hachette cloned its *Elle* fashion magazine for the United States, and Maxwell and Murdoch imported their British tabloid editors to reshape some of the American newspapers they bought. What can be said with certainty about media globalization is that it is occurring and that observers are divided about its consequences.

DEMASSIFICATION

Another contemporary economic phenomenon is *demassification*. The mass media are capable of reaching tremendous numbers of people, but most media today no longer try to reach the largest possible audience. They are demassifying, going after the narrower and narrower segments of the mass audience.

This demassification process, the result of technological breakthroughs and economic pressures, is changing the mass media dramatically. Radio demassified early, in the 1950s, replacing formats designed to reach the largest possible audiences with formats aimed at sectors of audience. Magazines followed in the 1960s and the 1970s, and today most of the 12,000 consumer magazines in the United States cater only to the special interests of carefully targeted groups of readers. Today, with dozens of television program services available via cable in most U.S. households, television also is going through demassification.

The effects of demassification are only beginning to emerge. At first, advertisers welcomed demassification because they could target their pitches to groups of their likeliest customers. Although demassification dramatically changed the mass media—network radio went into a decline, for example—the economic base of the mass media remained advertising. Local radio stations found new profitability from advertisers anxious to support demassified formats. Today, however, technology has found ways for advertisers to bypass the mass media to reach mass audiences. The

LECTURE RESOURCE I-H
Class Exercise: Students use *Writer's Market* to see how magazines are a demassified medium.

Alternative Media. Advertisers are putting more dollars into new media that reach consumers in the marketplace as they shop. The VideoCart Company, for example, makes a video screen that mounts on shopping carts and plays messages as shoppers wheel through aisles where certain products are shelved. Such place-based alternative media are a threat to traditional media, such as magazines, newspapers, radio and television, which are losing the near-monopoly they once held for reaching consumers with retail advertising.

latest trend in demassification has advertisers producing their own media to carry their messages by mail to potential customers who, through computer sorting and other mechanisms, are more precisely targeted than magazines, newspapers, television and radio could ever do. The new *alternative media*, as they are called, include:

- Direct mail catalogs and flyers to selected addresses.
- Television commercials at the point of purchase, such as screens in grocery store shopping carts.
- Place-based media, such as magazines designed for distribution only in physicians' waiting rooms.
- Telemarketing, in which salespeople make their pitches by telephone to households determined by statistical profiles to be good potential customers.

If advertisers continue their shift to these and other alternative media, the revenue base of magazines, newspapers, radio and television will decline. Wholly new ways to structure the finances of these media will be necessary, probably with readers, listeners and viewers picking up the bill directly rather than indirectly by buying advertised products, which is the case today.

MELDING

The seven primary mass media as we know them today are in a technological transition that is blurring the old distinctions that once clearly separated them. For example, newspapers are experimenting with electronic delivery via cable and telephone lines—"no paper" newspapers. Through personal computers, thousands of people have access to data banks to choose the news coverage they want. In the 1980s the Massachusetts Institute of Technology media lab developed *configurable video* systems that integrated printed articles and video segments that a person could read and view in any sequence desired. The MIT system was an integration of traditional print and electronic media with a new twist: An individual, sitting at a screen, could control the editing by passing unwanted portions and focusing on what was most valuable.

Some media melding has come about because competitors have recognized how partnerships could be mutually beneficial. When television became a media force in the 1950s, Hollywood lost millions of moviegoers and declared war on its new rival. For several years, the movie industry even forbade television from playing movies, and Hollywood developed distinctive technical and content approaches that television could not duplicate. The rivalry eased in time, and today Hollywood and the television industry are major partners. Hollywood produces a significant amount of programming for the television networks, and there are all kinds of joint ventures.

MASS COMMUNICATION PROCESS

STUDY PREVIEW   Mass communication is the process mass communicators use to send their mass messages to mass audiences. It is a process that is related to other kinds of communication but that also is distinctive. It is a process that is not well understood.

FOUR BASIC COMPONENTS

TEACHING OBJECTIVE 1-6
Mass media carry mass messages to mass audiences through mass communication.

The mass media are a relatively recent arrival in human experience. The oldest mass medium, the printed book, has been around more than 500 years, and the newest medium, television, only 50 years. These media affect us in many ways, but we know much less than we should about how they work. One way to understand how the mass media work is to define these different but related terms:

LECTURE RESOURCE 1-1
Slides: Timothy O'Keefe and Bill Thomas, *News Story*.

MASS MESSAGES.   A news item is a message, as are a movie, a novel, a recorded song and a billboard advertisement. The *message* is the most apparent part of our relationship to the mass media. The people who create messages include journalists, lyricists, scriptwriters, television anchors, radio disc jockeys, public relations practitioners, and advertising copywriters.

MASS MEDIA.   The *mass media* are the vehicles that carry messages. The primary mass media, as we have discussed, are books, magazines, newspapers, television, radio, sound recordings, and movies. Most theorists view media as neutral carriers of messages. The people who are experts at media include technicians who keep the presses running and who keep the television transmitters on the air. Media experts also are tinkerers and inventors who come up with technical improvements, such as compact discs, AM stereo radio and newspaper presses that can produce high-quality color.

MASS COMMUNICATION.   The process through which messages reach the audience via the mass media is called *mass communication*. This is a mysterious process about which we know far less than we should. Researchers and scholars have unraveled some of the mystery, but most of how it works remains a matter of wonderment. For example: Why do people pay more attention to some messages than to others? How does one advertisement generate more sales than another? Is behavior, including violent behavior, triggered through the mass communication process? There is reason to believe that mass communication affects voting behavior, but how does this work? Which is most correct—to say that people can be controlled, manipulated, or influenced by mass communication? Nobody has the answer.

MASS AUDIENCES.   The size and diversity of mass audiences add complexity to mass communication. Only indirectly do mass communicators learn whether their messages have been received. Mass communicators are never sure exactly of the size of audiences, let alone of the effect of their messages. Mass audiences are fickle. What attracts great attention one day may not the next. The challenge of trying to communicate to a mass audience is even more complex because people are tuning in and tuning out all the time, and when they are tuned in, it is with varying degrees of attentiveness.

MYSTERY OF MASS COMMUNICATION

The mass communication process is full of mystery. Major corporations commit millions of dollars to advertising a new product and then anxiously hope the promotional campaign works. Sometimes it does. Sometimes it doesn't. Even experts at mass communication, such as the people at advertising agencies, haven't unlocked the mysteries of the process, nor have scholars who try to understand the influence of mass communication on society and individuals. One of the enduring questions of our time is whether the media trigger violent behavior.

Despite the mystery and the uncertainties, there is no alternative to mass communication in modern society. Therefore, it is important for people who create mass media messages to learn all that can be known about the process. It is no less important that people who receive the messages have a sense of the process that is being used to inform, entertain and persuade them.

COMMUNICATION TYPES

The communication in which the mass media engage is only one form of communication. One way to begin understanding the process of mass communication is to differentiate it from other forms of communication:

INTRAPERSONAL COMMUNICATION.   We engage in *intrapersonal communication* when we talk to ourselves to develop our thoughts and ideas. This intrapersonal communication precedes our speaking or acting.

INTERPERSONAL COMMUNICATION.   When people talk to each other, they are engaging in *interpersonal communication*. In its simplest form, interpersonal communication is between two persons physically located in the same place. It can occur, however, if they are physically separated but emotionally connected, like lovers over the telephone.

The difference between the prefixes *intra-* and *inter-* is the key difference between intrapersonal and interpersonal communication. Just as *intrasquad* athletic games are within a team, *intrapersonal* communication is within one's self. Just as *intercollegiate* games are between schools, *interpersonal* communication is between individuals.

GROUP COMMUNICATION.   There comes a point when the number of people involved reduces the intimacy of the communication process. That's when the situation becomes *group communication*. A club meeting is an example. So is a speech to an audience in an auditorium.

MASS COMMUNICATION.   Capable of reaching thousands, even millions, of people is *mass communication*, which is accomplished through a mass medium like television or newspapers. Mass communication can be defined as the process of using a mass medium to send messages to large audiences for the purpose of informing, entertaining or persuading.

In many respects the process of mass communication and other communication forms is the same: Someone conceives a message, essentially an intrapersonal

MEDIA AND YOU

Failures to Communicate

When was the last time you misunderstood something you learned about from the mass media? Try to reconstruct the situation and identify what went wrong. Perhaps you had trouble following the plot of a television movie or could not determine the governor's position on some issue from a newspaper article. Ask yourself:

- Was encoding at fault? Decoding?
- Did channel, environmental or semantic noise interfere?

- Did filters interfere?
- Were gatekeepers at fault, giving you insufficient background or perhaps cluttering a message with irrelevancies that obscured the message?
- Was homophyly lacking?
- Would the misunderstanding have occurred if you had had an opportunity for immediate feedback with the source of the message that you misunderstood?

act. The message then is encoded into a common code, such as language. Then it's transmitted. Another person receives the message, decodes it and internalizes it. Internalizing a message is also an intrapersonal act.

In other respects, mass communication is distinctive. Crafting an effective message for thousands of people of diverse backgrounds and interests requires different skills than chatting with a friend across the table. Encoding the message is more complex because a device is always used—for example, a printing press, a camera or a recorder.

One aspect of mass communication that should not be a mystery is spelling the often-misused word "communication." The word takes no "s" if you are using it to refer to a *process*. If you are referring to a communication as *a thing*, such as a letter, a movie, a telegram or a television program, rather than a *process*, the word is "communication" in singular form and "communications" in plural. The term "mass communication" refers to a process, so it is spelled without the "s."

MASS COMMUNICATION MODELS

STUDY PREVIEW Scholars have devised numerous models that illustrate the communication process. These models identify elements of the process.

BASIC MODEL

Many ways have been devised to display the communication process to help explain how it works. One model was laid out in 1948 by two Bell telephone engineers, *Claude Shannon* and *Warren Weaver*, who were working on advanced computer applications in telephone systems. Shannon and Weaver needed a reference point for their research, so they devised a model that has become a standard baseline for describing the communication process.

STIMULATION. In the Shannon-Weaver model, communication begins with a source who is stimulated internally to want to communicate a message. The stimulation can result from many things. Emotions can be stimuli, as can something that is sensed—seeing a beautiful panorama, feeling a cold draft or hearing a child cry.

ENCODING. The second step is encoding. The source puts thoughts into symbols that can be understood by whomever is destined to receive the message. The symbols take many forms—for example, the written word, smoke signals or pictographs.

TRANSMISSION. The message is the representation of the thought. In interpersonal communication, the message is almost always delivered face to face. In mass communication, however, the message is encoded so that it is suitable for the equipment being used for transmission. Shannon and Weaver, being telephone engineers, offered the example of the sound pressure of a voice being changed into proportional electrical current for transmission over telephone lines. In technical terms, telephone lines were channels for Shannon and Weaver's messages. On a more conceptual basis, the telephone lines were the *media*, in the same way that the printed page or a broadcast signal is.

TEACHING OBJECTIVE 1-7
Models help explain the complex, mysterious mass communication process.

KEY PEOPLE
Claude Shannon and Warren Weaver developed early model of mass communication.

Classic Communication Model. This is the classic communication model to which people like Claude Shannon and Warren Weaver began adding the mechanical and electronic components of mass communication in the 1940s. In mass communication, the transmitter is not the human voice or a writing utensil but, in the case of a radio, a transmitter. The receiver is not a human ear but a radio receiver. The conception of a message by a sender and the internalization by the receiver remain human functions in mass communication. The terms *encoder* and *decoder* were added by scholar Wilbur Schramm.

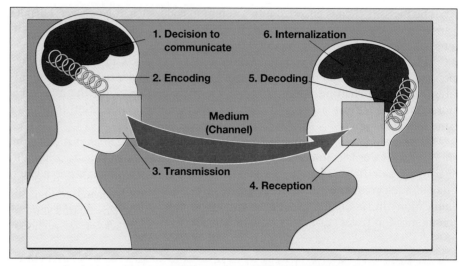

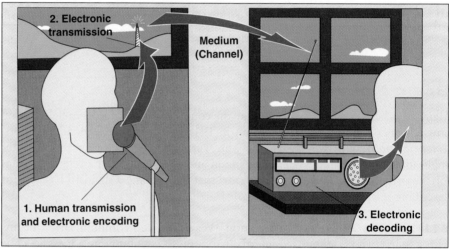

Claude Shannon   **Wilbur Schramm**

DECODING.   The receiver picks up signals sent by the transmitter. In interpersonal communication, the receiver is a person who hears the message or sees it, or both. An angry message encoded as a fist banging a table is heard and perhaps felt. An insulting message encoded as a puff of cigar smoke in the face is smelled. In mass communication, the first receiver of the message is not a person but the equipment that picks up and then reconstructs the message from the signal. This mechanical decoding is necessary so that the human receiver of the message can understand it. As Shannon and Weaver put it, "the receiver ordinarily performs the inverse operation that was done by the transmitter."

INTERNALIZATION.   In mass communication, a second kind of decoding occurs with the person who receives the message from the receiving equipment. This is an intrapersonal act, internalizing the message. For this second kind of decoding to work, the receiver must understand the communication form chosen by the source in encoding. Someone who reads only English will not be able to decode a message in Greek. Someone whose sensitivities are limited to punk rock will not understand Handel's water music. In other words, the source and the receiver must have enough in common for communication to occur. This common experience, which can be as simple as speaking the same tongue, is called *homophyly*. In mass communication, the encoder must know the audience well enough to shape messages that can be decoded accurately and with the intended effect.

NOISE.   If speakers slur their words, the effectiveness of their messages is jeopardized. Slurring and other impediments in the communication process are called *noise*. In mass communication, which is based on complex mechanical and electronic equipment, the opportunities for noise interference are countless because so many things can go wrong. Noise occurs in three forms. *Channel noise*, such as transmission static, faulty microphones and smudged pages, occurs in the transmission of messages. *Environmental noise*—a doorbell that interrupts someone's reading an article or shouting kids who distract a viewer from the 6 o'clock news—interferes with the decoding process. *Semantic noise*, such as sloppy wording, involves problems in crafting messages.

Mass communicators go to special lengths to guard against noise interfering with their messages. For example, in encoding, broadcast scriptwriters avoid "s" sounds as much as possible because they can hiss gratingly if listeners are not tuned precisely on the frequency. Because words can be unintentionally dropped in typesetting, newspaper reporters write that a verdict was "innocent" rather than "not guilty." It would be a serious matter if noise resulted in the deletion of "not."

To keep noise at a minimum, technicians strive to keep their equipment in topnotch condition. Even so, things can go wrong. Also, mass communicators cannot control noise that affects individual members of their audience—such as the siren of a passing fire truck, a migraine headache or the distraction of a pot boiling over on the stove. Clear enunciation, whether sharp writing in a magazine or clear pronunciation on the radio, can minimize such interference, but noise is mostly beyond the communicator's control.

Repetition is the mass communicator's best antidote against noise. If the message does not get through the first time, it is repeated. Rare is an advertisement that plays only once. Radio newscasters repeat the same major news stories every hour, although they rehash the scripts so they will not bore people who heard the stories earlier.

Semantic Noise. In every issue, the *Columbia Journalism Review* delights in reproducing bad headlines and other newspaper gaffes as a reminder to journalists to be more careful. These gaffes are examples of semantic noise, in which ambiguous wording and other poor word choices interfere with clear communication.

The Lower case

'Makes me feel good about where I live'
Crime in Severna Park jumps 2 percent   *The Capital (Annapolis, Md. 2/17/94*

Auto tag fees to aid animals sitting in bank
Sun-Sentinel (Fort Lauderdale, Fla.) 2/7/94

Ferguson Charged With Receiving Stolen Goods
Salem Man Also Accused of Murdering His Wife
Union Leader (Manchester, N.H.) 3/10/94

Parking lot floods when man bursts
Herald-Sun (Durham, N.C.) 2/4/94

Residential mortgage loan officer **Traci Weissmann** is now available at AnchorBank, Verona branch office, 845-6716.
The Capital Times (Madison, Wis.) 6/17/93

Clinton visits hurt soldiers
Sun-Sentinel (Broward County, Fla.) 3/26/94

OOPS OOPS OOPS OOPS OOPS
Due to an editing error, the October 22 story on the BCCP bonds read that Clif Ladd of Espey-Huston "said diddley squat" when asked to explain consultant recommendations on the BCCP. This should have read that we were unable to reach Ladd for comment. We apologize for the error.
Austin (Tex.) Chronicle 11/5/93

TV networks agree to police violence
New Orleans Times-Picayune 2/2/94

Man Who Made $1-Million Shot a Globetrotter
San Francisco Chronicle 1/17/94

■ Japanese tabloids are all atwitter that the wife of **Crown Prince Naruhito**—whose years-long search for a bride was exhaustively chronicled—might soon be a father.
The Washington Post 1/20/94

Trustee Named to Lead Troubled Executive Life
The Journal of Commerce 2/25/94

CIA agent donated to Dems
Rocky Mountain News 2/25/94

Humans have left Everglades dying of thirst
Kennebec Journal (Augusta, Me.) 1/29/94

Fiske Gets Off to Fast Start in Whitewater Probe By Moving Forward Aggressively on All Fronts
The Wall Street Journal 3/14/94
page A 16

The Fiske Coverup II
The Wall Street Journal 3/14/94
page A 14

FEEDBACK.   Because mass communication is not the one-way street that the Shannon-Weaver model indicated, later theorists embellished the model by looping the process back on itself. The recipient of a message, after decoding, responds. The original recipient then becomes the sender, encoding a response and sending it via a medium back to the original sender, who becomes the new destination and decodes the response. This reverse process is called *feedback*.

In interpersonal communication, you know if your listener does not understand. If you hear "Uhh?" or see a puzzled look, you restate your point. In mass communication, feedback is delayed. It might be a week after an article is published before a reader's letter arrives in the newsroom. Because feedback is delayed and because there usually is not very much of it, precise expression in mass communication is especially important. There is little chance to restate the point immediately if the television viewer does not understand. A mass communicator cannot hear the "Uhh?"

CONCENTRIC CIRCLE MODEL

The Shannon-Weaver model can be applied to all communication, but it misses some things unique to mass communication. In 1974 scholars *Ray Hiebert, Donald*

Ungurait and *Thomas Bohn* presented an important new model—a series of concentric circles with the encoding source at the center. One of the outer rings was the receiving audience. In between were several elements that are important in the mass communication process but less so in other communication processes.

GATEKEEPERS.   Mass communication is not a solo endeavor. Dozens, sometimes hundreds, of individuals are involved. A Stephen King thriller passes through several editors before being published. When it's adapted as a screenplay, substantial modifications are made by many other individuals, all expert in the medium of the movie. Later, when it is adapted for television, experts in television as a mass medium make further changes, and so might the network program standards office. Anyone who can stop or alter a message en route to the audience is a *gatekeeper.* Newscast producers are gatekeepers because they decide what is aired and what is not. They make decisions about what to emphasize and what to deemphasize. Magazine and newspaper editors do the same, sorting through hundreds of stories to choose the relatively few that will fit in their publications. When gatekeepers make a mistake, however, the communication process and also the message suffer.

REGULATORS.   The concentric circle model also recognizes *regulators* as a force that shapes and reshapes mass-communicated messages before they reach the

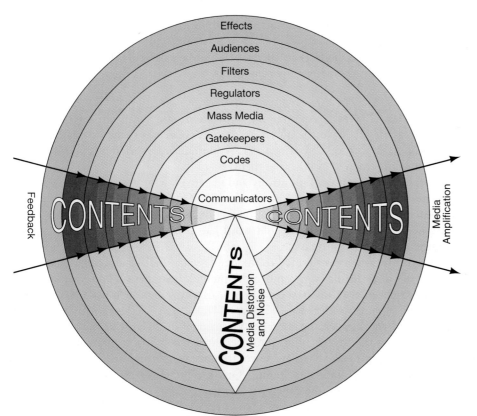

Concentric Circle Model.
The scholars who designed the concentric circle model suggest thinking of it as a pebble being dropped in still water. The ripples emanating outward from the communicator go through many barriers before reaching the audience or having any effect. The model takes note of feedback, media amplification, noise and distortion introduced by the media.

mass audience. Regulators are nonmedia institutions that influence media content. The Federal Communications Commission is a government agency that serves as a regulator when it levies fines on radio stations for indecencies on the "Howard Stern Show." Pressure groups like Action for Children's Television also have an effect. Peer pressure is institutionalized in trade and professional organizations. Other regulators include theater licensing procedures, libel laws and fair trade requirements in advertising.

FILTERS.   Hiebert, Ungurait and Bohn note that receivers are affected by a variety of filters in decoding a message. They call the language or symbols used for a message *informational filters*. If the sender and receiver are not in tune with the same symbols, the communication process is flawed. If you did not know how to read, an informational filter would be interfering right now with your understanding this sentence.

Physical filters exist when a receiver's mind is dimmed by fatigue.

If a receiver is a zealous animal rights activist, *psychological filters* likely will affect the reception of news on medical research involving animals. Being on a different wavelength can be a filter. Imagine two women friends going to the movie "Fatal Attraction" together. One woman is married and monogamous, the other is involved with a married man. Having different ideas on and experiences with marital fidelity, which is at the heart of the movie, the women hear the same words and see the same images, but they see two "different" movies.

EFFECTS.   A decoded message can do more than prompt verbal feedback. It can also affect how someone votes or even provoke a riot. The outermost ring of the concentric circle model, the effects of a message, goes beyond the Shannon-Weaver model to include this important point.

AMPLIFICATION.   An outgoing arrow in the concentric circle model points out that mass media have the ability to amplify, which is related to gatekeepers. Amplification is a process by which mass communication confers status to issues and personalities merely by covering them.

Status conferral can work positively and negatively. For example, some scholars claim that the U.S. government overreacted in 1980 to the 444-day Iran hostage situation because media coverage kept fueling public reaction. Oliver North's name would not have become a household word had it not been for saturation media coverage of the Iran-Contra issue.

Status conferral is not limited to the news media. Ballads and music, amplified through the mass media, can capture the public's imagination and keep an issue alive and even enlarge it. In World War I, catchy songs such as "Over There" helped rally support for the cause. Fifty years later, "An Okie From Muskogee" lent legitimacy to the hawkish position on Vietnam. Bob Dylan's 1975 song "Hurricane" reopened the investigation into the murder conviction of Reuben "Hurricane" Carter. Movies also have the power to move people and sustain issues. Sidney Poitier movies of the 1960s, including "Guess Who's Coming to Dinner," helped keep racial integration on the American agenda.

Narrative Model

Yale professor *Harold Lasswell*, an early mass communication theorist, developed a useful yet simple mass communication model. The Lasswell model is not diagrammed. Instead, it is in narrative form and poses four questions: Who says what? In which channel? To whom? With what effect?

You can easily apply the model. Pick any bylined story from the front page of a newspaper.

- Who says what? The newspaper reporter tells a story, often quoting someone who is especially knowledgeable on the subject.
- In which channel? In this case, the story is told through the newspaper, a mass medium.
- To whom? The story is told to a newspaper reader.
- With what effect? The reader decides to vote for Candidate A or B, or perhaps readers just add the information to their reservoir of knowledge.

Key Person

Harold Lasswell devised a narrative model of mass communication.

CHAPTER WRAP-UP

The mass media are the vehicles that carry messages to large audiences. These media—books, magazines, newspapers, records, movies, radio, television and sound and video recordings—are so pervasive in modern life that many people do not even notice their influence. Because of that influence, however, we should take time to understand the mass media so that we can better assess whether they are affecting us for better or worse.

The mass media are essential for democracy. By keeping people on top of current issues, the media enable people to participate intelligently in public policy discussion and decision making. The media also are the vehicles by which people debate the issues and try to persuade each other of different points of view. Even when they provide us with entertainment, the mass media are capable of portraying and shaping values that enrich our dialogue on social issues and public policy. Sometimes the media perform these functions well, sometimes not. Studying the media gives people the tools to know whether the media are living up to their potential as facilitators of democracy.

The mass media work through a process called mass communication. This is an important distinction: Mass media are *things*, mass communication is a *process*. The study of mass communication teaches a great deal about the influence of the mass media.

Technology is central to mass communication. Magazines and newspapers are possible only because the printing process was invented. Television, likewise, is dependent on electronic equipment. Because media technology is complex, mass communication is possible only through organizations that bring together many people with a range of specialized skills. These organizations include television networks, book publishers and newspaper chains, almost all of which exist only because they generate profits for their owners. A related approach to studying the mass media, therefore, involves examining the competitive economic context within which they operate.

QUESTIONS FOR **R**EVIEW

1. How are the mass media pervasive in our everyday lives?

2. What are the three technologies on which the primary mass media are built?

3. Explain three models that scholars have devised to explain the mass media.

4. How do mass media organizations make money to stay in business?

5. What are the major changes that the mass media are undergoing? And what are the effects?

6. How do these items relate to each other? Mass communicators, mass messages, mass communication, mass media, mass audiences.

7. Explain three models that scholars have devised to explain mass communication.

QUESTIONS FOR **C**RITICAL **T**HINKING

1. How is each of these types of communication—intrapersonal, interpersonal, group and mass—difficult to master?

2. All communication involves conceiving, encoding, transmitting, receiving and decoding, but some of these steps are more complicated for mass communication. In what way?

3. Some people were confused when Marshall McLuhan called electronic media cool and print media hot because, in their experience, radios and television sets heat up and newspapers are always at room temperature. What did McLuhan mean?

4. The effectiveness of messages communicated through the mass media is shaped by the technical limitations of each medium. A limitation of radio is that it cannot accommodate pictures. Is it a technical limitation that the *Wall Street Journal* does not carry photographs, or that the New York *Times* does not carry comics or that most radio news formats limit stories to 40 seconds? Can you provide examples of content limitations of certain media? What are the audience limitations inherent in all mass media?

5. For many years CBS television programs drew a generally older and more rural audience than the other

networks. Did that make CBS a niche-seeking mass media unit? Did it make the CBS audience any less heterogeneous?

6. Different mass communication models offer different insights into the mass communication process. Describe the different perspectives of these models: Shannon-Weaver, concentric circle and narrative.

7. Which mass media perform the informing purpose best? The entertaining purpose? The persuading purpose? Which of these purposes does the advertising industry serve? Public relations?

8. Why do revolutionaries try to take over the mass media right away?

9. Which is more important to the American mass media—profits or doing social good? What about the goals of supermarket tabloids like the *National Enquirer*?

10. Which mass media rely directly on consumer purchases for their economic survival? Advertising provides almost all the revenue for commercial radio and television stations, but indirectly consumer purchases are an important factor. In what way?

11. Are any types of mass media not dependent on advertising or consumer purchases?

FOR **F**URTHER **L**EARNING

Ken Auletta. *Three Blind Mice: How the TV Networks Lost Their Way* (Random House, 1991). Auletta takes a dim view of media conglomeration in this examination of the corporate takeovers of ABC, CBS and NBC in the 1980s.

Ben H. Bagdikian. "Special Issue: The Lords of the Global Village." *The Nation* 248 (June 12, 1989):23, 805–20. Bagdikian, a media critic, argues that the concen-

tration of media ownership into a few global conglomerates is diluting the vigor of news and other content.

Arthur Asa Berger. *Media USA: Process and Effect* (Longman, 1988). This is a collection of articles on media issues, including economic aspects of the mass media.

Stephen W. Littlejohn. *Theories of Human Communication*, 3rd ed. (Wadsworth, 1989). Professor Littlejohn traces developments in communication theory and synthesizes current research. One chapter focuses on mass communication.

Denis McQuail and Sven Windahl. *Communication Models for the Study of Mass Communication* (Longman, 1981). McQuail and Windahl show dozens of models from the first 30 years of mass communication research with explanatory comments. Included is discussion on the narrative, Shannon-Weaver and helix models.

Anthony Smith. *The Age of the Behemoths: The Globalization of Mass Media Firms* (Priority Press, 1991). In this brief volume, media scholar Smith details the recent growth of giant global media companies, including Bertelsmann, Sony and Time Warner, and discusses implications of this development.

Alexis S. Tan. *Mass Communication Theories and Research* (Macmillan, 1986). Drawing on the growing body of behavioral communication research, Professor Tan explains mass communication functions, processes and effects. Although it is written for serious students, the book requires no background in communication theory, methodology or statistics.

FOR KEEPING UP TO DATE

Scholarly discussion on the communication process can be found in *Communication Yearbook*, published since 1977, and *Mass Communication Review Yearbook*, published since 1986.

The Journal of Communication is a quarterly scholarly publication from Oxford University Press.

Many mass media developments abroad are tracked in the monthly London-based *Censorship Index*.

Newsmagazines including *Time* and *Newsweek* cover major mass media issues more or less regularly, as do the New York *Times*, the *Wall Street Journal* and other major newspapers.

Periodicals that track the mass media as business include *Business Week*, *Forbes*, and *Fortune*. *Forbes* and *Fortune* magazines rank major United States companies annually by numerous criteria, including sales, assets and profits. *Fortune* ranks industrial companies in April and service companies in May. The *Forbes* rankings are in April.

THE MASS PRODUCTION OF THE WRITTEN WORD IN THE 1400S FUNDAMENTALLY CHANGED HUMAN HISTORY

BOOKS TODAY FALL INTO TWO MAIN CATEGORIES: TRADE BOOKS AND TEXTBOOKS

A BOOK'S COMMERCIAL SUCCESS IS MEASURED IN SALES, BUT THESE ARE DIFFICULT TO CALCULATE ON AN ONGOING BASIS

THE BOOK INDUSTRY RANGES FROM GLOBAL CONGLOMERATES TO SMALL SPECIALTY PUBLISHERS

BOOKS ORIGINATE THROUGH AUTHOR SPECULATION, AUTHOR-PUBLISHER COLLABORATION AND PUBLISHER INITIATIVE

PUBLISHERS ARE INCREASINGLY SAVVY IN MARKETING BOOKS AND WRINGING PROFIT FROM SUBSIDIARY RIGHTS

THE ABSORPTION OF BOOK PUBLISHING COMPANIES INTO CONGLOMERATES HAS BROUGHT NEW PRESSURE FOR PROFITS

BOOK RETAILING IS TAKING NEW FORMS THAT CONCERN ELITISTS

PUBLISHERS ARE FOCUSING ON BOOKS WITH POTENTIAL FOR BLOCKBUSTER SUCCESS

chapter

Books

FIRST OF THE MASS MEDIA

Johannes Gutenberg was eccentric—a secretive tinkerer with a passion for beauty, detail and craftmanship. By trade, he was a metallurgist, but he never made much money at it. Like most of his fellow 15th-century Rhinelanders, he pressed his own grapes for wine. As a businessman, he was not very successful, and he died penniless. Despite his unpromising combination of traits, quirks and habits—perhaps because of them—Johannes Gutenberg wrought the most significant change in history: the mass-produced written word. He invented movable metal type.

Despite the significance of his invention, there is much we do not know about Gutenberg. Even to friends, he seldom mentioned his experiments, and when he did he referred to them mysteriously as his "secret art." When he ran out of money, Gutenberg quietly sought investors, luring them partly by the mystique he attached to his work. What we know about Gutenberg's "secret art" was recorded only because Gutenberg's main backer didn't realize the quick financial return he expected on his investment and sued. The litigation left a record from which historians have pieced together the origins of modern printing.

The date that Johannes Gutenberg printed his first page with movable type is unknown, but historians usually settle on 1446. Gutenberg's printing process was widely copied—and quickly. By 1500, presses all over western Europe had published almost 40,000 books.

First Mass-Produced Written Word. Johannes Gutenberg and his assistants could produce 50 to 60 imprints an hour with their modified wind press, but Gutenberg's real contribution was movable metal type. His moveable type expedited the putting together of pages and opened the age of mass communication.

Today, Gutenberg is remembered for the Bibles he printed with movable type. Two hundred Gutenberg Bibles, each a printing masterpiece, were produced over several years. Gutenberg used the best paper. He concocted an especially black ink. The quality amazed everybody, and the Bibles sold quickly. Gutenberg could have printed hundreds more, perhaps thousands. With a couple of husky helpers, he and his modified wine press could have produced 50 to 60 imprints an hour. However, Johannes Gutenberg, who never had much business savvy, concentrated instead on quality. Forty-seven Gutenberg Bibles remain today, all collector's items. One sold in 1978 for $2.4 million.

IMPORTANCE OF BOOKS

STUDY PREVIEW   Mass-produced books, first introduced in the mid-1400s, changed human history by accelerating the exchange of ideas and information among more people. Books have endured as a repository of culture. They are the primary vehicle by which new generations are educated to their society's values and by which they learn the lessons of the past.

BOOKS IN HUMAN HISTORY

TEACHING OBJECTIVE 2-1
Gutenberg changed human history with mass-produced written word.

The introduction of mass-produced books in the 15th century marked a turning point in human history. Before then, books were handwritten, usually by scribist monks who copied existing books onto blank sheets of paper letter by letter, one page at a time. These scribists could turn out only a few hand-lettered books in a lifetime of tedium.

KEY PERSON
Johannes Gutenberg.

In the mid-1400s, *Johannes Gutenberg*, a tinkerer in what is now Germany, devised an innovation that made it possible to print pages using metal letters. Printing itself was nothing new. Artisans in ancient China had been printing with a process that is still an art form:

- Impressions are carved in page-size wooden blocks.
- The blocks are laid on a flat surface and inked.
- A sheet of paper is carefully laid on the blocks.
- Pressure is brought down on the inked blocks.
- The carved-out niches in the block remain uninked, and the surface of the block becomes inked figures impressed on the paper.

Gutenberg's revolutionary contribution was in applying metallurgy to the process. The idea occurred to Gutenberg in the mid-1430s. Instead of wood, which often cracked in the pressing process, he experimented with casting individual letters in a lead-based alloy. He built a frame the size of a book's page and then arranged the metal letters into words. Once a page was filled—with letters and words and sentences—he put the frame into a modified wine press, applied ink, laid paper, and pressed. The process made it possible to produce dozens, even hundreds and thousands, of copies.

Gutenberg's impact cannot be overstated. The duplicative power of movable type put the written word into wide circulation and fueled quantum increases in literacy. One hundred years after Gutenberg, the state of communication in Europe had undergone a revolution. Elaborate postal systems were in place. Standardized maps produced by printing presses replaced hand-copied maps, with all their inaccuracies and idiosyncracies. People began writing open letters to be distributed far and wide. Newspapers followed. The exchange of scientific discoveries was hastened through special publications.

LECTURE RESOURCE 2-A
Slides: *Media Technology from Gutenberg to Videotex.*

LECTURE RESOURCE 2-B
Film: *Civilization: A Personal View by Kenneth Clark.*

Gutenberg Masterpiece. The craftsmanship that Johannes Gutenberg put into his Bibles made them sought after in the 1450s and still today. Of the 47 remaining, one sold at an auction for $2.4 million in 1978.

Scribist Monk. Until the invention of movable type by Johannes Gutenberg in the 1440s, books were produced one at a time by scribes. It was tedious work, production was slow and scribes were not always faithful to the original.

Johannes Gutenberg stands at a dividing point in the history of humankind. A *scribist* culture preceded him. The *age of mass communication* followed.

BOOKS IN NATIONAL DEVELOPMENT

Books were valued in the Colonial period. In Massachusetts in 1638, the pilgrims set up *Cambridge Press*, the first book producer in what is now the United States. Just as today, personal libraries were a symbol of the intelligentsia. *John Harvard* of Cambridge, Massachusetts, was widely known for his personal collection of 300 books, a large library for the time. When Harvard died in 1638, he bequeathed his books to Newtowne College, which was so grateful that it renamed itself for him. Today it's Harvard University.

William Holmes McGuffey's reading textbook series brought the United States out of frontier illiteracy. More than 122 million McGuffey's readers were sold beginning in 1836, coinciding with the boom in public-supported education as an American credo.

In the mid-1800s, American publishers brought out books that identified a distinctive new literary genre: the American novel. Still widely read are Nathaniel Hawthorne's *The Scarlet Letter* (1850), Herman Melville's *Moby Dick* (1851), Harriet Beecher Stowe's *Uncle Tom's Cabin* (1852), Mark Twain's *Huckleberry Finn* (1884) and Stephen Crane's *The Red Badge of Courage* (1895).

KEY PERSON
John Harvard.

KEY PERSON
William Holmes McGuffey.

James Fenimore Cooper.
Books were a major contributor to a distinctive American identity in the early days of nationhood. Authors like James Fenimore Cooper created stories that flowed from the American experience and gave United States citizens a feel for themselves as people with their own traditions. Cooper's stories, including *The Last of the Mohicans,* came out of the frontier—which was a uniquely American subject. The contributions of these early authors and the role of the early U.S. media has been enduring. Those works are still grist for media attention, including the 1992 movie *The Last of the Mohicans.*

James Fenimore Cooper

Today, most of the books that shape our culture are adapted to other media, which expands their influence. Magazine serialization put Henry Kissinger's memoirs in more hands than did the publisher of the book. More people have seen Carl Sagan on television than have read his books. Stephen King thrillers sell spectacularly, especially in paperback, but more people see the movie renditions. Books have a trickle-down effect through other media, their impact being felt even by those who cannot or do not read them. Although people are more in touch with other mass media day to day, books are the heart of creating American culture and passing it on to new generations.

DEFINING THE BOOK BUSINESS

STUDY PREVIEW   When most people think about books, fiction and nonfiction aimed at general readers come to mind. These are called *trade books,* which are a major segment of the book industry. Also important are *textbooks,* which include not only schoolbooks but also reference books and even cookbooks.

TRADE BOOKS

The most visible part of the $15-billion-a-year American book-publishing industry produces *trade books,* which include general-interest titles. Trade books can be incredible best-sellers:

TEACHING OBJECTIVE 2-2
Two main categories: tradebooks and textbooks.

- J. R. R. Tolkien's *The Hobbit,* 35 million copies since 1937.
- Margaret Mitchell's *Gone With the Wind,* 28 million since 1936.
- William Peter Blatty's *The Exorcist,* 12 million since 1972.

While publishing trade books can be extremely profitable when a book takes off, trade books have always been a high-risk proposition. One estimate is that 60 percent of them lose money, 36 percent break even and 4 percent turn a good profit, and only a few in the latter category become best-sellers and make spectacular money.

TEXTBOOKS

Although the typical successful trade book best-seller can be a spectacular money-maker for a few months, a successful *textbook* has a longer life with steady income. For example, Curtis MacDougall wrote a breakthrough textbook on journalism in 1932 that went through eight editions before he died in 1985. Now, the publisher has brought out a ninth edition, with Robert Reid bringing it up to date. This has given MacDougall's *Interpretative Reporting* a life span of more than 60 years. Although textbook publishers don't routinely announce profits by title, *Interpretative Reporting* undoubtedly has generated more income than most trade book best-sellers.

Textbooks are the biggest segment of the book market. Textbooks, a book industry category that includes reference and professional books, generate a little more than half of the industry's profits. About one-third of those profits are from lawyers, physicians, journalists, scholars, accountants, engineers and other professionals who need personal libraries for reference.

Reference books, such as dictionaries, atlases and encyclopedias, represent about 10 percent of textbook revenue. Over the years, the Bible and Noah Webster's dictionary have led reference books sales, but others also have had exceptional, long-term success that rivals leading trade books. For example:

- Benjamin Spock's *Baby and Child Care*, 32 million copies since 1946.
- *The Better Homes and Garden Cookbook*, 28 million since 1930.
- *Betty Crocker's Cookbook*, 21 million since 1950.
- Dale Carnegie's *How to Win Friends and Influence People*, 15 million since 1940.

PAPERBACKS

KEY PERSON
Allen Lane.

The modern paperback was the brainchild of *Allen Lane*. In 1935, in the middle of the Depression, Lane launched *Penguin Books* in London. He figured that low-cost books would find a following in poor times. It was a gamble. He printed only 20,000 copies of his first few books, popular novels and biographies. Then came a breakthrough. The Woolworth's dime store chain in the United States agreed to stock them.

KEY PERSON
Robert de Graff.

Imitators followed. In New York *Robert de Graff* introduced *Pocket Books*. They were unabridged best-sellers that fit easily in pocket or purse. They cost only 25 cents. In their first two months on the market, sales reached 325,000 books. Almost everybody could spring a quarter for a book. "The paperback democratized reading in America," wrote Kenneth Davis in his book, *Two-Bit Culture: The Paperbacking of America*. Today, paperback sales exceed 1 million copies a day. More than 120,000 titles are in print.

As the book industry has grown and become competitive in new ways, the traditional distinctions among trade, text and paperback books have broken down. Today, some trade books are released both in hard and soft covers. Some textbooks come out only in hard cover, some only in paper, some in both.

MEASURING COMMERCIAL SUCCESS

STUDY PREVIEW   One measure of a book's success is sales, but because some books cost a lot more to bring to market than others, a great number of sales do not necessarily mean profits for the publisher. Strange as it may seem, sales are not a strong indicator of whether a book is read. People buy books for all kinds of reasons besides reading them.

BEST-SELLERS

LECTURE RESOURCE 2-C
Class Exercise: Students compare
their reading with best-seller
books.

What makes a best-seller? Traditional successful subjects have been Abraham Lincoln, physicians and dogs, which prompted one wag to suggest that a book about Lincoln's doctor's dog couldn't help but make a fortune. Books on the Kennedy family have done well over the past 30 years. Controversy also sells. Watergate books had a ready audience, and so did the memoirs and insider accounts of key figures in the Iran-Contra scandal of 1986 and 1987. Inspirational books sell well, and so does just about any book with a title that starts with "How to." Gossipy books, including autobiographies by celebrities, tend to do well. Biographies by celebrities' estranged children can be blockbusters.

Usually publishers are pleased if a trade book sells more than 75,000 hardcover copies and 100,000 paperback copies—unless the book was part of a costly marketing program that required even more sales to break even. For James Clavell's *Whirlwind*, for example, the publishers gave the author such a large advance, $5 million, that they needed to sell 1 million hardcover and 3 million softcover copies to recoup the money and cover production and other expenses.

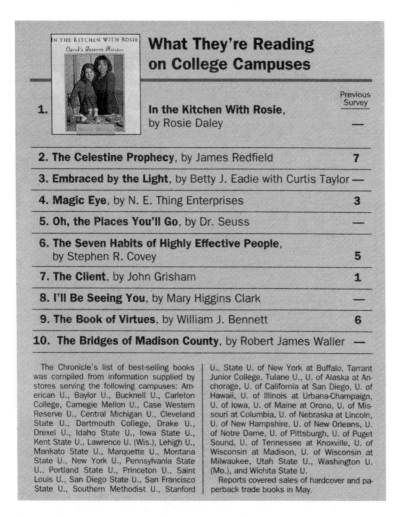

What They're Reading on College Campuses

		Previous Survey
1.	**In the Kitchen With Rosie,** by Rosie Daley	—
2.	**The Celestine Prophecy,** by James Redfield	7
3.	**Embraced by the Light,** by Betty J. Eadie with Curtis Taylor	—
4.	**Magic Eye,** by N. E. Thing Enterprises	3
5.	**Oh, the Places You'll Go,** by Dr. Seuss	—
6.	**The Seven Habits of Highly Effective People,** by Stephen R. Covey	5
7.	**The Client,** by John Grisham	1
8.	**I'll Be Seeing You,** by Mary Higgins Clark	—
9.	**The Book of Virtues,** by William J. Bennett	6
10.	**The Bridges of Madison County,** by Robert James Waller	—

The Chronicle's list of best-selling books was compiled from information supplied by stores serving the following campuses: American U., Baylor U., Bucknell U., Carleton College, Carnegie Mellon U., Case Western Reserve U., Central Michigan U., Cleveland State U., Dartmouth College, Drake U., Drexel U., Idaho State U., Iowa State U., Kent State U., Lawrence U. (Wis.), Lehigh U., Mankato State U., Marquette U., Montana State U., New York U., Pennsylvania State U., Portland State U., Princeton U., Saint Louis U., San Diego State U., San Francisco State U., Southern Methodist U., Stanford U., State U. of New York at Buffalo, Tarrant Junior College, Tulane U., U. of Alaska at Anchorage, U. of California at San Diego, U. of Hawaii, U. of Illinois at Urbana-Champaign, U. of Iowa, U. of Maine at Orono, U. of Missouri at Columbia, U. of Nebraska at Lincoln, U. of New Hampshire, U. of New Orleans, U. of Notre Dame, U. of Pittsburgh, U. of Puget Sound, U. of Tennessee at Knoxville, U. of Wisconsin at Madison, U. of Wisconsin at Milwaukee, Utah State U., Washington U. (Mo.), and Wichita State U.

Reports covered sales of hardcover and paperback trade books in May.

Campus Best-Seller List. The *Chronicle of Higher Education,* a weekly newspaper read mostly by college administrators and faculty, checks campus bookstores at selected universities for a regular best-seller list among college people. The list bears some semblance to the New York *Times* weekly best-seller list, but there are differences that reflect issues and subjects with special attraction for people who frequent campus shops.

For schoolbooks, both college and lower level, publishers gear their expectations to total national enrollments in the courses for which they are intended.

TEACHING OBJECTIVE 2-3
Book sales hard to calculate on ongoing basis.

WHY PEOPLE BUY BOOKS

Millions of books are printed in the United States every year. In a typical year, more than 50,000 titles, including follow-up editions, are issued. The numbers suggest that we are a literate society hungry for books, but the numbers are misleading. Half of all American adults read fewer than two books a year.

The biggest category of books sold is texts, professional books and references, all of which people are required to buy for school and work. Textbooks would not do well if it were not for the coerciveness of the syllabus. Professional books are needed by people in their work. Reference books, such as dictionaries and encyclopedias, are sourcebooks hardly designed to be read cover to cover.

Americans buy almost 300 million hardback general-interest books a year, which may seem like an enormous amount, but it averages only one book per citizen per year. While there are libraries and while people pass books along to their friends, the Gallup polling organization found that there are fewer books read per capita in the United States than in any other English-speaking country.

SPECIALTY PUBLISHERS

STUDY PREVIEW The U.S. Government Printing Office puts out more books than any other publisher, many of them best-sellers. Other less-recognized players in the book business are university presses, which concentrate on scholarly works, and the vanity press, which produces author-financed books.

U.S. GOVERNMENT PRINTING OFFICE

TEACHING OBJECTIVE 2-4
Book industry ranges from global conglomerates to specialty publishers.

Many major book publishers are household names—Doubleday, Random House, Simon & Schuster—but not many people think of the federal government as a major player. The fact is that the Government Printing Office is the biggest book producer in the nation.

The GPO, established in 1895 for the systematic distribution of government publications, has 27,000 titles in print, including a few best-sellers. A 108-page paperback called *Infant Care*, published first in 1914, has sold 14 million copies. *Your Federal Income Tax* is a perennial big seller as April 15 approaches.

When significant government documents are published, such as the Warren Commission report on the assassination of President John Kennedy, the Nixon tapes, the Surgeon General's report on smoking, or the Meese Commission report on pornography, the GPO can rival commercial publishing houses in the number of sales.

Because the GPO is a government operation designed to serve citizens and not to make a profit, its books are not protected through copyright. Many commercial publishers reprint popular GPO books without any acquisition expenses, move them through their distribution system to retail outlets, and make tidy profits.

SMALL PRESSES

Scholarly titles that commercial publishing houses couldn't consider for economic reasons often are published by universities, research institutions or museums, which generally are not in the book business primarily for profit. Books from the *university presses*, as these publishing houses are known collectively, are purchased mostly by libraries and scholars. Some end up as textbooks.

By some counts, there are 12,000 book-publishing companies in the United States. The catalogs of most contain only a few titles. Among these small presses are some important regional publishers that publish only low-volume books with a long life. For example, Caxton Press in Caldwell, Idaho, produces Pacific Northwest books, many of them on historical topics with a selling life that can run decades. Other small presses specialize in poetry and special subjects for limited audiences that wouldn't otherwise be served. It's almost impossible, for example, to find more than a few token poetry books in a chain store.

VANITY PRESS

It's easy for an author to get a book published—if the author is willing to pay all expenses up front. Family histories and club cookbooks are a staple in this part of the book industry. So are many who's-who books and directories, which list names and then are sold to those whose names are in the books.

Some book publishers, called *vanity presses*, go further by soliciting manuscripts and letting the author infer that the company can make it a best-seller. These companies direct their advertising at unpublished authors and promise a free manuscript review. A custom-addressed form letter then goes back to the author, saying, quite accurately no matter how good or how bad the manuscript, that the proposed book "is indicative of your talent." The letter also says the company would be pleased to publish the manuscript. Most vanity companies do little beyond printing, however. Their ability to promote and distribute a book is very limited, although an occasional best-seller emerges.

It can be argued that vanity publishers unscrupulously take advantage of unpublished authors who don't know how the book industry works. It can be argued too that a legitimate service is being provided. Ed Uhlan of Exposition Press, one of the largest vanity publishers, wrote an autobiographical book, *The Rogue of Publishers Row*, which details how slight the chance is that vanity press clients can make money. When he began including a free copy with the materials he sent inquiring authors, incredible as it seems, his business actually increased.

THE CREATION OF A BOOK

STUDY PREVIEW "I ought to write a book." That's something just about everybody says. Few do. Even so, most books come into being because someone had an idea and pursued it on speculation that a publisher might be found to market it. Books also originate at the initiative of the publisher and through a collaborative author-publisher process.

WRITING ON SPECULATION

There is no surefire formula for an author to get a book to market. Many books are written on speculation. The author has an idea, gets it on paper and then hunts for a publisher. That is how one of the continuing best-sellers of the past 20 years, Robert Pirsig's *Zen and the Art of Motorcycle Maintenance*, came to be.

LECTURE RESOURCE 2-D
Guest: Trade or textbook author.

Robert James Waller

Underdog Success. Most books are successful following major-league marketing promotions by their publisher. Occasionally an obscure book catapults to best-seller status by word-of-mouth. Such was the case in 1992 with Robert James Waller's romance, *Bridges of Madison County*. In fact, *Bridges* and a sequel, *Slow Waltz in Cedar Bend*, shared first and second on many best-seller lists in 1993 and 1994. An earlier underdog success was *Zen and the Art of Motorcycle Maintenance*, for which author Robert Pirsig tried to find a publisher for six years. Finally, Morrow put out the book but with only low expectations. To everyone's surprise, *Zen* took off. Today, a quarter century later, it still sells 100,000 copies a year.

Pirsig had not had any easy adulthood: mental breakdown, electric-shock treatment, itinerancy. He had grown up expecting more. A high point in his life was working out a relationship with his 11-year-old son. From his experiences emerged a gentle philosophy about life. There developed an idea in Pirsig's mind for a book that wrapped it all together.

Finding a publisher was difficult. For more than six years, Pirsig sent out his proposal 121 times. Publishing houses doubted its commercial potential. It was a meandering, sometimes confusing manuscript that operated at many levels. At one level, it was built around a motorcycle trip that Pirsig and his son had taken from Minnesota west. At another level, it was a highly cerebral exploration of values. Finally, the 122nd time that Pirsig mailed out his manuscript, it attracted the attention of James Landis, an editor at the William Morrow publishing house. The offbeat title was enticing, and Landis felt that the book had literary merit. Morrow took a flier and published it in 1974. *Zen and the Art of Motorcycle Maintenance* turned out to be the right book at the right time. Written from the heart in a soul-searching, soul-baring style, it touched readers emerging from the Haight-Ashbury flower child era. It became a best-seller, not just a flash sensation. For more than a decade, sales exceeded 100,000 copies a year.

Every year, by one estimate, 30,000 manuscripts written on speculation arrive at the nation's trade publishing houses. Many do not receive even a cursory review, and 9 out of 10 are rejected. Of the survivors, only a fraction make it to print.

PUBLISHER INITIATIVE

While many authors seek publishers, it can work the other way too. Publishing houses identify market niches and seek authors to write books to fill them. An example is Barbara Tuchman's Pulitzer-Prize–winning *Guns of August*, a book about the start of World War I. A publisher recognized a dearth of works on the war and went looking for an author. Tuchman, an accomplished journalist and historian, was an obvious choice, and she liked the proposal.

In the biggest publisher-initiated project in history, Warner Books went looking for an author for a sequel to Margaret Mitchell's *Gone With the Wind*. Warner knew there was a market. Since 1936 the book had sold an incredible 28 million copies and was selling 40,000 hardcover and 250,000 softcover copies a year. However, there was a risk. Many people felt that Margaret Mitchell had written the quintessential American novel, which could never be surpassed or even matched. Public expectations for a sequel could be so high that, no matter how good, it could be doomed to failure. Despite the risk, Warner poured unprecedented resources into the project. Warner scoured a list of proven authors, reportedly including Sidney Sheldon and John Jakes, and finally settled on Alexandra Ripley, who had written three solid Southern historical romances. Warner gave Ripley $4.9 million up front. When published in 1991, Ripley's *Scarlett* took the expected raps from critics, but shrewd promotion capitalizing on *Gone With the Wind* mania catapulted the book into a best-seller overnight.

It also is book publishers, not authors, who initiate *instant books*. Publishers discovered in the 1970s that they could gear up for books on topical issues and get them to the marketplace within a few days. After the daring 1976 Israeli raid on the Ugandan capital airport to rescue hostages, *24 Hours at Entebbe* was on bookshelves within days. Instant books also sprang up after the Jonestown Massacre, the Son of Sam killings, the slaying of Beatle John Lennon, the Oliver North testimony, the Persian Gulf War, and the O.J. Simpson murder case.

AUTHOR-PUBLISHER COLLABORATION

Collaboration between publisher and author is more and more common. Peter Benchley, a reporter and magazine writer, did not write his megaseller *Jaws* on speculation. Originally, over lunch with a Doubleday editor in 1971, Benchley was discussing an idea for a book on pirates and sunken treasure. The conversation turned to sharks. The dialogue continued over several weeks, and the editor seemed to prefer sharks to sunken treasure. Benchley submitted four chapters on a great white shark. Some of it the Doubleday editors liked, some they did not. Benchley, figuring Doubleday knew more about successful books than he, followed the editors' advice. The book, published in 1974, became a centerpiece in the national dialogue. A movie followed. The haunting theme song remains synonymous with uncertainty and terror. Then came another Benchley book, and another. Then the movie "Jaws II," then "Jaws III." A national fetish about sharks developed. Shark books flooded the market. Old shark documentaries were revived, and new ones were put together.

TEACHING OBJECTIVE 2-5
Books originate with authors, publishers and collaboration.

WHY AUTHORS NEED PUBLISHERS

A writer's talent is to write. Few writers have the knowledge, experience or interest to do the post-manuscript things necessary to get a book into print and to the marketplace. What publishers do is provide editing, design, typesetting, binding, illustrating, marketing and other services.

Most successful writers use *agents* who know the book industry well. An agent takes on only promising projects and tries to interest likely publishers. For example, a religious book has better chances at some publishing houses than others. The same is true with manuscripts for raunchy how-to books, short romances and epic Westerns. Agents generally charge 10 to 15 percent of an author's income from a book.

If a publisher decides to go with a proposal, the writer usually is given an advance payment. Robert Pirsig received $3,000 in advance against his percentage of the book's cover price. His editor, although he liked the book, was not optimistic about its prospects and cautioned Pirsig that there might be no further payments. In time, more than 3 million copies were sold. For already successful authors, advances may exceed $1 million.

Once a book sells, authors typically earn 10 percent of the cover price of trade books, minus the advance. For textbook authors, the amount is a bit less because it is calculated differently. The percentage is called a *royalty*. While 10 percent is typical, royalties are negotiable. A well-known author can bargain for more. If sales exceed a certain point, an author may earn an agreed-upon larger percentage. Royalties for paperbacks and juvenile books usually are less than 10 percent.

MARKETING BOOKS

STUDY PREVIEW   Trade publishers look to retail book chains like B. Dalton to make large prepublication purchases and then to push the book in their stores. A commercially successful book, however, does more than sell well. Publishers seek additional profits by recycling books through numerous outlets, including paperback publishers, movie studios and foreign distributors.

MASS MARKETING AND PROMOTION

LECTURE RESOURCE 2-E
Guest: Bookstore manager.

Book publishers once sent sample copies to influential magazines and newspapers and hoped for favorable reviews. They still do, but no longer is marketing so simple.

Retail chains have become key to a book's success. B. Dalton, Waldenbooks and other bookstore chains, with more than 2,300 stores nationwide, wield tremendous power. Enthusiastic about a title, a chain buyer might order thousands of copies and display them prominently, which attracts buyers. Doubtful about a title, the buyer might order only a few and provide no in-store promotion.

Authors on Television. Media exposure for a new book, especially on television, enhances sales, as talk-show producers can attest. Every day the major shows are deluged with proposals to interview authors of new books. Here, Amy Tan, author of the novels *The Joy Luck Club* and *The Kitchen God's Wife,* appears on the "Charlie Rose" show. This late night PBS program is considered one of the more literate, author-friendly shows on television.

Before the chains, publishers had sales representatives call on individual book-stores to pitch the latest titles. Sales reps still make those calls, but publishing houses now gear most of their marketing, and their choice of what books to publish, to what is most likely to do well in the shopping-mall environment of chain stores. Forty percent of all trade books today are sold through the big chains.

Today, newspaper and magazine reviews are less important than television and radio interviews. ABC White House correspondent Sam Donaldson went on the publicity trail to promote his book, *Hold On, Mr. President.* In a two-week whirl-wind, Donaldson hit 11 major cities, averaging six radio, television and newspaper interviews per city. There were appearances on the Johnny Carson, Joan Rivers and Larry King network programs. He also fielded 75 telephone interviews during the book's first few weeks on bookstore shelves and made other appearances that nobody tallied. Almost immediately, the Donaldson book was on best-seller lists. The major publishing houses have whole departments assigned to promotion, whose job is to line up time on major broadcast programs for their authors to hawk their latest books.

Advertising campaigns have become important in book marketing. If a publisher has decided to push a book with advertising, bookstore chains take greater interest. So do book clubs, another important retail outlet.

Books lend themselves to what advertising people call point-of-purchase displays—especially paperbacks, which often are impulse purchases. Countertop and freestanding promotional racks are used more than ever. Lascivious covers and hyped subtitles improve paperback sales at the racks. The excesses once prompted humorist Art Buchwald to suggest that *Snow White and the Seven Dwarfs* be subti-tled "The Story of a Ravishing Blonde Virgin Held Captive by Seven Deformed Men, All With Different Lusts." For *Alice in Wonderland*, he suggested "A Young Girl's Search for Happiness in a Weird, Depraved World of Animal Desires: Can She Ever Return to a Normal, Happy Life After Falling So Far?"

Controversy sells. After Stein & Day published Elia Kazan's *The Arrangement*, the Mount Pleasant, Iowa, Library Board sent it back as too racy for its shelves. Stein & Day's president mailed a letter to the Mount Pleasant *News*, offering a free copy to everyone in the community, urging them to read the book and decide for themselves and decrying the library board as censorious. Eight hundred people ordered their free copy, which created a bundle of publicity. Sales soared.

SUBSIDIARY RIGHTS

Trade book publishers make additional money from selling other companies the right to reprint books in paperback editions, in large-type editions for the visually impaired, in foreign editions and in other forms. There is income too in selling serialization, book club distribution and movie rights. Selling these *subsidiary rights*, as they are called, also raises more income for authors. In 1988, when Simon & Schuster was working out a deal to publish Ronald Reagan's memoirs, the book industry rumor mill reported that Reagan was guaranteed somewhere between $6 million and $8 million, undoubtedly a record that still stands. Of this money, Simon & Schuster reportedly hoped to recover $2.5 million from foreign publishers, $100,000 from book clubs, more from magazine or newspaper serialization and more later from selling paperback rights.

Serialization of a book in magazines, usually in condensed form, dates to 1936 when *DeWitt Wallace*, the founder of *Reader's Digest*, approached Harper & Bros.

TEACHING OBJECTIVE 2-6
Publishers emphasize marketing, subsidiary rights.

KEY PERSON
DeWitt Wallace.

Multimedia Books. Book publishers and software companies are working together to combine text, audio, graphics, still photos and video in digital CD-ROM format. The result is a multimedia platform expected to augment publisher's traditional book products and eventually replace certain categories of books as printed media. To date, the most successful books on CD-ROM have been reference works, including encyclopedias and directories requiring quick and easy search of entries.

with an idea. Wallace wanted to condense and reprint 50 pages from a new Harper book. He offered $1,000 for serialization rights. The proposition made no sense to Harper. The publishers supposed that condensation in a popular magazine would hurt book sales. Wallace argued the opposite, saying serialization would whet public interest, and he sweetened his offer to $5,000 if book sales did not increase after serialization began. Harper took him up on the deal, sales quadrupled, and the publishing house lost the $5,000. Today, publishing houses routinely figure income from magazine serialization into their budgets when planning a book. They know that serialization helps market the book.

Several theories exist on why serialization boosts book sales. One is that people who read a condensation then want to read the whole book. Another theory, which assumes human vanity, is that readers of a condensed version want the real book on their shelves to point to with pride as they talk about having read the book, even though they might never have opened the book itself.

Publishers also sell paperback rights. Bantam paid $75,000 at an auction to put out *Jaws* as a mass-marketed paperback. By the mid-1980s, mass-marketed paperback rights had skyrocketed for blockbusters. Judith Krantz's *Princess Daisy* drew a reported $3.2 million for paperback rights.

Other income can come from movie rights. Movie producers will pay handsomely for rights to a book, and there can be a profitable second wave of interest in a book after it has been made into a movie.

A book's financial success can be further assured if a publisher interests a book club in offering it to members as a monthly selection. Book club committees screen forthcoming books and then send them automatically to members, usually one a month, unless a member specifically rejects a book after reading the club's promotion for it. Book-of-the-Month Club, founded in 1926, is the oldest and largest club. During its history, BOMC has distributed 500 million books.

BOOK INDUSTRY CONGLOMERATION

STUDY PREVIEW   Whether the book industry can sustain its phenomenal growth is uncertain, especially considering that one out of every six Americans does not read much. The absorption of publishing houses into larger companies has created new profit opportunities but also severe pressure for profit. One result of the new pressure for profits, say critics, is less concern for literary quality.

SUSTAINING GROWTH

Since World War II, the number of new titles brought out by United States publishers has multiplied 10-fold to 50,000 a year, not counting 5,000 to 8,000 revised editions. The growth was triggered by the postwar baby boom demand for textbooks. Although baby boom population growth has leveled off, the demand for textbooks has increased as more people stay in school longer. Mass marketing through retail chains and book clubs also has fueled the growth, but, some experts suspect, the potential for expanding the market may be near its end because population growth has slowed.

Continuing the growth rests partly on cultivating a love for reading. Many Americans, perhaps 15 percent, can read but do not. These people, *aliterates*, never picked up a reading habit. They rely on the electronic media and interpersonal communication for information and entertainment. Incredible as it seems, among aliterates are some college graduates, who read what they must for their jobs but little more. *Illiterates*, who are unable to read, represent a much smaller percentage of the population.

POSITIVE EFFECTS OF CONGLOMERATION

At the end of World War II, the mainline book-publishing business was dominated by family-run publishing houses, all relatively small by today's standards. Although there still are hundreds of small publishers in the United States today, consolidation has reduced the industry to six giants. Depending on whom you ask, the

TEACHING OBJECTIVE 2-7
Conglomerates have brought new profit pressure.

Censored Books

How does censorship affect you? The American Library Association's Office for Intellectual Freedom receives reports on library materials that are most frequently challenged. The list in recent years has been led by:

- John Steinbeck's *Of Mice and Men.*
- Salman Rushdie's *The Satanic Verses.*
- J. D. Salinger's *The Catcher in the Rye.*

- Mark Twain's *Huckleberry Finn.*
- Maurice Sendak's *In the Night Kitchen.*
- Robert Cormier's *The Chocolate War.*
- *Playboy* magazine.
- All books on the occult.

How many of these materials have you read? Does your local library have them available to you? If not, what explanation do you receive when you ask for them?

MEDIA DATABANK

Corporate Connections

Book publishing in the United States once was dominated by small family-owned firms, most of which proudly bore the family name—Doubleday, Knopf, Random House. Today, the names remain, but through acquisitions and mergers most book companies are part of conglomerates with diversified interests. A sampler:

Book Company	Corporate Parents and Siblings
Doubleday	Bertelsmann of Germany, whose interests include Bantam Books, Dell publishing, RCA, and Arista records.
Harcourt Brace Jovanovich	General Cinema, whose interests include HBJ insurance; Holt, Rinehart & Winston books; W. B. Saunders books; Neiman Marcus department stores; specialty retail outlets; and movie theaters.
HarperCollins	News Corp., whose origins are in the Australian media empire of Rupert Murdoch and whose interests include Fox Television; Twentieth Century Fox movie studio; Ansett Airlines in Australia; the *New York Post*; newspapers in Australia, England, Hong Kong; a European satellite television network; and Australian television stations.
William Morrow	Hearst, whose interests include Avon books; Hearst newspapers; *Esquire, Cosmopolitan, Redbook* and other magazines; and television and radio stations.
G. P. Putnam's Sons	MCA, whose interests include Berkley Publishing; Universal movies; Decca, Kapp, Geffen and UNI records.
Random House	Newhouse, whose interests include Ballantine books, Fawcett books, Fodor's travel guides, Knopf books, Newhouse newspapers, Pantheon books and Vintage books.
Simon & Schuster	Viacom, whose interests include Allyn and Bacon books, Appleton & Lange books, Ginn books, Linden Press, Macmillan books, Prentice Hall books, and Silver, Burdett & Ginn books; Paramount movies; sports teams; Madison Square Garden; television stations; and movie houses.
Wadsworth	Thomson of Canada, whose interests include Delmar books, Linguistics books, South-Western books and Thomson newspapers.
Warner Books	Time Warner, whose interests include HBO; Time-Life books; *Life, People* and *Time* magazines; Whittle alternative media; Little, Brown books; local cable systems; Warner books; Warner Bros. movies; Warner Bros., Atlantic, Elektra, Reprise, Chappell records; Warner Home Video; Warner Amex and other cable television companies.

conglomeration has been a godsend or a disaster. Looking at the effects positively, the U.S. book industry is financially stronger:

- Parent corporations have infused cash into their new subsidiaries, financing expensive initiatives that were not financially possible before, including multi-million-dollar deals with authors.
- Because parent corporations often own newspapers, magazines and broadcast companies, book publishers have ready partners for repackaging books in additional media forms.
- Many of the new parent corporations own book companies abroad, which helps open up global markets.

Conglomeration, however, is not always good for book companies or other companies either. Richard MacDonald, who specializes in media deals as equity research director at First Boston, says there are two kinds of people who operate conglomerates: builder entrepreneurs and monster entrepreneurs.

BUILDER ENTREPRENEURS.   MacDonald, writing in the *Gannett Center Journal* in 1989, says the media and the public are well served by people who are "committed to the guts of the media business." He cites the late Bill Paley of CBS and David Sarnoff of RCA, who despite personal quirks were in the media business for the long haul and who recognized that attention to the quality of their product would pay dividends far into the future. MacDonald says contemporary media leaders of this sort include Rupert Murdoch, whose interests include HarperCollins, and Ted Turner of CNN. Among book publishers, these "builder entrepreneurs" would include *Alfred Knopf*, who emphasized outstanding European authors when he started a publishing house in 1915; *Bennett Cerf*, who cofounded Random House in 1927 to create "books of typographical excellence"; and *Barney Rosset*, founder of Grove Press, who waged numerous expensive battles against censorship of Henry Miller's *Tropic of Cancer*.

KEY PERSON
Alfred Knopf.

KEY PERSON
Bennett Cerf.

KEY PERSON
Barney Rosset.

MONSTER ENTREPRENEURS.   MacDonald uses the term "monster entrepreneurs" to describe people who are strictly in the media business for the money. They are motivated by greed, and, says MacDonald, they ask themselves: "How fast can I get the cash out?"

DUBIOUS EFFECTS OF CONGLOMERATION

One of the negative effects of conglomeration occurs when a parent company looks to its subsidiaries only to enrich conglomerate coffers as quickly as possible and by any means possible, regardless of the quality of products that are produced. This is especially a problem when a conglomerate's subsidiaries include widget factories, cherry orchards, funeral homes and, by the way, also some book companies. The top management of such diverse conglomerates is inclined to take a cookie-cutter approach that deemphasizes or even ignores important traditions in book publishing, including a sense of social responsibility. Many of these conglomerates focus myopically on profits alone. The result, according to many literary critics, has been a decline in the quality of books.

QUALITY SHORTCUTS.   In a revealing and controversial 1991 article in the *New Republic*, media critic Jacob Weisberg said that several major book publishers, including Simon & Schuster and Random House, had routinely eliminated important stages in the editing process to rush new titles to print and turn earlier profits. Weisberg lists these results:

- Factual errors, both major and minor, which in earlier times, he says, would have been caught by careful editing.
- Loose, flabby writing from deadline-pressured writers who once could rely on editors to tighten their work. Some books, Weisberg says, are running 100 pages longer than they should.

The issue of declining quality extends even to elementary and high school textbooks. In 1991 the Texas Board of Education found 250 errors, many of them glaring, in history books up for adoption. Among the errors:

■ The United States used the atomic bomb to end the Korean conflict.
■ Robert Kennedy and Martin Luther King Jr. were assassinated while Richard Nixon was president.
■ George Bush defeated Michael Dukakis in 1989.
■ Sputnik was the first intercontinental ballistic missile, and it carried a nuclear warhead.
■ The Wisconsin senator who was the 1950s namesake for *McCarthyism* was General Douglas MacArthur.

Shocked at such errors, the Texas board delayed certifying the books and told publishers to get their act together.

KEY PERSON
Robert Maxwell.

CORPORATE INSTABILITY.   Conglomeration also has introduced instability in the book business. Profit-driven corporate parents are quick to sell subsidiaries that fall short of profit expectations even for a short term or just to raise cash. An alarming example of the cash problem unfolded in 1991 after media magnate Robert Maxwell died, apparently of suicide. Within days of his death it was discovered that Maxwell had been illegally shuffling vast amounts of money around his subsidiaries to cover loans he had taken out to expand his empire, which included Macmillan, the prestigious U.S. book-publishing company. Maxwell was not alone among conglomerate builders who found themselves in deep trouble after overextending themselves financially. The problem was not only in the instability wrought by their miscalculations and recklessness, but also in the products that their media subsidiaries produced. Michael Lennie, a San Diego textbook author attorney, put the problem this way: "The industry continues to grow more and more concentrated with large debt-ridden publishers too preoccupied with serving crippling debt to pay attention to the publishing of quality texts."

With pressure from corporate parents for profits, many book companies have become obsessed with finding blockbuster projects that will make a killing in the marketplace. A result, although there are exceptions, is that publishers are less willing to take risks with authors who have not yet proven themselves in the marketplace. Today, it probably would take Robert Pirsig more than 121 trips to the post office before finding a publisher for *Zen and the Art of Motorcycle Maintenance*.

ANTI-INTELLECTUALISM.   Conglomeration worries book lovers because it means that conglomerate executives can use their chain-of-command authority to squash books they do not like and ramrod those they do into production. Generally these executives recognize that their professional expertise is in deal-making and management and leave judgments on literary quality and market potential to the editors at their book subsidiaries. Even so, the issue remains that the modern conglomerate structure of the American mass media, including the book industry, has created a whole new set of high-level gatekeepers who have unprecedented power to control media content.

THE MASS-MARKETING DEBATE

STUDY PREVIEW Shopping-mall bookstores have become essential in book retailing, which shapes what is published. Some people praise this phenomenon, noting that the book industry performs its best service when it provides great numbers of people what they want. Other people say that mass marketing detracts from the traditional literary and culture-enhancing role of books.

SHOPPING-MALL BOOK RETAILING

Traditionalists vilify the bookstore chains' focus on merchandising as pandering to low tastes. They see books and booklike products of transitory value displacing good literature and scholarship. The chain bookstores are vulnerable to the criticism, emphasizing books with mass appeal and little else—pop psychology, how-to's by the hundreds, celebrity titles, Gothic romances, and cookbooks. Journalism scholar Bruce Porter, researching for an article on the chains, noted this about a large B. Dalton store: "A recent visitor found nothing in the hardcover history section, for example, about Napoleon, Mao Tse-tung, Benjamin Franklin, the French and Russian Revolutions, or any of the British kings and queens. The only general American history book was the *Reader's Digest Story of America*. . . . In paperback, the Current Affairs/Political Science section was so sparsely stocked that *Das Kapital* and *On Revolution* by Hannah Arendt were lumped together with *Dog Days at the White House: Memories of the Presidential Kennel Keeper*. The store's Movie/TV section contained more books than the section for the History of Civilization."

When Porter asked B. Dalton merchandising director Dick Fontaine about the shift away from solid literature, Fontaine said: "I don't give a damn what starts people reading. If it's a sexual high, voyeurism, I say, 'Fine.' No one starts off by reading Proust."

POPULIST VERSUS ELITIST VIEWS

The mass-marketing debate can be boiled down to two contradictory traditions in American life. People in the *populist tradition* see the book industry and other mass media performing best when they satisfy the interests of the greatest number of people. The *elitist tradition* is not concerned with popularity or mass tastes but with quality. Elitists are not so unrealistic as to think that book publishers can survive by producing unpopular books. They emphasize, however, that the book industry has foresaken its traditional responsibility to produce books that are good for the society —not just those that sell well. Elitists tend to cast conglomeration in evil terms because parent corporations push their book subsidiaries to make ever greater profits, regardless of whether it is through publishing significant books or junk.

John Dessauer, a veteran publishing executive who is dismayed at what has happened, sounds a note of caution: "Publishers who consistently disrespect the demand for quality and worth in the manuscripts they publish will, despite temporary successes, find their enterprises dying of spiritual starvation in the end; just as publishers who consistently ignore the commercial needs of their establishments will find before long that cultural opportunities are negated by bankruptcy."

Critics of mass marketing may be overreacting. It has happened before when the book industry has gone in new directions. When Gutenberg introduced movable type, the Abbot of Sponheim exhorted his scribist monks to keep copying. He

TEACHING OBJECTIVE 2-8
Modern book retailing bothers elitists.

argued that it kept idle hands busy and encouraged diligence, devotion and knowledge of Scripture. When Robert de Graff introduced the 25-cent paperback, critics were concerned that the economics of the book industry would be so upset that the culture would be set back.

In a longer view, developments in the book industry all seem to have contributed to advances in the culture. Literacy, perhaps 10 percent in Gutenberg's time, is well past 90 percent in modern-day America. Not as many people are bookworms as might be, but more can read. Someday we may realize that the mass marketing of books has advanced literature and culture much as McGuffey's readers did in the 1800s, although in a different way. Perhaps Dick Fontaine, B. Dalton's merchandising chief, had a point when he said, "No one starts off by reading Proust."

BLOCKBUSTERS

STUDY PREVIEW   The competition for megaselling books has led many trade publishers to create a Hollywood-type star system for authors. Multimillion-dollar advances have reshaped book industry priorities, requiring a new emphasis on marketing. Inevitably, the concentration of resources on blockbuster book projects has dried up resources that could go to new and less known authors.

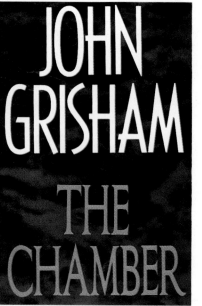

Blockbuster Authors. John Grisham, whose legal thrillers have been astoundingly successful, can command huge advances from his publisher. In turn, publishers can reap large profits on these authors' domestic, international and rights sales. The downside is that many publishers have become less interested in new or struggling authors.

AUTHORS IN STARRING ROLES

The competition for blockbusters approached frenzy in the late 1980s. Epic novelist James Clavell was given $5 million for his unwritten *Whirlwind* in 1985. It was an unprecedented risk that required sales of 1 million hardback and 3 million paperback copies for William Morrow and Avon Books, partners in the project, to break even. People who follow the book industry shuddered at the high stakes, but soon even the Clavell deal was eclipsed. Bursting with cash from corporate parents, other publishing houses upped the ante:

- Novelist Stephen King, $10 million from Viking Penguin and New American Library for each of his next four horror stories.
- Journalist Tom Wolfe, $7 million for a successor to his *Bonfire of the Vanities*. Out of loyalty to Farrar, Straus & Giroux, one of the few remaining independent houses, Wolfe turned down $15 million from a competing publisher.
- Southern author Alexandra Ripley, $4.9 million from Warner Books for a sequel to *Gone With the Wind*. Margaret Mitchell's advance for the 1936 original was $500.
- Mario Puzo, $4 million for an unwritten novel that Random House hoped would outdo *The Godfather.*
- Mary Higgins Clark, $32 million from Simon & Schuster in 1992 for her next six thrillers.
- Anne Rice, $17 million in 1993 for three new vampire books.
- Allan Folsom, $2 million for his first novel, *The Day After Tomorrow*, which publisher Little, Brown saw blockbuster potential.

Megabuck advances have been wonderful for proven authors, whose work is being rewarded in ways never possible for earlier generations of writers. The publishers who invest so heavily in these authors promote them as celebrities.

The author star system, however, has a negative side. The new blockbuster system concentrates the resources of publishing houses on a few major projects, which works against the richness that the book industry could contribute to the culture with a greater number of works. Brooks Thomas, president of Harper-Collins's predecessor company, acknowledged that the system centers attention on commercial books instead of books that may be better literature or stronger contributors to the culture and society. Said Thomas: "God help poetry or criticism."

Although book publishers have retreated from such huge advances to authors, the focus on blockbusters remains, as evident in unprecedented advertising campaigns. At the start of the 1990s, these budgets were averaging $200,000 for "brand name" authors, in contrast to only $10,000 for little-known authors. The biggest budgets were Viking Penguin's $750,000 for Stephen King's *Needful Things* and Warner's $600,000 for Alexandra Ripley's *Scarlett*.

TEACHING OBJECTIVE 2-9
Publishers focus resources on blockbuster projects.

MARKETING TOOLS VERSUS INFORMED INTUITION

Book companies are coming to rely more on market analysis than literary analysis in choosing what to publish. Using statistical models, publishing houses sift through the complex relationship of costs and revenues in their decision making. The models calculate printing and marketing costs and sales revenues and even variables such as paperback, movie, book club, serialization and foreign profits. The models even figure minute details many months in the future, such as timing the release of reprint editions to coincide with the release of a movie based on the book to capitalize on the movie's publicity. They even figure the cost of buying movie stills from the studios that put out the film to put on the cover of the second round of paperback reprints.

Missing from blockbuster projection models, note the critics, is a calculation for literary quality. Blockbuster publishers look for plots that can be redone into screenplays and for subjects and authors that lend themselves to promotion. Some publishers test prospective authors on how they come across in talk-show interviews. All this disturbs purists, who would rather that books rise or fall on their literary merit—not slick promotion. With projection models, according to these elitists, it doesn't matter if a book is good, mediocre or trash. What matters is whether the manuscript can be mass marketed.

CHAPTER WRAP-UP

Book publishing is a high-risk business, especially for works geared to general consumers. Most books do not make money, which means that publishing houses rely on best-sellers to offset the losses. Despite the risks, books can make enormous profits, which led many conglomerates to buy publishing houses in the 1980s. The new parent corporations pressed for more profitability. The result has been heightened competition for big-name authors and new attention to mass marketing. Multimillion-dollar advances to authors for popular, though not necessarily significant, works suggest that the book industry is backing away from its traditional role in furthering American culture and public enlightenment.

Conglomeration and increased pressure for profit are occurring in all mass media, and so is the question of cultural responsibility. The question is especially poignant for the book industry because it has been a central factor in American cultural values since the mid-19th century when a new literary genre, the American novel, emerged. These novels contributed to an American identity that was distinct from Europe's. With pride in their cultural contributions, major publishing houses integrated a profit consciousness with an explicit responsibility to publish worthy works for their own sake regardless of profit potential. There is evidence that the tradition is being lost with the new emphasis on mass marketing, which works almost exclusively with titles that sell quickly at mall bookstores.

QUESTIONS FOR REVIEW

1. How did the mass production of the written word fundamentally change human history?

2. What are the main categories of books today?

3. What makes a book a commercial success? How is this success measured?

4. Do small specialized book publishers still have a place?

5. Do the concepts for books originate with authors or publishers?

6. How do marketing and subsidiary rights reduce the risk in bringing out new books?

7. How has conglomeration changed the book industry?

8. Why do elitists worry about new forms of book retailing?

9. How does a publisher's focus on potential blockbusters affect other kinds of books?

QUESTIONS FOR CRITICAL THINKING

1. Trace the development of the book industry through the innovations of these persons: Johannes Gutenberg, William Holmes McGuffey, Allen Lane and Robert de Graff.

2. What invention doomed the scribist culture that preceded the age of mass communication?

3. How do subsidiary rights multiply the profit potential of trade books?

4. Distinguish trade books and textbooks in terms of profit potential, duration on the market, distribution systems and the effect of mass-marketed paperbacks.

5. Describe the relationship between an author and a publishing house in bringing a book to market, including the difference between writing on speculation and in collaboration. How do agents and royalties work? How has book retailing been affected by the bookstore chains, and has this been for better or worse?

6. Subsidiary rights have become a major revenue source for book publishers. Discuss three kinds of subsidiary rights and their effect on the book industry.

7. For most people, book publishing brings McGraw-Hill, Simon & Schuster, HarperCollins and other major companies to mind. Describe how the following entities fit into the industry: Government Printing Office, Iowa State University Press, Caxton Press and Exposition Press.

8. Is there a threat to quality literature from subsidiary rights? From mass marketing? From conglomeration? From the quest for blockbusters? From projection models?

9. What are ways the book industry can assure its continued growth? How can the book industry protect itself from the need to retrench if growth stalls?

10. Where is the U.S. book industry heading with electronic publishing?

FOR FURTHER LEARNING

John P. Dessauer. *Book Publishing: What It Is, What It Does*, 2nd ed. (R. R. Bowker, 1981). Dessauer, a veteran book publisher, is especially good on the organization of the book industry.

Ronald L. DiSanto and Thomas J. Steele. *Guidebook to "Zen and the Art of Motorcycle Maintenance"* (Morrow, 1990). DiSanto and Steele mostly discuss the underlying symbolism in Robert Pirsig's 1974 book, but they also deal with the difficulties he had in finding a publisher.

Wilson P. Dizard, Jr. *The Coming Information Age: An Overview of Technology, Economics and Politics* (Longman, 1982). Dizard, a futurist, explores the range of implications of postindustrialism, including the economics of media adaptation.

Elizabeth L. Eisenstein. *The Printing Press as an Agent of Change: Communications and Cultural Transformation in Early-Modern Europe*, 2 vols. (Cambridge University Press, 1980). Eisenstein offers a thorough examination of the advent of printing and how it changed even how we see ourselves.

Elizabeth A. Geiser and Arnold Dolin, with Gladys S. Topkis, eds. *The Business of Book Publishing: Papers by Practitioners* (Westview Press, 1985). Thirty articles comprise this primer on the book publishing process.

E. R. Hutchinson. *Tropic of Cancer on Trial* (Grove, 1968). Professor Hutchinson details the issues and the litigation trail of Grove Press's anticensorship battles in the 1960s on behalf of *Tropic of Cancer* by Henry Miller.

N. R. Kleinfield. "The Supermarket of Books." *New York Times Magazine* (November 9, 1986). Kleinfield takes a sprightly look at the Waldenbooks chain.

Richard J. MacDonald. "'Monster' Entrepreneurs and 'Builder' Entrepreneurs." *Gannett Center Journal* 3 (Winter 1989):1, 11–17. In this issue, devoted to news-media barons, MacDonald shares his experience as an investment banker who deals with people who make media acquisitions.

Ted Morgan. "Sharks: The Making of a Best Seller." *New York Times Magazine* (April 21, 1974). Morgan details *Jaws* from concept through every subsidiary rights deal.

Bruce Porter. "B. Dalton: The Leader of the Chain Gang." *Saturday Review* (June 9, 1979). Porter worries about the effect of bookstore chains on the quality of books that Americans are reading.

John Tebbel. *A History of Book Publishing in the United States*, Vols. 1–3 (R. R. Bowker, 1972–1977).

Jacob Weisberg. "Rough Trade." *New Republic* (June 17, 1991). Weisberg stirred a hornet's nest in criticizing major profit-eager book publishers for deemphasizing the editing process to cut costs and rush books to market to score earlier revenue returns. See also the letters to editors in the subsequent July 15 *New Republic*.

William Zinsser. *A Family of Readers* (Book-of-the-Month Club, 1986). Zinsser, general editor of Book-of-the-Month Club, offers a friendly history on club operations, including how titles are selected.

FOR **K**EEPING **U**P TO **D**ATE

Publisher's Weekly is the trade journal of the book industry.

Book Research Quarterly, published by Rutgers University, is a scholarly journal.

The Academic Author Newsletter, published by the Textana Academic Authors Association, deals with textbook issues from the authors' perspective.

Many general interest magazines, including *Time* and *Newsweek*, cover book industry issues when they are topical, as do the *New York Times*, the *Wall Street Journal* and other major newspapers.

In recent years, the *New Republic* has been especially enterprising in covering book industry practices as they change.

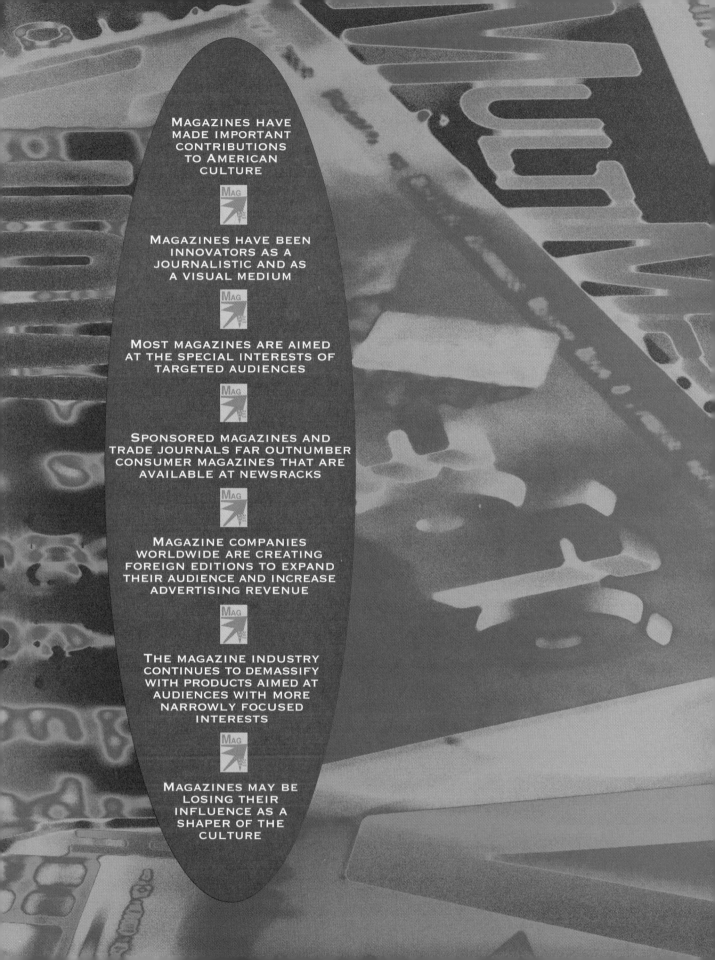

MAGAZINES HAVE
MADE IMPORTANT
CONTRIBUTIONS
TO AMERICAN
CULTURE

MAGAZINES HAVE BEEN
INNOVATORS AS A
JOURNALISTIC AND AS
A VISUAL MEDIUM

MOST MAGAZINES ARE AIMED
AT THE SPECIAL INTERESTS OF
TARGETED AUDIENCES

SPONSORED MAGAZINES AND
TRADE JOURNALS FAR OUTNUMBER
CONSUMER MAGAZINES THAT ARE
AVAILABLE AT NEWSRACKS

MAGAZINE COMPANIES
WORLDWIDE ARE CREATING
FOREIGN EDITIONS TO EXPAND
THEIR AUDIENCE AND INCREASE
ADVERTISING REVENUE

THE MAGAZINE INDUSTRY
CONTINUES TO DEMASSIFY
WITH PRODUCTS AIMED AT
AUDIENCES WITH MORE
NARROWLY FOCUSED
INTERESTS

MAGAZINES MAY BE
LOSING THEIR
INFLUENCE AS A
SHAPER OF THE
CULTURE

chapter 3

MAGAZINES
AN INNOVATIVE MASS MEDIUM

Despite its name, the *New Yorker* has a national, even a worldwide following. Once it was called "the best magazine there ever was." Certainly it was unique—a mix of superb reporting, whimsical cartoons and a rakish elegance that set it apart.

Founded in 1926, the *New Yorker* quickly became home for excellent reporting and writing. The magazine never carried news items, but it cemented its reputation for journalism when it introduced the lengthy personality profile in the 1920s. The *New Yorker* set no deadlines for reporters and did not expect on-scene stories on unfolding events. The assignment: "Take as long as you need. Talk to everybody. Learn what's really on their minds—what worries them, how they feel. Be complete, be vivid. No word limit. Make the writing good. We'll run it all."

Over the years, the magazine became important in American life by breaking new ground. In 1962, when nobody talked much about the environment, the magazine ran Rachel Carson's "Silent Spring." Her series, on the fragility of ecosystems, sensitized everybody to a major but overlooked issue and ushered in the environmental movement.

Fearful of Change at the New Yorker. Loyal readers of the *New Yorker* were concerned when Tina Brown was named editor in 1992 that she might import her eye-catching trendy style from *Vanity Fair.* The *New Yorker* was neither visually catchy nor trendy, and readers liked it that way. At *Vanity Fair,* Brown's reputation was linked to fawning celebrity features and arresting covers like the one for which actress Demi Moore posed pregnant. Brown's appointment to the *New Yorker* prompted *Advertising Age,* a trade journal, to speculate that Brown might do the same with the haughty Eustace Tilley, who has graced annual *New Yorker* covers since the 1920s. Brown did not go that far, making gradual changes in the New Yorker that drew new readers and assured profitability.

The *New Yorker* never followed trends. It set them. Media commentator Eric Utne hailed the magazine for "the courage to disagree with the conventional wisdom even as it defined it through genuine soul-searching rather than through politically correct polemic. In its coverage of the United States' involvement in Nicaragua, Guatemala and the Persian Gulf, the magazine asked tough questions that few other mainstream publications dared to ask, just as it had earlier about McCarthyism, civil rights and the Vietnam War."

The *New Yorker* went for timeless articles of enduring value. It didn't matter if they were read the day the magazine came out, or a month or even a year later. It avoided the topical, trendy thrust of other magazines.

The *New Yorker* even looked different. Disdaining the glitz of other magazines, layouts were forbiddingly gray. Masses of type were interrupted only by cartoons. There was no doubt that the *New Yorker* was word-driven. There were no photographs, no color. The dull appearance contributed to its cerebral tone and was part of the magazine's charm. There also was a tad of arrogance, captured by its trademark, the supercilious dandy Eustace Tilley.

The *New Yorker*'s only visually bright spot was its advertisements—lots of them for upscale perfumes, luxury automobiles and high fashion. Advertisers knew that despite its dowdy look, the *New Yorker* had readers with good educations and high incomes. But even with advertising, the *New Yorker* was different from other magazines. One of its influential editors, William Shawn, forbade ads in some sections of the magazine to avoid any suspicion that the magazine was beholden to advertisers when it came to decisions on what to report and how.

The *New Yorker*'s eccentricities made it successful, and in 1983 the Newhouse media conglomerate plunked down $168 million to buy the magazine. For a few years Newhouse left the magazine pretty much alone, and circulation hit a record 627,000 in 1991. Not all was well, however. The number of pages of advertising, a barometer of a magazine's financial health, had slipped badly. From a peak of 118 pages of advertising per weekly issue in 1966, the *New Yorker* was attracting only 39 ad pages by 1992. One analyst estimated losses at $15 million a year. At ad agencies, which decide where to place their clients' advertising, the word was that the *New Yorker* was admired but little read. Worse, the *New Yorker* audience was getting older. The average age was 44, and most advertisers were seeking people in their free-spending 30s.

This was all of great concern to Newhouse, which had no intention of presiding over the *New Yorker*'s demise. In 1992, Newhouse put a new editor in charge: Tina Brown, age 38, a British expatriate who had quadrupled the circulation of London's *Tatler* before moving stateside to take over the floundering *Vanity Fair.* The appointment staggered *New Yorker* loyalists who foresaw Brown using her proven formula of gushy celebrity profiles, articles on trendy subjects and provocative photos to remake the *New Yorker.*

To critics, Brown affirmed her respect for the *New Yorker* as a word-driven magazine and asserted that it would remain so—a home for good writing and reporting, not visual gimmickry. Her challenge, however, was to break new ground and to attract the younger readers advertisers wanted to reach and, at the same time, not lose the existing readership.

Brown hired an art director, which is common at magazines but which the *New Yorker* had never done. She put photographs into the magazine for the first time—color too. Some foreign correspondents were let go, and short columns on topical issues began appearing regularly. This marked the end of the magazine's historic total commitment to timeless as opposed to topical treatments of issues. Timeless stories remained part of the mix, but Brown pushed for what she called "hot, snappy" treatments.

She also mixed articles and ads, which earlier had been kept in distinct parts of the magazine. This drew criticism from loyalists who saw Madison Avenue buying favorable treatment in stories. Patti Hagen, who once worked at the *New Yorker,* put it this way: "I'm turned off by Marky Mark having sex in Calvin Klein's ads at the front of the magazine, followed a few weeks later by an interview with Marky Mark about his underwear ads. This would never have happened at the old *New Yorker.*"

Humorist Garrison Keillor left the magazine over Brown's changes, especially her shift to trendiness: "The *New Yorker* is a glorious and dear American institution, but Ms. Brown, like so many Brits, seems fascinated by the passing carnival and celebrity show in America. Fiction, serious reporting, the personal essay, criticism, all that made the *New Yorker* great, do not engage her interest apparently. She has redesigned it into a magazine that looks and reads an awful lot like a hundred other magazines."

Despite her critics, Brown is increasing the *New Yorker*'s audience. Some 20,000 copies are purchased on New York newsracks now, compared to 6,000 before. Also, in 1993, when many magazines were losing ad pages, Brown's *New Yorker* was scoring a 5 percent increase. The *New Yorker* is moving toward profitability, which pleases the $11 billion Newhouse conglomerate, whose interests include 29 newspapers, 14 magazines, Random House books and myriad local cable companies.

The story of Tina Brown and the *New Yorker* illustrates several key points about the magazine business. Magazines in general, including the *New Yorker,* have been significant contributors to American culture, but time doesn't stand still. As Si Newhouse said in appointing Brown: "Every magazine has to evolve. Readers change. Times change. Interests change. There is no such thing as a static magazine." The recent history of the *New Yorker* under Brown also demonstrates a fundamental reality of most American mass media: They must find the right audience to attract enough advertisers to be profitable to their owners.

- -

THE INFLUENCE OF MAGAZINES

STUDY PREVIEW Today, as through their whole history, magazines are a mass medium through which the distinctive American culture is brought to a national audience. The periodicals pack great literature and ideas into formats that, unlike books, almost anybody can afford. Magazines are also a national unifier because they offer manufacturers a nationwide audience for their goods.

CONTRIBUTING TO NATIONHOOD

The first successful magazines in the United States, in the 1820s, were much less expensive than books. People of ordinary means could afford them. Unlike newspapers, which were oriented to their cities of publication, early magazines created national audiences. This contributed to a sense of nationhood at a time when an American culture, distinctive from its European heritage, had not yet emerged. The American people had their magazines in common. The *Saturday Evening Post*, founded in 1821, carried fiction by Edgar Allan Poe, Nathaniel Hawthorne and

TEACHING OBJECTIVE 3-1
Magazines contribute to the national culture.

LECTURE RESOURCE 3-A
Video: *News Leaders.*

Harriet Beecher Stowe to readers who could not afford books. Their short stories and serialized novels flowed from the American experience and helped Americans establish a national identity.

With the *Postal Act of 1879*, Congress recognized the role of magazines in creating a national culture and promoting literacy—in effect, binding the nation. The law allowed a discount on mailing rates for magazines, a penny a pound. Magazines were being subsidized, which reduced distribution costs and sparked dramatic circulation growth. New magazines cropped up as a result.

A National Advertising Medium

TEACHING OBJECTIVE 3-2
Magazines helped create national markets.

Advertisers used magazines through the 1800s to build national markets for their products, which was an important factor in transforming the United States from an agricultural and cottage industry economy into a modern economy. This too contributed to a sense of nationhood. The other mass media could not do that as effectively. Few books carried advertisements, and newspapers, with few exceptions, delivered only local readership to advertisers.

Massive Magazine Audience

The American people have a tremendous appetite for magazines. According to magazine industry studies, almost 90 percent of U.S. adults read an average 10 magazine issues a month. While magazines are affordable for most people, the household income of the typical reader is 5 percent more than the national average. In general, the more education and higher income a person has, the greater the person's magazine consumption. A 1989 study by the Magazine Research Institute found:

- Of people who have been to college, 94 percent read at least one magazine issue a month, and, as a group, they average 11.1 issues a month.
- Of people whose annual household income exceeds $40,000, 93 percent read at least one issue a month and average 11.1 issues.
- Of people in professional and managerial jobs, 95 percent read at least one issue a month and average 13.3.

In short, magazines are a pervasive mass medium. Magazines, however, are not only for the upper crust. Many magazines are edited for "downscale" audiences, which means the medium's role in society is spread across almost the whole range of people with literacy skills. Even illiterates can derive some pleasure and value from magazines, which by and large are visual and colorful.

The massiveness of the audience makes the magazine an exceptionally competitive medium. About 12,000 publications vie for readers in the United States, ranging from general-interest publications like *Reader's Digest* to such specialized publications as *Chili Pepper,* for people interested in hot foods, and *Spur,* for racehorse aficionados. In recent years, 500 to 600 new titles have been launched annually, although only one in five survives into the third year. Even among major magazines, a huge following at the moment is no guarantee of survival. Of the 23 U.S. magazines with a circulation of more than 1 million in 1946, 10 no longer exist. Magazine publishing is a risky business.

MAGAZINES AS MEDIA INNOVATORS

STUDY PREVIEW   Magazines have led other media with significant innovations in journalism, advertising and circulation. These include investigative reporting, in-depth personality profiles and photojournalism.

INVESTIGATIVE REPORTING

Muckraking, usually called "investigative reporting" today, was honed by magazines as a journalistic approach in the first years of the 20th century. Magazines ran lengthy explorations of abusive institutions in the society. It was *Theodore Roosevelt,* the reform president, who coined the term "muckraking." Roosevelt generally enjoyed investigative journalism, but one day in 1906, when the digging got too close to home, he likened it to the work of a character in a 17th-century novel who focused so much on raking muck that he missed the good news. The president meant the term derisively, but it came to be a badge of honor among journalists.

Muckraking established magazines as a powerful medium in shaping public policy. In 1902 *Ida Tarbell* wrote a 19-part series on the Standard Oil monopoly for *McClure's.* Tarbell's revelations fueled the trust-busting thunder of the Roosevelt administration. *Lincoln Steffens* detailed municipal corruption, and reforms followed. Other magazines picked up investigative thrusts. *Collier's* took on patent medicine frauds. *Cosmopolitan,* a leading muckraking journal of the period, tackled dishonesty in the U.S. Senate. Muckraking expanded to books with *Upton Sinclair's The Jungle.* Sinclair shocked the nation by detailing filth in meat-packing plants. Federal inspection laws resulted. Later newspapers joined muckraking, but it was magazines that had led the way.

TEACHING OBJECTIVE 3-3
Many media innovations were pioneered by magazines.

KEY PERSON
Theodore Roosevelt coined the term *Muckraking.*

KEY PEOPLE
Among early muckrakers were Upton Sinclair, Lincoln Steffens and Ida Tarbell. See Index.

PERSONALITY PROFILES

The in-depth *personality profile* was a magazine invention. In the 1920s *Harold Ross* of the *New Yorker* began pushing writers to a thoroughness that was new in journalism. They used multiple interviews with a range of sources—talking not only with the subject of the profile but with just about everyone and anyone who could comment on the subject, including the subject's friends and enemies. Such depth required weeks, sometimes months of journalistic digging. It's not uncommon now in newspapers, broadcasting or magazines, but before Harold Ross, it didn't exist.

Under *Hugh Hefner, Playboy* took the interview in new directions in 1962 with in-depth profiles developed from a highly structured question-and-answer format. The *Playboy* Q-A format became widely imitated.

PHOTOJOURNALISM

Magazines brought *visuals* to the mass media in a way books never had. *Harper's Weekly* sent artists to Civil War battles, leading the way to journalism that went beyond words.

The young editor of the *National Geographic, Gilbert Grosvenor,* drew a map proposing a route to the South Pole for an 1899 issue, putting the *Geographic* on the road to being a visually oriented magazine. For subsequent issues, Grosvenor borrowed government plates to reproduce photos, and he encouraged travelers to submit their photographs to the magazine. This was at a time when most magazines scorned photographs. However, Grosvenor was undeterred as an advocate for

LECTURE RESOURCE 3-B
Slides: Charles Lewis, *Pictures of Past: Visual Reporting During Civil War.*

Photojournalism Innovator. The *National Geographic,* a sponsored membership magazine, has been a leader in photographic coverage. A 1903 photo of a bare-breasted Filipino woman irked some people, but the *Geographic* defended itself as showing the peoples of the world as the maga-

documentary photography, and membership in the National Geographic Society, a prerequisite for receiving the magazine, swelled. Eventually the magazine assembled its own staff of photographers and gradually became a model for other publications that discovered they needed to play catch-up.

Aided by technological advances involving smaller, more portable cameras and faster film capable of recording images under extreme conditions, photographers working for the *Geographic* opened a whole new world of documentary coverage to their readers. Among *Geographic* accomplishments were:

***Life* Defined America.** The giant general-interest magazines like *Life* gave meaning to the word "photojournalism." The grisliness of war was indelible in George Strock's shot of G.I.s felled in their steps on New Guinea in World War II. After the war, *Life* chronicled suburbanization of America with photo and text coverage of Leavittown.

zine found them. In 1911 the *Geographic* demonstrated with a dramatic 17-page foldout of the Canadian Rockies that format need not limit photojournalism's portrayal of the world. The magazine also has led in underwater color and dramatic aviation and space photography.

- A photo of a bare-breasted Filipino woman field-worker shocked some *Geographic* readers in 1903, but Grosvenor persisted against Victorian sensitivities to show the peoples of the world as they lived.
- The first photographs from Tibet, by Russian explorers, appeared in 1905 in an 11-page spread, extraordinary visual coverage for the time that confirmed photography's role in journalism.
- A 17-page, eight-foot foldout panorama of the Canadian Rockies in 1911 showed that photojournalism need not be limited by format.

Photojournalism Arrives. The oversize pages of *Life*, which opened to 13½ x 21 inches, did justice to great photography. Margaret Bourke-White's medieval tones captured the immensity of Fort Peck Dam under construction in Montana for the cover of the inaugural issue. Bourke-White became a star photographer for *Life*. She was among a handful of women journalists who covered World War II for American readers.

Margaret Bourke-White

■ The magazine's 100th anniversary cover in 1988 was the first hologram, a three-dimensional photograph, ever published in a mass-audience magazine. It was a significant production accomplishment.

Life magazine brought American photojournalism to new importance in the 1930s. The oversize pages of the magazine gave new intensity to photographs, and the magazine, a weekly, demonstrated that newsworthy events could be covered consistently by camera. *Life* captured the spirit of the times photographically and demonstrated that the whole range of human experience could be recorded visually. Both real life and *Life* could be shocking. A 1938 *Life* spread on human birth was so shocking for the time that censors succeeded in banning the issue in 33 cities.

CONSUMER MAGAZINES

STUDY PREVIEW The most visible category of magazines is general-interest magazines, which are available on newsracks and by subscription. Called *consumer magazines*, these include publications like *Reader's Digest* that try to offer something for everybody, as well as magazines edited for narrower audiences.

CIRCULATION LEADERS

TEACHING OBJECTIVE 3-4
To identify leading U.S. magazines.

LECTURE RESOURCE 3-C
Class exercise: Students inspect magazines to identify different audiences.

Reader's Digest is usually considered to have the largest circulation of any U.S. magazine, selling 16.4 million copies a month, not counting foreign editions. However, *Reader's Digest*'s lead in circulation is not technically correct because the circulation of the Sunday newspaper supplement *Parade* is twice that. Also, there have been periods, although none recently, when *TV Guide* outdid the *Digest*. In recent years, with the graying of America, the magazine *Modern Maturity*, which is sent to members of the American Association of Retired Persons every two months, has reached a circulation of 22.5 million, considerably ahead of *Reader's Digest*.

The common notion that *Reader's Digest* is the largest magazine stems from its attempt to serve a true mass audience. Unlike *Modern Maturity*, the *Digest*'s easy-to-read articles cut across divisions of age, gender, occupation and geography. *Reader's Digest* is a mass magazine in the truest sense of the word. It tries in every issue to have something for everybody. The Sunday newspaper supplements are also edited for a truly mass audience.

Led by *Reader's Digest*, about 1,200 magazines are published in the United States for newsrack and subscription sales. A few, including newsmagazines, deal with subjects of general interest. Most, however, have a narrower focus, such as *Motor Trend*, which is geared toward automobile enthusiasts; *Forbes*, which appeals to business people and investors; and *Family Circle*, which targets homemakers.

One thing that consumer magazines have in common is a heavy reliance on advertising. Exceptions include *Consumer Reports*, which wants to be above any suspicion that advertisers influence its reporting; the satire magazine *Mad*, whose editors like doing things their own way; the nondenominational magazine *Guideposts*; and the feminist *Ms.*, which lost advertising support in the late 1980s, shut down and then was revived as an ad-free magazine at $6 a copy, with readers picking up all the expenses.

NEWSMAGAZINES

Fresh out of Yale in 1923, classmates *Henry Luce* and *Briton Hadden* begged and borrowed $86,000 from friends and relatives and launched a new kind of magazine: *Time*. The magazine provided summaries of news by categories such as national affairs, sports and business. It took four years for *Time* to turn a profit, and some people doubted that the magazine would ever make money, noting that it merely rehashed what daily newspapers had already reported. Readers, however, came to like the handy compilation and the sprightly, often irreverent writing style that set *Time* apart.

The *Time* style, which came to be dubbed *Timespeak*, was carefully crafted by Luce and Hadden to give the magazine the tone of a single, knowledgeable, authoritative individual recapping the week's events and issues. *Timespeak*, which continues as part of *Time*'s personality, has two components:

- A snappy, informal, sometimes sassy writing style that includes calling people by unflattering nicknames, such as Scarface. To the consternation of English teachers everywhere, the style also took liberties with the English language, such as the reversed attributive "said Jones" instead of "Jones said." Testimony to *Time*'s impact on the culture is that reversed attributives are commonly accepted today in even the most formal writing.

TEACHING OBJECTIVE 3-5
Magazines are categorized by competitive categories, including news magazines, Sunday supplements, women's magazines.

KEY PERSON
Henry Luce founded *Time*, then *Life*, *Sports Illustrated* and *Fortune*. See Index.

KEY PEOPLE
DeWitt and Lila Wallace founded *Reader's Digest*.

MEDIA: PEOPLE

DeWitt and Lila Wallace

DeWitt and Lila Wallace had an idea, but hardly any money. The idea was a pocket-sized magazine that condensed informational, inspiring and entertaining nonfiction from other publications—a digest. With borrowed money, the Wallaces brought out their first issue of *Reader's Digest* in 1922.

The rest, as they say, is history. In 1947 the *Digest* became the first magazine to exceed a circulation of 9 million. Except for the Sunday newspaper supplement *Parade*, *Reader's Digest* has been the nation's largest-circulation magazine most of the time since then. In 1990, *Reader's Digest*'s circulation was 16.4 million—not counting an additional 12.2 million overseas in 18 languages.

The magazine has remained true to the Wallaces' successful formula. DeWitt and Lila Wallace, children of poor Presbyterian clergy, wanted "constructive articles," each with universal appeal. The thrust was upbeat but not Pollyanna. Digested as they were, the articles were quickly read. America loved it. More than 90 percent of *Reader's Digest* circulation is by subscription, representing long-term reader commitment.

For its first 33 years, *Reader's Digest* was wholly reader supported. It carried no advertising. Rising postal rates forced a change in 1955. There was scoffing about whether advertisers would go for "postage-stamp-sized ads" in *Reader's Digest* with its minipages, but the scoffers were wrong. The people who decide where to place advertisements never doubted that *Reader's Digest* was well read. Today, advertisers—except for cigarette manufacturers—pay more than $100,000 a page for a color advertisement. Consistent with the Wallaces' standards, cigarette advertisements are not accepted and never have been.

MEDIA DATABANK

Largest Magazines

These are the circulation leaders among United States magazines. The figures do not include foreign editions, which add substantial circulation for some magazines. *Reader's Digest*, for example, publishes 40 editions in 18 languages for 12.2 million copies a month in addition to 16.3 million in the United States.

Monthlies	
Reader's Digest	16.3 million
National Geographic	9.7 million
Better Homes & Gardens	8.0 million
Family Circle	5.3 million
Good Housekeeping	5.1 million
Consumer Reports	5.0 million
Ladies' Home Journal	5.0 million
Woman's Day	4.8 million
McCall's	4.7 million
Guideposts	3.6 million
Redbook	3.4 million
Playboy	3.4 million
Prevention	3.2 million
American Legion	3.0 million
Cosmopolitan	2.7 million
Highlights for Children	2.6 million
Southern Living	2.4 million
Smithsonian	2.2 million
Money	2.1 million
Field & Stream	2.0 million
Glamour	2.0 million
Ebony	1.9 million
Country Living	1.8 million
Home & Away	1.8 million
Life	1.8 million

Motorland	1.8 million
NEA Today	1.8 million
Penthouse	1.8 million
Popular Science	1.8 million
Seventeen	1.8 million
VFW Magazine	1.8 million
Bimonthlies	
Modern Maturity	22.9 million
Sunday Supplements	
Parade	36.3 million
USA Weekend	16.2 million
Biweeklies	
Rolling Stone	1.2 million
Weeklies	
TV Guide	14.5 million
Cable Guide	5.9 million
Time	4.2 million
People	3.5 million
National Enquirer	3.4 million
Sports Illustrated	3.4 million
Newsweek	3.2 million
U.S. News & World Report	2.3 million

■ *Time* articles at first were written by a relatively small group of editors who strived for a consistent style and tone. Even after the magazine built a staff of reporters and stationed them around the globe, reporters seldom wrote stories. Instead, they wrote memos on what they considered important, and those memos, chock full of information, quotations and comments, went to the magazine's editors in New York. The editors, after deciding what subjects to cover in the next issue, would put together stories from the reporter's field memos and other sources, such as newspaper and news service accounts. Still today, it is largely those editor-written stories, carefully controlled as to tone and style, that end up in the magazine.

A copycat, *Newsweek*, appeared in 1933. So did a third newsweekly, *U.S. News*, the forerunner to today's *U.S. News & World Report*. Despite the competition, *Time*, with 4 million copies weekly, has consistently led the newsmagazine field.

While *Time, Newsweek* and *U.S. News & World Report* cover a broad range of subjects, specialized newsmagazines focus on narrower subjects. The largest category is those featuring celebrity news, including the gossipy sort. The supermarket tabloid *National Enquirer* focuses on the rich and famous, hyped-up medical research and sensational oddball news and is an incredible commercial success.

While the *National Enquirer* treads the line between being a magazine and being a newspaper, its numerous imitators include publications that are distinctly magazines. In 1974 Time-Life created the consumer magazine *People*, aimed at the same supermarket checkout-line customers as the *National Enquirer*. *People*, however, concentrates on celebrities and avoids much of the *National Enquirer*'s blatant rumor mongering and sensationalism.

People proved a quick success and also spawned a slew of imitators. Even the New York Times Company joined the bandwagon with *Us*. Together the celebrity-focused magazines robbed circulation from the sensationalistic tabloids. By 1992 *People*'s circulation was 3.4 million. The *National Enquirer* remained ahead at 3.8 million, but that was down from its 5 million-plus peak.

SUNDAY NEWSPAPER SUPPLEMENTS

Sometimes overlooked as magazines are *Parade* and *USA Weekend*, the independently produced supplements that newspapers buy and stuff inside their Sunday editions. They are designed for general family reading.

The Sunday supplements have built-in advantages over other magazines. Readers neither subscribe nor buy them directly. The supplements need only convince a newspaper to carry them, and they have instant circulation. *Parade*'s circulation exceeds 36 million, which, technically speaking, makes it easily the largest magazine in the nation. *USA Weekend* has a circulation in excess of 16 million.

WOMEN'S MAGAZINES

The first U.S. magazine edited to interest only a portion of the mass audience, but otherwise to be of general interest, was *Godey's Lady's Book*. It was started by *Sarah Josepha Hale* in 1830 to uplift and glorify womanhood. Its advice on fashions, morals, taste, sewing and cooking developed a following, which peaked with a circulation of 150,000. The *Godey's* tradition is maintained today in seven competing magazines known as the *Seven Sisters* because of their female following: *Better Homes & Gardens, Family Circle, Good Housekeeping, Ladies' Home Journal, McCall's, Redbook* and *Woman's Day*. While each sister can be distinguished from her siblings, there is a thematic connection: concern for home, family and quality living from a traditional woman's perspective.

An eighth sister is *Cosmopolitan*, although more aptly it is a distant cousin. Under Helen Gurley Brown, *Cosmopolitan* has geared itself to a subcategory of women readers—young, unmarried and working. It's the most successful in a large group of women's magazines seeking narrow groups. Among them are *Elle*, focusing on fashion; *Playgirl*, with its soft pornography; *Mirabella*, which mixes fashion and social issues; *Essence*, for black women; *Seventeen*, for teenage girls; and *Self*, for women of the "me generation."

LECTURE RESOURCE 3-D
Slides: Barbara Reed, *Women's Magazines in 1970's.*

KEY PERSON
Sarah Josepha Hale launched first women's magazine.

KEY PERSON
Helen Gurley Brown was innovator in demassifying women's magazines.

MEN'S MAGAZINES

Founded in 1933, *Esquire* was the first classy men's magazine. It was as famous for its pin-ups as its literary content, which over the years has included articles from Ernest Hemingway, John Dos Passos and Gay Talese. Fashion has also been a cornerstone in the *Esquire* content mix.

Hugh Hefner learned about magazines as an *Esquire* staff member, and he applied those lessons when he created *Playboy* in 1953. With its lustier tone, *Playboy* quickly overtook *Esquire* in circulation. At its peak, *Playboy* sold 7 million copies a month. The magazine emphasized female nudity but also carried journalistic and literary pieces whose merit attracted many readers. Readers embarrassed by their carnal curiosity could claim they bought the magazine for its articles. Critics sniped, however, that *Playboy* published the worst stuff of the best writers.

Playboy imitators added raunch—some a little, some a lot. The most successful, Bob Guccione's *Penthouse*, has never attracted as many readers or advertisers as *Playboy*, but it has been a success.

Social observers credit Hefner with capitalizing on the post–World War II sexual revolution in the United States and fanning it. A moral backlash developed in the mid-1980s, and *Playboy* and other sex-oriented men's magazines suffered. The major blow was the 1986 decision by 7-Eleven convenience stores to discontinue selling *skin magazines*. Seven-Eleven was the largest among retail outlets that responded to pressure from moralists and the presidential Meese Commission on Pornography. The 7-Eleven decision especially hurt *Penthouse*, which relied on newsrack sales more than *Playboy*, but *Playboy* was hurt too. *Playboy*'s circulation dipped to 3.5 million and *Penthouse*'s to 1.8 million. Both have recovered some circulation but still are far short of their peaks. With less circulation, they have had to adjust advertising rates downward. Also, they have lost some advertisers who had been attracted by the earlier large circulations.

Not all men's magazines dwell on sex. The outdoor life is exalted in *Field & Stream*, whose circulation tops 2 million. Fix-it magazines, led by *Popular Science* and *Popular Mechanics*, have a steady following.

MAGAZINES FOR THE INTELLIGENTSIA

Magazines such as *Harper's* and *Atlantic* that approach issues cerebrally are *high-brow slicks*. Articles are exploratory and essayish. Fiction is included. The nonfiction focuses in depth on literary, cultural and political issues. Both *Harper's* and *Atlantic* have grand traditions going back to the 1850s, but their recent financial history has been weak. *Harper's* has survived only with cash infusions from philanthropists.

Ideologues can choose among many *opinion magazines*, none of which have achieved great circulation but whose influence has been as a forum for dialogue in pressing various issues. The *New Republic, Nation* and *Progressive* have liberal traditions, William Buckley's *National Review* a conservative one. For opinion magazines, making ends meet is difficult. Buckley's *National Review* typically loses $100,000 a year.

NON-NEWSRACK MAGAZINES

STUDY PREVIEW   Many organizations publish magazines for their members. While these sponsored magazines, including *National Geographic, Modern Maturity* and *Smithsonian,* resemble consumer magazines, they generally are not available at newsracks. In fact, consumer magazines are far outnumbered by sponsored magazines and by trade journals.

SPONSORED MAGAZINES

The founders of the National Geographic Society decided in 1888 to put out a magazine to promote the society and build membership. The idea was to entice people to join by bundling a subscription with membership and then to use the dues to finance the society's research and expeditions. Within a few years, the *National Geographic* had become a phenomenal success both in generating membership and as a profit center for the National Geographic Society. Today, more than 100 years old and with U.S. circulation near 10 million, the *Geographic* is the most widely recognized sponsored magazine in the nation. Other sponsored magazines include *Modern Maturity*, published by the American Association of Retired People for its members. Its circulation exceeds 22 million. Other major membership magazines include *Smithsonian*, by the Smithsonian Institute; *VFW*, by the Veterans of Foreign Wars; *American Legion;* and *Elks*, by the Elks Lodge.

Many sponsored magazines carry advertising and are financially self-sufficient. In fact, the most successful sponsored magazines compete aggressively with consumer magazines for advertising. In 1991 *National Geographic's* advertising staff put together an elaborate pitch to the Ford Motor Company for more of its ads. Impressed with the *Geographic's* readership data, Ford increased its *Geographic* advertising for 1992 models by 250 percent—at a time when Ford was cutting back overall in magazine advertising. It is not unusual for an issue of *Smithsonian* to carry 100 pages of advertising.

While advertising has made sponsored magazines into profit centers for their parent organizations, others come nowhere near breaking even. Typical is *Quill*,

TEACHING OBJECTIVE 3-6
To distinguish consumer magazines from sponsored magazines and trade journals.

which the Society of Professional Journalists publishes as an organizational expense for the good of its membership. The society seeks advertising for *Quill*, but the magazine's relatively small readership has never attracted as much volume or the type of advertising as the *National Geographic*, the *Smithsonian* or *Modern Maturity*.

Many sponsored magazines do not seek advertising. These include many university magazines, which are considered something that a university should publish as an institutional expense to disseminate information about research and scholarly activities and, not incidentally, to promote itself. Other sponsored magazines that typically do not carry advertising include publications for union members, in-house publications for employees, and company publications for customers. These publications, which number more than 11,000 nationwide, do not have the public recognition of consumer magazines, but many are as slick and professional as consumer magazines. All together, they employ far more editors, photographers and writers than consumer magazines.

TRADE JOURNALS

LECTURE RESOURCE 3-E
Video: *Editorial Careers in Specialized Business Press*.

Everyone in a profession or trade has at least one magazine for keeping abreast of what is happening in the field. In entertainment, *Billboard* provides a solid journalistic coverage on a broad range of subjects in music: new recording releases, new acts, new technology, new merger deals and so forth. *Billboard*, a trade journal, is essential reading for people in the industry. About 4,000 trade journals cover a mind-boggling range of businesses and trades. Consider the diversity in these titles: *Rock and Dirt, Progressive Grocer, Plastics Technology, Hogs Today* and *Hardware Age*.

Like consumer magazines, the "trades" rely mostly on advertising for their income and profits. Some charge for subscriptions, but many are sent free to a carefully culled list of readers whom advertisers want to reach. As an example, listed below are major advertisers in *Broadcasting*, a trade journal for people with radio, television and cable jobs:

- King World, promoting "Jeopardy," the television game show, which it sells to television stations.
- Americom, a brokerage and financing company for radio station buyers.
- Sony, promoting industrial-quality video equipment for on-air editing and field production.

Many trade magazines are parts of companies that produce related publications, some with overlapping staffs. McGraw-Hill, the book publisher, produces more than 30 trade journals, including *Chemical Week* and *Modern Hospital*. Another trade magazine company is Crain Communications, whose titles include *Advertising Age, AutoWeek, Electronic Media* and two dozen other trades.

CRITICISM OF TRADE MAGAZINES

Many trade magazine companies, including McGraw-Hill and Crain, have reputations for honest, hard-hitting reporting of the industries they cover, but the trades have a mixed reputation. Some trade magazines are loaded with puffery exalting their advertisers and industries. For years, *Body Fashions*, formerly *Corset and Underwear Review*, unabashedly presented ads as news stories. As many trade journals do, it charged companies to run stories about them and covered only companies that were also advertisers. At some trades, the employees who solicit ads write news stories that echo the ads. These trades tend to be no more than boosters of the industries they pretend to cover. Kent MacDougall, writing in the *Wall Street Journal*, offered this especially egregious example: *America's Textile Reporter*, which promoted the textile industry from a management perspective, once dismissed the hazard of textile workers' contracting brown lung disease by inhaling cotton dust as "a thing brought up by venal doctors" at an international labor meeting in Africa, "where inferior races are bound to be afflicted by new diseases more superior people defeated years ago." At the time, in 1972, 100,000 U.S. textiles workers were afflicted with brown lung. Many trade magazines persist today in pandering to their trades, professions and industries, rather than approaching their subjects with journalistic truth-seeking and truth-telling.

Responsible trade journals are embarrassed by some of their brethren, many of which are upstarts put out by people with no journalistic experience or instincts. Because of this, and also because it takes relatively little capital to start a trade magazine, many bad trade magazines thrive. Several trade magazine professional organizations, including the American Business Press and the Society of Business Press Editors, work to improve both their industry and its image. Even so, as former ABP President Charles Mill said, trades continue to be plagued "by fleabag outfits published in somebody's garage."

Trade magazines covering the mass media include reputable, journalistically respectable *Advertising Age*, from Crain; *AdWeek*, from McGraw-Hill; *Billboard*, for the music industry; *Broadcasting/Cable; Editor & Publisher*, for the newspaper industry; *Folio*, for the magazine industry; *Publisher's Weekly*, for the book industry; and *Variety*, for the entertainment industry.

MAGAZINE GLOBALIZATION

STUDY PREVIEW Many magazines are seeking readers and revenue beyond their national borders. Some have created foreign editions, each with distinctive editorial content and advertising. More magazines are establishing foreign editions, and the growing number of multinational media companies is accelerating the trend.

EXPORTED MAGAZINES

With their *Reader's Digest* a phenomenal success in the United States and with a growing list of subscribers abroad, DeWitt and Lila Wallace decided in 1938 to set up a London office and launch a foreign edition. By the end of World War II, *Digest* circulation reached 9 million in the United States and 4 million overseas. Meanwhile, *National Geographic* also found an international following.

The potential of foreign editions was not lost on other major U.S. magazines, and today *Cosmopolitan, Newsweek* and *Time* derive substantial revenue from international editions. With the development of the global economy, *Business Week, Fortune* and *Forbes* have gone with a variety of editions to build an international audience, and the *Playboy* and *Penthouse* men's magazines have increased their readership with international editions. In 1991 Hearst bought out United Kingdom editions of *Esquire* and *Vanity Fair*. The leader, however, remains *Reader's Digest*, which is published in 18 languages and sells more than 12.2 million copies abroad.

TEACHING OBJECTIVE 3-7
Global magazine conglomeration is occurring.

MEDIA ABROAD

Spanish Celebrity Magazine

In the darkest period of Spanish fascism, Antonio Sanchez Gomez wanted to start a magazine, but the intolerant, humorless Franco dictatorship was an obstacle. What kind of magazine would survive the government's scrutiny? Sanchez settled on a four-page gossip sheet with upbeat stories on celebrities. Called *¡Hola!,* the colorful sheet introduced a bit of gaiety into the drab Spanish life of late World War II, albeit a fantasy version of celebrity life. Quickly it found a following.

Today, *¡Hola!* remains true to its original formula, fawning over movie stars, royalty and jet-setters with incessant flattery. Typically selling 600,000 copies, *¡Hola!* pulls in more advertising revenue than any other Spanish weekly.

Now *¡Hola!* is being exported. A British edition that began in 1990 has a 450,000 circulation and is growing, and the current publisher, Eduardo Sanchez Junco, is testing the waters for an edition in the United States. In 1993, Sanchez placed

ads in New York and Los Angeles newspapers, offering a free copy of the British edition, which had an at-home interview with actress Elizabeth Taylor, to anyone who wrote in. Sanchez says 30,000 people responded. That fueled his enthusiasm for a possible joint venture with a U.S. magazine company.

There is no question that celebrity coverage sells, as seen in the commercial success of the *National Enquirer* and *People* magazines. But *¡Hola!* is different. *¡Hola!*'s coverage skips the naughty escapades and scandals that are the bread and butter of most celebrity magazines and puts a glamorous although not balanced spin to its stories. Roula Khalaf, writing in *Forbes* magazine, said: "Like a fawning portrait painter who omits warts and bumps, *¡Hola!* paints only sweet, flattering accounts of celebs who never sweat and are always in good taste."

Foreign editions are not mere rehashes or translations of U.S. editions. *Reader's Digest* discovered early that some articles of interest to American readers were offensive abroad. In the 1960s, many U.S. articles on the civil rights movement, including "Why Negroes Riot," did not go into the edition for racially segregated South Africa. In deference to Roman Catholicism, *Digest* editions in heavily Catholic areas, including France, Germany, Ireland, Italy, Latin America and French Canada, did not carry articles on birth control. The *Digest's* fervent anti-Communism, a mainstay in home editions, was skipped in the Finland edition, whose readers, not to mention the government, feared their Soviet neighbor.

Newsweek and *Time* also offer distinctive content in their foreign editions. Editors boil down domestic U.S. news and carry more coverage from their foreign staffs. The rules on advertising acceptability are geared to local mores. Liquor and certain pharmaceutical ads are not accepted for some editions.

TRANSNATIONAL MAGAZINE OWNERSHIP

The international ownership of a growing number of media companies can be expected to bring more foreign magazines to the United States and also to send more U.S. magazines abroad. The French company Hachette, which publishes 74 magazines in 10 countries, entered the U.S. magazine business in 1988 by buying CBS's magazines, including *Woman's Day* with a circulation of 4.4 million. Soon Hachette launched a U.S. edition of its French *Elle* fashion magazine and followed it with *Elle Home*. Twenty-five foreign companies either own outright or have an ownership interest in U.S. magazines, more than a 10-fold increase since 1980. Among the most significant is Hachette, whose U.S. titles, besides *Woman's Day* and *Elle*, include *Car & Driver*, *Road & Track*, *Popular Photography*, *Stereo Review* and *Home*. Gruner & Jahr, a subsidiary of the German media conglomerate Bertelsmann, publishes *Parents* and *YM* (formerly *Young Miss*). News Corp., owned by Australian-born *Rupert Murdoch*, publishes *TV Guide*. Until 1991 Murdoch owned eight other U.S. magazines, including *Automobile*, *Premiere*, *Seventeen* and *Soap Opera Digest*, but then, overextended and needing cash, he sold them to a U.S. investment group.

COOPERATIVE INTERNATIONAL ARRANGEMENTS

To gain experience in new markets and to reduce risk, magazine companies go into joint ventures. Time Warner and Hachette have teamed for a French edition of *Fortune*. Time Warner joined with a Milan company for an Italian edition of *Time*. Hachette is in a joint agreement with a Shanghai publishing house for the Chinese edition of *Elle* in Chinese and with a Moscow publishing house for a Russian-language edition of *Paris Match* (without the prefix *Paris*). The Hungarian edition of *Penthouse* is published under license to a Swiss company. With a Hong Kong company, *Forbes* is producing an edition aimed at the 40 million Chinese who do not live on the still-closed mainland. *Newsweek* has an arrangement with the Australian newsmagazine *Bulletin*.

The first U.S. and Western European magazines into the former Soviet Union during the perestroika reforms had to forge special arrangements because dealings had to be in rubles, which could not be taken out of the country. The Russian-language edition of *Scientific American* was published through a royalty arrangement with a government agency. The Russian-language *Business Week* is a joint venture with a Moscow publisher.

Major magazine publishers worldwide are anxious to position themselves as the choice of advertisers for internationally marketed goods. The potential is obvious with the democratization and capitalistic reforms in the former Soviet bloc, the economic unification of Europe and the growing international commerce in consumer goods.

Reader's Digest in Russian

One hundred thousand people in the Ukrainian city of Kharkov opened their mail in August 1991 to find a four-page flier announcing that "the world's most popular journal" soon would be available. The flier marked the entry of *Reader's Digest,* that homey embodiment of conservative, middle-class American values, into areas that were once part of the closed Soviet empire. A few days later, 50,000 copies of the 160-page debut issue were delivered to newsracks in Kharkov, Kiev, St. Petersburg and Moscow, and they sold out. The people liked the mix of brief articles on international life, health and psychology. The press run soon was increased to 100,000.

Although the Russian-language *Reader's Digest* sells for the ruble equivalent of $1.50, twice as much as most Russian magazines, the Reader's Digest Association of Pleasantville, New York, was not seeking early profits. Start-up and distribution costs were high, and the inaugural issue carried a mere five pages of advertising—from Coca-Cola, Colgate toothpaste, Pepsi-Cola, Smirnoff vodka and Toshiba televisions.

The marketing-savvy *Reader's Digest* organization viewed the Russian-language edition as an investment. The company wanted to learn how to reach mass audiences in the former Soviet Union with the goal eventually of selling not only magazines but also books, music and other products.

Mass mailing, a key to the success of *Reader's Digest* elsewhere, is a special challenge in the former Soviet republics. Not only are the mails slow and unreliable, but the remnants of the notorious Soviet black market system include the postal structure, which swallows attractive products, including slick, colorful magazines, before they reach addressees. Instead of being mailed to subscribers, Russian *Reader's Digests* are sent to newsracks individually, where clerks hold copies for subscribers.

Thievery in the postal system even cuts into mailings of subscription offers, which prompted the decision to stick to black-and-white fliers for advertising *Reader's Digest.* To distribute books, tapes and other products at some future date, the company assumes it may need to go with unadorned plain brown wrappers.

A key to the Reader's Digest Association's marketing success with mass mailing elsewhere has been computerized, cross-indexed mailing lists that match people with the products they are likeliest to order. In the former Soviet Union, where consumer mailing lists are virtually nonexistent, that aspect of marketing is starting from scratch.

While early issues produced hardly any advertising revenue—only $6,000 a page—the Reader's Digest Association was not unmindful that the introduction of capitalism in the old Soviet Union meant advertising could become a profit center some day.

MAGAZINE DEMASSIFICATION

STUDY PREVIEW Giant mass-audience magazines, led by *Life*, were major influences in their heyday, but television killed them off by offering larger audiences to advertisers. Today, the magazine industry thrives through demassification, the process of seeking audiences with narrow interests. Critics feel demassification has changed the role of magazines in society for the worse.

HEYDAY OF MASS MAGAZINES

Magazines once were epitomized by *Life*. Henry Luce used the fortune he amassed from *Time* to launch *Life* in 1936. The magazine exceeded Luce's expectations. He had planned on an initial circulation of 250,000, but almost right away it was 500,000. *Life* was perfect for its time. At 10 cents a copy, *Life* was within the reach of almost everyone, even during the Great Depression. It had quality—fiction from the best authors of the day. It had daring—flamboyant photography that seemed to jump off huge, oversize pages. The term "photo essay" was a *Life* creation.

Imitators followed. *Look*, introduced in 1937, was a knockoff in the same oversize dimension as *Life*. The historic *Saturday Evening Post* and *Collier's* were revamped as oversize magazines.

TEACHING OBJECTIVE 3-8
To understand how magazine industry survived losses to television.

ASSAULT FROM TELEVISION

The oversize mass-audience magazines do not exist today, at least not as they did in the old days. *Collier's*, bankrupt, published its final issue in 1956. Hemorrhaging money despite a circulation of 4 million, *Saturday Evening Post* ceased in 1969. In 1971 *Look* died. *Life* was not even able to capitalize on the fact that it suddenly had less competition, and it went out of business the next year. It has lost $30 million over the previous three years. What had happened to the high-flying, oversize, mass-audience magazines? In a single word: television.

At its peak, *Life* had 8.5 million circulation, but in the 1950s the television networks had begun to deliver even bigger audiences. The villain for the giant magazines was not merely television's audience size, but *CPM*, advertising jargon for *cost per 1,000* readers, listeners or viewers (the *M* standing for the Roman numeral for 1,000). In 1970 a full-page advertisement in *Life* ran $65,000. For less, an advertiser could have one minute of network television and reach far more potential customers. CPM-conscious advertising agencies could not conscientiously recommend *Life's* $7.75 CPM when the networks' CPM was $3.60, and advertisers shifted to television.

CROSS-REFERENCE
See index for demassification.

A NARROWER FOCUS

With the demise of *Life*, doomsayers predicted that magazines were a dying breed of media. The fact, however, was that advertisers withdrew only from magazines with broad readerships. What advertisers discovered was that although it was less expensive to use television to peddle universally used products like detergents, grooming aids and packaged foods, television, geared at the time for mass audiences, was too expensive for products appealing to narrow groups. Today, relatively few magazines seek a truly mass audience. These include *Reader's Digest*, the Sunday magazine supplements and *Life*, which has been resurrected as a smaller-format monthly.

Special-interest magazines, whose content focused on limited subjects and whose advertising rates were lower, fit the bill better than either television or the giant mass-audience magazines for reaching customers with special interests. For manufacturers of $3,000 stereo systems, for example, it made sense to advertise in a narrowly focused audiophile magazine like *Stereo Review*. In the same way, neither mass-audience magazines nor television was a medium of choice for top-of-the-line racing skis, but ski magazines were ideal. For fancy cookware, *Food & Wine* made sense.

Among new magazines that emerged with the demassification in the 1960s were regional and city magazines, offering a geographically defined audience to advertisers. Some of these magazines, which usually bore the name of their city or region, including *New York*, *Texas Monthly*, *Washingtonian*, offered hard-hitting journalistic coverage of local issues. Many, though, focused on soft life-style subjects rather than antagonize powerful local interests and risk losing advertisers. Indeed, hypersensitivity to advertisers is a criticism of today's demassified magazines.

CRITICS OF DEMASSIFICATION

Norman Cousins, once editor of the high-brow *Saturday Review of Literature*, criticized demassified magazines for betraying their traditional role of enriching the culture. Cousins said specialization had diluted the intellectual role of magazines in the society. Advertisers, he said, were shaping magazines' journalistic content for their commercial purposes—in contrast to magazine editors independently deciding content with loftier purposes in mind.

Scholar Dennis Holder put this "unholy alliance" of advertisers and readers this way: "The readers see themselves as members of small, and in some sense, elite groups—joggers, for example, or cat lovers—and they want to be told that they are terribly neat people for being in those groups. Advertisers, of course, want to reinforce the so-called positive self-image too, because joggers who feel good about themselves tend to buy those ridiculous suits and cat lovers who believe lavishing affection on their felines is a sign of warmth and sincerity are the ones who purchase cute little cat sweaters, or are they cat's pajamas." Magazine editors and writers, Holder said, are caught in the symbiotic advertiser-reader alliance and have no choice but to go along.

Norman Cousins and Dennis Holder were right that most consumer magazines today tend to a frothy mix of light, upbeat features, with little that is thoughtful or hard-hitting. However, most readers want to know about other people, particularly celebrities, and a great many trendy topics, and advertisers want to reach those readers, avoiding controversies that might hurt sales. So profitability for most magazines and their advertisers is locked into providing information their target audiences are interested in rather than serving an undefinable "public interest." The emphasis on profits and demassification saddens a number of people who believe that magazines have a higher calling than a cash register. These critics would agree with Cousins, who warned that emphasizing the superficial just because it sells magazines is a betrayal of the social trust that magazine publishers once held. "The purpose of a magazine," he said, "is not to tell you how to fix a leaky faucet, but to tell you what the world is about."

There is no question that demassification works against giving readers any kind of global view. In demassified magazines for auto enthusiasts, as an example, road test articles typically wax as enthusiastically as the advertisements about new cars. These demassified magazines, edited to target selected audiences and thereby attract advertisers, make no pretense of broadening their readers' understanding of substantive issues by exploring diverse perspectives. The narrowing of magazine editorial content appears destined to continue, not only because it is profitable but

Calvin and Hobbes   by Bill Watterson

Magazine Demassification. Advertisers favor magazines that are edited to specific audience interests that coincide with the advertisers' products. Fewer and fewer magazines geared to a general audience remain in business today.

also because new technologies, like Time Warner's geodemographic TargetSelect program, make it possible for magazine publishers to identify narrower and narrower segments of the mass audience and then to gear their publications to those narrower and narrower interests.

MAGAZINE CHALLENGES

STUDY PREVIEW Magazines face new challenges as cable television becomes a demassified advertising medium. Other problems include fickle audiences for narrowly focused magazines, finding a balance between newsrack and subscription sales and ever-rising costs.

HAZARDS OF DEMASSIFICATION

While many magazines have prospered through demassification by catering to special interests, serving a niche of readers has its hazards. One problem is that a narrow audience may turn out to be transitory. Citizen's band radios were the rage in the 1970s, and CB magazines suddenly cropped up, only to die as public interest in CBs waned.

A second problem stems from the fact that, in coming years, specialized magazines may feel competition from other media, which are going through their own belated demassification. Radio is already demographically divided, with stations using formats designed for narrow audiences, and the narrowing is continuing. At the start of the 1990s, major cities had stations that aired only comedy, only financial news and only motivational talk. Specialized magazines were losing their monopoly on narrow audience segments.

TEACHING OBJECTIVE 3-9
Magazines have shifted away from broad issues.

NEW COMPETITION

Another ominous sign for magazines is the cable television industry, which is eating into magazine advertising with an array of demassified channels, such as the ESPN sports channel, the Arts & Entertainment network, and the CNBC financial and consumer news network. The demassified cable channels are picking up advertisers that once used magazines almost exclusively to reach narrow slices of the mass audience with a presumed interest in their products and services.

CROSS REFERENCE
For television's impact on other media, see Chapter 4 on newspapers, Chapter 6 on movies, Chapter 7 on radio and Chapter 8 on television.

MEDIA: PEOPLE

Jann Wenner

Jann Wenner was a student at the University of California's Berkeley campus as the hippie movement of the mid-1960s was flowering across the bay in San Francisco. Wenner dabbled in the loose, bohemian Haight-Ashbury life-style himself, including the drugs, but it was the music of the new generation that intrigued him the most—and he wanted to write about it.

In his second year at Berkeley, Wenner persuaded the editors of the campus newspaper, the *Daily Californian,* to give him a music column. In many ways, the column was a preview of Wenner's yet-to-come *Rolling Stone* magazine. Amid obscure egocentric references, Wenner reported music news seriously with a focus on his favorites: Bob Dylan, Mick Jagger, the Beatles. There were literary allusions, particularly to F. Scott Fitzgerald, and he found ways to tie the emerging psychedelic drug culture into politics. "One of these days," he wrote, "Lyndon Johnson is going to find out why the 'leaders of tomorrow' are hung up on LSD instead of LBJ."

Wenner gave up the column when he dropped out of college, but he tried to continue writing. The problem was that nobody would print his work. *Stereo Review* turned him down. So did the San Francisco dailies. Wenner went to London to propose covering the San Francisco music scene for *Melody Maker,* but that editor too said no.

Wenner decided to start his own magazine.

From friends, Wenner picked up venture capital totaling $6,500, and when his father gave him $1,000 in stock for his 21st birthday, he sold it to help fund the magazine. It was enough for Wenner, age 21, to launch *Rolling Stone.* That was in 1967. Within two years, *Rolling Stone* was widely regarded as the most authoritative rock 'n' roll magazine. It also became the voice for a new generation—not just the flower children of Haight-Ashbury but young people disenchanted with President Lyndon Johnson, the Vietnam war and the Establishment in general, and later with Richard Nixon and Watergate.

There were other magazines aimed at young people, but only Wenner realized that music was what bound the new generation together. Always at *Rolling Stone's* core, amid the fiction and political coverage, was rock 'n' roll.

The magazine became home for great writers of the new generation. Gonzo journalist Hunter Thompson

Jann Wenner

was an early *Rolling Stone* regular, and later there were Truman Capote, Tom Wolfe and P. J. O'Rourke. Wenner encouraged writers to uninhibited truth-seeking and truth-telling. In his history of the magazine, Robert Draper wrote: "Wenner urged his writers to scrape away the bullshit. If the President lies, call him a liar; if Dylan is a poet, call him one."

By its sixth year, 1973, *Rolling Stone* turned profitable. No longer just "a little rock 'n' roll newspaper in San Francisco," as Wenner fondly referred to it in the early days, *Rolling Stone* has grown to maturity along with its original 1960s generation readership. The focus remains rock 'n' roll but without the beads and other symbols of the psychedelic era. In middle age, *Rolling Stone* now is edited in New York. The instinctive seat-of-the-pants approach to editing that marked the early San Francisco days now is tempered by audience analysis from people who are comfortable in pin-stripe suits. The magazine's new mainstream respectability was cemented in 1985 when David Black won a National Magazine Award for a pioneering and explosive series on AIDS.

Today, circulation is 1.2 million. Wenner's company, Straight Arrow Publishers, is worth $250 million—more than 30,000 times the initial 1967 capitalization. Wenner himself is worth an estimated $100 million, not bad for a college dropout who started out with only $7,500 and a vision.

Another drain on magazine revenue is the growth of direct-mail advertising. Using sophisticated analysis of potential customer groups, advertisers can mail brochures, catalogs, fliers and other material, including video pitches, directly to potential customers at their homes or places of business. Every dollar that goes into direct-mail campaigns is a dollar that in an earlier period went into magazines and other traditional advertising media.

CUTTING COSTS

Besides the soft advertising situation, magazines are facing rising costs. Hikes in paper costs prompted the once-oversize *Ladies' Home Journal* and *Esquire* to trim their page size. In 1991 even the fashion magazines *Elle* and *Mirabella*, whose fashion ads erupted off huge, oversize pages, abandoned the large European formats that had been standard for fashion magazines. The change allowed the magazines to fit better into newsrack slots, and, conceded publisher Grace Mirabella, "to save precious dollars on expensive paper." Trimming down also saves mailing costs, one of a magazine's largest expenses. When *Premiere* reduced the page dimensions, its weight dropped 2 percent, which was hardly insignificant at the postal meter.

NEWSRACKS OR SUBSCRIPTIONS

A magazine's financial health can hinge on finding the right balance between single-copy sales at newsracks and subscriptions. Subscriptions represent long-term reader commitment, but they are sold at deep discounts. Newsrack sales generate more revenue. Finding the right balance is complicated because advertisers have different points of view on which delivery system is better for reaching potential customers. Some advertisers reason that readers who pay cash for individual issues are more attentive to the content than people who routinely receive every issue via mail. Other advertisers are impressed by the loyalty implicit in subscriptions. Also, there are advertisers who flip-flop on the question.

To find the right balance, magazines manipulate their subscription rates and newsrack prices. When its advertisers shifted to a newsstand preference, *Cosmopolitan* lowered its single-copy price and hiked subscription rates until 95 percent of its circulation was through newsracks. The shift helped make the magazine attractive to advertisers.

Single sales benefit magazines in another way. They are more profitable than subscriptions, which means that magazines can keep their advertising rates down because readers pick up more of the bills. In general, the shift through the 1970s and 1980s was toward single-copy sales. The shift helped magazines improve their competitive stance against television.

CHAPTER WRAP-UP

Magazines have been an adaptable medium, adjusting with the times and with changing audience interests. *Cosmopolitan*, an especially good example of adaptability, was founded in 1886 as a home magazine, became a leading muckraking journal, switched into a general women's magazine, and now is a specialized women's magazine. The adaptability of magazines is clear in the medium's long history of innovations which, in time, other media have copied. These include in-depth personality profiles, photojournalism and muckraking.

The magazine industry once was defined by giant general-interest magazines, epitomized by *Life*, that offered something for everybody. Advertisers soured on these oversize giants when television offered more potential customers per advertising dollar. Magazines shifted to more specialized packages, and the focused approach worked. Magazines found advertisers who were seeking readers with narrow interests. Now, as other media, particularly television, are demassifying, magazines stand to lose advertisers, which poses new challenges.

A troubling question about contemporary magazines is whether they are still enriching American culture. Through most of their history, starting in the 1820s, magazines have made significant literature and ideas available at reasonable cost to the general public. Critics worry that many of today's specialized magazines have lost a sense of society's significant issues. Troubling too, say critics, is that these magazines have forsaken detached, neutral journalistic approaches in an enthusiasm for their specialized subjects, in effect selling out to the commercial interests of their advertisers rather than pursuing truth.

QUESTIONS FOR REVIEW

1. How have magazines contributed to American culture?
2. How have magazines been innovative as a journalistic and as a visual medium?
3. Why are most magazines edited for the special interests of targeted audiences?
4. How do sponsored magazines and trade journals differ from the consumer magazines available at newsracks?

5. Why are magazine companies worldwide creating foreign editions?
6. What is the status of demassification in the magazine industry?
7. Are magazines losing their influence as a shaper of the culture? Explain your answer.

QUESTION FOR CRITICAL THINKING

1. What characteristics does Jann Wenner have in common with these magazine founders: Sarah Josepha Hale, Henry Luce, and DeWitt and Lila Wallace?
2. When American magazines came into their own in the 1820s, they represented a mass medium that was distinct from the existing book and newspaper media. How were magazines different?
3. How was the American identity that emerged in the 19th century fostered by magazines?
4. To some people, the word "muckraking" has a negative tone. Can you make the case that it should be regarded positively? Can you also argue the opposite?
5. Discuss the role of these innovators in contributing to magazines as a visual medium: Gilbert Grosvenor, Margaret Bourke-White and Henry Luce.

6. Can you name three consumer magazines in each of these categories: newsmagazines, Seven Sisters magazines, skin magazines, giant magazines and specialized magazines?
7. Considering that *Playboy* magazine relies less on newsrack sales than *Penthouse*, which would you as an advertiser prefer if all other things, including circulation, were equal?
8. The late Norman Cousins, a veteran social commentator and magazine editor, worried that trends in the magazine industry are undermining the historic role that magazines have had in enriching the culture. What is your response to Cousins's concerns?

FOR FURTHER LEARNING

James L. Baughman. *Henry R. Luce and the Rise of the American News Media* (Tawyne, 1987). Baughman, a historian, traces the influence of Luce on the presentation of news in other media through his innovations at *Time* and other magazines.

Reginald Bragonier, Jr., and David J. Fisher. *The Mechanics of a Magazine* (Hearst, 1984). This lavishly illustrated book details every facet of the creation of an issue of *Popular Mechanics*.

Walter M. Brasch. *Forerunners of Revolution: Muckrakers and the American Social Conscience* (University of America Press, 1990). Professor Brasch distinguishes muckraking from investigative reporting. Muckrakers, he says, seek to expose misdeeds that undermine the social fabric of society, while investigative reporters focus on abuses of the public trust and schemes that bilk people.

J. William Click and Russell N. Baird. *Magazine Editing and Production*, 5th ed. (Wm. C. Brown, 1990). This textbook focuses on the mechanics of producing a magazine.

Robert Draper. *Rolling Stone Magazine: The Uncensored History* (Doubleday, 1990). In this lively and colorful account, Draper is enthusiastic about the early days of the music magazine *Rolling Stone* but less so about its founder, Jann Wenner, and what the magazine has become.

Otto Friedrich. *Decline and Fall* (Harper & Row, 1969). Friedrich, a *Saturday Evening Post* editor, details the power struggle that made drama of the magazine's demise.

Douglas H. George. *The Smart Magazines: 50 Years of Literary Revelry and High Jinks at Vanity Fair, the New Yorker, Life, Esquire and the Smart Set.* (Archon Books, 1991). George, an English professor, offers lively, anecdote-laden accounts of magazines whose appeal was giving readers a sense of participation in society's upper crust. The magazines are profiled separately.

Dennis Holder, Robert Love, Bill Meyers and Roger Piantadosi, contributors. "Magazines in the 1980s." *Washington Journalism Review 3* (November 1981):3, 28–41. Holder's article, "The Decade of Specialization," looks at social implications of magazines seeking market niches.

M. Thomas Inge, ed. *Handbook of American Popular Culture*, 2nd ed. (Greenwood, 1989). Inge includes a thoroughly annotated article on magazines.

Amy Janello and Brennon Jones. *The American Magazine* (Harry N. Abrams, 1991). Janello and Jones focus on magazines as a creative medium, editorially and visually. The book includes essays by magazine people and more than 500 illustrations, including many magazine covers and spreads.

A. Kent MacDougall. *The Press: A Critical Look From the Inside* (Dow Jones Books, 1972). In this collection of reprints from the *Wall Street Journal*, MacDougall has included his article on the dark side of trade magazines. The article details trade magazine boosterism of their subjects and pandering to advertisers, rather than journalistic coverage.

Richmond M. McClure. *To the End of Time: The Seduction and Conquest of a Media Empire* (Simon & Schuster, 1992). McClure, a former Time Inc. executive with many inside sources, chronicles the deal-making that merged Henry Luce's Time-Life empire into the Time Warner media conglomerate. Luce's vision was lost in the process, and McClure is not sympathetic.

Alan and Barbara Nourie. *American Mass-Market Magazines* (Greenwood, 1990). The Nouries offer histories of 106 current and defunct consumer magazines.

Theodore Peterson. *Magazines in the Twentieth Century* (University of Illinois Press, 1964).

Sam G. Riley, ed. *Corporate Magazines in the United States* (Greenwood Press, 1992). This is a pioneering attempt at an overview of the publications that corporations produce for free circulation among employees, customers and other groups. The diversity of these publications makes a profile difficult. Sometimes called "public relations magazines," these publications employ many more people than the more visible consumer magazines.

Sam G. Riley and Gary W. Selnow, eds. *Regional Interest Magazines of the United States* (Greenwood Press, 1991). Riley and Selnow profile city and regional magazines, including *Arizona Highways, Southern Living, Texas Monthly, Chicago* and *Philadelphia*.

Ted Curtis Smythe. "Special Interest Magazines: Wave of the Future or Undertow." In Michael Emery and Smythe. *Readings in Mass Communication*, 6th ed. (Wm. C. Brown, 1986). Smythe examines trends in the magazine industry.

W. A. Swanberg. *Luce and His Empire* (Scribners, 1972). Swanberg, a biographer of major journalists, is at his best with Henry Luce of Time-Life.

William H. Taft. *American Magazines for the 1980s* (Hastings House, 1982). In this overview, Professor Taft describes the American magazine industry and trends at the start of the 1980s.

John Tebbel and Mary Ellen Zuckerman. *The Magazine in America, 1741–1990* (Oxford University Press, 1991). Tebbel and Zuckerman provide a great amount of information, much of it colorful, on the evolution of magazines in the United States. They make the case that magazines have been a major shaper of American life.

Eric Utne. "Tina's *New Yorker*." *Columbia Journalism Review* 31 (March/April 1993):6, 31–37. Utne, a self-described magazine junkie, is far from convinced that the commercial-driven changes that Tina Brown is bringing to the *New Yorker* are making a better magazine.

FOR KEEPING UP TO DATE

Folio is a trade journal on magazine management. Among major newspapers that track magazine issues in a fairly consistent way are the *New York Times*, the *Wall Street Journal* and *USA Today*.

NEWSPAPERS
ARE THE
MAJOR SOURCE
OF NEWS FOR
MOST AMERICANS

MOST U.S. NEWSPAPERS
ARE OWNED BY CHAINS, FOR
BETTER OR WORSE

THE UNITED STATES IS LARGELY A
NATION OF LOCAL AND REGIONAL
NEWSPAPERS, WITH ONLY THREE
NATIONAL DAILIES

MOST OF THE LEADING U.S.
NEWSPAPERS ARE METROPOLITAN
DAILIES, WHICH HAVE DWINDLED
IN NUMBER WITH POPULATION AND
LIFE-STYLE SHIFTS

TELEVISION AND RETAILING
CHANGES HAVE CUT INTO
NEWSPAPER DISPLAY ADVERTISING,
AND NEWSPAPERS MAY LOSE THEIR
DOMINANCE AS AN ADVERTISING
MEDIUM

COMMUNITY NEWSPAPERS,
ESPECIALLY SUBURBAN
WEEKLIES, ARE BOOMING AS
PEOPLE CONTINUE MOVING
OUT OF CORE CITIES

THRIVING
NEWSPAPERS INCLUDE
COUNTER-CULTURE,
GAY AND SPANISH-
LANGUAGE PAPERS
AIMED AT NARROW
SEGMENTS OF
READERS

chapter
NEWSPAPERS
A MEDIUM FOR NEWS

4

Cousins Joseph Patterson and Robert McCormick, heirs to the McCormick reaper and Chicago *Tribune* fortunes, went off to fight in World War I. Little did they expect to see each other during the war, but one day during a lull in a battle they met. Full of war stories, Captain Patterson and Colonel McCormick stretched out on a dried-out manure pile behind a French farm house to catch up on each other's recent experiences.

The conversation turned to journalism, and Patterson described the flashy tabloids he had seen in London. There was nothing like them in the United States, and they seemed to be making lots of money. Then and there, the cousins decided to start a tabloid in New York after the war. Using Chicago *Tribune* money, they launched the New York *Daily News* in 1919. Patterson ran the *Daily News*, while McCormick stayed in Chicago with the *Tribune*.

In 1919, when the *Daily News* was founded, there already were 18 dailies in New York. Within four years it was in the lead. Daily circulation broke through 2 million in 1944 and then climbed up to 2.4 million daily and more than 3 million Sunday—the largest in the nation.

Joseph Patterson

Sold-out Edition. Perhaps the most famous news photograph of all time was Tom Howard's shot of the electric chair execution of murderer Ruth Snyder. Knowing the Sing Sing warden wouldn't agree to a photo, Howard strapped a tiny camera to his ankle and, at the right moment, lifted his trouser leg and snapped the shutter with a trip wire. The exclusive photo goosed street sales of the New York *Daily News*, which had followed the lurid trial of Snyder and her lover for killing her husband. Such stories and a focus on photo coverage, typical of the *Daily News* under founder Joseph Patterson, boosted the newspaper's circulation to more than 2 million, the largest in the nation, in the 1940s.

From the beginning, Patterson's *Daily News* was an irreverent, borderline-tawdry tabloid. It had detractors who delighted in noting that it was a newspaper conceived on a dung heap—that dried-out manure pile back in France.

The *Daily News* was a paper for common people. Patterson followed the theory: "Tell it to Sweeney! The Stuyvesants will take care of themselves." In fact, the paper pointed out to advertisers that common people, taken all together, had tremendous buying power.

The newspaper screamed to be picked up with snappy heads on sensational stories: "Maid Back With Baby and Rape Tale" and "Trial Expected to Hear Lovelord Today." The *Daily News* called itself "New York's Picture Paper" and went after photos aggressively. When Ruth Snyder was electrocuted for murder at Sing Sing in 1928, prison officials barred cameras, but Tom Howard of the *Daily News* strapped a tiny camera to his leg and lifted his pant leg and snapped the shutter at the moment the current surged through the woman's body. The *Daily News* ran the picture as a full-page cover.

The *Daily News* had a sense of humor anyone could appreciate, whether a Sweeney or a Stuyvesant. When an Italian prosecutor accused actress Gina Lollobrigida of indecency in a film, the head read: "Charges Gina Was Obscena on La Screena."

The gee-whiz, sometimes offbeat style endeared the *Daily News* to readers, at least until recent years. Today, there are doubts whether the *Daily News* can survive.

Despite its circulation, the New York *Daily News* never was a great newspaper, at least not in the sense of the serious, somber New York *Times,* and in the late 1960s circulation dropped precipitously. So did advertising and profits. As many *Daily News* readers moved upscale, with more education and more income, the *Daily News* no longer was their kind of newspaper. There were fewer Sweeneys in New York.

The Tribune Company in Chicago, which still owned the *Daily News,* put the paper up for sale in the 1980s, but there were no takers. Labor turmoil further weakened the paper, and many readers, sympathetic to the unions, boycotted the paper. At one low point, circulation reportedly slipped to 350,000. With losses mounting at $700,000 a day, the Tribune Company announced that it would shut down the paper.

Three days before the scheduled shutdown, British press tycoon Robert Maxwell agreed to buy the newspaper. But when he died a few weeks later, it was learned he was a world-class crook who had been raiding his employees' pension funds and committing other financial shenanigans. The *Daily News* went to Maxwell's creditors.

Although the future of the *Daily News* is unclear, the story of its rise and decline illustrates several fundamental realities of today's newspaper business. One is that many people love hyped news. In this sense, the *Daily News* could be considered the U.S. progenitor of today's supermarket tabloids. At the same time, people generally are more educated and sophisticated today than when the the *Daily News* peaked. This has reduced markets for local gee-whiz scandal sheets. Also, television has cut into newspaper readership and led to a shakeout in the newspaper industry. Only the strongest newspapers survive.

The most fundamental lesson from the saga of the New York *Daily News* is that newspapers prosper when they attract a large audience that advertisers want to reach. When the audience diminishes or becomes an audience that advertisers aren't interested in, a newspaper is in trouble. If advertisers perceive that a newspaper doesn't reach the "right readers," they go elsewhere. So do the profits.

IMPORTANCE OF NEWSPAPERS

STUDY PREVIEW Newspapers are the primary mass medium from which people receive news. In most cities, no other news source comes close to the local newspaper's range and depth of coverage. This contributes to the popularity and influence of newspapers.

NEWSPAPER INDUSTRY DIMENSIONS

The newspaper industry dwarfs other news media by almost every measure. Nearly one out of two people in the United States reads a newspaper every day, far more than tune in the network news on television in the evening. The data are staggering:

TEACHING OBJECTIVE 4-1
Newspapers are major source of news.

- About 1,570 daily newspapers put out 60 million copies a day, more on Sundays. Because each copy is passed along to an average of 2.2 people, daily newspapers reach 132 million people a day.
- Weekly newspapers put out 50 million copies. With their pass-along circulation of four people a copy, these newspapers reach somewhere around 200 million people a week.

Perhaps because television has stolen the glitz and romance that newspapers once had, the significance of newspapers is easy to miss. But the newspaper industry is large by every measure. In an article marveling at an issue of a newspaper as "the daily creation," the Washington *Post*'s Richard Harwood, writing about his own newspaper, said: "Roughly 11,000 people are involved in the production and distribution each day, enough bodies to fill all the billets of an Army light infantry division." Although Harwood stretched to include even the delivery boys and girls in his startling number, his point is valid: In Washington and everywhere else, newspapers far outdistance other news media in the number of people who gather, edit and disseminate news.

Newspapers are the medium of choice for more advertising than competing media. For local advertising, daily newspapers attracted $27.1 billion in 1992. Over-air television stations and cable systems were a distant second at $8.4 billion. Nationwide, including network television's tremendous advertising revenue, newspapers still lead with $30.7 billion in advertising revenue to television's $29.4 billion.

Except for brief downturns in the overall economy and an occasional exceptional situation, daily newspapers have been consistently profitable enterprises through the 20th century. Less than double-digit returns on investment are uncommon. As a mass medium, the newspaper is not to be underrated.

CONTENT DIVERSITY AND DEPTH

In most communities, newspapers cover more news at greater depth than competing media. A metropolitan daily like the Washington *Post* typically may carry 300 items, much more on Sundays—more than any Washington television or radio station and at greater length. City magazines in Washington, for example, offer more depth on selected stories, but the magazines are published relatively infrequently and run relatively few articles. Nationally, no broadcast organization comes close to the number of stories or the depth of the two major national newspapers, the *Wall Street Journal* and *USA Today*.

Newspapers have a rich mix of content—news, advice, comics, opinion, puzzles and data. It's all there to tap into at will. Some people go right for the stock market tables, others to sports or a favorite columnist. Unlike radio and television, you don't have to wait for what you want.

People like newspapers. Some talk affectionately of cuddling up in bed on a leisurely Sunday morning with their paper. The news and features give people something in common to talk about. Newspapers are important in people's lives, and as a medium they adapt to changing lifestyles. The number of Sunday newspapers, for example, grew from 600 in the 1970s to almost 900 today, reflecting an increase in people's weekend leisure time for reading and shopping. Ads in Sunday papers are their guide for shopping excursions.

LECTURE RESOURCE 4-A
Slide: *History in Front Pages*.

All this does not mean that the newspaper industry is not facing problems from competing media, new technology and ongoing lifestyle shifts. But to date, newspapers have reacted to change with surprising effectiveness. To offset television's inroads, newspapers put new emphasis on being a visual medium and shed their drab graphics for color and aesthetics. To accommodate the work schedule transition of Americans over recent years from factory jobs starting at 7 a.m. to service jobs starting at 9 a.m., newspapers have emphasized morning editions and phased out afternoon editions. Knowing that the days of ink-on-paper technology are limited, the newspaper industry is examining electronic delivery methods for the 21st century.

News Habits

The Scripps-Howard newspaper chain has a long tradition of sponsoring spelling bees. It seemed a good thing to do, and it also contributed in a small way to Scripps-Howard's self-interest by improving the society's sensitivity to one fundamental of literacy: People who can't spell won't read newspapers.

Those spelling bees seem a quaint way to handle the readership problem that is shaping up today for the U.S. newspaper industry. Confirming what was widely suspected, a 1990 study found that young people by and large don't read newspapers. According to the study, sponsored through the Los Angeles *Times*, only 30 percent of people under 35 read a newspaper the day before. Twenty-five years earlier, the Gallup polling people found the rate was 67 percent.

Newspaper executives have cause to worry. Unless they entice young readers, their medium will decline as older people, the bulk of their audience, die. But the problem may be even more serious. The Los Angeles *Times* study found that it isn't just newspapers that young people are avoiding but news itself. Of respondents between ages 18 and 29, 40 percent are less likely than their elders to be able to identify significant figures

in the news, and 20 percent said they were less likely to follow even major events.

The study overturned the notion that young people prefer television to newspaper for news. Only four of every 10 respondents under age 35 had watched television news the day before. Twenty-five years earlier it was five of 10. Except for sports and issues that affect them directly, like abortion, young people are less and less interested in news.

Conduct your own informal survey to test whether the younger generation in your community also has less interest in newspapers and in news. Ask these questions to a dozen people under 35 and another dozen people over 35:

- Did you read a newspaper yesterday?
- Did you watch a television newscast yesterday?
- Did you follow the NAFTA debate closely?
- Are you following events in Serbia and Croatia closely?

If you were a newspaper editor or a television news executive, what would you do to attract more people to your product?

Some problems are truly daunting, like the aversion of many young people to newspapers. Also, chain ownership has raised fundamental questions about how well newspapers can do their work and still meet the profit expectations of distant shareholders.

NEWSPAPER CHAIN OWNERSHIP

STUDY PREVIEW   Through the 20th century, newspapers have been incredibly profitable, which, for better or worse, encouraged chain ownership. Today, chains own most U.S. newspapers.

TREND TOWARD CHAINS

Reasoning that he could multiply profits by owning multiple newspapers, *William Randolph Hearst* put together a chain of big-city newspapers in the late 1880s. Although Hearst's chain was not the first, his empire became the model in the public's mind for much that was both good and bad about newspaper chains. Like other chains, Hearst also expanded into magazines, radio and television. The trend toward chain ownership continues, and today 160 chains own four of every five

TEACHING OBJECTIVE 4-2
Most U.S. newspapers owned by chains.

KEY PERSON
William Randolph Hearst.

dailies in the United States. Chain ownership is also coming to dominate weeklies, which had long been a bastion of independent ownership.

Newspaper profitability skyrocketed in the 1970s and 1980s, which prompted chains to buy up locally owned newspapers, sometimes in bidding frenzies. Single-newspaper cities were especially attractive because no competing media could match a local newspaper's large audience. It was possible for new owners to push ad rates up rapidly, and local retailers had to go along. The profit potential was enhanced because production costs were falling dramatically with less labor-intensive back-shop procedures, computerized typesetting and other automation. Profits were dramatic. Eight newspaper companies tracked by *Forbes* magazine from 1983 to 1988 earned the equivalent of 23.9 percent interest on a bank account. Only soft drink companies did better.

Federal tax law also accelerated the shift from family-owned to chain-owned newspapers in two ways. Inheritance taxes made it easier for families that owned independent newspapers to sell the papers than to leave them to their heirs. Also, chains were very eager to acquire more newspapers because they could avoid paying tax on income from their existing properties if they reinvested it in new holdings.

The Gannett media conglomerate's growth typifies how newspapers became chains and then grew into cross-media conglomerates. In 1906 the chain was six upstate New York newspapers. By 1982 Gannett had grown to almost 90 dailies, all profitable medium-size newspapers. Swimming in money, Gannett launched *USA Today*. Gannett not only absorbed *USA Today's* tremendous start-up costs for several years but also had enough spare cash to outbid other companies for expensive metropolitan newspapers. In 1985 and 1986 Gannett paid $1.4 billion for the Detroit *News*, Des Moines *Register* and Louisville *Courier-Journal*. Along the way, Gannett acquired Combined Communications, which owned 20 broadcasting stations. Today Gannett owns 82 daily newspapers, 39 weeklies, 16 radio and 8 television stations, the largest billboard company in the nation, and the Louis Harris polling organization. It renamed and beefed up a national Sunday newspaper magazine supplement. No longer just a newspaper chain, Gannett has become a mass media conglomerate.

ASSESSING CHAIN OWNERSHIP

Is chain ownership good for newspapers? The question raised in Hearst's time was whether diverse points of view were as likely to get into print if ownership were concentrated in fewer and fewer hands. That concern has dissipated as chains have become oriented more to profits than to participating in public dialogue. Executives at the headquarters of most chains focus on management and leave editorials to local editors. While local autonomy is consistent with American journalistic values, a corporate focus on profits raises a dark new question: Are chains so myopic about profits that they forget good journalism? The answer is that the emphasis varies among chains.

LECTURE RESOURCE 4-B
Video: *The Knight-Ridder Promise.*

JOURNALISTIC EMPHASIS.   Some chains, such as Knight-Ridder, whose properties include the Miami *Herald*, the Philadelphia *Enquirer* and the Detroit *Free Press*, are known for a strong corporate commitment to quality journalism. In 1988 Knight-Ridder newspapers won 6 of the 14 Pulitzer Prizes, including one by the Charlotte *Observer* for revealing the misuse of funds by the PTL ministry that opened up the televangelism scandals.

MEDIA DATABANK

Newspaper Chains

Here are the largest U.S. newspaper chains, ranked by circulation, with a sample of their major properties:

	Daily Circulation	Number of Dailies		Daily Circulation	Number of Dailies
Gannett	5.5 million	82	Dow Jones	2.4 million	8
USA Today			*Wall Street Journal*		
Des Moines *Register*			Ottaway Newspapers		
Detroit *News*			New York Times	1.7 million	26
Louisville *Courier-Journal*			New York *Times*		
Knight-Ridder	3.6 million	27	Florida dailies		
Charlotte *Observer*			Scripps Howard	1.6 million	21
Detroit *Free Press*			Albuquerque *Tribune*		
Miami *Herald*			Columbus *Citizen-Journal*		
Philadelphia *Inquirer*			Cincinnati *Post*		
Seattle *Times*			Denver *Rocky Mountain News*		
Newhouse	2.9 million	26	El Paso *Herald-Post*		
Cleveland *Plain Dealer*			Memphis *Commercial Appeal*		
Newark *Star-Ledger*			Pittsburgh *Press*		
New Orleans *Times-Picayune*			Thomson Newspapers	1.5 million	90
Portland *Oregonian*			Small dailies		
Tribune Company	2.6 million	8	News America Corp.	1.3 million	3
Chicago *Tribune*			Boston *Herald*		
Times-Mirror	2.5 million	22	San Antonio *Express-News*		
Los Angeles *Times*					
Hartford *Courant*					
Denver *Post*					
New York *Newsday*					

BALANCED EMPHASIS.   Most chains are known for undistinguished though profitable newspapers. This is an apt description for Gannett, the largest United States chain, measured by circulation.

PROFIT EMPHASIS.   Several chains, including Thomson, Donrey and American Publishing, have a pattern of cutting costs aggressively, reducing staffs and trimming news coverage. It is not uncommon for a new chain owner to fire veteran reporters and editors, in some cases almost halving the staff. To save newsprint, some chains cut back the number of pages. They hire inexperienced reporters right out of college, pay them poorly, and encourage them to move on after a few months, so they can be replaced by other eager but inexperienced, and cheap, new reporters. The result is a reporting staff that lacks the kind of local expertise that is necessary for good journalism. Only the shareholders benefit.

In general, the following realities of chain ownership work against strong local journalistic enterprise:

ABSENTEE OWNERSHIP.   Newspaper chain executives, under pressure at corporate headquarters to run profitable enterprises, do not live in the communities that are shortchanged by decisions to deemphasize good, aggressive journalism.

TRANSIENT MANAGEMENT.   The local managers of newspapers owned by chains tend to be career climbers who have no long-term stake in the community their newspaper serves. These people generally are not promoted from within a newspaper but are appointed by corporate headquarters, and generally they have short-term goals to look good to their corporate bosses so they can be promoted to better-paying jobs with more responsibility at bigger newspapers in the chain.

WEAK ENTRY-LEVEL SALARIES.   The focus of newspaper chains on enhancing profits to keep costs down has worked against strong salaries for journalists. The result is a "brain drain." Many talented reporters and editors leave newspapers for more lucrative jobs in public relations and other fields. In a report in *Quill* magazine, Wendy Govier and Neal Pattison offered this 1991 random collection of entry-level reporter salaries:

- St. Paul, Minnesota, *Pioneer Press*, owned by Knight-Ridder, circulation 200,000, $23,556 a year.
- Bremerton, Washington, *Sun*, owned by John P. Scripps Newspapers, circulation 41,500, $22,360 a year.
- Indianapolis *Star*, owned by Central Newspapers, circulation 244,000, $21,632 a year.

Congratulations, and Here's $25. Betty Gray of the Washington, North Carolina, *Daily News* unearthed a major scandal that public officials knew about carcinogen-contaminated water and did nothing about it. Gray's work earned her a 1989 Pulitzer Prize—and a $25-a-week pay raise, which brought her annual salary to $15,000. The deplorable salary typifies the dubious success of many newspapers at boosting profits by keeping costs down.

HIGH NEWSROOM TURNOVER. Cost-conscious policies at many chain newspapers encourage newsroom employees to move on after a few pay raises, so they can be replaced by rookies at entry-level salaries. This turnover can denude a newsroom of people knowledgeable about the community the newspaper services, thus eroding coverage.

NATIONAL DAILIES

STUDY PREVIEW Although the United States is a country of mostly local newspapers, three dailies have national circulation. *The Wall Street Journal* is the most solidly established with most of its readership anchored in business and finance. Prospects for the flashy *USA Today* and the dowdy but respected *The Christian Science Monitor* are less certain.

THE WALL STREET JOURNAL

The Wall Street Journal, the nation's largest newspaper, began humbly. *Charles Dow* and *Edward Jones* went into business in 1882, roaming the New York financial district for news and then scribbling notes by hand, which they sent by courier to their clients. As more information-hungry investors signed up, the service was expanded into a newsletter, and in 1889 *The Wall Street Journal* was founded. Advertisers eager to reach *Journal* readers bought space in the newspaper, which provided revenue to hire correspondents in Boston, Philadelphia and Washington. By 1900 circulation reached 10,000, and it grew to 30,000 by 1940.

The Wall Street Journal might have remained a relatively small albeit successful business paper had it not been for the legendary *Barney Kilgore*, who joined the newspaper's San Francisco bureau in 1929. Within two years, Kilgore was the *Journal*'s news editor and in a position to shift the newspaper's journalistic direction. Kilgore's formula was threefold:

- Simplify the *Journal*'s business coverage into plain English without sacrificing thoroughness.
- Provide detailed coverage of government but without the jargon that plagued much of Washington reporting.
- Expand the definition of the *Journal*'s field of coverage from "business" to "everything that somehow relates to earning a living."

The last part of the formula, expanded coverage, was a risk. Critics told Kilgore that the newspaper's existing readers might switch to other papers if they felt the *Journal* was slighting business. Kilgore's vision, however, was not to reduce business coverage but to seek business angles in other fields and cover them. It worked. Under Kilgore's leadership, *Journal* circulation reached 100,000 in 1947. When Kilgore died in 1967, a year after retiring as chairman of Dow Jones, publisher of the *Journal*, circulation had passed 1 million. Today, with circulation approaching 2 million, the *Journal* is the largest U.S. daily and, among the three national dailies, the most financially secure.

Although the *Journal* is edited for a general audience as well as for traditional business readers, it does not pander to a downscale audience. It carries no comics or horoscope columns, and its sports and entertainment coverage tends to focus on the front office and the box office. A mark of the *Journal* is its grayness. The only art on Page 1 is an occasional one-column etching. Inside, advertisements are lavish with photography, but line art dominates the news sections. In 1991 the *Journal* began accepting limited color in advertisements, but even so, the visual impression, a correct one, is that the *Journal* is a newspaper for readers to take seriously. Advertisers take the *Journal* seriously too, knowing its readers' average household income is $146,300 a year. No other newspaper comes close to delivering such a prosperous audience.

The *Journal* puts significant resources into reporting. It is not unusual for a reporter to be given six weeks for research on a major story. This digging gives the *Journal* big breaks on significant stories. In 1988, as an example, the *Journal* reported in a lengthy biographical piece on evangelist Pat Robertson, who was seeking the Republican presidential nomination, that one of his children was conceived out of wedlock. It was a revelation that affected the course of the campaign, especially in view of Robertson's moral posture on family issues. While a serious newspaper, the *Journal* is neither stodgy nor prudish. Lengthy Page 1 pieces range from heavy-duty coverage of national politics to such diverse and unexpected stories as a black widow spider outbreak in Phoenix, archaeological research into human turds to understand life-styles of lost civilizations, and how the admiral of landlocked Bolivia's navy keeps busy.

The Wall Street Journal has 500 editors and reporters, but not all are at the newspaper's Manhattan headquarters. The *Journal* has 11 foreign and 14 domestic bureaus, and its European and Asian editions have their own staffs.

The domestic U.S. editions are edited in New York, and page images are transmitted via orbiting satellite to 17 printing plants across the nation, so the paper is on the street and in the mail on the day of publication. Advertisers may pick and choose the editions in which they want their ads to appear.

The European and Asian editions are edited separately but lean heavily on the domestic U.S. edition for stories. The foreign editions are printed in Hong Kong, Japan, Singapore, England, the Netherlands and Switzerland.

The challenge for the *Journal* has been finding a balance between its original forte, covering business, and its expanding coverage of broader issues. It is a precarious balance. Numerous business publications, including *Business Week* and the Los Angeles-based *Investor's Daily*, vie for the same readers and advertisers with compacter packages, and numerous other national publications, including the newsmagazines, offer general coverage. So far, the *Journal* has succeeded with a gradual broadening of general coverage without losing its business readers.

In brief, here are distinctive features of *The Wall Street Journal*:

BUSINESS COVERAGE.   The *Journal* is more consistently thorough in its coverage of business and finance than any other newspaper. The coverage, it is said accurately, "moves markets." The third section of the newspaper, typically 24 pages, is dominated by stock and financial tables.

EXPLORATORY REPORTING.   The *Journal* seeks out stories that might not be told unless a journalist went after them. This exploratory reporting includes what Kilgore called *leaders*, Page 1 in-depth stories on current events, trends and issues but not necessarily breaking news.

COMMENTARY.   The editorial section is influential in political circles. Columnists represent a wide range of views. The *Journal's* book, film, drama and other critics are widely followed and respected.

Barney Kilgore

WRITING STYLE. Under Kilgore, the *Journal* encouraged writers to be simple, although not simplistic, in dealing with complex subjects. Part of the technique is a conversational tone, now widely used, that even includes contractions like "don't" and "we've."

STORY ORGANIZATION. Many longer *Journal* articles begin with the personification of the subject, a story-telling technique that has been dubbed "dow-jonesing," after the *Journal's* parent corporation. This too was a Kilgore innovation. He encouraged writers to hook the reader at the start of a complex story by explaining how individual human beings are affected by the subject. It is an especially effective approach to financial subjects that would bore most readers if told in the traditional "just the facts, ma'am" kind of reporting common in many newspapers before Barney Kilgore's time. Today, dow-jonesing is widely employed in print and broadcast journalism.

USA TODAY

A strict format, snappy visuals and crisp writing give *USA Today* an air of confidence and the trappings of success, and the newspaper has its strengths. In less than a decade, circulation has reached 1.6 million, behind only *The Wall Street Journal*, and Gannett executives exude sureness about long-term prospects. The optimism is underscored by the confident if not brash Page 1 motto: "The Nation's Newspaper."

The fact, however, is that except for an occasional profitable month, *USA Today* lost money over its first 11 years of publication, and Gannett has come

USA Today Graphics. When the Challenger exploded after take-off, *USA Today* demonstrated how graphics can tell some stories better than words alone. Most of Page 1 was turned over to a team of artists and reporters who explained through pictures and very few words what had happened. One of the influences of *USA Today* has been to revive interest in newspapers as a visual medium.

nowhere near recouping the startup costs, reported as high as $40 million. In 1993, analysts thought the newspaper might have its first profitable year, even though the company declined to break out financial details of *USA Today* operations for either the public or its shareholders.

Whatever the financial situation at *USA Today*, the newspaper has had a significant impact. Like *The Wall Street Journal*, *USA Today* seeks well-heeled readers, although in different ways. *USA Today* has relatively few subscribers, going instead after single-copy sales mostly to business people who are on the run and want a quick fix on what the news is. Many of *USA Today's* sales are at airport newsracks, by which corporate executives and middle-management travelers pass. Gannett offers deep discounts to upscale hotels to buy the papers in bulk and slip free under guests' doors as a morning courtesy. Stories strain to be lively and upbeat to make the experience of reading the paper a positive one. In contrast to *The Wall Street Journal*, almost all *USA Today* stories are short, which diverts little of a reader's time from pressing business. The brevity and crispness of *USA Today*, combined with the enticing graphics, has led some critics to liken the newspaper to fast food and dub it "McNewspaper"—not bad for you but not as nourishing as, say, *The Wall Street Journal*.

Despite its critics, *USA Today* has been true to founder *Al Neuharth's* original concept. Neuharth wanted to create a distinctive newspaper positioned below *The Wall Street Journal* and the *New York Times*, both of which are available nationally, and yet provide a kind of coverage not available in the metropolitan dailies. Because many corporate travelers change jobs fairly often and make career moves from state to state, Neuharth decided to provide two to three news and sports items every day from every state in the union. Not uncommon, for example, are

MEDIA: PEOPLE

Allen Neuharth

Many people were sure that *Al Neuharth* had made a rare blunder. It was 1982, and Neuharth, chief of the enormously successful *Gannett* media conglomerate, was announcing that Gannett would launch a national daily newspaper—*USA Today.* Under Neuharth, Gannett had become a leading newspaper chain with more than 80 newspapers. Its profitability record was among the strongest of all American corporations, not just newspapers. But with Neuharth's *USA Today* announcements, Gannett stock tumbled on Wall Street. Within three days, the stock lost almost 1.8 percent of its value.

The doubters had cause. Historically the United States was a nation of *provincial newspapers,* reflecting the country's enormity, which made national distribution of a daily newspaper prohibitively expensive.

A second reason for the local thrust of U.S. newspapers is the nation's multi-layered, decentralized system of government. Many political decisions affecting people's lives are made at local levels, so naturally, newspapers track local issues. In contrast, most other nations, with strong central governments and not much local autonomy, have national newspapers.

Despite the provincial tradition and the conventional wisdom, Neuharth convinced Gannett directors that *USA Today* could be profitable. "Give me five years," he said. Four and one-half years later, Neuharth's daringly distinctive newspaper had its first profitable month. Even though the red ink returned the next month, Gannett executives were sure by then that the paper eventually could be a consistent money-maker, and they never wavered publicly on their commitment to keep it going. In 1993, in fact, some financial analysts figured that *USA Today* might break into black ink for the whole year for the first time—11 years after the newspaper was founded.

Neuharth, who was 58 when *USA Today* was born, had learned the newspaper business the hard way. After college and two years with the Associated Press in his

Old-Fashioned Way. After retiring from day-to-day operations at the Gannett chain, which owns *USA Today,* Al Neuharth, who created the national newspaper, took up reporting again. Neuharth trotted the globe in a Gannett corporate jet for a regular column that *USA Today* carried as "JetCapade." Ironic as it seems, the man who created the glitzy *USA Today* could not give up his Royal manual typewriter.

native South Dakota, Neuharth and a friend started a weekly tabloid they called *SoDak Sports.* Two years later and $50,000 in debt, they acknowledged that the paper was a failure and shut it down. However, lessons were learned. Years later, Neuharth told an interviewer, "Getting really bloodied as I did there at the age of 28, 29, was a tremendous stroke of good fortune for me. I thought I was a red-hot journalist then, a sportswriter who thought he ran great prose through the typewriter. And I thought if you did that, you would automatically succeed with a publication. Then I found out without advertising and other revenues, you couldn't pay the rent, no matter how much you and your friends enjoyed what you were writing and publishing."

MEDIA ABROAD

Australia's Transcontinental Newspaper

When his father died in 1955, Rupert Murdoch, who was 21 years old, inherited a second-rate newspaper in Adelaide, Australia. Through mergers and acquisitions, young Murdoch parlayed his inheritance into a company that included papers in five of Australia's six state capital cities. Ever growth-minded, Murdoch set his sights on a new kind of newspaper in 1964: a national daily to be circulated coast to coast. It would be a radical departure. At the time, Australia was a nation with provincial newspapers that had only local circulation. The expanse of the nation, almost 3,000 miles coast to coast, had precluded the kinds of national papers that existed in relatively small countries.

Rupert Murdoch

Murdoch established the *Australian* in Canberra, the national capital, where editors could be on top of federal news that would be of nationwide interest. For the newspaper's second staple, foreign news, he arranged for news agencies and set up a modest foreign staff. Murdoch hoped that local circulation and advertising income in Canberra would keep the paper going until it attracted a national readership and advertising.

To deliver the paper nationally, whole pages were photographed and converted into lightweight printing plates. These plates were flown overnight to the major cities of Sydney and Melbourne, each 200 miles away, where Murdoch-owned presses printed copies for local distribution the next morning. Meanwhile, editions were printed in Canberra for air delivery to cities coast to coast.

It was an exciting time in Murdoch's life, not just because of the unprecedented scope and risk of the endeavor but because of Canberra's notorious fog. Stories abound about Murdoch on the fog-shrouded tarmac at Canberra in his pajamas, egging pilots on by telling them that it really wasn't fog, just a light mist.

Today, the paper is printed in Sydney, Melbourne and Brisbane, the nation's largest cities, none of which have Canberra's fog problem. Besides local distribution, copies are dispatched throughout the continent by airplane.

Although the *Australian* became the crown jewel of Rupert Murdoch's Australian newspaper media empire, it did not keep his attention. Next he expanded into Australian television, and then British newspapers, and today his interests include the Fox Television network, *TV Guide* and HarperCollins books in the United States. At various times, Murdoch has owned the Boston *Herald,* Chicago *Sun-Times,* New York *Post,* and the San Antonio *News* and *Express.* His attempt at a national newspaper in the United States was the racy scandal sheet *Star.*

KEY PERSON
Rupert Murdock began global media empire with Australian innovations.

items on Little League baseball championships in Idaho, if that happens to be the major sports event in Idaho on a particular day. Such tidbits from home are valuable to business travelers who have been on the road for days and cannot find such home-state items in local dailies or on television. Also for business people, the newspaper has a separate business section, which lacks the depth of *The Wall Street Journal* but which includes several pages of stock data and stories, usually short, on breaking business news.

Neuharth's goal of tapping into a corporate readership with the kind of discretionary income that attracts advertisers has succeeded in part. Gannett claims that one out of four readers has a $50,000-plus annual household income, unusually high for a newspaper but less than half the average of all *Journal* readers.

Despite financial questions and despite its critics, *USA Today* has been a major innovator, especially in news and information packaging, and its techniques have caught on with many local newspapers. Innovations include:

HIGH STORY COUNTS. Most stories run no more than 10 sentences, which creates room for many more stories per issue than in other newspapers. Even lengthier pieces, limited to only four per issue, are capped at 35 sentences. Among journalists, this is known as a "high story count."

SPLASHY DESIGN. *USA Today* emphasizes color photographs and illustrations, moving away from words alone to tell the news and explain issues.

GRAPHS, TABLES, CHARTS. The newspaper offers data graphically, not just accompanying stories but standing alone in separate displays.

The introduction of *USA Today* came at a time when most newspapers were trying to distinguish themselves from television news with longer, exploratory and interpretive stories. While some major newspapers like the New York *Times* and the Los Angeles *Times* were unswayed by *USA Today*'s snappy, quick-to-read format, many other newspapers moved to shorter, easily digested stories, infographics and more data lists. Color became standard. *USA Today* has influenced today's newspaper style and format.

THE CHRISTIAN SCIENCE MONITOR

Mary Baker Eddy, the influential founder of the Christian Science faith, was aghast at turn-of-the-century Boston newspapers. The Boston dailies, as in other major American cities, were sensationalistic, overplaying crime and gore in hyperbolic battles to steal readers from each other. Entering the fray, Eddy introduced a newspaper with a different mission. Eddy's *The Christian Science Monitor*, founded in 1908, sought to deal with issues and problems on a high plane and to help the world come up with solutions.

KEY PERSON
Mary Baker Eddy founded *The Christian Science Monitor*.

Constructive Journalism. Since its 1908 founding, *The Christian Science Monitor* has emphasized solution-oriented journalism. The *Monitor*, based in Boston, began as an antidote to sensationalistic newspapers, emphasizing accurate and truthful coverage to help people address serious problems facing humankind.

Nobody, least of all Mary Baker Eddy, expected such an intellectually oriented newspaper to make money, at least not right away, so the church underwrote expenses when subscriptions, newsstand sales and advertising revenue fell short. The *Monitor* sought subscriptions nationwide and abroad, and it developed a following. While edited in Boston, the *Monitor* was conceived as an international, not a local, newspaper, and it became the first national daily newspaper in the United States.

The *Christian Science Monitor* tries to emphasize positive news, but it also deals with crime, disaster, war and other down-beat news, and it has won Pulitzer Prizes for covering them. The thrust, though, is interpretive, unlike the sensationalistic newspapers to which Mary Baker Eddy wanted an alternative. The *Monitor* does not cover events and issues to titillate its readers. Rather, as veteran *Monitor* editor Erwin Canham explained, the newspaper's mission is "to help give humankind the tools with which to work out its salvation." The *Monitor* is not preachy; in fact, only one plainly labeled religious article appears in each issue. It seeks to lead and influence by example.

A few seasoned foreign correspondents provide the backbone of the *Monitor's* respected international coverage, and their stories are backed up with stories from reporters who work for other news organizations but who moonlight for the *Monitor*. A staff in Washington anchors domestic coverage. The cultural coverage and editorials are widely read.

Circulation peaked at 239,000 in 1971, the year when the *Monitor* joined several leading newspapers, including the New York *Times*, in printing secret Pentagon documents over the objections of the Nixon administration. By then, the *Monitor* was being printed at plants near Boston, Chicago, Los Angeles and New York for same-day mail delivery to much of the nation, as well as at a plant near London for foreign distribution. Since the 1971 peak, however, circulation has deteriorated to less than 140,000. Failing to find a sufficient following among national advertisers, the *Monitor* has shrunk from a full-size newspaper to a thinner and thinner tabloid. A handicap in finding advertising revenue is the church's doctrine-based refusal to accept ads for alcoholic beverages, tobacco products and drugs.

It is unclear how much longer the church, whose membership has dwindled to 150,000 and whose overall income is estimated at only $85 million a year, can afford to carry out Mary Baker Eddy's goal for a strong Christian Science presence in the news media.

HOMETOWN NEWSPAPERS

STUDY PREVIEW   The United States has 1,570 daily newspapers, most oriented to covering hometown news and carrying local advertising. Big-city dailies are the most visible hometown newspapers, but medium-size and small dailies have made significant strides in quality in recent decades and eroded the metros' outlying circulation.

METROPOLITAN DAILIES

TEACHING OBJECTIVE 4-4
U.S. is a nation of local and regional newspapers.

In every region of the United States, there is a newspaper whose name is a household word. These are metropolitan dailies with extensive regional circulation. In New England, for example, the Boston *Globe* covers Boston but also prides itself on extensive coverage of Massachusetts state government, as well as coverage of neighboring states. The *Globe* has a Washington bureau, and it sends reporters abroad on special assignments.

When experts are asked to list the nation's best newspapers, the lists are dominated by these high-visibility metropolitan dailies. The New York *Times* perennially leads these lists, but others with a continuing presence include the Baltimore *Sun*, Chicago *Tribune*, Dallas *Morning News*, Houston *Chronicle*, Los Angeles *Times*, Miami *Herald*, Minneapolis *Star Tribune*, Philadelphia *Inquirer*, St. Louis *Post Dispatch* and Washington *Post*.

Here are snapshots of three leading metro dailies:

NEW YORK *TIMES*. Not a librarian anywhere would want to be without a subscription to the New York *Times*, which is one reason that the *Times* boasts at least one subscriber in every county in the country. Since its founding in 1851, the *Times* has had a reputation for fair and thorough coverage of foreign news. A large, widely respected staff covers Washington. It is a newspaper of record, printing the president's annual state of the union address and other important documents in their entirety. The *Times* is an important research source, in part because the *Times* puts out a monthly and annual index that lists every story. The editorials are among the most quoted.

The news sections are somber and gray, but inside sections, although without color, have become dazzling graphic displays in recent years. However, in March of 1994, color was added to the *Arts and Leisure* section and to the *Book Review*. The Sunday edition includes the glitzy New York *Times Magazine*, a serious book review magazine, and one of the world's most followed crossword puzzles. Unusual for an American newspaper, especially one with a large Sunday edition, the *Times* carries no comics.

LECTURE RESOURCE 4-D
Video: *News Leaders*.

LECTURE RESOURCE 4-E
Video: *Special to the Times*.

New York *Times*. The New York *Times* was founded in 1851 as a serious newspaper, a reputation it has maintained. The *Times* even looks serious, with its somber Page 1 design. Inside, though, Sunday readers find the splashy, colorful New York *Times Magazine*, a serious book review and one of the world's most followed crossword puzzles. The newspaper is especially noted for foreign and Washington coverage and its influential, often-quoted editorial section.

While the *Times* prints a national edition at remote plants for same-day delivery to much of the country, most of its circulation is in the New York metropolitan area. Because it is edited primarily for its own area and because it does not seek advertising for a national audience, the *Times* is not truly a national newspaper.

LOS ANGELES *TIMES*.   The Los Angeles *Times* edged out the declining New York *Daily News* in 1990 as the nation's largest metropolitan daily when circulation reached 1.3 million. By many measures, the *Times* is huge. A typical Sunday edition makes quite a thump on the doorstep at four pounds and 444 pages.

The *Times* has 1,300 editors and reporters, some in 27 foreign bureaus and 13 U.S. bureaus. Fifty-seven reporters cover the federal government in Washington alone. To cover the 1991 war against Iraq, the *Times* dispatched 20 reporters and photographers to the Gulf region, compared to 12 for the New York *Times* and 10 for the Washington *Post*, the traditional leading U.S. metro dailies for foreign coverage. Critics say the Los Angeles *Times* is sometimes disappointing in local coverage, but it is applauded for the coverage to which it channels resources.

WASHINGTON *POST*.   The Washington *Post* cemented its reputation for investigative reporting by breaking revelation after revelation in the 1972 Watergate scandal, until finally Richard Nixon resigned the presidency in disgrace. The *Wall Street Journal*, New York *Times* and Los Angeles *Times*, all with large Washington staffs, compete aggressively with the *Post* for major federal stories, but the *Post* remains the most quoted newspaper for government coverage.

With the demise of the afternoon Washington *Daily News* and the *Star*, the *Post* was left the only local newspaper in the nation's capital, which upset critics who perceived a liberal bias in the *Post*. This prompted the Unification Church of the Reverend Sun Myung Moon to found the Washington *Times* as a rightist daily. The *Times* has only a fraction of the *Post*'s 772,000 circulation, but its scrappy coverage inserts local excitement into Washington journalism, as does its incessant sniping at the *Post* and *Post*-owned *Newsweek* magazine.

HOMETOWN DAILIES

With their aggressive reporting on national and regional issues, the metro dailies receive more attention than smaller dailies, but most Americans read hometown dailies. By and large, these locally oriented newspapers, most of them chain-owned, have been incredibly profitable while making significant journalistic progress since World War II.

Fifty years ago, people in small towns generally bought both a metropolitan daily and a local newspaper. Hometown dailies were thin and coverage was hardly comprehensive. Editorial pages tended to offer only a single perspective. Readers had few alternative sources of information. Since then, these smaller dailies have hired better-prepared journalists, acquired new technology and strengthened their local advertising base.

Hometown dailies have grown larger and more comprehensive. The years between 1970 and 1980 were especially important for quantum increases in news coverage. The space available for news, called the *news hole*, increased more than 25 percent. Many hometown dailies also gave much of their large news holes to bigger and more diverse opinion sections. Most editorial sections today are smorgasbords of perspectives.

MEDIA DATABANK

Newsroom Salaries

Reporters, photographers and copyeditors at 134 U.S. and Canadian newspapers are represented in contract negotiations by the Newspaper Guild, a union affiliated with the AFL-CIO. Reporters at the New York *Times* had the most lucrative guild contract in 1992, almost $1,200 a week, $62,000 a year, for reporters and photographers with two years of experience. Many reporters earn more for merit, in bonuses and for working odd hours.

The lowest guild salary for experienced reporters was $340 a week at the Newport News, Virginia, *Daily Press* and *Times-Herald.*

The U.S. guild average was $685 a week, $35,620 a year. National averages that include non-union newsrooms are hard to calculate because there's no reliable data-gathering mechanism.

Weekly salaries negotiated by the Newspaper Guild and also by the Wire Service Guild for member reporters and photographers are listed below, rounded off. Desk editors under these contracts typically earned $30 to $40 more per week, although at the Washington *Post* it was $85.

New York *Times*	$1,190 after two years
New York *Daily News*	1,010 after six years
Philadelphia *Inquirer* and *Daily News*	1,000 after five years
Chicago *Sun-Times*	940 after five years
Reuters	910 after four years
Baltimore *Sun* and *Evening Sun*	890 after five years
Honolulu *Advertiser* and *Star-Bulletin*	890 after five years
San Francisco *Chronicle* and *Examiner*	890 after six years
San Jose, Calif., *Mercury-News*	890 after six years
San Mateo, Calif., *Times*	890 after three years
Washington *Post*	890 after four years
St. Paul, Minn., *Pioneer Press*	880 after five years
Buffalo, N.Y., *News*	870 after five years
Pittsburgh *Post-Gazette*	870 after five years

Associated Press (New York and Washington)	$860 after five years
Cleveland *Plain Dealer*	850 after four years
Denver *Post*	840 after five years
Denver *Rocky Mountain News*	840 after five years
Minneapolis *Star Tribune*	840 after five years
Providence, R.I., *Journal-Bulletin*	840 after four years
San Diego *Union-Tribune*	830 after six years
Long Beach, Calif., *Press-Telegram*	820 after five years
Toledo, Ohio, *Blade*	820 after four years
Monterey, Calif., *Herald*	800 after six years
Santa Rosa, Calif., *Press Democrat*	800 after six years
Boston *Herald*	790 after four years
Eugene, Ore., *Register Guard*	780 after five years
Akron, Ohio, *Beacon-Journal*	770 after four years
Seattle *Times* and *Post-Intelligencer*	760 after four years
Detroit *Free Press* and *News*	750 after four years

Many metro dailies have lost circulation to upstart newspapers in the suburbs. The Los Angeles *Times* is an example. While becoming a world-class newspaper with extensive foreign and national coverage, to the neglect of local coverage, the *Times* lost thousands of readers in suburban areas to the Orange County *Register.*

In some cities, metro dailies went into niche marketing to keep suburban readers and advertisers. The Chicago *Tribune* stalled a threat from a well-financed north suburban chain by creating five new sections with news about specific suburban areas. The new sections went only to the designated areas, and suburban businesses could buy space in any zoned section they chose. This made it possible for small-budget advertisers, like neighborhood hardware stores and bakeries, to place their ads in the *Tribune* rather than a suburban paper. Today, the Chicago *Tribune*'s zoning is so sophisticated that advertisers may choose among 360 different neighborhoods in which preprints may be inserted in the newspaper.

Among papers that have stemmed circulation declines have been the Atlanta *Constitution and Journal.* In an assault on the Atlanta dailies, the New York Times

MEDIA DATABANK

Daily Newspaper Circulation

	Daily	Sunday		Daily	Sunday
Wall Street Journal	1.8 million		Philadelphia *Inquirer*	487,000	944,000
USA Today	1.5 million		Newark *Star Ledger*	473,000	704,000
New York *Times*	1.1 million	1.8 million	Houston *Chronicle*	413,000	606,000
Los Angeles *Times*	1.0 million	1.5 million	Minneapolis *Star Tribune*	411,000	696,000
Washington *Post*	814,000	1.2 million	Cleveland *Plain Dealer*	396,000	543,000
New York *Daily News*	764,000	927,000	New York *Post*	394,000	
Long Island *Newsday*	747,000	825,000	Miami *Herald*	387,000	509,000
Chicago *Tribune*	690,000	1.1 million	San Diego *Union-Tribune*	383,000	455,000
Detroit *Free Press*	556,000	1.2 million	Detroit *News*	367,000	1.2 million
San Francisco *Chronicle*	544,000	705,000	Phoenix *Republic*	348,000	547,000
Chicago *Sun-Times*	535,000	524,000	Orange County *Register*	344,000	303,000
Boston *Globe*	508,000	814,000	Denver *Rocky Mountain News*	342,000	425,000
Dallas *Morning News*	494,000	814,000			

Company bought the suburban Gwinett, Georgia, *Daily News* and poured $40 million into new presses, cut the newsrack price from 25 cents to 10 cents a copy, and slashed advertising rates. The Atlanta *Constitution* and *Journal* responded with a daily section of Gwinett news, matched the suburban rival's cut-rate subscriptions and advertising rates and promoted itself through telephone solicitations several times a year to every Gwinett household that didn't subscribe. Five years later the battle ended. Forty-eight million dollars lost, the New York *Times* shut down the Gwinett *Daily News*.

The Philadelphia *Inquirer*, using zoned editions, has aggressively resisted suburban threats. In an interview for *Forbes* magazine, *Inquirer* Editor Maxwell E.P. King said the survival of metro dailies requires combating reader losses at the suburban fringes of their circulation areas: "If readers are going to take only one paper, we have to make damn sure it's us."

CHALLENGES FOR DAILY NEWSPAPERS

STUDY PREVIEW   Daily newspaper circulation in the United States is stagnant, and other media are eroding the dominance of the newspaper as an advertising medium. Even so, the newspaper industry is financially strong, and newspapers have inherent advantages over competing media.

CIRCULATION PATTERNS

Despite the profitability of the U.S. newspaper industry overall, all is not well. Many metropolitan and non-metro dailies face problems. Overall, circulation growth has stalled after peaking at 62.8 million in 1988. More seriously, market penetration has declined sharply. The 1960 census found that the average American household subscribed to 1.12 newspapers. By 1990 the average was fewer than 0.7 subscription per household. Fewer people are reading newspapers.

The circulation decline has been heaviest among evening newspapers. Television is largely responsible. As television became the dominant evening activity in the nation, Americans spent less time with evening newspapers and eventually dropped their subscriptions. The decline in evening newspapers, called *PMs*, has been especially severe in blue-collar towns, where most families once built their life-style around 7 a.m. to 3 p.m. factory shifts. Today, as the United States shifts from an industrial to a service economy, more people work 9-to-5 jobs and have less discretionary time in the afternoon and evening to read a newspaper. Predictably, advertisers have followed readers from evenings to mornings, and one by one afternoon newspapers in two-newspaper cities folded. In many places, afternoon newspapers have followed their readers' life-style changes and converted to the morning publication cycle.

ADVERTISING PATTERNS

Even morning papers are having advertising problems. The heady days when newspapers could count on more advertising every year seem over. Projections for the rest of the 1990s indicate that newspaper advertising will be lucky to hold its own. Television's growth is a factor, but other media, including ads distributed by mail, are eating into the historic dominance of the newspaper as an advertising medium. In 1980 daily newspapers led all media with 27.6 percent of the total advertising pie. By 1992 the newspaper slice was down to 23.4 percent. The situation varied from city to city, but overall newspaper advertising was flattening out.

Besides television, daily newspaper advertising revenue has taken a hit from the consolidation of retailing into fewer albeit bigger companies. Grocery, discount

CNN Electronic Newspapers
More than 600 newspapers provide news and information via the telephone for subscribers who want updates more often than the next edition. The Newspaper Association of America, a trade group, is confident, however, that the ink-on-paper newspapers as we know them, will be around for a good, long time. This segment, reported by CNN's Mark Sheerer, aired June 10, 1992.

TEACHING OBJECTIVE 4-5
Newspapers may lose dominance as advertising medium.

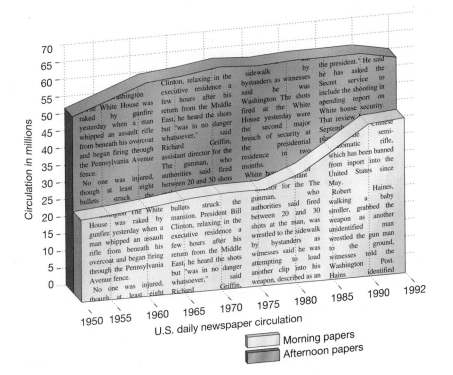

Death in the Afternoon.
American newspaper circulation is almost stagnant at 60 million a day. Growth leveled off in the 1970s as evening television newscasts drew people away from afternoon newspapers. Some major afternoon newspapers folded; others switched to morning publication. Afternoon newspaper circulation, which peaked at 36.2 million in 1965, slipped to 17.7 million in 1972.

Morning papers
Afternoon papers

U.S. daily newspaper circulation

and department store mergers cut down on advertising revenue. Fewer competing retail chains meant fewer ads.

This was a major loss because the grocery, discount and department stores were newspapers' largest source of income. The Los Angeles *Times* estimated it lost $12 million in ad revenue because of mergers in 1989 alone.

A growing advertising practice, bypassing the traditional mass media and sending circulars and catalogs directly to potential customers, also is cutting into newspaper advertising income. This *direct mail* trend took off in the 1970s and accelerated into the 1990s. Today, direct mail advertising accounts for 14 percent of the money spent nationwide by advertisers. To win back advertisers who switched to direct mail, newspapers are willing to tuck preprinted advertising circulars, mostly from large retailers, inside the regular paper. In one sense, *preprints*, as they are called, represent lost revenue because in the days before direct mail those ads would have been placed in the regular pages of the newspaper at full ad rates. Newspaper preprint rates are discounted deeply to compete with postal rates.

PROSPECTS FOR THE DAILY PRESS

While daily newspapers, both metros and smaller dailies, face problems, hardly are they on the verge of extinction. While competing media have taken away some newspaper retail advertising, the want ads, formally called *classified advertising*, may not be glamorous to anybody except newspaper owners. At some newspapers, classifieds generate more than half of the revenue. The national average exceeds 40 percent. Television and radio have not found a way to offer a competing service, and not even free-distribution papers devoted to classified advertising have reversed the growth in daily newspaper classified revenue.

Also, the newspaper remains the dominant advertising medium for most major local advertisers: grocery stores, department stores, automobile dealerships and discount stores.

On the downside, daily newspapers have suffered major losses over the years in national advertising, mostly to magazines and network television. Despite the losses, newspapers have not given up on national advertising. Every newspaper has a broker, called a *national representative*, whose business is to line up national advertising for its client newspapers.

Daily newspapers have inherent advantages that competing media cannot match, at least not now.

PORTABILITY.   Newspapers are a portable medium. People can pick up a newspaper any time and take it with them, which is hardly possible with newspaper's biggest rival for advertisers, television. In the long term, as television sets are installed in more places and with the arrival of miniaturized, battery-operated television receivers, this newspaper advantage may erode.

VARIETY.   A newspaper has more room to cover a greater variety of events and provide a greater variety of features than competing media units. The entire script for a 30-minute television newscast can fit on a fraction of a single newspaper page. This advantage may dissipate as people have greater access to new specialized television services and zip and zap among them: the Weather Channel on cable, sports channels, consumer information channels, ticker-tape streamers on cable. Also, 900-number telephone services offer scores, game details and sports news on demand, although they are more expensive than buying a newspaper.

INDEXED CONTENT.   Newspapers remain quick sources of information, ideas and entertainment. Readers can quickly find items that interest them by using headlines as an indexing device. With television, people have to wait for the items they want.

DEPTH COVERAGE.   Newspapers have room for lengthy, in-depth treatments, which most contemporary broadcast formats preclude. Rare are radio newscasts with stories longer than 120 words, and most television focuses only on highlights.

These traditional advantages that accrue to the newspaper as a medium are being eroded, but the newspaper remains the only package that has them all. In general, newspaper companies are in a good position to survive because of an asset that competing media lack: the largest, most skilled newsroom staffs in their communities. Television stations have relatively minuscule news-gathering staffs, and they lack the tradition and experience to match the ongoing, thorough coverage of newspapers. The strength of newspaper companies is their news-gathering capability, not their means of delivery. Since the 1970s newspapers have experimented with facsimile and television text delivery, gaining familiarity with alternate technology for disseminating their main product, which is news, not newsprint.

WEEKLY NEWSPAPERS

> **STUDY PREVIEW**   Many community weekly newspapers, especially in fast-growing suburbs, are thriving, while others, especially rural weeklies, have fallen on hard times. In all areas, free-distribution advertising sheets called *shoppers* have attracted strong followings.

COMMUNITY WEEKLIES

Weekly newspapers are making strong circulation gains, especially in suburban communities, and some have moved into publishing twice a week. In all, almost 8,000 weekly newspapers are published in the United States, with circulation approaching 45 million. Weeklies are received in almost 60 percent of the nation's households, up almost one-third from 1970.

To the detriment of metro dailies, many advertisers are following their customers to the suburban weeklies. Advertisers have found that they can buy space in weeklies for less and reach their likeliest customers. Ralph Ingersoll, whose weeklies give fits to the daily Long Island *Newsday* in New York, explained it this way in an interview with *Forbes:* "If you're an automobile dealer on Long Island, you can pay, say, $14,000 for a tabloid page in *Newsday*, most of which is wasted because the people that get it will never buy a car in your neck of the woods, or you can go into one of the weekender publications and pay a few hundred dollars and reach just the people likely to drive over to your shop."

Some weeklies, particularly those in upscale suburbs, offer sophisticated coverage of community issues. Others feature a homey mix of reports on social events such as who visited whom for Sunday dinner. The success of these weeklies sometimes is called "telephone book journalism" because of the emphasis on names, the somewhat ·overdrawn theory being that people buy papers to see their names in print. Weeklies have in common that they cover their communities with a detail that metro dailies have neither staff nor space to match. There is no alternative to keeping up with local news.

TEACHING OBJECTIVE 4-6
Community newspapers booming.

Rural weeklies generally have fallen on rough times. Part of their problem is the diminishing significance of agriculture in the national economy and the continuing depopulation of rural America. In communities that remain retail centers, rural weeklies can maintain a strong advertising base. However, the Main Street of many small towns has declined as improved roads and the construction of major retail stores like Wal-Mart draw customers from 40 to 50 miles away. In earlier days, those customers patronized hometown retailers, who placed significant advertising in hometown weeklies. Today many of these Main Street retailers, unable to compete with giant discount stores, are out of business.

SHOPPERS

Free-distribution papers that carry only advertisements have become increasingly important as vehicles for classified advertising. In recent years, *shoppers* have attracted display advertising that earlier would have gone to regular newspapers. Almost all shoppers undercut daily newspapers on advertising rates. The number of shoppers has grown to about 1,500 nationwide, and they no longer are merely an ignorable competitor for daily newspapers for advertising.

By definition, shoppers are strictly advertising sheets, but beginning in the 1970s some shoppers added editorial content, usually material that came free over the transom, such as publicity and occasional self-serving columns from legislators. Some shoppers have added staff members to compile calendars and provide a modicum of news coverage. Most of these papers, however, remain ad sheets with little that is journalistic. Still, their news-gathering efforts and expenses are minuscule compared to those of a daily newspaper.

ALTERNATIVE AND MINORITY NEWSPAPERS

STUDY PREVIEW   Most newspapers attempt broad coverage for a broad audience, but more specialized newspapers are important in the lives of many people. These include counter-culture, gay, black and Spanish-language newspapers, many of which are expanding and prospering today.

COUNTER-CULTURE NEWSPAPERS

TEACHING OBJECTIVE 4-7
Counter-culture, gay and Spanish language papers booming.

KEY PEOPLE
Norman Mailer and Don Wolf helped invent *Village Voice*.

A group of friends in the Greenwich Village neighborhood of New York, including novelist Norman Mailer and Don Wolf, decided to start a newspaper. Thus in 1955 was born the *Village Voice*, a free-wheeling weekly that became a prototype for a 1960s phenomenon called the *alternative press* and that has continued to thrive.

In its early days, the *Village Voice* was a haven for bohemian writers of diverse competence who volunteered occasional pieces, some lengthy, many rambling. Many articles purported to be investigative examinations of hypocritical people and institutions, but, as *Voice* veteran Nat Hentoff has noted, nobody ever bothered to check "noisome facts," let alone the "self-righteous author." The *Voice* seemed to scorn traditional, detached, neutral reporting. Despite its flaws, the amateurism gave the *Voice* a charm, and it picked up readership.

The *Voice* today is more polished and journalistically serious. The characteristics that made it distinctive in its early history, and which were picked up by other counter-culture newspapers, include:

- Antiestablishment political coverage with a strong antimilitary slant.
- Cultural coverage that emphasizes contrarian music and art and exalts sex and drugs.
- Interpretive coverage focusing more on issues of special concern to alienated young people.
- Extensive entertainment coverage and listings of events.
- Conversational, sometimes crude style that includes four-letter words and gratuitous expletives for their shock value.
- Extensive personals for dating and sex liaisons.

By delivering a loyal readership that was hard to reach through mainstream media, many counter-culture newspapers became fat with advertising. Today, about 100 alternative newspapers are published in the United States, and many are prospering. With a circulation of 172,000, the *Village Voice* is widely available in big-city newsracks and by mail throughout the country.

Phoenix-based New Times, Inc., started by college dropouts Michael Lacey and James Larkin in 1970, exemplifies the success of latter-day counter-culture newspapers. Their company owns the Dallas *Observer*, Denver *Westward*, Miami *New Times* and Phoenix *New Times*, with a combined circulation of 410,000. The flagship *New Times* paper in Phoenix averages 144 pages a week, reaches about one in four Phoenix adults, and challenges the daily Phoenix *Gazette* and *Arizona Republic* for advertising. Like many counter-culture newspapers, the New Times papers are give-aways left on newsracks for passersby to take.

GAY NEWSPAPERS

Jim Michaels began publishing the nation's first gay newspaper, the Los Angeles *Advocate*, out of his living room in 1967. Today, 125 gay newspapers have a total circulation of more than 1 million. Most are free papers distributed at gay bars, nightclubs and businesses, and many are financially marginal. However, mainstream advertisers are beginning to take notice of the loyalty of gay readers to their newspapers. In 1990 the Columbia CD Club tested a membership ad offering eight discs for $1 in 12 gay newspapers. The response rate was so high that the club began placing the ad in 70 gay papers within a year.

The success of the Columbia ad confirmed a 1988 study that found unexpected affluence among readers of eight major gay newspapers. Individual incomes averaged $36,800, which was three times the national average, and household incomes averaged $55,430, which was 2½ times the national average. The number of college graduates, 60 percent, and the number of people in professional and managerial jobs, 49 percent, was three times the national average. Other national advertisers followed Columbia into the gay press.

KEY PERSON
Jim Michael founded first gay newspaper.

BLACK NEWSPAPERS

The ongoing integration of black and white people in American society has eroded the role of black newspapers since World War II, but 172 black newspapers remain in publication. In all, the black newspapers have a circulation of 3.6 million, a ratio of about 1:10 to the nation's black population. At their peak after World War II, black newspapers included three nationally distributed dailies, from Baltimore, Chicago and Pittsburgh, whose combined circulation approached 600,000. The

LECTURE RESOURCE F
The Black Media.

black dailies today, the Atlanta *Daily World*, Chicago *Daily Defender* and New York *Daily Challenge*, together have a circulation of 106,000, almost all local.

Black newspapers have been important in the U.S. civil rights movement, beginning in 1827 with *John Russwurm* and *Samuel Cornish's Freedom's Journal*, the first black newspaper. *Frederick Douglass's North Star*, founded in 1847, was a strident abolitionist sheet before the Civil War, and *W. E. B. Du Bois's Crisis*, founded in 1910, was a militant voice for black advancement. Today, some black newspapers, like *A. M. Journal*, founded by American Muslim *Malcolm X* in 1961, crusade for causes in the tradition of their early predecessors. In the early 1990s, the Chicago *Defender* was alone among U.S. news media in covering the Haitian refugee situation until others picked up the issue and forced public attention on it. In general, though, black newspapers focus on neighborhood social, church and sports events, and the tone is moderate.

Prospects for black newspapers generally do not appear strong. Only 15 percent of the advertising placed in black media, including television, radio and magazines, goes to newspapers. Media scholar James Tinney found that middle-income blacks look to establishment rather than black newspapers for information, even while relying on other black institutions, like the church and universities, for intellectual stimulation.

FOREIGN-LANGUAGE NEWSPAPERS

Through every wave of immigration, newspapers in foreign languages have sprouted to serve newcomers to the United States in their native tongue. In 1914, there were 140 foreign-language dailies published in the United States. About one-third were German, led by New York *Vorwarts* with a circulation of 175,000. The U.S. German-language press withered during World War I when its loyalty was challenged, but, like other foreign-language newspapers, it undoubtedly would have eventually disappeared anyway as the immigrants assimilated into the mainstream culture.

Today, the fast-growing Hispanic minority represents about 1 of every 15 Americans, and although most are bilingual, 6 daily newspapers and about 150 weeklies are published in Spanish. In general, these newspapers are thriving. The Knight-Ridder newspaper chain publishes *El Herald* as a daily Spanish-language companion to its Miami *Herald* and sells 67,000 copies a day. In New York, the Gannett chain operates the 63,000-circulation daily *El Diario-La Prensa*. Most Spanish-language newspapers are owned by Hispanics, but the presence of the gigantic, profitable Knight-Ridder and Gannett chains bespeaks the commercial viability of these papers.

The profitability of Spanish-language newspapers is fueled partly by the desire of many national advertisers to tap into the large Hispanic market. The newspapers' penetration, however, is not especially high. In heavily Hispanic Los Angeles, *La Opinion* has a circulation of only 55,000 a day. In Miami the competing *El Herald* and *Diario Las Americas* together sell only 130,000 copies a day. In New York *El Diario-La Prensa* and *Noticias del Mundo* together have a circulation of less than 130,000 in a metropolitan area with 2.5 million Hispanic people.

Whether Spanish-language newspapers will disappear as did earlier foreign-language newspapers is uncertain. While assimilation is occurring, many Hispanics are intent on maintaining their distinctive cultural identity and resist adopting English. Also, there is more sympathy for multiculturalism in the society than in the past. For the foreseeable future, Spanish-language newspapers will have a strong following among the continuing influx of people from Latin America and

Spanish-Language Newspapers. As the percentage of Spanish-speaking people in the United States has increased, so has the circulation of Spanish-language newspapers. Whether this growth will be sustained depends on the assimilation process. Earlier foreign-language newspapers went through explosive growth that accompanied immigration patterns and then withered as immigrants eased into the mainstream language and life-styles. The Spanish-language press in the United States today includes six daily newspapers and 150 weeklies.

the Caribbean. With this immigration and a high fertility rate, the U.S. Hispanic population is growing about 4 percent a year.

Some analysts feel the Spanish-language media have peaked as Hispanics assimilate into the dominant U.S. culture. Frank Welzer, president of Sony's Latin music company, was quoted in a *Forbes* magazine analysis: "Hispanics watch as much English-language television as anyone else. It's only recent arrivals and the elderly who use Spanish media exclusively." Sigfredo Hernandez, a specialist in Hispanic marketing at Rider College in New Jersey, was quoted in the same article: "If you're trying to reach younger Hispanics, they've got to be addressed in English." Christopher Palmeri and Joshua Levine, who wrote the *Forbes* analysis, concluded: "Of course, there will always be a market for specialized advertising aimed at recent immigrants. Just recall the lively German, Italian and Yiddish language media of yore. But it is beginning to dawn on advertisers that the idea of a vast and unassimilated 'Hispanic market' is just a myth fostered by professional multiculturists and hucksters."

CHAPTER WRAP-UP

Numerous, once powerful newspapers have disappeared since the middle of the century, among them the Chicago *Daily News*, Los Angeles *Herald Examiner*, New York *Herald Tribune*, Philadelphia *Bulletin* and Washington *Star*. U.S. dailies, which numbered 1,745 in 1980, were down to 1,570 by 1993. Other media, particularly television and its evening newscasts, have siphoned readers away from evening newspapers. Also, while newspapers remain the largest U.S. advertising medium, television is making gains.

Can newspapers survive? Even if people were to stop buying newspapers tomorrow, newspaper organizations would survive because they have an asset that competing media lack: the largest, most skilled newsroom staffs in their communities. The presses and the ink-on-newsprint medium for carrying the message may not have a long future, but newspapers' news-gathering capability will endure. Already newspapers have experimented with facsimile and television text delivery, gaining familiarity with alternate technology for disseminating their main product, which is news, not newsprint.

Besides the daily national, metro and hometown newspapers, the United States has thousands of weekly community newspapers and special-interest papers. By focusing on audiences with special interests, many of these newspapers are attracting more advertisers and either solidifying their existing financial base or building strong new foundations for the future.

QUESTIONS FOR **REVIEW**

1. Describe how newspapers are important in the lives of most Americans.

2. Explain the rise of newspaper chains. Have they been good for readers?

3. Why is the United States a nation mostly of provincial newspapers?

4. Many metropolitan daily newspapers have lost circulation and some have shut down. Why?

5. What challenges to their dominance as a news and advertising medium do newspapers face?

6. Community newspapers, especially suburban weeklies, are booming. Why?

7. What kinds of newspapers aimed at narrow audience segments are prospering?

QUESTIONS FOR **CRITICAL THINKING**

1. The United States is called a nation of provincial newspapers. Is the label correct? Do the *Wall Street Journal, USA Today* and the *Christian Science Monitor* fit the provincial characterization?

2. How can you explain the declining number of U.S. newspapers and their losses in market penetration in view of the newspaper industry's profitability?

3. How have newspapers met challenges to their advertising revenue from radio, television, direct mail and shoppers?

4. Can you explain why a greater percentage of American newspapers are published for morning reading, not afternoon?

5. Identify advantages and disadvantages in the consolidation of U.S. newspapers, daily and weekly, into chains and cross-media conglomerates.

6. Can you identify how *USA Today* has changed American newspapers by comparing your hometown paper today with an issue from the 1970s?

7. How have improvements in American newspapers led to fewer households taking more than a single newspaper?

8. Considering the business orientation that makes newspaper chains so profitable, does it seem unusual that someone like Al Neuharth, whose background was in journalism rather than business, led Gannett through its incredible and profitable growth?

FOR **FURTHER LEARNING**

Bill Bishop. "A Warning from Smithville: Owning Your Own Weekly," *Washington Journalism Review* 10 (May 1988):4, 25–32. Bishop offers a first-person case study on how chains are consolidating the weekly newspaper industry. He deals with the pleasure and pain of publishing an independent rural weekly.

Leo Bogart. *Preserving the Press: How Daily Newspapers Mobilized to Keep Their Readers* (Columbia University Press, 1991). Bogart, a newspaper industry analyst, describes the strengths and weaknesses of newspapers in times of changing technology, reader life-style changes and preferences, and new options for advertisers through other media.

Ellis Cose. *The Press* (Morrow, 1989). Cose profiles the Washington *Post;* Times Mirror, owner of the Los Angeles *Times;* the New York *Times;* and the Gannett and Knight-Ridder chains.

Jonathan Curiel. "Gay Newspapers," *Editor & Publisher* 224 (August 3, 1991):32, 14–19. Curiel, a San Francisco *Chronicle* reporter, gives a history of gay newspapers and their growing attractiveness as an advertising medium.

Francis X. Dealy. *The Power and the Money: Inside the Wall Street Journal* (Birch Lane Press, 1993). Dealy, a former Dow Jones employee, claims the *Journal* has gone soft, citing a lack of investigative fervor on the 1980s' excesses in American business. Dealy argues that the newspaper missed scandals that would not have escaped its attention in an earlier era.

Edwin Diamond. *Behind the Times: Inside the New York* Times (Villard Books, 1994). Diamond, media columnist for *New York* magazine, updates Gay Talese's classic 1969 study of the most prestigious newspaper in the United States.

Ernest C. Hynds. *American Newspapers in the 1980s* (Hastings House, 1980). Hynds, a journalism professor, offers a snapshot of all aspects of the newspaper industry.

Lauren Kessler. *Against the Grain: The Dissident Press in America* (Sage, 1984). Kessler surveys the newspapers of minority and persecuted groups through U.S. history.

Michael Leapman. *Arrogant Aussie: The Rupert Murdoch Story* (Lyle Stuart, 1985). Leapman, who worked at two newspapers at the time of Murdoch's takeovers, offers an unfriendly portrait of how Murdoch's media empire was built.

Barbara Matusow. "Allen H. Neuharth Today," *Washington Journalism Review* 8 (August 1986):8, 18–24. Media commentator Matusow traces Neuharth's career, quirks and all, to the eve of his retirement as chief executive officer of the Gannett media chain.

Courtland Milloy. "The Black Press: A Victim of Its Own Crusade," *Washington Journalism Review* 6 (June 1984):5, 50–53. Milloy, a Washington *Post* reporter, profiles the bleak state of black newspapers.

Al Neuharth. *Confessions of an S.O.B.* (Doubleday, 1989). Neuharth, who created *USA Today*, explains his controversial newspaper management style in this sprightly autobiography.

Christopher Palmeri and Joshua Levine. "No Habla Espanol." *Forbes* (December 24, 1991), 140–142. These *Forbes* reporters conclude that the idea of a vast, unassimilated Spanish-language media market in the United States is "a myth fostered by professional multiculturists and hucksters."

Edward E. Scharfe. *Worldly Power: The Making of the* Wall Street Journal (Beaufort, 1986). Traces the history of the *Journal* with emphasis on its editorial leadership since World War II.

William Shawcross. *Murdoch* (Simon & Schuster, 1993). Shawcross chronicles the rise of Rupert Murdoch as a global media baron and attempts to explain what motivates the man. Shawcross, a British journalist, relies extensively on interviews with people around Murdoch and Murdoch himself.

James D. Squires. *Read All About It! The Corporate Takeover of America's Newspapers* (Times Books, 1993). Squires, a former Chicago *Tribune* executive, makes a case that newspaper managers are preoccupied with advertising and profits. As a result, the traditional separation of advertising and news staffs has been eroded, which in turn has led to news coverage that is compromised by newspapers' financial interests.

Jim Strader. "Black on Black," *Washington Journalism Review* 14 (March 1992):2, 33–36. Strader, a Pittsburgh reporter, discusses the decline of national black newspapers and their hopes to beef up local coverage to restore their influence.

Times Mirror Center for The People and The Press. *The Age of Indifference* (Times Mirror Company, 1990). This major study found that young people have significantly less interest in news than the generations before them. They read fewer newspapers and watch less news on television.

■**F**OR **K**EEPING **U**P TO **D**ATE

Editor & Publisher is a weekly trade journal for the newspaper industry.

NewsInc. is a monthly trade journal on newspaper management.

Newspaper Research Journal is a quarterly dealing mostly with applied research.

Presstime is published monthly by the American Newspaper Publishers Association.

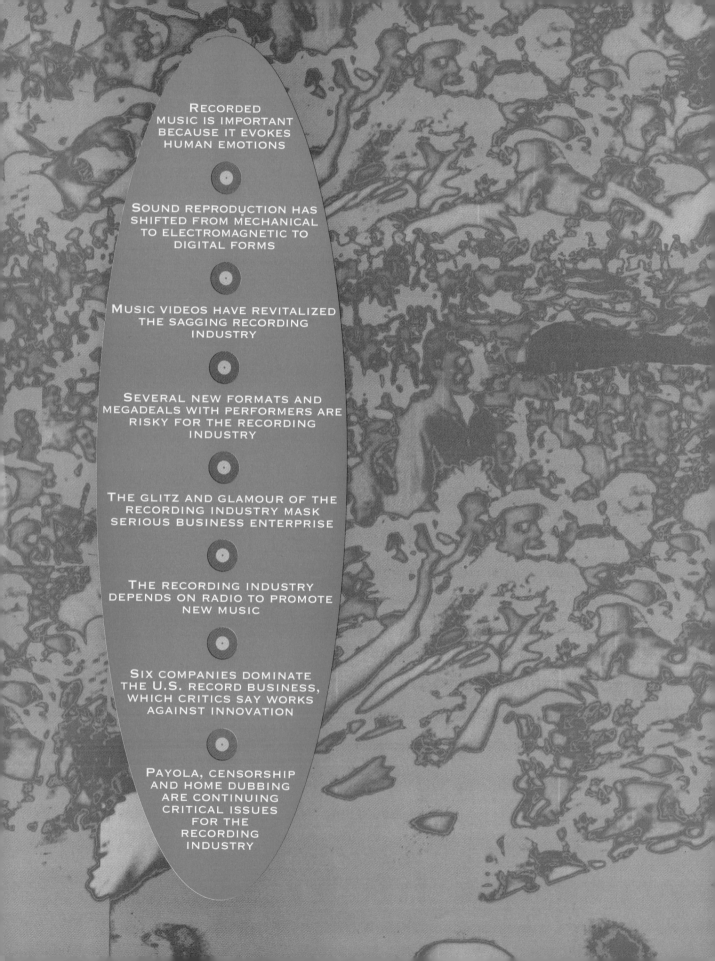

RECORDED MUSIC IS IMPORTANT BECAUSE IT EVOKES HUMAN EMOTIONS

SOUND REPRODUCTION HAS SHIFTED FROM MECHANICAL TO ELECTROMAGNETIC TO DIGITAL FORMS

MUSIC VIDEOS HAVE REVITALIZED THE SAGGING RECORDING INDUSTRY

SEVERAL NEW FORMATS AND MEGADEALS WITH PERFORMERS ARE RISKY FOR THE RECORDING INDUSTRY

THE GLITZ AND GLAMOUR OF THE RECORDING INDUSTRY MASK SERIOUS BUSINESS ENTERPRISE

THE RECORDING INDUSTRY DEPENDS ON RADIO TO PROMOTE NEW MUSIC

SIX COMPANIES DOMINATE THE U.S. RECORD BUSINESS, WHICH CRITICS SAY WORKS AGAINST INNOVATION

PAYOLA, CENSORSHIP AND HOME DUBBING ARE CONTINUING CRITICAL ISSUES FOR THE RECORDING INDUSTRY

chapter 5

SOUND RECORDINGS

SPINNING THE MUSIC

Alan Freed had always liked music. At Ohio State University, Freed played trombone in a jazz band called the Sultans of Swing. After an army stint during World War II, he landed an announcing job at a classical radio station in Pennsylvania. Later Freed went to Cleveland and became host for a late-night radio show. He played records by Frank Sinatra, Jo Stafford, Frankie Laine and other popular performers of the day.

That was before rock 'n' roll. In 1951 Cleveland record store owner Leo Mintz, who sponsored Freed's "Record Rendezvous" on WJW, decided one day to show Freed his shop. Neither the radio nor the record industry was ever the same again. Freed saw Mintz's shop full of white teenagers. They weren't listening to Perry Como or Rosemary Clooney. They were dancing in the aisles to rhythm 'n' blues—"Negro music," as it was called then. And they were buying it.

Freed went back to WJW and talked management into a new show, "Moon Dog House." With the new show and a variety of promotions, Freed built a white audience for black music in Cleveland. Word spread. Soon Freed was syndicated on faraway stations with music he called "rock 'n' roll." Within three years he was the top disc jockey in New York City. Rock 'n' roll was here to stay, and the U.S. record industry would be shaken to its roots.

Alan Freed. On his "Moon Dog House" radio show in Cleveland, Alan Freed laid the groundwork for rock 'n' roll in the early 1950s. By the time he reached New York, Freed was a major influence in the success of young, new performers.

Alan Freed embodied the best and the worst of the intertwined businesses of music, records and radio. He was an innovator at a pivotal point in music history. The rock 'n' roll he played transformed musical tastes almost overnight. Critics charged that his rock 'n' roll was corrupting a generation of teenagers, the same kind of controversy that still plagues the record business today. For Freed, as with many people in the music industry, life was in the fast lane. He became involved in shady deals with record-makers eager for him to play their music on the air, and he was prosecuted—some say persecuted—in the first of many payola scandals. Like many in the faddish record and music industry, Freed rose fast and died young, in 1965 at age 43.

RECORDED MUSIC AS A SOCIAL FORCE

STUDY PREVIEW Music is a potent form of human expression that can mobilize hearts and minds. Think about the effects of hymns and anthems, martial music and love songs. For better or worse, these powerful effects are magnified by the technology of sound recording.

RALLYING POWER

TEACHING OBJECTIVE 5-1
Recorded music important because it evokes human emotions.

LECTURE RESOURCE 5-A
Speaker: Pop culture professor.

Released in 1984, "We Are the World" right away was the fastest-climbing record of the decade. Four million copies were sold within six weeks. Profits from the record, produced by big-name entertainers who volunteered, went to the USA for Africa project. The marketplace success paled, however, next to the social impact. The record's message of the oneness of humankind inspired one of the most massive outpouring of donations in history. Americans pumped $20 million into USA for Africa in the first six weeks the record was out. Within six months, $50 million in medical and financial support was en route to drought-stricken parts of Africa. "We Are the World," a single song, had directly saved lives.

The power of recorded music is not a recent phenomenon. In World War I, "Over There" and other records reflected an enthusiasm for American involvement in the war. Composers who felt strongly about the Vietnam war wrote songs that put their views on vinyl. "The Green Berets" cast American soldiers in a heroic vein, "An Okie From Muskogee" glorified blind patriotism, and there were antiwar songs, dozens of them.

Political speech writers know the political value of tapping into popular music. It was no accident in the 1992 primaries when George Bush paraphrased a Nitty Gritty Dirt Band song to a New Hampshire crowd: "If you want to see a rainbow, you've got to stand a little rain." In his state-of-the-union message, the president borrowed from Paul Simon's "Boy in the Bubble" to make a point on the economy: "If this age of miracles and wonders has taught us anything, it's that if we can change the world, we can change America."

In short, music has tremendous effects on human beings, and the technology of sound recording amplifies these effects. The bugle boy was essential to Company B in earlier times, but today reveille is on tape to wake the troops. Mothers still sing Brahms's lullaby, but more babies probably are lulled to sleep by Brahms on tape. For romance, lovers today lean more on recorded music than their own vocal cords. The technology of sound recording gives composers, lyricists and performers far larger audiences than would ever be possible through live performances.

BRINGING ABOUT CHANGE

Besides explicit advocacy and its immediate, obvious effects, recorded music can have subtle impact on the course of human events. *Elvis Presley*, "the white boy who sang colored," hardly realized in the mid-1950s that his music was helping pave the way for American racial integration. It was the black roots of much of Presley's music, as well as his suggestive gyrations, that made him such a controversial performer. Whatever the fuss, white teenagers liked the music, and it blazed a trail for many black singers who became popular beyond the black community. A major black influence entered mainstream American culture. There also was a hillbilly element in early rock, bringing the concerns and issues of poor, rural whites—another oppressed, neglected minority—into the mainstream consciousness. Nashville ceased to be an American cultural ghetto.

REFLECTION OF CHANGING VALUES

While recorded music has the power to move people to war and peace, to love and to sleep, it also reflects changing human values. In 1991, as U.S. troops were massing at the Persian Gulf to reclaim Kuwait, American record-makers issued music that reflected public enthusiasm for the war. Arista records put Whitney Houston's Super Bowl version of "The Star Spangled Banner" on a single, which sold 750,000 audio copies in only eight days. It was the fastest-selling single in Arista's history. In addition, Arista sold more than 100,000 videos. Boston Dawn's remake of the Shirelle's oldie "Soldier Boy," expressing a woman's love for her soldier overseas, included some rap lines from the soldier. It was very much a song of the times, and the record company, American Sound, had 25,000 back orders for the record almost as soon as it was released.

The Persian Gulf war also had protest music, of a sort. The Rolling Stones' "Highwire," a single issued two weeks ahead of the U.S.-led ground war in Iraq, blamed the war on the industrialized world's greed for oil. Even the protest music was largely in sync with mainstream American opinion. In "Highwire," for example, the chorus was in the background singing support for the troops as Mick Jagger attacked the war. When "Highwire" was included in an album released a month after the coalition victory, it went mostly unnoticed in the public's war euphoria.

LECTURE RESOURCE 5-B
Exercise: Black influence on U.S. music.

KEY PERSON
Elvis Presley.

LEARNING RESOURCE 5-C
Speaker: Record store manager.

SOUND RECORDING TECHNOLOGY

STUDY PREVIEW The recording industry, as with all mass media, has been built on technological advances and breakthroughs, beginning with Thomas Edison's mechanical phonograph. Today, the technology is all electrical and digital.

VIBRATION-SENSITIVE RECORDING

TEACHING OBJECTIVE 5-2
Sound reproduction: first mechanical, then electromagnetic, today digital.

KEY PERSON
Thomas Edison.

For years scientific journals had speculated on ways to reproduce sound, but not until 1877 did anyone build a machine that could do it. That was when American inventor *Thomas Edison* applied for a patent for a talking machine. He used the trade name *Phonograph*, which was taken from Greek words meaning "to write sound."

The heart of Edison's invention was a cylinder wrapped in tin foil. The cylinder was rotated as a singer shouted into a large metal funnel. The funnel channeled the voice against a diaphragm, which fluttered to the vibrations. A *stylus*, which most people called a "needle," was connected to the diaphragm and cut a groove in the foil, the depth of the groove reflecting the vibrations. To listen to a recording, you put the cylinder on a player and set a needle in the groove that had been created in the recording process. Then you placed your ear to a megaphone-like horn and rotated the cylinder. The needle tracked the groove, and the vibrations created by the varying depths of the groove were fed through the horn.

KEY PERSON
Emile Berliner.

Edison's system contained a major impediment to commercial success: a recording could not be duplicated. In 1887 *Emile Berliner* introduced a breakthrough. Rather than recording on a cylinder covered with flimsy foil, as Edison did, Berliner used a sturdy metal disc. From the metal disc, Berliner made a mold and then poured a thermoplastic material into the mold. When the material hardened, Berliner had a near-perfect copy of the original disc—and he could make hundreds of them. Berliner's system, called the *gramophone*, led to mass production.

Thomas Edison. Prolific U.S. inventor Thomas Edison devised a machine that took sound waves and etched them into grooves on a foil drum. When the drum was put on a replacing mechanism and rotated, you could hear the recorded sound. Edison's *Phonograph*, as he called it, was never a commercial success because his recordings could not be duplicated. It was a later inventor, Emile Berliner, who found a way to mass produce recorded music.

ELECTROMAGNETIC RECORDING

In the 1920s, the Columbia and Victor record companies introduced records based on an electrical system perfected by *Joseph Maxwell* of Bell Laboratories. Metal funnels were replaced by microphones, which had superior sensitivity. For listening, it was no longer a matter of putting an ear to a mechanical amplifying horn that had only a narrow frequency response. Instead, loudspeakers amplified the sound electromagnetically.

Magnetic tape was developed in Germany and used to broadcast propaganda in World War II. In 1945 American troops brought the German technology home with them. Ampex began building recording and playback machines. The 3M Company perfected tape. Recording companies shifted from discs to magnetic tape to record master discs. An advantage of tape was that bobbles could be edited out. Creative editing became possible.

While magnetic tape suggested the possibility of long-playing records, the industry continued to use brittle shellac discs that revolved 78 times a minute. One problem with the 10-inch 78-rpm disc was that it could accommodate only three to four minutes of sound on a side.

KEY PERSON
Joseph Maxwell.

VINYL RECORDS AND MICROGROOVES

One day *Peter Goldmark*, chief engineer at Columbia Records, was listening to a 78-rpm recording of Brahms's Second Piano Concerto, Arturo Toscanini conducting. The concerto was divided onto six discs, 12 sides. Fed up with flipping discs, Goldmark got out his pencil and calculated whether a slower spin and narrower grooves could get the whole concerto on one disc. It was possible, although it would take both sides. At least the break could come between movements.

In 1948 Goldmark's long-playing record was introduced. Each side had 240 *microgrooves* per inch and contained up to 25 minutes of music. Offering several

KEY PERSON
Peter Goldmark.

Early Mechanical Recording.
Band music was popular in the early days of sound recording. Brass sounds picked up well on the primitive mechanical recording equipment. In recording's early days, John Philip Sousa recorded hundreds of cylinders because the technology did not permit duplicating copies from masters. Each cylinder sold to a customer was an original. Some recording studios had up to 10 recording horns—which allowed 10 cylinders to be made at once. Still, recording was time-consuming.

advantages, LPs soon replaced the 78-rpm record. Not only did each record have more music, but also the sound was better. The records were of vinyl plastic, which meant less hissing and scratching than shellac records. Also, vinyl discs were harder to break than the brittle 78s.

Refusing to be upstaged, RCA, which earlier had dabbled unsuccessfully with 33⅓-rpm records, introduced extended-play records called EPs. They were small 45-rpm discs with a large spindle. Thus was launched the *battle of the speeds*, which pitted RCA and Columbia against each other. RCA, which manufactured phonographs, included only 78-rpm and 45-rpm speeds on its machines—no 33⅓-rpm. The battle was costly. Unsure which would prevail, the public hesitated to buy phonographs and records. Record sales slumped by $50 million.

A truce came, finally, when conductor Arturo Toscanini took RCA boss *David Sarnoff* aside and pointed out the obvious—that Brahms's Second Piano Concerto could not fit even on two sides of an RCA 45-rpm disc. Toscanini convinced Sarnoff to add a 33⅓ speed to RCA phonographs for classical music. The 45-rpm disc, meanwhile, became the standard for pop music, with one song on each side. Discs sold for a dollar, within the means of the teenagers who ushered in the rock 'n' roll era in the 1950s.

KEY PERSON
David Sarnoff.

THE STEREO AND DIGITAL REVOLUTIONS

Technical progress until the late 1970s produced nothing as revolutionary as the microgroove, but the improvements, taken all together, made for dramatically better sound. Anyone who has grown up with the B-52s would hardly believe that record-buyers accepted the sound quality of Bill Haley records only 30 years earlier. Better fidelity, called high fidelity, or *hi-fi*, was introduced in the early 1950s. The full audio range of the human ear could be delivered to listeners exactly as it was recorded. *Stereo* came in 1961. Multiple microphones recorded on separate tracks. Records played the sound back through two speakers, simulating the way people hear—through their left and their right ears. Consumers went for the new quality. FM stereo radio was introduced about the same time.

Except for tapes, Edison's 1877 technology, refined by Maxwell half a century later, was at the heart of sound recording for 101 years. The technology was called *analog recording* because it converted the waves that were physically engraved in the grooves of the record into electrical pulses that coincided analogously with the waves in the grooves. It worked this way:

- As the record rotated, a stylus suspended from an arm over the record tracked waves embedded in the grooves.
- A gizmo called a *transducer*, located in the arm, converted the physical energy created by the stylus moving through the grooves into electrical energy.
- The resulting electrical pulses moved through an *amplifier* and then to a loudspeaker.
- The *loudspeaker* converted the pulses back into physical energy, which took the form of sound waves moving through the air.

Record-makers developed a technological revolution in 1978: the *digital recording*. No longer were continuous sound waves inscribed physically on a disc. Instead, sound waves were captured at millisecond intervals, and each wave was logged in computer language as an isolated on-off binary number. When discs were played back, the digits were translated back to the sound at the same millisecond intervals they were recorded. The intervals would be replayed so fast that the sound would seem continuous, just as the individual frames in a motion picture become a moving blur that is perceived by the eye as continuous motion.

By 1983 digital recordings were available to consumers in the form of *compact discs*, silvery 4.7-inch platters. The binary numbers were pits on the disc that were read by a laser light in the latest version of the phonograph: the *CD player*. The player itself converted the numbers to sound.

Each disc could carry 70 minutes of uninterrupted sound, more than Peter Goldmark dared dream. Consumers raved about the purity. Some critics argued, however, that there was a sterility in digital recording. The sound was too perfect, they said. Instead of reproducing performances, said the critics, compact discs produced a quality more perfect than a performance. Traditional audiophiles had sought to reproduce live music perfectly, not to create a perfection that could never be heard in a live performance.

BUMPY ECONOMIC PROGRESS

STUDY PREVIEW If a single word could describe the economic history of the record industry, it would be "volatile." In the beginning, there was a struggle to determine whether recorded sound could even turn a profit. Booms were spectacular, but not even the industry giants like RCA and Columbia escaped the bad times.

FINDING A MARKET

At first, nobody realized the economic potential of sound recordings. When Thomas Edison's hand-cranked phonograph was taken on tour, it attracted attention on the vaudeville circuit and in lecture halls, but not even the inventive and entrepreneurial Edison foresaw its home entertainment possibilities.

Seeking commercial applications, entrepreneur *Jesse Lippincott* bought the Edison and a passel of other phonograph patents in 1888 and formed the *Columbia Phonograph Co.* Times were tough, and Lippincott almost went under. At a crucial moment an aide suggested installing phonographs at arcades and charging people who wanted to listen. At a nickel a song, Lippincott was rescued. The nickelodeons whetted consumer interest. Eventually sales picked up.

Emile Berliner went into business with his superior disc technology. The sound was better than cylinders, and discs were far easier to store. In 1896 the Berliner gramophone and some other patents were combined in a commercial venture, the *Victor Talking Machine Co.*, which aimed at a home entertainment market and eventually became RCA. In time, Columbia abandoned cylinders and introduced its own disc machine.

TEACHING OBJECTIVE 5-3
Music videos have revitalized recording industry.

KEY PERSON
Jesse Lippincott.

BOOM AND BUST

The recording business received a big boost in 1913 when a dance craze hit America. Then World War I songs became popular, further fueling demand. Record production, 27 million discs in 1914, quadrupled to 107 million in 1919. The boom continued into the early 1920s, but in 1924 sales of records and record players dropped 50 percent as a mushrooming number of radio stations drew customers away from records.

Then came the 1929 stock market crash. The *jukebox* helped keep the recording industry going through the difficult 1930s. The machines were installed in restaurants, saloons and soda fountains. By 1940, a total of 250,000 jukeboxes, each with 60 records, were taking nickels throughout the land. Jukeboxes kept the public interested in recorded music.

More setbacks were ahead, however. During World War II the government diverted shellac production from civilian to military purposes. Because shellac was an essential ingredient in records of the period, record production plummeted. In another crippling setback, the *American Federation of Musicians* prohibited its members from cutting records in 1942. The union wanted royalties on all recorded music, arguing that jukeboxes and other record-playing equipment were putting musicians out of work. The ban virtually shut down the recording industry. Within a few months, Decca capitulated, agreeing to assign up to 5 cents from every record sold to a fund for out-of-work musicians. A year later RCA and Columbia followed.

THE ROCK 'N' ROLL JOLT

When shellac was scarce during World War II, the major record-makers gave up the small black rhythm 'n' blues market. After the war, these major companies expected big profits from contracts with proven performers like Bing Crosby and Frank Sinatra. When rock 'n' roll came along in the 1950s, the major record-makers ignored it as a momentary flash. How wrong they were. Almost overnight, the small companies were swamped with orders. The Sun label, now almost forgotten, put out such enduring stars as Elvis Presley, Roy Orbison, Johnny Cash and Carl Perkins. From 1955 to 1957 the number of records on the trade journal *Billboard*'s Top 10 charts from independent companies quintupled from 8 to 40.

Even though they were losing market share, the major record-makers were slow to respond. In one cautious reaction, they issued toned-down remakes of rock 'n' roll songs that were catching on, a practice they called *covering*. As profits plummeted, they tightened their business practices. They streamlined their systems for getting records to customers. Some formed music publishing companies. Some even bought retail outlets. The result was that their music passed through fewer hands to get to market. Fewer intermediaries meant more profits.

Despite their success, the scrappy independents had relatively small repertoires and lacked the resources to put together competitive distribution systems. One at a time, as the major recordmakers realized that rock 'n' roll was here to stay, the independents sold out to them. Giant Warner, for example, first bought independents Atlantic and Reprise, and then Elektra, another independent, was merged into the company. These acquisitions and mergers shaped today's recording industry, which is dominated by a handful of giant companies.

The emergence of rock 'n' roll, from Bill Haley and the Comets to Elvis Presley and then the Beatles, pushed the record industry to unprecedented profitability. Record sales outpaced even movies by the mid-1970s. In 1974 Americans spent $2.2 billion on rock 'n' roll records and tapes. On movies they spent only $1.7 billion.

HORRIFIC 1979

Record companies released extraordinary hits in the late 1970s. The "Rumours" album by Fleetwood Mac sold 13 million copies. The "Saturday Night Fever" and "Grease" soundtracks did spectacularly. In 1978 sales were a record $4.1 billion.

The King. Exuberant fans welcome Elvis Presley at a 1956 outdoor concert in his hometown of Tupelo, Mississippi. Elvis was among early rockabillies who blended black rhythm 'n' blues with rural, white grassroots music form that became a social force. The new rock 'n' roll fueled a period of fantastic growth in the record industry.

While things looked good on the surface, there was a big problem. Except for the mega-hits, sales were flat—a fact masked by the big sellers and a $1-per-album price hike.

The year 1979 produced no megahits. Worse, sales were off because teenagers were plugging quarters into video games, not saving them to buy records. At the same time, an oil shortage sparked huge increases in the price of petroleum, a raw material used in record manufacturing. The industry's problems went even deeper. Wrongly assuming that their earlier spectacular growth would continue, the companies had overexpanded. With sales down and manufacturing costs rising, the industry had no choice but to scale back. Here is how the industry retrenched:

- **Layoffs.** Record companies laid off an estimated 5,000 people.
- **Contracts.** Lavish long-term contracts like Stevie Wonder's $13 million and Elton John's $8 million deals became rarer.
- **Focused marketing.** Fewer records were released. In lusher times, the companies put out a lot of new recordings, knowing that most would flop. The idea, called the *buckshot philosophy*, was to throw dozens of releases "up against the wall to see which stuck." Not anymore. By 1984 record-makers had halved the number of releases.
- **Fewer artists.** The number of artists under contract was reduced, which allowed companies to focus reduced resources on their remaining artists.
- **Inventories.** Companies reduced their inventory in the distribution chain. Previously, retailers could return any unsold records they had ordered. Now returns were limited to 20 percent.

Leaner, the industry survived to rise again.

RESURGENCE IN THE 1980s

Promotional and technical innovations led a record industry revival that cannonballed through the 1980s. By 1990 U.S. record-buyers were shelling out some $7.5 billion a year for recorded music. The key factors were music videos and digital technology.

MUSIC VIDEOS.   Because strictly regulated European radio does not play much pop music, record-makers there needed to be especially innovative in promoting new music. In the 1970s, seeking new ways to interest young people in their products, European record companies created videos that featured recording artists acting out their music. Dance clubs played the videos, and record sales picked up. American record-makers, desperate to reverse slumping sales, borrowed the idea and made videos available to cable television channels to play between movies. The videos developed a following.

In 1981 the Warner media conglomerate, whose divisions included Warner records, gambled that a full-time music video cable channel would attract enough viewers to interest advertisers and make money, while simultaneously promoting records. At first there were doubters, but by 1984 the *Music Television Channel, MTV* for short, claimed 24 million viewers, more than any other cable channel. Warner was right too about a correlation between music videos on television and record sales. The MTV audience was mostly teenagers and young adults, the same people who buy most records. It was no surprise when surveys found that almost three out of four record-buyers reported that MTV influenced their choices at the record shop.

DIGITAL TECHNOLOGY.   The record industry gave itself another shot in the arm in the 1980s by switching to compact disc digital playback equipment and software. The quality of CD sound attracted attention, and many people began replacing their tape and record collections with CDs. By the mid-1980s, the record industry was clearly out of its slump.

UNCERTAINTIES AHEAD

STUDY PREVIEW   New digital disc and tape formats, introduced in the 1990s, are intended to spur hardware and software sales, but doubters fear that consumers might hold off buying music until one or two formats emerge as dominant. There is concern too that the industry might again be overextending itself with megabuck deals with performers.

NEW DISC AND TAPE FORMATS

TEACHING OBJECTIVE 5-4
New formats, megadeals are risky.

By 1995 only a few tiny, obscure record companies were still pressing vinyl discs, and most record shops had given up stocking 33⅓ LPs. The transition to digital technology, however, had just begun. The Japanese manufacturers next introduced digital audio tape (DAT) playback machines in the United States. DAT had the clarity of the CD with the additional feature of a dubbing capacity. Compact discs had been designed for listening only. With DAT, people could record as well as listen. It seemed at first that the process of people replacing their music collections with a new format would repeat itself, again bolstering sales not only of recordings but also the equipment to play them. In their first year on the U.S. market, however, DAT machines were bought by only 30,000 people, less than one-third of the manufacturers' expectation. The expanded variety of formats had given too many choices to consumers, reminiscent of the RCA-CBS battle of the speeds in the late 1940s when people put off purchasing phonographs and records rather than be stuck with an orphaned format. Again, people were sitting out the "war" to see who would win.

The format confusion worsened in 1992 when playback manufacturers expanded the options. Besides CDs and DATs, there suddenly was Philips's DCC, short for *digital compact cassette*, which lacked DAT's audio range but which could play both digital and ordinary tapes. Sony simultaneously introduced *Mini Disc* (MD), a small 2½-inch CD onto which 70 minutes of music could be crammed, albeit with some quality loss. The MD was the logical successor to Sony's portable Walkman, which played only traditional tapes. Just as in the LP versus the EP war between CBS and RCA, the new 1990s competition was taking form as a war to the finish. On its side, Philips lined up fellow hardware manufacturer Matsushita and the Radio Shack retail chain, and it sent the rock group Dire Straits on a 300-city global tour to promote DCCs. As both a music software and hardware company, Philips had plenty of muscle to push DCCs in both audio equipment stores and record stores. On behalf of MDs, Sony had the muscle not only in its traditional strength and hardware, but also in its 1988 acquisition of CBS Records, itself a major force in music software.

PERFORMER MEGADEALS

Big star megadeals became the fashion again in the 1990s, despite the experience of 1979 when the bottom fell out of the music business and record companies found themselves locked into extravagant commitments. Michael Jackson signed a long-term deal with Sony in 1991 for $65 million, five times more than Stevie Wonder's deal that typified the record industry's earlier overextension. Sony guaranteed Jackson not only $65 million but also a 50-50 split on profits. Next, Time Warner inked a similar 50-50 deal with Madonna, with her guarantee reported to be $75 million, a new benchmark. Among groups, the heavyweight hard-rock Aerosmith's $50 million deal with Sony eclipsed a $28 million Rolling Stones contract.

The scale of the new megadeals reflected the corporate mergers that were consolidating the mass media into the hands of fewer but bigger companies. Sony had just bought CBS Records and Columbia Pictures and was eager to lock up proven talent like Michael Jackson for its new software enterprises. With Sony flashing so much cash, the newly created Time Warner media conglomerate felt it had little choice but to sweeten its deal with Madonna to keep her from straying. The contract kept Madonna on Sire records and in Warner films. Her percentage of the retail price of recordings went from 18 to 30 percent.

With the biggest names under long-term agreements, the record companies eased away from megadeals in the mid-1990s. There was also the experience of Michael Jackson's problems, with both Sony and Jackson backing off from several of their anticipated projects.

MAKING AND SELLING RECORDS

STUDY PREVIEW Record companies spend a lot of energy on the glitzy aspects of their business, including celebrity artists, but much more is involved in bringing recorded music to market.

ARTISTS AND REPERTOIRES

Record companies have *A&R*, short for *artist and repertoire departments*, to work with stars. Before rock 'n' roll, A&R people signed new artists and even arranged their music and supervised recording sessions. They nurtured performing styles, worked on grooming and wardrobe to make a performer salable, arranged inter-

TEACHING OBJECTIVE 5-5
Glitz of recording industry masks serious business enterprise.

views and worried about things like overexposing their stars. In his book *Solid Gold*, Serge Denisoff quotes a former Capitol executive about how the A&R system once worked: "The company would pick out 12 songs for Peggy Lee and tell her to be at the studio Wednesday at 8, and she'd show up and sing what you told her. And she'd leave three hours later and Capitol'd take her songs and do anything it wanted with them. Her art was totally out of her—the artist's—hands. . . . That was a time when the artist was supposed to shut up and put up with anything the almighty recording company wanted."

Today, performers do not lean nearly so much on A&R people. Many insist on producing their own work, some in their own studios with their own producers. A&R people still scout the country for talent, checking small clubs and colleges, but most A&R activity today is office work: listening to *demo tapes* sent in by aspiring musicians and tending to contract details.

RECORDING STUDIOS

Making records is a complex process that occurs in a recording studio. Based on preliminary discussions with A&R people, record producers and the recording artists, engineers set up the studio. Dozens of microphones can be used, sometimes one for every performer or instrument. Baffles separate different sound sources to keep spillover minimal. Days can go into *miking* a studio. No matter how experienced the engineers, there is an element of trial and error in choosing the right microphones, placing them for best effect and adjusting settings.

Once a recording session begins, the producer is in charge. In an ideal session, everything goes perfectly the first time. That happens rarely. The producer might insist that a song be done over and over. Tapes may be played back so that performers can hear deficiencies that concern the producer. Not infrequently, arrangements are modified during a recording session.

A recording may include three or four dozen tracks, each from a separate microphone. The tracks are consolidated onto two tracks in a complicated process called *mix-down*. In mixing-down, some tracks can be emphasized and others deemphasized or even deleted. Special effects can be dubbed in. Decisions are made concerning which sounds go on the right and the left tracks.

AIRPLAY AND MARKETING

Record companies ship new releases free to radio stations in hope of airplay. Few make it. Stations are inundated with more records than they can possibly audition. Also, most stations stick to a playlist of already popular music rather than risk losing listeners by playing untried records. To minimize the risk and yet offer some fresh sounds, most radio station music directors rely heavily on *charts* of what music is selling and being played elsewhere. The most-followed charts appear in the trade journal *Billboard*. There also are *tip sheets*, which leading disc jockeys and music directors put out as a sideline and sell by subscription.

Airplay is valuable because it is the way in which most people are first exposed to new releases that they might go out and buy. Also, airplay is efficient for record-makers because it is free except for the cost of shipping the sample records.

Promotion also includes advertising campaigns. Record companies place ads on television and radio and in magazines to promote their records and performers.

The Mophead Four. The Beatles from Liverpool, England, as they appeared on Ed Sullivan's television show in New York in the 1960s.

Because an estimated 13 percent of record purchases are on impulse, promotional point-of-purchase displays also are important.

Tours can generate enthusiasm for an album, but interest in tours has declined among performers unless a record company is willing to pick up the expenses. Costs have skyrocketed, not only for special effects and backups but also for security. When Larry Gatlin gave up recording in 1991, he blamed the exhaustion of touring and the expenses. Overexuberant fans take their toll too, especially when a concert goes sour. Guns n' Roses won few friends or fans after a melee at a St. Louis concert that ended with 60 people injured, $200,000 in damages, and numerous lawsuit threats.

A variation on concert tours was pioneered by CBS Records in 1990. With nothing to lose, CBS sent little-known Mariah Carey on a low-budget nationwide tour singing in record stores. Within weeks and with virtually no airplay, her debut album reached Number 1. Next, Musicland, the 1,000-store U.S. record retailer, stocked its stores with the meandering, synthesized New Age album of Yanni and asked him to perform in stores. The album sold 900,000 copies, not bad for a hitherto obscure Greek-born musician whose music received hardly any airplay.

MEASURES OF COMMERCIAL SUCCESS

Discount stores account for 50 percent of U.S. record sales; 25 percent are through department stores; and 15 to 20 percent are through record stores, including chains like Musicland. Mail-order outlets, including record clubs, account for the rest.

In-Store Promotion. An HMV megastore in Manhattan includes a performance area for recording artists to give customers a live sample of albums for sale. Whether this new marketing approach works in the long term could determine whether the record industry continues to rely so much on radio airplay to promote new music. Here the jazz group Special FX hopes its HMV performance will generate the kind of success that folk singer Suzanne Vega achieved for her album *Days of Open Hand*. Without much airplay at all, it sold almost 1 million copies.

About half the records sold in the United States today are pop, a broad category that ranges from Barry Manilow's mellow sentimentalism to Mötley Crüe's hard-edged rock. The rest are country, classical, jazz and the other musical genres, as well as children's records and the minor although growing category of recorded literature and self-help cassettes.

The measure of success in the record-making business is the *gold record*. Once a single sells 1 million or an album sells 500,000 copies, the Recording Industry Association of America confers a gold-record award. A *platinum record* is awarded for 2 million singles sold or 1 million albums. RCA's Tchaikovsky treatment by the pianist Van Cliburn is one of only two classical recordings ever to receive a gold record.

INTERDEPENDENCE WITH RADIO

STUDY PREVIEW   The radio and record industries need each other. Record companies rely on the publicity that comes when radio stations play their records, and radio stations rely on the record industry as a source of low-cost programming.

RECORD–RADIO PARTNERSHIP

TEACHING OBJECTIVE 5-6
Recording industry depends on radio to promote new music.

LECTURE RESOURCE 5-D
Speaker: Radio station music director.

KEY PERSON
Alan Freed.

The radio and record industries are intimately connected. In the 1940s, when records by performers like Bing Crosby and Frank Sinatra were promoted over the radio, sales soared. The relationship of the record and radio industries assumed a new dimension in the 1950s when *Alan Freed*, the Cleveland disc jockey who turned white teens on to rock 'n' roll music, demonstrated that records could attract new audiences. One by one, radio stations also discovered that they could both build audiences and cut costs by building more and more programming around records. Spinning records was far less expensive than the big-name productions that had been radio's main programming.

The relationship between the radio and record industries was a two-way street. Not only did radio stations need records, but record-makers needed Freed and other pace-setting jockeys to air their products. Records that won airplay were almost assured success. Record companies scrambled to curry favor with leading disc jockeys. This interdependence expanded to television in the 1980s when cable television services, like MTV and VH-1, built their programming on video versions of popular music.

PAYOLA

The relationship between the radio and record industries has had problems. Alan Freed was at the heart of one: the first *payola* crisis. In 1958 the grapevine was full of stories about record companies' bribes to disc jockeys to play certain records. One audit found that $263,000 in "consulting fees" had been paid to radio announcers in 23 cities. The Federal Trade Commission filed unfair competition complaints against record companies. Radio station managers, ever conscious that their licenses from the Federal Communications Commission could be yanked for improprieties, began demanding signed statements from disc jockeys that they had not accepted payola. Dozens of disc jockeys in major markets quietly left town. Alan Freed did not go quietly. He refused to sign an affidavit requested by ABC, which owned a New York station running one of Freed's programs. He called the request a slur on his reputation. ABC fired him. Freed maintained he had done nothing unethical, and some observers contend that the news media overplayed the payola question.

Whether legitimate or hyped, payola scandals did not end with the 1950s. Competition for airplay has continued to tempt record promoters to "buy" airtime under the table. There were indictments again in the 1970s. And in 1988 two independent promoters were charged with paying $270,000 to program directors at nine widely imitated radio stations to place records on their playlists. One station executive was charged with receiving $100,000 over two years. Some payola bribery involved drugs.

Payola scandals illustrate the relationship that has taken shape between the record and radio industries. It is an interdependent relationship, but radio holds the upper hand. It is the record industry's need for airplay that precipitates the scandals.

HOME-DUBBING REVENUE DRAIN

The lopsidedness of the relationship between the radio and record industries became obvious in another way in the 1970s. Instead of buying records and tapes at $9 each, people began sharing records and dubbing them onto relatively inexpensive blank tapes. Phonograph manufacturers offered machines that not only could dub tapes from records but also could record from the air at the flick of a toggle. Many FM stereo radio stations catered to home dubbers by announcing when they would play uninterrupted albums.

The economic effect of home dubbing on the record industry is hard to measure precisely, but the Recording Industry Association of America estimates that the industry loses $1.5 billion a year, one-fifth of its sales.

Recording Piracy. Pirating operations in Bangkok are so well organized that illegal copies of music and videotapes find their way into local shops ahead of their release through legal channels. A tape of the movie *Pretty Woman* went for $5 in a blank cassette box weeks before the U.S. distributor put it on the market.

Record companies tried to dissuade stations from playing albums uninterrupted, but it did not work. Stations were not about to give up the audience they had cultivated for their made-for-dubbing programs. The record companies had no recourse. Cutting off pre-releases to radio stations would mean throwing away free airplay, and airplay was too important. Again, the record industry's dependence on radio was clear. Record-makers were powerless to close a major drain on their revenues.

The dependence of the record industry on radio again was demonstrated in the 1980s when many radio stations shifted to oldies. Traditionally, the record industry derived most of its profits from new music, whose marketing was boosted by radio airplay. In the 1980s, however, stations played more old songs to reach the huge audience of baby boomers who grew up in the 1950s and 1960s and who, like generations before them, preferred the music that was popular when they were young. The change in radio programming worked against the record industry, which, although it was in an economic partnership with radio, was not in control of the relationship.

While record-makers were unable to strike a deal with the radio industry to plug the home-dubbing revenue drain, progress was made on another front in 1991. The record-makers and their long-time foe on the home-dubbing issue, the manufacturers of home electronic equipment, agreed on a "taping tax." Anyone purchasing a blank tape would pay a 1 percent fee to be passed on to songwriters, music publishers and others who lose royalty income from home dubbing. Congress approved the taping tax in 1992.

AUDIO AND VIDEO PIRACY

Criminal *piracy* involves dubbing records and videos and selling the dubs. An estimated 18 percent of the records and tapes sold are from shadowy pirate sources, mostly in Asia but also in other countries, including Saudi Arabia. These pirate operations have no A&R, royalty or promotion expenses. They dub tapes produced by legitimate companies and sell them through black-market channels. Their costs are low, and their profits are high.

These pirate operations are well financed and organized. It is not uncommon for a Bangkok pirate operation to have 100 "slave" tape-copying machines going simultaneously 24 hours a day and even to ship illegal copies before the official release by the U.S. distributor. Both the Recording Industry Association of America and the Motion Picture Association of America spend millions of dollars a year on formal trade complaints and private investigations in Bangkok and other piracy centers, but with limited success. Local authorities have other priorities and antipiracy laws are weak. In an interview with *Fortune* magazine, Frank Knight, a Bangkok investigator who specializes in these cases, said: "Anybody who's been involved in past mischief, such as drug exports, finds this to be a highly lucrative crime that's easier and less punishable." Knight has tracked exports of illegal tapes to South Africa, to the Indian subcontinent, throughout the Asian Rim, and to the United States. The RIAA estimates that $1.5 billion in music revenue is lost to pirates every year, and the MPAA estimates the loss to filmmakers at $1.2 billion a year.

- -

A CONSOLIDATED INDUSTRY

STUDY PREVIEW   The U.S. record industry is concentrated in six major companies. This consolidation worries cultural sociologists, who say that the industry's size and bent for profits discourage musical innovation.

MAJORS AND INDIES

Records, like the other mass media, are big business. Six companies dominate the U.S. recording industry with 90 percent of the market. Each of these *majors* is, in turn, part of a larger media conglomerate:

TEACHING OBJECTIVE 5-7
Critics say conglomeration works against innovation.

- CBS Records is owned by Sony, the Japanese electronic hardware company, which purchased it in 1988 from CBS Inc. Labels include Columbia, Epic and WTG.
- Capitol is owned by Electrical and Musical Instruments of England and Paramount Communications of the United States. Labels include Chrysalis.
- MCA, formerly Music Corporation of America, is owned by Matsushita Electrical Industrial Corp. of Japan. It has numerous media interests, including Universal Pictures. Labels include MCA, Decca, Kapp, Geffen and UNI.
- PolyGram is part of a London-based company owned by Philips of the Netherlands. Labels include A&M, Deutsche Grammophon, Island, Mercury and Motown.
- RCA Records is a subsidiary of the German media giant Bertelsmann, which purchased it in 1988 from General Electric. RCA labels include Arista.
- Warner Music is owned by Time Warner, the conglomerate that resulted from the 1989 merger of Warner Communications, whose interests included Warner movies and Time-Life, the magazine giant. Labels include Atco, Atlantic, East West, Elektra, Giant, Nonesuch, Reprise, Sire and Warner Brothers.

The remaining 10 percent of the U.S. record market is held by independent companies. Although many *indies* are financially marginal, they are not to be written off. Some indies prosper in market niches. Windham Hill succeeded with high-tech jazz recordings in the 1980s, as did 415 Records with its own brand of rock. A single hit can propel an independent label from a relatively obscure market niche into a *major independent.* For Rounder Records, it was releases by George Thorogood and the Destroyers in the late 1970s. For Windham Hill, it was a hit by pianist George Winston. IRS scored with the group R.E.M.

CULTURAL ISSUES

Many media critics bemoan the concentration of the music industry in a few big companies. One result, they say, is *cultural homogenization.* In their book *Rock 'n' Roll is Here to Pay*, Steve Chapple and Reebee Garofalo argue that the greatest creativity in pop music comes from lean and hungry independent companies, not the fat majors. They note, for example, that the rockabilly innovators of the mid-1950s, like Elvis Presley, Bill Haley and Carl Perkins, recorded for scrappy little risk-taking companies. These companies contributed new richness and diversity to the culture. Chapple and Garofalo contrast the rockabilly innovations with "the Philadelphia schlock" of slick packager *Dick Clark*, who watered down the work of the innovators into commercially safe pap that would sell to a mass audience. An example, from the 1950s, was a song by the Midnighters, an obscure black group, with the suggestive title, "Work With Me, Henry." Major label pop singer Georgia

KEY PERSON
Dick Clark.

MEDIA DATABANK

Conglomeration and Globalization

The major record companies are all part of larger corporations with diverse interests. Japan-based Sony, which acquired CBS Records in 1988 and Columbia Pictures in 1989, represents the extent to which media conglomeration and globalization is occurring. Here is a thumbnail list of Sony's U.S. units, excluding its subsidiaries elsewhere, and a sampler of their products:

CBS Records	Michael Jackson
Digital Audio Disc Corp.	Compact discs
Sony Magnetic Products Group	Video- and audiotape
Sony Engineering and Manufacturing	Television, video, audio hardware
Columbia Pictures	First-run movies
Tri-Star Pictures	First-run movies
Columbia Pictures Television	"Wheel of Fortune"
Columbia Tri-Star Home Video	Recycled movies for home video
Loews theaters	Movie houses
Sony Electronic Publishing	Electronic games
SVS	Video distribution
Material Research Corp.	Semiconductors
Sony Trans Com Corp.	In-flight entertainment

Gibbs changed the title to "Dance With Me, Henry" and toned down the lyrics, and it became a big hit. This process of modifying a song to pander to vanilla mass market tastes, called *covering*, has been repeated hundreds of times. Each time, say cultural historians, artistic authenticity is compromised. The financial rewards and lures go to homogenization, not originality. Art that springs from the grassroots, they say, doesn't have much of a chance with mass marketers, and the result is that authentic culture is co-opted.

Cultural homogenization became a high-visibility issue in the 1990s when many music reviewers panned the record industry's Grammy Awards for favoring *derivative artists* who may be popular, as was Georgia Gibbs, but whose artistic merits are second rate. The issue erupted in 1990 when Rob Pilatus and Fab Morvan, who performed as Milli Vanilli, were embarrassed into surrendering a Grammy when it was learned that somebody else recorded their popular records and they lip-synced the videos.

The cultural homogenization issue became more focused when Sinéad O'Connor, considered an especially talented rock artist, announced that she would boycott the 1991 Grammy ceremony. The awards, she said, were merely the record industry's hype to promote sales and had little to do with authentic artistry. Her point was underscored by reviewers who noted that previous Grammy winners had included such dubious talents as Debby Boone and the group Toto.

The biggest factor in cultural homogenization is the major record companies, whose quest for marketplace success often supersedes any sense of responsibility to foster artistic contributions. Music commentator David Hadelman, writing in

Kurt Cobain. The Seattle rocker and his band Nirvana created music in which a new generation of alienated teenagers found identity. The defining moment, according to Anthony DeCurtis when writing Cobain's obituary for *Rolling Stone* was the 1991 release "Smells Like a Teen Spirit." The message was an anticommercial, antipolitical and resentful reaction to the self-indulgence and greed of the 1980s. Cobain shot himself to death in 1994.

Growing PolyGram Web

Dutch-owned, London-based PolyGram is a power-house in global entertainment, except in the United States. But in the last few years PolyGram has been buying up U.S. entertainment companies and acquiring part ownership in others in hope of becoming a major player in the United States also. PolyGram epitomizes the globalization of the mass media, especially in delivering entertainment.

The German company Siemens and the Dutch company Philips founded PolyGram in 1962. Their goal was to diversify into the software end of the recorded music industry. Already, they were in the hardware business with several lines of record players. Fifteen years later, in 1987, Philips bought out Siemens's stake. In the meantime, PolyGram had become one of the world's largest music companies, with popular acts under contract throughout Europe and Asia. But in the United States, the world's largest entertainment market, PolyGram was an also-ran known mostly for its classical records. U.S. sales accounted for less than one-quarter of PolyGram's sales.

Alain Levy, a Frenchman with a business degree from Pennsylvania's Wharton School, is aggressively trying to carve out a bigger stake for PolyGram in the United States. His base was small to begin with—Mercury Records. But since 1989, Poly-Gram has acquired Island and A&M records. In 1993, PolyGram paid $325 million for the Motown label. The bevy of Poly-Gram artists has grown to include Bryan Adams, Elton John, Jon Bon Jovi, INXS, Aaron Neville, Sting and U2. Thirty PolyGram albums went platinum in 1993.

Levy, who is PolyGram's chief executive, plans now to capitalize on existing U.S. resources. These plans include starting a chain of Motown cafés. The ambiance would be the Detroit sound that made the label famous.

Levy also is moving into Hollywood, so far one small step at

a time to test the waters. In the 1980s, PolyGram put $140 million into a number of independent film projects. The projects lost money overall, but the company picked up experience in moviemaking and now has acquired Working Title, the British company that put out *My Beautiful Laundrette,* and Interscope, the U.S. company that put out *Three Men and a Baby.* Poly-Gram has also gone into the movie distribution business for Disney, MGM and Universal. In 1993 and 1994, PolyGram released seven feature films of its own, including *Four Weddings and a Funeral, Backbeat* and *The Air Up There.*

There has been talk that PolyGram may buy part or all of MGM. Levy hopes movies will represent 25 percent of PolyGram's business within a few years, much of it in the United States.

PolyGram also is moving into U.S. television. It has purchased Propaganda, the company that produced the television series "Twin Peaks." New shows are in the works. PolyGram also is involved in a joint venture to launch a music video channel that will compete with MTV.

PolyGram is beefing up its Broadway investments. Since 1991 it has owned 30 percent of Andrew Lloyd Webber's company, which produced *The Phantom of the Opera.* PolyGram also produced the recent musicals *Jelly's Last Jam* and *Damn Yankees.* Those soundtracks, of course, are on Poly-Gram labels—and which fast-emerging U.S. movie company would you think will produce the movie versions eventually?

In 1993 alone, PolyGram's U.S. income doubled. With its recent U.S. record label acquisitions, PolyGram is running with Time Warner and EMI to be the largest music company in the world. Alain Levy's goal is to be an equally heavy player in the whole range of the entertainment business, including movies, television, live entertainment and home video.

Alain Levy

Gangsta Rap. For Charles Broadus, escaping his past seemed too big a task. As gangsta rapper Snoop Doggy Dogg, Broadus rapped about his gang roots in Long Beach, California, but just as his career was about to take off, he was arrested. The night of the 1993 MTV Awards, where he made a presentation, Broadus was arrested and charged with first-degree murder. Police said his bodyguards fired two bullets into the back of a man Broadus claimed had threatened him. As *Newsweek* commented: "Authenticity was his asset and his downfall."

Rolling Stone, made the point this way: "It's no revelation that teenybopper acts like Abdul, the New Kids, Milli Vanilli, Rick Astley and Kylie Minogue are primarily poster-ready hunks and babes and barely singers at all. In this age of the producer-auteur, their vocals are the last element added to a record." About the Grammys, *Time* music critic Jay Cocks said: "The Grammys have the most unfortunate reputation for often making saccharine choices that toady shamelessly to the marketplace." Joe Smith, president of Capitol records, was unwittingly revealing about the profit-over-art orientation of the major record companies when he defended the televised Grammy awards by saying: "They get good ratings. This is not the International Red Cross."

Record industry critics say that cultural homogenization has accelerated since the 1950s, coinciding with the disappearance of many independent record companies. The major labels have acquired most of the independents, which prided themselves on distinctive music. These include the black label *Motown,* known once for a distinctive "Detroit sound" but which moved to Los Angeles and went for the mass market before being swallowed up by a major label in 1988. *Arista,* the last so-called *major independent,* was bought by a major, Time Warner, in 1989.

LECTURE RESOURCE 5-E
Exercise: Discuss cultural homogenization.

RECORD CENSORSHIP

STUDY PREVIEW   A perennial problem for record-makers is pressure to sanitize lyrics to protect young listeners. Some would-be censors are at the reactionary and radical fringes of society, but others have received serious attention from congressional committees. By and large, the record industry has headed off government sanctions with voluntary labels on records.

OBJECTIONABLE MUSIC

Campaigns to ban records are nothing new. In the Roaring '20s, some people saw jazz as morally loose. White racists of the 1950s called Bill Haley's rock "nigger music." War protest songs of the Vietnam period angered many Americans.

TEACHING OBJECTIVE 5-8
Payola, censorship and home dubbing are critical issues.

Government attempts to censor records have been rare, yet the Federal Com-munications Commission indirectly keeps some records off the market. The FCC can take a dim view of stations that air objectionable music, which guides broad-casters toward caution. Stations do not want to risk their licenses. Because the record industry is so dependent on airplay, hardly any music that might offend makes it to market.

The FCC has been explicit about obnoxious lyrics. In 1971 the commission said stations have a responsibility to know "the content of the lyrics." Not to do so, said the commission, would raise "serious questions as to whether continued opera-tion of the station is in the public interest." The issue at the time was music that glorified drugs.

The politically active radical right affects what record-makers do. The radical right has campaigned against specific artists and records in protests to Congress and the FCC, boycotts against stations and record-burning rallies. The flavor of these campaigns is reflected in the titles of books by David Noebel of evangelist Billy James Hargis's Christian Crusade: *Communism, Hypnotism and the Beatles: An Analysis of the Communist Use of Music; The Beatles: A Study in Drugs, Sex and Revolu-tion;* and *Rhythm, Riots, and Revolution,* which Noebel announced he would retitle *The Marxist Minstrels.* Televangelist Jimmy Swaggart and coauthor Robert Lamb kept up the same theme with their 1987 book *Religious Rock 'n' Roll: A Wolf in Sheep's Clothing.*

What effect have the FCC and the radical right had on the recording industry? In his book *Solid Gold,* Serge Denisoff says, "Depending upon geography and polit-ical climate, both the Right and the FCC have influenced musical fare in America. Fear of these entities forced CBS to remove Bob Dylan's 'Talking John Birch Society Blues' from his second album and from the Ed Sullivan Show. Pete Seeger was blacklisted from commercial radio and television for nearly 17 years. Ed Sullivan changed the title of the Rolling Stones' 'Let's Spend the Night Together' to 'Let's Spend Some Time Together.' Barry McGuire's 'Eve of Destruction' and Crosby, Stills, Nash and Young's 'Ohio' were blacklisted in many parts of the country."

RECORD LABELING

In the 1980s complaints about lyrics narrowed to drugs, sexual promiscuity and violence. A group led by Tipper Gore and wives of several other influential mem-bers of Congress, *Parents' Music Resource Center,* claimed links between explicit rock music and teen suicide, teen pregnancy, abusive parents, broken homes, and other social ills. The group objected to lyrics like Prince's "Sister," which extolls incest; Mötley Crüe's "Live Wire," with its psychopathic enthusiasm for strangulation; Guns n' Roses' white racism; and Ice T and other rap artists' hate music.

The Parents' Music Resource Center argued that consumer protection laws should be invoked to require that records with offensive lyrics be labeled as dangerous, like cigarette warning labels or the movie industry's rating system. After the group went to the FCC and the National Association of Broadcasters, record companies began labeling potentially offensive records: "Explicit Lyrics—Parental Advisory." In some cases, the companies printed lyrics on album covers as a warning.

LYRICS AND YOUNG PEOPLE

Despite countless studies, it is unclear whether mores are affected by lyrics. Two scholars from California State University at Fullerton found that most high school students are hazy on the meaning of their favorite songs. Asked to explain Bruce Springsteen's "Born in the U.S.A.," about the hopelessness of being born in a blue-collar environment, many teenagers were simplistically literal. "It's about the town Bruce Springsteen lives in," said one. Led Zeppelin's "Stairway to Heaven" has been criticized for glorifying drug or sexual rushes, but many teenagers in the study were incredibly literal, saying the song was about climbing steps into the sky. What does this mean? Professor Lorraine Prinsky of the Fullerton study concluded that teenagers use rock music as background noise. At most 3 percent, she said, are fully attentive to the lyrics.

Critics, however, see an insidious subliminal effect. Some songs repeat their simple and explicitly sexual messages over and over, as many as 15 to 30 times in one song. Said a spokesperson from the Parents' Music Resource Center: "I can't believe it's not getting through. It's getting into the subconscious, even if they can't recite the lyrics."

CHAPTER WRAP-UP

Prospects for the record industry are upbeat, as long as record-makers stay in tune with the changing tastes of the young people comprising their major market. Citing huge profits, analyst Allan Dodds Frank says, "Gold hasn't flowed from black vinyl disks in such quantities in many years." Compact discs have caught on, and profits are high. The discs cost $3 each to make, not including $1 or so in royalties, and sell for $8 wholesale and $13 to $15 retail. Record-makers clear $4 a disc, which makes for happy shareholders.

Technological advances continue to create new profit opportunities by rendering old formats obsolete. Just as record-makers reissued old 78-rpm music on EP and LP when the microgroove was introduced, they later added stereo versions. Then they went to eight-track tapes, which eventually lost favor to cassette tapes, which later were replaced by CDs. As consumers buy improved playback equipment, they need to update their music collections with recordings in the new formats. While this can churn profits for record companies, promoters of new formats run a risk with the introduction of so many competing formats: Customers may shy away from buying any of them until they know which will survive. It is doubtful, for example, that over the long haul CD, DAT, DCC and MD equipment will all find a sufficient marketplace following to justify record companies' manufacturing in all the formats or record stores' stocking them all.

The future has other challenges. Home-dubbing equipment could be an unstoppable leak on profits. There also are antitrust questions about whether the public or our culture would be better served by a less concentrated recording industry.

The long-term future of the recording industry, however, rests more on each new generation of young people than anything else. Since the turn of the century, when a separate youth culture began taking form, teenagers have looked to new music to set their generation apart. They have bought records that irritated their parents, that represented the social causes of the day and that were fun to listen to. Today almost 50 percent of recording industry sales are to people under the age of 25.

But young people can be fickle. When record sales plummeted in 1924, young people were turning on the radio. In 1979 they played video games and sent the record industry into depression. For the most part, though, young people have been a loyal, growing market, and they will continue to be as long as recordings are an affordable vehicle to identify their generation, to celebrate their values, to demonstrate youthful rebellion and to dance to.

QUESTIONS FOR REVIEW

1. Why is recorded music important?

2. How did mechanical sound reproduction work? How about electromagnetic reproduction? How about digital reproduction?

3. What effect did music videos have on the recording industry when they were introduced?

4. What is the effect of new formats and megadeals with performers on the recording industry?

5. Is making money easy in the recording industry?

6. What is the relationship of the recording and radio industries?

7. Does conglomeration in the recording business affect innovation?

8. What is the effect of payola, censorship and home dubbing on the recording business?

QUESTIONS FOR CRITICAL THINKING

1. Three principal methods for storing sound for replaying have been developed. Distinguish each type, explain the advantages of each and place them in a historical perspective. The methods are mechanical media, like the phonograph disc; magnetic media, like cassette tapes; and digital media, like compact discs.

2. Two types of piracy are plaguing the United States recording industry. Describe illegal copying of both records and tapes for resale and home dubbing, and discuss what can be done.

3. Of the major technological developments in sound recording, which was the most significant? Support your case. Consider but do not limit yourself to these developments: the Phonograph of Thomas Edison in 1877, electromagnetic applications by Joseph Maxwell in 1924, the 33⅓ LP by Peter Goldmark and the compact disc.

4. The year 1979 was disastrous for the U.S. recording industry. Of the industry's problems that year, which have been addressed successfully? Which have not? What lies ahead? Is it realistic to expect continued growth? Consider home dubbing and piracy, a loose distribution system for getting products to consumers and megabuck contracts with star performers.

5. What are the common and the distinguishing characteristics of the six major U.S. recording companies? They are Capitol, CBS, MCA, PolyGram, RCA and Warner.

6. Discuss the relationship of the independent recording companies and the majors, with particular attention to Windham Hill, Rounder and Motown. Consider that Motown was acquired by a major label in 1988.

7. Historically, the direction of radio has had major effects on the U.S. recording industry. Discuss the effects brought about by Alan Freed's record programs in the 1950s, FCC authorization of FM stereo in 1961, and demographics-based programming shifts from a teenage to an older, larger audience.

8. Some historians divide the recording industry into periods. Using information in this chapter, cite specifics on what characterizes each of these periods: the age of discovery (1877–1924), the age of electrical recording (1925–1945), the age of the LP and rock 'n' roll (1948–1960), the age of maturing rock and high profits (1960–1978), the age of retrenchment (1979–1984) and the age of video and digital resurgence (1985 on).

9. What criteria would make sense to protect teenagers from the records to which Parents' Music Resource Center objects? Do teenagers need to be protected? Are cover labels enough? Does printing lyrics on album covers make a difference?

10. Explain how the record-making industry and the manufacturers of playback equipment came to be divided on the home-dubbing issue. How did conglomeration, including Sony's purchase of CBS Records, ease this antagonism?

11. What kind of solution is the taping tax to the revenue drain that home dubbing represents for the recording industry? How can the taping tax encourage more creative activity among lyricists and musical performers?

FOR FURTHER LEARNING

Iain Chambers. *Urban Rhythms: Pop Music and Popular Culture* (St. Martin's, 1985). Chambers, a British scholar, sees post–World War II pop music as a liberator for the masses of people against traditional cultural forces.

Steve Chapple and Reebee Garofalo. *Rock 'n' Roll Is Here to Pay: The History and Politics of the Music Industry* (Nelson-Hall, 1977). This interpretive look at the music industry is built on the premise that authentic cultural contributions are co-opted by profit motives.

R. Serge Denisoff with William Schurk. *Tarnished Gold: The Record Industry Revisited* (Transaction Books, 1986). Denisoff, a sociologist, examines the recording industry by accepting popular music as a cultural phenomenon within a commercial framework. This is an update of his 1975 book, *Solid Gold.*

Peter Fornatale and Joshua E. Mills. *Radio in the Television Age* (Overlook Press, 1980). This interestingly written account of radio from the 1950s through the 1970s suggests that the payola scandals were overplayed in the media because of other events of the time.

Roland Gelatt. *The Fabulous Phonograph: From Tin Foil to High Fidelity* (J.B. Lippincott, 1955). This is a comprehensive history through the battle of the speeds and the demise of the 78-rpm record.

Barry L. Sherman and Joseph R. Dominick. "Violence and Sex in Music Videos: TV and Rock 'n' Roll." *Journal of Communication* 36 (Winter 1986):1, 79–93. Scholars Sherman and Dominick tackle the influence of music videos from numerous perspectives. Their report is part of a 68-page special music video section in this issue of the *Journal of Communication.*

Dick Weissman. *The Music Business: Career Opportunities and Self-Defense* (Crown Publishers, 1979). After 20 years of learning the ropes of the music business as a performer, Weissman wrote this excellent primer for anyone aspiring to a career in music.

FOR KEEPING UP TO DATE

Consumer magazines that track popular music and report on the record industry include *Rolling Stone* and *Spin.*

Entertainment Weekly has a regular section on music.

MOVIES HAVE
POWERFUL IMPACT

THE TECHNOLOGICAL
BASIS OF MOVIES IS
PHOTOGRAPHY CHEMISTRY

MOVIES HAD THEIR HEYDAY
AS A MASS MEDIUM IN
THE 1940S

TELEVISION WAS A SERIOUS
THREAT TO HOLLYWOOD
BEGINNING IN THE LATE 1940S

HOLLYWOOD TODAY IS A MAJOR
PRODUCER OF TELEVISION
PROGRAMMING

THE MOVIE EXHIBITION BUSINESS
FACES CHALLENGES FROM HOME
VIDEO

MOVIEMAKERS ARE IN AN
EXPENSIVE, HIGH-RISK BUSINESS

HOLLYWOOD HAS OPTED
FOR SELF-POLICING TO
QUELL CENSORSHIP
THREATS

THE U.S. AND GLOBAL
MOVIE BUSINESS IS
BECOMING MORE
CONCENTRATED

chapter 6

MOVIES
A GLAMOUR MEDIUM

Steven Spielberg was infected young with a love for movies—not just seeing them but making them. When he was 12, he put two Lionel toy trains on a collision course, turned up the juice to both engines and made a home movie of the crash. By that time, he already had shot dozens of short movies. For one of them, he coaxed his mother into donning a pith helmet and Army surplus uniform, and then he rolled the film as she bounced the family Jeep through backhill potholes near Phoenix. That was his family war movie.

Imagine Steven Spielberg's excitement, at age 17, when a family visit to Los Angeles included a tour of the Universal studios. Imagine his disappointment when the tour bus bypassed the sound stages. At the next break, he gave the tour group the slip and headed straight back to the sound stages, somehow managed to get in, and ended up chatting for an hour with editorial head Chuck Silvers. The next day, with a pass signed by Silvers, Spielberg was back to show him four of his 8-millimeter home movies. Silvers liked what he saw but told the young Spielberg that he could not issue another pass for the next day. Undaunted, Spielberg put on a suit and tie the next day and, carrying his father's briefcase, walked through the Universal gates, faking a familiar wave to the guard. It worked. Spielberg spent the whole summer in and out of Universal, hanging around as movies were being made.

Today, Spielberg is one of the world's best-known moviemakers. His 1993 movie, *Jurassic Park,* has earned more money than any other movie in history. The gross topped $900 million in less than a year and was heading toward $1 billion with home video and other after-market releases. That surpassed 1982's *E.T.: The Extra-Terrestrial,* another Spielberg film, which had been the top Hollywood moneymaker. Spielberg's *Indiana Jones: Last Crusade* is fifth and *Jaws* eighth. His *Raiders of the Lost Ark, Indiana Jones and the Temple of Doom* and *Close Encounters of the Third Kind* all are in the top 20. In all, his 15 movies have grossed more than $4 billion.

Steven Spielberg

Steven Spielberg. Perhaps no other moviemaker can project stories so compellingly across such a diverse range as Steven Spielberg. His *Jurassic Park,* which raised questions about DNA preservation of extinct life forms, became the most profitable movie in history, surpassing *E.T.* by over $165 million. *Schindler's List,* which depicts one aspect of the World War II Holocaust, etched powerful, not-to-be-forgotten images into viewers' consciousness.

CNN *Schindler's List*

Even anti-Semites and bigots were deeply moved by Steven Spielberg's movie *Schindler's List.* CNN reporter Jeanne Moos tells about early screenings and special showings that were intended to ease hatred and bigotry. A question raised by the segment is whether the media can be effective in undermining aberrant human attitudes. This segment aired February 28, 1994.

Steven Spielberg's work embodies a whole range of qualities that tell us a lot about Hollywood and the role of movies in our culture. He is a wonderful, audience-oriented storyteller: "I want people to love my movies, and I'll be a whore to get them into theaters," he once said.

Spielberg's films also represent the glitz and glamour of Hollywood. Most are spectacularly filmed with dazzling special effects. And their box-office success has helped fuel the extravagances that are part of the image Hollywood cultivates for itself.

But Spielberg is deeper than that. He entwines observations from his personal life into film commentary on fundamental human issues. The fantasy *E.T.* centers on a boy growing up alienated in a broken home who identifies with the alien E.T. Movie analysts see the boy as a metaphorical stand-in for Spielberg, who was taunted as a Jew when he transferred into a new high school and found himself alienated for something over which he had no control.

Moviegoers entranced by Spielberg's adventure stories sometimes forget his serious works. His 1985 *The Color Purple,* adapted from Alice Walker's Pulitzer Prize–winning book, was a painful, insightful account of a southern African-American family during the first half of the century. *Schindler's List,* his acclaimed 1993 account of the Holocaust, flows from his own heritage. These movies, some say Spielberg's best, represent the potential of the medium to help us individually and collectively to sort through the dilemmas of the human condition.

Schindler's List swept the Oscars in 1993, casting Spielberg in a whole new light as director. Until then, Spielberg's critical success seemed to count against him at Oscar time, and even critics who liked his work for its seamless craft and visceral punch dismissed him as a serious director. Though he had tackled serious themes before, he always seemed uncomfortable with the material, as if he were trying too hard to make a point. All that changed with *Schindler's List*. The film, from the novel by Thomas Keneally, has been universally praised as one of the great films of the decade, and with it Spielberg has assured himself a place in film history not only as the highest-grossing director of all time, but as one of the great U.S. directors of the post-war period.

In this chapter, you also will learn how the movie industry is structured, including the historical influences that have reshaped the industry. You also will learn about issues that will shape Hollywood in the years ahead.

IMPORTANCE OF MOVIES

STUDY PREVIEW The experience of watching a movie, uninterrupted in a darkened auditorium, has entranced people since the medium's earliest days. It is an all-encompassing experience, which has given movies a special power in shaping cultural values.

OVERWHELMING EXPERIENCE

Movies have a hold on people, at least while they are watching one, that is more intense than any other medium. It is not unusual for a movie reviewer to recommend taking a handkerchief, but never will you hear such advice from a record reviewer and seldom from a book reviewer. Why do movies have such powerful effects? It is not movies themselves. With rare exception, these evocative efforts occur only when movies are shown in a theater. The viewer sits in a darkened auditorium in front of a giant screen, with nothing to interrupt the experience. The rest of the world is excluded. Movies, of course, can be shown outdoors at drive-in theaters and on television, but the experience is strongest in the darkened cocoon of a movie house.

People have been fascinated with movies almost from the invention of the technology that made it possible, even when the pictures were nothing more than wobbly, fuzzy images on a whitewashed wall. The medium seemed to possess magical powers. With the introduction of sound in the late 1920s, and then color and a host of later technical enhancements, movies have kept people in awe. Going to the movies remains a thrill—an experience unmatched by other media.

HOLLYWOOD'S CULTURAL INFLUENCE

When Clark Gable took off his shirt in the 1934 movie *It Happened One Night* and revealed that he was not wearing anything underneath, American men in great numbers decided that they too would go without undershirts. Nationwide, undershirt sales plummeted. Whether men prefer wearing underwear is trivial compared to some concerns about how Hollywood portrays American life and its influence:

■ Sociologist Norman Denzin says the treatment of drinking in American movies has contributed to a misleading bittersweet romanticism about alcoholism in the public consciousness.

TEACHING OBJECTIVE 6-1
Movies influence contemporary culture.

MEDIA: PEOPLE

Robert Flaherty

KEY PERSON
Robert Flaherty produced *Nanook* documentary.

Explorer *Robert Flaherty* took a camera to the Arctic in 1921 to record the life of an Eskimo family. The result was a new kind of movie: the *documentary*. While other movies of the time were theatrical productions with scripts, set and actors, Flaherty tried something different —recording reality.

His 57-minute *Nanook of the North* was compelling on its own merits when it started on the movie house circuit in 1922, but the film received an unexpected macabre boost a few days later when Nanook, the father of the Eskimo family, died of hunger on the ice. News stories of Nanook's death stirred public interest and attendance at the movie, which helped establish the documentary as an important new film genre.

Flaherty's innovative approach took a new twist in the 1930s, when propagandists saw reality-based movies as a tool to promote their causes. In Germany the Nazi government produced propaganda films, and other countries followed. Frank Capra directed the vigorous five-film series *Why We Fight* for the U.S. War Office in 1942.

After World War II, there was a revival of documentaries in Flaherty's style—a neutral recording of natural history. Walt Disney produced a variety of such documentaries, including the popular *Living Desert* in the 1950s.

Today, documentaries are unusual in American movie houses, with occasional exceptions like *Mother Teresa* in 1986 and movies built on rock concerts.

The CBS television network gained a reputation in the 1950s and 1960s for picking up on the documentary tradition with "Harvest of Shame," on migrant workers, and "Hunger in America." In the same period, the National Geographic Society established a documentary unit, and French explorer Jacques Cousteau went into the television documentary business.

Such full-length documentaries mostly are relegated to the Public Broadcasting Service and cable networks today. The major networks, meanwhile, shifted most documentaries away from full-length treatments. Typical was CBS's "60 Minutes," a weekly one-hour program of three minidocumentaries. These new network projects, which included ABC's "20/20," combined reality programming and entertainment in slick packages that attracted larger audiences than traditional documentaries.

Robert Flaherty

Nanook of the North. The documentary became a film genre with explorer Robert Flaherty's *Nanook of the North* in 1921. This film was an attempt to record reality—no actors, no props. The film was especially potent not only because it was a new approach and on a fascinating subject but also because, coincidentally, Nanook died of starvation on the ice about the time that it was released.

Reality Bites. Young adults in their 20s, dubbed "Generation X" by novelist Douglas Coupland, have been the subject of several recent films, including 1993's *Reality Bites*. X-ers (a.k.a. "Slackers," from the Richard Linklater film of the same name) complain that their cultural image is entirely media-created, and in fact is meaningless, except as a convenient demographic category for advertisers.

- Scholars using content analysis have found exponential increases in movie violence that far outpace violence in real life but that nonetheless correspond with perceptions that violence is a growing problem in modern life.
- Utility company executives were none too pleased with the widespread public concern about nuclear power created by James Bridges's 1979 movie, *The China Syndrome*.
- Political leaders express concern from time to time that movies corrupt the morals of young people and glamorize deviant behavior. Congressman Parnell Thomas once raised questions that Hollywood was advocating the violent overthrow of the government.

Movies are part of our everyday lives in more ways than we realize. Even the way we talk is loaded with movie metaphors. The *New Yorker* magazine noted this introducing an issue on Hollywood: "Our personal scenarios unspool in a sequence of flashbacks, voice-overs and cameos. We zoom in, cut to the chase, fade to black."

Because of the perceived influence of movies, some real, some not, it is important to know about the industry that creates them. This is especially true now that television entertainment programming has been largely subsumed by Hollywood and that the book, magazine and sound recording industries are closely tied into it.

TECHNICAL HERITAGE OF MOVIES

STUDY PREVIEW   Motion picture technology is based on the same chemical process as photography. The medium developed in the 1880s and 1890s. By the 1930s movie houses everywhere were showing "talkies."

AN ADAPTATION FROM PHOTOGRAPHY

The technical heritage of motion pictures is photography. The 1727 discovery that light causes silver nitrate to darken was basic to the development of motion picture technology. So was a human phenomenon called *persistence of vision*. The human eye retains an image for a fraction of a second. If a series of photographs captures something in motion and if those photographs are flipped quickly, the human eye will perceive continuous motion.

TEACHING OBJECTIVE 6-2
Photographic technology is basis of movies.

LECTURE RESOURCE 6-A
Film: *Facts About Film.*

LECTURE RESOURCE 6-B
Film: *ABC's of Fllm Direction.*

LECTURE RESOURCE 6-C
Video: *Before Hindsight.*

KEY PERSON
Eadweard Muybridge demonstrated persistence of vision.

KEY PERSON
William Dickson developed movie camera.

KEY PERSON
George Eastman devised photo technology used for movies.

The persistence of vision phenomenon was demonstrated photographically in 1877 by *Eadweard Muybridge* in California. Former Governor Leland Stanford had found himself in a wager on whether horses ever had all their legs off the ground when galloping. It was something the human eye could not perceive. All anyone could make out of the legs of a galloping horse was a blur. Stanford asked Muybridge if photography could settle the question. Muybridge stationed 24 cameras along a track with trip strings to open the shutters. The galloping horse hit the strings, and Muybridge had 24 sequential photographs that showed that galloping horses take all four legs off the ground at the same time. Stanford won his $25,000 bet.

More significant to us was that the illusion of a horse in motion was possible by flipping Muybridge's photographs quickly. The sequential photographic images, when run rapidly by the human eye, made it appear that the horse was moving. All that was needed was the right kind of camera and film to capture about 16 images per second. Those appeared in 1888. *William Dickson* of Thomas Edison's laboratory developed a workable motion picture camera. Dickson and Edison used celluloid film perfected by *George Eastman*, who had just introduced his Kodak camera. By 1891 Edison began producing movies.

MEDIA ABROAD

High-Brow Movies

European movie directors, especially the Swede *Ingmar Bergman,* have been favorites of a high-brow American moviegoing crowd since the 1950s. These directors looked to film as a sophisticated literary form, not escapist entertainment. Among Bergman's 50 films, several explored the turbulent relationship he witnessed as a child between his depression-prone father and his emotionally cool mother. The Italian director *Federico Fellini*'s *La Dolce Vita* in 1960 commented with poetic abstraction on human rituals.

High-brow foreign movies never attracted huge American audiences, but they developed a loyal, influential following. They also reminded entertainment-oriented Hollywood of the artistic and literary possibilities of film as a medium. Bergman's 1982 *Fanny and Alexander* won four of Hollywood's Academy Awards.

Occasionally, foreign art films find their way into major movie houses, but usually they are exhibited at small specialized theaters in major cities and near universities. These movies also are popular at film society meetings.

The Remains of the Day. The Ismail Merchant and James Ivory producer-director team created a series of high-brow films, most with a small but intense following. *The Remains of the Day* in 1993, starring Anthony Hopkins and Emma Thompson, dealt with class, politics, and repressed desire in England between the wars. Earlier Merchant-Ivory films, adapted from English novels, included *A Room with a View* and *Howard's End.*

Edison movies were viewed by looking into a box. In France, brothers *Auguste* and *Louis Lumière* brought projection to motion pictures. By running the film in front of a specially aimed powerful lightbulb, the Lumières projected movie images on a wall. In 1895 they opened an exhibition hall in Paris—the first movie house. Edison recognized the commercial advantage of projection, and himself patented the *Vitascope* projector, which he put on the market in 1896.

ADDING SOUND TO PICTURES

Dickson at Edison's lab came up with a sound system for movies in 1889. In the first successful commercial application, Fox used sound in its 1922 Movietone newsreels. But it was four upstart moviemakers, the brothers *Albert, Harry, Jack* and *Sam Warner*, who revolutionized movies with sound. In 1927 the Warners released *The Jazz Singer* starring Al Jolson. There was sound for only two segments, but it caught the public's fancy. By 1930, 9,000 movie houses around the country were equipped for sound.

KEY PEOPLE
Auguste and Louis Lumière projected movie images on wall.

KEY PERSON
Thomas Edison perfected projector. See Index.

KEY PEOPLE
Albert, Harry, Jack and Sam Warner developed "talkies."

THREE CRISES THAT RESHAPED HOLLYWOOD

STUDY PREVIEW In quick succession, Hollywood took three body blows in the late 1940s. Right-wing political leaders sent some directors and screenwriters to jail in 1947 and intimidated moviemakers into creative cowardice. In 1948 the U.S. Supreme Court broke up the economic structure of the movie industry. Then television stole people from the box office.

THE HOLLYWOOD 10

Hollywood had a creative crisis in 1947 when Congressman *Parnell Thomas*, chair of the House Un-American Activities Subcommittee, began hearings on communists in Hollywood. Thomas summoned 47 screenwriters, directors and actors and demanded answers to accusations about leftist influences in Hollywood and the Screen Writers Guild. Ten witnesses who refused to answer insulting accusations went to jail for contempt of Congress. It was one of the most highly visible manifestations of *McCarthyism*, a post–World War II overreaction to Soviet communism as a national threat.

The Thomas hearings had longer deleterious effects. Movie producers, afraid the smear would extend to them, declined to hire the *Hollywood 10*. Other careers were also ruined. One expert identified 11 directors, 36 actors, 106 writers and 61 others who suddenly were unwelcome in their old circles and could not find work.

Among the Hollywood 10 was screenwriter *Dalton Trumbo*. His powerful pacifist novel *Johnny Got His Gun* made Trumbo an obvious target for the jingoist Thomas committee. After Trumbo refused to answer committee questions, he was jailed. On his release, Trumbo could not find anybody who would accept his screenplays, so he resorted to writing under the pseudonym Robert Rich. The best he could earn was $15,000 per script, one-fifth his former rate. When his screenplay for *The Brave One* won an Academy Award in 1957, Robert Rich did not dare show up to accept it.

In a courageous act, *Kirk Douglas* hired Trumbo in 1959 to write *Spartacus*. Then *Otto Preminger* did the same with *Exodus*. Besides Trumbo, only screenwriter *Ring Lardner Jr.* rose from the 1947 ashes. In 1970, after two decades on the blacklist, Lardner won an Academy Award for *M*A*S*H*.

TEACHING OBJECTIVE 6-3
Political and economic crises reshaped movie industry in 1940s.

KEY PERSON
Parnell Thomas led hunt for Hollywood communists.

KEY PERSON
Dalton Trumbo blacklisted as screenwriter.

KEY PERSON
Screenwriter Ring Lardner Jr. overcame 1947 blacklist.

The personal tragedies resulting from the Thomas excesses were bad enough, but the broader ramification was a paucity of substantial treatments of major social and political issues. Eventually, moviemakers rallied with sophisticated treatments of controversial subjects that, it can be argued, were more intense than they might otherwise have been. It was an anti-McCarthy backlash, which did not occur until the mid-1950s, when Hollywood began to reestablish movies as a serious medium. By the 1970s, there were even cinematic exposés of this vicious period in American political history, including *The Way We Were*, a 1973 film starring Robert Redford and Barbra Streisand, and *The Front*, a 1976 satire starring Woody Allen and Zero Mostel.

COURT BANS ON VERTICAL INTEGRATION

KEY PERSON
Adolph Zukor built Paramount as a vertically integrated company.

The government has acted twice to break up the movie industry when it became so consolidated that there was no alternative to preventing abuses. *Adolph Zukor*'s Paramount became a major success as a producer and distributor of feature films in the 1920s, but Zukor wanted more. He began buying movie houses, and eventually owned 1,400 of them. It was a classic case of *vertical integration*, a business practice in which a company controls its product all the way from inception to consumption. Paramount not only was producing and distributing movies but also, through its own movie houses, was exhibiting them. It was profitable, and soon other major Hollywood studios also expanded vertically.

Still not satisfied with his power and profits, Zukor introduced the practice of *block booking*, which required non-Paramount movie houses to book Paramount films in batches. Good movies could be rented only along with the clunkers. The practice was good for Zukor because it guaranteed him a market for the failures. Exhibitors, however, felt coerced, which fueled resentment against the big studios.

The U.S. Justice Department began litigation against vertical integration in 1938, using Paramount as a test case. Ten years later, in 1948, the U.S. Supreme Court told Paramount and four other major studios to divest. They had a choice of selling off either their production or distribution or exhibition interests. Most sold their theater chains.

The effect shook the whole economic structure on which Hollywood was based. No longer could the major studios guarantee an audience for their movies by booking them into their own theaters, and what had come to be known as the *studio system* began to collapse. There was now risk in producing movies because movie houses decided what to show, and there was also a hitherto missing competition among studios.

Movie scholars say the court-ordered divestiture, coming when it did, had a more damaging effect than the Justice Department and the courts foresaw. It was about this time that Parnell Thomas and his congressional committee were bashing producers, which undermined Hollywood's creative output. Now the whole way in which the industry operated was required to change overnight. Hollywood was coming apart.

THE CHALLENGE FROM TELEVISION

Movie attendance in the United States peaked in 1946 at 90 million tickets a week. Every neighborhood had a movie house, and people went as families to see the latest shows, even those that were not very good. Movies, rivaled only by radio, had become the nation's dominant entertainment medium.

Then came television. The early television sets were expensive, and it was a major decision in many families whether to buy one. In many households there were family conferences to decide whether to divert the weekly movie budget to buying a television. By 1950 movie attendance plummeted to 60 million a week and then 46 million by 1955.

Not only had the movie industry been pummeled by Congress into creative timidity, and then been broken up by the courts, but also it had lost the bulk of its audience. Doomsayers predicted an end to Hollywood.

- -

HOLLYWOOD'S RESPONSE TO TELEVISION

STUDY PREVIEW Ironic as it seems, television has been the greatest force shaping the modern movie industry. When television began eroding movie attendance in the 1950s, moviemakers responded with technical innovations such as wraparound screens. There also were major shifts in movie content, including treatments of social issues that early television would not touch.

TECHNICAL INNOVATION

When television began squeezing movies in the late 1940s, moviemakers scrambled for special effects to hold their audience. Color movies had been introduced in the 1930s. In the 1950s they came to be the standard—something that early television could not offer. Other technical responses included wraparound Cinerama screens, which put images not only in front of audiences but also in their peripheral vision. Television's small screen could not match it. Cinerama also permitted moviemakers

TEACHING OBJECTIVE 6-4
Hollywood survived audience losses to television.

CROSS-REFERENCE
For more on effect of television, see Chapters 3, 4 and 7.

to outdo television with sweeping panoramas that were lost on small television screens. Offsetting its advantages, Cinerama was a costly attempt to increase audience involvement. It required multicamera production, and theaters had to be equipped with special projectors and remodeled for the curved screens. Cinema-Scope gave much the same effect as Cinerama but less expensively with an image 2½ times wider than it was high, on a flat screen. CinemaScope did not fill peripheral vision, but it seemed more realistic than the earlier squarish screen images. Gimmicky innovations included *three-dimensional pictures*, which gave viewers not only width and height but also depth. Smellovision was a dubious, short-lived technique. Odors wafted through movie houses to enhance the audience's sensual involvement.

CONTENT INNOVATION

Besides technical innovations, moviemakers attempted to regain their audiences with high-budget movies, with innovative themes and, finally, by abandoning their traditional mass audiences and appealing to subgroups within the mass audiences.

High-budget movies called *spectaculars* became popular in the 1950s. How could anybody, no matter how entranced by television, ignore the epic *Quo Vadis*, with one scene using 5,500 extras? There were limits, however, to luring Americans from their television sets with publicity-generating big-budget epics. The lavish *Cleopatra* of 1963 cost $44 million, much of which Twentieth Century-Fox lost. It just cost too much to make. Even so, moviemakers continued to risk occasional big-budget spectaculars. No television network in the 1960s would have put up $20 million to produce the profitable *The Sound of Music*. Later, the *Star Wars* movies by George Lucas were huge successes of the sort television could not contemplate.

Television's capture of the broad mass audience was a mixed blessing. Television was in a content trap that had confined movies earlier. To avoid offending big sections of the mass audience, television stuck with safe subjects. Moviemakers, seeking to distinguish their products from television, began producing films on serious, disturbing *social issues*. In 1955 *Blackboard Jungle* tackled disruptive classroom behavior, hardly a sufficiently nonthreatening subject for television. Also in 1955 there was *Rebel Without a Cause*, with James Dean as a teenager seeking identity. Marital intimacy and implied homosexuality were elements in the movie adaptation of Tennessee Williams's *Cat on a Hot Tin Roof*, starring Paul Newman and Elizabeth Taylor.

Television continued to be squeamish about many social issues into the 1960s, but movies continued testing new waters, notably with violence and sex. The slow-motion machine-gun deaths of bank robbers Bonnie and Clyde in Arthur Penn's 1967 classic left audiences awed in sickening silence. Nevertheless, people kept coming back to movies with graphic violence. Sex was taboo on television but not at the movies. It was the theme in *Bob and Carol and Ted and Alice*, *Carnal Knowledge* and *I Am Curious, Yellow*. Sex went about as far as it could with the hard-core *Deep Throat* of 1973, which was produced for porno houses but achieved crossover commercial success in regular movie houses.

Movies came to be made for a younger crowd. By 1985, regular moviegoers fell into a relatively narrow age group—from teenagers through college age. Fifty-nine percent of the tickets were purchased by people between the ages of 12 and 24.

Movies of India

At 13 cents a seat, people jam Indian movie houses in such numbers that some exhibitors schedule five showings a day starting at 9 a.m. Better seats sell out days in advance in some cities. There is no question that movies are the country's strongest mass medium. Even though per capita income is only $206 a year, Indians find enough rupees to support an industry that cranks out 800 movies a year, four times more than American moviemakers. Most are B-grade formula melodramas and action stories. Screen credits often include a *director of fights*. Despite their flaws, Indian movies are so popular that it is not unusual for a movie house in a Hindi-speaking area to be packed for a film in another Indian language that nobody understands. Movies are produced in 15 Indian languages.

The movie mania centers on stars. Incredible as it may seem, M. G. Ramachandran, who played folk warriors, and M. R. Radha, who played villains, got into a real-life gun duel one day. Both survived their wounds, but Ramachandran exploited the incident to bid for public office. He campaigned with posters that showed him bound in head bandages and was elected chief minister of his state. While in office, Ramachandran continued to make B-grade movies, always as the hero.

Billboards, fan clubs and scurrilous magazines fuel the obsession with stars. Scholars Erik Barnouw and Subrahmanyam Krishna, in their book *Indian Film,* characterize the portrayals of stars as "mythological demigods who live on a highly physical and erotic plane, indulging in amours." With some magazines, compromising photos are a specialty.

A few Indian moviemakers have been recognized abroad for innovation and excellence, but they generally have an uphill battle against B-movies in attracting Indian audiences. Many internationally recognized Indian films, such as those by *Satyajit Ray,* flop commercially at home.

India Fan Mags. Prolific moviemakers in India crank out movies (most of them not very good) in 15 languages to meet a seemingly insatiable public demand. Fans track the off-screen antics of their favorite stars in celebrity magazines like these in English, Gujerato and Hindi.

Even so, the industry did not produce exclusively for a young audience. Moviemakers recognized that the highest profits came from movies with a *crossover audience.* These were movies that attracted not only the regular box-office crowd but also infrequent moviegoers. Essential, however, was the youth audience. Without it, a movie could not achieve extraordinary success. The immensely profitable *E.T.* was an example. It appealed to the youth audience, to parents who took their small children, and to film aficionados who were fascinated with the special effects.

MELDING OF MOVIES AND TELEVISION

STUDY PREVIEW   Hollywood's initial response to television was to fight the new medium, an effort that had mixed results. Next Hollywood adopted the idea that if you can't beat them, join them. Today, most of the entertainment fare on television comes from Hollywood.

RECONCILIATION OF COMPETING INDUSTRIES

TEACHING OBJECTIVE 6-5
Hollywood became producer of television programming.

Despite Hollywood's best attempts to stem the erosion in attendance caused by television, the box-office sales continued to dwindle. Today, an average of only 16 million tickets are sold a week, one-fifth of attendance at the 1946 box-office peak. Considering that the U.S. population has grown steadily during the period, the decline has been an even more severe indication of television's impact on movie attendance.

Despite a near 50-year slide in box-office traffic, Hollywood has hardly lost its war with television. The movie industry today, a $4 billion a year component of the U.S. economy, is so intertwined with television that it is hard to distinguish them. Three-quarters of the movie industry's production today is for television.

There remains, however, an uneasy tension between the exhibitors who own movie houses and television. Theater traffic has not recovered, and while moviemakers and distributors are profiting from new distribution channels, especially home videos, these new outlets are hurting theater traffic.

FIRST RUNS AND AFTER-MARKETS

When moviemakers plan films today, they build budgets around anticipated revenues that go beyond first runs in movie houses. Unlike the old days, when movies either made it or didn't at the box office, today moviemakers earn more than 17 percent of their revenue from pay television services like HBO after the movie has played itself out in movie houses. Another 8 percent comes from selling videotapes.

For most movies, foreign release is important. Movies are usually released in the United States and abroad simultaneously. Foreign distribution revenues can be significant. The box-office revenue from U.S. movies abroad, in fact, is significant in balance-of-trade figures with other nations.

After-market revenue comes from pay-per-view television channels and the home video market.

MOVIE EXHIBITORS

STUDY PREVIEW   Most moviegoers today go to multiscreen theaters that show a wide range of movies. These multiplexes are a far cry from the first commercially successful exhibition vehicles, peep show machines that only one viewer at a time could watch. Intermediate exhibition vehicles ranged from humble neighborhood movie houses to downtown palaces.

EARLY EXHIBITION FACILITIES

TEACHING OBJECTIVE 6-6
Development of movie exhibition facilities.

In the early days, movie patrons peered into a box as they cranked a 50-foot loop over sprockets. These were called *peep shows*. When Thomas Edison's powerful incandescent lamp was introduced, peep show parlors added a room for projecting movies on a wall. Business thrived. Typical admission was a nickel. By 1908 just about every town had a *nickelodeon*, as these early exhibition places were called.

Exhibition parlors multiplied and became grander. In 1913 the elegant *Strand Theater*, the first of the movie palaces, opened in New York. By the early 1940s there were more than 20,000 movie houses in the United States. Every neighborhood had one.

As television gained prominence in the 1950s, many movie houses fell into disrepair. One by one they were boarded up. *Drive-in movies* eased the loss. At their peak, there were 4,000 drive-ins, but that did not offset the 7,000 movie houses that had closed. Furthermore, drive-ins were hardly 365-day operations, especially in northern climates.

MULTISCREEN THEATERS

Since a nadir in 1971, when annual attendance dropped to 875 million, the exhibition business has evolved into new patterns. Exhibitors have copied the European practice of *multiscreen theaters*—and they built them mostly in suburbs. The new multiscreen theaters allow moviegoers to choose among several first-run movies, all nearby in a multiplex theater with as many as 12 screens. A family can split up in the lobby—mom and dad to one screen, teenagers to another, and the little kids to a G-rated flick.

Showing rooms are smaller today, averaging 340 seats compared with 750 in 1950. Most multiplexes have large and small showing rooms. An advantage for exhibitors is that they can shift popular films to their bigger rooms to accommodate large crowds and move other films to smaller rooms.

Multiplex theaters have lower overhead. There might be 12 projectors, but only one projectionist, one ticket taker and one concession stand. The system has been profitable. Today there are more than 23,000 screens in the United States—more than double the number in 1970 and more than the total number of theaters when movies were the only game in town. In the 1990s, ticket sales have fluctuated from year to year, but the trend in attendance has been downward.

Edison's Kinetoscope. Among the earliest mechanisms for watching movies was inventor Thomas Edison's kinetoscope. A person would look through a peephole as a strip of film was wound over a light bulb. The effect was shaky. Later, Edison borrowed a technique from the Lumière brothers of Paris for the Vitascope system of projecting images on a wall.

Movies from the Front Seat. Drive-in theaters, with speakers that attach to the car window, were especially popular with teenagers, who often refer to them as "passion pits." Today, the number of drive-ins has diminished to less than 900.

BOX-OFFICE INCOME

Movie houses usually split box-office receipts with a movie's distributors. The movie house percentage is called the *nut.* Deals vary, but a 50-50 split is common the first week. *Exhibitors,* as the movie houses are called, take a higher percentage the longer the run. A frequent formula is 60 percent the second week and 70 percent the third, and sometimes more after that. Besides the nut, the concession stand is an important revenue source for exhibitors. Concessions are so profitable that exhibitors sometimes agree to give up their nut entirely for a blockbuster and rely on popcorn and Milk Duds to make money. Movie-house markups on confections are typically 60 percent, even more on popcorn.

The *distributors* that market and promote movies claim a share of movie revenue, taking part of the nut from exhibitors and charging booking fees plus expenses to the moviemakers. Distribution expenses can be significant. Advertising and marketing average $6 million per movie. Making multiple prints, 1,200 copies at $1,200 apiece, and shipping them around the country is expensive too. Distributors also take care of after-markets, including foreign exhibition, videocassette distributors and television—for a fee plus expenses.

With some movies not enough box-office income is generated for the producers to recoup their production expenses. These expenses can be staggering, about $24 million on average. However, when production budgets are kept low and the movie succeeds at the box office, the return to the producers can be phenomenal.

FINANCING FOR MOVIES

STUDY PREVIEW The financing of movies is based more on hardball assessments of their prospects for commercial success than on artistic merit. The money to produce movies comes from major movie studios, banks and investment groups. Studios sometimes draw on the resources of their corporate parents.

THE LESSON OF *INTOLERANCE*

The great cinematic innovator *D. W. Griffith* was riding high after the success of his 1915 Civil War epic, *The Birth of a Nation.* Griffith poured the profits into a new venture, *Intolerance.* It was a complex movie that examined social injustice in ancient Babylon, Renaissance France, early 20th-century America and the Holy Land at the time of Christ. It was a critical success, a masterpiece, but film audiences had not developed the sophistication to follow a theme through disparate historical periods. At the box office it failed.

Intolerance cost $2 million to make, unbelievable by 1916 standards. Griffith had used huge sets and hundreds of extras. He ended up broke. To make more movies, Griffith had to seek outside financing. The result, say movie historians, was a dilution in creativity. Financiers were unwilling to bankroll projects with dubious prospects at the box office. Whether creativity is sacrificed by the realities of capitalism remains a debated issue, but there is no doubt that moviemaking is big business.

ARTISTIC VERSUS BUDGET ISSUES

Today, finding financial backing is easier for some moviemakers than others. Producer-actor Clint Eastwood has no problem because of his record for producing not only popular but also low-cost films, always within budget. Steven Spielberg,

MEDIA DATABANK

Top-Earning Movies

These are the top-earning movies of all time.

Movie	Director	Gross	Year
Jurassic Park	Steven Spielberg	$870 million	1993
E.T.: The Extra-Terrestrial	Steven Spielberg	$702 million	1982
Ghost	Jerry Zucker	$520 million	1990
Star Wars	George Lucas	$510 million	1977
Indiana Jones: Last Crusade	Steven Spielberg	$500 million	1989
Terminator 2	James Cameron	$490 million	1991
Home Alone	Chris Columbus	$480 million	1990
Jaws	Steven Spielberg	$460 million	1975
Pretty Woman	Garry Marshall	$450 million	1990
Batman	Leslie Martinson	$420 million	1989

who produces big-budget movies like *Jurassic Park*, has an almost Eastwoodlike reputation for careful planning, good organization and delivering projects close to budget.

Raising money is harder for producers known for overspending. Michael Cimino reached an extreme with *Heaven's Gate*, a western budgeted originally at $10 million for production. Cimino spent $45 million in pursuing his compulsion for historical detail. The film ended up a masterpiece by many standards, every scene a cinematographic postcard. It also almost put United Artists out of business.

Francis Ford Coppola has a similar reputation for refusing to compromise on detail, whatever the budget implications. For his war movie *Apocalypse Now*, Coppola asked the Pentagon to provide troops and equipment. The Pentagon declined, concerned about Coppola's focus on bizarre sideshows of the Vietnam War. So Coppola built his own army—an expensive artistic decision. In contrast, when the Army objected to a scene of trainee brutality in Clint Eastwood's *Heartbreak Ridge*, Eastwood dropped the scene and received the military support he wanted—a budget-conscious decision.

FINANCING SOURCES

Just as in D. W. Griffith's time, movies are expensive to make—about $24 million on average. Then there are the big-budget movies. Depending on how the expenses are tallied, the 1991 movie *Terminator 2* cost $90 million to $110 million to make. The 1987 box-office flop *Ishtar* ran up bills of $40 million. *Who Framed Roger Rabbit?* exceeded $60 million. Where does the money come from?

MAJOR STUDIOS.   Major studios finance many movies with profits from their earlier movies. Most movies, however, do not originate with major studios but with *independent producers*. While these producers are autonomous in many respects, most of them rely on major studios for their financing. The studios hedge

The Oscars. Anna Paquin won an Academy Award for best supporting actress for the 1993 movie *The Piano.* The Oscar is recognized as a mark of accomplishment because it is the film industry itself, the Academy of Motion Picture Arts and Sciences, who selects the winners.

their risks by requiring that they distribute the movies, a profitable enterprise involving rentals to movie houses and television, home video sales and merchandise licensing.

The studios, as well as other financial backers, do more than write checks. To protect their investments, some involve themselves directly in film projects. They examine budgets and production schedules in considering a loan request. It's common for them to send representatives to shooting sites to guard against budget overruns.

Major studios that are part of conglomerates can draw on the resources of their corporate parents. In 1952 giant MCA acquired the ailing Universal studio and plowed its record business profits into the studio. Universal turned profitable, and

MEDIA: PEOPLE

Spike Lee

Spike Lee, a bright, clever young film director, was in deep trouble in 1992. He had persuaded Warner Brothers, the big Hollywood studio, to put up $20 million for a film biography of controversial black leader Malcolm X, one of his heroes. Lee insisted on expensive foreign shooting in Cairo and Soweto, and now, not only was the $20 million from Warner gone but so was $8 million from other investors. To finish the movie, Lee put up his own $3 million up-front salary to pay, he hoped, all the production bills.

The crisis was not the first for Lee, whose experience as a moviemaker illustrates several realities about the American movie industry, not all of them flattering:

- Hollywood is the heart of the American movie industry, and it is difficult if not impossible for feature filmmakers to succeed outside of the Hollywood establishment.
- Hollywood, with rare exception, favors movies that follow themes that already have proven successful rather than taking risks on innovative, controversial themes.
- Fortunes come and go in Hollywood, even studio fortunes. Although Warner is a major studio and often flush with money, it was on an austerity binge when Spike Lee came back for more money in 1992.
- The American movie industry has been taken over by conglomerates, which, as in the case of Warner Brothers, a subsidiary of Time Warner, was being pressured in 1992 to maximize profits to see the parent company through a difficult economic period.

To hear Spike Lee tell it, his problem also was symptomatic of racism in the movie industry. Addressing the Los Angeles Advertising Club during the *Malcolm X* crisis, Lee, who is black, was blunt: "I think there's a ceiling on how much money Hollywood's going to spend on black films or films with a black theme."

Although studio executives would deny Lee's charge, his perceptions were born of experience in making five movies, all critically acclaimed and all profitable but all filmed on shoestring budgets and with little or no studio promotion.

As a student at Morehouse College, Spike Lee had dabbled in film, and when he graduated he decided to commit herself fully to making movies. He enrolled in the film program at New York University. As his master's thesis he put together *Joe's Bed-Stuy Barbershop: We Cut Heads*. It won a 1982 student Academy Award and became the first student film ever shown in the Lincoln Center's new films series in New York.

That would seem to make a young filmmaker a sought-after talent in Hollywood, but such would not be Lee's experience. Despite the acclaim for *Joe's Bed-Stuy Barbershop*, which called for an awakening of American black consciousness, Lee could not interest Hollywood in financing any of his ideas for more black-oriented films. On his own, Lee raised $175,000 in 1986 to produce *She's Gotta Have It*, a sharp, witty movie that upset Hollywood's conventional wisdom by making $8 million.

Bristling with ideas for more films, Lee again went hat in hand to Hollywood, but the response was lukewarm. For lack of financing, he put his movie ideas on a back burner and kept busy as a filmmaker with an Anita

MCA became even stronger by having another profitable subsidiary. The Gulf and Western conglomerate later did the same with Paramount. Coca-Cola acquired Columbia in 1982 with a promise to help Columbia through the rough times that had beset the movie company.

In the 1980s several studios acquired new corporate parents, which made it easier to finance movies. The Japanese electronics giant Sony bought Columbia in 1989. At $3.4 billion, it was the biggest Japanese takeover of an American corporation in history. The size of the deal was a sign of the new resources Columbia could tap to make movies. By the early 1990s three of the largest U.S. studios were owned by giant foreign companies with the ability to generate cash from other enterprises to strengthen their new U.S. movie subsidiaries.

"Public Enemy." Between movie projects, Spike Lee produces television commercials and videos, including the popular "Public Enemy." There have been many slow periods between movies for Lee, who finds Hollywood money hard to come by for his work, even though he is acclaimed as one of his generation's great moviemakers. Lee blames racism among those who control Hollywood purse strings.

Baker music video, the "Horn of Plenty" short for "Saturday Night Live," and the "Hangtime" and "Cover" ads for Nike, with basketball star Michael Jordan and himself playing his Mars Blackmon streetwise hustler character from *She's Gotta Have It*.

The videos won awards, and the Nike ads sold a lot of shoes, which finally enabled Lee to persuade Columbia Pictures to put up some money for a new movie, *School Daze,* although only one-third the studio's usual commitment for a movie. Columbia's hesitancy was understandable from a commercial perspective. The movie seemed risky. Not only did it delve into sensitive racial issues, including social stratification between light-skinned and dark-skinned blacks, but also, being a musical, it had complex production numbers that might confound a young director, even one as promising as Spike Lee.

Columbia's hesitancy, it turned out, was misplaced. Despite weak studio publicity, *School Daze* turned out to be Columbia's top-grossing movie of 1988. Especially significant about *School Daze* was that Columbia had given Lee complete creative control, unusual even for many veteran filmmakers. That, of course, made the movie's success even a greater credit to Lee, and in 1989 *Newsweek* magazine proclaimed Lee one of the nation's 25 leading innovators.

Lee followed *School Daze* with *Do the Right Thing, Mo' Better Blues* and *Jungle Fever*. None had strong studio financial backing. He remained an outsider. Not only was he a black person in a white-dominated business, but he also insisted on living in the New York neighborhood where he grew up.

When he proposed *Malcolm X,* Warner put up $20 million, unprecedented for a black film, but still short of the whole budget. Lee was sent out to raise the remainder of the $28 million budget from other sources, and then, when the cost overruns came in, he found himself putting his own salary into the project to pay the bills and keep the project alive.

INVESTOR GROUPS.   Special investment groups sometimes are put together to fund movies for major studios. Among them is Silver Screen Partners, which provided millions of dollars in financing for Disney projects at a critical point in Disney's revival in the 1980s.

Less proven producers, or those whose track records are marred by budget overruns and loose production schedules, often seek financing from *risk investors*, who include venture capitalists, tax-shelter organizers and foreign distributors. Risk investors often take a bigger share of revenue in exchange for their bigger risk. It sometimes is a surprise who puts up the money. For *Willie Wonka and the Chocolate Factory*, it was Quaker Oats.

BANKS.   To meet front-end production expenses, studios go to banks for loans against their assets, which include their production facilities and warehouses of vintage films awaiting rerelease. By bankrolling movies, California-based Bank of America grew into one of the nation's biggest banks.

- -

MOVIE CENSORSHIP

| STUDY PREVIEW | The movie industry has devised a five-step rating system that alerts people to movies they might find objectionable. Despite problems inherent in any rating scheme, the NC-17, R, PG-13, P, and G system has been more successful than earlier self-regulation attempts to quiet critics. |

MORALITY AS AN ISSUE

TEACHING OBJECTIVE 6-8
Movie self-regulation has quieted would-be censors.

It was no wonder in Victorian 1896 that a movie called *Dolorita in the Passion Dance* caused an uproar. There were demands that it be banned—the first but hardly last such call against a movie. In 1907 Chicago passed a law restricting objectionable motion pictures. State legislators across the land were insisting that something be done. Worried moviemakers created the *Motion Picture Producers and Distributors of America* in 1922 to clean up movies. *Will Hays*, a prominent Republican who was an elder in his Presbyterian church, was put in charge. Despite his efforts, movies with titillating titles continued to be produced. A lot of people shuddered at titles such as *Sinners in Silk* and *Red Hot Romance*, and Hollywood scandals were no help. Actor William Ried died from drugs. Fatty Arbuckle was tried for the drunken slaying of a young actress. When the Depression struck, many people linked the nation's economic failure with "moral bankruptcy." Movies were a target.

KEY PERSON
Will Hays enforced early movie code.

Under pressure, the movie industry adopted the *Motion Picture Production Code* in 1930, which codified the kind of thing that *Will Hays* had been doing. There was to be no naughty language, nothing sexually suggestive and no bad guys going unpunished.

KEY PEOPLE
Father Daniel Lord and Martin Quigley led decency crusade.

Church people led intensified efforts to clean up movies. The 1930 code was largely the product of *Father Daniel Lord*, a Roman Catholic priest, and *Martin Quigley*, a Catholic layperson. In 1934, after an apostolic delegate from the Vatican berated movies in an address to a New York church convention, United States bishops organized the *Legion of Decency*, which worked closely with the movie industry's code administrators.

The legion, which was endorsed by religious leaders of many faiths, moved on several fronts. Chapters sprouted in major cities. Some chapters boycotted theaters for six weeks if they showed condemned films. Members slapped stickers marked "We Demand Clean Movies" on car bumpers. Many theater owners responded, vowing to show only approved movies. Meanwhile, the industry itself added teeth to its own code. Any members of the Motion Picture Producers and Distributors of America who released movies without approval were fined $25,000.

MOVIES AND CHANGING MORES

In the late 1940s the influence of the policing agencies began to wane. The 1948 Paramount court decision was one factor. It took major studios out of the exhibition business. As a result, many movie houses could rent films from independent producers, many of whom never subscribed to the code. A second factor was the movie *The Miracle*, which became a First Amendment issue in 1952. The movie was about a simple woman who was sure St. Joseph had seduced her. Her baby, she felt, was Christ. Critics wanted the movie banned as sacrilege, but the Supreme Court sided with exhibitors on grounds of free expression. Filmmakers became a bit more venturesome.

At the same time, with mores changing in the wake of World War II, the influence of the Legion of Decency was slipping. In 1953 the legion condemned *The Moon Is Blue*, which had failed to receive code approval for being a bit racy. Despite the legion's condemnation, the movie was a box-office smash. The legion contributed to its own undoing with a series of incomprehensible recommendations. It condemned significant movies like Ingmar Bergman's *The Silence* and Michaelangelo Antonioni's *Blow-Up* in the early 1960s while endorsing the likes of *Godzilla vs. the Thing*.

CURRENT MOVIE CODE

Moviemakers sensed the change in public attitudes in the 1950s but realized that audiences still wanted guidance they could trust on movies. Also, there remained some moralist critics. In 1968 several industry organizations established a new rating system. No movies were banned. Fines were out. Instead, a board representing movie producers, distributors, importers and exhibitors, the *Classification and Rating Administration Board*, placed movies in categories to help parents determine what movies their children should see. The categories, as modified through the years, are:

- **G:** Suitable for *general audiences* and all ages.
- **PG:** *Parental guidance* suggested because some content may be considered unsuitable for preteens.
- **PG-13:** *Parental guidance* especially suggested *for children younger than 13* because of partial nudity, swearing or violence.
- **R:** *Restricted* for anyone younger than 17 unless accompanied by an adult.
- **NC-17:** *No children under age 17* should be admitted.

Whether the rating system is widely used by parents is questionable. One survey found two out of three parents couldn't name a movie their teenagers had seen in recent weeks.

ONGOING ISSUES

STUDY PREVIEW   Movie companies have taken advantage of the federal government's hands-off attitude toward business, which began in the Reagan administration, and integrated themselves vertically. Critics fret that this integration has the same potential for abuse as earlier consolidations that were broken up by the government.

VERTICAL INTEGRATION

TEACHING OBJECTIVE 6-9
Current Hollywood issues, including conglomeration.

Despite the U.S. Supreme Court's 1948 Paramount decision, movie studios clearly are back in the exhibition business, resurrecting vertical integration. Tri-Star Pictures, 23 percent of which was owned by Columbia Pictures, bought the Loew's movie-house chain in 1986. Within months the Cannon Group, Paramount, MCA and Warner also bought exhibition chains either directly or through their corporate parents.

These acquisitions raised questions about whether the 1948 Paramount decision against vertical integration was being violated. Entering the 1990s, the government was not in a trust-busting mood. The Reagan and Bush administrations, in office from 1981 to 1993, eased government regulation of business activities, and there was even discussion about reversing or at least modifying the 1948 Paramount decision.

At the same time, some people, concerned that Hollywood was again too powerful, were advancing the same kinds of arguments that led to the 1948 divestiture. These trust-busting arguments noted not only that vertical integration had returned but also that the coerciveness of Zukor's block booking had never disappeared. Distribution companies, some owned by studios, had taken to selling movies to television in batches, winners being available only with clunkers.

The new vertical integration could go even further. The technology is available for movie distribution companies to move directly into exhibition by beaming movies via satellites to local movie houses. It sounds like Zukor's outlawed Paramount vertical integration, albeit with electronic impulses, not celluloid, as the vehicle to streamline the intermediary distribution step.

COMMERCIAL VERSUS ARTISTIC PRIORITIES

Moviemakers are expanding their supplemental incomes by charging other companies to use movie characters, themes and music for other purposes. This has raised questions about whether commercial imperatives have more priority than artistic considerations.

MERCHANDISE TIE-INS.   Fortunes can be made by licensing other companies to use characters and signature items from a movie. In one of the most successful *merchandise tie-ins,* Twentieth Century-Fox and George Lucas licensed Ewok dolls, R2D2 posters and even *Star Wars* bed sheets and pillowcases. By 1985, seven years after the movie's release, tie-ins had racked up sales of $2 billion. The licensing fee typically is 10 percent of the retail price of the merchandise. *Batman* tie-ins rang up $500 million in sales in 1989, within six months of the movie's release, and Warner Bros. was earning 20 percent of the retail revenue on some products. The totals aren't in yet from the dinosaur mania that followed the 1993 release of *Jurassic Park* or the cave life mugs, T-shirts and trinkets that followed the 1994 release of *The Flintstones.*

Tie-ins are not new. Music, for example, was a revenue source for moviemakers even before talkies. Just about every early movie house had a piano player who kept one eye on the screen and hammered out supportive mood music, and sheet-music publishers bought the rights to print and sell the music to musicians who wanted to perform it on their own. This was no small enterprise. D. W. Griffith's *The Birth of a Nation* of 1915 had an accompanying score for a 70-piece symphony.

Today, music has assumed importance besides supporting the screen drama. It has become a movie-making profit center. *Saturday Night Fever* was the vehicle for a host of hit songs. *Urban Cowboy* was as much a film endeavor as a recording industry enterprise.

PRODUCT PLACEMENT.   Moviemakers also have begun building commercial products into story lines in a subtle form of advertising. It was no coincidence that Tom Cruise downed Pepsi in *Top Gun*. Some movie producers work brand names into their movies for a fee. When the alien E.T. was coaxed out of hiding with a handful of candy, it was with Reese's Pieces. The Hershey company, which makes Reese's, paid to have its candy used. Sales soared in the next few months. Producers first offered the Mars company a chance for the candy to be M&Ms, but Mars executives were squeamish about their candy being associated with anything as ugly as E.T. They did not realize that moviegoers would fall in love with the little alien.

After *E.T.*, the product placement business boomed. Miller beer paid to have 21 references in *Bull Durham*. The same movie also included seven references for Budweiser, four for Pepsi, three for Jim Beam, and two for Oscar Meyer. A simple shot of a product in the foreground typically goes for $25,000 to $50,000. Some advertisers have paid $350,000 for multiple on-screen plugs.

Critics claim that *product placements* are sneaky. Some want them banned. Others say the word "advertisement" should be flashed on the screen when the products appear. Movie people, on the other hand, argue that using real products adds credibility. In the old days, directors assiduously avoided implicit endorsements. In a bar scene, the players would drink from cans marked "beer"—no brand name. Today, says Marvin Cohen, whose agency matches advertisers and movies, "A can that says 'Beer' isn't going to make it anymore." The unanswered question is how much product-placement deals affect artistic decisions.

CHAPTER WRAP-UP

Movies passed their 100th birthday in the 1980s as an entertainment medium with an especially strong following among young adults and teenagers. From the beginning, movies were a glamorous medium, but beneath the glitz were dramatic struggles between competing businesspeople whose success depended on catching the public's fancy.

The most dramatic period for the movie industry came at midcentury. Fanatic anti-communists in Congress intimidated moviemakers into backing away from cutting-edge explorations of social and political issues, and then a government antitrust action forced the major studios to break up their operations. Meanwhile, television was siphoning people away from the box office. Movie attendance fell from 90 million to 16 million per week.

It took a few years, but the movie industry regrouped. More than ever, political activism and social inquiry have become themes in American movies. Moviemakers met the threat from television by becoming a primary supplier of TV programming. In response to the antitrust orders, the big studios sold their movie houses and concentrated on financing independent productions and then distributing them. In short, the movie industry has proved itself remarkably resilient and adaptive.

The movie industry has three primary components: production, marketing and exhibition. Most movie fans follow production, which involves stars, screenplays and big money. Major studios control most production, either by producing movies themselves or by putting up the money for independent producers to create movies, which the studios then market. Marketing, called "distribution" in the trade, involves promotion and profitable after-markets like television and home video sales. Since the 1948 antitrust action, exhibition has been largely independent of Hollywood, although the corporations that own the major studios have again begun moving into the movie-house business.

Throughout their history, movies have been scrutinized by moralists who fear their influence. Today, the critics seem fairly satisfied with the NC-17, R, PG-13, PG, and G rating system that alerts parents to movies that they might find unsuitable for their children.

QUESTIONS FOR REVIEW

1. Why do movies as a mass medium have such a strong impact on people?

2. How does the technological basis of movies differ from the other primary mass media?

3. Why did movies begin fading in popularity in the 1940s?

4. What was Hollywood's initial response to television?

5. What is the relationship of Hollywood and the television industry today?

6. How has the movie exhibition business changed over the years?

7. How do moviemakers raise cash for their expensive, high-risk projects?

8. How has Hollywood responded to criticism of movie content?

9. What was the effect of the Reagan administration's relaxed posture toward business?

QUESTIONS FOR CRITICAL THINKING

1. How would you describe the success of these innovations—Cinerama, CinemaScope, 3-D and Smellovision—in the movie industry's competition against television?

2. Epic spectaculars marked one period of moviemaking, social causes another, sex and violence another. Have these genres had lasting effect?

3. Can you explain why films geared to baby boomers, sometimes called teen films, dominated Hollywood in the 1970s and well into the 1980s? Why are they less important now?

4. How did Eadweard Muybridge demonstrate persistence of vision, and how did that lead to early moviemaking? Cite the contributions of William Dickson, George Eastman and the Lumière brothers.

5. Explain how these three developments forced a major change in Hollywood in the 1950s: the 1947 Thomas hearings, the 1948 Paramount court decision and the advent of television.

6. Once the number of movie exhibitors in the nation was measured in terms of movie houses. Today it is measured by the number of screens. Why?

7. Explain how moviemakers finance their movies. What are the advantages and disadvantages of each method?

8. What has been the role of these institutions in shaping movie content: Motion Picture Producers and Distributors of America, Legion of Decency, and Classification and Rating Administration Board?

9. Describe government censorship of movies in the United States.

FOR FURTHER LEARNING

Thomas W. Bohn and Richard L. Stromgren. *Light and Shadows: A History of Motion Pictures* (Alfred Publishing, 1975). This is a lively, comprehensive examination.

Larry Ceplair and Steven Englund. *The Inquisition in Hollywood: Politics in the Film Community, 1930-1960* (Doubleday, 1980). Ceplair and Englund examine the 1947 congressional smear that depopulated Hollywood of some of its most talented screenwriters and directors.

Norman K. Denzin. *Hollywood Shot by Shot: Alcoholism in American Cinema* (de Gruyter, 1991). Denzin, a sociologist, tracks Hollywood portrayals of alcoholism from 1932 to 1989 for trends to interpret how they came to be and their effects.

Joan Didion. "In Hollywood." *The White Album* (Pocket, 1979). Didion discredits the notion that the major studios are dying with the emergence of independent producers. The studios both bankroll and distribute independent films and, she says, make lots of money in the process.

Douglas Gomery. *The Hollywood Studio System* (St. Martin's, 1986). Gomery examines the movie industry of the 1930s and 1940s, a period when Hollywood moved into mass production, global marketing and a centralized distribution system.

Thomas Guback. "The Evolution of the Motion Picture Theater Business in the 1980s." *Journal of Communication* 37 (Spring 1987):3, 70–77. Why are so many new movie screens being built in the United States even though a smaller percentage of the population goes to movies? Guback lays out an array of economic factors from popcorn prices to new vertical integration schemes.

Garth Jowett and James M. Linton. *Movies as Mass Communication* (Sage, 1980). Jowett and Linton examine the social impact of movies and the economic determinants of the movie industry in this brief, scholarly book.

Lary May. *Screening Out the Past: The Birth of Mass Culture and the Motion Picture Industry* (Oxford University Press, 1980). A thoroughly documented early history.

Victor Navasky. *Naming Names* (Viking, 1980). This is another treatment of the congressional investigation into the film industry.

Murray Schumach. *The Face on the Cutting Room Floor: The Story of Movie and Television Censorship* (Da Capo, 1974).

FOR KEEPING UP TO DATE

People serious about movies as art will find *American Film* and *Film Comment* valuable sources of information.

Trade journals include *Variety* and *Hollywood Reporter.*

Among consumer magazines with significant movie coverage are *Premiere, Entertainment Weekly,* and *Rolling Stone.*

The *Wall Street Journal, Business Week, Forbes* and *Fortune* track the movie industry.

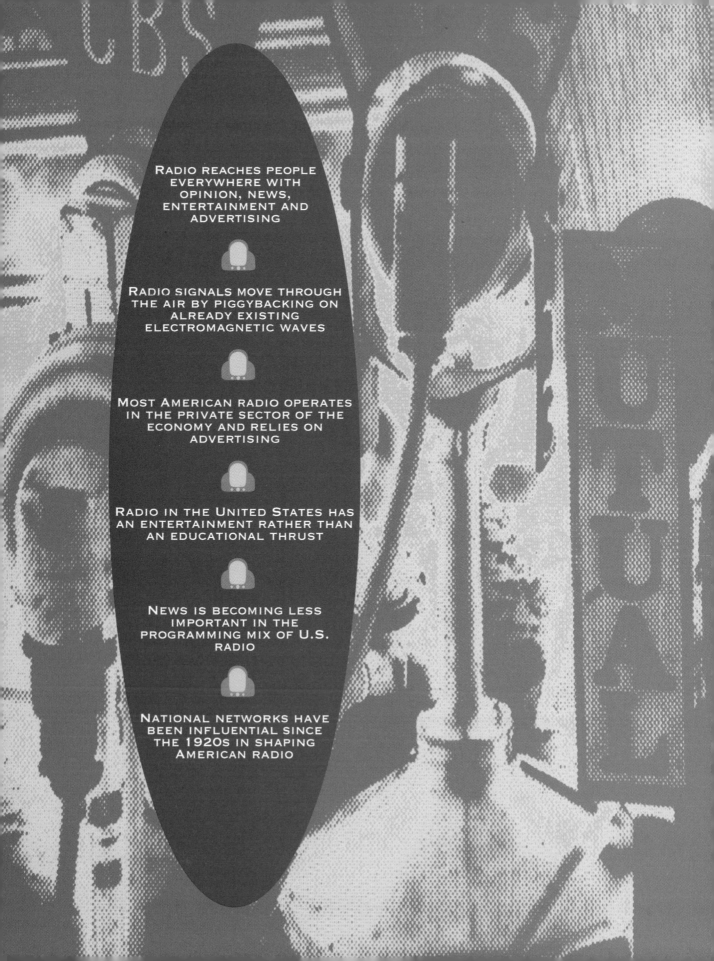

RADIO REACHES PEOPLE EVERYWHERE WITH OPINION, NEWS, ENTERTAINMENT AND ADVERTISING

RADIO SIGNALS MOVE THROUGH THE AIR BY PIGGYBACKING ON ALREADY EXISTING ELECTROMAGNETIC WAVES

MOST AMERICAN RADIO OPERATES IN THE PRIVATE SECTOR OF THE ECONOMY AND RELIES ON ADVERTISING

RADIO IN THE UNITED STATES HAS AN ENTERTAINMENT RATHER THAN AN EDUCATIONAL THRUST

NEWS IS BECOMING LESS IMPORTANT IN THE PROGRAMMING MIX OF U.S. RADIO

NATIONAL NETWORKS HAVE BEEN INFLUENTIAL SINCE THE 1920S IN SHAPING AMERICAN RADIO

With his butterscotch voice, Garrison Keillor purred Hank Snow's "Hello Love" into a radio microphone one Saturday night in 1974. Twenty years after live drama, comedy and theater had departed the airwaves, replaced by disc jockeys and records, Keillor was inaugurating a radio show that brought back the good old days for many Americans and intrigued a whole younger generation with gentle stories about Norwegian bachelor farmers, poems and homey music.

The show, "A Prairie Home Companion," soon went national, attracting 4 million listeners a week, becoming a cult hit among sophisticated noncommercial radio listeners, and landing Keillor on the cover of *Time* magazine. Except for a two-year sabbatical, Keillor has been on the air ever since with stories from his fictional Lake Wobegon, somewhere in Minnesota, "where all the men are strong, all the women are good looking and all the children are above average." Today, the two-hour broadcasts remain a staple at 350 noncommercial radio stations around the country on Saturday nights—an unlikely time, it would seem, to amass great numbers of people around their radios.

A lot of "APHC," as it's called in the trade, is unlikely. There are the tongue-in-cheek commercials from Wobegon merchants:

- Ralph's Pretty Good Grocery: "If you can't find it at Ralph's, you probably can get along without it."
- Fearmonger's Shoppe, "serving all your phobia needs since 1954."
- Bertha's Kitty Boutique.

And then there are the "ads" for Powdermilk Biscuits "with that whole-wheat goodness that gives shy persons the strength to get up and do what needs to be done."

Live Radio. Garrison Keillor and his radio company perform "A Prairie Home Companion" on stage live at the old Globe Theater in downtown St. Paul, Minnesota, before a studio audience. The show, reminiscent of old-time radio, began in 1974. Quickly a cult hit, the show always sold out the 900-seat theater, and 4 million people tuned in weekly. Now slightly updated and revised, the show emanates from New York, still with a live audience and still with its small-town, agrarian romanticism.

Keillor weaves those whimsical commercials into his 20-minute monologues about Lake Wobegon's Lutherans and Catholics, old Plymouths, picnics at the lake and, inevitably, those Norwegian bachelor farmers.

The success of "APHC," now reincarnated as "Garrison Keillor's American Radio Company of the Air," may rest on its nostalgic feel. As in radio's early days, the show is aired live before an audience. It has spontaneity. It's down-home, not slick—just like local radio used to be. It has a powerful intimacy and immediacy, putting listeners' imaginations to work as they conjure up impressions from the drowsy voices of Keillor and his companions and their old-fashioned sound effects.

Lake Wobegon, "the little town that time forgot and the decades cannot improve," is everybody's hometown. It is rustic, cozy, warm—a refuge in Americana. It is also radio at its traditional old-time best.

In this chapter, you will learn that radio's heyday was dominated by live bands, drama and comedy, like Garrison Keillor's show today. You will also learn why radio dropped all that in the 1950s, almost instantly switching to canned music and formulaic disc jockey patter. And you will learn where radio is likely headed, which probably is not back to Lake Wobegon.

SIGNIFICANCE OF RADIO

> **STUDY PREVIEW**   Radio is an important medium for opinion, news, entertainment and advertising. The portability of radio means it is everywhere in our daily lives.

RADIO AS A MOTIVATOR

TEACHING OBJECTIVE 7-1
Discuss radio's ubiquitous reach.

Radio can motivate people to action. When members of Congress were mulling a 51 percent pay hike for themselves in 1988, radio talk-show host Jerry Williams decided it was time for another Boston tea party. He stirred his Boston listeners to send thousands of tea bags to Congress as a not-so-subtle reminder of the 1765 colonial frustration over taxes that led to the Revolutionary War. Talk-show hosts elsewhere joined the campaign, and Congress, swamped with tea bags, scuttled the pay raise proposal.

Recording companies know the power of radio. Without radio stations playing new music, a new record release is almost certainly doomed. Airplay spurs people to go out and buy a record.

Advertisers value radio to reach buyers. Only newspapers, television and direct mail have a larger share of the advertising dollars spent nationwide, and radio's share is growing. From $7 billion in 1986, radio ad revenue soared almost 30 percent to beyond $9 billion in 1992.

UBIQUITY OF RADIO

Radio is everywhere. The signals piggyback on naturally occurring waves in the electromagnetic spectrum and reach every nook and cranny. Hardly a place in the world is beyond the reach of radio.

There are 6.6 radio receivers on average in U.S. households. Nineteen of 20 automobiles come with radios. People wake up with clock radios, jog with headset radios, party with boomboxes, and commute with car radios. People listen to sports events on the radio, even if they're in the stadium. Thousands of people build their day around commentators like Paul Harvey. Millions rely on hourly newscasts to be up to date. People develop personal attachments to their favorite announcers and disc jockeys.

Statistics abound about radio's importance:

- Arbitron, a company that surveys radio listenership, says teenagers and adults average 22 hours a week listening to radio.
- People in the United States own 520 million radio sets. Looked at another way, radios outnumber people 2:1.
- More people receive their morning news from radio than from any other medium.

SCOPE OF THE RADIO INDUSTRY

More than 11,000 radio stations are on the air in the United States. Communities as small as a few hundred people have stations.

Although significant as a $9 billion a year industry, the financial health of radio overall is uneven. It was estimated in 1991 that half the stations in the nation were losing money, and in that year 153 stations signed off the air for the final time. At the same time, radio can be incredibly profitable. Pretax profits were running 37 percent in the early 1990s. The biggest player in the industry, CBS, derived $205 million in radio revenue in 1992, followed by Westinghouse at $201 million and Cap Cities/ABC with $199 million.

The potential for profits is driving the selling price for some stations to astronomical levels. In 1989 a Los Angeles classical music station, KFAC, sold for $55 million, 70 percent more than three years earlier. That was all the more amazing because classical stations have relatively few listeners. Sports station WFAN-AM in New York went for $70 million.

Word Power. For more than 30 years, cantankerous Jerry Williams has demonstrated the power of radio to mobilize people. From his microphone at WRKO, Williams once helped gather 40,000 petition signatures to repeal Massachusetts' mandatory seat-belt law. The law was repealed. In 1988, Williams sparked a national drive against proposed congressional pay increases. Thousands of radio listeners mailed tea bags to Congress as a latter-day symbol of the Boston Tea Party of 1765. Congress decided against the raise.

TECHNICAL DEVELOPMENT

STUDY PREVIEW Human mastery of the electromagnetic spectrum, through which radio is possible, is only a century old. In 1895 an Italian physicist and inventor, Guglielmo Marconi, was the first to transmit a message through the air. Later came voice transmissions and better sound.

ELECTROMAGNETIC SPECTRUM

TEACHING OBJECTIVE 7-2
Explain how radio signals piggyback on electromagnetic waves.

KEY PERSON
Gugielmo Marconi was first to send radio message.

Radio waves are part of the physical universe. They have existed forever, moving through the air and the ether. Like light waves, they are silent—a part of a continuing spectrum of energies, the *electromagnetic spectrum*. As early as 1873, physicists speculated that the electromagnetic spectrum existed, but it was a young Italian nobleman, *Guglielmo Marconi*, who made practical application of the physicists' theories.

Young Marconi became obsessed with the possibilities of the electromagnetic spectrum and built equipment that could ring a bell by remote control—no strings, no wires. The Marconi device shaped a radio wave in such a way that another device could intercept it and decipher a message from the wave's shape. In 1895, when he was 21, Marconi used his wireless method to transmit codes for more than a mile on his father's Bologna estate. Marconi patented his invention in England, and his mother, a well-connected Irish woman, arranged British financing to set up the Marconi Wireless Telegraph Co. Soon ocean-going ships were equipped with Marconi radiotelegraphy equipment to communicate at sea, even when they were beyond the horizon, something never possible before.

Before Tape Recorders. It was no small task when radio stations arranged remote broadcasts in the early days. Staff members at noncommercial station KUOM at the University of Minnesota packed a lot into this sedan for a field production.

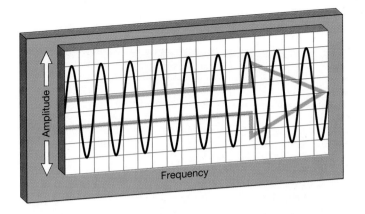

Unmodulated Wave. If you could see electromagnetic waves, they would look like the cross-section of a ripple moving across a pond, except they would be steady and unending. Guglielmo Marconi figured out how to hitch a ride on these waves to send messages in 1895.

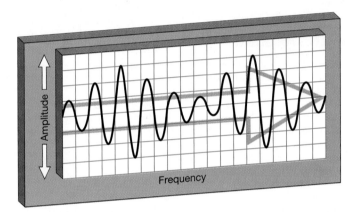

Amplitude-Modulated Wave. Lee De Forest discovered how to adjust the height of electromagnetic waves to coincide with the human voice and other sounds. De Forest's audion tube made voice transmission possible, including an Enrico Caruso concert in 1910.

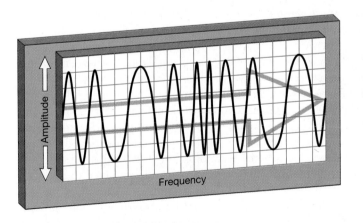

Frequency-Modulated Wave. FM radio transmissions squeeze and expand electromagnetic waves without changing their height. Edwin Armstrong introduced this form of broadcasting, which had superior clarity and fidelity, in the 1930s. Not even lightning interferes with transmission.

Bounce-Back Effect. When AM electromagnetic waves are transmitted, many of them follow the contour of the earth, which extends their range beyond the line-of-sight from the transmitter. Some AM waves go upward, and many of these are bounced back to earth by reflective layers in the ionosphere, which further extends a station's range. The bounce-back effect is weaker during the day when the sun warms the ionosphere and reduces its reflective properties. FM transmissions have a shorter range than AM because the signals move in straight lines and tend not to adhere to the earth's contours. Also, upward-moving FM waves pass through the ionosphere rather than being reflected back.

TRANSMITTING VOICES

KEY PERSON
Lee De Forest invented audion tube and made voice transmissions possible. See Index.

Breakthroughs came quickly. In 1901 a message was sent across the Atlantic. In 1906 *Lee De Forest* created the *audion tube*, which made voice transmissions possible. Radio's entertainment potential was demonstrated in 1910 when De Forest broadcast a magnificent performance by the tenor Enrico Caruso from the New York Metropolitan Opera House.

Technical development stalled during World War I. Military and civilian research concentrated on other things, and work on the newfangled wireless was put off. After the war, Americans were wary as never before about the dangers of dependence on foreign goods. They worried about being cut off if another war disrupted transoceanic commerce. The worry extended to patents, even those in friendly countries, like Marconi's British wireless patent. At the urging of the federal government, three American companies, General Electric, Westinghouse and American Telephone & Telegraph, pooled their resources in 1919 and bought Marconi's American subsidiary and patents. Although the consortium broke up within a few years, it helped to refine the technology further. In this same period, physics department experiments at many United States colleges added to the technology, which gave further impetus to radio's development.

KEY PERSON
Edwin Armstrong invented FM radio.

LECTURE RESOURCE 7-A
Video: *Empire of the Air.*

Static-free transmission was developed by *Edwin Armstrong*, a Columbia University researcher. In 1939 Armstrong built an experimental station in New Jersey using a new system called *frequency modulation*, FM for short. FM's system, piggybacking sound on airwaves, was different from the older *amplitude modulation*, or AM method. In time, Armstrong developed FM stereo with two soundtracks, one for each ear, duplicating the sensation of hearing a performance live.

CHARACTERISTICS OF AMERICAN RADIO

STUDY PREVIEW The radio industry established itself early in the private, free enterprise sector of the economy. It also chose entertainment, rather than news, information and education, as its main programming thrust.

RADIO IN THE PRIVATE SECTOR

A Pittsburgh engineer, *Frank Conrad*, fiddled with radiotelegraphy in his home garage, playing music as he experimented. People with homemade receivers liked what they heard from Conrad's transmitter, and soon he had a following. When Conrad's Westinghouse bosses learned that he had become a local celebrity, they saw profit in building receivers that consumers could buy at $10 a set and take home to listen to. To encourage sales of the receivers, Westinghouse built a station to provide regular programming of news, sports and music—mostly music. That station, KDKA, became the nation's first licensed commercial station in 1920.

The licensing of KDKA was important because it demonstrated the United States' commitment to placing radio in the private sector. In Europe, broadcasting was a government monopoly. KDKA's entertainment programming also sent American broadcasting in a certain direction. In many other countries, radio was used mostly for education and high culture, not mass entertainment.

TEACHING OBJECTIVE 7-3
Discuss the economic basis of U.S. radio.

KEY PERSON
Frank Conrad prompted Westinghouse to put first licensed, commercial station on the air.

"Radio" Becomes a Household Word. When the *Titanic* sank in 1912, newspapers relied on young radio operator David Sarnoff for information on what was happening in the mid-Atlantic. For 72 hours Sarnoff sat at his primitive receiver, which happened to be on exhibit in a department store, to pick up details from rescue ships. The newspaper coverage of the disaster made "radio" a household word, which paved the way for consumer acceptance over the next few years.

ROLE OF ADVERTISING

Westinghouse never expected KDKA itself to make money, only to spur sales of $10 Westinghouse home receivers. The economic base of KDKA and the rest of American broadcasting changed in 1922 when WEAF in New York accepted $50 from a real estate developer and allowed him 10 minutes to pitch his new Long Island apartments. Then the Gimbel's department store tried radio advertising. Within months, companies were clamoring for air time. The Lucky Strike Orchestra produced programs, as did the Taystee Loafers from the Taystee bread company, and the A&P Gypsies, the Goodrich Silvertown Orchestra, and the Interwoven Pair from the sock company.

In those first few years of the 1920s, American radio took on these distinctive traits:

- Private rather than state ownership of the broadcast system.
- An entertainment thrust to programming that emphasized popular culture.
- An economic foundation based on selling time to advertisers who needed to reach a mass audience of consumers.

NONCOMMERCIAL RADIO

American radio was already solidly established as a commercially supported medium when Congress established a regulatory agency in 1927, the Federal Radio Commission. To assure that radio's potential as an educational medium was not lost, the FRC reserved some licenses for noncommercial stations. These went mostly to stations operated by colleges and other institutions that would finance their operation without advertising. Today, about 10 percent of the nation's radio stations hold

MEDIA DATABANK

Radio Formats

Commercial radio stations, dependent on advertising revenue, change formats to find the large, profitable niches of listeners. Classification of formats is tricky because so many overlap. By the mid-1990s, however, it was clear that a mix of adult and light rock, usually called "adult contemporary," had displaced country, the 1980s leader. The leading formats:

Format	Stations	Percentage	Format	Stations	Percentage
Adult contemporary	2,014	18.3 percent	Spanish	451	4.1 percent
Top 40	1,310	11.9 percent	Adult standard	385	3.5 percent
News and talk	1,607	14.6 percent	Classic rock	363	3.3 percent
Country	1,211	11.0 percent	Easy listening	275	2.5 percent
Album-oriented rock	1,001	9.1 percent	Adult alternative	231	2.1 percent
Urban contemporary	968	8.8 percent	Religious	220	2.0 percent
Oldies	693	6.3 percent	Classical	188	1.7 percent

noncommercial licenses. Many of these are low-power stations that colleges operate as training facilities.

In 1967 Congress passed the *Public Broadcasting Act* to create a national noncommercial radio system. Every major city and most college towns have a public radio station, most of which carry specialized programs that do not have large enough audiences to attract advertisers. Classical music, news and documentaries are programming mainstays at most public stations.

Many noncommercial stations are affiliates of *National Public Radio*, a network that went on the air in 1970. NPR was created with support from the *Corporation for Public Broadcasting*, a quasi-governmental agency that channels federal funds into the national public radio system. Two NPR news programs, "Morning Edition" and "All Things Considered," have earned a loyal following. NPR offers about 50 hours of programming a week to affiliate stations. Since 1981 *American Public Radio* of St. Paul, Minnesota, also has offered programs to noncommercial stations.

Neither noncommercial stations nor their networks carry advertising, but supporting foundations and corporations are acknowledged on the air as underwriters. In recent years some of these acknowledgements have come to resemble advertising but without exhortations, which the FCC prohibits.

RADIO AS ENTERTAINMENT

STUDY PREVIEW Radio stations today are known by a wide range of formats, each geared to attracting narrow segments of the population. In earlier times, radio stations sought broader mass audiences with programs that had wide appeal. The programming was a culturally unifying influence on the nation. Today's more segmented programming came about when radio began losing the mass audience to television in the 1950s.

EARLY MASS PROGRAMMING

In the early days, most stations were on the air at night with hotel tea-time music. It was pleasant programming, offensive to no one. Sandwiched among the *potted-palm* music, as it was called, were occasional soloists, poets and public speakers. As broadcasting expanded into the daytime, stations used more recordings, which introduced a bit more variety. In the 1930s, evening programming became more varied. Potted-palm music gave way to symphonies and big bands. Guy Lombardo, the Dorsey Brothers and Benny Goodman all found that radio helped promote their record sales.

With more varied programs, radio attracted a true mass audience in the 1930s. Fred Waring and His Pennsylvanians demonstrated that variety shows could attract large audiences. Jack Benny, Milton Berle and Bob Hope did the same with comedy. George Burns and Gracie Allen put together the first continuing situation comedy. Drama series were introduced—murders, soap operas, Westerns, thrillers. Quiz shows became part of the mix. Many early radio programs remain popular today on cassettes. "The Lone Ranger," "The Whistler" and "The Shadow," among dozens of others, are available at record shops.

The early radio programming, geared to attract large audiences, was a culturally unifying factor for the nation. Almost everyone had a common experience in the radio programs of the time.

LECTURE RESOURCE 7-B
Film: *Radio.*

TEACHING OBJECTIVE 7-4
Discuss the programming forms.

Assessing Hometown Radio

The demassification of radio has led to a great many formats, each designed to appeal to a segment of the mass audience. The shape of demassification varies from region to region, reflecting different interests. You can assess the flavor of radio programming in your area by listening to all the daytime signals you can pick up and categorizing them by these criteria:

- **Formats.** What percentage of stations falls into major format categories? Almost everywhere, the adult contemporary format is dominant, but in some regions other formats are unusually strong—like country in the South, ethnic in big cities, and polka in Wisconsin. You may find some stations dabble in so many programming genres that they are difficult to categorize. Generally, though, one type of content best characterizes a station.

- **Audience.** What age group is each station most appealing to? Top 40 tends to be a teenage audience, classical much older. Are some formats more appealing to women? All-sports stations have strong male followings.

- **Market.** Listen to local advertisements to determine what socioeconomic level each station is geared to. Ads on all-news stations will show that advertisers believe they have listeners with higher incomes than most other formats. Stations that carry advertisements for luxury products, like Cadillacs, have wealthier audiences than stations that carry ads from muffler shops.

It is important to do this exercise during the daytime because many AM signals at night are from distant cities that won't reflect your area's distinctiveness.

FORMATS FOR SPECIFIC AUDIENCES

Comedies, dramas and quiz shows moved to television beginning in the late 1940s, and so did the huge audience that radio had cultivated. The radio networks, losing advertisers to television, scaled back what they offered stations. As the number of listeners dropped, local stations played more recorded music, which was far cheaper than producing programs.

Although most stations in the pre-television period offered diversity, a few stations emphasized certain kinds of programming. Country music stations dotted the South. Some stations carried only religious programs. In the 1950s, Cleveland announcer Alan Freed introduced rock 'n' roll, which became the fare at hundreds of stations and began wide-scale fragmentation in radio programming. Today, hardly any station tries to offer something for everyone, but everyone can find something on the radio to like. There is a format for everyone.

After Freed came the *Top 40* format, in which the day's top songs were repeated in rotation. The wizard of radio formatting, *Gordon McLendon*, perfected the format at KLIF in Dallas, Texas, by mixing fast-paced newscasts, disc jockey chatter, lively commercials and promotional jingles, and hype with the music. It was catchy, almost hypnotizing—and widely imitated. McLendon designed *beautiful music* as a format at KABL, San Francisco, in 1959; *all-news* at XTRA, Tijuana, Mexico, aimed at southern California, in 1961; *all-classified ads* at KADS, Los Angeles, 1967. In all of his innovations, McLendon was firm about a strict structure. In Top 40, for example, there were no deviations from music in rotation, news every 20 minutes, naming the station by call letters twice between songs, upbeat jingles and no dead-pan commercials. McLendon's classified-ad format bombed, but the others have survived.

KEY PERSON
Gordon McLendon pioneered strictly formatted radio.

Spanning Generations. Newscaster and commentator Paul Harvey, reportedly the highest-paid person in radio, survived the change from radio's heyday to today's specialized programming with his touch for the ironic. His clipped delivery and signature items, like his drawn-out "good day," have made his ABC programs a fixture in the lives of millions of people.

Radio's fragmented programming has reduced its role as a culturally unifying factor. Almost everyone listens to radio, but listening to a hard-rock station gives a person hardly anything in common with people who listen to public affairs-oriented stations, or soul stations, or beautiful-music stations. Today, the shared experience of radio does not extend beyond narrow segments of the population.

Here are terms used to distinguish radio's major music formats:

ADULT CONTEMPORARY.   Many advertisers like adult contemporary stations because so many people in the big-spending 25 to 40 age group listen. One in five U.S. stations is in this category, sometimes called "light rock" or "adult rock."

TOP 40.   Top 40, also called "CHR," short for "contemporary hits radio," emphasizes current rock but not as strictly as McLendon insisted. These stations target teenagers.

NEWS AND TALK.   As FM stations drew listeners away from AM with its superior sound for music, many AM stations switched to news and talk programming. One in seven stations uses this format.

COUNTRY.   Once called "country and western" or "CW" for short, the format goes back to the WSM "Grand Old Opry" program from Nashville, Ten-

CNN Top 40 Radio
The venerable Top 40 radio format that Gordon McLendon pioneered in the 1950s is fragmenting. CNN reporter Palmer Cameron says rap and country have been the major factors, and today fewer than 500 Top 40 stations remain. This is an example of the demassification that continues in radio programming. This segment aired July 27, 1993.

Casey's Hits. For almost a quarter century, honey-voiced Casey Kasem has been counting down the Top 40 hits on a nationally syndicated weekly radio show. About 8 million people tune in. Analysts say it's more than the music that draws listeners. An editor at the trade journal *Billboard,* Paul Grein, told a *Newsweek* interviewer: "Countdown shows are very orderly, very ritualistic, and people love a ritual." Today, more than a dozen syndicated countdown shows, built on Kasem's concept, are available to local stations. All together, these programs bring in $50 million in national advertising revenue. It is estimated that local stations earn an additional $100 million by dropping local ads into the programs.

nessee, in 1925. Today, one in 10 U.S. stations is country. The music varies significantly from twangy western ballads to what's called "urban country."

ALBUM-ORIENTED ROCK.   AOR formats offer songs from the 100 best-selling albums. A casual listener might confuse AOR with Top 40, but album stations go back a couple of years for wider variety. Audiences tend to be aged 18 to 24.

OLDIES.   Oldies stations play music that the 30-something generation grew up with, mostly music of the 1960s and 1970s. Sometimes it's called "classic hits."

MIDDLE OF THE ROAD.   Some radio people still use the term "MOR," but this traditional format has been largely subsumed by newer categorizations. MOR avoids the extremes of potted-palm music and hard rock, not concerned about being on top of the latest hits and not hesitant about older music as long as it's not too hard, not too soft.

BEAUTIFUL MUSIC.   Modern variations on this McLendon format provide lavishly orchestrated standards that many people like as background music. This format, sometimes called "musical wallpaper" and "elevator music," was popular in the 1970s and 1980s, especially with women 18 to 45, but much of that audience has switched to "lite" or easy-listening stations that meld MOR and AOR.

ETHNIC.   Most ethnic formats are geared either to a black or to a Spanish-speaking audience. Black stations originated in the 1950s with the soul format of rhythm 'n' blues, jazz and gospel music and black performers. In news, ethnic stations concentrate on their ethnic communities instead of news of broader interest.

CLASSICAL.   This format offers the basic repertoire of enduring music since the Baroque era, although some classical stations also play experimental symphonies, operas and contemporary composers. Because high-brow music has a limited following, most classical stations are supported not by advertising but by listener donations and by universities and other institutions.

RELIGIOUS.   Inspirational music is the programming core of religious stations. The music is interspersed with sermons from evangelists who buy time for their programs, seeking both to proselytize and to raise funds to support ministries.

RADIO NEWS

STUDY PREVIEW   Radio became a significant news source for many Americans during World War II. Today, a few large cities have at least one excellent all-news station, but in general radio has declined as a news medium. Listener call-in programs have become a popular format that has potential as a forum on public issues.

TEACHING OBJECTIVE 7-5
Chronicle the rise, decline of radio news.

KEY PERSON
Lee De Forest aired 1916 and 1920 election returns—first radio news. See Index.

PIONEER RADIO NEWS

Radio news preceded radio stations. In November 1916, *Lee De Forest* arranged with a New York newspaper, the *American*, to broadcast election returns. Hundreds of people tuned in with home-built receivers to an experimental transmission to hear De Forest proclaim: "Charles Evans Hughes will be the next president of the

United States." In November 1920, when KDKA in Pittsburgh became the nation's first licensed commercial station, it began by reporting returns in the Harding-Cox presidential race as they were being counted at the Pittsburgh *Post*. This time radio had the winner right.

The Detroit *News* began regular newscasts with its WWJ a few months later. While the *News* and some other newspapers built radio stations to promote interest in news and strengthen circulations, the newspaper industry was not enthusiastic. Worried that radio might steal away readers, the industry tried to deny stations access to far-away news from the Associated Press. In 1933 the AP, which was controlled by newspapers, offered its news to stations only if they agreed to limit newscasts to five minutes twice a day. Furthermore, the morning newscast could be aired only after 9:30 a.m. and the evening newscast only after 9 p.m. to protect morning and evening newspaper sales. No single story could exceed 30 words. Bulletins on breaking stories were banned, as were commercial sponsors for newscasts. The restrictions fell apart within two years as the NBC and CBS networks set up their own news-gathering organizations. "CBS World News Roundup" began in 1938, with correspondents reporting from five European cities.

Radio news came into its own in World War II, when the networks sent their first correspondents abroad. Americans, eager for news from Europe, developed the habit of listening to the likes of *Edward R. Murrow* for first-person accounts of what was happening. Murrow's reporting compared to the best that newspapers were offering. Consider the potency of this 1940 Murrow report from London: "Today I went to buy a hat. My favorite shop had gone, blown to bits. The windows of my shoe store were blown out. I decided to have a haircut. The windows of the barbershop were gone, but the Italian barber was still doing business. 'Some day', he said, 'we smile again, but the food it doesn't taste so good since being bombed.'"

McLendon Influence

Local radio news improved after the war when reporters began using audiotape recorders to interview and to capture the sounds of the news. It was the innovation of tape that gave Gordon McLendon's KLIF newscasts the you-are-there quality that helped propel the station to the top of the ratings in the 1950s. After XTRA in Tijuana turned profitable in the early 1960s, McLendon took over a Chicago station, renamed it WNUS and converted it to all-news. He used the same low-budget approach that worked at XTRA—a skeletal announcing staff reading wire copy. Taking notice, the Group W broadcasting chain began converting to all-news in 1965, but with strong local coverage by station reporters. CBS followed in 1967 with some of the stations it owned. Unlike McLendon, Group W and CBS went beyond spot news and invested in well-known commentators and included features. It worked. An estimated 35 percent of all New York listeners tuned in to either Group W's WINS or CBS's WCBS at least once a week. So successful were Group W and CBS that McLendon surrendered the all-news market in Chicago to CBS's WBBM and in Los Angeles to Group W's KFWB in 1968.

In 1975 NBC established an all-news network, *News and Information Service*. The new network was unable to attract enough affiliates in major markets, where Group W and CBS had all-news footholds, or in smaller markets, where the audience was not large enough to sustain an all-news station. Two years after its launch, the 24-hour news service was aborted. Some NIS affiliates, however, retained a heavy news diet in programming and added talk and listener call-in programs.

Gordon McLendon. The views of radio programming guru Gordon McLendon were widely sought in the 1950s. It was McLendon who created the Top 40 and all-news formats that enabled radio to survive massive audience losses to television.

BBC: "This Is London"

All over the world, people listen to their radios for the premier British Broadcasting Company program, "This Is London." It goes out in 39 languages to an estimated 75 million people, some listening to shortwave signals direct from BBC transmitters, others to their local stations, which relay the program. The popularity of "This Is London," which offers news, culture and entertainment, rests in part with the respect the BBC gained in World War II for consistent and reliable foreign coverage. Later, BBC's international reputation was strengthened by quality television documentaries and dramas, which were exported widely.

BBC's quality sometimes is attributed to the fact that it need not be overly concerned with ratings. Overseas services are funded by Parliament and domestic services through a Parliament-approved tax on the sale of radio and television sets. BBC takes no advertising. Although its financial base is dependent on Parliament, the BBC functions through a governance structure that buffers it from political pressure.

The BBC went on the air in 1922, and five years later received a royal charter as a nonprofit public corporation. By 1939 the BBC was operating a number of shortwave services to other Commonwealth nations in addition to foreign language services to other countries.

BBC held a home monopoly until 1954, when Parliament authorized a second domestic broadcast system. Even though the new ITV television and ILR radio networks use advertising as their revenue base, the British never embraced commercial broadcasting of the American sort. All advertisements are placed before or after programs—never in the middle—so they will not interrupt.

DECLINE OF RADIO NEWS

When the United States launched the air war against Iraq on January 16, 1991, ABC radio did not even try to cover what was happening. That whole evening, the network plugged its radio affiliates into the audio of the ABC television coverage being anchored by Peter Jennings. It was a telling moment, and a sad one, in the history of American radio as a news medium. Instead of leading the way in originating coverage, ABC and other traditional radio networks gave a poor showing of themselves throughout the Persian Gulf war, mostly picking up audio from official briefings and sandwiching it inside brief scripts rewritten from the AP and other news services.

By the 1990s, radio had become primarily an entertainment medium with low-cost programming based on playing records. Even the historic KDKA in Pittsburgh, which aired the first news reports as early as 1920, had by 1991 suspended local newscasts after 8 p.m. Many metropolitan stations had cut news to minimal local staffs, sometimes using just one or two people who anchored brief newscasts during commuting hours, and relied for global and national coverage on brief network summaries. Some stations don't even commit a person full-time to local news.

Today, only four networks offer extended newscasts:

- **"The CBS World News Roundup."** Twice daily, CBS airs this 15-minute program, which tries to maintain a proud tradition that goes back to 1938. But bowing to declining affiliate interest in news, the "roundup" has been reformatted so affiliates can break away at various points—after three, five and eight minutes. The program has 14 million listeners in the "cumes," a radio ratings measure of people who tune in at least once a week.

Radio Martí

Six years after Fidel Castro took over Cuba and allied himself with the Soviet Union, the U.S. government set up a radio station, Radio Martí, to blanket the Caribbean island, 90 miles off Key West, with news, commentary and entertainment. Outraged, Castro countered with a super-powered station of his own that drowned out some U.S. commercial stations, including one as far away as WHO in Des Moines, Iowa.

Radio Martí, founded in 1985 and funded at $20 million a year, broadcasts 24 hours a day. It has 165 employees, all Spanish-speaking. The signal goes out on shortwave from the government-operated U.S. Information Agency's Voice of America headquarters in Washington. Two Miami AM stations also carry Martí programming an hour a day.

In 1990, USIA added TV Martí, a $13 million a year, 80-staff operation that beams 2½ hours of programming a day at Cuba from a balloon antenna tethered above the Florida Straits.

Martí has been controversial not only with Castro. As with earlier U.S. government-sponsored transnational broadcast services, Radio Free Europe and Radio Liberty, there are continuing charges of political bias. The U.S. Information Service defends Martí news and commentary as dispassionate, albeit from a U.S. perspective.

Part of the suspicion about Martí stems from U.S. government lies about Radio Free Europe and Radio Liberty, which were set up after World War II to reach into the Soviet Union and its Central Europe satellite countries. Both services were ostensibly operated by private interests, but it was later discovered that the CIA funded them.

At their peak, various Radio Free Europe and Radio Liberty transmitters were beaming 1,000 hours a week of programming behind the Iron Curtain. Reporting every bungle and misstep of the communist governments, the U.S.-funded stations clearly were fomenting dissent. The Soviet Union countered by building 1,000 transmitters that broadcast shrieks and howls to drown out the incoming signals. When the United States objected, the Soviet Union pointed to a 1936 international agreement treaty that condemned broadcasts calculated "to incite the population of any territory to acts incompatible with internal order."

The Soviet Union had its own international propaganda service, Radio Moscow, which pumped out almost 2,000 hours of shortwave programming a week in 64 languages.

- **"Morning Edition" and "All Things Considered."** NPR has attracted a steadily growing audience on noncommercial stations with these 60- and 120-minute programs, and almost all affiliates carry these programs in their entirety. The audience has grown from 3.1 million in the cumes in 1976 to 12.1 million.
- **"America in the Morning."** This 60-minute program is fed before dawn to affiliates of the Mutual Broadcasting System, all of which are commercial stations.
- **"Monitor."** This 60-minute daily newscast draws on the *Christian Science Monitor*'s global reporting staff. It is offered to noncommercial stations via the Minnesota-based American Public Radio network.

Despite these programs, each distinctive and first-rate in its own way, the commercial networks, including CBS and Mutual, no longer are putting their energy into gathering news for radio. Former congressional correspondent Edward Connors, writing in *Washington Journalism Review* in 1991, reported that radio network reporters in the nation's capital seldom go out after a story any more. Instead they spend most of their time in studios, picking up audio feeds and watching coverage of scheduled events on the C-SPAN public affairs television network. ABC was down to four full-time radio reporters in Washington. CBS had only two. Every radio network except CBS subscribes to an audio-feed service which, for fees starting at $31,000 a year, provides raw coverage from which newscasters extract a few sentences to combine with boiled-down copy from the AP or UPI script service.

This remote coverage lacks the advantages of having a reporter at the scene. For example, when confirmation hearings for Supreme Court Justice David Souter were under way in 1990, newscasters in remote studios had no idea from their audio feeds that a demonstration had broken out in the back of the hearing room. They heard only the official exchange from microphones fixed to pick up senators' questions and Souter's responses. Incredible as it seems, only one radio reporter was at the hearing, Louise Schiavone of the AP. Schiavone scrambled with her recorder to the back of the room and had the only sound on a significant aspect of a major story.

Another disadvantage to remote coverage is that if reporters aren't present, they cannot ask questions to follow up on the official dialogue or to seek added perspective. David Oziel, UPI Radio news director, put it this way: "You are there to see expressions on people's faces and other human elements that can only be described by a reporter on the scene."

The decline in radio news coverage at all levels is a result of station program managers, strapped to cut expenses, trimming their labor-intensive news departments until, in many cases, nothing is left. News coverage is reduced to brief networks newscasts and occasional state stories read by local announcers from the AP wire. Some stations even replaced the AP with the new ZAP news service that provided one- or two-page summaries to stations via fax a few times a day.

Despite the decline of radio news, there are two bright spots:

NATIONAL PUBLIC RADIO.   The biggest radio network reporting staff in the nation's capital, with 12 people, is noncommercial National Public Radio. NPR has many of the sources of the commercial networks—news services like AP and audio services—but it is different in the emphasis it places on staffing events. The reporters also approach stories differently. Instead of keeping stories to 25 seconds, a recommended maximum at commercial networks, NPR allows reporters the airtime to tell their stories thoroughly and in depth.

Alone among the radio networks, NPR offers extended newscasts in the tradition of commercial networks in radio's heyday—"Morning Edition" and "All Things Considered." NPR's staff beyond Washington is limited, however, and the network leans heavily on the BBC for international coverage and its noncommercial affiliates for coverage beyond the Potomac. Occasionally NPR sends reporters abroad and into the hinterlands of the United States, but with no advertising base, NPR has perennial budget problems that limit its full inheritance of the tradition of Edward R. Murrow and other radio news pioneers.

ALL-NEWS STATIONS.   All-news stations have prospered in a few major cities. New York and some other cities have sustained two all-news stations. In Chicago, for example, Westinghouse's WMAQ and CBS's WBBM are all-news rivals with large reporting staffs that provide on-scene competitive coverage that newspapers and television newsrooms monitor routinely to avoid being skunked. Such news operations maintain the tradition of radio news at its best—instantaneous, informed and intelligent coverage of a sort that other media cannot match.

Some all-news stations, however, are *all-news* in name only and provide scant local coverage amid piped-in network newscasts, like the 24-hour CNN audio network. So-called all-news stations in many markets actually run mostly listener call-in and lengthy interviews, and they originate less local coverage than some competitors who, although not all-news, have kept a stronger commitment to news.

TALK FORMATS

LECTURE RESOURCE 7-G
Listening: Compare talk shows.

Talk formats that feature live listener telephone calls emerged as a major genre in American radio in the 1980s. The Mutual network found a growing audience for talk-show host Larry King at night. ABC launched its TalkRadio network. Local talk shows prospered.

Call-in formats were greeted enthusiastically at first because of their potential as forums for discussion of the great public issues, but there was a dark side. Many stations with music-based formats used the advent of news and talk stations to reduce their news programming. In effect, many music stations were saying, "Let those guys do news and talk, and we'll do music." The rationale really was a profit-motivated guise to get out of news and public affairs, which is expensive. Playing records is cheap. The result was fewer stations offering serious news and public affairs programming.

Disturbing too was that talk formats failed to live up to expectations that they would be serious forums on public policy. While talk shows provided opportunities for immediate listener feedback, many of the most popular ones degenerated into advice programs on hemorrhoids, psoriasis, face-lifts and psychoses. Sports trivia went over big. Talk shows gave an illusion of being news, but in fact they were low-brow entertainment. The call-in shows that focused on public issues, mostly late at night, attracted many screwballs and hate-mongers who diminished the quality of public dialogue on the great issues. The shows were vulnerable to people who tried to divide communities. A Denver talk show host, Alan Berg, who was Jewish, was

Shock Jock. Blunt and uninhibited on the air, radio personality Howard Stern is the epitome of the "shock jock." He has expanded into television on the E! channel, and in 1993 he wrote a best-selling autobiographical book. Although his New York-based program has strong listenership, Stern's crude humor is not universally popular. Fox television boss Rupert Murdoch got cold feet about creating a program for Stern in 1994, and the FCC has fined stations that carry his radio program $1.2 million.

MEDIA: PEOPLE

Howard Stern

No wonder they call Howard Stern a "shock jock." The New York disc jockey is outrageous, cynical and vulgar. But people listen to his bathroom-wall jokes and his topless female studio guests. Not surprisingly, the Federal Communications Commission, which regulates U.S. broadcast stations, doesn't cotton well to Stern's brand of humor. That hasn't bothered Stern much. In fact, he told listeners he was praying that the prostate cancer of FCC Chairman Alfred Sikes would spread.

No matter how obnoxious, Stern has a following. In fact, he is the crown jewel air personality of Infinity Broadcasting, the nation's fourth largest radio company, which syndicates Stern's show coast to coast. The company had $150 million in revenue in 1992, up 11 percent from the year before.

Stern has been expensive for Infinity Broadcasting, not just because he commands top dollar in salary but because the FCC has fined stations carrying Stern $1.2 million for his "references to sexual and excretory activities and functions." Infinity can afford to pay the fine, but it is fighting it on First Amendment grounds. Infinity's president, Mel Karmazin, calls it a harassing attempt at censorship of something that thousands of

people want to hear. Those who don't like it can listen elsewhere, Karmazin says: "That's why they make on-off buttons."

Howard Stern has known controversy a long time. At Boston College, he worked at the campus radio station— until they fired him for a show on Godzilla going to Harlem. Later at WNBC in New York, a bit called "Bestiality Dial-a-Porn" got him fired again.

At WXRK in New York, Stern proved he could draw listeners. The station shot from number 21 to number 1 in morning ratings after he signed on in 1985. At his current Infinity home, the blue humor, as well as his racism, sexism, homophobia, misogyny and bad taste, continue to attract a large, profitable audience.

Depending on who you talk to, Howard Stern represents the best in American radio, meeting the interests and needs of a mass audience, or the worst, pandering to the lowest instincts in the society and getting rich in the process.

His autobiographical 1993 book, *Private Parts,* was further evidence of his commercial success. Publisher Simon and Schuster was into a sixth printing within weeks of the release. At that point, sales were 750,000 and climbing.

shot to death by an anti-Semite who became fired up over what he heard on the radio. In Houston, talk shows encouraged the airing of a rash of antigay sentiments. Talk shows, by their nature, lend themselves to misinformation, even disinformation, from crackpots, fanatics and ignoramuses.

RADIO NETWORKS

STUDY PREVIEW Although the major networks, ABC, CBS, NBC and Mutual, have different roots, they all contributed to the shaping of the American broadcasting industry. They were at the heart of radio in its heyday. Today, the networks are leaders in demographic programming.

FOUR TRADITIONAL NETWORKS

NBC. The Radio Corporation of America station in Newark, New Jersey, WJZ, and a station in Schenectady, New York, linked themselves by telegraph line and simultaneously carried the same broadcast of the 1923 World Series. It was the first network. More linkups with more stations followed. RCA recognized the commercial potential of networks and formed the *National Broadcasting Company* in 1926 as a coast-to-coast service to local stations.

TEACHING OBJECTIVE 7-6 Explain networks' role in shaping U.S. broadcast system.

Meanwhile, *American Telephone & Telegraph* developed a 27-station network that stretched as far west as Kansas City. However, in 1926, just as NBC was being formed, AT&T decided to get out of radio. AT&T was aware that the government was looking at restraint-of-trade issues and could break up the company. Also, the company wanted to concentrate on activities that promised more profit than it foresaw in radio. AT&T sold the network to NBC, which operated it as a separate enterprise.

ABC.   Although NBC operated the two networks independently, the Federal Communications Commission became increasingly doubtful about "chain broadcasting," as it was called. Under government pressure, NBC sold the old AT&T network in 1943 to *Edward Nobel*, who had made a fortune with Lifesavers candy. Nobel named his new corporation the *American Broadcasting Company*, and the ABC network was born with 168 stations.

CBS.   The new ABC network was in competition not only with the scaled-down NBC but also with the *Columbia Broadcasting System*. CBS had its roots in a 1927 experiment by *William S. Paley*, who was advertising manager for his father's Philadelphia cigar company. To see if radio advertising could boost sales, young Paley placed advertisements on United Independent Broadcasters, a 16-station upstart network. Within six months sales skyrocketed from 400,000 to 1 million cigars a day. Impressed, Paley bought the network, called it CBS, and remained at the helm almost 50 years.

MUTUAL.   When NBC and CBS signed up local affiliates, they guaranteed that no competing station would be given the network's programs, which put independent stations without popular network programs at a disadvantage. To compete, independents exchanged programs and sometimes linked up for one-shot coverage of events. In 1934, independent stations led by WGN in Chicago and WOR in New York created a new kind of network, the *Mutual Broadcasting System*. Any station could pick up Mutual programs no matter who else was airing them. Furthermore, in a departure from policy at NBC and CBS, Mutual stations were not required to carry programs they did not want. Many independent stations tapped into Mutual, and the network eventually claimed more affiliates than the other networks, although few stations carried all that Mutual made available.

AFFILIATE–NETWORK RELATIONS

The early networks were attractive vehicles to advertisers seeking a national audience, which is how the networks made their money and how they still do. Networks base their fees for running commercials on the size of their huge multistation audiences. In general, the more affiliate stations and the larger the audience, the higher a network's revenue.

ABC, CBS and NBC each owns a few stations called *o-and-o's*, short for *network owned and operated*, but most of a network's strength is in its affiliates. That is why networks look to popular local stations to carry their programs and advertisements. Affiliate–network relationships are mutually advantageous. Local stations profit from network affiliations in two ways. Networks pay affiliates for running their national advertisements. These network payments average about 5 percent of the station's income. Also, strong network programs are audience builders. The larger a station's audience, generally, the more it can charge local advertisers to carry their messages.

A network and an affiliate define their relationship in a contract that is subject to periodic renegotiation and renewal. In radio's heyday, which ran into the early 1950s, network affiliations were so attractive and profitable to local stations that the networks could dictate terms. As television displaced radio as the preferred national entertainment medium, however, the networks relaxed exclusivity and other requirements. Today, local stations are in a stronger position in negotiating affiliation contracts and terms. There are also more possible affiliations because, with the economies possible through satellite hook-up, so many networks have come into existence. About 40 percent of American stations have a network affiliation.

EFFECTS OF TELEVISION

NBC led the way in television after World War II, followed by CBS and ABC. One by one, the networks' variety shows, mysteries and comedies were converted to television. By the 1960s, about all the networks had to offer their radio affiliates was newscasts, commentaries and short features—and that was about all local stations wanted. Stations had given up trying to steal the general mass audience back from television and were specializing with demographic programming. The specialized programming, sometimes called *narrowcasting*, sought audience segments that could be defined by age, educational levels, economic status and even gender, giving target audiences to advertisers.

Was network radio dead? In 1968, recognizing what was happening, ABC divided itself into four radio networks, each with newscasts styled to fit a particular music format. Here is how it worked:

- American Information Network emphasized foreign, domestic and economic news for stations with strong public affairs programming and a generally middle-aged and older, well-educated, relatively well-heeled audience.
- American Contemporary Network focused on domestic news and pocketbook issues in short, fast-paced programs for young adults.
- American FM Network geared for rock stations and college-aged listeners. It emphasized news affecting careers, in a pace that was consistent with typical FM rock formats. The tone was sophisticated and aware.
- American Entertainment Network was slower paced to fit middle-of-the-road music formats. Paul Harvey, whose commentaries had developed a Middle America following since 1951, was in the lineup.

With multiple networks, ABC could sign up four stations per market and still guarantee stations that no competitor would have access to the same programs. The number of ABC affiliates grew from 400 to 1,500 in 12 years. Advertisers liked targeting their messages demographically. A pimple-cream company would find more potential customers per advertising dollar on the American FM Network than on NBC, CBS or Mutual. For the same reason, luxury-car manufacturers would go with the American Information Network.

Meanwhile, Mutual had established a network for black stations with newscasts emphasizing information of interest to black listeners. Mutual later put together a Spanish-language network. NBC established *The Source*, a news network for rock 'n' roll stations. CBS eventually did the same.

CNN **Howard Stern the Candidate** When shock jock Howard Stern tried to translate his on-air popularity into political hay, he created a fundamental problem for stations. The problem was this: In New York, where Stern's program runs four hours a day, his four opponents could have demanded a total of 16 hours a day on the stations. As CNN reporter Jill Brooks points out, Stern dropped out of the race before the issue came to the fore. This segment aired April 25, 1994.

CNN **Howard Stern Popularity** CNN reporter Mark Watts documents the popularity of Howard Stern by covering a book signing at a Las Vegas store. People slept the night in 30-degree weather to be in line when the store opened. In all, 8,000 fans bought his book, *Private Parts*, and stood in line for him to autograph their copies. This happened earlier in New York, where 125,000 people lined up, and also in Los Angeles. This segment aired December 16, 1993.

The proliferation continued. United Press International and the Associated Press expanded their own radio news networks, which had been established in the 1970s. Unlike other networks, *UPI Audio* and *AP Radio* neither carried advertising nor paid stations to carry their programs. Stations paid for the services and were free to plug local advertising into newscasts at will.

CHAPTER WRAP-UP

The proliferation in radio programming can be expected to continue with stations narrowcasting into more and more specialized niches. Broadcast industry commentator Erik Zorn predicts hundreds of formats, some as narrow as all-blues music stations, business news stations, Czech-language stations and full-time stations for the blind. In this new world of *demand programming*, any listener will be able to choose among literally hundreds of programs at any time—a far cry from pre-television days when mainstream radio was truly a mass medium and sought the whole audience with every program.

Technology has created problems. The advent of FM stereo drew listeners away from AM in the 1980s. With its superior quality of sound, FM held more than 70 percent of the U.S. radio audience by the 1990s. Many AM stations shifted to news and talk formats, which did not require stereo transmissions to attract an audience, but these audiences were smaller and AM ended up with fewer listeners. The resale value of AM stations sank, even for old-line big-name stations. Some AM stations entered bankruptcy.

There is no question that radio will continue as a strong medium of mass communication, but the shape of the radio industry is less certain. As in the past, government regulation, technological innovation and competition from other mass media will be major players in determining radio's future.

QUESTIONS FOR REVIEW

1. Why is radio called a ubiquitous and influential medium?
2. How does radio move invisibly through on electromagnetic waves?
3. What are characteristics of the radio industry in the United States?

4. Why has U.S. radio historically had an entertainment rather than educational thrust?
5. What is the status of news in U.S. radio today?
6. How have the national networks shaped American radio?

QUESTIONS FOR CRITICAL THINKING

1. The telegraph was invented by Samuel Morse in 1844. Roughly 50 years later Guglielmo Marconi introduced radio wireless telegraphy. What was the difference?
2. Lee De Forest was a technical and programming innovator. Explain the significance of his audion tube and his 1916 broadcast of election returns.

3. A new way of transmitting radio was developed by Edwin Armstrong in the 1930s, and by the 1980s it had left the nation's original AM broadcast system in economic peril. Discuss Armstrong's invention and how it has reshaped American radio.
4. American radio was shaped by the networks in the 1920s and 1930s and reshaped by the advent of televi-

sion in the 1950s. Explain these influences, and be sure to cite radio's transition from literal *broadcasting* toward *narrowcasting*. What about the influence of Gordon McLendon? What of the future?

5. Explain the significance of KDKA of Pittsburgh, WEAF of New York, WOR of New York and WGN of Chicago.

6. How does demographic programming today differ from the potted-palm music of early radio? From newscasts of the 1930s when the networks set up their own reporting staffs? From newscasts of the late 1950s when AM stations improved local coverage?

FOR FURTHER LEARNING

Erik Barnouw. *A Tower in Babel, A History of Broadcasting in the United States to 1933* (Oxford, 1966); *The Golden Web, A History of Broadcasting in the United States, 1933–1953* (Oxford, 1968); *The Image Empire, A History of Broadcasting in the United States, 1953–On* (Oxford, 1970). Barnouw's trilogy is thorough and readable.

John R. Bittner. *Broadcast Law and Regulation* (Prentice Hall, 1982).

Gerald Carson. *The Roguish World of Dr. Brinkley* (Holt, Rinehart & Winston, 1960). Carson's lightly written account tells how the Goat Gland Surgeon took the issue of broadcast regulation to court and lost.

Lynne Schafer Gross. *Telecommunications: An Introduction to Radio, Television and Other Electronic Media*, 2nd ed. (Wm. C. Brown, 1986). Professor Gross's survey of broadcasting includes an excellent explanation of how the electromagnetic spectrum works.

Murray B. Levin. *Talk Radio and the American Dream* (D.C. Heath, 1987). Levin, a political scientist, argues that talk radio programs are unique in the American mass media as a voice of common people.

Erik Zorn. "Radio Lives!" *Esquire* 101(March 1984):3, 45–54; "The Specialized Signals of Radio News," *Washington Journalism Review* 8(June 1986):6, 31–33. Zorn, a news reporter whose beat is radio and television, tracks changes in broadcasting.

"The Fowler Years: A Chairman Who Marches to His Own Drummer," *Broadcasting* 112(March 23, 1987): 12, 51–54. An analytical summary of the FCC's deregulation policy under commission chair Mark Fowler.

FOR KEEPING UP TO DATE

The weekly trade journals *Broadcasting* and *Electronic Media* keep abreast of news and issues.

Other news coverage can be found in the *Wall Street Journal*, the New York *Times*, the Los Angeles *Times* and other major daily newspapers.

Scholarly articles can be found in the *Journal of Broadcasting, Electronic Media, Journal of Communication* and *Journalism Quarterly*.

On regulation, see the *Federal Communications Law Journal*.

CNN video case study

HOWARD STERN AND THE FEDERAL COMMUNICATIONS COMMISSION

Howard Stern regularly tweaks the federal agency that regulates broadcasting. The syndicated New York shock jock's antics continually raise fundamental questions about whether the government should be in the business of regulating broadcasting. Whether by intention or otherwise, Stern raises these issues:

- Should the Federal Communications Commission be permitted to muzzle a broadcast performer because he or she is suggestive and lewd on the air?
- Should the FCC be able to deny people access to a broadcast performer because of the content of the show?
- Should the FCC be able to punish stations that carry popular programming that some people find objectionable?
- Should the FCC be able to bar a company from purchasing a station because its other stations carry objectionable programming?

These are First Amendment questions that have been shrugged off by the government and also most broadcasters for 70 years, but Stern is bringing them to the fore. This is the heart of the issue:

- **First Amendment.** The First Amendment to the U.S. Constitution, which dates to 1791, guarantees free expression. This includes freedom of speech and freedom of the press, which everyone agrees applies to radio and television even though the authors of the amendment thought only in terms of the print media.
- **1927 Federal Radio Act.** Congress put the government into the business of regulating broadcasting in 1927 when it created an agency that eventually became the FCC. The agency decides who can own a station and go on the air by licensing companies with the best potential to contribute to the "public interest." Some companies are denied a

license because the FCC sees less potential in them to serve this public interest.

The conflict between the First Amendment and the 1927 Radio Act sneaked up on many people. In 1927, the U.S. radio industry was a mess. There was room for only 568 stations on the air, but many more stations were broadcasting. Stations, none of them regulated, could broadcast at whatever signal strength they wanted. Signals overlapped. When a station was squeezed off a certain frequency by more powerful signals, it moved to another frequency. The radio industry tried to sort out the problem, but could not, so it turned to Congress for government regulation.

Through the 1927 Federal Radio Act, Congress created the Federal Radio Commission. The agency's duties included assigning frequencies to stations that would broadcast in "the public interest, convenience and necessity." There needed to be some standard to decide who could be on the air and who could not, and public service seemed a good one.

The inherent First Amendment conflict emerged soon thereafter. The FRC refused to renew the license of a Los Angeles church station that aired a hate-mongering preacher. The commission also refused renewal to a station owned by a quack medicine man in Kansas who hawked his cures over the air. Both stations argued that the FRC was taking away their electronic megaphones because of what they put on the air, which, they said, was censorship.

The issue was difficult. On the one hand, regulation was needed if radio was to be a useful medium. Otherwise, cacophony and confusion would rule the airwaves. On the other hand, government licensing meant some people got licenses and some people did not. With content a factor in deciding who was licensed, and with government issuing the licenses, government was in a position to decide what it liked and did not like on the air and to issue licenses accordingly. That surely smacks of censorship.

The courts danced on the issue. An appellate court, in 1931, in the Kansas quack doctor case, endorsed past programming as a criterion in deciding license renewals. Invoking a biblical injunction, the court said: "By their fruits ye shall know them." The court went even further to claim, however dubiously, that this was not censorship: "In considering the question whether the public interest, convenience or necessity will be served by a renewal [of] appellant's license, the Commission has merely exercised its undoubted right to take note of appellant's past conduct, which is not censorship."

That sanction for government regulation has been a time bomb, and Howard Stern is the fuse—and so is technology, which has exponentially expanded the number of stations that can fit onto the electromagnetic spectrum.

The underlying justification for government regulation is that there are not enough frequencies to go around. Because of this scarcity of channels, somebody must dole them out, and the government, as representative of the people, is in the best position to do this.

Over the years, as technology has increased the number of available frequencies, the scarcity rationale has been unraveling. In 1927, when the FRC was created, there was room for 568 stations. Today, the United States has about 12,000 radio stations and hundreds of television stations. In fact, in the 1990s, this proliferation has resulted in more stations than the market in some cities can accommodate. Some have thus gone into bankruptcy, and others have gone silent.

Instead of scarcity, a new way of looking at the relationship of government and broadcasters has emerged since the Reagan administration in the 1980s—the marketplace model. Reagan argued that the people, not government, should regulate the industry through the marketplace. The people he appointed to the FCC began applying this principle, backing off on a lot of traditional regulation. They said let the marketplace decide what is on the air. Stations without listeners will not survive economically, because they will not be able to find advertisers that want to buy time. The marketplace concept is taking increasing hold but is not fully in place. If it were, station managers would be free to let audience ratings decide what goes on the air, and Howard Stern, whose popularity is incredible in several major cities, could be as suggestive and lewd as his audience would tolerate.

In the meantime, though, the transition from scarcity to the marketplace model is still occurring— and Howard Stern may end up caught in the transition. So might Infinity Broadcasting, whose flagship station in New York is where Stern's radio show originates. The FCC has fined Stern stations $123,000 for his on-air vulgarity. The FCC also has delayed Infinity's applications to buy additional stations. The issue is what the federal courts said in 1931 was properly within the purview of regulators: "the appellant's past conduct."

Technology, besides upending the scarcity rationale for broadcast regulation, has made cable television possible. Because cable, for most purposes, is free of federal content regulation, Stern has been on cable hassle-free with his blue jokes, double entendres and racial slurs. Cable uses private lines to send signals to receivers rather than the airwaves, which Congress says belong to the public and thereby are subject to government regulation. However, what is the point of government regulation to stifle if not silent Howard Stern when he can use the medium of cable, which is growing explosively, to reach his audiences? As Stern argues it, government broadcast regulation is a dinosaur whose extinction is overdue.

TELEVISION
CAN INFLUENCE
PEOPLE IN THE
SHORT TERM AND
THE CULTURE IN
THE LONG TERM

TELEVISION RELIES ON
ELECTRONIC TECHNOLOGY,
IN CONTRAST TO MOVIES, A
CHEMICAL-BASED MEDIUM

THE STRUCTURE FOR AMERICAN
TELEVISION WAS BUILT AROUND
LOCAL OVER-AIR STATIONS

RADIO WAS A ROLE MODEL FOR
EARLY TELEVISION PROGRAMMING

TELEVISION HAS EVOLVED
INTO AN EFFICIENT PURVEYOR OF
INFORMATION

LOCAL STATIONS AFFILIATED WITH
NETWORKS CAN PLAY A MAJOR
ROLE IN NETWORK PROGRAMMING

THE FOUR PRIMARY SOURCES
OF AMERICAN TELEVISION
PROGRAMMING ARE
NETWORKS, MOTION PICTURE
COMPANIES, INDEPENDENT
PRODUCTION COMPANIES,
LOCAL STATIONS

NEW TECHNOLOGIES AND
PROGRAMMING SERVICES
ARE CRACKING THE BIG
THREE NETWORKS'
MONOPOLY

chapter

TELEVISION
ELECTRONIC MOVING
PICTURES

8

Skeptics were everywhere when Fox television went on the air. A lot of people had romantic notions about launching a fourth U.S. television network, but nobody had ever succeeded. Rupert Murdoch, the global media giant, took the plunge in 1987 with Fox. It was a ragtag network of second-tier stations with only a few programs a week, but there was excitement about it. Part of the excitement was a David and Goliath tilting at the three dominants in the field—ABC, CBS and NBC.

In charge was Barry Diller. As president of Fox, he charted a shrewd course: Build a base with Sunday night programming, then Saturday night, then weeknights. His strategy was to keep costs low with programs that would attract audiences but not cost much to produce. A lot of programs had fast-paced cops and robbers themes with lots of on-scene and amateur footage. He avoided a costly news operation.

Fox grew. In fact, under Diller's strategy, the network had profitable periods when the Big Three were losing tremendous amounts of money. Proud of his success and feeling he deserved greater reward, Diller went to Rupert Murdoch and proposed that he be allowed to buy into the ownership of the network. Murdoch said no. Diller quit.

Where Next? In 1987 skeptics doubted that Rupert Murdoch's new Fox network would make it. Veteran network program wonderworker Barry Diller, who was in charge, proved them wrong. A few years later, Diller asked Murdoch if he could buy into the company and Murdoch said no. Diller quit. Next he surfaced as the prime figure at the QVC shopping network and worked to improve its image and profitability. In 1994 Diller made an offer to merge QVC with CBS. The deal fell apart, but television industry observers expect Diller will find another high-profile niche to work his magic at putting successful TV operations together.

Barry Diller

That began a sabbatical for Diller. He spent months exploring opportunities for applying his skills and creativity. Diller-watchers were surprised when he announced in 1992 that he had put $25 million into the QVC home-shopping network. Although QVC was into 44 million homes at the time, home shopping had a shoddy, huckster image that didn't excite most television people. But, then, Diller began making things happen:

■ QVC and rival Home Shopping Network agreed to merge.
■ QVC created an upscale network, Q2, with entertainment and how-to programs to sell products. Viewers know when to tune in to what interests them: cooking, exercise, gardening, home decorating, home entertaining, travel.
■ QVC began displacing the wall-to-wall pitches with packaged features, like "Shopping for Your Girlfriend" and "Pulling Together the Ultimate Dinner Party."
■ QVC entered discussions with the Prodigy computer network to create an on-line home shopping service. This would be truly interactive because computer users could place orders via their modems rather than having to order by phone.

The Diller touch brought glamour to home shopping. Some expect home shopping will grow 100-fold over the next 10 years. Advertising consultant R. Fulton Macdonald told the trade journal *Advertising Age*: "Diller has the edge. Everyone else is waiting in the wings, and Barry's clearly getting the jump position."

IMPACT OF TELEVISION

STUDY PREVIEW In a remarkably short period, television became the most popular U.S. medium for entertainment and later for news. Older media were muscled out of their former prominence and had to adapt with whatever audience and advertising segments were left. Today, television has become so central in modern culture that it is almost impossible for anyone looking at society to ignore it.

TEACHING OBJECTIVE 8-1
Television influences people and society in short and long term.

KEY PERSON
Ted Turner created cable services.

MASS MEDIA SHAKE-UP

In a brash moment in 1981, television tycoon *Ted Turner* predicted the end of newspapers within 10 years. The year 1991 came and went, and, as Turner had predicted, television was even more entrenched as a mass medium—but newspapers too were still in business. Turner had overstated the impact of television, but he was right that television would continue taking readers and advertisers from newspapers, just as it had from the other mass media.

Since its introduction in the early 1950s, the presence of television has reshaped the other media. Consider the following areas of impact:

BOOKS. The discretionary time people spend on television today is time that once went to other activities, including reading, for diversion and information. To stem the decline in reading, book publishers have responded with more extravagant promotions to draw attention to their products. A major consideration with fiction manuscripts at publishing houses is their potential as screenplays, many of which end up on television. Also, in deciding which manuscripts to accept, some publishers even consider how well an author will come across in television interviews when the book is published.

NEWSPAPERS. Evening television newscasts have been a major factor in the steady decline of afternoon newspapers, many of which have ceased publication or switched to mornings. Also, newspapers have lost almost all of their national advertisers, primarily to television. Most newspaper redesigns today, including Gannett's *USA Today*, attempt to be visual in ways that newspapers never were before television.

MAGAZINES. Television took advertisers from the big mass circulation magazines like *Life*, forcing magazine companies to shift to magazines that catered to smaller segments of the mass audience that television could not serve.

RECORDINGS. The success of recorded music today hinges in many cases on the airplay that music videos receive on television.

MOVIES. Just as magazines demassified after television took away many of their advertisers, Hollywood demassified after television stole its audience. Today, savvy moviemakers plan their projects for both the big screen and for reissuing to be shown on television, via the networks and for home video rental. These after-markets, in fact, have come to account for far more revenue to major Hollywood studios than their moviemaking.

RADIO. Radio too demassified with the arrival of television. The television networks first took radio's most successful programs and moved them to television.

Ted Turner

When his father died, Ted Turner inherited a floundering Atlanta television station that hardly anybody watched. Back then, in 1963, many televisions sets could not pick up channels higher than 13, which meant that Turners' WTGC, like other UHF stations, was nonexistent in many households. Advertising revenue was thin, and it was not easy to make the rent for the decrepit building that housed the studios. Only 60 people were on the payroll. Fumigators sprayed for fleas weekly.

Young Turner threw himself energetically into making something of the inheritance. He did everything himself, even stocking the soda machine. More important, he recognized that WTGC was condemned to a shoe string future unless he could offer viewers more than old B movies and sitcom reruns. Desperate to diversify programming, Turner borrowed enough money to buy the cellar-dwelling Atlanta Braves and Atlanta Hawks teams in the mid-1970s. The purchases spread Turner's finances even thinner, but they gave WTGC something distinctive to offer.

Turner then turned to his other major problem—WTGC's obscure UHF channel. Learning that HBO was planning to beam programs to an orbiting satellite for retransmission to local systems nationwide, he decided to do the same. Turner redubbed his station WTBS in 1976, bought satellite time and persuaded cable systems to add his "superstation" to their package of services. Overnight, Turner multiplied the audience for his old movies, sitcom reruns, and Atlanta pro sports. WTBS began attracting national advertising, something WTGC never could.

Ted Turner stopped refilling the soda machine himself, but he still worked hard. He kept an old bathrobe at his office and slept on the couch when he worked late. His mind never stopped. He considered a second cable network—a 24-hour television news service. In 1980, again stretching his finances to the limit, Turner bought an old mansion, outfitted it with the latest electronic news-gathering and editing equipment, hired a couple dozen anchors and launched *Cable News Network*. A few months later, with CNN still deep in red ink, Turner learned that ABC and Westinghouse were setting up the Satellite News Channel, which would compete with CNN. To discourage cable systems from picking up the competitor, Turner decided over a weekend to establish a second news network himself, and *Headline News* was born. The gamble worked, and ABC and Westinghouse sold their news network to Turner, who promptly shut it down.

There were setbacks. Turner started a rock 'n' roll cable network, but it could not compete with MTV, so he sold it. Detractors found the stogie-puffing Turner easy to criticize. He was called "the Mouth of the South" for his brash outspokenness. Operating at the edge financially, making major decisions alone and sometimes impulsively, he seemed to be an entrepreneurial loose cannon. Or was it genius? Or luck? The mystique was fueled by Turner's high profile, including his defense of the America's Cup sailing championship. His strongest detractors, local television station executives, called him unscrupulous, charging that he was leasing old movies and sitcoms for WTBS at the going rate for a local station while making a killing by charging national ad rates. They called on the FCC to reinstate the syndex rule, which had guaranteed local exclusivity to stations buying syndicated programs. Because WTBS was running the same syndicated programs as over-air stations, the move was clearly aimed at drying up Turners' program supply. The syndicating companies also felt burned by how Turner was exploiting his rental agreements.

Turner's previous successes had been masterstrokes—buying pro sports teams to create programming, using satellites to make himself a national television presence and establishing an around-the-clock television news channel. Now, facing a programming crisis if the syndex rule were restored, Turner looked for another masterstroke. He decided in 1985 to buy CBS, which not only could generate lots of programming but also would put him firmly in both the new cable and the traditional broadcasting industries. The buyout plan backfired, and Turner lost $21 million. Worse, he still did not have the new programming supply he needed.

A few days later, a Hollywood financier who knew Turner's programming predicament called him and offered to sell MGM/United Artists including the MGM movie library. Turner agreed on the spot, not even challenging the exorbitant $1.4 billion asking price. He mortgaged TBS to the hilt, but even then he could not raise enough. Facing foreclosure, Turner managed, barely, to keep the MGM films by selling off the rest of MGM/UA bit by bit. With MGM's 3,700 movies, including *Gone With the Wind, Casablanca* and *Citizen Kane,* Turner had significant programming that could be run and rerun forever. It was a buffer against program vendors, which turned out to be important when the syndex rule was reinstated in 1989.

On the downside, the CBS and MGM ventures left Turner so debt-ridden that he had no choice but to sell

Ted Turner. Atlanta television station owner Ted Turner saw orbiting satellites as an inexpensive way to beam his Atlanta stations to local cable systems that were hungry for programming in the early 1980s. Almost overnight Turner's WTBS became a superstation available to viewers nationwide. CNN, Headline News and TNT followed, making Turner Broadcasting a major player in the U.S. television industry. Turner was named *Time* magazine's Man of the Year in 1992.

chunks of TBS. Sensation-mongering media mogul Rupert Murdoch expressed interest. General Electric, which recently had bought NBC, also inquired. Cable companies, however, did not want control of WTBS, CNN and Headline News to go to outside interests. The Turner networks had become essential parts of the cable companies' packages for subscribers. John Malone, chief of the giant TeleCommunications cable company, pulled together 31 cable chains to bail out Turner. They put up $562 million. Said Malone: "If we hadn't rescued Ted Turner, TBS would have been bought by Rupert Murdoch, and CNN now would be running 'Murder of the Week.'"

In exchange for the cash infusion, Turner agreed to share control and operate less impulsively, but his mind kept going. To capitalize on the MGM film library, he proposed a fourth cable service. In 1988 *Turner Network Television,* TNT for short, began transmitting to 17 million cable households—five times more than any previous cable network. TNT began mostly with old MGM movies, but TBS's new directors budgeted $280 million to produce miniseries, made-for-TV movies, and high-profile events to go up against the traditional over-air networks. Turner hoped to bid against the major networks for events like the World Series, Rose Bowl, Indianapolis 500 and Academy Awards.

Almost overnight in 1991, a lynch pin in Turner's vision came to fruition. CNN leaped to industry dominance with its 24-hour coverage of the Persian Gulf War. Government and industry leaders worldwide watched it for quicker and better information than they could obtain through their own sources. Not infrequently, other news organizations ended up quoting CNN because they couldn't match the network's no-holds-barred commitment to thoroughness and timeliness. Turner's audience swelled, as each day CNN earned greater and wider respect. Back when it went on the air, CNN had been laughed at as "Chicken Noodle News." No more.

Ted Turner's odyssey from WTGC in 1963 embodies ongoing dynamics in the television industry:

- The expansion of satellite-delivered and cable-delivered programming, like Turner networks.
- The fragile state of even the oldest, proudest television organizations, demonstrated by upstart Turner's takeover run on CBS.
- The important role of program vendors in network and local programming.
- The constant need for programmers to find and air programs, demonstrated by Turner's acquisition of the MGM library.

After losing its traditional programming strengths, radio then lost both the mass audience and advertisers it had built up since the 1920s. For survival, individual radio stations shifted almost entirely to recorded music and geared the music to narrower and narrower audience segments.

PERVASIVE MEDIUM, PERSUASIVE MESSAGES

Ninety-eight percent of American households have at least one television set. On average, a set is on seven hours a day in these households. There is no question that television has changed American lifestyles, drawing people away from other diversions that once occupied their time. Churches, lodges and neighborhood taverns once were central in the lives of many people, and today they are less so. For 26 million people, "60 Minutes" is a Sunday night ritual that was not available three generations ago.

Television can move people. Revlon was an obscure cosmetic brand before it took on sponsorship of the "$64,000 Question" quiz show in the 1950s. Overnight, Revlon became a household word and an exceptionally successful product. In 1992 Procter & Gamble spent $995 million advertising its wares on television; Philip Morris, $795 million (for its noncigarette products); and General Motors, $664 million.

The role of television in riveting the nation on serious matters was demonstrated in 1962, when President John Kennedy spoke into the camera and told the American people that the nation was in a nuclear showdown with the Soviet Union. People rallied to the president's decision to blockade Cuba until the Soviet Union removed the ballistic missiles it was secretly installing. Today, it is rare for a candidate for public office not to use television to solicit support:

- Bill Clinton, running for president in 1992, tried to defuse the slanderous stories about his extramarital dallying by granting an extended, live interview on the CBS program "60 Minutes."
- Ross Perot chose CNN's "Larry King Live" talk show to test the waters for his long-shot presidential bid, and he returned to the show again and again to take viewer calls live.
- George Bush knew the television cameras were rolling when he made his no-new-taxes, "read my lips" pledge in 1988. It was a memorable campaign moment, which analysts saw as a key to Bush's election, and, later, as part of his 1992 undoing when, in fact, he found no recourse but to raise taxes.

Fictional television characters can capture the imagination of the public. Perry Mason did wonders for the reputation of the law profession. Mary Tyler Moore showed that women could succeed in male-dominated industries. Alan Alda was the counter-macho model for the bright, gentle man of the 1970s. In this same sense, Bart Simpson's bratty irreverence toward authority figures sent quivers through parents and teachers in the 1990s. Then came the alarm that Beavis and Butt-head's fun with matches might lead kids from all over the country to set everything in sight on fire.

CULTURAL IMPACT

While television can be effective in creating short-term impressions, there also are long-term effects. Today, a whole generation of children is growing up with Teenage Mutant Ninja Turtles as part of their generational identity. These long-term effects exist at both a superficial level, as with Teenage Mutant Ninja Turtles, and at a serious level. Social critic *Michael Novak* puts the effect of television in broad terms: "Television is a molder of the soul's geography. It builds up incrementally a psychic structure of expectations. It does so in much the same way that school lessons slowly, over the years, tutor the unformed mind and teach it how to think."

What are the "lessons" to which Novak refers? Scholars *Linda and Robert Lichter* and *Stanley Rothman*, who have surveyed the television creative community, make a case that the creators of television programs are social reformers who build their political ideas into their scripts. The Lichters and Rothman identify the television creative community as largely secular and politically liberal. Among program creators whom they quote is Garry Marshall, the creative force behind "Happy Days" and later "Mork and Mindy": "The tag on 'Mork' is almost like the sermon of the week. But it doesn't look like that. It is very cleverly disguised to look like something else, but that's what it is." In many ways, Norman Lear, the creator of Archie Bunker, is the archetype program creator for the Lichter-Rothman profile. And Lear's liberal political and social agenda doesn't go away. He was back with a summer series in 1994, "133 Houser Rd." set in the Bunker house—new characters, same issues.

Scholars have different views on the potency of television's effect on the society, but they all agree that there is some degree of influence. Media scholar George Comstock, in his book *Television in America*, wrote: "Television has become an unavoidable and unremitting factor in shaping what we are and what we will become."

KEY PERSON
Michael Novak sees television as broad shaper of issues.

KEY PEOPLE
Linda and Robert Lichter, Stanley Rothman see television as reformist.

LECTURE RESOURCE 8-A
Video: *The Television Makers.*

LECTURE RESOURCE 8-B
Class Exercise: Media role in fads, trends, fashion.

TECHNOLOGICAL DEVELOPMENT

> **STUDY PREVIEW** Television is based on electronic technology. Light-sensitive cameras scan a scene with incredibly fast sweeps across several hundred horizontally stacked lines. The resulting electronic blips are transmitted to receivers, which recreate the original image by sending electrons across horizontally stacked lines on a screen.

ELECTRONIC SCANNING

In the 1920s *Vladimir Zworykin*, a Westinghouse physicist, devised a vacuum tube that could pick up moving images and then display them electronically on a screen. Zworykin's main inventions, the *iconoscope* and the *kinescope*, sent electrons repeatedly across stacked horizontal lines on a tiny screen, each pass following the previous one so fast that the screen showed the movement as picked up by a camera. As with the motion picture, the system froze movement at fraction-of-a-second intervals and then replayed it to create an illusion of movement, but there was a significant difference. Motion pictures used chemical-based photographic processes. Zworykin used electronics, not chemicals, and the image recorded by a camera was transmitted instantly to a receiving tube. Zworykin's picture quality was not sharp, with electrons being shot across only 30 horizontal lines on the screen compared to 525 today, but the system worked.

Westinghouse, RCA and General Electric pooled their television research in 1930, and Zworykin was put in charge of a team of engineers to develop a national television system. In 1939 RCA flamboyantly displayed the Zworykin invention at the New York World's Fair. Although the British had introduced a system three years earlier, RCA had superior picture quality. Soon, 10 commercial stations were licensed and several companies were manufacturing home receivers. Then came World War II. The companies that were developing commercial television diverted their research and other energies to the war effort.

TEACHING OBJECTIVE 8-2
Television technology is electronic.

KEY PERSON
Vladimir Zworykin invented television tube.

INTEGRATED STANDARDIZATION

Even after the war, there were delays. The Federal Communications Commission, wanting to head off topsy-turvy expansion that might create problems later, halted further station licensing in 1948. Not until 1952 did the FCC settle on a comprehensive licensing and frequency allocation system and lift the freeze. The freeze gave the FCC time to settle on a uniform system for the next step in television's evolution: color. RCA wanted a system that could transmit to both existing black-and-white and new color sets. CBS favored a system that had superior clarity, but people would have to buy new sets to pick it up, and even then they would not be able to receive black-and-white programs. Finally, in 1953, the FCC settled on the RCA system.

STRUCTURE OF AMERICAN TELEVISION

STUDY PREVIEW   The American television system was built on both a local and a national foundation. As it did with radio, the FCC licensed local stations with the goal of a diversified system. At the same time, networks gave the system a national character.

DUAL NATIONAL SYSTEM

TEACHING OBJECTIVE 8-3
U.S. television has national and local tiers.

Congress and the Federal Communications Commission were generally satisfied with the American radio system that had taken form by the 1930s, and they set up a similar structure for television. The FCC invited people who wanted to build stations in local communities to apply for a federal license. As a condition of their FCC license, station owners raised the money to build the technical facilities, to develop an economic base and to provide programming. These stations, which broadcast over the airwaves, the same as radio, became the core of a locally based national television system. It was the same regulated yet free-enterprise approach that had developed for radio. By contrast, governments in most other countries financed and built centralized national television systems.

Even though the FCC regulated a locally based television system, the American system soon had a national flavor. NBC and CBS modeled television networks on their radio networks and provided programs to the new local television stations.

Talk Shows. When CBS put David Letterman opposite the venerable "Tonight" show, the network had a lot at stake. The success of the show depended on how many of the network's affiliates would air it on a scheduled basis. Many CBS affiliates had earlier found it more profitable to play old movies and sitcom reruns than CBS's previous attempts to compete with "Tonight." Affiliates decide which network programs to carry. For CBS, the Letterman gamble paid off—his offbeat humour attracted a large following.

Today, American television still has a backbone in the networks. Of 900 local commercial stations, two-thirds are affiliates of one of the three major networks, ABC, CBS or NBC. In almost every city, it is the network-affiliated stations that have the most viewers.

The American national television system began to undergo major changes in the 1980s. Dozens of new networks, led by HBO, Turner and other cable program services, bypassed FCC-licensed local stations, delivering programs via satellite and local cable systems into individual homes.

NETWORK–AFFILIATE RELATIONS

A network affiliation is an asset to local stations. Programs offered by the networks are of a quality that an individual station cannot afford to produce. With quality network programs, stations attract larger audiences than they could on their own. Larger audiences mean that stations can charge higher rates for local advertisements in the six to eight minutes per hour the networks leave open for affiliates to fill. Stations also profit directly from affiliations. The networks share their advertising revenue with affiliates, paying each affiliate 30 percent of the local advertising rate for time that network-sold advertisements take. Typically almost 10 percent of a station's income is from the network.

Network–affiliate relations are not entirely money-making bliss. The networks, whose advertising rates are based on the number of viewers they have, would prefer that all affiliates carry all their programs. Affiliates, however, sometimes have sufficient financial incentives to preempt network programming. Broadcasting a state basketball tournament can generate lots of local advertising. The networks would also prefer that affiliates confine their quest for advertising to their home areas, leaving national ads to the networks. Local stations, however, accept national advertising on their own, which they schedule inside and between programs, just as they do local advertising.

The networks have learned to pay more heed to affiliate relations in recent years. Unhappy affiliates have been known to leave one network for another. Television chains like Group W or Gannett have a major bargaining chip with networks because, with a single stroke of a pen, they can change the affiliations of several stations. This happened in 1994 when Fox lured 12 stations away from the big three networks, eight of them from CBS alone.

Also, affiliates are organized to deal en masse with their networks. In 1982 the affiliates forced CBS and NBC to abandon plans to expand the evening network newscasts to 60 minutes. An hour-long newscast would have lost lucrative station slots for local advertising. One estimate is that the stations would have lost $260 million a year in advertising revenue, far more than network payments would have brought in.

Networks once required affiliates to carry most network programs, which guaranteed network advertisers a large audience. Most stations were not bothered by the requirement, which dated to network radio's early days, because they received a slice of the network advertising revenue. Even so, the requirement eventually was declared coercive by the FCC, which put an end to it. There remains pressure on affiliates, however, to carry a high percentage of network programs. If a station does not, the network might transfer the affiliation to a competing station. At the same time, the FCC decision increased the opportunities for affiliates to seek programming from nonnetwork sources, which increased pressure on networks to provide popular programs.

ENTERTAINMENT PROGRAMMING

STUDY PREVIEW   Early national television networks patterned their programs on their successful radio experience, even adapting specific radio programs to the screen. Until "I Love Lucy" in 1951, programs were aired live. Today, most entertainment programming is taped and then polished by editing.

RADIO HERITAGE

TEACHING OBJECTIVE 8-4
Radio was model for early television programming.

KEY PEOPLE
Desi Arnaz and Lucille Ball introduced taping.

In the early days of television, the networks provided their affiliate stations with video versions of popular radio programs, mostly comedy and variety shows. Like radio, the programs originated in New York. With videotape still to be invented, almost everything was broadcast live. Early television drama had a live theatrical on-stage quality that is lost with today's multiple taping of scenes and slick editing. Comedy shows like Milton Berle's and variety shows like Ed Sullivan's, also live, had a spontaneity that typified early television.

Desi Arnaz and *Lucille Ball*'s "I Love Lucy" situation comedy, introduced in 1951, was significant not just because it was such a hit, but because it was not transmitted live. Rather, multiple cameras filmed several takes. Film editors then chose the best shots, the best lines, and the best facial expressions for the final production. Just as in movie production, sequences could be rearranged in the cutting room. Even comedic pacing and timing could be improved. Final responsibility for what went on the air shifted from actors to editors. Taping also made possible the libraries of programs that are reissued by syndicates for rerunning.

The Innovative "I Love Lucy." The long-running television series "I Love Lucy," starting in 1951, was taped and then edited for polish. This practice was a departure from other television programs, which, being broadcast live, lacked "Lucy's" slickness. The program also was significant because Desi Arnaz and Lucille Ball, who created the series, refused to live in New York where most television programs were being produced. The show thus became a Hollywood production and marked the beginning of the shift of television entertainment program production to California.

"I Love Lucy" also marked the start of television's shift to Hollywood. Because Desi and Lucy wanted to continue to live in California, they refused to commute to New York to produce the show. Thus, "Lucy" became television's first Los Angeles show. Gradually, most of television's entertainment production went west.

Entertainment programming has grown through phrases. Cowboy programs became popular in the 1950s, later supplemented by quiz shows. The cowboy genre was replaced by cop shows in the late 1960s. Through the changes, sitcoms have remained popular, although they have changed with the times, from "Father Knows Best" in the 1950s through "All in the Family" in the 1970s to "Home Improvement" and "Full House" in the 1990s.

CHANGING PROGRAM STANDARDS

Vulgar lines and risqué scenes once were verboten on the television networks. Critics complained that the networks' prudery was stifling creative license, but the networks had two overriding concerns. One was that they wanted to avoid putting their affiliates at risk. Offended viewers might object to the FCC, which could revoke affiliate licenses. Also, network people also talked of decency for decency's sake. Each network maintained a *Standards and Practices Department* to review all entertainment programs and commercials. The "censors," as they were called, insisted that Rob and Laura Petrie of "The Dick Van Dyke Show" sleep in separate beds, sent suggestive commercials back to agencies for revising, and even banned Smothers Brothers's antiwar jibes at President Lyndon Johnson.

LECTURE RESOURCE 8-C
Guest: Station manager, news director, program director.

Melrose Place. In 1987, the Fox television network began with a handful of programs two evenings a week and gradually expanded. With hits like "Beverly Hills 90210" and "Melrose Place," Fox became the most profitable network, primarily with low-cost entertainment shows and by not going against the Traditional Big Three networks with a full schedule of programming. Also, Fox didn't rush into expensive news programming. Behind Fox are the financial resources of international media mogul Rupert Murdoch.

"NYPD Blue." Even before Steven Bochco's "NYPD Blue" was on the air, moralists rallied against it because of reports that the script was heavy with vulgarities and skin. Despite pressure on advertisers to back away from sponsorship, ABC stuck to its position that the program was high-caliber drama. The protest withered. Audiences loved the show, and it won numerous awards.

In the 1980s, with FCC deregulation lessening license worries and with society generally more tolerant of vulgarity and licentiousness, local stations began offering nonnetwork programs that ventured into areas the network never had. These independent programs included lurid recreations of crimes, as on "America's Most Wanted"; frank examinations of once-taboo subjects on Phil Donahue and other syndicated talk shows; and unbridled blue humor on comedy club programs. Local stations found audiences for what detractors called "tabloid journalism" and "trash TV," and the FCC let it continue.

Suddenly concerned about their programs being bypassed by affiliates for racier programs available from independent sources, networks reassessed their standards. Also figuring into the reassessment was that cable, which operated beyond FCC content control, was siphoning viewers to programs that Standards and Practices reviewers would never approve. Also, viewers were being lost to home videos that even included smutty movies. Amid encroachments on their traditional viewership, the networks acquired new corporate parents, all profit-conscious in ways that network bosses had never been. In the ensuing overhauls of their management structures, CBS and NBC abolished their Standards and Practices Departments, putting the "censors" in other departments with greatly diminished power. ABC cut its standards staff drastically.

The issue of network tastes peaked in 1988 when NBC aired a two-hour Geraldo Rivera special on satanism. The network drew the line at ritualistic draining and drinking of human blood, but the program included dismembered corpses, bloody orgies and programmed child abuse. Ratings were high.

Now, network sitcom couples no longer sleep in separate beds, and hardly ever in pajamas.

TELEVISION NEWS

STUDY PREVIEW The television networks began newscasts in 1947 with anchors reading stories into cameras, embellished only with occasional newsreel clips. Networks expanded their staffs and programming over the years. Documentaries, introduced in the 1950s, demonstrated that television could cover serious issues in depth.

TALKING HEADS AND NEWSREELS

The networks began news programs in 1947, CBS with "Douglas Edwards and the News" and NBC with John Cameron Swayze's "Camel News Caravan." The 15-minute evening programs rehashed AP and UPI dispatches and ran film clips from movie newsreel companies. The networks eventually built up their own reporting staffs and abandoned the photogenic but predictable newsreel coverage of events like beauty contests and ship launchings. With on-scene reporters, network news focused more on public issues. In 1963 the evening newscasts expanded to 30 minutes with NBC's Chet Huntley–David Brinkley team and CBS's Walter Cronkite in nightly competition for serious yet interesting accounts of what was happening. When Walter Cronkite retired in 1981, surveys found him the most trusted man in the country—testimony to how important television news had become. Although news originally was an unprofitable network activity, sometimes referred to as a "glorious burden," it had become a profit center by the 1980s as news programs attracted larger audiences, which in turn attracted more advertisers.

Television's potential as a serious news medium was demonstrated in 1951 when producer *Fred W. Friendly* and reporter *Edward R. Murrow* created "See It Now," a weekly investigative program. Television gained new respect when Friendly and Murrow exposed the false, hysterical charges of Senator Joseph McCarthy about Communist infiltration of federal agencies.

TEACHING OBJECTIVE 8-5
Television news evolved into significant service.

KEY PERSON
Douglas Edwards, a pioneer anchor.

KEY PERSON
John Cameron Swayze, a pioneer anchor.

KEY PEOPLE
Chet Huntley and David Brinkley with first 30-minute newscast.

KEY PERSON
Walter Cronkite, best-known anchor.

KEY PEOPLE
Fred Friendly and Edward R. Murrow showed power of television news.

Walter Cronkite on a 1952 Set. More than anyone else, Walter Cronkite is associated with the rise of television as a news medium. He began his career with a series of newspaper, radio station and news-service jobs, and then he became well known for his United Press stories from Europe in World War II. He joined CBS in 1950 and began anchoring the network's evening television news in 1962. Surveys found him to be the most trusted person in the nation in the 1960s and 1970s, primarily for his centrist approach to news. He retired from full-time anchoring in 1981.

LOCAL NEWS

LECTURE RESOURCE 8-D
Video: *News Leaders.*

LECTURE RESOURCE 8-E
Slides: *TV News Gathering at Local Level.*

Local television news imitated network formats in the early days, but by the 1970s many innovations were occurring at the local level. Local reporting staffs grew, and some stations went beyond a headline service to enterprising and investigative reports. Many stations were quick to latch onto possibilities of satellite technology in the 1980s to do their own locally oriented coverage of far-away events. This reduced the dependence of stations on networks for national stories. Today, large stations send their own reporters and crews with uplink vans to transmit live reports back home via satellite. At the 1992 Democratic and Republican National Conventions, for example, viewers could see local delegates being interviewed by local reporters who know local issues, which was something the networks, always looking for broad, general stories, could not do.

TELEVISION NETWORKS TODAY

STUDY PREVIEW   The dominance of ABC, CBS and NBC in American television is being challenged. Public television and independent stations have nibbled away at network audiences. So have new programming sources and delivery systems. Today more than half of the nation's households are wired for cable, which can deliver more channels than are available over the air.

THE TRADITIONAL NETWORKS

TEACHING OBJECTIVE 8-6
Affiliate–network relations in flux.

LECTURE RESOURCE 8-F
Film: *Story of Television.*

KEY PERSON
Allen DuMont pioneered fourth network, failed.

Television had four networks to begin with, but few cities had more than two stations. Because NBC and CBS both had been household words since the early days of radio, they were the first choices of local stations in lining up an affiliation. Upstart ABC, in the radio business only since 1943, survived in television through a cash infusion that accompanied a 1953 merger with United-Paramount Theaters. The DuMont Network, namesake of picture-tube developer *Allen DuMont*, folded in 1955. Meanwhile, as more cities acquired a third station, ABC grew and eventually rivaled the other networks for viewers. In the late 1970s, ABC unseated CBS as the ratings leader with youth-oriented comedies and Monday night football. In 1985, with the Bill Cosby sitcom and "Miami Vice," NBC displaced ABC. Today, the three networks are well matched in their affiliate bases and resources.

CNN PBS Funding
The debate goes on between supporters of governmental funding for PBS programming and others who object to governmental funds to support programming that they find objectionable. This report by Anne McDermott aired March 3, 1992.

With federal funding provided in 1967, the *Public Broadcasting Service* began providing programs to noncommercial stations. While PBS has offered some popular programs, such as "Sesame Street," commercial stations did not see it as much of a threat. In fact, with its emphasis on informational programming such as the "MacNeil-Lehrer News Hour," "Nova" and quality drama and arts, PBS relieved public pressure on commercial stations for less profitable high-brow programming. Even so, relations between commercial and noncommercial stations were never warm, and they cooled in the 1980s when the FCC allowed public stations to acknowledge their supporters with on-air messages that come close to all-out advertising. In effect, public stations were free to join the competition for local advertising dollars.

KEY PERSON
Rupert Murdoch launched the network.

Media baron *Rupert Murdoch* launched a fourth network in 1987 after buying seven nonnetwork stations in major cities and the Twentieth Century-Fox Film Corporation, which gave him production facilities and a huge movie library. Murdoch's new Fox network recruited affiliates among other independent stations nationwide with a late-night talk show, then Sunday night programming, and then Saturday night shows. By 1994, with a full prime-time lineup and having outbid CBS for NFL football, Fox raided eight stations from CBS.

MEDIA: PEOPLE

Christine Craft

Kansas City television anchor Christine Craft was stunned. Her boss, the news director, had sat her down in his office and announced he was taking her off the anchor desk. He flashed a consultant's report at her. "We've just gotten our research back," he said. "You are too old, too unattractive, and not sufficiently deferential to men." He went on, "When the people of Kansas City see your face, they turn the dial."

Christine Craft was incredulous. During her few months at KMBC, in 1981, the station had climbed to number one for the first time in three years. She was an experienced television journalist who had anchored in her hometown, at KEYT in Santa Barbara; reported in San Francisco, at KPIX; and anchored a sports show on the CBS network. At 36, she was hardly over the hill. What did her news director mean that she was "not sufficiently deferential to men"? He explained that she had not played second fiddle to male co-anchors. "You don't hide your intelligence to make the guys look smarter. People

don't like that you know the difference between the American and the National league."

Angry, Chris Craft sued. She charged that KMBC was demoting her on sexist grounds, claiming that male anchors were not held to the same standards in age, appearance or deference. Further, she said, the station had paid her unfairly, $38,500 compared to $75,000 for her male co-anchor. It was an important moment in American television, triggering an overdue sensitivity to equal opportunity and treatment for women and men.

Craft won her jury trial and even an appeal trial before a second jury. In further appeals, the Metromedia conglomerate, which owned KMBC, prevailed, but Craft had made her point on behalf of women broadcasters throughout the land.

Within two years, Craft was back as an anchor and happy at KRBK in Sacramento. Then she was named news director and managing editor, the first woman to hold the positions at a Sacramento television station.

Today, the older networks—ABC, CBS and NBC—each have about 200 affiliates. Fox, with about 180, is catching up, but many Fox stations don't have evening newscasts to draw viewers into a whole evening of programming, which means Fox has far fewer viewers than the other networks. Also, most Fox affiliates are UHF stations which, in general, have fewer viewers than stations in the VHF lower-end of the television spectrum.

THE CABLE CHALLENGE

Today the major commercial networks, which deliver programming via over-the-air local affiliates, face a significant challenge from cable television. It was not always so. In the late 1940s, the networks were pleased that communities beyond the range of television stations built master antennas that would catch distant signals and then distribute the signals house to house by wire.

In 1972 the networks watched helplessly as a new company, Home Box Office, began providing movies and special sports events by microwave relay to local cable

LECTURE RESOURCE 8-G
Video: *Ted Turner and the News War.*

LECTURE RESOURCE 8-H
Video: *Broadcasting/Cablecasting Interface.*

companies, which set up a separate channel and charged subscribers an extra fee to tune in to the programs. HBO made hardly a dent in network viewership, but in 1975 the company switched to an orbiting satellite to relay its programs, which made the service available to every cable system in the country and 265,000 homes. HBO itself still was hardly a threat to the Big Three networks, but within months the owner of an independent station in Atlanta, Ted Turner, began beaming his signal to an orbiting satellite that retransmitted the signal to subscribing cable systems—the start of Superstation WTBS. This increasing variety of cable-delivered programming, plus the wiring of more and more communities for cable in the 1970s, began draining viewers from the traditional networks.

Today, cable is available in more than 20,000 communities in the United States. Six out of 10 U.S. households, representing 180 million people, subscribe,

Ken Burns

Ken Burns and the Civil War. The Public Broadcasting System again demonstrated its unique place in American television with Ken Burns's "Civil War" series in 1991. It was the kind of serious, high-quality television to which commercial networks give little attention, yet it drew massive numbers of viewers, skunking the traditional fare on the other networks night after night.

MEDIA DATABANK

Changing Face of Television

The television networks that supply programming to over-air local stations have lost significant audience in recent years, as more households have hooked up with cable. The Cabletelevision Advertising Bureau offered these comparisons of audience share changes between 1985 and 1986 and 1992 and 1993 in television-equipped households:

	ABC/CBS/NBC	Fox, PBS, Independents	Basic Cable
Early morning	− 8.4 percent	− 3.4 percent	+11.8 percent
Daytime	−13.0 percent	− 0.7 percent	+13.7 percent
Early fringe	− 8.6 percent	− 2.2 percent	+10.8 percent
Prime time	−16.4 percent	+ 2.8 percent	+13.6 percent
Late night	−16.1 percent	− 0.4 percent	+15.5 percent
Weekend	−13.9 percent	− 3.6 percent	+17.5 percent
TOTAL	−13.5 percent	− 0.8 percent	+14.3 percent

CNN HDTV
Consumers may want the better quality television pictures that HDTV brings but not at current prices. The networks and stations also will have to make a heavy investment, and this too is delaying the arrival of HDTV. This report, by CNN's Bonnie Anderson aired February 25, 1994.

and the number is growing. This has hurt the traditional networks, whose local affiliates are losing viewers to cable.

The Big Three were also losing viewers to nonnetwork stations. In the early days, most television sets were designed to pick up only the *VHF* channels, 2 to 13, which meant most people could not receive independent stations, which tended to be on higher frequencies. In 1962 the FCC ruled that all new sets had to be able to receive the *UHF* channels, 2 to 83. Gradually, as people replaced their old sets, the audience potential for independent stations grew.

In some markets, independent stations established their own news departments and became serious competitors for viewers. Some major-market nonnetwork stations pooled their resources to create the Independent News Network, offering an alternative to network stations. Others tapped into CNN and other sources for national and international newscasts. Also many independents boosted ratings by signing with Rupert Murdoch's new Fox network, which built viewership with several popular programs, including "Married . . . With Children," "America's Most Wanted" and "Melrose Place."

INTERACTIVE TELEVISION

Television is being put to new uses. Amid talk and speculation about a future of *interactive television*, in which people can send and receive messages through their television sets, home-shopping networks are doing it now. It is true that viewers don't order merchandise by using their television set, which would be truly interactive, but viewers do react immediately to television pitches for products on home-shopping networks by placing their orders by telephone. Home shopping has tremendous potential. Today it is a mainstay in the $2 billion a year electronic retailing industry.

PROGRAM SOURCES

STUDY PREVIEW   The networks and local stations produce almost all of their own news, sports and public-affairs programming, but most entertainment programming originates with outside sources.

PRODUCING NEWS PROGRAMS

TEACHING OBJECTIVE 8-7
Program Sources: Networks, Hollywood, independent companies, local stations.

Because of the prestige associated with quality news programs, the networks and local stations produce their own programs, each with its own stamp: "*ABC* World News Tonight," "*Channel 4* Eyewitness News," "The *CBS* Evening News." For spot news when their own reporters are not at the scene, the networks buy videotape and stills from free-lancers and even amateurs. However, the networks hardly ever risk the reputations of their news operations by farming out newscast and news documentary production to outsiders. For the same reason, most stations produce all their own news programs, although some stations occasionally air a documentary by an independent producer.

The role of free-lance television producers is limited mostly to contracted projects. For example, the PBS documentary program "Nova" is built on free-lance projects. For its specials, the National Geographic issues contracts to producers to cover specific subjects.

At local stations, little programming besides news, sports and public affairs is produced. Local variety and quiz shows, even dramas, were attempted in the 1950s, but they were amateurish compared to network shows. Only in big markets where stations have major resources available are local entertainment programs produced anymore.

PRODUCING ENTERTAINMENT PROGRAMS

The networks produce some entertainment programs themselves, but because of FCC regulations that limited network profits for their own programs over many years, the networks rely mostly on independent companies for their shows. The independent companies create prototype episodes called "pilots" to entice the networks to buy the whole series, usually a session in advance. When a network buys a series, the show's producers work closely with network programming people on details. Because networks are responsible for the programs they feed their affiliates, the networks have standards and practices people who review every program for content acceptability. They order changes to be made. Although it is gatekeeping, not true censorship, these people who control the standards and practices sometimes are called "censors."

At all three major networks, the "censorship" units have been downsized in recent years—in part because of greater audience and government acceptance of risqué language and forthright dramatizations. This does not mean there are no limits. In 1993, ABC pushed some people's tolerance with the new "NYPD Blue" program. Many advertisers were first cautious about signing up for the program. The criticism, mostly from the religious right, led by the Reverend David Wildmon, was offset by the critical acclaim the program received. The program also drew large audiences. Many advertisers, despite the criticism, couldn't pass up "NYPD Blue" as an effective vehicle to air their messages. Undeterred, in 1994 Wildmon and his followers launched a $3 million campaign against the program,

Media Use

The Nielsen audience research company tracks how much time people spend watching television. Using this partial breakdown of Nielsen data, which are divided by age groups into hours and minutes of viewing, how do your viewing patterns coincide with national averages? What patterns do you see in these data, and how do you explain these patterns?

	Women			Men		
	18–24	25–54	55 up	18–24	25–54	55 up
Monday–Friday 10 a.m.–4:30 p.m.	5:41	5:43	8:04	3:11	2:58	5:35
Monday–Friday 4:30 p.m.–7:30 p.m.	3:50	4:20	7:08	2:51	3:19	6:09
Monday–Friday 8 p.m.–11 p.m.	1:08	1:28	1:34	1:21	1:24	1:26
Monday–Sunday 11:30 p.m.–1:30 a.m.	7:05	9:26	12:19	6:06	8:58	11:32
Saturday 7 a.m.–1 p.m.	:40	:44	:38	:35	:41	:39

the network and the sponsors, but decision makers, including regulators, weren't listening.

Besides buying programs from independent producers, networks buy motion pictures from Hollywood, some that have already been on the movie-house circuit and on pay television, and others made expressly for the networks. Hollywood studios are among the largest producers of network entertainment programs.

Like the networks, stations buy independently produced entertainment programs. To do this, stations go to distributors, called *syndicators*, who package programs specifically for sale to individual stations, usually for one-time use. Syndicators also sell programs that previously appeared on the networks. These *off-network programs*, as they are called, sometimes include old episodes of programs still playing on the networks. "Murder, She Wrote," a successful CBS program, went off-net in 1987 to the USA cable network even while new episodes were still being produced for CBS. Local stations, like the networks, also buy old movies from motion picture companies for one-time showing.

PRODUCING ADVERTISEMENTS

Many television stations have elaborate facilities that produce commercials for local advertisers. In some cities, stations provide production services free, but the general practice is to charge production fees. These fees, usually based on studio time, vary widely but can run hundreds of dollars an hour. They can be a significant revenue source for stations. Except in the smallest markets, stations do not have a monop-

Japanese Television

Anyone who owns a television set in Japan can expect a knock on the door every couple of months. It is the collector from NHK, the Japan Broadcast Corporation, to pick up the $16 reception fee. This ritual occurs six times a year in 31 million doorways. The reception fee, required by law since 1950, produces $2.6 billion annually to support the NHK network.

NHK is a Japanese tradition. It went on the air in 1926, a single radio station whose first broadcast was the enthronement of Emperor Hirohito. Today, NHK operates three radio and two domestic television networks. It also runs Radio Japan, the national overseas shortwave, which transmits 40 hours of programs a day in 21 languages.

The primary NHK television network, Channel One, offers mostly high-brow programming, which gives NHK its reputation as the good gray network. Medieval samurai epics have been a long-term staple.

NHK also is known for programs like the 1980 "Silk Road," 30 hours total. which traced early Europe-Japan trade across Asia. NHK airs about 600 hours a year of British and American documentaries and dramas from the BBC and PBS. The network prides itself on its news.

Some NHK programs, such as the 15-minute Sunday morning "Serial Novel," have huge followings. Ratings regularly are 50 percent. Most Japanese viewers, however, spend most of their television time with stations served by four networks, all with headquarters in Tokyo: Fuji, NHK, NTV and Tokyo Broadcasting System. A few independent stations complete Japan's television system.

The commercial stations all offer similar fare: comedies, pop concerts and videos, quiz shows, sports and talk shows. In recent years news has gained importance in attracting viewers and advertisers, encroaching on one of NHK's traditional strengths.

oly on producing commercials. Independent video production houses are also available to advertisers to put together commercials, which then are provided ready-to-play to stations.

GOVERNMENT PROGRAMS

Although government agencies in some countries are responsible for television programming and even some production, the U.S. government does not produce programs for domestic stations. Government agencies do offer public service announcements, but it is up to individual stations whether to carry them.

FRAGMENTING AUDIENCE

STUDY PREVIEW Innovations in delivering television programs are dividing the audience into more and more segments. New and coming services have changed the vocabulary of television with terms and acronyms like PPV (pay-per-view), superstations, LPTV (low-power television), DBS (direct broadcast satellite) and STV (subscriber television).

TEACHING OBJECTIVE 8-8
New technology reduces affiliate dependence on networks.

KEY PERSON
Gerald Levin offered HBO to cable systems.

CABLE INNOVATIONS

Television entered a new era in 1975 when *Gerald Levin* took over *Home Box Office*, a Time Inc. subsidiary. HBO had been offering movies and special events, such as championship fights, to local cable systems, which sold the programs to subscribers willing to pay an extra fee. It was a *pay-per-program* service. Levin converted HBO to a *pay-per-month* service offering 24 hours a day of programming, mostly movies. To make the expanded system work, Levin needed somehow to cut the tremendous expense of relaying HBO programs across the country from microwave tower to microwave tower. It occurred to Levin that he could bypass microwaving if the HBO signal could be sent instead to an orbiting satellite, which then could send it back in one relay to every local cable company in the country. Levin put up $7.5 million to use the Satcom 1 satellite, which allowed him to cut microwave costs while expanding programming and making HBO available to more of the country.

It was a significant development. Until then, most television viewers had a choice only of three network-affiliated stations; one, possibly two independent stations; and a PBS station. ABC, CBS and NBC stations easily dominated. Suddenly, HBO was a widely available alternative. Although HBO made hardly a dent in ABC, CBS and NBC ratings, the Levin innovation opened the way for other satellite-delivered cable networks. The potential of HBO's satellite delivery was not lost on Ted Turner, who put his nonnetwork Atlanta station on a satellite and called it a superstation. Others followed—WGN of Chicago, WWOR of New York, KPIX of San Francisco, KTLA of Los Angeles, and KTVT of Fort Worth, Texas. By 1990 cable subscribers had access to more than 60 cable networks, most of them specializing in program niches that the Big Three networks, in the quest for general audiences, could not match.

NETWORK BELT-TIGHTENING

The effect was profound on the three traditional commercial networks. The networks had claimed 93 percent of the nation's viewers in 1978, before cable networks began offering alternatives. Within six years, ABC, CBS and NBC together drew only 77 percent. With fewer viewers, the traditional commercial networks inevitably faced declining advertising revenue. The networks responded by cutting back on expenses. At CBS the news division was cut from 1,400 to 1,000 employees in one swoop. Similar cuts followed at ABC and NBC.

The networks also tried to establish footholds in the growing cable industry with their own networks. Some early efforts failed, including CBS Cable, which featured serious concerts, opera and drama; and Satellite News Network, an all-news venture of ABC and Westinghouse, which never overcame CNN's head start. ABC did better with its stake in the ESPN cable sports network and the low-budget USA entertainment network. NBC has found success with its CNBC consumer-oriented business network, which went up against the Financial News Network in a niche it had created. NBC eventually bought out FNN.

EVEN MORE CHANNELS

More fragmentation of the television audience seems inevitable. In 1980 the FCC invited applications for licenses for *low-power television* stations to serve neighborhoods and small communities. Hundreds of LPTVs are now on the air, some with their own programming, others merely relaying bigger stations.

Then there is DBS, short for *direct broadcast satellite* service, which could be cable's own comeuppance. DBS, authorized by the FCC in 1982, allows companies to transmit an array of channels directly to subscribers who have special antenna dishes—bypassing local cable companies. Early DBS experiments had mixed results, but DBS companies, without the expense of wiring communities, seem to

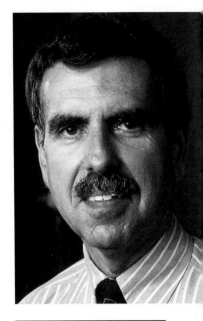

Gerald Levin. Television was revolutionized in the mid-1970s when Gerald Levin put HBO on satellite, giving local cable systems relatively inexpensive access to the service. Previously, television signals were transmitted via microwave towers spaced a few miles apart. With hundreds of relays across the countryside, the microwave system was expensive and prone to failure. With a satellite, however, it was one beam up and one beam down. Levin eventually moved up the ranks of HBO's parent corporation, Time-Life, and in 1992, was put in charge of the successor corporation, Time Warner.

CNN 500-Channel Future
The TCI cable giant is putting 500-channel services into operation for backyard downlink customers. Eventually, this diversity will be available for cable subscribers. Skeptics aren't sure whether expanded services will improve programming. "Five-hundred channels and nothing to watch," they say. This segment, reported by CNN's Steve Young, aired April 12, 1993.

Satellite Repair Job. Although satellites are highly reliable for relaying television and radio signals, when something does go wrong it is a major project to repair it. In 1992, astronauts Richard Hieb, Tom Akers and Pierre Thuot from the spacecraft Endeavor went space walking to capture the Intelsat VI satellite for repairs. While the Intelsat was out of commission, broadcast transmissions were channeled to alternate satellites.

LECTURE RESOURCE 8-1
Class Exercise: How commercials coincide with dayparts.

have the potential to undercut cable company rates and further fragment the television market.

Telephone companies, meanwhile, are upgrading their lines with *fiber-optic* cables. These cables can carry a great number of high-quality signals, including video, which means that telephone companies have the potential to compete with cable companies in delivering television services. Because far more homes are wired for telephone than for cable, especially in rural areas, today's cable companies may face stiff new competition from the telephone companies.

PAY SERVICES

Meanwhile, other pay services joined HBO. These included Showtime, Cinemax, Disney and Playboy, which further divided the television audience. In addition, pay-per-view services, offered by cable companies to subscribers who are charged for each program they watch, were coming into their own. The largest PPV, Viewer's Cable, is available in more than 2.5 million homes.

A PPV variation that does not deliver programming through cable companies is subscriber television—called *STV*. STV companies send scrambled signals through the air directly to subscribers who rent a decoder from the STV company. STV has worked in populous areas not yet wired for cable, but because STV offers only one channel, it is disadvantaged once cable reaches a neighborhood. It is also susceptible to piracy. Decoding boxes are easily copied and sold on the black market.

CHAPTER WRAP-UP

American television patterned itself after radio. From the beginning, television was a dual national system of locally owned commercial stations and national networks. Companies that were heavily involved in radio were also the television heavyweights. Even television's programming mimicked radio's. The Big Three networks, NBC, CBS and ABC, were the most powerful shapers of television, leading in entertainment programming and news. They also pioneered many of the technological advances. Today, program packaging and further technical innovations are challenging the Big Three dominance, and the television industry is undergoing a major restructuring.

Gerald Levin and then Ted Turner led the restructuring when they realized that they could deliver programs to local cable companies via orbiting satellite. Levin's HBO and Turner's WTBS, both movie services, became unique features of cable companies in the 1970s. The threat to local over-air stations and the Big Three networks was minor at first, but cable companies began wiring more neighborhoods, and additional cable networks came to be, among them Turner's 24-hour news service. With cable into more than 60 percent of the nation's homes today, the cable networks are siphoning major advertising from the Big Three, and many local cable companies are going after local advertisers. In some cities, independent local stations have become major players for advertising, which further contributes to the restructuring.

Satellite technology is contributing to major changes in a second way. Network affiliates discovered in the 1980s that they could use their new downlink equipment, which received network transmissions from satellites, to pick up programming from other sources. Suddenly, these stations could pick and choose programs, even news video, as never before. Many stations expanded their newscasts and assembled their own far-away coverage with video from a variety of network and nonnetwork sources. Larger stations acquired mobile uplink equipment and sent crews great distances to cover news. It was not unusual for some stations to send crews abroad several times a year. No longer were local over-air stations so dependent on their networks to succeed.

QUESTIONS FOR REVIEW

1. How does television influence people and society in the short term and the long term?

2. How is television technology different from movie technology?

3. How was radio the role model for early television programming?

4. How has television news evolved into its present format?

5. Why does the United States have a two-tier structure for the television industry?

6. What role do affiliates have in network programming?

7. What are the main sources of television programming in the United States?

8. How are the traditional U.S. television networks being affected by new technology that is available to their affiliates?

9. What developments in television are threatening the traditional over-air stations and the networks that supply much of their programming?

QUESTIONS FOR CRITICAL THINKING

1. How did Vladimir Zworykin's iconoscope and kinescope employ electronics to pick up moving images and relay them to far-away screens? Explain the difference between television and film technology.

2. What was the relationship of radio and early television programming? You might want to review Chapter 7 to explain the effect of television on radio.

3. Trace the development of television news from the newsreel days. Include the heyday of documentaries and explain what happened to them. What was the contribution of Fred Friendly and Edward R. Murrow? Explain expanded network newscasts and the importance of Walter Cronkite. What contribution has PBS made? Include magazine and talk-show programs in your answer.

4. Outline the development of television networks. Besides the three major networks, include Allen DuMont's, Ted Turner's and Rupert Murdoch's networks. Explain challenges faced today by the major networks, including how independent stations have become stronger, the innovation pioneered by Gerald Levin, the effect of FCC deregulation, expanded program production by syndicators, and new technologies (LPTV, PPV, DBS, STV, cable and home video). How do you regard the observation of some critics that the Big Three networks will not exist in their present form by the year 2000?

5. Historically, why have television stations sought affiliations with ABC, CBS and NBC? Discuss changes in network–affiliate relations. Is a network affiliation as attractive today as it was 20 years ago? Why or why not?

6. What happened to network Standards and Practices Departments in the late 1980s? Why?

7. How is the television industry funded? Remember that the financial base is different for the commercial networks, network–affiliated stations, independent stations, noncommercial networks and stations, superstations, cable networks, cable systems, and subscriber services.

8. How does the career of Ted Turner epitomize the emergence of new program and delivery systems as a challenge to the traditional structure of television in the United States?

FOR FURTHER LEARNING

Erik Barnouw. *Tube of Plenty: The Evolution of American Television* (Oxford, 1975). Barnouw, the preeminent biographer of television, deals with evolutions in network programming and the powerful personalities that shaped the industry.

Warren Bennis and Ian Mitroff. *The Unreality Industry* (Carol Publishing 1989). Professors Bennis and Mitroff claim that television has turned America into a "24-hour entertainment society." It is for the worse, they say. By treating complex issues in slick 15-, 30-, and 60-second segments of information, television has lulled viewers into believing that the modern world can be understood with hardly any effort.

Mary Lu Carnevale. "Untangling the Debate over Cable Television." *Wall Street Journal* 71 (March 19, 1990):107, B1, B5, B6. The *Journal* offers a package on the status of the cable industry, including competition from fiber-optic networks owned by telephone companies and from direct-to-home satellite services.

Mark Christensen and Cameron Stauth. *The Sweeps* (Morrow, 1984). An examination of special network programs, including miniseries and scandal reports, to attract viewers during ratings periods when advertising rates are set.

Christine Craft. *Too Old, Too Ugly, and Not Deferential to Men* (Dell, 1988). An anchorwoman recounts the sad emphasis on image over journalistic substance at a profitable, tight-fisted metropolitan station. It is a personal story that details her removal as an anchor because her bosses did not think she was young or pretty enough.

Ed Joyce. *Prime Times, Bad Times* (Doubleday, 1988). A former president of CBS News explains network television journalism from the inside, up to the economic crunch of the late 1980s.

Joshua Meyrowitz. *No Sense of Place: The Impact of the Electronic Media on Social Behavior* (Oxford, 1985). Meyrowitz summarizes research on television's effects on human behavior, concluding that the effect has been powerful.

Lucas A. Powe, Jr. *American Broadcasting and the First Amendment* (University of California Press, 1987). Powe challenges the premise that broadcasting must be regulated to serve the public interest.

John P. Robinson and Mark R. Levy. *The Main Source* (Sage, 1986). Robinson and Levy argue that television news programs leave viewers with a false sense that they have been informed. The core problem, they say, is deficiencies inherent in the medium, rather than programs.

Hank Whittemore. *CNN: The Inside Story* (Little, Brown, 1990). This is an enthusiastic account about Ted Turner and a small group of visionaries who proved that television had more potential as a news medium than the three major networks had shown.

■F OR KEEPING UP TO DATE

Broadcasting is a weekly trade journal for the radio, television and cable industries.

Channels is a monthly trade journal.

Journal of Broadcasting and Electronic Media is a quarterly scholarly journal published by the Broadcast Education Association.

Television/Radio Age is a trade journal.

Consumer magazines that deal extensively with television programming include *Entertainment* and *TV Guide*.

Newsmagazines that report television issues more or less regularly include *Newsweek* and *Time*.

Business Week, Forbes and *Fortune* track television as a business.

Major newspapers with strong television coverage include the Los Angeles *Times*, the New York *Times* and the *Wall Street Journal*.

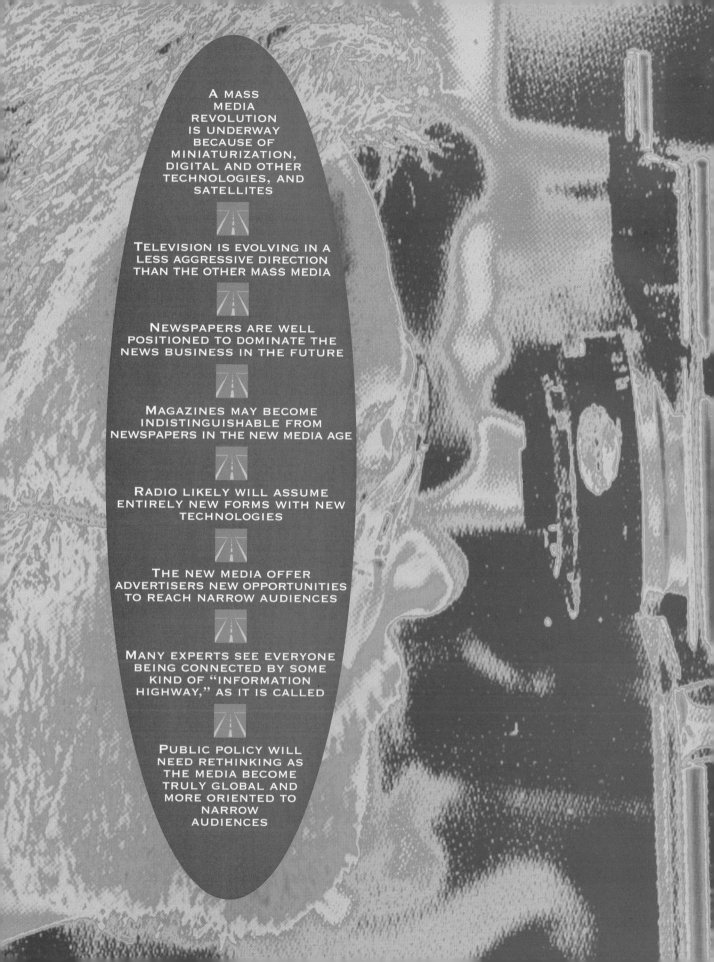

A MASS MEDIA REVOLUTION IS UNDERWAY BECAUSE OF MINIATURIZATION, DIGITAL AND OTHER TECHNOLOGIES, AND SATELLITES

TELEVISION IS EVOLVING IN A LESS AGGRESSIVE DIRECTION THAN THE OTHER MASS MEDIA

NEWSPAPERS ARE WELL POSITIONED TO DOMINATE THE NEWS BUSINESS IN THE FUTURE

MAGAZINES MAY BECOME INDISTINGUISHABLE FROM NEWSPAPERS IN THE NEW MEDIA AGE

RADIO LIKELY WILL ASSUME ENTIRELY NEW FORMS WITH NEW TECHNOLOGIES

THE NEW MEDIA OFFER ADVERTISERS NEW OPPORTUNITIES TO REACH NARROW AUDIENCES

MANY EXPERTS SEE EVERYONE BEING CONNECTED BY SOME KIND OF "INFORMATION HIGHWAY," AS IT IS CALLED

PUBLIC POLICY WILL NEED RETHINKING AS THE MEDIA BECOME TRULY GLOBAL AND MORE ORIENTED TO NARROW AUDIENCES

chapter 9

MASS MEDIA TOMORROW

When Roger Fidler was growing up in Eugene, Oregon, in the 1950s, he did what a lot of other 11-year-old kids did then. He had a paper route and delivered newspapers house to house. Fidler remembers those days with a bemused nostalgia. But it bothers him today, in this electronic age with all kinds of other delivery possibilities for news and pictures, that newspapers still rely on 11-year-old kids to hand-deliver a 15th-century, ink-on-paper product to their customers.

Fidler now heads the Knight-Ridder Information Design Laboratory in Boulder, Colorado. His job is to look at technology for better ways for newspapers to do their business. He knows more efficient, less expensive and more reliable means for delivering newspapers are possible. That makes him shudder every time he hears that a newspaper has spent millions of dollars for new presses. New presses are such a major investment that it takes 30 to 40 years to pay for them. That's great for the next couple of generations of 11-year-old kids who want paper routes, but it locks newspapers into archaic technology. To Fidler, that makes no sense.

Roger Fidler, now in his mid-40s, has seen the newspaper business from many perspectives. He has been a reporter, a science columnist and a newspaper art director. When Knight-Ridder, a leading U.S. newspaper chain, went into a joint venture to produce graphics, Fidler was put in charge. The venture became a multimillion-dollar enterprise, supplying digitized graphics to newspapers and video animations to television stations. From there, Fidler became head of the Knight-Ridder Design Lab and began to identify routes newspapers could take to capitalize on new technology to survive, even thrive, into the 21st century.

Fidler is convinced that newspapers will dominate other mass media into the future because of their capacity to produce word-based messages that are quick to read and have a precision impossible with video-dominated media.

But as Fidler sees it, many newspaper executives may be their own worst enemy. Speaking at a forum at Columbia University, he said: "The executives in the glass offices grew up before computers had a dominant role in newspapers. They know presses. They know how the newspaper business was run in the 1950s and 1960s. It is very difficult for them to deal with a future that may not involve the printing press."

Fidler's vision, his nostalgia notwithstanding, does not include 11-year-old kids bicycling through neighborhoods tossing the afternoon edition toward porches, sometimes hitting their mark, sometimes not. He foresees people having an electronic clipboard, roughly 8½ by 11 inches, half an inch thick, weighing less than a pound. The surface would be a computerlike screen on which people call up the latest edition any time and browse through stories, reading what they want, passing by the rest. Delivery could be by fiber-optic lines, with people plugging into an outlet for the latest update, or by some kind of over-air delivery. These media tablets could also deliver entertainment of many sorts. Eleven-year-old kids would have to find other jobs.

In this chapter, you will explore the media of tomorrow as Roger Fidler and other futurists see them. Everything is changing.

MASS MEDIA REVOLUTION

STUDY PREVIEW A mass media revolution is underway because of miniaturization, digital and other new technologies and satellites. An important key in new media forms is the ability to compress messages for storage and transmission.

MINIATURIZATION

TEACHING OBJECTIVE 9-1
Identify the technological developments since 1947 that are leading to the forms that the mass media will take in the future.

Until the 1950s, home radios were delicate pieces of equipment that glowed with lightbulblike tubes that amplified broadcast signals so they could be heard. Even the smallest radios, called "table models," were pieces of furniture. Then, in the 1950s, came a technological marvel: handheld battery-powered transistor radios that people could carry anywhere. While revolutionary in themselves, these transistor radios were only the beginning of an age of technological miniaturization.

The revolution began in 1947 when researchers at AT&T's Bell Laboratories developed the first semiconductor switch. They took pieces of glasslike silicon, really just pieces of sand, and devised a way to make them respond to a negative or positive charge. These tiny slivers of sand, called semiconductors, could function as on-off switches. The implications of semiconductors for the electronic mass media were quickly evident because they could solve problems inherent in the technology of radio at the time. For one thing, radios and their tubes were fragile. The tubes got hot and eventually burned out. Also, they consumed massive amounts of electricity. Semiconductors, on the other hand, could amplify broadcast signals without any heat, and they used hardly any electricity. Important too, semiconductors were much, much smaller than tubes. That's why transistor radios were portable, unlike the radios before them.

Miniaturization has been important not only because equipment can be smaller and more reliable but also because it can be much less expensive. The first computers in the 1940s, based on tube technology, were so big it took entire buildings to house them and large staffs of technicians to operate them. According to a National Academy of Science estimate, it cost $130,000 to make 125 multiplications with those computers. By 1970 the cost was a mere $4. Today it can be done for pennies.

Wilbur Schramm, in his book *The Story of Human Communication*, cited a Marquardt Corporation estimate that all the information recorded in the last 10,000 years could be stored in a cube 6 feet by 6 feet by 6 feet. All 12 million books in the Library of Congress would take less than 2 cubic inches. Miniaturization through semiconductors has brought us a long way.

DIGITAL AND OTHER TECHNOLOGIES

Telephones today are mostly point-to-point communication tools for one person to talk to another person or for the one-way transmission of data. Mass media, in contrast, allow one person to talk to hundreds if not millions of people. This distinction, however, is disappearing as telephone companies, capitalizing on semiconductor and other technologies, develop the capacity to carry messages to multiple parties. This technological revolution, making telephone systems into mass media, is based on several developments:

- **Semiconductors.** The rapid on-off switching of semiconductors allows more voices to be carried simultaneously on a single cable.

- **Optical fiber cable.** Glass fiber cable technology, often called *fiber optics*, has vastly greater capacity to carry messages than old copper cables, with better quality at less cost. In the early days of semiconductor on-off switching, people marveled that 51 calls could be carried at the same time on a copper cable. Today, with semiconductor switching combined with optical fiber cable, a single line can carry 60,000 calls simultaneously.

- **Digitization.** An outgrowth of semiconductor technology has been the digitization of data, even voices and video, for storage and transmission. A message, whether a voice on a phone line or music on a compact disc, is reduced to millions and millions of on-off signals. Miniaturization has made it possible to record a tremendous number of these on-off signals for transmission and replay. Hence, as Wilbur Schramm noted, all human knowledge could fit in a 36-square-foot cube.

SATELLITES

Orbiting satellites are platforms that relay messages worldwide, including both entertainment and news. Combined with other technologies that are transforming the mass media, satellites are making the world a very small place. Not a spot on the globe is beyond the media's reach. These technologies are creating vast global commercial opportunities to supply news and entertainment without regard to national borders.

TELEVISION AND TELECOMPUTERS

STUDY PREVIEW   The over-air television industry is working to improve picture clarity with high-definition screens. Other media, meanwhile, are leapfrogging HDTV and going on to even better on-screen images. These include images with easily read text.

HIGH-DEFINITION TELEVISION

The over-air television industry is developing new enhanced-picture systems known variously as *HDTV,* short for high-definition television, and *ATV,* short for advanced television. Television screens in the United States today have 525 inter-laced horizontal lines with every other line filled in at rapid intervals. This fools the eye into seeing motion, although the image is fuzzy close up and on oversize screens. The European 625-line screens are a bit sharper, and the Japanese 1,124-line HDTV screens sharper yet. But not even the Japanese system handles text well. If a whole newspaper page is transmitted, viewers can make out only the headlines. For a story to be read, the camera must zoom in on a single narrow column of type.

For HDTV, the National Television Standards Committee, which decides such things, has set 62 dots per inch as the new television transmission standard. That is wholly adequate for producing the image quality of today's 525-line screens and even HDTV screens of the future. But compared to the telecomputer standards that other media are developing, 62 dots per inch doesn't measure up at all.

You Choose the Shot. An experiment with interactive television involved 130 Springfield, Massachusetts, house-holds. With a remote control–type device, viewers chose which camera they wanted to see as a New England Patri-ots football game progressed: go to an end zone camera; zoom in on a tackle; zoom back on a long pass; or go to the scoreboard. Interactive media allow the consumer to send messages back to the source. The introduction of high-capacity optical fiber cable is opening the way to entirely new structures of media programming and presentation. Possibilities include on-demand music, much like a jukebox.

TELECOMPUTERS

For on-screen images, computers use at least a 200-dot-per-inch standard, or, put another way, 40,000 dots per square inch, for fully readable text—more than 30 times what television people are planning for HDTV.

The other mass media, particularly newspapers, appear to be leapfrogging television by adapting standards developed by the computer industry to create, transmit and display readable messages. This technology involves compressing those tiny on-screen dots, called *pixels*. Television's upcoming 62-dot standard doesn't come close to the level needed for delivering text. One current computer standard for pixels, the 72 dots per inch that Apple uses for its laptop computers, is one-third sharper than the 62-dot NTSC standard. But even the laptop's 72 dots aren't sharp enough. In tests with people reading from standard books and from laptops, those using laptops moved through the material 25 percent more slowly.

As engineers discover new miniaturization techniques and ways to squeeze more capacity into computer chips, pixels will be packed more and more densely on screens. This means that superb-image, lightweight compact screens will be coming along. The term *telecomputer* is often used to distinguish this new, sharper image medium from television.

FLAT SCREENS

Technology is making flat screens possible. We see flat screens today on laptop and other small computers. These telecomputer screens contrast with the thick cathode-ray tubes of television sets, which are neither lightweight nor compact. The cost of producing television picture tubes is about as low as it will go, whereas flat screen production costs are destined to drop significantly.

Today high-density telecomputer screens cost $10 per square inch to manufacture, but with the price of computer chip technology dropping by half every 18 months, manufacturers expect high-density pixel screens to drop to $1 per square inch. This means that compact computer screens with the resolution of the best laser printers could be manufactured for $100 or less.

If the future of mass media is in personal compact reception equipment, as many futurists foresee, then the future will be with telecomputer systems because they have the flexibility people want. These screens can handle both images and text, and they are light, compact and cheap and becoming more so. The relative bulkiness and cost of television screens means they won't compete. George Gilder, a leading media technologist, is blunt: "Computers will soon blow away the broadcast television industry." Gilder says major broadcast companies that are committing themselves to television's over-air technology rather than going the telecomputer route are "in a kind of elephants' waltz into the sunset."

VIRTUAL RETINA DISPLAYS

Even before flat screens make it to market they may be obsolete. University of Washington technologists and Micro Vision, a Seattle company, are developing a system that displays electronic images directly on the human retina. People would wear something resembling a pair of glasses that would project three-dimensional photographic-quality images with the eyeball itself as the screen. These eyeball projectors, called *virtual retina displays*, would leapfrog the competition between cathode ray tubes and flat screens.

The Eyeball as a Screen. A Seattle company, Micro Vision, is hoping to market a device that projects images directly onto the human eyeball. The VRD, short for "virtual retina display," will be small enough to mount on a pair of eyeglasses and it will give a sharper image than a 70-millimeter IMAX screen. With the VDR, people would not need television or computer screens. Micro Vision says this device eventually can be made for less than $100.00. The technology is being developed in the Human Interface Technology Laboratory at the Washington Technology Center.

Micro Vision demonstrated VRDs in 1994 and planned to have a black-and-white model available by 1996. Color VRDs would follow. The price is projected eventually at $100 a unit, which is less than conventional telecomputer screens and one-tenth of HDTV screens.

TOMORROW'S NEWS MEDIA

STUDY PREVIEW   Newspaper companies are well positioned to dominate the news business in the future and to expand into services beyond news. In the not too distant future, people will be able to call up the news they want in as much detail as they want. In effect, everyone would be able to create custom, individual news packages from massive arrays of information that will be available.

NEWSPAPERS' FUTURE

TEACHING OBJECTIVE 9-3
Explain why newspapers are well positioned to dominate the news business in the future.

Newspapers are well into the electronic age in every way except final production and delivery. Writers do their stories on computers, and editors use advanced digital equipment to edit the copy, lay it out and make it ready for printing. The actual printing, however, is on monstrous presses whose technological heritage can be traced to Johannes Gutenberg's movable type of the 1400s. Also, just as it was 500 years ago, the product is still ink on paper—barrels and barrels of ink and tons and tons of paper. And just as it has been for almost two centuries, the delivery of newspapers is mostly in the hands of youngsters who trot from house to house to drop the papers on doorsteps. There is a quaint irony in trusting boys and girls to deliver a million-dollar product, like an edition of a metropolitan daily, to the customers.

Do newspapers have a future? The obituary for newspapers was written prematurely twice before. Publishers once feared radio would put them out of business. It didn't happen. Later, television was a threat, and in fact television stole newspaper readers, especially in the evening, and this prompted speculation that the end for newspapers was near. That speculation is fading, however, and many futurists believe today's newspaper companies are well positioned to dominate the news business in the 21st century.

EFFICIENCY AND EFFECTIVENESS

Newspapers are a medium based on words. For the most part, visuals in newspapers and also magazines are mere enhancements to written messages. Those people who see the communication of the future as primarily video have missed the fact that video works better than words for only an extremely narrow range of messages. Media technologist George Gilder puts it this way: "Video is most effective in conveying shocks and sensations and appealing to prurient interests of large miscellaneous audiences. Images easily excel in blasting through to the glandular substances of the human community; there's nothing like a body naked or bloody or both to arrest the eye." Human communication, however, goes far beyond shock scenes and sensual appeals. People communicate mostly through words.

Television technology today, with only 525 lines on a screen, is not a good medium for written messages. Nor is television an efficient medium for relaying information. News anchors and reporters talk on air at 140 to 160 words a minute. That is not an efficient rate to communicate messages, especially considering that most people read at least 700 words a minute. Veteran network anchor Walter Cronkite once noted that the script for one edition of the CBS Evening News would take up only half the front page of the *New York Times*. Think about how many pages of the *Times* or any other newspaper you could read in the time it takes to watch a half-hour newscast.

COMPUTER DELIVERY

The ability of computer networks to relay digitized text, images and even voice almost instantly will be the heart of tomorrow's news media. There will be no morning or afternoon newspapers. With delivery through computer networks

Digital Delivery. The La Crosse, Wisconsin, *Tribune*, began experimenting with expanded coverage via home fax machines in 1993. Readers with fax capabilities can call an automated phone number to request longer stories, in-depth movie reviews, complete financial tables and other features from an index published every day in the paper. They can request as many articles as they want. Lee Enterprises, which owns the *Tribune*, is ready to expand the service to other newspapers if the La Crosse experiment works financially.

directly to readers, news people can update their stories as events warrant and as articles are written and as visual and sound packages are produced. The product can be delivered in real time, just like television with reporters and photographers at the scene live—but with crisper telecomputer video than with television and text.

The news media of tomorrow will also have other advantages over television as we know it today, including unlimited space and time. Also, the audience will have an ability to choose individually what stories to follow instead of being forced to wait, as with today's television, for stories that interest them to come up in the newscast.

NEWS HOLE. People will have access to far more information than today. The "news hole" no longer will be limited by the space available in an edition or the time available in a newscast. Readers can see the headlines and then, with their screen controls, choose to go into depth with more background stories, with stories from previous days, with maps, charts and photos, and with video segments with voices and sound of news events as they happened. It will be possible to read the texts of important speeches, rather than merely read summaries, or to listen to the whole speech as it was delivered. It will be possible even to watch the actual interviews on which stories are based.

PIXELS. Television today has a built-in disadvantage in displaying on-screen text. The current on-screen pixel density does not give the crisp resolution that is needed for people to read from their screens, except for oversized, headline-type messages. If you see words on a television screen today, they usually are bottom-of-the-screen streamers with four or five words per line at most. To show a piece of writing on screen, television producers have to zoom in so close that only a fragment of a line shows. The alternative, scrolling or panning over a written message, works for a brief message but is as distracting as would be turning the pages of a newspaper every few words.

The television industry has committed itself to relatively modest improvements in pixel density. Even with the higher resolution of HDTV, with roughly double the horizontal lines, the image will not be crisp enough to deliver text. In the meantime, newspapers plan to deliver news to telecomputer screens, which use thousands more pixels to create images. Besides text, telecomputer screens can present moving images—and do it more sharply than television. In short, telecomputer newspapers are in a good position to displace television as a medium for news.

Over-air television won't disappear as a medium all at once. It will remain satisfactory for watching movies and simple visual presentations, but because it doesn't work for texts and because telecomputer screens will do everything better, over-air television eventually will be displaced by cable-delivered media—unless sharper over-air transmission standards are adopted.

BROWSING. Newspapers today lend themselves to browsing. People scan headlines and photos to decide what interests them. Tomorrow's on-screen newspaper also will allow browsing. With a click of a key or a mouse or button, or perhaps a voice command, readers will move to another page or even turn pages by uttering a voice command: "Next screen, please." "Sports now, please." "More photos, please." "How about those Dodgers?"

This browsing capacity is something that television, as it now exists, does not have. With television, if you are interested in a particular story, you have to sit through other stories until what you want comes up. This makes television a dull news medium. It also has made television a superficial medium: So viewers don't get bored waiting for the items they're interested in, television people have devised formats with short stories. Many stations and networks have a two-minute cap on stories. The result is stories that touch only on the surface of a subject.

READER CONTROL. 　With telecomputer systems, people will be able to call up from newspaper databanks the news and information that interests them. Unlike over-air radio and television, people will not be compelled to watch live coverage if something else interests them more. People can create their own sequences of stories and skip ones that don't interest them. On-screen newspapers, then as now, will be a personal medium over which the reader has control. George Gilder put it this way: "Newspapers rely on the intelligence of the reader. Although the editors select and shape the matter to be delivered, readers choose, peruse, sort, queue and quaff the news and advertising copy at their own pace and volition."

Gilder offers this telling analogy: "Newspapers differ from television stations in much the way automobiles differ from trains. With the car (and the newspaper), you get in and go pretty much where you want when you want." In short, newspapers put the decision-making power in the hands of readers. Readers interact with the product, which they shape to their own needs and interests.

MAGAZINES AND BOOKS

STUDY PREVIEW 　Magazines may become indistinguishable from newspapers in the new media age. Both magazine and book publishers already are dabbling in digitized nonpaper delivery.

MELDING MAGAZINES AND NEWSPAPERS

Like newspapers, magazines can be delivered digitally. This is happening already, with numerous magazines available on CD-ROM discs that people can play on computers and read on screen. But the future for magazines as a distinct mass medium is not clear.

TEACHING OBJECTIVE 9-4
Discuss the fate of magazines and books in the coming media convergence.

Interim to Tomorrow.
Magazines have experimented with television editions and also delivery by on-line computer services, but the economics aren't quite right. Time Warner is trying CD-ROM packages distilled from its magazines that retail at $29.95. *Time* reporters are getting a taste of work in the multimedia world because editors ask them to lug handheld video cameras to interviews.

MEDIA: PEOPLE

The Mondo 2000 Crew

The convergence of the old, distinct mass media into wholly new structures confuses people. Is television no longer television if it is delivered on a telecomputer rather than a television screen? Does a newspaper cease being a newspaper if it isn't printed on paper but is delivered electronically? Does a book have to be bound between cover boards to be a book?

Alison Kennedy, who likes calling herself "Queen Mu," took an inheritance in 1988 and founded a magazine that not only tracks a lot of what is happening in media technology but also tries to get inside it. The magazine, *Mondo 2000,* has been called the *Rolling Stone* of the new cyberpunk generation, which dabbles in drugs, science fiction, computer hacking and a lot of at-the-edge stuff that sends traditionalists climbing the walls. In recent issues:

- How to buy drugs designed to make you smarter.
- Experiencing sex via computer.
- Breaking into automated teller machines.
- A history of transsexuals.

Amid the cyberpunk subjects, *Mondo 2000* explores where the mass media are headed as they shift from old print and analog technology to newer technology.

Comparisons between *Mondo 2000* and *Rolling Stone* are easy to make. *Rolling Stone* started from scratch to become the banner of the music-obsessed

generation that came of age in the 1970s. *Mondo 2000* is capturing the imagination of a growing computer-crazed segment of the new generation. Both began in the San Francisco Bay area, *Mondo* being published out of an old Victorian mansion in Berkeley. Both have strong-willed, imaginative people at the helm.

On *Mondo*'s masthead, Alison Kennedy calls herself "Queen Mu, Domineditrix," a computerese-inspired creation that won't be found in any dictionary but whose meaning is clear to both cyberpunks and fuddy-duddies. Icon-at-large is Ken Goffman, who lists himself R.U. Sirius, and the art director is Bart Nagel, who gives the magazine an overcaffeinated, MTV look.

Writing in *Time* magazine, analyst Paul Saffo said this of *Mondo 2000:* "This is the kind of magazine that engineers read in their teens and influences what they build 20 years later. It's an idea time bomb."

As newspapers offer more and more coverage of specialized events and allow readers to browse through an incredible choice of detail and perspectives, magazines will lose their role as a specialized medium catering to special tastes and interests. For example, why would a ski enthusiast subscribe to a ski magazine if a newspaper offers unlimited access to all the information available on skiing?

Some futurists see magazines and newspapers melding into a single medium. When *Roger Fidler*, of Knight-Ridder's Information Design Laboratory, speaks of the newspaper of tomorrow, he talks about multiple layers of coverage. Readers, he says, can tap into conventional general news coverage of unfolding events by browsing through headlines to find what interests them, and, if they want more depth and detail, they can plunge into deeper levels of the subject. These deeper levels would include the kind of thorough, focused and specialized treatment we find in today's magazines. The same is true for nonnews subjects. The knitting columns in today's newspapers, to take one example, can have so many sublayers of detail and instruction and options that they could rival today's specialized magazines on knitting. If Fidler is correct, a melding of today's newspapers and magazines seems inevitable.

This melding is already beginning. In fact, if you review metropolitan daily newspapers and magazines today, you will find a lot of the content is much the same. Newspapers generally offer more background and depth in coverage than ever before, and they have a wide range of commentary on the issues of the day. Many magazines package their articles for republication by newspapers. What most separates newspapers and magazines today is presentation. Magazines are slicker and bound. Those physical distinctions will disappear when both newspapers and magazines are delivered on-screen.

KEY PERSON

Roger Fidler exploring electronic newspaper formats and delivery.

ELECTRONIC BOOKS

Book publishers are dabbling with electronic delivery. Many best-sellers are read onto cassette tapes and sold to people who want to hear books, not read them, as they commute to work and go about their chores. The next step is for publishers to put books into digitized storage banks. Readers could then call them up on demand for reading on their telecomputer screens or listening via new telecomputers with voice capabilities. Publishers already sell digitized versions of books that can be read on computers. These versions could easily be installed in computer networks for readers to call up on demand.

- -

TOMORROW'S RADIO

STUDY PREVIEW New transmission techniques could bring digital clarity to radio listening. This could shake up the economic structure of the U.S. radio industry. So could proposed national stations that might displace today's locally based broadcast system.

DIGITAL RADIO

Music lovers who were in awe at the sound quality when FM stereo began playing compact discs in the 1980s are in for a big surprise. The next improvement in radio technology will use digital transmitters. Instead of taking the 0s and 1s of a CD computer code and converting them to analog signals for transmission, as stations

TEACHING OBJECTIVE 9-5

Discuss the hazards ahead for radio as we know it.

do today, the new equipment would send the 0s and 1s themselves. Listeners with digital receivers would hear the sound as precisely and clearly as a CD on a home player.

Digital signals would be transmitted in a now-unused portion of the broadcast spectrum. A policy question for the Federal Communications Commission is whether to allocate the new digital frequencies to existing stations. If the FCC remains true to its historic commitment to diverse ownership of the nation's radio industry, the digital signals would go to new stations. The result, if listeners buy digital receivers, is that today's AM and FM station owners could find themselves as out of date as the horse and buggy.

The National Association of Broadcasters, a trade association of station owners, is lobbying the FCC to give existing stations the first chance at digital licenses. Even if existing stations prevail with the FCC, going digital could be risky. If only audiophiles buy the new digital receivers, the stations may find themselves saddled with expensive digital transmission equipment and very few listeners. That sort of thing happened in the 1980s when some AM stations began transmitting in stereo. Hardly any listeners bought the new AM stereo receivers.

If the FCC decides to diversify station ownership by granting digital licenses only to new stations, existing stations could lose out entirely if listeners are so mesmerized by digital radio that nobody listens to AM or FM anymore.

NATIONAL STATIONS

Today's AM and FM station owners worry that the FCC might abandon its traditional preference to license stations to localities. There are proposals to allow new stations to transmit directly from orbiting satellites to listeners. The new stations could cover the whole nation. While radio networks offer national program services today, they reach listeners only through local stations that retransmit the signals and insert local advertising. If such programming services could bypass local transmission, then local stations could lose their present source of revenue for high-quality, low-cost programming.

Even more threatening to local stations, national advertisers might opt to place their ads on the new satellite stations. That would cut off an important revenue source for local stations.

INTERACTIVE THREAT

The digital transmission technology that excites so many radio people today may eventually lead to the radio industry's demise. Technology is finding ways to compress digital signals so more and more messages, including music and news, can be squeezed down for transmission. It is this compression that will allow people to have on-demand programming via their fiber-optic lines. Instead of waiting for your favorite song or the latest sports, you could call up what you want and it would be instantly played for you—just for you when you want it. It is the telephone and cable television companies, which now are wiring the nation and the world, that will offer these on-demand services.

Radio would still have a role for people on the go, commuting or at the beach, where they can't plug in, but that is a much smaller audience segment than radio has today. In the distant future, digital compression may reach the point that wireless over-air communication can be truly interactive, with so many messages squeezed onto the electromagnetic spectrum that on-demand services can be delivered over the air. It may still be radio stations that deliver these services, but the programming would be listener-determined, not station-determined. Radio would be like a giant jukebox. This raises fundamental questions about the structure of tomorrow's radio industry: How will advertising fit in? Will it fit in at all? Who would want to listen to happy idiot disc jockeys if they could get the music they want whenever they want it? Or the latest sports or news?

In short, the kinds of services offered by radio today will likely be subsumed in the broader media services that are being created by companies installing interactive cable links.

FINANCING THE NEW MEDIA

STUDY PREVIEW The new media present new opportunities for advertisers to reach highly defined, narrow audiences. If advertisers shift to new media, the current economic foundation of the magazine, newspaper, radio and television industries would be upended.

REACHING NARROW AUDIENCES

In the mid-1950s, when many magazines and radio stations demassified to find narrower audience segments, advertising shifted to the narrower media. The huge mass-oriented magazines lost advertising, and most, including *Life* and the venerable *Saturday Evening Post*, went out of business. For advertisers, it was economics pure and simple: "Where can the greatest number of potential buyers of my products or services be reached for the least cost?" Advertisements for men's products shifted to media that geared themselves to male audiences. Cadillac ads went to upscale outlets, muffler ads to downscale outlets. Ads for pimple potions reached more potential customers in teen outlets than mass outlets like *Life*.

Now, technology has introduced a whole new ability for the mass media to reach narrower audience segments. The major television networks are losing huge segments of their audience and the major portion of their advertising to the multitude of specially focused cable channels. Newspapers have lost advertising to direct mail, which aims at audiences as narrowly defined as physicians who live in neighborhoods with home prices averaging $800,000. Magazines also have lost advertising to direct mail.

The advertising industry will have to learn whole new ways to target sales pitches to specialized audiences. This learning may not come easily. In the 1990s, some Madison Avenue agencies turned away clients who wanted to shift from network television to direct mail. These agencies, locked into creating network television ads, hadn't developed any expertise at direct mail. To survive in an age of new, narrowly defined mass media, Madison Avenue agencies will need to adapt. Otherwise, they will shrink as new, more flexible agencies take over clients that see financial advantages in new media.

TEACHING OBJECTIVE 9-6
Identify advantages that advertisers will find in the coming media revolution.

RESTRUCTURING MEDIA ECONOMICS

The current financial structure of the mass media may be turned topsy-turvy by the new media. If advertisers go to new media geared to narrower, more defined niches, media outlets that today offer massive heterogeneous audiences will lose their largest source of revenue. *Time* magazine, as an example, could not survive in its present form if advertisers shifted to newsmagazines that offered them narrower slices of the mass market that better fit their products and services. Current mass media units like *Time* would need to restructure themselves. That restructuring could mean more rounds of demassification, shifting the financial base of magazines, newspapers, television and radio from advertisers to consumers, or shutting down.

DEMASSIFY.   Just as magazines have been doing since the dawn of television, mass media could reposition themselves to seek the narrow audience segments that advertisers want to reach. In the case of *Time*, the magazine might narrow its focus to business or the arts or the biosciences. The problem for large-audience media units like *Time* is that narrowly focused publications already have staked out the demassified territory.

A variation on demassification would be splitting existing mass media outlets into numerous demassified entities. *Time*, for example, could have one edition for businesspeople, one for arts people, one for bioscientists, and many others. This already has occurred on a relatively modest scale. The newsmagazines have special editions with bulked-up coverage for certain audience segments like college students, and those editions carry advertising aimed at those audience segments.

TRANSFER COSTS.   A popular mass media unit, like *Time*, could remain in largely its present form by transferring its costs from advertisers to its audience. In effect, *Time* readers would be asked to pick up a greater share of the expense of running the operation. This might mean a $10 cover price, perhaps more, to offset declining advertising revenue.

Some media observers like the idea of media consumers paying all the cost of the media directly because it purifies the media–consumer relationship. Media people then edit their messages for the audience without worrying about whether they might offend advertisers. In some media operations, say these critics, advertisers influence and taint the content.

While $10, perhaps more, for a copy of *Time* may seem like a lot, consumers already are paying the whole costs of producing the magazine, but they do it indirectly. The advertising dollars that *Time* now collects are really the dollars readers pay for the products they buy after seeing advertisements in *Time*. Those dollars end up back at the magazine anyway when advertisers pay for the space their ads occupied. The idea of consumers paying the whole cost of running the mass media directly has attractions in being so straightforward.

SHUT DOWN.   Media operations that don't reposition themselves or find alternate revenue sources when advertisers leave them will not survive. This is what happened to the oversize mass magazines like *Life* in the 1960s and 1970s when their advertisers gravitated to network television. A major shakeout could occur again as more narrowly focused media outlets attract advertisers.

ADVERTISING AND DIGITAL MEDIA

Many media futurists believe today's advertising-dependent media can adapt to the digital future. One of the newspaper mockups that Knight-Ridder's Roger Fidler has put together has ads along the bottom of the screen. By touching the ad, the reader activates screen changes and gains access to more information about the product—in words, images, motion and sound. As Fidler sees it, newspaper ads can be more alive with digital delivery than the present delivery on paper, like a television picture. The reader, in control, can open up more and more screens for more information, delving deeper into information about the advertised product.

If it's an automobile advertisement, the reader could call up an index for competing brands to do a kind of comparison that's not easily done today. Or a reader could delve immediately into independent product reviews. With interactive communication, readers could easily register their interest in a product, perhaps to have a new automobile dropped off for a test drive, by clicking a key or touching a box on the screen. Automatically and instantly, the advertiser is informed about the potential customer. By touching another box, the reader could send the credit card number and address, which had been encrypted into the screens, to order a product immediately.

The new digitized media probably would not charge advertisers by the column inch, as newspapers and magazines do today. Rate structures might instead be based on electronically measured circulation, or on how well ever-changing audience demographics coincide with advertised products, or even on how long readers spend with a particular advertisement. Whatever the new structure, say futurists like Knight-Ridder's Roger Fidler, there is no reason to believe that these future newspapers and magazines will surrender any of their current advertising revenues, which today typically total more than 80 percent of their income.

If Fidler is wrong and the new digital media lose advertisers, the means are available for media consumers themselves to pay all the costs. Today's forerunners of digitized media, database services like America OnLine, CompuServe and Prodigy, charge subscription fees for people who use them. This is equivalent to the subscription price or cover price of today's magazines and newspapers, and it would not be difficult for digital media to have similar subscription fees.

INFORMATION HIGHWAY

STUDY PREVIEW Many experts see everyone being connected by some kind of "information highway," as they call it. The Internet and numerous on-line commercial networks exist today. These are forerunners of what is being called the *information superhighway* of tomorrow. The superhighway could displace today's mass media for delivering information and entertainment to mass audiences.

THE INTERNET

Some historians say the most important contribution of Dwight Eisenhower's presidency in the 1950s was the U.S. interstate highway system. It was a massive project, easily surpassing the scale of such previous human endeavors as the pyramids, the Great Wall of China and the Panama Canal. Like the railroads a century earlier, Eisenhower's interstate highways bound the nation together in new ways and facilitated major economic growth by making commerce less expensive. Today, what is called the *information highway* is being built—an electronic network that connects libraries, corporations, government agencies and individuals.

The information highway had its origins in a 1969 U.S. Defense Department computer network that allowed military contractors and universities doing military research to exchange information. In the 1980s, the National Science Foundation, whose mandate is to promote science, created a network to give researchers access to costly supercomputers at Cornell, Illinois, Pittsburgh and San Diego. The network, comprised of high-capacity telephone lines, microwave relay systems, lasers, fiber optics and satellites, was inexpensive compared to buying more of the $10 million computers.

TEACHING OBJECTIVE 9-7
Define the term *information highway* and explain what role this plays in the new media.

The National Science Foundation network attracted more and more users, many of whom had their own internal networks. For example, most universities that joined the NSF network had intracampus computer networks. The National Science Foundation network became a backbone connecting hundreds of other networks operated by educational institutions, government agencies and research organizations. People at Internet institutions are able to communicate via the Internet from their local network to other local networks. More than 2 million people nationally exchange information with each other. The cost of the backbone network is borne by the National Science Foundation. Member institutions fund the cost of their local networks, including the cost of outsiders who come into their system from outside. It is the whole system that is called the *Internet*.

NERN—The Next Step

The Internet is undergoing significant upgrading. In 1992 President George Bush signed the High-Performance Computing Act into law, authorizing $3 billion to develop and install computers at leading research centers so they can exchange information. This enhanced Internet, called the National Education and Research Network, *NERN* for short, will permit the exchange of more and lengthier material, even full-motion video. What kinds of things can be done via NERN?

- Physicians will be able to send X rays and CAT scans instantly to faraway experts for analysis.
- Students will be able to zip through the entire collection of the Library of Congress and have whole books transmitted back to them.
- Farmers will be able to receive detailed geographic maps from satellite photos to make decisions on planting and harvesting.

Vice President *Al Gore*, who championed the NERN legislation through Congress when he was in the Senate, predicts that the information highway will "revolutionize almost every facet of business and commerce and communication in the United States." Also, he says, it will allow the United States to leapfrog other nations, notably the Germans and Japanese, in developing an information infrastructure.

NERN will use the high-capacity fiber-optic networks that telephone and cable television companies are laying nationwide. Information will move at least 100 times faster than Internet messages.

Commercial On-Line Services

The information highway is more than the Internet, however. Commercial enterprises, including America OnLine, CompuServe, Delphi, GEnie and Prodigy, provide packages of information and entertainment to subscribers for a fee. America OnLine, for example, offers *U.S. News and World Report*, the Associated Press and oodles of games for $8.95 a month. CompuServe and other on-line services have gateways to the National Science Foundation backbone that allows their subscribers to send and receive electronic mail, called *e-mail*, on the NSF network.

Media and Information Highways

The mass media as we know them today may be replaced by the information highway. Many companies are scrambling to position themselves on the ground floor of this developing technology. Telephone companies and cable companies are merging and entering cooperative ventures to build delivery systems to every household and business. These companies and ventures also are seeking other partners to develop packages of information and entertainment for their customers. In effect, these new ventures will be able to do what the mass media today are doing—but instead of a newspaper delivering news, it will come electronically via the information highway. The same will also be true with books, magazines, radio, television, sound recording and perhaps even movies.

Subscribers to commercial on-line services today pay for the long-distance time they use when they are plugged into the service. This may well change if the analogy between the Eisenhower interstate highway system and the new information highway comes into general acceptance over the coming years. Just as the government-financed interstate highway system is available to anyone who wants to travel, the government-financed information highway would be too.

At one time, the Internet tried to keep commercial interests off the network, but those restrictions are softening. The thinking is shifting toward accepting anyone who can contribute to a stronger Internet. This doesn't mean anybody and everybody is welcome. A Hollywood movie studio, for example, would be kept from transmitting feature-length movies to home viewers. The network doesn't have that kind of capacity. But futurists, noting with certainty that technology will increase the information highway's capacity exponentially over the years, believe it is destined to become an open carrier—moving from a toll road to a freeway.

In time, the information highway will not only be a vehicle for mass media companies to send their products to their consumers, but its capacity also will permit consumers to talk back. The information highway will be the backbone of the interactive mass media that will allow on-call services whenever people want them: movies on-call, news on-call, your favorite song on-call. People also will be able to place orders instantly for products they want by return message.

INFORMATION HIGHWAY IMPLICATIONS

It will make possible the national, electronic town meetings that presidential aspirant Ross Perot talked about in the 1992 campaign, with the people being able to register their preferences in ongoing referendums. People will be able to review catalogs delivered by merchants via the information highway.

PUBLIC POLICY AND NEW MEDIA

STUDY PREVIEW   Public policy will need rethinking as the media become truly global and more oriented to narrow audiences. A transition from government to conglomerate and marketplace control is already well under way.

GLOBALIZATION AND CONGLOMERATION

Nations once assumed control over the mass media within their boundaries. Dictators took absolute control. Even in democracies, governments legislated certain controls on the mass media, particularly in broadcasting. The ability of government to control media has always been vulnerable. In Henry VIII's time, Dutch news sheets were still smuggled into England despite his ban. And the U.S.-sponsored propaganda services, including Radio Free Europe, penetrated behind the Soviet Union's Iron Curtain during the Cold War. But today, with transnational communication exploding on many fronts, there is less and less governments can do.

TEACHING OBJECTIVE 9-8
Explore the public policy implications posed by media convergence.

The driving force behind transnational communication today is not so much political as economic. Transnational communication once was mostly for political reasons. Those 16th-century Dutch corantos advanced libertarian ideas that the English monarchy feared. Radio Free Europe encouraged internal revolts and new ways of thinking in Central Europe and the Soviet Union. In contrast, today it is global media conglomerates that are creating the international publishing deals and the satellite linkups that transcend national borders. Their motivations are economic—to amass huge audiences that advertisers want to reach.

With only a few exceptions, like China, governments don't feel threatened by these global media enterprises, and therefore they are less inclined to regulate them closely. By and large, the marketplace is more an influence on what these global media companies disseminate than governments are. People, not governments, are deciding whether to tune in.

SCARCITY ISSUE

In the early days of radio, the major justification for government to regulate broadcasting was scarcity. Because the electromagnetic spectrum didn't have enough room for everybody, somebody had to police the airwaves to ensure that the public interest was served in the best possible way. So Congress, in 1927, created a forerunner to the Federal Communications Commission. At that time, the airwaves had room for roughly 600 stations. Today, thanks to improved technology, 11,000 AM and FM stations are on the air in the United States. In addition to these signals, many FM stations are embedding other programming in their signals for listeners with special decoders. Some FM stations carry as many as nine "subcarriers," as they are called.

While once there was scarcity on the airwaves, today we may be at the point of too many stations. In fact, some cities have many unprofitable stations. Some have entered bankruptcy, something inconceivable back when the scarcity of frequencies limited the number of stations on the air. In those days, an FCC license was called "a license to make money." Today, it can be argued, we have opened more room in the electromagnetic spectrum than we need. Even so, technology marches on, and it is certain that we soon will be able to compress digital signals so that even more stations can be on the air. In fact, technology may bring us to the point where everyone could be transmitting.

Government may still have a role in assigning frequencies and seeing that people don't use other people's frequencies, but the rationale for the government to regulate ownership and over-the-air content would have vaporized. The marketplace—the audience—will be the primary determinant of content.

MEDIA CONSUMER IDENTIFICATION

So people can tap into the new media networks and use these networks to communicate with one another and to call up on-demand media services and also be billed for the services they use, some kind of personal identification will be necessary. It would be something like a telephone number either that government could assign, perhaps at birth like a Social Security number, or that media companies could agree to, like the standard format for credit card numbers that banks have come up with. Whoever does the assigning, these numbers would make everyone reachable through personal media receptors any time, anywhere.

Already, people who subscribe to existing communication networks have *ISDN numbers*, short for "integrated services digital network." The ISDN system could be expanded as more channels of information come into being and more people take advantage of them.

WHOLE NEW MEDIA WORLD

STUDY PREVIEW The mass media are in a technology-driven transformation that will change how we inform and entertain ourselves. Despite the changes ahead, mass communicators will still be preparing mass messages for mass audiences.

MELDING MEDIA

Johannes Gutenberg brought mass production to books, and the other primary print media, magazines and newspapers, followed. People have never had a problem recognizing the differences among books, magazines and newspapers. When sound recording and movies came along, they too were distinctive, and later so were radio and television.

Now get ready for a whole new media world in which the old, familiar distinctions will be disappearing. Technology already is influencing how media organizations deliver messages. Many of the changes so far, like satellite delivery, still rely on traditional reception equipment. People watch HBO, for example, on the same kind of television set they always did. Coming soon, however, are fundamentally new reception mechanisms.

THE MEDIA TABLET

Transport yourself 100 years into the future to, say, North Dakota for a look at how college students will be living their lives differently in a new mass media age:

When Jamal and Suzy, high school classmates in Bismarck, head off to college at the University of North Dakota, 200 miles away, they won't need a mail subscription to the *Bismarck Tribune* to keep up with what's happening at home. Whether they're at the UND home campus in Grand Forks or one of the new national branch campuses, they can check their media tablet to learn the latest Bismarck news. Everybody has one. Any time of the day, Jamal and Suzy can pull out the clipboard-like tablets, tap in a few keypad characters and hear the headlines from the *Tribune* newsroom. Back in 1995, it might have been called on-call radio.

For items they want to know more about, they can hit a key for greater detail, or, if they wish, give an oral command to the tablet. The tablet listens as well as talks. If Jamal is especially interested in the day's big high school football game, he can call up even minor details that never would have made the newspaper or any sportscast back in 1995, such as who the water boy was, how many hot dogs were sold, and who attended. Interviews with everybody involved in the game are available too, on call.

Jamal and Suzy aren't restricted to audio accounts. With the media tablet, they can call up video reports of varying length and detail, including artists' renditions of key plays, player biographies and statistical analysis. It's all available on the tablet's high-resolution, razor-thin color screen.

The media tablet allows Jamal and Suzy to tap into thousands of events reported live all over the world—football, baseball and rugby games; meetings of Congress,

TEACHING OBJECTIVE 9-9
Discuss the future of people in mass media careers in view of technological changes.

Today's Media Tablet. A precursor of tomorrow's personal media tablet is the Newton Messagepad that the Apple Computer Company introduced in 1993. The handheld Newton, which weighs less than a pound, can send a scribbled note, sketch or fax; receive messages; and tap into on-line information services like CompuServe and Prodigy. Although the base Newton model costs less than $1,000, questions remain about whether everyone will be able to afford to participate in the coming new media age.

MEDIA AND YOU

Interactive Media

Hooked on the mass media, we allow them to shape how we put our daily lives together. If the network airs "Home Improvement" at 8 p.m., millions of people make it a point to be there to see it. We choose one car over another because it's equipped with a tape player. We choose a route to work that goes past a newsstand to pick up the morning paper. We haul the radio outside to listen while we wash our cars. Millions of people are sure to be free at noon to hear Paul Harvey on the radio.

Some cracks in this slavery to the mass media have already been introduced through technology. Home VCRs, for example, permit the automatic taping of television programs for later replay. And video rentals free us from the showing times at the local cinema.

New technology will ease even more of our slavery to media schedules and also give us new options to improve our lives. Consider:

- How do you decide today what brand of sneakers you want to buy? How could your personal interactive media, like the media tablet, change how you make your decision?
- To read a best-selling book today, most people go to a bookstore or library, join a book club or borrow the book from a friend. Could there be a more convenient way for you to acquire the book when interactive media are available?
- When you want the latest news in the evening now, you tune to a newscast on television or radio. Then you wait for what you're interested in. How would this change with interactive media?
- Futurists have been talking about the "cashless society" for years. Could interactive media make the cashless society possible?

the British Parliament, the Japanese Diet; scholarly seminars, jury trials, the latest human expedition to Neptune. Latter-day versions of MTV allow them to call up their favorite videos at will: no waiting.

If they remember to do it by 5:55 p.m., Jamal and Suzy can specify what they want at the campus cafeteria for dinner at 6. Besides the evening's menu, the media tablet will give them access to thousands of catalogs from which they can do all their shopping.

If they want a printed account of a news event or a catalog entry or a page from *Macbeth*, Jamal and Suzy can plug their tablets into a toaster-size unit in their dorm rooms or into outlets all over campus. As soon as they enter the right instructions, a paper copy emerges from the unit, much like a sheet from those bulky fax machines back in the 1990s. Depending on what Jamal and Suzy specify, the hard copy on the Bismarck football game can be a single-page word-only account, a hardboard photo-filled memory book all in dazzling color, or any number of variations. Suzy chooses a midsize 16-page account that her uncle narrates. He's a popular artist-reporter for the *Tribune* known for his gaudy graphics and stinging wit. Jamal prefers the stark style of another *Tribune* reporter-artist known for her no-nonsense delivery.

On most reports, Jamal and Suzy can choose from among 20 *Tribune* information packagers, each of whom has a distinctive style. They also can choose reports from the *Tribune*'s competitors. These are companies that once operated Bismarck's radio and television stations, but that, like the *Tribune*, converted long ago to media tablet technology.

The media tablet isn't just for news. Jamal can call up the Mass three Sundays ago at his St. Mary's parish church if he wishes, or the one two weeks ago, or one week ago. Suzy can do the same for her church. She can even hear—or see, if she wishes—any church service in Bismarck as far back as 2001, when services were first video recorded for archival purposes.

Suzy can call her pastor for advice on her homesickness. A minicamera in the tablet picks up her image so Pastor Nelson sees her as she talks. She, of course, can see him too. It's a face-to-face telephone conversation of the sort that television interviewer Ted Koppel pioneered more than 100 years earlier on ABC's "Nightline." Jamal and Suzy can use the media tablet to call anybody anywhere—mom, dad, cousins, old heartthrobs.

The media tablet is essential for studies. It delivers homework assignments for them, including text readings, some supplemented with moving video as well as audio and video lessons. As they study, Jamal and Suzy are tested on their understanding. Their responses are assessed immediately and, depending on their progress, they're channeled into remedial material or advanced to the next lesson.

Through the media tablet, Jamal and Suzy have access to every library in the world. Aristotle, Mark Twain and Ayn Rand, even Tom Clancy and Danielle Steel, can be retrieved instantly anywhere. So can the university's learning packages, which began replacing textbooks in the waning days of the 20th century.

The media tablet is also where Jamal and Suzy do their assignments, which are transmitted to their professors' media tablets and stored until the profs have time to review them. They can communicate directly with their professors through the media tablet, even showing them their work as they discuss it.

Penmanship is a lost art. Bismarck schools abandoned it in 2010, about the time that media tablets added voice activation to supplement the keyboards that were used in earlier versions.

Media tablets, about the size of an 8½ by 11 inch sheet of paper, can be folded over to fit into a shirt pocket when not in use. They can be taken anywhere. They communicate by radio wave with information centers like the *Tribune* in Bismarck. When a user wants a copy on paper, it's necessary to plug the tablet into a unit that stores paper and contains a printing mechanism. The units are everywhere. Otherwise, tablets are self-contained with internal power supplies.

ESSENTIALS THAT WILL REMAIN

Whatever dazzling changes are ahead for the mass media, the essentials will remain the same as today: *mass communicators* preparing *mass messages* for delivery via the process of *mass communication* to *mass audiences*. We cannot anticipate all that new technology will bring, but we can be certain that the human need for information and entertainment, and the need for us to have forums to exchange our views, are undeniable elements of the human condition.

CHAPTER WRAP-UP

The mass media as we know them today are about to meld in a technological convergence in which the technological differences among the media will disappear. This convergence is fueled by accelerated miniaturization of equipment and the ability to compress data into tiny digital bits for storage and transmission. And all the media, whether they traditionally have relied on print, electronic or photographic technology, are involved in the convergence. *USA Today's* Kevin Mania, writing in *Quill* magazine, put it this way: "All the devices people use for communicating and all the kinds of communication have started crashing together into one massive mega-media industry. The result is that telephone lines will soon carry TV shows. Cable TV will carry telephone calls. Desktop computers will be used to watch and edit movies. Cellular phone-computers the size of a notepad will dial into interactive magazines that combine text, sound and video to tell stories."

These changes represent a media revolution because they will affect the fundamental relationship between the media and their audiences. Two-way communication will be possible for the first time, with people being able to extract what they want from the media when they want it. This interactive relationship, as it is called, will enable people to check on a Yankees score, a fire raging down the road or an obscure bill in the state legislature by hitting a few buttons on a remote control, rather than waiting for the morning newspaper or scanning through TV and radio channels hoping to catch a report. Movies, market data and the latest John Grisham novel will be on tap too.

There may be fewer media, but there will be more messages than ever. This means that messages will be going to narrower and narrower segments of the mass audience. This will be a nightmare for advertising people, who will have thousands more channels to choose from in deciding where to place their clients' ads. Advertisers themselves, however, will welcome the ability to zero in on their likeliest potential customers and thereby save dollars they waste today in sending messages to large audiences that include people with scant interest in the product.

At the heart of the melded media are the fiber-optic lines that telephone and cable companies are laying to transmit massive amounts of data. A single strand can carry 50 copies of a medium-size novel in a second—hundreds of times faster than the existing copper cable television lines and thousands of times faster than copper telephone lines. Fiber-optic lines, which have many strands, are the backbone of the coming information highways. Already, 2 million people a day use the Internet information highway, which connects hundreds of computer networks. Coming soon is the NERN network, sometimes called the "information superhighway." The NERN system will link more people with greater capacity than the Internet.

Public policy will need rethinking as the media converge. The old regulatory distinctions between print and broadcast media, which involve fundamental First Amendment issues, will need to be reassessed. There also are global implications because of the virtual impossibility of stopping media signals, particularly those relayed by satellite, at national borders. With the new media, authoritarian governments will find their traditional controls of media content won't work any more.

Whatever changes are ahead, however, the heart of mass communication remains with trained and talented people preparing messages for mass audiences. The work of mass communicators is in gathering, digesting and packaging information, whether it be news, entertainment or persuasion. Newspapers as we know them may disappear, and so may television and books and the other traditional media. But the demand for creating media messages of all kinds will grow as technology enables the mass media to cater to more specific audience segments. For mass communicators, the future is in the content, not the hardware.

QUESTIONS FOR **R**EVIEW

1. What technologies are fueling the mass media revolution?

2. Why are other mass media set to leapfrog television technologically?

3. Why are newspapers well positioned to dominate the news business in the future?

4. Why are magazines probably going to be subsumed by newspapers in the new media age?

5. What are the prospects for radio in the near and distant future?

6. What new opportunities do the new media present advertisers?

7. What will the information highway do?

8. Why is media technology forcing a rethinking of public policy?

9. How will new media forms affect the fundamental structure of media people preparing media messages for dissemination through the mass communication process to mass audiences?

QUESTIONS FOR **C**RITICAL **T**HINKING

1. Will it be possible to condense all human knowledge smaller than the 36-square-foot cube cited by media scholar Wilbur Schramm in his book *The Story of Human Communication*?

2. Why is the television industry hesitant about moving to the pixel-dense screens the computer industry and other media are developing?

3. Why would media scholar George Gilder disagree with the notion that pictures are more important than words—and even the old adage that a picture is worth a thousand words?

4. How can books make the shift from being a print medium to being an electronic medium? Should they?

5. How are digital radio, national radio and interactive radio all risks for people now in the radio business?

6. How will the economics of the mass media be reshaped as technology makes it possible to narrow even more closely to specific audiences?

7. What improvements for the Internet information highway are coming in the years ahead?

8. One traditional justification for government regulation of the broadcast media is being wiped out by emerging marketplace realities. How so?

9. What makes books, magazines, newspapers, sound recordings, movies, radio and television different from one another? What will become of these distinctions in coming years?

FOR **F**URTHER **L**EARNING

George Gilder. *Life after Television: The Coming Transformation of Media and American Life* (Norton, 1992). Gilder is excellent at explaining the contrasting technology of television and the telecomputer. Gilder writes regularly for the *Forbes* magazine supplement *ASAP.*

Joshua Eddings. *How the Internet Works* (Ziff-Davis Press, 1994). An excellent primer.

Roger Fidler. *Mediamorphosis* (forthcoming). Fidler, a technologist for Knight-Ridder newspapers, makes a case that it is newspapers that are positioned to dominate the mass media of the future.

Martha FitzSimons, editor. *Media, Democracy and the Information Highway* (Freedom Forum Media Studies Center, 1993). This conference report on national information policy is an excellent starting point on the major issues involving rapidly changing technology.

John R. Levine and Carol Naroudi. *The Internet for Dummies* (IDG Books, 1993). This how-to for beginning Internet users is loaded with information on the backbone of the emerging information highway.

Robert Lucky. *Silicon Dreams* (St. Martin's, 1989). Lucky argues that words are more important in mass communication than images. This is fortunate, he notes, because more words can be stored digitally than photographs.

Kevin Maney. "Will the Techno Tsunami Wash Us Out?" *Quill* 82 (March 1994):2, 16–18. Maney, a newspaper reporter, discusses career implications of media convergence on the careers of media people. This issue of *Quill* has additional articles on the subject.

John V. Pavlik and Everette E. Dennis, editors. *Demystifying Media Technology* (Mayfield, 1993).

Jack Lyle and Douglas B. McLeod. *Communication, Media and Change* (Mayfield, 1993).

Wilbur Schramm. *The Story of Human Communication* (Harper & Row, 1988). In this work, which capped his distinguished career of scholarship, Schramm covers the whole sweep of communication history, with peeks at where it is headed.

CNN video case study

THE CORPORATE SCRAMBLE TO GET ON THE INFORMATION SUPERHIGHWAY

The interconnected, digital, multimedia world of tomorrow, comprehensively wired, is coming too fast for anyone to figure out. The components are plain enough—the conventional technologies of the telephone, the television and the computer—but, to quote *The Economist*, they "are being whirled into an extraordinary whole." Millions of dollars are to be made by whoever figures out how to marshal these three traditionally distinct enterprises. At this point, no single company has all the assets to bring it together. Because nobody wants to be left out, the corporate jockeying for a stake in the fuzzy, multimedia future makes high drama. The unanswered question, which heightens the drama, is whether people will be willing to fork out the money to tap into new multimedia services.

The costs are astronomical, as some players have learned. The Knight-Ridder newspaper chain lost its shirt on an on-line information service it established in the 1980s. The public wasn't ready, and Knight-Ridder, at least a decade ahead of its time, aborted the enterprise. There have been dozens of corporate casualties.

The multimedia future is hard to chart because the major components—the telephone, television and computer industries—have grown up separately. In fact, the U.S. government has kept many of them apart. Until recently, telephone companies were barred from being more than carriers of other people's messages. Cable companies were barred from adding two-way communication to their systems. Government restrictions made it uneconomical for television networks to produce series that could be recycled through syndication.

While restrictions are being eased, federal regulators remain a major player in shaping the multimedia future. In 1994, for example, the giant TCI cable company and the Bell Atlantic telephone company proposed the biggest merger in history to capitalize on each other's assets and become a multimedia leader. The companies cancelled the marriage when the Federal Communications Commission changed cable company rules in a way that was expected to depress TCI's earnings for a while. The economics of going into the uncharted multimedia future are so dicey that even a temporary interruption of a company's cash flow can derail a deal.

While the government has funded the Internet backbone for multimedia communication, private companies are putting together their own networks. All the systems are designed to connect and interlace, which adds to the complexity of the whole. Many companies have bits of tomorrow's mass media, but nobody has enough pieces to go it alone.

The vision for tomorrow's media is built on digital technology, which converts words and pictures into digital form for transmission by wire. Movies, books, news, games and information, and entertainment of all sorts can be so compressed that home viewers will be able to tap 500 channels. The fiber-optic cables that will permit such volumes of material can also accommodate two-way communication—putting music and movies and news on call, permitting people to order merchandise from their screens, play on-screen games with people all over the word, tap into long-distance learning and provide immediate feedback to the originators of programming.

But will people pay for multimedia services? Cable television now costs about $20 to $30 a month, a newspaper about $15 a month and an occasional rental video about $3.50 each. Basic interactive services are expected to be approximately $80 or $90 a month. Companies that have moved too aggressively into the multimedia future, like Knight-Ridder, got stung.

These are the essential components of the coming interconnected media world:

CONTENT. Book publishers, movie studios, independent television production companies, newspapers and electronic game companies have tremendous amounts of material to feed people, but they don't have the means of delivery. Disney, for example, is a mill for producing popular programming, but it relies on other companies, like local cable systems and movie distributors and exhibitors, to deliver the product. Disney's stake in interactive delivery is modest.

DELIVERY. Telephone companies have wired the nation and already are carriers for on-line services that are the heart of our future media, but telephone companies are mere carriers of other people's messages. AT&T, for example, doesn't produce informational and educational material to deliver on its system.

AUDIENCE. Most people today use the traditional mass media: television, newspapers and books. The companies that own these media outlets have found ways to assemble huge audiences, but their means of delivery hardly dovetail with the potential of multimedia delivery. The New York *Times*, for example, still distributes many of its newspapers door to door by carrier. The ABC, CBS and NBC television networks use the airwaves, which don't fit into the wired, digital future. Nor do book, video and record shops.

Because no company is positioned to pull the opportunities of the interconnected future together, there is a mad scramble for joint ventures in which companies find synergies that build on each other's strengths. The trade journal *Digital Media* took a tally of multimedia joint ventures and alliances in 1993 and found a dizzying 348. The number is growing exponentially. Meanwhile, companies are struggling to strengthen their own assets to bring more to the table in talks with possible suitors and partners. The players include not only the traditional media companies but also computer makers and telephone companies. Here is a sampler of major players:

TIME WARNER. Time Warner, the result of a merger of Time-Life and Warner Brothers, has powerful programming assets in its magazine, book, movie, HBO and record enterprises. The company owns cable television systems, which are being upgraded with fiber-optic cable that will allow massive amounts of information to be delivered to individuals and which will also allow interactive, two-way communication. A frustration for Time Warner is that its cable systems, local and scattered, are far from being a comprehensive distribution network for the company's diverse, competitive content.

TCI. Tele-Communications Inc., the largest U.S. cable company with 10 million subscribers, has Time Warner's problem of owning many cable systems that don't constitute a comprehensive whole. TCI has moved into programming with Liberty Media, which is positioned to provide substantial content, and the company has a big stake in CNN. These are all parts of the puzzle but don't complete the picture.

DISNEY. Disney solidified its role as a powerhouse in entertainment programming when it bought the Miramax studio in 1993, but it has no entrée into interactive delivery. Disney has been eyeing NBC and CBS, which were unofficially for sale. While both networks have huge audiences, neither is positioned strongly for interactive delivery.

VIACOM. Viacom, a television program producer, bought Paramount Communications and its Simon & Schuster subsidiary in 1993 and instantly became a mega-producer of content. Now the company needs partners to help reach audiences in the new interactive way. One joint venture with America On-Line, called College On-Line, gives college students, professors and textbook authors a forum for on-line discussion that, Viacom hopes, will spur S&S textbook sales.

MANY MASS
MEDIA PRACTICES
ORIGINATED
DURING MAJOR
PERIODS IN
AMERICAN HISTORY

JOURNALISTS RELY LARGELY
ON INDIVIDUAL JUDGMENT
IN DECIDING WHAT TO REPORT

MANY VARIABLES BEYOND A
JOURNALIST'S CONTROL AFFECT
WHAT ENDS UP BEING REPORTED

JOURNALISTS BRING MANY
PERSONAL, SOCIAL AND POLITICAL
VALUES TO THEIR WORK

STUDIES HAVE FOUND THAT
JOURNALISTS IDENTIFY
THEMSELVES AS MIDDLE OF THE
ROAD POLITICALLY

NEWS IS CONCERNED WITH
CHANGE, WHICH GIVES CURRENCY
TO THE CHARGE THAT NEWS HAS A
LIBERAL SLANT

FACTORS OUTSIDE THE
NEWSROOM INFLUENCE HOW
NEWS IS REPORTED

GATEKEEPING IS BOTH
ESSENTIAL AND HAZARDOUS
IN THE NEWS PROCESS

NEWS ORGANIZATIONS
RELY HEAVILY ON
COMMON SOURCES,
LIKE NEWS
SERVICES AND
SYNDICATES

chapter 10

JOURNALISM
GATHERING AND
TELLING NEWS

The top Marine general in the Persian Gulf, Walter Boomer, invited six reporters to his forward command post to report the ground war to reclaim Kuwait first hand. This was in the hectic final, climactic days of the war, and many editors wanted their reporters elsewhere. Only Molly Moore of the Washington *Post* took up Boomer's offer. Moore, it turned out, was going to have an exclusive picture window on the war. In fact, over the next few days, Molly Moore would be the only reporter in the Persian Gulf war to accompany a senior commander leading his troops to battle.

How does a journalist prepare for war? Molly Moore was in a Dhahran hotel when Boomer, a three-star general, issued his invitation. Here's what she did: "I tossed the rucksack on the bed and wedged in extra notebooks and pens in one pocket, my miniature tape recorder and extra batteries in another. A handful of granola bars, Snicker's candy bars, and tea bags fit in another empty pouch. I wrapped a few extra pairs of underwear and socks and a spare turtleneck sweater inside a plastic zip-lock freezer bag and stuffed them in a small canvas duffel bag. I'd learned the plastic-bag trick from the troops who used them to protect clothes from sand and water. I packed only the most necessary toiletries in another plastic freezer bag, and crammed a wool ski sweater into the last remaining inches of space."

Before continuing, she called her parents and her fiancé. "After the calls, I pulled on a clean pair of khaki pants, a black turtleneck sweater, two pairs of socks, and a pair of L.L. Bean fleece-lined hiking boots. I tied a gray bandanna around my neck, slipped into the oversized green military parka, and plopped the tan desert bush hat over my hair. I shoved a small automatic Olympus camera and six rolls of film into the canvas case that held my laptop computer. I hefted the rucksack on my shoulder and grabbed the computer case and duffel bag."

A Woman at War. The Washington *Post's* senior military correspondent, Molly Moore, was driven by the most significant journalistic imperative, curiosity, when she chose a frontline combat vantage to report the Persian Gulf war. Moore was the only reporter to see the war from inside a Marine general's command post and to go with the general everywhere he did in the combat zone. Moore now is the *Post's* bureau chief in New Delhi.

Molly Moore was off to cover frontline combat.

Her preparation actually had begun years earlier. Her high school journalism teacher had encouraged her into a $1.60 an hour part-time job writing obits for her hometown newspaper, The Lake Charles, Louisiana, *American Press*. It didn't take long for her to get a nickel an hour raise and a promotion to the weekend police beat. She chose Georgetown University for college and went home summers to cover the Louisiana Legislature. Her senior year, she landed a low-level newsroom side job at the Washington *Post*. That plus her Lake Charles experience led to a job on graduation at the New Orleans *Times-Picayune*. Three years later the *Post* took her on to cover suburban schools and later suburban politics. Her big career break came in 1986 when she applied for a vacancy at the Pentagon, and she became the *Post's* first woman military correspondent. It was only natural that she would be back and forth to the Persian Gulf as the United States amassed troops for the war to reclaim Kuwait from Iraq.

In the final days of the war, Moore witnessed the largest armored assault since World War II—a 100-hour allied ground attack in which tens of thousands of Iraqi troops surrendered and Kuwait was retaken, all with hardly any U.S. or allied casualties. She dodged through minefields in the general's truck, tasted the acrid smoke from burning oil wells, and wondered all the while whether desperate Iraqis would try nerve gas and whether her mask and antidotes would work.

She covered every aspect—the headquarters planning, the drama in the field, the human dimension. And as is often the case in reporting a confused, breaking military situation, with censors calling many of the shots and with telephone and radio communication failing for all kinds of reasons, few of Moore's stories got back to the *Post*. Those that made it through to her editors added an important dimension to the war coverage, and some led to questions of Washington officials about the accuracy at headquarters. She witnessed the confusion and disarray attendant to anything as complex as a major military operation. She saw the drama, the tension, the exhilaration.

When the war was over, General Boomer waved goodbye to Moore as an aide drove her to a hotel in Jabail. "You were a great trooper," he said.

Moore's reporting had the qualities that make up good journalism—an honest, energetic quest for information and truth whatever the circumstances and difficulties, and a commitment to telling those truths accurately, fully and interestingly. In this chapter, you will read about the values journalists bring to their work, about the historic roots of those values, and about how journalists succeed at their work and, also, sometimes fail.

NEWS MEDIA TRADITIONS

STUDY PREVIEW United States journalism has evolved through four distinctive eras—the colonial, partisan, penny and yellow press periods. Each of these periods made distinctive contributions to contemporary news media practices.

COLONIAL PERIOD

Benjamin Harris published the first colonial newspaper, *Publick Occurrences*, in Boston in 1690. He was in hot water right away. Harris scandalized Puritan sensitivities, alleging that the king of France had dallied with his son's wife. In the colonies just as in England, a newspaper needed royal consent. The governor had not consented, and Harris was put out of business after one issue.

Even so, Harris's daring was a precursor for emerging press defiance against authority. In 1733 *John Peter Zenger* started a paper in New York in competition with the existing Crown-supported newspaper. Zenger's New York *Journal* was backed by merchants and lawyers who disliked the royal governor. From the beginning the newspaper antagonized the governor with items challenging his competence, and finally the governor arrested Zenger. The trial made history. Zenger's attorney, *Andrew Hamilton*, argued that there should be no punishment for printing articles that are true. The argument was a dramatic departure from the legal practice of the day, which allowed royal governors to prosecute for articles that might undermine their authority, regardless of whether the articles were true. Hamilton's argument prevailed, and Zenger, who had become a hero for standing up to the Crown, was freed. To the governor's chagrin, there was great public celebration in the streets of New York that night.

Zenger's success against the Crown foreshadowed the explosive colonial reaction after Parliament passed a stamp tax in 1765. The colonies did not have elected representatives in Parliament, so the cry was a defiant "No taxation without representation." The campaign, however, was less ideological than economic. Colonial printers, who stood to lose from the new tax, which was levied on printed materials, led the campaign. Historian *Arthur Schlesinger* has called it the *newspaper war on Britain*. The newspapers won: the tax was withdrawn. Having seen their potential to force the government's hand, newspapers then led the way in stirring other ill feelings against England and precipitating the American Revolution.

These traditions from the colonial period remain today:

- The news media, both print and broadcast, relish their independence from government censorship and control.
- The news media, especially newspapers and magazines, actively try to mold government policy and mobilize public sentiment. Today this is done primarily on the editorial page.

TEACHING OBJECTIVE 10-1
Many news practices rooted in colonial, partisan, penny and yellow press periods.

LECTURE RESOURCE 10-A
Slides: *People in Journalism.*

KEY PERSON
Ben Harris started first colonial newspaper.

KEY PERSON
John Peter Zenger defied authorities with his newspaper.

LECTURE RESOURCE 10-B
Film: *Mightier Than the Sword: Zenger and Freedom of the Press.*

KEY PERSON
Andrew Hamilton urged truth as defense for libel.

LECTURE RESOURCE 10-C
Slides: *Newspapers and the Revolution.*

KEY PERSON
Arthur Schlesinger argued newspapers fueled revolution against Britain.

When Words Failed, 1798-Style. The partisanship during the crude partisan period peaked in 1798 when Roger Griswold impugned the war record of fellow congressman Matthew Lyons. Lyons spat in Griswold's eye. The next day, on the floor of the U.S. House of Representatives, Griswold went after Lyons with his cane, and Lyons beat him back with a handy set of fire tongs. This political cartoon, one of the first, captured the hand-to-hand combat. Later, after Lyons mildly insulted President Adams in print, the Federalists put him in jail.

- Journalists are committed to seeking truth, which was articulated as a social value in Zenger's "truth defense."
- The public comes down in favor of independent news media when government becomes too heavy-handed, as demonstrated by Zenger's popularity.
- In a capitalistic system, the news media are economic entities that sometimes react in their own self-interest when their profit-making ability is threatened.

PARTISAN PERIOD

After the Revolution, newspapers divided along partisan lines. What is called the Federalist period in American history is also referred to as the *partisan period* among newspaper historians. Intense partisanship characterized newspapers of the period, which spanned roughly 50 years to the 1830s.

Initially the issue was over a constitution. Should the nation have a strong central government or remain a loose coalition of states? James Madison, Alexander Hamilton, Thomas Jefferson, John Jay and other leading thinkers exchanged ideas with articles and essays in newspapers. The *Federalist Papers*, a series of essays printed and reprinted in newspapers throughout the nation, were part of the debate. Typical of the extreme partisanship of the era were journalists who reveled in nasty barbs and rhetorical excesses. It was not unusual for an ideological opponent to be called "a spaniel" or "a traitor."

After the Constitution was drafted, partisanship intensified, finally culminating lopsidedly when the Federalist party both controlled the Congress and had their leader, John Adams, in the presidency. In firm control and bent on silencing their detractors, the Federalists ramrodded a series of laws through Congress in 1798. One of the things these laws, the *Alien and Sedition Acts*, prohibited was "false, scandalous, malicious" statements about government. Using these laws, the Federalists made 25 indictments, which culminated in 10 convictions. Among those indicted was *David Bowen*, a Revolutionary War veteran who felt strongly about free expression. He put up a sign in Dedham, Massachusetts, that said: "No stamp tax. No sedition. No alien bills. No land tax. Downfall to tyrants of America. Peace and retirement to the president [the Federalist John Adams]. Long live the vice president [the Anti-Federalist Thomas Jefferson] and the minority [the Anti-Federalists]. May moral virtues be the basis of civil government." If only critics of recent presidents were so mild! But the Federalists were not of a tolerant mind. Bowen was fined $400 and sentenced to 18 months in prison.

Federalist excesses were at their most extreme when *Matthew Lyon*, a member of Congress, was jailed for a letter to a newspaper editor that accused President Adams of "ridiculous pomp, foolish adulation, selfish avarice." Lyon, an anti-Federalist, was sentenced to four months in jail and fined $1,000. Although he was tried in Rutland, Vermont, he was sent to a filthy jail 40 miles away. When editor Anthony Haswell printed an advertisement to raise money for Lyon's fine, he was jailed for abetting a criminal. The public was outraged at Federalist heavy-handedness. The $1,000 was quickly raised, and Lyon, while still in prison, was re-elected by a two-to-one margin. After his release from prison, Lyon's supporters followed his carriage for 12 miles as he began his way back to Philadelphia, the national capital. Public outrage showed itself in the election of 1800. Jefferson was elected president, and the Federalists were thumped out of office, never to rise again. The people had spoken.

Here are traditions from the partisan period that continue today:

- Government should keep its hands off the press. The First Amendment to the Constitution, which set a tone for this period, declared that "Congress shall make no law . . . abridging freedom . . . of the press."
- The news media are a forum for discussion and debate, as newspapers were in the *Federalist Papers* dialogue on what form the Constitution should take.
- The news media should comment vigorously on public issues.
- Government transgressions against the news media will ultimately be met by public rejection of those committing the excesses, which has happened periodically throughout American history.

PENNY PERIOD

In 1833, when he was 22, the enterprising *Benjamin Day* started a newspaper that changed American journalism: the New York *Sun*. At a penny a copy, the *Sun* was within reach of just about everybody. Other papers were expensive, an annual subscription costing as much as a full week's wages. Unlike other papers, distributed mostly by mail, the *Sun* was hawked every day on the streets. The *Sun*'s content was different too. It avoided the political and economic thrust of the traditional papers, concentrating instead on items of interest to common folk. The writing was simple, straightforward and easy to follow. For a motto for the *Sun*, Day came up with "It Shines for All," his pun fully intended.

Day's *Sun* was an immediate success. Naturally, it was quickly imitated, and the *penny press period* began. Partisan papers that characterized the partisan period continued, but the mainstream of American newspapers came to be in the mold of the *Sun*.

Merchants saw the unprecedented circulation of the penny papers as a way to reach great numbers of potential customers. Advertising revenue meant bigger papers, which attracted more readers, which attracted more advertisers. A snowballing momentum began that continues today with more and more advertising being carried by the mass media. A significant result was a shift in newspaper revenues from subscriptions to advertisers. Day, as a matter of fact, did not meet expenses by selling the *Sun* for a penny a copy. He counted on advertisers to pick up a good part of his production cost. In effect, advertisers subsidized readers, just as they do today.

Several social and economic factors, all resulting from the Industrial Revolution, made the penny press possible:

- **Industrialization.**   With new steam-powered presses, hundreds of copies an hour could be printed. Earlier presses were hand operated.
- **Urbanization.**   Workers flocked to the cities to work in new factories, creating a great pool of potential newspaper readers within delivery range. Until the urbanization of the 1820s and 1830s, the U.S. population had been almost wholly agricultural and scattered across the countryside. Even the most populous cities had been relatively small.
- **Immigration.**   Waves of immigrants arrived from impoverished parts of Europe. Most were eager to learn English and found that penny papers, with their simple style, were good tutors.
- **Literacy.**   As immigrants learned English, they hungered for reading material within their economic means. Also, literacy in general was increasing, which contributed to the rise of mass circulation newspapers and magazines.

Penny Press Period. When Benjamin Day launched the New York *Sun* in 1833 and sold it for one cent a copy, he ushered in an era of cheap newspapers that common people could afford. The penny press period also was marked by newspapers with stories of broad appeal, as opposed to the political and financial papers of the preceding party period.

A leading penny press editor was *James Gordon Bennett*, who, in the 1830s, organized the first newsroom and reporting staff. Earlier newspapers had been either sidelines of printers, who put whatever was handy into their papers, or projects of ideologues, whose writing was in an essay vein. Bennett hired reporters and sent them out on rounds to gather information for readers of his New York *Herald*.

Horace Greeley developed editorials as a distinctive journalistic form in his New York *Tribune*, which he founded in 1841. More than his competitors, Greeley used his newspaper to fight social ills that accompanied industrialization. Greeley's *Tribune* was a voice against poverty and slums, an advocate of labor unions, and an opponent of slavery. It was a lively forum for discussions of ideas. Karl Marx, the communist philosopher, was a *Tribune* columnist for a while. So was Albert Brisbane, who advocated collective living. Firm in Greeley's concept of a newspaper was that it should be used for social good. He saw the *Tribune* as a voice for those who did not have a voice; a defender for those unable to articulate a defense; and a champion for the underdog, the deprived and the underprivileged.

In 1844, late in the penny press period, *Samuel Morse* invented the telegraph. Within months, the nation was being wired. When the Civil War came in 1861, correspondents used the telegraph to get battle news to eager readers. It was called *lightning news*, delivered electrically and instantly. The Civil War also gave rise to a new convention in writing news, the *inverted pyramid*. Editors instructed their war correspondents to tell the most important information first in case telegraph lines failed—or were snipped by the enemy—as a story was being transmitted. That way, when a story was interrupted, editors would have at least a few usable sentences. The inverted pyramid, it turned out, was popular with readers because it allowed them to learn what was most important at a glance. They did not have to wade through a whole story if they were in a hurry. Also, the inverted pyramid helped editors fit stories into the limited confines of a page—a story could be cut off at any paragraph and the most important parts remained intact. The inverted pyramid remains a standard expository form for telling event-based stories in newspapers, radio and television.

Several New York newspaper publishers, concerned about the escalating expense of sending reporters to gather far-away news, got together in 1848 to share stories. By together sending one reporter, the newspapers cut costs dramatically. They called their cooperative venture the *Associated Press*, a predecessor of today's giant global news service. The AP introduced a new tone in news reporting. So that AP stories could be used by member newspapers of different political persuasions, reporters were told to write from a nonpartisan point of view. The result was a fact-oriented kind of news writing often called *objective reporting*. It was widely imitated and still is the dominant reporting style for event-based news stories in all the news media.

There are traditions of today's news media, both print and electronic, that can be traced to the penny press period:

- Inverted pyramid story structures.
- Coverage and writing that appeals to a general audience, sometimes by trying to be entertaining or even sensationalistic. It's worth noting that the egalitarian thinking of Andrew Jackson's 1829–1837 presidency, which placed special value on the "common man," coincided with the start of the penny press and its appeal to a large audience of "everyday people."

- A strong orientation to covering events, including the aggressive ferreting out of news.
- A commitment to social improvement, which included a willingness to crusade against corruption.
- Being on top of unfolding events and providing information to readers quickly, something made possible by the telegraph but that also came to be valued in local reporting.
- A detached, neutral perspective in reporting events, a tradition fostered by the Associated Press.

YELLOW PERIOD

The quest to sell more copies led to excesses that are illustrated by the Pulitzer-Hearst circulation war in New York in the 1890s.

Joseph Pulitzer, a poor immigrant, made the St. Louis *Post-Dispatch* into a financial success. In 1883, Pulitzer decided to try a bigger city. He bought the New York *World* and applied his St. Louis formula. He emphasized human interest, crusaded for worthy causes, and ran lots of promotional hoopla. Pulitzer's *World* also featured solid journalism. His star reporter, *Nellie Bly,* epitomized the two faces of the Pulitzer formula for journalistic success. For one story, Bly feigned mental illness, entered an insane asylum and emerged with scandalous tales about how patients were treated. It was enterprising journalism of great significance. Reforms resulted. Later, showing the less serious, show biz side of Pulitzer's formula, Nellie Bly was sent out to circle the globe in 80 days, like the fictitious Phineas Fogg. Her journalism stunt took 72 days.

In San Francisco, Pulitzer had a young admirer, *William Randolph Hearst.* With his father's Nevada mining fortune and mimicking Pulitzer's New York formula, Hearst made the San Francisco *Examiner* a great success. In 1895 Hearst decided

Yellow Journalism's Namesake. The Yellow Kid, a popular cartoon character in New York newspapers, became the namesake for the sensationalist "yellow journalism" of the 1880s and 1890s. Many newspapers of the period, especially in New York, hyperbolized and fabricated the news to attract readers. The tradition remains in isolated areas of modern journalism, such as the supermarket tabloids and trash documentary programs on television.

Stunt Journalism. When newspaper owner Joseph Pulitzer sent reporter Nellie Bly on an around-the-world trip in 1890 to try to outdo the fictional Phineas Fogg's 80-day trip, stunt journalism was approaching its peak. Her feat took 72 days.

to go to New York and take on the master. He bought the New York *Journal* and vowed to "out-Pulitzer" Pulitzer. The inevitable resulted. To outdo each other, Pulitzer and Hearst launched crazier and crazier stunts. Not even the comic pages escaped the competitive frenzy. Pulitzer ran the *Yellow Kid*, and then Hearst hired the cartoonist away. Pulitzer hired a new one, and both papers ran the yellow character and plastered the city with yellow promotional posters. The circulation war was nicknamed *yellow journalism*, and the term came to be a derisive reference to sensational excesses in news coverage.

The yellow excesses reached a feverish peak as Hearst and Pulitzer covered the growing tensions between Spain and the United States. Fueled by hyped atrocity stories, the tension eventually exploded in war. One story, perhaps apocryphal, epitomizes the no-holds-barred competition between Pulitzer and Hearst. Although Spain had consented to all demands by the United States, Hearst sent the artist Frederic Remington to Cuba to cover the situation. Remington cabled back: "Everything is quiet. There is no trouble here. There will be no war. Wish to return." Hearst replied: "Please remain. You furnish the pictures. I'll furnish the war."

Yellow journalism had its imitators in New York and elsewhere. It is important to note, however, that not all American journalism went the yellow route. *Adolph Ochs* bought the New York *Times* in 1896 and built it into a newspaper that avoided sideshows to report and comment seriously on important issues and events. The *Times*, still true to that approach, outlived the Pulitzer and Hearst newspapers in New York and today is considered among the best newspapers in the world.

KEY PERSON
Adolph Ochs kept *New York Times* on serious course.

Joseph Pulitzer

William Randolph Hearst

Journalistic Sensationalism. Rival New York newspaper publishers Joseph Pulitzer and William Randolph Hearst tried to outdo each other daily with anti-Spanish atrocity stories from Cuba, many of them trumped up. Some historians say the public hysteria fueled by Pulitzer and Hearst helped precipitate the Spanish-American War, especially after the U.S. battleship *Maine* exploded in Havana harbor. Both Pulitzer and Hearst claimed it was a Spanish attack on an American vessel, although a case can be made that the explosion was accidental.

LECTURE RESOURCE 10-D
Film: *Stop, Thief!*

LECTURE RESOURCE 10-E
Film: *The Tiger's Tail.*

The yellow tradition, however, still lives. The New York *Daily News*, founded in 1919 and almost an immediate hit, ushered in a period that some historians characterize as *jazz journalism*. It was just Hearst and Pulitzer updated in tabloid form with an emphasis on photography. Today, newspapers like the commercially successful *National Enquirer* are in the yellow tradition. So are a handful of metropolitan dailies, including Rupert Murdoch's San Antonio, Texas, *Express-News*. It is obvious too in tabloid television programs like "Hard Copy" and "A Current Affair" and interview programs like Donahue, Oprah and Geraldo, which pander to the offbeat and the sensational.

While not as important in forming distinctive journalistic traditions as the earlier penny papers, yellow newspapers were significant in contributing to the growing feeling of nationhood in the United States, especially among the diverse immigrants arriving in massive numbers. Journalism historian Larry Lorenz put it this way: "The publishers reached out to the widest possible audience by trying to find a common denominator, and that turned out to be the human interest story. Similarities among groups were emphasized rather than differences. Readers, in their quest to be real Americans, seized on those common elements to pattern themselves after, and soon their distinctive characteristics and awareness of themselves as special groups began to fade."

PERSONAL VALUES IN NEWS

STUDY PREVIEW Journalists make important decisions on which events, phenomena and issues are reported and which are not. The personal values journalists bring to their work and that therefore determine which stories are told, and also how they are told, generally coincide with mainstream American values.

ROLE OF THE JOURNALIST

After years of wrestling to come up with a definition for *news*, NBC newscaster Chet Huntley threw up his hands and declared: "News is what I decide is news." Huntley was not being arrogant. Rather, he was pointing out that events that go unreported aren't news. Regardless of an event's intrinsic qualities, such as the prominence of the people involved and the event's consequence and drama, it becomes news only when it's reported. Huntley's point was that the journalist's judgment is indispensable in deciding what's news.

Huntley's conclusion underscores the high degree of autonomy that individual journalists have in shaping what is reported. Even a reporter hired fresh out of college by a small daily newspaper and assigned to city hall has a great deal of independence in deciding what to report and how to report it. Such trust is unheard of in most other fields, which dole out responsibility to newcomers in small bits over a lengthy period. Of course, rookie journalists are monitored by their newsroom superiors, and editors give them assignments and review their stories, but it is that city hall reporter, no matter how green, who is the news organization's expert on city government.

The First Amendment guarantee of a free press also contributes to the independence and autonomy that characterize news work. Journalists know they have a high level of constitutional protection in deciding what to report as news. While

TEACHING OBJECTIVE 10-2
Journalists' personal values affect what is reporting.

Peter Arnett in Baghdad. CNN's Peter Arnett provided exclusive coverage from Baghdad during the 1991 Persian Gulf war. The coverage troubled many Americans and some journalists who, in their ethnocentrism, saw Arnett as being used by the enemy. While the Iraqis controlled much of Arnett's access to information, he wrote his own dispatches. He consistently reminded viewers of the conditions under which he was gathering information, including that Iraqi officials were his primary source.

Mainstream Values. Although the most powerful news media in the nation are located in New York, Washington, D.C., and other urban, cosmopolitan areas, studies by sociologist Herbert Gans have found that journalists for these organizations bring mainstream values to their work. Among these values is a fascination with rural life and small-town pastoralism. CBS correspondent Charles Kuralt built a following by criss-crossing the country for stories about common people doing interesting things, mostly in small-town and rural settings.

most reporters will agree on the newsworthiness of some events and issues, such as a catastrophic storm or a tax proposal, their judgments will result in stories that take different slants and angles. On events and issues whose newsworthiness is less obvious, reporters will differ even on whether to do a story.

JOURNALISTS' PERSONAL VALUES

The journalistic ideal, an unbiased seeking of truth and an unvarnished telling of it, dictates that the work be done without partisanship. Yet as human beings, journalists have personal values that influence all that they do, including their work. Because the news judgment decisions that journalists make are so important to an informed citizenry, we need to know what makes these people tick. Are they left-wingers? Are they ideological zealots? Are they quirky and unpredictable? Are they conscientious?

A sociologist who studied stories in the American news media for 20 years, *Herbert Gans*, concluded that journalists have a typical American value system. Gans identified primary values, all in the American mainstream, that journalists use in making their news judgments:

KEY PERSON
Herbert Gans examined sociology of journalism.

ETHNOCENTRISM.   American journalists see things through American eyes, which colors news coverage. In the 1960s and 1970s, Gans notes, North Vietnam was consistently characterized as "the enemy." American reporters took the view of the American government and military, which was hardly detached or neutral. This ethnocentricity was clear at the end of the war, which American media headlined as "the *fall* of South Vietnam." By other values, Gans said, the Communist takeover of Saigon could be considered a *liberation*. In neutral terms, it was a *change in government*.

This ethnocentrism creates problems as the news media become global. During the Persian Gulf war in 1991, CNN discovered that the commonly used word "foreign," which to American audiences meant anything non-American, was confusing to

CNN audiences in other countries. Eager to build a global audience, CNN boss Ted Turner banned the word "foreign" and told anchors and scriptwriters that they would be fired for uttering the word. "International" became the substitute word, as awkward as it sometimes sounded to American ears. The semantic change was cosmetic, however, for the CNN war coverage continued, inevitably, to be largely from the American perspective, just as Gans found in his earlier studies. It is hard for all people, including journalists, to transcend their own skins.

COMMITMENT TO DEMOCRACY AND CAPITALISM.

Gans found that American journalists favor democracy of the American style. Coverage of other governmental forms dwells on corruption, conflict, protest and bureaucratic malfunction. The unstated idea of most U.S. journalists, said Gans, is that other societies do best when they follow the American ideal of serving the public interest.

Gans also found that American journalists are committed to the capitalist economic system. When they report corruption and misbehavior in American business, journalists treat them as aberrations. The underlying posture of the news coverage of the U.S. economy, Gans said, is "an optimistic faith" that businesspeople refrain from unreasonable profits and gross exploitation of workers or customers while competing to create increased prosperity for all. In covering controlled foreign economies, American journalists emphasize the downside.

It may seem only natural to most Americans that democracy and capitalism should be core values of any reasonable human being. This sense itself is an ethnocentric value, which many people do not even think about but which nonetheless shapes how they conduct their lives. Knowing that American journalists by and large share this value explains a lot about the news coverage they create.

SMALL-TOWN PASTORALISM.

Like most of their fellow citizens, American journalists romanticize about rural life. Given similar stories from metropolitan Portland and tiny Sweet Home, Oregon, editors usually opt for the small town.

Cities are covered as places with problems; rural life is celebrated. Suburbs are largely ignored. This small-town pastoralism, said Gans, helps explain the success of Charles Kuralt's long-running "On the Road" series on CBS television.

INDIVIDUALISM TEMPERED BY MODERATION.

Gans found that American journalists love stories about rugged individuals who overcome adversity and defeat powerful forces. This is a value that contributes to a negative coverage of technology as something to be feared because it can stifle individuality. Gans again cited "On the Road," noting how Charles Kuralt found a following for his pastoral features on rugged individuals.

Journalists like to turn ordinary individuals into heroes, but there are limits. Rebels and deviates are panned as extremists who go beyond another value—moderation. To illustrate this propensity toward moderation, Gans noted that "the news treats atheists as extremists and uses the same approach, if more gingerly, with religious fanatics. People who consume conspicuously are criticized, but so are people such as hippies who turn their backs on consumer goods. The news is scornful both of the overly academic scholar and the over simplifying popularizer; it is kind neither to high-brows nor to low-brows, to users of jargon or users of slang. College students who play when they should study receive disapproval, but so do 'grinds.' Lack of moderation is wrong, whether it involves excesses or abstention."

In politics, Gans says, both ideologues and politicians who lack ideology are treated with suspicion: "Political candidates who talk openly about issues may be described as dull; those who avoid issues entirely evoke doubts about their fitness for office."

LECTURE RESOURCE 10-F
Slides: *Man and Nature: An Editor's Dilemma.*

SOCIAL ORDER.   Journalists cover disorder—earthquakes, industrial catastrophes, protest marches, the disintegrating nuclear family, and transgressions of laws and mores. This coverage, noted Gans, is concerned not with glamorizing disorder but with finding ways to restore order. To critics who claim that the news media concentrate on disruption and the negative, Gans noted a study of television coverage of the 1967 race riots: Only 3 percent of the sequences covered the riots, and only 2 percent dealt with injuries and deaths. A full 34 percent of the coverage focused on restoring order. *Newsweek*'s coverage, according to the same study, devoted four times as many words to police and Army attempts to restore order as to describing the disturbances.

The journalistic commitment to social order also is evident in how heavily reporters rely on persons in leadership roles as primary sources of information. These leaders, largely representing the Establishment and the status quo, are the people in the best position to maintain social order and to restore it if there's a disruption. This means government representatives often shape news media reports and thus their audiences' understanding of what is important, "true" or meaningful. No one receives more media attention than the president of the United States, who is seen, said Gans, "as the ultimate protector of order."

JOURNALISTIC BIAS

Critics of the news media come in many colors. Conservatives are the most vocal, charging that the media slant news to favor liberal causes. Liberal critics see it in the opposite light. The most recurrent charge, however, is that the media are leftist, favoring Democrats over Republicans, liberals over conservatives, and change over the status quo.

MEDIA: PEOPLE

The Composite Journalist

Here is a look at American journalists, drawn from numerous studies in recent years:

- **Age.** Journalism is more a young person's line of work than most career areas, probably because of stresses from deadlines, uncooperative news sources and difficult reporting assignments. Forty-five percent are 25 to 34 years old, compared to 28 percent for the civilian U.S. workforce.
- **Gender.** Women comprise 53 percent of the new reporters hired by the media. Many women leave the field, however. Among long-term reporters, 65 percent are men. The number of women in manage-

ment is increasing but remains small. Of managing editors, 26 percent are women; of editors, 16 percent; of general managers, 8 percent; of publishers, 6 percent.
- **Education.** Most young journalists hold college degrees in journalism or mass communication, and gradually such degrees are increasing. Among television journalists, the percentage of journalism and mass communication degrees is 63 percent; daily newspapers, 56 percent; news services, 53 percent; radio, 53 percent; weekly newspapers, 50 percent; and newsmagazines, 26 percent.

The fact is that journalists generally fall near the political center. A landmark 1971 survey by *John Johnstone* found 84.6 percent of journalists considered themselves middle-of-the-road or a little to the left or right. In 1983 *David Weaver* and *Cleveland Wilhoit* found 91.1 percent in those categories. At the same time, Gallup surveys put 90 percent of Americans at the center or a little left or right. The breakdown is as follows:

Political Leanings	Journalists 1971	Journalists 1983*	U.S. Adults 1982
Pretty far left	7.5	3.8	0.0
A little left	30.5	18.3	21.0
Middle of road	38.5	57.6	37.0
A little right	15.6	16.3	32.0
Pretty far right	3.4	1.6	0.0
No answer	4.5	2.5	10.0

*Percentages add up to 100.1 due to rounding.

The number of journalists who claimed to be a little leftist dropped considerably during the 12 years. Journalists had moved even more to the middle politically.

On party affiliation, Weaver and Wilhoit found that journalists identify themselves as independents more than the general population:

Political Affiliation	Journalists 1971	Journalists 1983*	U.S. Adults 1982
Democrat	33.5	38.5	45.0
Independent	32.5	39.1	30.0
Republican	25.7	18.8	25.0
Other	5.8	1.6	0.0
No answer	0.5	2.1	0.0

*Percentages add up to 100.1 due to rounding.

Despite such evidence, charges persist that journalists are biased. The charges are all the stranger considering that most American news organizations pride themselves on a neutral presentation and go to extraordinary lengths to prove it. To avoid confusion between straight reporting and commentary, opinion pieces are set apart in clearly labeled editorial sections. Most journalists, even those with left or right leanings, have a zealous regard for detached, neutral reporting. Although they see their truth-seeking as unfettered by partisanship, they recognize that their news judgments often are made in confusing situations against deadline pressure, and they are the first, in self-flagellating postmortems, to criticize themselves when they fall short of the journalistic goals of accuracy, balance and fairness.

Considering the media's obsession with avoiding partisanship, how do the charges of bias retain any currency? First, critics who paint the media as leftist usually are forgetting that news, by its nature, is concerned with change. Everybody, journalists and media consumers alike, is more interested in a volcano that is blowing its top than in one that remains dormant. This interest in what is happening, as opposed to what is not happening, does not mean that anyone favors volcanic eruptions. However, the fact is that change almost always is more interesting than the status quo, although it is often more threatening and less comfortable. When journalists spend time on a presidential candidate's ideas to eliminate farm subsidies, it is not that the journalists favor the change, just that the topic is more interesting than stories about government programs that are unchallenged. Because conservatives favor the status quo, it is natural that they would feel threatened by news coverage of change and proposals for change, no matter how disinterested and dispassionate the coverage, but this is hardly liberal bias.

The news media also are criticized because of an American journalistic tradition that is implicit in the U.S. Constitution: a belief that democracy requires the press to serve a watchdog function. Since the founding of the Republic, journalists have been expected to keep government honest and responsive to the electorate by reporting on its activities, especially on shortcomings. Unless the people have full reports on the government, they cannot intelligently discuss public issues, let alone vote intelligently on whether or not to keep their representatives. Sometimes to the dismay of those in power, the news media are part of the American system to facilitate change when it is needed.

In short, journalists' concern with change is not born of political bias. It is inherent in the nature of their work.

VARIABLES AFFECTING NEWS

STUDY PREVIEW   The variables that determine what is reported include things beyond a journalist's control, such as how much space or time is available to tell stories. Also, a story that might receive top billing on a slow news day might not even appear on a day when an overwhelming number of major stories are breaking.

NEWS HOLE

TEACHING OBJECTIVE 10-3
Variables beyond journalists' control affect news.

LECTURE RESOURCE 10-G
Slides: *Current Newspaper Leaders—Sunday.*

LECTURE RESOURCE 10-H
Slides: *Best Newspaper Design.*

LECTURE RESOURCE 10-I
Video: *A Newspaper Career and You.*

A variable affecting what ends up being reported as news is called the *news hole*. In newspapers the news hole is the space left after the advertising department has placed all the ads it has sold in the paper. The volume of advertising determines the number of total pages, and generally, the bigger the issue, the more room for news. Newspaper editors can squeeze fewer stories into a thin Monday issue than a fat Wednesday issue.

In broadcasting, the news hole tends to be more consistent. A 30-minute television newscast may have room for only 23 minutes of news, but the format doesn't vary. When the advertising department doesn't sell all the seven minutes available for advertising, it usually is public service announcements, promotional messages and program notes—not news—that pick up the slack. Even so, the news hole can vary in broadcasting. A 10-minute newscast can accommodate more stories than a 5-minute newscast, and, as with newspapers, it is the judgment of journalists that determines which events make it.

NEWS FLOW AND STAFFING

Besides the news hole, the flow of news varies from day to day. A story that might be played prominently on a slow news day can be passed over entirely in the competition for space on a heavy news day.

On one of the heaviest news days of all time, in 1989, death claimed Iran's Ayatollah Khomeini, a central figure in United States foreign policy; Chinese young people and the government were locked in a showdown in Tiananmen Square; the Polish people were voting to reject their one-party Communist political system;

and a revolt was under way in the Soviet republic of Uzbekistan. That was a heavy news day, and the flow of major nation-rattling events preempted stories that otherwise would have been news.

Whether reporters are in the right place at the right time can affect coverage. A newsworthy event in Nigeria will receive short shrift if the network correspondent for Africa is occupied with a natural disaster in next-door Cameroon. A radio station's city government coverage will slip when the city hall reporter is on vacation or if the station can't afford a regular reporter at city hall. When Iraq invaded Kuwait by surprise in August 1990, it so happened that almost all the U.S. and European reporters assigned to the Persian Gulf were on vacation or elsewhere on assignment. An exception was Caryle Murphy of the Washington *Post*. Like everyone else, Murphy hadn't expected the invasion, but she had decided to make a routine trip from her Cairo bureau for a first-hand look at Kuwaiti affairs. Only by happenstance did Murphy have what she called "a front-row seat for witnessing a small nation being crushed." Competing news organizations were devoid of eyewitness staff coverage until they scrambled to fly people into the region.

PERCEPTIONS ABOUT AUDIENCE

How a news organization perceives its audience affects news coverage. The *National Enquirer* lavishes attention on unproven cancer cures that the *New York Times* treats briefly if at all. The *Wall Street Journal* sees its purpose as news for readers who have special interests in finance, the economy and business. NBC's Consumer News and Business Channel was established to serve an audience more interested in quick market updates, brief analysis and trendy consumer news than the kind of depth offered by the *Journal*.

The perception that a news organization has of its audience is evident in a comparison of stories on different networks' newscasts. CNN may lead newscasts with a coup d'état in another country, while CNBC leads with a new government economic forecast, MTV with the announcement of a rock group's tour, and "A Current Affair" with a six-month-old gory homicide that none of the others covered at all.

AVAILABILITY OF MATERIAL

The availability of photographs and video also is a factor in what ends up being news. Television is often faulted for overplaying visually titillating stories, such as fires, and underplaying or ignoring more significant stories that are not photogenic. Newspapers and magazines also are partial to stories with strong accompanying visuals, as shown in an especially poignant way when a Boston woman and child sought refuge on their apartment's balcony when the building caught fire. Then the balcony collapsed. The woman died on impact; the child somehow survived. The tragedy was all the more dramatic because it occurred just as firefighters were about to rescue the woman and child. Most journalists would report such an event, but in this case the coverage was far more extensive than would normally be the case because Stanley Forman of the Boston *Herald-American* photographed the woman and child plunging to the ground. On its own merits, the event probably would not have been reported beyond Boston, but with Forman's series of dramatic photographs, clicked in quick succession, the story was reported in visual media—newspapers, magazines and television—around the world.

MEDIA AND YOU

The Price of Diversity

Listen to a few local radio stations for national news or pick up half a dozen newspapers from around your state, and you will find the same stories, often word for word from the Associated Press. Check the editorial pages, and you will find many of the same columnists in paper after paper.

This sameness bothers media critics, who say that democracy would be better served with coverage and commentary from a greater range of sources. Also, some critics say the news services and syndicates work insidiously against good local coverage because penny-pinching media owners find stories from Timbuktu and Ulan Bator less costly than hiring local reporters. The result: Mali and Outer Mongolia are sometimes better covered than city hall.

The other side of the argument is that news services and syndicates provide a quantity and quality of coverage that hardly any local newspapers or broadcast stations could afford on their own.

How do you see this issue?

Radio news people revel in stories when sound is available, which influences what is reported and new. A barnyard interview with a farm leader, with cows snorting in the background, is likelier to make the air than the same farm leader saying virtually the same thing in the sterile confines of a legislative committee chamber.

COMPETITION

One trigger of adrenalin for journalists is landing a scoop and, conversely, being scooped. Journalism is a competitive business, and the drive to outdo other news organizations keeps news publications and newscasts fresh with new material.

Competition has an unglamorous side. Journalists constantly monitor each other to identify events that they missed and need to catch up on to be competitive. This catch-up aspect of the news business contributes to similarities in coverage, which scholar Leon Sigal calls the *consensible nature of news*. It also is called "pack" and "herd" journalism.

In the final analysis, news is the result of journalists scanning their environment and making decisions, first on whether to cover certain events and then on how to cover them. The decisions are made against a backdrop of countless variables, many of them changing during the reporting, writing and editing processes.

NONNEWSROOM INFLUENCES ON NEWS

STUDY PREVIEW While journalists are key in deciding what to report and how, nonnewsroom forces in news organizations sometimes play a role too. These forces include advertiser-sensitive executives, who do not always share the truth-seeking and truth-telling agendas of journalists.

EXECUTIVE ORDERS

TEACHING OBJECTIVE 10-4
External pressures including advertisers affect news.

While reporters have significant roles in deciding what makes news, news organizations are corporate structures. The people in charge have the final word on matters big and small. It is publishers and general managers and their immediate lieutenants who are in charge. Some of these executives make self-serving decisions on coverage that gall the journalists who work for them, but such is how chains of command work.

An egregious example of front-office meddling in news judgments was alleged in a 1990 complaint to the Federal Communications Commission by radio station KCDA in Coeur d'Alene, Idaho. The station charged that the local newspaper, the Coeur d'Alene *Press*, lavished news coverage on the radio station owned by the newspaper's owner but ignored KCDA despite KCDA's extensive participation in community activities that were as newsworthy as the activities that garnered coverage for the newspaper-owned station. In one *Press* story in which mentioning KCDA was unavoidable, it was referred to only as "an obscure local radio station."

Also appalling is excessive pandering to advertiser interests. It is impossible to catalog the extent to which journalistic autonomy is sacrificed to curry favor from advertisers, but it can occur even at generally respected news organizations. The Denver *Post*, a metro daily, once offered a shopping mall 1,820 column inches of free publicity, equivalent roughly to 72,000 words, a small book, as a bonus if the mall bought 30 pages of advertising. The puffery cut into space that might have been used for substantive news.

Some news organizations obsequiously lean over backwards not to alienate advertisers, which also can undermine journalistic autonomy. NBC once invited Coca-Cola, a major advertiser, to preview a television documentary that reported the company benefited from exploited migrant agricultural workers. NBC then acceded to Coca-Cola's requests to drop certain scenes.

Such policy decisions are more common among smaller, less financially solid news organizations, whose existence can be in jeopardy if they lose advertisers. To

Trailing of O. J. Simpson. News reporters sometimes operate in packs. This is because most reporters use the same values in deciding what their audiences want to know. They are surrogates who ask questions for their readers, viewers and listeners. During the O. J. Simpson case, reporters were seeking information and asking questions that the public wanted to know.

avoid rankling advertisers, the Las Cruces, New Mexico, *Sun-News*, as an example, once had a policy against naming local businesses that were in the news in an unsavory way. When police raided a local hotel room, the *Sun-News* offered not even a hint of which hotel was the site of the raid.

Rarely do media owners acknowledge that they manipulate news coverage to their own economic interests, which is why it is difficult to document the frequency of these abuses. Sociologists who have studied newsrooms note that publishers hire managers whose thinking coincides with their own, and these managers hire editors and reporters of the same sort. The result is that decisions made by reporters do not differ much from those the publisher would make in the same situation. With the sociology of the newsroom shaped by largely like-minded people, seldom does anyone need to order manipulation explicitly. This means most instances of slanting coverage to the wishes of advertisers or other special interests are neither recorded nor reported.

In fairness, it must be said that media owners generally are sensitive to their truth-seeking and truth-telling journalistic responsibilities and assiduously avoid calling the shots on news coverage. Those who answer to a call other than journalistic soundness are within their court-recognized First Amendment rights, which allow media people to exercise their freedom responsibly as well as irresponsibly. Journalists who are bothered by wrong-headed news decisions have three choices: persuade wayward owners of the wrongness of their ways, comply with directives, or quit and go work for a respectable journalistic organization.

ADVERTISER PRESSURE

Special interests try to exert influence on coverage, such as squelching a story or insisting on self-serving angles. Advertiser pressure can be overt. The managing editor of the Laramie, Wyoming, *Boomerang* complied with a request from the newspaper's own advertising manager not to carry a state agency's news release warning people that Bon Vivant vichyssoise, possibly tainted with lethal botulism bacteria, had been found on the shelves at a local grocery. The ad manager was fearful of losing the store's advertising. In fact, the store did yank its advertising from a Laramie radio station when it aired the story, and the station's news director reported that he was warned to back off from the story and later fired.

Generally, advertiser clout is applied quietly, as when Ralph's grocery chain cancelled a $250,000 advertising contract with the Los Angeles *Herald Examiner* after a story on supermarket overcharging and shortweighting. From a journalistic perspective, the sinister result of cancelling advertising is the possible chilling effect on future coverage.

Advertiser pressure can be even more subtle. Many airlines insist that their ads be deleted from newscasts with stories about airline crashes. This is reasonable from an airline's perspective, but it also is a policy that has the effect of encouraging stations, especially financially marginal stations, to omit crash stories, even though these stories would contribute to listeners' having a clearer sense about air safety.

To their credit, most news organizations place allegiance to their audiences ahead of pleasing advertisers, as Terry Berger, president of an advertising agency representing the Brazilian airline Varig, found out from *Condé Nast's Traveler*, a travel magazine. After an article on air pollution in Rio de Janeiro, Berger wrote the magazine: "Is your editorial policy then to see how quickly you can alienate present and potential advertisers and at the same time convince your readers to stick closer to home? I really think that if you continue with this kind of editorial information, you are doing both your readers and your advertisers a disservice. For this kind of information, people read the *New York Times*. I therefore find it necessary to remove *Condé Nast's Traveler* from Varig's media schedule." Unintimidated, the magazine's editor, Harold Evans, did not recant. Not only did Evans print the letter but he followed with this comment: "Mrs. Berger is, of course, entitled to use her judgment about where she advertises Brazil's national airline. I write not about that narrow commercial issue, but about her assertion that it is a disservice to readers and advertisers for us to print true but unattractive facts when they are relevant. This goes to the heart of the editorial policy of this magazine. . . . We rejoice in the enrichments of travel, but our aim is to give readers the fullest information, frankly and fairly, so they can make their own judgments."

PRESSURE FROM SOURCES

Journalists sometimes feel external pressure directly. At the court house, valuable sources turn cold after a story appears that they don't like. A tearful husband begs an editor not to use the name of his wife in a story that points to her as a bank embezzler. A bottle of Chivas Regal arrives at Christmas from a sports publicist who says she appreciates excellent coverage over the past year. Most journalists will tell you that their commitment to truth overrides external assaults on their autonomy. Even so, external pressures exist.

The relationship between journalists and publicists can be troublesome. In general, the relationship works well. Publicists want news coverage for their clients and provide information and help reporters line up interviews. Some publicists, however, are more committed to advancing their clients than to advancing truth, and they work to manipulate journalists into providing coverage that unduly glorifies their clients.

Staging events is a publicity tactic to gain news coverage that a cause would not otherwise attract. Some staged events are obvious hucksterism, such as Evel Knievel's ballyhooed motorcycle leaps across vast canyons in the 1970s and local flagpole-sitting stunts by celebrity disc jockeys. Covering such events usually is part of the softer side of news and, in the spirit of fun and games and diversion, is relatively harmless.

Of more serious concern are staged events about which publicists create a mirage of significance to suck journalists and the public into giving more attention than they deserve. For example, consider:

■ The false impression created when hundreds of federal workers are released from work for an hour to see an incumbent's campaign speech outside a government office building.

■ The contrived "photo opportunity" at which people, props and lighting are carefully, even meticulously arranged to create an image on television.

■ Stunts that bring attention to a new product and give it an undeserved boost in the marketplace.

Staged events distort a balanced journalistic portrayal of the world. Worse, they divert attention from truly significant events.

GATEKEEPING IN NEWS

STUDY PREVIEW The individual reporter has a lot of independence in determining what to report, but news work is a team effort. No individual acts entirely alone, and there are factors, such as gatekeeping, that affect what ends up on the printed page or over the air.

GATEKEEPERS' RESPONSIBILITIES

TEACHING OBJECTIVE 10-5
Gatekeepers have a high level of responsibility for news.

LECTURE RESOURCE 10-J
Speaker: Newspaper wire editor.

News dispatches and photographs are subject to changes at many points in the communication chain. At these points, called *gates*, gatekeepers delete, trim, embellish and otherwise try to improve messages.

Just as a reporter exercises judgment in deciding what to report and how to report it, judgment also is at the heart of the gatekeeping process. Hardly any message, except live reporting, reaches its audience in its original form. Along the path from its originator to the eventual audience, a message is subject to all kinds of deletions, additions and changes of emphasis. With large news organizations, this process may involve dozens of editors and other persons.

The gatekeeping process affects all news. A public relations practitioner who doesn't tell the whole story is a gatekeeper. A reporter who emphasizes one aspect of an event and neglects others is a gatekeeper. Even live, on-scene television coverage involves gatekeeping because it's a gatekeeper who decides where to point the camera, and that's a decision that affects the type of information that reaches viewers. The C-SPAN network's live, unedited coverage of Congress, for example, never shows members of Congress sleeping or reading a newspaper during debate, even though such happens.

CNN Agenda Setting
This segment, reported by CNN's Jamie McIntyre, examines the influence of the media in deciding what people will be regarding as important on any given day. The context is the 1992 Clinton presidential campaign, when Clinton's media advisers had a difficult time shaping the agenda. One point in the report is that the media's agenda is really the agenda that reporters think coincides with their audience's interests. This segment aired September 5, 1992.

Gatekeeping can be a creative force. Trimming a news story can add potency. A news producer can enhance a reporter's field report with file footage. An editor can call a public relations person for additional detail to illuminate a point in a reporter's story. A newsmagazine's editor can consolidate related stories and add context that makes an important interpretive point.

GATEKEEPERS AT WORK

Most gatekeepers are invisible to the news audience, working behind the scenes and making crucial decisions in near-anonymity on how the world will be portrayed in the evening newscast and the next morning's newspaper. Here, slightly updated, is how mass communication scholar Wilbur Schramm explained gatekeeping in 1960: "Suppose we follow a news item, let us say, from India to Indiana. The first gatekeeper is the person who sees an event happen. This person sees the event selectively, noticing some things, not others. The second gatekeeper is the reporter who talks to this 'news source.' Now, of course, we could complicate this picture by giving the reporter a number of news sources to talk to about the same event, but in any case the reporter has to decide which facts to pass along the chain, what to write, what shape and color and importance to give to the event. The reporter gives his message to an editor, who must decide how to edit the story, whether to cut or add or change. Then the message goes to a news service where someone must decide which of many hundreds of items will be picked up and telegraphed to other towns, and how important the story is, and therefore how much space it deserves.

MEDIA: PEOPLE

Susan Zirinsky

Susan Zirinsky never appears on the air, but, as a CBS field producer, she is as influential as any reporter in deciding what appears on "The CBS Evening News." Zirinsky coordinates White House coverage and decides what video footage to use to illustrate the reporter's script. During the 1984 presidential campaign, the Washington *Post* gave this account of Zirinsky at work:

"She and CBS White House correspondent Bill Plante have spent the day with the President, and after three cities in eight hours the story she has to edit and send to New York is still stacked in cassettes on the floor. Plante is writing his narration at a table, trying to find a nugget of news. She wants to include some Reagan hecklers in the piece; Plante thinks there weren't enough to be important. She appeals to New York, loses, then looks at Plante's stand-up, a shot of him talking in front of Air Force One. She tells him she's going to make it shorter. 'It's only a sentence,' he grumps. 'How much are you going to cut?'"

At the time, Zirinsky was 32. Already she had been with CBS 10 years. In college, she landed a job answering phones in the CBS Washington bureau once a week. She was typing scripts for the evening news by her senior year. After graduation she became a researcher, and at age 24, she was named an associate producer. By the time Walter Mondale was challenging Ronald Reagan for the presidency in 1984, Zirinsky had been covering the White House almost four years.

Here is how one day went on the 1984 campaign trail:

8:30 a.m. On board a charter plane, Zirinsky issues four pages of notes to her staff of 12. They tell where every camera crew and reporter will be and when. They list numbers for dozens of telephones that Zirinsky has had installed at airports, speech sites and other locations on this one-day, three-city Reagan campaign trip.

10:25 a.m. In Pennsylvania, as the president is speaking at the Millersville University gym, one of Zirinsky's photographers catches a protester yelling and being dragged off by two Reagan supporters.

1:00 p.m. From a third-floor window of the white-columned Media, Pennsylvania, courthouse, photographers tape powerful panoramas of 13,000 people jamming a dead-end street to hear the president.

1:30 p.m. Zirinsky is on a bus for the president's third campaign stop. Plante calls from a helicopter, en route to the same speech, to say that the president took a few minutes to chat with reporters while catching his own helicopter at Media. Nothing worth reporting was said, Plante reports.

6:15 p.m. After the president's third stop, in Parkersburg, Pennsylvania, Zirinsky is slaving over her computerized editing equipment set up on a teacher's desk at a local school. Zirinsky finishes splicing crowd and speech shots into Plante's stand-up. It is dispatched to New York, a whole 15 minutes before Dan Rather begins the evening newscast.

8:00 p.m. Zirinsky's charter flight lands back in Washington. Her day is done.

Covering Politics. Most journalists have a keen interest in covering government and political process because those are the vehicles through which the people in a democracy create public policy. Diane Sawyer at the 1992 Democratic National Convention interviewed party leaders and delegates as the party's platform took shape. That platform proved to be the basis for the Clinton presidency.

"At a further link in the chain, this story will come to a United States news service and here again an editor must decide what is worth passing on to the American newspapers and broadcasting stations. The chain leads us on to a regional and perhaps a state news service bureau, where the same decisions must be made; always there is more news than can be sent on—which items, and how much of the items, shall be retained and retransmitted? And finally when the item comes to a local newspaper, an editor must go through the same process, deciding which items to print in the paper.

"Out of news stories gathered by tens of thousands of reporters around the world, only a few hundred will pass the gatekeepers along the chains and reach a local newspaper editor, who will be able to pass only a few dozen of those on to the newspaper reader."

GLOBAL GATEKEEPING: THE NEWS AGENCIES

STUDY PREVIEW   Because gathering news is expensive, especially when it comes from far away, news organizations set up agencies, usually called wire services, news services, or networks to reduce the cost and then share the resulting stories. Today, global news services, led by the Associated Press, have more influence than most people realize on what is reported and how it is told.

COMPETITION FOR FAR-AWAY NEWS

Sam Gilbert took great pride in his coffee house. At seven stories, it was the tallest building in the United States. It dominated the Boston waterfront. Gilbert's was a popular place, partly because of an extensive collection of the latest European newspapers that he maintained in a reading room. In 1811, with a second war imminent with Britain, Gilbert announced that his patrons no longer would have to wait for ships to dock to have the latest news. Forthwith, he said, an employee would row out to ships waiting to enter the harbor and rush back with packets of the latest news. Newspapers up and down the seaboard picked up Gilbert's idea, and publishers scrambled to outdo each other by buying the fastest sloops.

In time, complex courier systems caught ships arriving at Halifax, Nova Scotia, and rushed news by pony and sloop to Boston and New York. Competition escalated, especially after Samuel Morse invented the telegraph in 1844 and coastal cities began to be linked by wire.

ASSOCIATED PRESS

The competition was spirited, especially in New York, where 10 newspapers raced to beat each other with foreign dispatches. The competition escalated costs, and in 1846, one of New York's scrappiest news merchants, *David Hale* of the *Journal of Commerce*, brought five of his competitors together to discuss combining their efforts in order to reduce expenses. The concept was simple. Competing newspapers would rely on a common organization, Harbor News Association, and share both the material and the expenses. The name evolved into the *Associated Press*.

Today the Associated Press is the world's largest news-gathering organization, with bureaus in 71 countries. In the United States, the AP has 142 bureaus in state capitals and major cities. Like its predecessor organization, it remains a nonprofit cooperative. Member newspapers each own a share based on circulation and numerous other factors. Each newspaper is obligated to furnish its local stories to the AP for distribution to other member newspapers. The AP also has its own staff, 1,100 journalists in the United States and 480 abroad, to generate stories for all members. Periodically the expense of operating the AP is tallied, and members are billed for their share. The budget is about $300 million. Policies are set by member newspapers, which meet regularly.

The AP sells its news to magazines and even government agencies, and it operates profit-making news script, audio and video services for radio and television newsrooms. Only newspapers, however, are full members with a controlling voice in the organization's policies.

These numbers give a sense of the AP's size:

- 3,000 employees nationwide, including journalists, management and support personnel.
- 1,700 United States newspapers, including 1,460 daily newspaper members.
- 6,000 television, cable and station outlets.
- 1,000 radio subscribers to AP Network News, which is the largest single radio network in the United States.
- 8,500 foreign subscribers in 112 countries.

UNITED PRESS INTERNATIONAL

As the AP evolved, it limited membership to one newspaper per city. The policy upset newspaper-chain owner *E. W. Scripps*, who was denied AP membership for the new papers he was founding in the 1880s because older papers already had exclusive AP franchises. In 1907 Scripps founded the *United Press* for newspapers that the AP shut out. The heart of Scripps's new service was his own newspapers, but the service also was a profit-seeking enterprise available to any and all newspapers willing to subscribe.

William Randolph Hearst followed in 1909 with the *International News Service*. Both UP and INS tried to match the comprehensive Washington and foreign service of the Associated Press, but the AP proved impossible to derail. Even when the AP suffered a major setback, losing a 1945 U.S. Supreme Court decision that

LECTURE RESOURCE 10-K
Film: *The Associated Press: One of a Kind.*

KEY PERSON
David Hale organized first AP forerunner.

KEY PERSON
E. W. Scripps founded UP.

KEY PERSON
William Randolph Hearst founded INS.

Reuter's Pigeon Service

Much of Europe had been linked by telegraph by the late 1840s, but a 100-mile gap remained between the financial centers of Brussels in Belgium and Aachen in Prussia. Young *Paul Julius Reuter* established a carrier pigeon service, with the birds carrying dispatches tied to their legs, and he immediately attracted banking customers. Reuter then moved to London to pick up the latest American news from the new trans-Atlantic cable for his pigeon delivery. In 1858 he offered his service to newspapers via telegraph.

Paul Julius Reuter

In 1984, after years of being owned by newspapers in Britain, Australia and New Zealand, Reuters became a publicly traded company. Newly aggressive, the company beefed up its financial market reporting and expanded its domestic U.S. service. Today, Reuters serves 6,500 media organizations worldwide, including 290 in the United States. Including clients in the business and financial community, Reuters has 27,000 subscribers worldwide. The service is offered in 11 languages.

Besides Reuters, AP and UPI, two other news services have extensive global networks:

■ **Agence France-Presse.** Paris-based AFP was founded by *Charles Havas* in 1835. Using carrier pigeons, Havas supplied Paris newspapers by noon with news that had happened that same morning in London and Brussels. It was from Havas that young Paul Julius Reuter learned the carrier pigeon business before setting off on his own.

Today, AFP has 2,000 people in 150 bureaus worldwide, including 850 full-time journalists. Text, photo, audio and video services are transmitted in Arabic, English, French, German, Spanish and Portuguese to 500 newspaper, 350 radio and 200 television clients, and to 99 national news agencies that pass AFP stories on to more media outlets. AFP has more than 50 U.S. media clients.

■ **TASS.** This Moscow-based news agency was founded in 1918, just after the Bolshevik Revolution. Today TASS supplies reports in Russian, English, French, German, Spanish and Arabic to 5,500 media and nonmedia subscribers.

Until the Communist party was disbanded in 1991, TASS's editorial direction was from the party's central committee. The fall of Soviet communism left TASS in disarray about its mission. It continues, however, as the global news service of choice in some of the former Soviet bloc.

forced it to abandon exclusivity, the result spurred AP growth. Non-AP newspapers joined the co-op by the dozen, which hurt United Press and Hearst's INS.

In 1958 UP and INS merged to form the *United Press International*, but the new company, in reality a subsidiary of the Scripps-Howard newspaper chain, failed to meet profit expectations and eventually went on the selling block. Nobody wanted it. The British news service *Reuters*, anxious for a toehold in the United States, surveyed UPI's assets and decided against buying. In the 1980s UPI went through a series of owners. There were attempts at corporate reorganization, technological economies and sales blitzes, but several owners later the service was anything but secure.

SUPPLEMENTAL SERVICES

One UPI problem was the emergence of supplemental news services in the 1960s. The New York *Times* began packaging its stories, opinion pieces and columnists for other newspapers. The Washington *Post* and Los Angeles *Times* followed. By the mid-1970s, many newspapers that had used both AP and UPI were being tempted to drop one of them and buy one of the supplementals for distinctive, in-depth reporting, top-flight opinion pieces and colorful columnists—things that were strengths of neither AP nor UPI. It was UPI that usually got the ax. The reasoning was that AP and UPI were largely duplicates. Both had large worldwide news-gathering systems, but the AP had more correspondents in more bureaus. Both provided state and regional coverage, but again, in most states, AP had more staff. Neither missed major events, which meant that one was expendable.

VIDEO NEWS SERVICES

The three major American television networks prided themselves on covering the world with their own staffs until the late 1980s, when they cut back their foreign news staffs and even shut down some bureaus to save costs. To fill more and more gaps in their own coverage, ABC, CBS and NBC leaned on independent video news services. The largest such service, *Visnews*, claims its network and station clients reach almost every television set in the world.

SYNDICATE INFLUENCE ON NEWS

STUDY PREVIEW News organizations buy ready-to-run features, including political columns, from organizations called *syndicates*. Because syndicates sell the same features to many organizations, their influence is substantial.

NEWSPAPER SYNDICATES

After Union recruiters swept through Baraboo, Wisconsin, and signed up the local boys for the Civil War, *Ansel Kellogg* lacked the staff to get out his four-page Baraboo *Republic*, so he took to borrowing the inside pages of another newspaper. The practice not only saw Kellogg through a staffing crisis but also sparked an idea to save costs by supplying inside pages at a fee to other short-handed publishers. By 1865 Kellogg was in Chicago providing ready-to-print material for newspapers nationwide. In journalism history, Kellogg is remembered as the father of the newspaper syndicate.

In the 1880s *S. S. McClure* had a thriving syndicate, putting out 50,000 words a week in timeless features on fashion, homemaking, manners and literature. McClure and other syndicators charged subscribing newspapers a fraction of what each would have to pay to generate such material with its own staff. Features, poetry, opinion and serialized stories by the period's great literary figures, including Jack London, Rudyard Kipling, George Bernard Shaw, Robert Louis Stevenson and Mark Twain, became standard fare in many newspapers through syndication.

Today, syndicates offer a wide range of material, usually on an exclusive basis. In major cities with competing newspapers, some features go to the highest bidder. Generally, rates are based on circulation. A small daily might spend $150 a week for 30 to 50 syndicated features. A metropolitan newspaper might spend $500 a week for a single comic strip.

Here are the major features distributed by syndicates, some of which are important as news and commentary, others of which are pure diversion:

■ **Political Columns.** Commentator *David Lawrence* introduced the syndicated political column in 1916, providing modest-budget local newspapers with a low-

TEACHING OBJECTIVE 10-7
Syndicates low cost, usually high quality content.

KEY PERSON
Ansel Kellogg founded first syndicate.

KEY PERSON
S. S. McClure expanded syndicate concept.

Lincoln Weeps. Bill Mauldin's editorial cartoon captured the sorrow of the nation when President Kennedy was shot fatally in 1963. The cartoon needed no caption. Americans everywhere recognized the figure of Lincoln from the District of Columbia memorial, and everyone understood Mauldin's portrayal.

cost tie to Washington. *Walter Lippmann*, the most influential columnist in U.S. history, appeared in hundreds of newspapers as a syndicated feature from 1929 into the 1960s.

- **Political Cartoons.** *Bill Mauldin*'s powerful World War II cartoons received a nationwide audience by syndication. Look at political cartoons on your local newspaper's editorial page, and you will see a note that identifies the cartoonist's home newspaper and, unless the cartoonist is local, the name of the syndicate that distributed it.

- **Comics.** Early syndicates offered stand-alone cartoons. In 1907 "Mutt and Jeff" became the first daily strip. Comics were packed on a single page in the 1920s and became a major circulation builder. In 1984 *Charles Schultz*'s "Peanuts" established a landmark as the first strip to appear in 2,000 newspapers.

- **Lovelorn Columns.** Writing as *Dorothy Dix*, Elizabeth Meriwether Gilmer became "Mother Confessor" to millions in 1916 with the first column to the lovelorn. It was predecessor to today's columns by sisters *Abigail Van Buren* and *Ann Landers*. In the 1920s Gilmer earned an unheard-of $90,000 a year from syndication, more than any single newspaper could have paid a columnist.

- **How-to Columns.** Among available columns are "Shelby Lyman on Chess," and June Roth's "Nutrition Hotline."

- **Reviews.** Book, movie, television and video reviews are provided by syndicates. They range from high-brow criticism to the low-brow "Joe Bob Goes to the Drive-In."

- **Games.** Syndicates offer dozens of crosswords, games and puzzles. Horoscopes and astrology columns are other staples.

- **Literature.** Some syndicates buy serialization rights to memoirs and books, giving newspapers that sign up for them a truncated prepublication series. Leading magazines supply stories to newspapers through syndicates.

Syndicates also offer picture, graphics and art services. Many syndicates offer all the editorial copy that's needed for topical advertising supplements, such as spring car-care tabloids and September back-to-school issues.

JOURNALISM TRENDS

STUDY PREVIEW News has taken two divergent paths in content in recent years. Some news organizations have moved into sophisticated, interpretative and investigative reporting. Others have emphasized superficial, tantalizing news.

EXPLORATORY REPORTING

Norman Cousins acquired his reputation as a thinker when he edited the magazine *Saturday Review*. A premier journal under Cousins, the magazine tackled issues in depth and with intelligence. A few years later, Cousins said he couldn't find much of that kind of journalism in magazines any more: "The best magazine articles in the U.S. today are appearing not in magazines but in newspapers." Cousins was taking note of a profound late 20th-century change in the concept of news. Newspapers and to a lesser extent television were tackling difficult issues that earlier were almost the exclusive provinces of magazines. Cousins especially admired the Los Angeles *Times*, which runs thoroughly researched, thoughtful pieces. It is not unusual for the Los Angeles *Times* to commit weeks, even months, of reporters' time to develop major stories, nor is that unusual at other major newspapers and some smaller ones.

Investigative Journalism. Dogged pursuit of meticulous factual detail became a new wrinkle in 20th-century journalism after Washington *Post* reporters Carl Bernstein and Bob Woodward unearthed the Watergate scandal. For months they pursued tips that a break-in at the Democratic Party national headquarters in the Watergate hotel, office, and apartment complex in Washington, D.C., had been authorized high in the Republican White House and that the White House then had tried to cover it up. In the end, for the first time in American history, a president resigned.

Although American newspapers have never been devoid of in-depth coverage, the thrust through most of their history has been to chronicle events: meetings, speeches, deaths, catastrophes. The emphasis began changing noticeably in the 1960s as it dawned on journalists that chronicling easily identifiable events was insufficient to capture larger, more significant issues and trends.

The failure of event-based reporting became clear when northern cities were burning in race riots in the late 1960s. Journalists had missed one of the 20th century's most significant changes: the northward migration of southern blacks. Had journalists covered the migration and provided information on the festering social divisions that resulted, there might have been a chance to develop public policies before frustration over racial injustices blew up with heavy losses of life and property and great disruption.

The superficiality of mere chronicling was underscored in early coverage of the Vietnam War. By focusing on events, journalists missed asking significant questions about the flawed policies until it was too late.

Newspapers expanded significantly beyond a myopic focus on events in the 1970s for three reasons:

- Recognition that old ways of reporting news were not enough.
- Larger reporting staffs that permitted time-consuming enterprise reporting.
- Better-educated reporters and editors, many with graduate degrees.

Newspapers, profitable as never before, were able to hire larger staffs that permitted them to try more labor-intensive, exploratory kinds of journalism. Instead of merely responding to events, newspapers, particularly big ones, began digging for stories. Much of this investigative journalism was modeled on the Washington *Post*'s doggedness in covering Watergate, the White House-authorized break-in at the Democratic national headquarters during the 1972 presidential campaign. Twenty years earlier, the Watergate break-in scandal probably would not have gone beyond three paragraphs from the police beat. In 1972, however, the persistence of *Post* reporters Carl Bernstein and Bob Woodward posed so many questions about morality in the White House that eventually President Nixon resigned and 25 aides went to jail.

As late as 1960, many daily newspapers were still hiring reporters without college degrees. By 1970 that had changed, and many newspaper reporters were acquiring advanced degrees and developing specialties. Major newspapers hired reporters with law degrees for special work and encouraged promising reporters to go back to college for graduate work in science, business, medicine and the environment. The result was a new emphasis on proactive reporting in which journalists did not wait for events to happen but went out looking, even digging, for things worth telling.

SOFT NEWS

The success of the *National Enquirer*, whose circulation began to skyrocket in the 1960s, was not unnoticed, and when Time, Inc. launched *People* magazine and the New York *Times* launched *Us* magazine, gossipy celebrity news gained a kind of respectability. In this period, the newspaper industry began sophisticated research to identify what readers wanted, then fine-tuned the content mix that would improve market penetration. As a result, many dailies added "People" columns. The news services began receiving requests for more off-beat, gee-whiz items of the sensational sort. Newspapers had always run such material, but more is being printed today to appeal to a broader audience. Many newspapers today also carry more consumer-oriented stories, life-style tips, and entertainment news. This is called *soft news*.

Traditionalists decry the space that soft news takes in many newspapers today, but soft news generally has not displaced hard news. Rather, newspapers fit additional hard news, as well as soft news, into larger newspapers. The *news hole*, the space left after advertisements are put in a newspaper, increased from 19 pages on average in 1970 to 24 pages today.

CHAPTER WRAP-UP

Journalism is an art, not a science. Judgments, rather than formulas, determine which events and issues are reported and how—and no two journalists approach any story exactly the same way. This leaves the whole process of gathering and telling news subject to second-guessing and criticism. Journalists ask themselves all the time if there are ways to do a better job. All journalists can do is try to find truth and to relate it accurately. Even then, the complexity of modern news-gathering—which involves many people, each with an opportunity to change or even kill a story—includes dozens of points at which inaccuracy and imprecision can creep into a story that started out well.

The hazards of the news-gathering process are most obvious with foreign coverage. Even if the reporter is able to gather information and put it into a meaningful context, the story passes through many gatekeepers, all of whom can modify it, before it reaches an American newsroom. Then copy editors, headline writers, photo editors, caption writers and others can take even more cracks at a story.

It is no wonder that the coverage that ends up in print and on the air does not please everyone. At the same time, the news media receive some unfair criticism. The most frequent is the charge that the media slant coverage. The fact, according to respected surveys, is that the political orientation of American journalists largely coincides with that of the rest of the American people. Other studies have found that the values that journalists bring to their work are mainstream cultural values, including ethnocentrism and faith in democracy and capitalism.

The consolidation of news-gathering, through services like the Associated Press, has created great economies in covering far-away events and issues. These services permit local newspapers and broadcast stations to offer more thorough coverage than they could with their own resources. The flip side is that far-away coverage is less expensive than hiring local reporters, which raises serious questions about the appropriate balance between hometown and far-away coverage. The same questions can be raised about syndicates, which provide high-quality political commentary, cartoons, comics and other materials inexpensively to local newspapers and stations.

QUESTIONS FOR REVIEW

1. What contemporary news practices are rooted in the colonial, partisan, penny, and yellow periods of U.S. history?

2. What personal values do journalists bring to their work? Does this affect what is reported and how?

3. What variables beyond journalists' control affect news?

4. What external pressures, from outside the media, affect news reporting?

5. What responsibilities do journalists have as gatekeepers?

6. What is the relationship between global news services and the newspapers you read and the newscasts you hear?

7. What is the relationship between syndicates and the newspapers you read?

8. Is there a contradiction between the two contemporary journalistic trends of exploratory reporting and soft news?

QUESTIONS FOR CRITICAL THINKING

1. The 19-year-old son of the premier of a troubled Central American country in which the CIA has deep involvement died, perhaps of a drug overdose, aboard a Northwest Airlines plane en route from Tokyo to Singapore. On the plane was a young female country-western singer, his frequent companion in recent weeks. The plane was a Boeing 747 manufactured in Washington state. Northwest's corporate headquarters is in Minnesota. The death occurred at 4 a.m. Eastern time. Consider the six elements of news—proximity, prominence, timeliness, consequence, currency and drama, and discuss how this event might be reported on morning television newscasts in Miami, Minneapolis, Nashville, Seattle and the District of Columbia. How about in Managua? Singapore? Tokyo? Rome? Istanbul? Johannesburg? What if the victim were an ordinary college student? What if the death occurred a week ago?

2. Explain news judgment.

3. How do news hole and news flow affect what is reported in the news media?

4. *Time* and *Newsweek* carry cover stories on the same subject one week. Does this indicate that executives of the magazine have conspired, or is it more likely to be caused by what Leon Sigal calls the *consensible nature of news*?

5. How does the nature of news provide ammunition to conservatives to criticize the news media as leftist promoters of change?

6. Discuss whether the American news media reflect mainstream American values. Do you see evidence in your news media of an underlying belief that democracy, capitalism, rural small-town life, individualism and moderation are virtues?

7. Do you feel that the mass media revel in disorder? Consider Herbert Gans's view that the media cover disorder from the perspective of identifying ways to restore order.

8. If a college president calls a news conference and makes a major announcement, who are the gatekeepers who determine how the announcement is covered in the campus newspaper?

9. The five major global news services are the Agence France-Presse, the Associated Press, Reuters, TASS and United Press International. Discuss their similarities and differences.

10. Consider the advantages and disadvantages of your local daily newspaper running both the Ann Landers and the Dear Abby advice columns.

FOR FURTHER LEARNING

L. Brent Bozell III and Brent H. Baker, eds. *And That's the Way It Isn't: A Reference Guide to Media Bias* (Media Research Center, 1990). Bozell and Baker compile a great amount of evidence, much of it circumstantial, to demonstrate a leftist tilt in the U.S. mass media.

Daniel J. Czitrom. *Media and the American Mind: From Morse to McLuhan* (University of North Carolina Press, 1982). Czitrom explores the effect of technological innovations, particularly the telegraph, movies and radio, and popular and scholarly responses to them.

Hazel Dicken-Garcia. *Journalistic Standards in the Nineteenth Century* (University of Wisconsin Press, 1989). Dicken-Garcia traces the idea that the press should be a purveyor of information, not only a forum for partisanship, back to the time before the penny press period.

Edwin and Michael Emery. *The Press and America*, 4th ed. (Prentice Hall, 1984). The Emerys offer an encyclopedic chronology of American mass media back to its roots in authoritarian England.

Mark Fishman. *Manufacturing the News* (University of Texas Press, 1980). Fishman argues that the conventions of gathering news shape what ends up being reported as much as events themselves.

Thomas L. Friedman. *From Beirut to Jerusalem* (Farrar, Straus & Giroux, 1989). Friedman, of the New York *Times*, reveals a lot about being a foreign correspondent in this insightful look at anarchy in Beirut, Arab-Israeli tensions and Arab politics.

Herbert J. Gans. *Deciding What's News: A Study of CBS Evening News, NBC Nightly News, Newsweek and*

Time (Pantheon, 1979). A sociologist examines how the values journalists bring to their work affect the news that is reported.

Jane T. Harrigan. *Read All About It! A Day in the Life of a Metropolitan Newspaper* (Globe Pequot Press, 1987). Harrigan, a journalist, tracks hundreds of newspaper people from 6 a.m. through midnight as they produce an issue of the Boston *Globe*. Along the way, she explains how journalists decide which events to report.

Norman E. Isaacs. *Untended Gates: The Mismanaged Press* (Columbia University Press, 1986). Isaacs, who has edited several major American dailies, argues that the lapses of media ethics can be blamed on top-level managers who are reluctant to involve themselves in newsroom decisions.

Brooke Kroeger. *Nellie Bly: Daredevil, Reporter, Feminist* (Random House, 1994). Kroeger, a former news reporter, unearthed court documents and lost letters for this meticulous, detailed account of an innovative reporting pioneer.

Molly Moore. *A Woman at War: Storming Kuwait With the U.S. Marines* (Scribner's, 1993). Moore, a Washington *Post* reporter, explains the difficulties of getting breaking stories back to the newsroom when military personnel control your movement and access. Moore is especially good at recounting the psychological impact of pending combat on soldiers.

Michael Parenti. *Inventing Reality: The Politics of the Mass Media* (St. Martin's, 1988).

Michael Schudson. *Discovering the News: A Social History of American Newspapers* (Basic Books, 1978). Schudson chronicles the development of journalism as a profession in the United States, focusing on changing concepts of news values and objectivity along the way.

Pamela J. Shoemaker with Elizabeth Kay Mayfield. *Building a Theory of News Content: A Synthesis of Current Approaches* (*Journalism Monographs*, No. 103, June 1987). Shoemaker and Mayfield attempt to bring coherence to the leading theories on the factors that contribute to events being reported.

David H. Weaver and G. Cleveland Wilhoit. *The American Journalist: A Portrait of U.S. News People and Their Work*, 2nd ed. (Indiana University Press, 1991). This comprehensive profile updates the authors' 1986 work and an earlier 1971 study, which also bears reading: John W. C. Johnstone, Edward J. Slawski and William W. Bowman. *The News People: A Sociological Portrait of American Journalists and Their Work* (University of Illinois Press, 1976).

■F OR KEEPING UP TO DATE

Among publications that keep current on journalistic issues are *Columbia Journalism Review, Quill, American Journalism Review, Editor & Publisher, Media* and *News Inc.*

Bridging the gap between scholarly and professional work is *Newspaper Research Journal.*

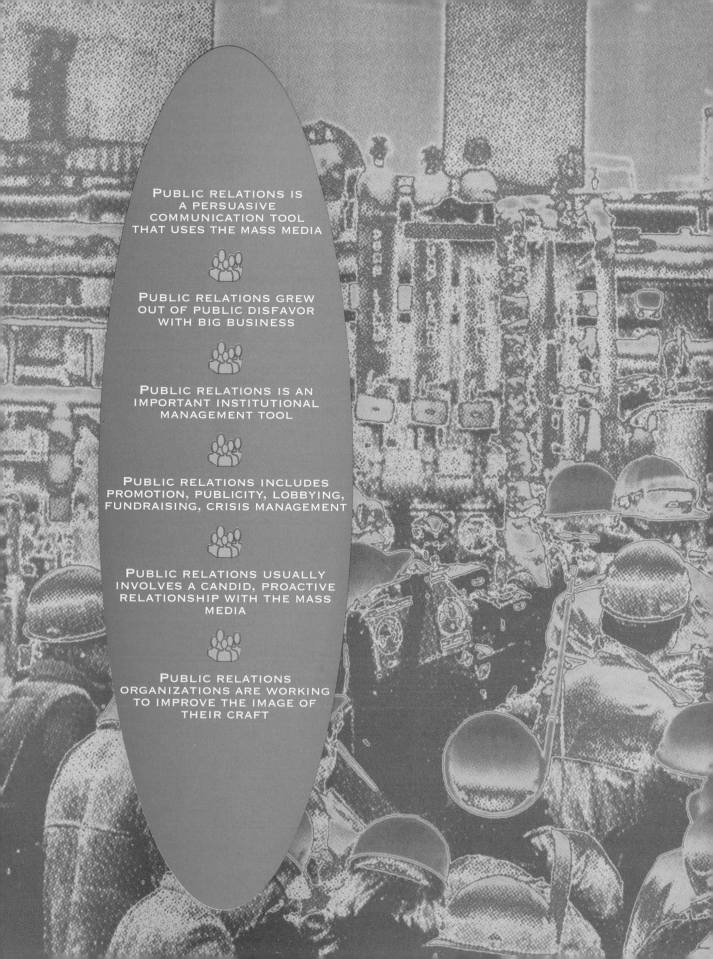

PUBLIC RELATIONS IS
A PERSUASIVE
COMMUNICATION TOOL
THAT USES THE MASS MEDIA

PUBLIC RELATIONS GREW
OUT OF PUBLIC DISFAVOR
WITH BIG BUSINESS

PUBLIC RELATIONS IS AN
IMPORTANT INSTITUTIONAL
MANAGEMENT TOOL

PUBLIC RELATIONS INCLUDES
PROMOTION, PUBLICITY, LOBBYING,
FUNDRAISING, CRISIS MANAGEMENT

PUBLIC RELATIONS USUALLY
INVOLVES A CANDID, PROACTIVE
RELATIONSHIP WITH THE MASS
MEDIA

PUBLIC RELATIONS
ORGANIZATIONS ARE WORKING
TO IMPROVE THE IMAGE OF
THEIR CRAFT

chapter 11

PUBLIC RELATIONS WINNING HEARTS AND MINDS

In tearful and dramatic testimony, a 15-year-old Kuwaiti girl told a congressional committee that she had witnessed horrible atrocities when Iraqi troops invaded her homeland. She described soldiers pulling babies out of hospital incubators and leaving them on the floor to die. This was October 1990, while U.S. President George Bush was engaged both in massive military build-up to retake Kuwait from the Iraqis and in a massive campaign at home to convince Congress and the American people that military intervention was justified.

The horrible Iraqi deeds described by the Kuwaiti girl helped President Bush win the battle at home. Over the next few days, he cited her testimony in at least 10 speeches. On one occasion he even took some literary license to whip up public feeling against the Iraqis by saying they "scattered babies like firewood."

Within a few days, Congress voted narrowly to let President Bush proceed with the war preparations. Of course, much more than the girl's testimony shaped public feelings, but for many people her account was riveted indelibly in their minds. Also, the testimony, as well as the U.S. military intervention, marked a huge success for the giant Hill and Knowlton public relations company.

Tearful and Compelling. Fourteen-year-old Nayirah al-Sabah told Congress that she had witnessed Iraqi troops committing atrocities in her Kuwaiti homeland. Her testimony, it was learned later, was arranged by the Hill and Knowlton public relations agency, and her claims were wildly exaggerated in an attempt to arouse U.S. public sentiment against the Iraqi invaders so they would intervene militarily. Critics have raised serious questions about the appropriateness of Hill and Knowlton's role in trying to influence U.S. public policy on behalf of Kuwaiti clients.

After the Iraqi blitzkrieg into Kuwait in August 1990, well-heeled Kuwaiti leaders who had fled their country founded a group called Citizens for a Free Kuwait to generate U.S. support for their cause. They hired Hill and Knowlton, which has 290 employees in Washington alone, to send lobbyists to Congress to make their client's case. The company arranged for Kuwaiti sympathizers to give television, radio, newspaper and magazine interviews. Fact sheets and updates were widely distributed, Hill and Knowlton even arranged for Citizens for a Free Kuwait to make a $50,000 gift to a private foundation operated by one member of Congress.

Hill and Knowlton was engaged in classic public relations activities: advising a client on how to present the best possible case to groups it wants to win over to its view and then helping the client accomplish its purposes. For Hill and Knowlton's services, the exiled Kuwaiti government paid $11.9 million. It was a bargain, to whatever extent the expenditure contributed to the multination military and diplomatic mobilization against Iraq and the eventual expulsion of Iraqis from Kuwaiti soil. The Kuwaitis got the most bang for their buck, however, from the testimony of 15-year-old Nayirah al-Sabah.

Early in October, two months after the Iraqi invasion, officials from the Kuwaiti embassy in Washington escorted Nayirah to the Hill and Knowlton office to tell her story. The potential for the girl's story was clear right away to Lauri Fitz-Pegado, a senior H&K vice president. The agency contacted House member Tom Lantos, co-chair of the congressional Human Rights Caucus, and set up a hearing for Nayirah to testify. The news media were advised to be there for dynamite revelations. Then Fitz-Pegado began coaching Nayirah for the appearance.

The hearing lived up to Hill and Knowlton's advance billing. Nayirah choked back tears as she explained that she had been working as a volunteer at the hospital under an assumed name, and then she told about the dreadful infanticides. Among other atrocities she described was how teen-age friends had been tortured with electricity. CNN carried the testimony live, evening newscasts led with it, newspapers bannered it, and magazines featured it. Amnesty International, which tracks political terrorism worldwide, reported the baby massacre based on Nayirah's testimony, and the Red Crescent cited it before the United Nations.

Later, it turned out that Hill and Knowlton may have been duped. Although many Iraqi atrocities occurred in Kuwait, investigators were never able, even after the war, to corroborate Nayirah's story of the baby massacre. Furthermore, journalists raised questions about a cozy connection between H&K and Congressman Tom Lantos, who arranged the hearing at which Nayirah testified. Questions were raised whether Citizens for a Free Kuwait was a legitimate grassroots organization or a front manufactured for Kuwaiti interests by Hill and Knowlton. Additional doubts surfaced when it was learned that Nayirah was actually the daughter of the Kuwaiti ambassador, which had not been announced at the hearings. To that issue, Hill and Knowlton said it had needed to protect her and her family members from Iraqi death squads.

Some observers minimized the fuss, which came three months after Nayirah's mesmerizing testimony, as part of the rough-and-tumble reality of big-league adversarial American politics. Anyone involved in the process, including public relations agencies, is going to get bloodied from time to time. Through it all, H&K defended its performance on behalf of Citizens for a Free Kuwait by saying it never had any reason to doubt Nayirah's veracity. No one doubted that Hill and Knowlton had succeeded at a crucial point in winning support for the United States to go to war against Iraq.

CNN Kuwait PR Flap

Hill and Knowlton, one of the largest U.S. public relations firms, had a front group for the Kuwaiti government as a client during the buildup for the Persian Gulf war. Critics say the Hill and Knowlton campaign influenced the American people on whether to enter the war, which raises questions about the manipulation of the public on major issues like war and peace. This report, by CNN's Bob Franken, aired December 20, 1990.

IMPORTANCE OF PUBLIC RELATIONS

STUDY PREVIEW Public relations is a persuasive communication tool that people can use to motivate other people and institutions to help them achieve their goals.

DEFINING PUBLIC RELATIONS

It's unfortunate, but the term *public relations* sometimes is used loosely. Some people think it means backslapping, glad-handing and smiling prettily to make people feel good. It's not uncommon for a secretary or receptionist to list "public relations" on a résumé. The fact, however, is that public relations goes far beyond good interpersonal skills. A useful definition is that public relations is a management tool for leaders in business, government and other institutions to establish beneficial *relationships* with other institutions and groups. Four steps are necessary for public relations to accomplish its goals:

IDENTIFY EXISTING RELATIONSHIPS. In modern society, institutions have many relationships. A college, for example, has relationships with its students, its faculty, its staff, its alumni, its benefactors, the neighborhood, the community, the legislature, other colleges, accreditors of its programs, perhaps unions. The list could go on and on. Each of these constituencies is called a *public*—hence the term *public relations*.

TEACHING OBJECTIVE 11-1
Public relations is persuasive communication tool that uses mass media.

EVALUATE THE RELATIONSHIPS.   Through research, the public relations practitioner studies these relationships to determine how well they are working. This evaluation is an ongoing process. A college may have excellent relations with the legislature one year and win major appropriations, but after a scandal related to the president's budget the next year, legislators may be downright unfriendly.

DESIGN POLICIES TO IMPROVE THE RELATIONSHIPS. The job of public relations people is to recommend policies to top management to make these relationships work better, not only for the organization but also for the partners in each relationship. *Paul Garrett*, a pioneer in corporate relations, found that General Motors was not seen in friendly terms during the Great Depression, which put the giant auto-maker at risk with many publics, including its own employees. GM, he advised, needed new policies to seem neighborly—rather than as a far-removed, impersonal, monolithic industrial giant.

KEY PERSON
Paul Garrett devised "enlightened self-interest" concept.

IMPLEMENT THE POLICIES.   Garrett used the term *enlightened self-interest* for his series of policies intended to downsize GM in the eyes of many of the company's publics. Garrett set up municipal programs in towns with GM plants, and grants for schools and scholarships for employees' children. General Motors benefited from a revised image and, in the spirit of enlightened self-interest, so did GM employees, their children and their communities.

Public relations is not a mass medium itself, but PR uses the media as tools to accomplish its goals. To announce GM's initiatives to change its image in the 1930s, Paul Garrett issued news releases that he hoped newspapers, magazines and radio stations would pick up. The number of people in most of the publics with which public relations practitioners need to communicate is so large that it can be reached only through the mass media. The influence of public relations on the news media is extensive. Half of the news in many newspapers originates with formal statements or news releases from organizations that want something in the paper. It is the same with radio and television.

PUBLIC RELATIONS IN A DEMOCRACY

Misconceptions about public relations include the idea that it is a one-way street for institutions and individuals to communicate *to* the public. Actually, the good practice of public relations seeks two-way communication between and among all the people and institutions concerned with an issue.

A task force established by the Public Relations Society of America to explore the stature and role of the profession concluded that public relations has the potential to improve the functioning of democracy by encouraging the exchange of information and ideas on public issues. The task force made these points:

- Public relations is a means for the public to have its desires and interests felt by the institutions in our society. It interprets and speaks for the public to organizations that otherwise might be unresponsive, and it speaks for those organizations to the public.
- Public relations is a means to achieve mutual adjustments between institutions and groups, establishing smoother relationships that benefit the public.

Crisis Management. Something went wrong at a Union Carbide chemical factory at Bhopal, India, and more than 2,000 people died. It was the worst industrial accident in history. Union Carbide fumbled at first in dealing with media inquiries. Company guards denied access to a reporter who wanted to visit a Union Carbide plant in West Virginia that manufactured the same chemical as the Bhopal plant. A few days later, however, the company invited reporters inside the gates en masse. The turnaround represented a realization that shutting out the news media was engendering public suspicions about Union Carbide's culpability in the Bhopal disaster. In contrast, openness can inspire public confidence.

- Public relations is a safety valve for freedom. By providing means of working out accommodations, it makes arbitrary action or coercion less likely.
- Public relations is an essential element in the communication system that enables individuals to be informed on many aspects of subjects that affect their lives.
- Public relations people can help activate the social conscience of the organizations for which they work.

ORIGINS OF PUBLIC RELATIONS

STUDY PREVIEW Many big companies found themselves in disfavor in the late 1800s for ignoring the public good to make profits. Feeling misunderstood, some moguls of industry turned to Ivy Lee, the father of public relations, for counsel on gaining public support.

TEACHING OBJECTIVE 11-2
Public relations originated when Big Business worried about public disfavor.

KEY PERSON
William Henry Vanderbilt: "Public be damned."

MOGULS IN TROUBLE

Nobody would be tempted to think of *William Henry Vanderbilt* as very good at public relations. In 1882, it was Vanderbilt, president of the New York Central Railroad, who said, "The public be damned," when asked about the effect of changing train schedules. Vanderbilt's utterance so infuriated people that it became a banner in the populist crusade against robber barons and tycoons in the late 1800s. Under populist pressure, state governments set up agencies to regulate railroads. Then the national government established the Interstate Commerce Commission to control freight and passenger rates. Government began insisting on safety standards. Labor unions formed in the industries with the worst working conditions, safety records and pay. Journalists added pressure with muckraking exposés on excesses in the railroad, coal and oil trusts; on meat-packing industry frauds; and on patent medicines.

The leaders of industry were slow to recognize the effect of populist objections on their practices. They were comfortable with *social Darwinism*, an adaptation of *Charles Darwin*'s survival-of-the-fittest theory. In fact, they thought themselves forward-thinking in applying Darwin's theory to business and social issues. It was only a few years earlier, in 1859, that Darwin had laid out his biological theory in *On the Origin of Species by Means of Natural Selection*. To cushion the harshness of social Darwinism, many tycoons espoused a paternalism toward those whose "fitness" had not brought them fortune and power. No matter how carefully put, the paternalism seemed arrogant to the "less fit."

George Baer, a railroad president, epitomized both social Darwinism and paternalism in commenting on a labor strike: "The rights and interests of the laboring man will be protected and cared for not by labor agitators but by the Christian men to whom God in His infinite wisdom has given the control of the property interests of the country." Baer was quoted widely, further fueling sentiment against big business. Baer may have been sincere, but his position was read as a cover for excessive business practices by barons who assumed superiority to everyone else.

Meanwhile, social Darwinism came under attack as circuitous reasoning: economic success accomplished by abusive practices could be used to justify further abusive practices, which would lead to further success. Social Darwinism was a dog-eat-dog outlook that hardly jibed with democratic ideals, especially not as described in the preamble to the U.S. Constitution, which sought to "promote the general welfare, and secure the blessings of liberty" for everyone—not for only the chosen "fittest." Into these tensions at the turn of the century came public relations pioneer Ivy Lee.

THE IDEAS OF IVY LEE

Coal mine operators, like the railroad magnates, were held in the public's contempt at the turn of the century. Obsessed with profits, caring little about public sentiment or even the well-being of their employees, the mine operators were vulnerable in the new populist wave. Mine workers organized, and 150,000 in Pennsylvania went out on strike in 1902, shutting down the anthracite industry and disrupting coal-dependent industries, including the railroads. The mine operators snubbed reporters, which probably contributed to a pro-union slant in many news stories and worsened the operators' public image. Not until six months into the strike, when President Theodore Roosevelt threatened to take over the mines with Army troops, did the operators settle.

Shaken finally by Roosevelt's threat and recognizing Roosevelt's responsiveness to public opinion, the mine operators began reconsidering how they went about their

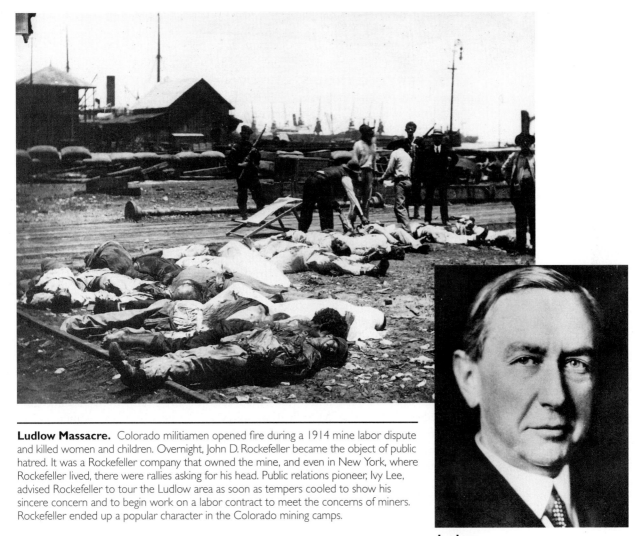

Ludlow Massacre. Colorado militiamen opened fire during a 1914 mine labor dispute and killed women and children. Overnight, John D. Rockefeller became the object of public hatred. It was a Rockefeller company that owned the mine, and even in New York, where Rockefeller lived, there were rallies asking for his head. Public relations pioneer, Ivy Lee, advised Rockefeller to tour the Ludlow area as soon as tempers cooled to show his sincere concern and to begin work on a labor contract to meet the concerns of miners. Rockefeller ended up a popular character in the Colorado mining camps.

Ivy Lee

business. In 1906, with another strike looming, one operator heard about *Ivy Lee*, a young publicist in New York who had new ideas about winning public support. He was hired. In a turnabout in press relations, Lee issued a news release that announced, "The anthracite coal operators, realizing the general public interest in conditions in the mining regions, have arranged to supply the press with all possible information." Then followed a series of releases with information attributed to the mine operators by name—the same people who earlier had preferred anonymity and refused all interview requests. There were no more secret strike strategy meetings. When operators planned a meeting, reporters covering the impending strike were informed. Although reporters were not admitted to the meetings, summaries of the proceedings were given to them immediately afterward. This relative openness eased long-standing hostility toward the operators, and a strike was averted.

KEY PERSON
Ivy Lee laid out fundamentals of public relations.

Lee's success with the mine operators began a career that rewrote the rules on how corporations deal with their various publics. Among his accomplishments were:

CONVERTING INDUSTRY TOWARD OPENNESS.   Railroads had notoriously secretive policies not only about their business practices but even about accidents. When the Pennsylvania Railroad sought Ivy Lee's counsel, he advised against suppressing news—especially on things that inevitably would leak out anyway. When a train jumped the rails near Gap, Pennsylvania, Lee arranged for a special car to take reporters to the scene and even take pictures. The Pennsylvania line was applauded in the press for the openness, and coverage of the railroad, which had been negative for years, began changing. A "bad press" continued plaguing other railroads that persisted in their secretive tradition.

TURNING NEGATIVE NEWS INTO POSITIVE NEWS.   When the U.S. Senate proposed investigating International Harvester for monopolistic practices, Lee advised the giant farm implement manufacturer against reflexive obstructionism and silence. A statement went out announcing that the company, confident in its business practices, not only welcomed but also would facilitate an investigation. Then began a campaign that pointed out International Harvester's beneficence toward its employees. The campaign also emphasized other upbeat information about the company.

PUTTING CORPORATE EXECUTIVES ON DISPLAY.   When workers at a Colorado mine went on strike, company guards fired machine guns and killed several men. More battling followed, during which two women and 11 children were killed. It was called the *Ludlow Massacre*, and John D. Rockefeller Jr., the chief mine owner, was pilloried for what had happened. Rockefeller was an easy target. Like his father, widely despised for the earlier Standard Oil monopolistic practices, John Jr., tried to keep himself out of the spotlight, but suddenly mobs were protesting at his mansion in New York and calling out "shoot him down like a dog." Rockefeller asked Ivy Lee what he should do. Lee began whipping up articles about Rockefeller's human side, his family and his generosity. Then, on Lee's advice, Rockefeller announced he would visit Colorado to see conditions himself. He spent two weeks talking with miners at work and in their homes and meeting their families. It was a news story that reporters could not resist, and it unveiled Rockefeller as a human being, not a far-removed, callous captain of industry. One myth-shattering episode occurred one evening when Rockefeller, after a brief address to miners and their wives, suggested that the floor be cleared for a dance. Before it was all over, John D. Rockefeller Jr. had danced with almost every miner's wife, and the news stories about the evening did a great deal to mitigate antagonism and distrust toward Rockefeller. Back in New York, with Lee's help, Rockefeller put together a proposal for a grievance procedure, which he asked the Colorado miners to approve. It was ratified overwhelmingly.

AVOIDING PUFFERY AND FLUFF.   Ivy Lee came on the scene at a time when many organizations were making extravagant claims about themselves and their products. Circus promoter *P. T. Barnum* made this kind of hyping a fine art in the late 1800s, and he had many imitators. It was an age of puffed-up advertising claims and fluffy rhetoric. Lee noted, however, that people soon saw through

KEY PERSON
P. T. Barnum known for hype.

hyperbolic claims and lost faith in those who made them. In launching his public relations agency in 1906, he vowed to be accurate in everything he said and to provide whatever verification anyone requested. This became part of the creed of good practice in public relations, and it remains so today.

PUBLIC RELATIONS ON A NEW SCALE

The potential of public relations to rally support for a cause was demonstrated on a gigantic scale in World War I and again in World War II. In 1917 President Woodrow Wilson, concerned about widespread antiwar sentiment, asked *George Creel* to head a new government agency whose job was to make the war popular. The Creel Committee cranked out news releases, magazine pieces, posters, even movies. A list of 75,000 local speakers was put together to talk nationwide at school programs, church groups and civic organizations about making the world safe for democracy. More than 15,000 committee articles were printed. Never before had public relations been attempted on such a scale—and it worked. World War I

KEY PERSON
George Creel successful with public relations on mammoth scale.

War Popular. Contrary to myth, World War I did not begin as a popular cause with Americans. In fact, there were antidraft riots in many cities. This prompted President Woodrow Wilson to ask journalist George Creel to launch a major campaign to persuade Americans that the war was important to make the world safe for democracy. Within months, Americans were financing much of the war voluntarily by buying government bonds. This poster was only one aspect of Creel's work, which demonstrated that public relations principles could be applied on a massive scale.

George Creel

became a popular cause even to the point of inspiring people to buy Liberty Bonds, putting up their own money to finance the war outside the usual taxation apparatus.

When World War II began, an agency akin to the Creel Committee was formed. Veteran journalist *Elmer Davis* was put in charge. The new *Office of War Information* was public relations on a bigger scale than ever before.

The Creel and Davis committees employed hundreds of people. Davis had 250 employees handling news releases alone. These staff members, mostly young, carried new lessons about public relations into the private sector after the war. These were the people who shaped corporate public relations as we know it today.

KEY PERSON
Elmer Davis applied public relations with success in World War II.

STRUCTURE OF PUBLIC RELATIONS

STUDY PREVIEW In developing sound policies, corporations and other institutions depend on public relations experts who are sensitive to the implications of policy on the public consciousness. This makes public relations a vital management function. Besides a role in policymaking, public relations people play key roles in carrying out institutional policy.

TEACHING OBJECTIVE 11-3
Public relations is essential management tool.

KEY PERSON
Arthur Page established public relations role in top management.

POLICY ROLE OF PUBLIC RELATIONS

When giant AT&T needed somebody to take over public relations in 1927, the president of the company went to magazine editor *Arthur Page* and offered him a vice presidency. Before accepting, Page laid out several conditions. One was that he have a voice in AT&T policy. Page was hardly on an ego trip. He had seen too many corporations that regarded their public relations arm merely as an executor of policy. Page considered PR itself as a *management function.* To be effective as vice president for public relations, Page knew that he must contribute to the making of high-level corporate decisions as well as executing them.

Perrier Is Back. In 1990, when traces of cancer-causing benzene were found in Perrier, the bottled French mineral water, Perrier's reputation was in jeopardy. So were sales of $100 million a year in the United States alone. The company acted promptly to meet this challenge. First, release all available information about the contamination. Second, explain there was no significant health risk from the minute amounts of benzene. Third, point out that the company voluntarily recalled 160 million bottles from distribution channels worldwide because it did not meet their standards. Fourth, relaunch the product. Fifth, put Perrier President Ronald V. Davis in touch with the public vouching for Perrier's purity and quality controls. Photographs of Davis quaffing Perrier were soon in the news media everywhere. This was all followed, three weeks after the recall, by an advertising campaign, "Perrier Is Back." Sales rebounded.

Today, experts on public relations agree with Arthur Page's concept: When institutions are making policy, they need to consider the effects on their many publics. That can be done best when the person in charge of public relations, ideally at the vice presidential level, is intimately involved in decision-making. The public relations executive advises the rest of the institution's leaders on public perceptions and the effects that policy options might have on perceptions. Also, the public relations vice president is in a better position to implement the institution's policy for having been a part of developing it.

HOW PUBLIC RELATIONS IS ORGANIZED

No two institutions are organized in precisely the same way. At General Motors, 200 people work in public relations. In smaller organizations, PR may be one of several hats worn by a single person. Except in the smallest operations, the public relations department usually has three functional areas of responsibility:

EXTERNAL RELATIONS. This involves communication with groups and people outside the organization, including customers, dealers, suppliers and community leaders. The external-relations unit usually is responsible for encouraging employees to participate in civic activities. Other responsibilities include arranging promotional activities like exhibits, trade shows, conferences and tours.

Public relations people also lobby government agencies and legislators on behalf of their organization, keep the organization abreast of government regulations and legislation, and coordinate relations with political candidates. This may include fund-raising for candidates and coordinating political action committees.

In hospitals and nonprofit organizations, a public relations function may include recruiting and scheduling volunteer workers.

INTERNAL RELATIONS. This involves developing optimal relations with employees, managers, unions, shareholders and other internal groups. In-house newsletters, magazines and brochures are important media for communicating with organizations' internal audiences.

MEDIA RELATIONS. Communication with large groups of people outside an organization is practicable only through the mass media. An organization's coordinator of media relations responds to news media queries, arranges news conferences and issues news releases. These coordinators coach executives for news interviews and sometimes serve as their organization's spokesperson.

PUBLIC RELATIONS AGENCIES

Even though many organizations have their own public relations staff, they may go to public relations agencies for help on specific projects or problems. In the United States today, hundreds of companies specialize in public relations counsel and related services. It is a big business. Income at global PR agencies like Burson-Marsteller runs about $200 million a year.

The biggest agencies offer a full range of services on a global scale. Hill and Knowlton has offices in Cleveland, its original home; Dallas; Frankfurt; Geneva; London; Los Angeles; New York, now its headquarters; Paris; Rome; Seattle; and

MEDIA DATABANK

Major Public Relations Agencies

These are the largest U.S.-based public relations agencies. Because some agencies are part of larger companies that don't break out data on their subordinate units, some data here are estimates.

Company	Income Worldwide	Employees Worldwide	Company	Income Worldwide	Employees Worldwide
Burson-Marsteller	$204 million	2,100	Fleishman-Hillard	59 million	600
Shandick	166 million	1,900	Ketchum	45 million	400
Hill and Knowlton	149 million	1,600	Rowland	44 million	500
Omnicon	66 million	1,000	Ogilvy Adams & Rinehart	36 million	300
Edelman	60 million	700	Manning, Selvage & Lee	31 million	300

Washington, D.C. The agency will take on projects anywhere in the world, either on its own or by working with local agencies.

Besides full-service agencies, there are specialized public relations companies, which focus on a narrow range of services. For example, clipping services cut out and provide newspaper and magazine articles and radio and television items of interest to clients. Among specialized agencies are those that focus exclusively on political campaigns. Others coach corporate executives for news interviews. Others coordinate trade shows.

Some agencies bill clients only for services rendered. Others charge clients just to be on call. Hill and Knowlton, for example, has a minimum $5,000-a-month retainer fee. Agency expenses for specific projects are billed in addition. Staff time usually is at an hourly rate that covers the agency's overhead and allows a profit margin. Other expenses are usually billed with a 15 to 17 percent markup.

PUBLIC RELATIONS SERVICES

STUDY PREVIEW   Public relations deals with publicity and promotion, but it also involves less visible activities. These include lobbying, fund-raising and crisis management. Public relations is distinct from advertising.

ACTIVITIES BEYOND PUBLICITY

TEACHING OBJECTIVE 11-4
Public relations includes crisis management, fundraising, lobbying, promotion, publicity.

Full-service public relations agencies provide a wide range of services built on two of the cornerstones of the business: *publicity* and *promotion*. These agencies are ready to conduct media campaigns to rally support for a cause, create an image or turn a problem into an asset. Publicity and promotion, however, are only the most visible services offered by public relations agencies. Others include:

LOBBYING.   Every state capital has hundreds of public relations practitioners whose specialty is representing their clients to legislative bodies and government agencies. In North Dakota, hardly a populous state, more than 300 persons are registered as lobbyists in the capital city of Bismarck.

Lobbying has been called a "growth industry." The number of registered lobbyists in Washington, D.C., has grown from 3,400 in 1976 to almost 10,000 today. In addition, there are an estimated 20,000 other people in the nation's capital who have slipped through registration requirements but who nonetheless ply the halls of government to plead their clients' interests.

In one sense, lobbyists are expediters. They know local traditions and customs, and they know who is in a position to affect policy. Lobbyists advise their clients, which include trade associations, corporations, public interest groups and regulated utilities and industries, on how to achieve their goals by working with legislators and government regulators. Many lobbyists call themselves "government relations specialists."

POLITICAL COMMUNICATION.   Every capital has political consultants whose work mostly is advising candidates for public office. Services include campaign management, survey research, publicity, media relations and image consulting. Political consultants also work on elections, referendums, recalls and other public policy issues.

IMAGE CONSULTING.   Image consulting has been a growing specialized branch of public relations since the first energy crisis in the 1970s. Oil companies, realizing that their side of the story was not getting across, turned to image consultants to groom corporate spokespersons, often chief executives, to meet reporters one on one and go on talk shows. The groomers did a brisk business, and it paid off in countering the stories and rumors that were blaming the oil companies for skyrocketing fuel prices.

Jacqueline Thompson, author of the *Directory of Personal Image Consultants*, listed 53 entries in 1981 and has been adding up to 157 new entries a year since then. About these consultants, said Thompson: "They will lower the pitch of your voice, remove your accent, correct your 'body language,' modify your unacceptable behavior, eliminate your negative self-perception, select your wardrobe, restyle your hair, and teach you how to speak off the cuff or read a speech without putting your audience to sleep."

FINANCIAL PUBLIC RELATIONS.   Financial public relations dates to the 1920s and 1930s, when the U.S. Securities and Exchange Commission cracked down on abuses in the financial industry. Regulations on promoting sales of securities are complex. It is the job of people in financial PR to know not only the principles of public relations but also the complex regulations governing the promotion of securities in corporate mergers, acquisitions, new issues and stock splits.

FUND-RAISING.   Some public relations people specialize in fund-raising and membership drives. Many colleges, for example, have their own staffs to perform these functions. Others look to fund-raising firms to manage capital drives. Such an agency employs a variety of techniques, from mass mailings to phonathon soliciting, and charges a percentage of the amount raised.

CONTINGENCY PLANNING.   Many organizations rely on public relations people to design programs to address problems that can be expected to occur. Airlines, for example, need detailed plans for handling inevitable plane crashes—situations requiring quick, appropriate responses under tremendous pressure. When a crisis occurs, an organization can turn to public relations people for advice on dealing with it. Some agencies specialize in *crisis management*, which involves picking up the pieces either when a contingency plan fails or when there was no plan to deal with a crisis.

POLLING.   Public-opinion sampling is essential in many public relations projects. Full-service agencies can either conduct surveys themselves or contract with companies that specialize in surveying.

EVENTS COORDINATION.   Many public relations people are involved in coordinating a broad range of events, including product announcements, news conferences and convention planning. Some in-house public relations departments and agencies have their own artistic and audio-visual production talent to produce brochures, tapes and other promotional materials. Other agencies contract for those services.

PUBLIC RELATIONS AND ADVERTISING

Both public relations and advertising involve persuasion, but most of the similarities end there. Public relations has responsibility in shaping an organization's policy. It is a management activity. Advertising is not. The work of advertising is much narrower.

Taking on the Media. After ABC television reported that tobacco companies spiked cigarettes to make them more addictive, R.J. Reynolds responded with a multiprong campaign to tell its side. The tobacco company sued ABC. The company also ran advertorials in the *Wall Street Journal* and elsewhere featuring the chairman of the company. Adversarial responses to the media are not mainstream public relations, but they are becoming more frequent. General Motors used adversarial public relations against NBC after the network rigged a GM truck to explode in order to support a claim that they were prone to fires in collisions. GM filed a suit and went public with evidence that NBC's video was staged. After extracting an apology from a humiliated NBC, GM dropped its suit.

It focuses on selling a service or product after all the management decisions have been made. Public relations "sells" points of view and images, which are intangibles and therefore hard to measure. In advertising, success is measurable with tangibles, like sales, that can be calculated from the bottom line.

When an organization decides it needs a persuasive campaign, there is a choice between public relations and advertising. One advantage of advertising is that the organization controls the message. By buying space or time in the mass media, an organization has the final say on what it says in its advertising messages.

In public relations, in contrast, an organization tries to influence the media to tell its story its way, but the message that goes out is actually up to the media. A news reporter, for example, may lean heavily on a public relations person for information about an organization, but the reporter may also gather information from other sources, and, in the end, it is the reporter who writes the story. The result, usually, is that a news story carries more credibility than advertisements with mass audiences. The disadvantage to an organization is the risk that comes with surrendering control over the message that goes to the public.

For many persuasive campaigns, organizations use both public relations and advertising. Increasingly, public relations and advertising people find themselves working together. This is especially true in corporations that have adopted *total marketing plans*, which attempt to coordinate advertising as a marketing tool with promotion and publicity of the sort that pubic relations experts can provide. Several major advertising agencies, aware of their clients' shift to total marketing, have acquired or established public relations subsidiaries to provide a wider range of services under their roof.

It's this overlap that has prompted some advertising agencies to move more into public relations. The WWP Group of London, a global advertising agency, has acquired both Hill and Knowlton, the third-largest public relations company in the United States, and the Ogilvy PR Group, the ninth largest. The Young & Rubicam advertising agency has three public relations subsidiaries: Burson-Marsteller, the largest; Cohn & Wolf, the 13th; and Creswell, Munsell, Fultz & Zirbel, the 50th. These are giant enterprises, which reflect the conglomeration and globalization of both advertising and public relations.

Public relations and advertising also overlap in *institutional advertising*, which involves producing ads not to sell goods or services but to promote an institution's image or position on a public issue.

MEDIA RELATIONS

STUDY PREVIEW Public relations people generally favor candor in working with the news media. Even so, some organizations opt to stonewall journalistic inquiries. An emerging school of thought in public relations is to challenge negative stories aggressively and publicly.

OPEN MEDIA RELATIONS

The common wisdom among public relations people today is to be open and candid with the mass media. It is a principle that dates to Ivy Lee, and case studies abound to confirm its effectiveness. A classic case study on this point is the Tylenol crisis.

Johnson & Johnson had spent many years and millions of dollars to inspire public confidence in its product Tylenol, and by 1982 the product was the leader in

TEACHING OBJECTIVE 11-5
Public relations usually involves candid, proactive mass media relations.

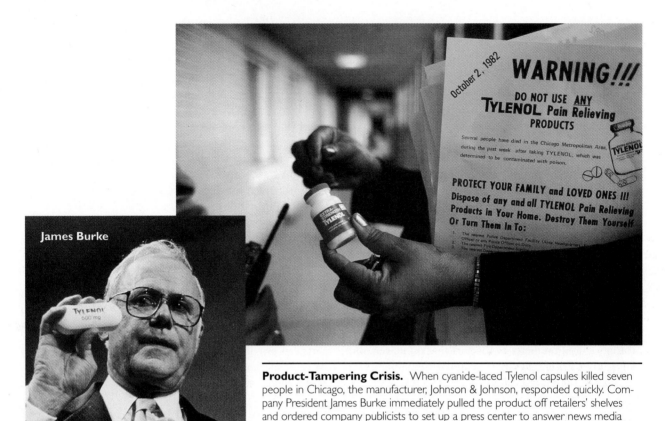

Product-Tampering Crisis. When cyanide-laced Tylenol capsules killed seven people in Chicago, the manufacturer, Johnson & Johnson, responded quickly. Company President James Burke immediately pulled the product off retailers' shelves and ordered company publicists to set up a press center to answer news media inquiries as fully as possible. Burke's action and candor helped restore the public's shaken confidence in Tylenol, and the product resumed its significant market share after the crisis ended. It turned out that it had been a crazy person outside Johnson & Johnson's production and distribution system who had contaminated the capsules rather than a manufacturing lapse.

TEACHING OBJECTIVE 11-4
Public relations organizations are
working to improve their image.

a crowded field of headache remedies with 36 percent of the market. Then disaster struck. Seven people in Chicago died after taking Tylenol capsules laced with cyanide. James Burke, president of Johnson & Johnson, and Lawrence Foster, vice president for public relations, moved quickly. Within hours, Johnson & Johnson:

■ Halted the manufacture and distribution of Tylenol.
■ Removed Tylenol products from retailers' shelves.
■ Launched a massive advertising campaign requesting people to exchange Tylenol capsules for a safe replacement.
■ Summoned 50 public relations employees from Johnson & Johnson and its subsidiary companies to staff a press center to answer media and consumer questions forthrightly.
■ Ordered an internal company investigation of the Tylenol manufacturing and distribution process.
■ Promised full cooperation with government investigators.
■ Ordered the development of tamper-proof packaging for the reintroduction of Tylenol products after the contamination problem was resolved.

Investigators determined within days that an urban terrorist had poisoned the capsules. Although the news media exonerated Johnson & Johnson of negligence, the company nonetheless had a tremendous problem: how to restore public confidence in Tylenol. Many former Tylenol users were reluctant to take a chance, and the Tylenol share of the analgesic market dropped to 6 percent.

To address the problem, Johnson & Johnson called in the Burson-Marsteller public relations agency. Burson-Marsteller recommended a media campaign to capitalize on the high marks the news media had given the company for openness during the crisis. Mailgrams went out inviting journalists to a 30-city video teleconference to hear James Burke announce the reintroduction. Six hundred reporters turned out, and Johnson & Johnson officials took their questions live.

To stir even wider attention, 7,500 *media kits* had been sent to newsrooms the day before the teleconference. The kits included a news release and a bevy of supporting materials: photographs, charts and background information.

The resulting news coverage was extensive. On average, newspapers carried 32 column inches of copy on the announcement. Network television and radio as well as local stations also afforded heavy coverage. Meanwhile, Johnson & Johnson executives, who had attended a workshop on how to make favorable television appearances, made themselves available as guests on the network morning shows and talk shows such as "Donahue" and "Nightline." At the same time, Johnson & Johnson distributed 80 million free coupons to encourage people to use Tylenol again.

The massive media-based public relations campaign worked. Within a year, Tylenol had regained 80 percent of its former market share, and today, in an increasingly crowded analgesic field, Tylenol is again the market leader with annual sales of $670 million, compared with $520 million before the cyanide crisis.

PROACTIVE MEDIA RELATIONS

Although public relations campaigns cannot control what the media say, public relations people can help shape how news media report issues by taking the initiative. In the Tylenol crisis, for example, Johnson & Johnson reacted quickly and decisively and took control of disseminating information, which, coupled with full disclosure, headed off false rumors that could have caused further damage.

PROACTIVE CRISIS RESPONSES.   A principle in crisis management is to seize leadership on the story. This involves anticipating what journalists will want to know and providing it to them before they even have time to formulate their questions. Ivy Lee did this time and again, and Johnson & Johnson did it in 1982.

For successful crisis management, public relations people need strong ongoing relationships with an organization's top officials. Otherwise, when a crisis strikes, they likely will have difficulty rounding up the kind of breaking information they need to deal effectively with the news media. During the 1991 Persian Gulf war, Pentagon spokesperson Pete Williams received high marks as a public relations person for shaping news coverage of the conflict. Williams did this by tapping his close working relationships with Defense Secretary Dick Cheney and the Joint Chiefs of Staff for information favorable to the war effort. At regular news briefings, sometimes several a day, Williams provided so much grist for the journalistic mill that reporters were overwhelmed putting it together for stories, which reduced the time available for them to go after stories on their own. The war was reported largely as the Pentagon wanted.

ONGOING MEDIA RELATIONSHIPS.   Good media relations cannot be forged in the fire of a crisis. Organizations that survive a crisis generally have a history of solid media relations. Their public relations staff people know reporters, editors and news directors on a first-name basis. They avoid hyping news releases on routine matters, and they work hard at earning the trust of journalists.

Many public relations people, in fact, are seasoned journalists themselves, and they understand how journalists go about their work. It is their journalistic background that made them attractive candidates for their PR jobs. Pete Williams, for example, was a television news reporter in Wyoming before making a midcareer shift to join Dick Cheney's staff in Washington when Cheney was first elected to Congress from Wyoming.

SOUND OPERATING PRINCIPLES.   An underlying strength that helped see Johnson & Johnson through the Tylenol crisis was the company's credo. The credo was a written vow that Johnson & Johnson's first responsibility was to "those who use our products and services." The credo, which had been promoted in-house for years, said: "Every time a business hires, builds, sells or buys, it is acting *for the people* as well as *for itself*, and it must be prepared to accept full responsibility."

With such a sound operating principle, Johnson & Johnson's crisis response was, in some respects, almost reflexive. Going silent, for example, would have run counter to the principles that Johnson & Johnson people had accepted as part of their corporate culture for years.

AMBIVALENCE IN MEDIA RELATIONS

Despite the advantages of open media relations, there are companies that choose not to embrace that approach. The business magazine *Fortune* has listed these major corporations as notorious for not even returning phone calls when journalists call:

- Amerada Hess, the huge crude oil and natural gas company.
- Winn-Dixie, the southern supermarket chain.
- Texas Instruments, the semiconductor company, which felt stung by 1983 media coverage of a $145 million loss.

Some corporations take a middle ground, currying media coverage selectively. Giant IBM, which receives 30,000 media queries a year, frets that news coverage would underscore its sheer size and invite federal antitrust scrutiny. IBM turns away questions on many issues, including the company's long-term planning. The corporation's PR chief, Seth McCormick, spurns Ivy Lee's maxim that corporate executives should be "on display." In an interview, McCormick told *Fortune:* "We control what is said about the company through the sparsity of heads for the outside world to talk to. We like it that way."

Although IBM ignores the common wisdom about media relations, the corporation shows up frequently in rankings of the most respected companies in the nation. An imponderable question is whether IBM's reputation is due to its posture on media relations or in spite of it.

Joseph Hazelwood

Lawrence Rawl

Messing Up. The Exxon public-relations operations bungled badly when a tanker went aground off Alaska in 1989, causing a gigantic environmental disaster. Exxon Chairman Lawrence Rawl remained silent for a week. Exxon was slow to mobilize its cleanup crews and then blamed Coast Guard and state authorities for delays. Also, Exxon tried to handle media inquiries with a one-person press center, which was hardly sufficient. Things worsened. Amid media finger-pointing at the captain of the ship, Joseph Hazelwood, Exxon publicly abandoned him. Public sympathy shifted to the captain when it turned out that the media had given him a worse rap than he was due.

Procter & Gamble is another major U.S. company that generally is tight-lipped about how it conducts its business, with the notable exception of product promotions. Another notable exception was Procter & Gamble's full-scale public relations campaign in the 1980s to squelch persistent rumors that its corporate symbol—the moon and stars—had roots in Satanism.

ADVERSARIAL PUBLIC RELATIONS

KEY PERSON
Herb Schmertz developed adversarial public relations for Mobil.

LECTURE RESOURCE 11-A
Class Exercise: Identify local media decision makers.

Public relations took on aggressive, even feisty tactics when Mobil Oil decided in the 1970s not to take media criticism lightly any more. *Herb Schmertz*, vice president for Mobil's public affairs, charted a new course by:

- Filing formal complaints with news organizations when coverage was unfair in the company's view.
- Taking Mobil's case directly to the general public with paid advertising, *advertorials* as they are called, a splicing of the words "advertising" and "editorial," that explained the company's views.
- Sending corporate representatives on media tours to spread Mobil's side to as many constituencies as possible.

Schmertz's energetic counterattacks were a departure from conventional wisdom in pubic relations, which was to let criticism go unanswered or, at most, to complain privately to executives of news organizations about negative coverage as

Mobil Avertorial. Many public relations practitioners seek to avoid confrontation, but Herb Schmertz of Mobil bought space in newspapers and magazines beginning in the 1970s to lay out his company's positions on controversial issues and even to be confrontational. Schmertz tackled the news media when he felt Mobil had not received a fair shake in coverage. These position statements are called "advertorials" because they are in space purchased as advertising and their content is like an editorial.

Herb Schmertz

unwarranted. The conventional wisdom was that a public response would only bring more attention to the negative coverage.

In abandoning passivity, Mobil was adapting what sports fans call the Red Auerbach technique. Auerbach, the legendary coach of the Boston Celtics, was known for criticizing referees. He realized they would never change a call, but he believed that refs would be less inclined to make questionable calls against the Celtics if they knew that Auerbach would jump all over them. Mobil President Rawleigh Warner Jr. explained the new Mobil policy this way: "People know that if they take a swipe at us, we will fight back."

Schmertz employed the full range of PR tools in 1974 when ABC aired a television documentary that raised critical questions about the U.S. oil industry. Mobil objected first to ABC and then fired off a formal complaint to the National News Council, a volunteer media watchdog group. Mobil claimed 32 inaccuracies and instances of unfairness and requested that the council investigate. Mobil also issued an unusually lengthy news release, quoting from the documentary and offering point-by-point rebuttals.

Six Mobil executives were given a crash course on giving good interviews and sent out to meet the news media. In two years, the executives and other Mobil representatives appeared on 365 television and 211 radio shows and talked with 80 newspaper reporters. Schmertz encouraged them to take the offensive. To counter the ABC impression that the oil industry still engaged in the bad practices of its past, Schmertz told executives to stress that such information was outdated. "Put the shoe on the other foot," he said, advising the Mobil executives to say the impression left by the ABC documentary was "comparable to Mobil's producing a documentary about today's television industry and pointing to a 1941 FCC decree requiring RCA to rid itself of one of its networks as evidence of a current conspiracy."

Advertorials were part of Mobil's initiatives. Under Schmertz, as much as $6 million a year went into newspaper and magazine ads, explaining the company's position. Mobil also began producing its own television programs on energy issues and providing them free to stations. The programs had a journalistic tone, and many stations ran them as if they were actual documentaries rather than part of Mobil's media campaign.

The jury is still out on whether Schmertz's aggressive sparring is good policy. Most organizations continue to follow the traditional thinking that taking on the media only generates more attention on the original bad news. On the other hand, Schmertz's approach has been tried by some major corporations. Bechtel, Illinois Power and Kaiser Aluminum all have called for independent investigations of stories that reflected badly on them.

Another adversarial approach, although not recommended by most public relations people, is for an offended organization to sever relations with the source of unfavorable news—an information boycott. In 1954, in a spectacular pout, General Motors cut off contact with *Wall Street Journal* reporters and withdrew advertising from the newspaper. This approach carries great risks:

- By going silent, an organization loses avenues for conveying its message to mass audiences.
- An organization that yanks advertising to punish detractors is perceived negatively for coercively wielding its economic might.
- An organization that quits advertising in an effective advertising medium will lose sales.

A boycott differs from Schmertz's adversarial approach in an important respect. Schmertz responds to negative news by contributing to the exchange of information and ideas, which is positive in a democratic society. An information boycott, on the other hand, restricts the flow of information. Today, GM's policy has returned to the conventional wisdom of not arguing with anyone who buys paper by the ton and ink by the barrel.

PROFESSIONALIZATION

STUDY PREVIEW Public relations has a tarnished image that stems from shortsighted promotion and whitewashing techniques of the late 1800s. While some dubious practices continue, PR leaders are working to improve standards.

A TARNISHED HERITAGE

LECTURE RESOURCE 11-B
Guest Speaker: Publicist for local sports team.

Unsavory elements in the heritage of public relations remain a heavy burden. P. T. Barnum, whose name became synonymous with hype, attracted crowds to his stunts and shows in the latter 1800s with extravagant promises. Sad to say, some promoters still use Barnum's tactics. The claims for snake oils and elixirs from Barnum's era live on in commercials for pain relievers and cold remedies. The early response of tycoons to muckraking attacks, before Ivy Lee came along, was *whitewashing*—covering up the abuses but not correcting them. It is no wonder that the term "PR" sometimes is used derisively. To say something is "all PR" means it lacks substance. Of people whose apparent positive qualities are a mere façade, it may be said that they have "good PR."

Although journalists rely heavily on public relations people for information, many journalists look with suspicion on PR practitioners. Not uncommon among seasoned journalists are utterances like: "I've never met a PR person I couldn't distrust." Such cynicism flows partly from the journalists' self-image as unfettered truth seekers whose only obligation is serving their audiences' needs. PR people, on the other hand, are seen as obligated to their employers, whose interests do not always dovetail with the public good. Behind their backs, PR people are called "flaks," a takeoff on the World War II slang for antiaircraft bursts intended to stop enemy bombers. PR *flakkers*, as journalists use the term, interfere with journalistic truth seeking by putting forth slanted, self-serving information, which is not necessarily the whole story.

The journalism-PR tension is exacerbated by a common newsroom view that PR people try to get free news hole space for their messages rather than buy airtime and column inches. This view may seem strange considering that 50 to 90 percent of all news stories either originate with or contain information supplied by PR people. It is also strange considering that many PR people are former news reporters and editors. No matter how uncomfortable PR people and journalists are as bedfellows, they are bedfellows nonetheless.

Some public relations people have tried to leapfrog the negative baggage attached to the term "PR" by abandoning it. The U.S. military shucked "PR" and tried *public information*, but it found itself still dogged by the same distrust that surrounded "public relations." The military then tried *public affairs*, but that was no solution either. Many organizations have tried *communication* as a way around the problem. Common labels today include the military's current *public affairs* offices and businesses' *corporate communication* departments.

STANDARDS AND CERTIFICATION

The *Public Relations Society of America*, which has grown to 12,000 members, has a different approach: improving the quality of public relations work, whatever the label. In 1951, the association adopted a code of professional standards. In a further professionalization step in 1965, PRSA established a certification process. Those who meet the criteria and pass exams are allowed to place *APR*, which stands for *accredited public relations professional*, after their names. The criteria are:

- Being recommended by an already accredited PRSA member.
- Five years of professional experience.
- Passing an eight-hour written examination on public relations principles, techniques, history and ethics.
- Passing an oral exam conducted by three professionals.

The process is rigorous. Typically, a third of those who attempt the examination fail it the first time. Once earned, certification needs to be renewed through continuing education, and the right to use "APR" can be taken away if a member violates the PRSA code. About 3,800 PRSA members hold APR certification.

The PRSA set of professional standards, intended to encourage a high level of practice, says a member shall:

- Deal fairly with clients or employees, past, present or potential; with fellow practitioners; and with the general public.
- Conduct his or her professional life in accord with the public interest.
- Adhere to truth and accuracy and to generally accepted standards of good taste.
- Not engage in any practice that tends to corrupt the integrity of channels of communication or the process of government.
- Not intentionally communicate false or misleading information.

PRSA is not alone in encouraging the practice of public relations at a high level. The *International Association of Business Communicators*, with 125 chapters, also keeps dialogue going on professional issues with seminars and conferences. Some professional groups are highly specialized, like the Library Public Relations Council, the Bank Marketing Association and the Religious PR Council. The International Public Relations Association, with members in 60 countries, sponsors the World Congress of Public Relations every third year. The student arm of PRSA, the *Public Relations Student Society of America*, works through 145 campus chapters at improving standards.

CHAPTER WRAP-UP

When Ivy Lee hung up a shingle in New York for a new publicity agency in 1906, he wanted to distance himself from the huckstering that marked most publicity at the time. To do that, Lee issued a declaration of principles for the new agency and sent it out to editors. Today, Lee's declaration remains a classic statement on the practice of public relations. It promised that the agency would deal only in legitimate news about its clients, and no fluff. It invited journalists to pursue more information about the agency's clients. It also vowed to be honest and accurate.

Here's Lee's declaration: "This is not a secret press bureau. All our work is done in the open. We aim to supply news. This is not an advertising agency; if you think any of our matter ought properly to go to your business office, do not use it. Our matter is accurate. Further details on any subject treated will be supplied promptly, and any editor will be assisted most cheerfully in verifying directly any statement of fact. Upon inquiry, full information will be given to any editor concerning those on whose behalf an article is sent out. In brief, our plan is, frankly and openly, on behalf of the business concerns and public institutions, to supply to the press and the public of the United States prompt and accurate information concerning subjects which is of value and interest to the public to know about."

The declaration hangs in many public relations shops today.

QUESTIONS FOR REVIEW

1. What is public relations? How is public relations connected to the mass media?

2. Why did big business become interested in the techniques and principles of public relations beginning in the late 1800s?

3. How is public relations a management tool?

4. What is the range of activities in which public relations people are involved?

5. What kind of relationship do most people strive to have with the mass media?

6. Why does public relations have a bad image? What are public relations professionals doing about it?

QUESTIONS FOR CRITICAL THINKING

1. When Ivy Lee accepted the Pennsylvania Railroad as a client in 1906, he saw the job as "interpreting the Pennsylvania Railroad to the public and interpreting the public to the Pennsylvania Railroad." Compare Lee's point with Arthur Page's view of public relations as a management function.

2. A federal grand jury indicted the Chrysler Corporation in 1987 for disconnecting odometers from 60,000 new vehicles, giving them to company executives to drive, sometimes hundreds of miles, then reconnecting the odometers and selling the cars as new. Chrysler Chairman Lee Iacocca called a news conference, admitted the practice "went beyond dumb and reached all the way to stupid," promised it would not happen again, and offered to compensate people who bought the "new" cars. Would Ivy Lee endorse how Iacocca dealt with the situation?

3. How would a corporate leader of the 1880s have handled the Chrysler odometer tampering?

4. How are public relations practitioners trying to overcome the complaints from journalists that they are flakkers interfering with an unfettered pursuit of truth?

5. What was the contribution of the Committee on Public Information, usually called the Creel Committee, to public relations after World War I?

6. How do public relations agencies turn profits?

7. When does an institution with its own in-house public relations operation need to hire a PR agency?

8. Explain the concept of enlightened self-interest.

9. How did the confluence of the following three phenomena at the turn of the century contribute to the emergence of modern public relations?

The related concepts of social Darwinism, a social theory; laissez-faire, a government philosophy; and paternalism, a practice of business.

Muckraking, which attacked prevalent abuses of the public interest.

Advertising, which had grown since the 1830s as a way to reach great numbers of people.

10. Showman P. T. Barnum epitomized 19th-century press agentry with extravagant claims, like promoting the midget Tom Thumb as a Civil War general. To attract crowds to a tour by an unknown European soprano, Jenny Lind, Barnum labeled her "the Swedish Nightingale." Would such promotional methods work today? Keep in mind that Barnum, explaining his methods, once said, "There's a sucker born every minute."

FOR FURTHER LEARNING

Scott M. Cutlip, Allen H. Center and Glen M. Broom. *Effective Public Relations*, 6th ed. (Prentice Hall, 1985). This widely used introductory textbook touches all bases.

Ray Eldon Hiebert. *Courtier to the Crowd: The Story of Ivy Lee and the Development of Public Relations* (Iowa State University Press, 1966). Professor Hiebert's flattering biography focuses on the enduring public relations principles articulated, if not always practiced, by Ivy Lee.

George S. McGovern and Leonard F. Guttridge. *The Great Coalfield War* (Houghton Mifflin, 1972). This account of the Ludlow Massacre includes the success of the Ivy Lee–inspired campaign to rescue the Rockefeller reputation but is less than enthusiastic about Lee's corporate-oriented perspective and sometimes shoddy fact gathering.

Kevin McManus. "Video Coaches." *Forbes* 129 (June 7, 1982). McManus provides additional background on the emerging field of image consulting.

Lael M. Moynihan. "Horrendous PR Crises: What They Did When the Unthinkable Happened." *Media History Digest* 8 (Spring–Summer 1988):1, 19–25. Moynihan, a consumer relations specialist, details eight major cases of crisis management through proven public relations principles.

Herbert Schmertz and William Novak. *Good-bye to the Low Profile: The Art of Creative Confrontation* (Little, Brown, 1986). Combative Herb Schmertz passes on the lessons he learned as Mobil Oil's innovative public relations chief, including how-tos for advertorials and preparation of executives for interviews with journalists.

Perry Dean Young. *God's Bullies: Power Politics and Religious Tyranny* (Henry Holt, 1982). Young provides a quick look at contemporary image consulting.

FOR KEEPING UP TO DATE

The trade journal *O'Dwyer's PR Services* tracks the industry on a monthly basis.

Other sources of ongoing information are *Public Relations Journal*, *Public Relations Quarterly* and *Public Relations Review*.

OF all the ills that flesh is heir to few cause more intense suffering than earache. Not only to children, but to grown people it seems as if malignant sprites were at work tormenting the most sensitive organ of the body.

Salva-cea,

(TRADE-MARK)

the new lubricant, is just the remedy for such cases. A little in the ear will give instant relief and permit quiet rest. It will accomplish the same result with Neuralgia, Lumbago, Convulsions, Paralysis, Bruises, Pains in the Joints, Aches and Sprains, Eczema, Burns, Toothache, Boils, Ulcers, Stings,

and all kindred complaints. It is in truth the most powerful healing agent ever discovered.

Only quite recently has this marvellous remedy been before the public. During this short time the numerous cures that have been effected, and the numerous important testimonials that have been received, have been absolutely unprecedented in the history of the world. Salva-cea forms a medicine chest in itself, and is absolutely invaluable in every household.

Salva-cea should be in every Home, Workshop, Police-Station, Hospital, and Institution—and wherever a Pain-Relieving, Soothing, and Curative Lubricant is likely to be required. No discovery in the world of Healing Remedies has had such high testimony.

ADVERTISING CONTRIBUTES TO PROSPERITY, FINANCES MOST OF THE MASS MEDIA, AND FACILITATES INTELLIGENT CONSUMER DECISION MAKING

MOST ADVERTISING MESSAGES ARE CARRIED THROUGH THE MASS MEDIA

ADVERTISING AGENCIES CREATE AND PLACE ADS FOR ADVERTISERS

ADVERTISEMENTS ARE CAREFULLY PLACED IN MEDIA TO REACH APPROPRIATE AUDIENCES FOR PRODUCTS AND SERVICES

TACTICS INCLUDE BRAND NAMES, LOWEST COMMON DENOMINATORS, POSITIONING, REDUNDANCY

ADVERTISING USES PSYCHOLOGY TO TAP AUDIENCE INTERESTS

A GLOBALIZATION OF THE ADVERTISING INDUSTRY HAS CREATED OPPORTUNITIES AND PROBLEMS

ADVERTISING MESSAGES HAVE SHIFTED FROM "BUYER BEWARE" TO "SELLER BEWARE"

ADVERTISING PEOPLE NEED TO SOLVE PROBLEMS CREATED BY AD CLUTTER AND CREATIVE EXCESSES

chapter 12

ADVERTISING
SELLING GOODS AND SERVICES

Chris Whittle and Phillip Moffitt were college buddies at the University of Tennessee. Like a lot of young people, they had big ideas. One was to start a national college magazine. The major obstacle was bankrolling the project: The magazine would need advertisers. After a lot of head-scratching Whittle and Moffitt pitched their idea to Toyota, the Japanese car maker, and Toyota bought it. The magazine seemed a perfect vehicle for reaching college seniors who, nearing graduation, wallets depleted after four years of tuition, needed cheap wheels. Toyota not only manufactured low-cost vehicles but also was especially eager to expand its U.S. sales by finding market niches. In 1966 Toyota became the major sponsor of the magazine, *13–30,* and its ads dominated the magazine's pages.

Even before graduating, Whittle and Moffitt were rolling in dough, mostly from Toyota. Within a few years, in 1979, they had the resources to buy *Esquire,* the classy men's magazine, and score new profits. Seven years later, wanting to try new adventures, they sold *Esquire* to the Hearst media conglomerate and dissolved their partnership to go their separate ways.

During the *Esquire* years, Whittle had dallied with a sideline enterprise that created information-loaded packages aimed at audiences that advertisers had difficulty reaching through traditional media. It was an enterprise that harkened back to the *13–30* concept that brought Toyota together with a new generation of car buyers.

Chris Whittle. As an alternative to traditional media vehicles, Chris Whittle offers ways for advertisers to target audiences that are especially responsive to certain products. His *Special Reports* magazines, displayed in fancy wooden cases in physician's waiting rooms, are among Whittle's media. He also has launched a video service that beams programs—and advertisements—into waiting rooms.

Now on his own and back in Knoxville with the *Esquire* experience behind him, Whittle hatched what seemed an audacious idea: a glossy, oversize magazine for physician's waiting rooms. The magazine would go free to the doctors if they agreed to cancel their waiting-room subscriptions to all other magazines. To potential advertisers, Whittle extolled the fact that people waiting to see the doctor would be a captive audience. Furthermore, he guaranteed to advertisers that no competing products could buy space in the magazine. To physicians, he provided a classy wooden display rack for six current issues and promised that a representative would drop by personally once a month with fresh copies so the issues would never become dog-eared and worn. In 1988 the first issues of *Special Report* appeared, loaded with articles on family, health, personality and sports topics—and advertising.

It was the first initiative in what Chris Whittle called his "guerrilla media." Since then, he has launched other alternative vehicles for advertisers. And advertisers, buffeted by the recession of the early 1990s, proved especially eager to experiment with new approaches to recoup lost sales.

Although not all of Whittle's enterprises have succeeded, he has been a leader in developing alternatives to the traditional media for reaching people whom advertisers want to reach. Among Whittle's enterprises:

- **Channel One.** Whittle beams a 12-minute daily newscast for children to watch at school. This captive audience, estimated at 6.6 million young people aged 12 to 17, is three times larger than the most popular television shows among teenagers. Not surprisingly, Whittle has no problem lining up advertisers, even at $150,000 for a 30-second slot. Some educators and parents object, however, that Channel One commercializes the schoolhouse.
- **Larger Agenda.** Whittle publishes the Larger Agenda series of books on major public policy issues. They are distributed free only to business executives. Sumptuously bound and graphically lavish, these books feature articles by people prominent in their fields and advertising from a single corporate sponsor.
- **Special Reports Television.** Whittle has replaced his *Special Reports* waiting-room magazines with a video service with short items of general interest and ads from companies that view people waiting to see their physician as potential customers.

Whittle is at the cutting edge of *alternative media,* but he is not alone in offering advertisers access to narrowly targeted potential customers. Turner Broadcasting has a video service for airport waiting rooms. NBC has ad-loaded video programming for grocery store checkout lines. Future possibilities include television for breaks during professional meetings and seminars.

New technology will expand the possibilities for alternative media. By the year 2010, as Whittle sees it, written advertising messages will no longer be in the printed media but on discs that can be played in book-sized computers. His vision also includes some old-fashioned peddling techniques, including a return of door-to-door sales reps who make the pitch one on one with customers.

All this is a serious threat to traditional media companies whose products, especially magazines and television, are geared to being read and watched at home. Whittle and other alternative-media companies are reaching people not just at home but wherever they are, and the advertising that these *place-based* media take is advertising that once went into *home-based* media.

IMPORTANCE OF ADVERTISING

STUDY PREVIEW Advertising is key in a consumer economy. Without it, people would have a hard time even knowing what products and services are available. Advertising, in fact, is essential to a prosperous society. Advertising also is the financial basis of important contemporary mass media.

ADVERTISING AND CONSUMER ECONOMIES

Advertising is a major component of modern economies. In the United States, the amount that advertisers spend to promote their wares is about 2 percent of the gross national product. When the GNP is up, so is advertising spending. When the GNP falters, as it did in the early 1990s, many manufacturers, distributors and retailers pull back their advertising expenditures.

Place-Based Media. Advertisers are dabbling with alternatives to the traditional media for delivering their messages. Newspapers stand to lose grocery advertising to in-store coupon dispensers like this Actmedia device, located right on the shelf near the advertised product. Advertisers using Actmedia pay to have the devices stocked with up to 1,500 coupons a month.

The essential role of advertising in a modern consumer economy is obvious if you think about how people decide what to buy. If a shoe manufacturer were unable to tout the virtues of its footwear by advertising in the mass media, people would have a hard time learning about the product, let alone knowing that it is what they want.

ADVERTISING AND PROSPERITY

Advertising's phenomenal continuing growth has been a product of a plentiful society. In a poor society with a shortage of goods, people line up for necessities like food and clothing. Advertising has no role and serves no purpose when survival is the question. With prosperity, however, people have not only discretionary income but also a choice of ways to spend it. Advertising is the vehicle that provides information and rationales to help them decide how to enjoy their prosperity.

Besides being a product of economic prosperity, advertising contributes to prosperity. By dangling desirable commodities and services before mass audiences, advertising can inspire people to greater productivity, so that they can have more income to buy the things that are advertised.

Advertising also can introduce efficiency into the economy by allowing comparison shopping without in-person inspections of all the alternatives. Efficiencies also can result when advertising alerts consumers to superior and less costly products and services, which displace outdated, outmoded and inefficient offerings.

Said Howard Morgens when he was president of Procter & Gamble: "Advertising is the most effective and efficient way to sell to the consumer. If we should ever find better methods of selling our type of products to the consumer, we'll leave advertising and turn to these other methods." Veteran advertising executive David Ogilvy made the point this way: "Advertising is still the cheapest form of selling. It would cost you $25,000 to have salesmen call on a thousand homes. A television commercial can do it for $4.69." McGraw-Hill, which publishes trade magazines, has offered research that a salesperson's typical call costs $178, a letter $6.63, and a phone call $6.35. For 17 cents, says McGraw-Hill, an advertiser can reach a prospect through advertising. Although an advertisement does not close a sale, it introduces the product and makes the salesperson's job easier and quicker.

ADVERTISING AND DEMOCRACY

Advertising took off as a modern phenomenon in the United States more than elsewhere, which has given rise to a theory that advertising and democracy are connected. This theory notes that Americans, early in their history as a democracy, were required by their political system to hold individual opinions. They looked for information so that they could evaluate their leaders and vote on public policy. This emphasis on individuality and reason paved the way for advertising: Just as Americans looked to the mass media for information on political matters, they also came to look to the media for information on buying decisions.

In authoritarian countries, on the other hand, people tend to look to strong personal leaders, not reason, for ideas to embrace. This, according to the theory, diminishes the demand for information in these nondemocracies, including the kind of information provided by advertising.

Advertising has another important role in democratic societies in generating most of the operating revenue for newspapers, magazines, television and radio. Without advertising, many of the media on which people rely for information and for the exchange of ideas on public issues would not exist as we know them.

LECTURE RESOURCE 12-A
Video: *Mastering the Media.*

LECTURE RESOURCE 12-B
Video: *Yellow Pages Advertising.*

LECTURE RESOURCE 12-C
Video: *The 30-Second President.*

- -

ORIGINS OF ADVERTISING

STUDY PREVIEW   Advertising is the product of great forces that have shaped modern society, beginning with Gutenberg's movable type that made mass-produced messages possible. Without the mass media, there would be no vehicle to carry advertisements to mass audiences. Advertising also is a product of the democratic experience; of the Industrial Revolution and its spin-offs, including vast transportation networks and mass markets; and of continuing economic growth.

STEPCHILD OF TECHNOLOGY

Advertising is not a mass medium, but it relies on media to carry its messages. *Johannes Gutenberg's* movable type, which permitted mass production of the printed word, made mass-produced advertising possible. First came flyers, then advertisements in newspapers and magazines. In the 1800s, when technology created high-speed presses that could produce enough copies for larger audiences, advertising used them to expand markets. With the introduction of radio, advertisers learned how to use electronic communication. Then came television.

Flyers were the first form of printed advertising. The British printer *William Caxton* issued the first printed advertisement in 1468 to promote one of his books. In America, publisher *John Campbell* of the Boston *News-Letter* ran the first advertisement in 1704, a notice from somebody wanting to sell an estate on Long Island. Colonial newspapers listed cargo arriving from Europe and invited readers to come, look and buy.

TEACHING OBJECTIVE 12-2
Mass media carry most advertising.

KEY PERSON
Johannes Gutenberg was progenitor of advertising media.

KEY PERSON
William Caxton printed first advertisement.

KEY PERSON
John Campbell ran first advertisement in British North American colonies.

INDUSTRIAL REVOLUTION SPIN-OFFS

The genius of *Ben Day*'s New York *Sun*, in 1833 the first penny newspaper, was that it recognized and exploited so many changes spawned by the *Industrial Revolution*. Steam-powered presses made large press runs possible. Factories drew great numbers of people to jobs within geographically small areas to which newspapers could be distributed quickly. The jobs also drew immigrants who were eager to learn—from newspapers as well as other sources—about their adopted country. Industrialization also created unprecedented wealth, giving even laborers a share of the new prosperity. A consumer economy was emerging, although it was primitive by today's standards.

A key to the success of Day's *Sun* was that, at a penny a copy, it was affordable for almost everyone. Of course, Day's production expenses exceeded a penny a copy. Just as the commercial media do today, Day looked to advertisers to pick up the slack. As Day wrote in his first issue: "The object of this paper is to lay before the public, at a price within the means of everyone, all the news of the day, and at the same time afford an advantageous medium for advertising." Day and imitator penny press publishers sought larger and larger circulations, knowing that merchants would see the value in buying space to reach so much buying power.

National advertising took root in the 1840s as railroads, another creation of the Industrial Revolution, spawned new networks for mass distribution of manufactured goods. National brands developed, and their producers looked to magazines, also delivered by rail, to promote sales. By 1869 the rail network linked the Atlantic and Pacific coasts.

PIONEER AGENCIES

By 1869 most merchants recognized the value of advertising, but they grumbled about the time it took away from their other work. In that grumbling, a young Philadelphia man sensed opportunity. *Wayland Ayer*, age 20, speculated that merchants, and even national manufacturers, would welcome a service company to help them create advertisements and place them in publications. Ayer feared, however, that his idea might not be taken seriously by potential clients because of his youth

---

MEDIA DATABANK

Advertising Spending

Here are the biggest-spending advertisers in the United States. One way to put these figures in everyday terms is to think about the percentage of the price of products that is spent on advertising. Procter & Gamble, for example, spends about $1 on advertising for every $6.70 in sales. Looked at another way, 25 cents of the $1.69 you spend for a tube of Procter & Gamble toothpaste goes into advertising.

Procter & Gamble	$2.2 billion	Ford	800 million
Philip Morris	2.0 billion	Warner-Lambert	760 million
General Motors	1.3 billion	Chrysler	760 million
Sears, Roebuck	1.2 billion	McDonald's	740 million
PepsiCo	930 million	Nestlé	730 million

and inexperience. So when Wayland Ayer opened a shop, he borrowed his father's name for the shingle. The father was never part of the business, but the agency's name, *N. W. Ayer & Son*, gave young Ayer access to potential clients, and the first advertising agency was born.

The Ayer agency had forerunners in space brokers who, beginning in 1842 with *Volney Palmer*, bought large blocks of newspaper space at a discount, broke up the space, and resold it to advertisers at a markup, usually 25 percent. Space brokers, however, did not create advertisements. The Ayer agency not only created ads but also offered the array of services that agencies still offer clients today:

KEY PERSON
Volney Palmer a pioneer space broker.

- Counsel on selling products and services.
- Design services, that is, actually creating advertisements and campaigns.
- Expertise on placing advertisements in advantageous media.

ADVERTISING AGENCIES

STUDY PREVIEW Central in modern advertising are the agencies that create and place ads on behalf of their clients. These agencies are generally funded by the media in which they place ads. In effect, this makes agency services free to advertisers.

AGENCY STRUCTURE

Full-service advertising agencies conduct market research for their clients, design and produce advertisements, and choose the media in which the advertisement will run. The 500 leading U.S. agencies employ 120,000 people worldwide. In the United States, they employ about 73,000. The responsibilities of people who work at advertising agencies fall into these broad categories:

TEACHING OBJECTIVE 12-3
Advertising agencies create, place ads.

CREATIVE POSITIONS. This category includes copywriters, graphics experts and layout people. These creative people generally report to creative directors, art directors and copy supervisors.

CLIENT LIAISON. Most of these people are *account executives*, who work with clients. Account executives are responsible for understanding clients' needs, communicating those needs to the creative staff, and going back to clients with the creative staff's ideas.

MEDIA BUYING. Agency employees called *media buyers* determine the most effective media in which to place ads and then place them.

MARKET RESEARCH. Agency research staffs generate information on target consumer groups, data that can guide the creative and media staffs.

Many agencies also employ technicians and producers who turn ideas into camera-ready proofs, colorplates, videotape, and film and audio cartridges, although a lot of production work is contracted to specialty companies. Besides full-service agencies, there are creative boutiques, which specialize in preparing messages; media buying houses, which recommend strategy on placing ads; and other narrowly focused agencies.

AGENCY-MEDIA RELATIONS

Because agencies are so influential in deciding where advertisements are placed, the mass media give them a 15 percent discount. A newspaper that lists $100 per column inch as its standard rate charges agencies only $85. The agencies, however, bill their clients the full $100 and keep the 15 percent difference. This discount, actually a *commission system*, is available only to agencies. Besides the 15 percent commission, agencies receive an additional 2 percent discount from media units by paying cash for space and time. Because these media discounts are offered only to ad agencies, advertisers themselves would not receive them if they did their advertising work in-house.

The commission system causes a problem for agencies because their income is dependent on the frequency with which advertisements are placed. The fluctuations can be great, which makes it difficult for the agencies to meet their regular payroll. To even out their income, some agencies have shifted to a *fee system*. Arrangements vary, but it is common for the client to be billed for the agency's professional time and research plus an agreed-on percentage. The fee system reduces gigantic fluctuations in agency income when clients change their media spending because revenue is derived from fees for services, not a percentage of space and time purchases. Another advantage of the fee system is that clients who pay fees for services are not suspicious that their agencies are being self-serving when they recommend bigger and bigger campaigns.

MEDIA ROLE IN CREATING ADVERTISING

Agencies are the most visible part of the advertising industry, but more advertising people work outside agencies than for agencies. The media themselves have advertising staffs that work with agency media buyers on placing advertisements. These staffs, comprised of *ad reps*, also design and produce material for smaller advertisers. Broadcast networks, magazines and radio and television stations also have their own sales staffs.

An extension of media advertising staffs are *brokers* who solicit national advertising and pass it on to their newspaper and station clients at a fee. Many broker agencies are specialized. For example, if an advertiser needs to reach the campus market, it might look to Cass Communications, which represents most college newspapers.

ADVERTISER ROLE IN ADVERTISING

Most companies, although they hire agencies for advertising services, have their own advertising expertise among the in-house people who develop marketing strategies. These companies look to ad agencies to develop the advertising campaigns that will help them meet their marketing goals. For some companies, the *advertising director* or *advertising manager* is the liaison between the company's marketing strategists and the ad agency's tacticians. Large companies with many products have in-house *brand managers* for this liaison.

Although it is not the usual pattern, some companies have in-house advertising departments and rely hardly at all on agencies.

PLACING ADVERTISEMENTS

STUDY PREVIEW The placement of advertisements is a sophisticated business. Not only do different media have inherent advantages and disadvantages in reaching potential customers, but so do individual publications and broadcast outlets.

MEDIA ADVERTISING PLANS

Agencies create *media plans* to insure that advertisements reach the right target audience. Developing a media plan is no small task. Consider the number of media outlets available: 1,600 daily newspapers in the United States alone, 8,000 weeklies, 1,200 general-interest magazines, 10,000 radio stations and 1,000 television stations. Other possibilities include direct mail, billboards, blimps, skywriting and even printing the company's name on pencils.

Media buyers have formulas for deciding which media are best for reaching potential customers. The most common formula is called *CPM*, short for *cost per thousand*. If airtime for a radio advertisement costs 7.2 cents per thousand listeners, and if space for a magazine advertisement costs 7.3 cents per thousand readers, and if both can be expected to reach equally appropriate target audiences, and if all other things are equal, radio—with the lower CPM—will be the medium of choice.

Media buyers have numerous sources of data to help them decide where advertisements can be placed for the best results. The *Audit Bureau of Circulations*, created by the newspaper industry in 1914, provides reliable information based on independent audits of the circulation of most newspapers. Survey organizations like *Nielsen* and *Arbitron* conduct surveys on television and radio audiences. *Standard Rate and Data Service* publishes volumes of information on media audiences, circulations and advertising rates.

Placing advertisements involves more than just calculating CPM. Even if the numbers favor the *National Enquirer* over the *New Yorker*, advertisements for $80-an-ounce perfumes and world cruises would be wasted in the *Enquirer*, just as ads for high-grade barley seed would be pointless on an urban radio station, no matter how much less expensive on a CPM basis than a strong farm station in the Midwest.

TEACHING OBJECTIVE 12-4
Ads are placed to reach appropriate audiences for advertised products and services.

MEDIA FOR ADVERTISING

Here are the pluses and minuses of major media as advertising vehicles:

NEWSPAPERS. The hot relationship that media theorist Marshall McLuhan described between newspapers and their readers attracts advertisers. Newspaper readers are predisposed to consider information in advertisements seriously. Studies show that people, when ready to buy, look more to newspapers than to other media. Because newspapers are tangible, readers can refer back to advertisements just by picking up the paper a second time, which is not possible with ephemeral media like television and radio. Coupons are possible in newspapers. Newspaper readers tend to be older, better educated and higher earning than television and radio audiences. Space for newspaper ads usually can be reserved as late as 48 hours ahead, and 11th-hour changes are possible.

However, newspapers are becoming less valuable for reaching young adults with advertising messages. To the consternation of newspaper publishers, there has been an alarming drop among these people in recent years, and it appears that, unlike their parents, young adults are not picking up the newspaper habit as they mature.

Another drawback to newspapers as an advertising medium is that, being printed on cheap paper, the ads do not look as good as in slick magazines. Also, most people recycle their newspapers within a day or so, which means that, unlike magazines, there is not much opportunity for readers to happen upon an ad a second or third time.

MAGAZINES.   As another print medium, magazines have many of the advantages of newspapers, plus longer *shelf life*, an advertising term for the amount of time that an advertisement remains available to readers. Magazines remain in the home for weeks, sometimes months, which offers greater exposure to advertisements. People share magazines, which give them high *pass-along circulation*. Magazines are more prestigious, with slick paper and splashier graphics. With precise color separations and enameled papers, magazine advertisements can be beautiful in ways that newspaper advertisements cannot. Magazines, specializing as they do, offer more narrowly defined audiences than newspapers.

On the downside, magazines require reservations for advertising space up to three months in advance. Opportunities for last-minute changes are limited, often impossible.

RADIO.   Radio stations with narrow formats offer easily identified target audiences. Time can be bought on short notice, with changes possible almost until airtime. Comparatively inexpensive, radio lends itself to repeated play of advertisements to drive home a message introduced in more expensive media like television. Radio lends itself to jingles that can contribute to a lasting image.

However, radio offers no opportunity for a visual display, although the images listeners create in their minds from audio suggestions can be more potent than those set out visually on television. Radio is a mobile medium that people carry with them. The extensive availability of radio is offset, however, by the fact that people tune in and out. Another negative is that many listeners are inattentive. Also, there is no shelf life.

TELEVISION.   As a moving and visual medium, television can offer unmatched impact, and the rapid growth of both network and local television advertising, far outpacing other media, indicates its effectiveness in reaching a diverse mass audience.

Drawbacks include the fact that production costs can be high. So are rates. The expense of television time has forced advertisers to go to shorter and shorter advertisements. A result is *ad clutter*, a phenomenon in which advertisements compete against each other and reduce the impact of all of them. Placing advertisements on television is a problem because demand outstrips the supply of slots, especially during prime hours. Slots for some hours are locked up months, even whole seasons, in advance. Because of the audience's diversity and size, targeting potential customers with any precision is difficult with television—with the exception of emerging narrowly focused cable services.

SATURATION ADVERTISING

An emerging twist on advertisement placement is *saturation advertising*, which Chris Whittle has pioneered through some of his alternative media publications, including the Larger Agenda books and his video services. With this approach, an advertiser selects a media vehicle that seems right for its products or services and then buys all the ad space that is available. Besides saturating a targeted audience, this approach blocks out the competition.

Asked how he would spend General Motors's $13 billion advertising budget through the 1990s, Whittle, applying the saturation idea, said he would advise GM to:

- Become sole sponsor of the summer and winter Olympics ($2.6 billion).
- Buy all the ad space for one week in every newspaper and magazine and on every television and radio station, as well as every billboard and milk carton, to advertise GM cars ($2 billion).
- Hire 8,000 bright college graduates to take the 8 million people who bought Fords the previous year to a $100 lunch to explain the virtue of GM cars ($2 billion).
- Send the 8,000 bright college grads back to their lunch partners three years later with a new GM car to drive for a week ($2 billion).
- Build showrooms in the nation's 300 largest indoor malls and allow shoppers to inspect new cars without being hassled by salespeople and to book a test drive ($1 billion).
- Buy every commercial slot on Cable News Network for a whole year.
- Buy every commercial slot on ABC, CBS and NBC during the 25th anniversary of Earth Day in 1995 and sponsor environmental television programs ($200 million).
- Engage filmmaker Steven Spielberg to create an adventure trilogy to be shown at special screenings for the 10 million Americans who bought a Japanese car the previous year ($200 million).

PITCHING MESSAGES

STUDY PREVIEW When the age of mass production and mass markets arrived, common wisdom in advertising favored aiming at the largest possible audience of potential customers. These are called lowest common denominator approaches, and such advertisements tend to be heavy-handed, so that no one can possibly miss the point. Narrower pitches, going for segments of the mass audience, permit more deftness, subtlety and imagination.

IMPORTANCE OF BRANDS

A challenge for advertising people is the modern-day reality that mass-produced products aimed at large markets are essentially alike: Toothpaste is toothpaste is toothpaste. When a product is virtually identical to the competition, how can one toothpaste-maker move more tubes?

TEACHING OBJECTIVE 12-5
Advertising pitches include brand names, lowest common denominators, positioning, redundancy.

BRAND NAMES. By trial and error, tactics were devised in the late 1800s to set similar products apart. One tactic, promoting a product as a *brand name*, aims to make a product a household word. When it is successful, a brand name becomes almost the generic identifier, like *Coke* for cola and *Kleenex* for facial tissue.

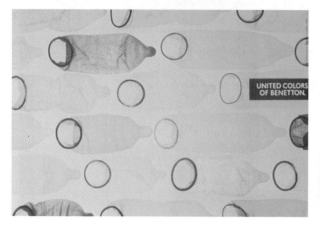

Benetton with Message. For years Benetton, the global casual clothing retailer, has run controversial ads drawing attention to social issues more than the company's products. A 1994 campaign in 25 countries featured a bloody military uniform from Bosnia, recovered from the family of a young man who died in combat. It was a haunting photo. Oliviero Toscani, Benetton's creative director who shoots the company's ads, says the goal is to position Benetton as a socially conscious marketer. The attention-getting 1991 "flying condoms" ad, said Toscani,, was aimed to combat the disease AIDS. Even so, in the United States, *Self, Mademoiselle* and *Cosmopolitan* rejected it for fear of offending readers. There were objections also with a follow-up campaign that Benetton claimed celebrated love, but which some cautious publications thought tread too closely on taboos.

Oliviero Toscani

Techniques of successful brand name advertising came together in the 1890s for an English product, Pears' soap. A key element in the campaign was *multimedia saturation*. Advertisements for Pears' were everywhere, in newspapers and magazines and on posters, vacant walls, fences, buses and street posts. Redundancy hammered home the brand name. "Good morning. Have you used Pears' today?" became a good-natured greeting among Britons that was still being repeated 50 years later. Each repetition reinforced the brand name.

BRAND IMAGE.   *David Ogilvy*, who headed the Ogilvy & Mather agency, developed the *brand image* in the 1950s. Ogilvy's advice: "Give your product a first-class ticket through life."

Ogilvy created shirt advertisements with the distinguished Baron Wrangell, who really was a European nobleman, wearing a black eye patch—and a Hathaway shirt. The classy image was reinforced with the accoutrements around Wrangell: exquisite models of sailing ships, antique weapons, silver dinnerware. To some, seeing Wrangell's setting, the patch suggested all kinds of exotica. Perhaps he had lost an eye in a romantic duel or a sporting accident.

LECTURE RESOURCE 12-D
Slides: *Advertising Themes and Slogans.*

LECTURE RESOURCE 12-E
Film: *60-Second Spot.*

KEY PERSON
David Ogilvy worked on brand imaging.

The man from Schweppes is here

First-Class Ticket. In one of his most noted campaigns, advertising genius David Ogilvy featured the distinguished chair of the company that bottled Schweppes mixers in classy locations. Said Ogilvy: "It pays to give products an image of quality—a first-class ticket." Ogilvy realized how advertising creates impressions. "Nobody wants to be seen using shoddy products," he said.

Explaining the importance of image, Ogilvy once said: "Take whisky. Why do some people choose Jack Daniel's, while others choose Grand Dad or Taylor? Have they tried all three and compared the taste? Don't make me laugh. The reality is that these three brands have different images which appeal to different kinds of people. It isn't the whisky they choose, it's the image. The brand image is 90 percent of what the distiller has to sell. Give people a taste of Old Crow, and tell them it's Old Crow. Then give them another taste of Old Crow, but tell them it's Jack Daniel's. Ask them which they prefer. They'll think the two drinks are quite different. They are tasting images."

LOWEST COMMON DENOMINATOR

Early brand-name campaigns were geared to the largest possible audience, sometimes called an *LCD*, or *lowest common denominator*, approach. The term "LCD" is adapted from mathematics. To reach an audience that includes members with IQs of 100, the pitch cannot exceed their level of understanding, even if some people in the audience have IQs of 150. The opportunity for deft touches and even cleverness is limited by the fact they might be lost on some potential customers.

Lowest common denominator advertising is best epitomized in contemporary advertising by *USP*, short for *unique selling proposition*, a term coined by *Rosser Reeves* of the giant Ted Bates agency in the 1960s. Reeves's prescription was simple: Create a benefit of the product, even if from thin air, and then tout the benefit authoritatively and repeatedly as if the competition doesn't have it. One early USP campaign flaunted that Schlitz beer bottles were "washed with live steam." The claim sounded good—who would want to drink from dirty bottles? However, the fact was that every brewery used steam to clean reusable bottles before filling them again. Furthermore, what is "live steam"? Although the implication of a competitive edge was hollow, it was done dramatically and pounded home with emphasis, and it sold beer. Just as hollow as a competitive advantage was the USP claim for Colgate toothpaste: "Cleans Your Breath While It Cleans Your Teeth."

Perhaps to compensate for a lack of substance, many USP ads are heavy-handed. Hardly an American has not heard about fast-fast-fast relief from headache remedies or that heartburn relief is spelled R-O-L-A-I-D-S. USP can be unappealing, as acknowledged even by the chairman of Warner-Lambert, which makes Rolaids, who once laughed that his company owed the American people an apology for insulting their intelligence over and over with Bates's USP slogans. Warner-Lambert was also laughing all the way to the bank over the USP-spurred success of Rolaids, Efferdent, Listermint and Bubblicious.

A unique selling proposition, however, need be neither hollow nor insulting. *Leo Burnett*, founder of the agency bearing his name, refined the USP concept by insisting that the unique point be real. For Maytag, Burnett took the company's slight advantage in reliability and dramatized it with the lonely Maytag repairman.

MARKET SEGMENTS

Rather than pitching to the lowest common denominator, advertising executive *Jack Trout* developed the idea of *positioning*. Trout worked to establish product identities that appealed not to the whole audience but to a specific audience. The cowboy image for Marlboro cigarettes, for example, established a macho attraction beginning in 1958. Later, something similar was done with Virginia Slims, aimed at women.

Positioning helps distinguish products from all the LCD clamor and noise. Advocates of positioning note that there are more and more advertisements and that they are becoming noisier and noisier. Ad clutter, as it is called, drowns out individual advertisements. With positioning, the appeal is focused and caters to audience segments, and it need not be done in such broad strokes.

Campaigns based on positioning have included:

- Johnson & Johnson's baby oil and baby shampoo, which were positioned as an adult product by advertisements featuring athletes.
- Alka-Seltzer, once a hangover and headache remedy, which was positioned as an upmarket product for stress relief among health-conscious, success-driven people.

REDUNDANCY TECHNIQUES

Advertising people learned the importance of *redundancy* early on. To be effective, an advertising message must be repeated, perhaps thousands of times. Redundancy, however, is expensive. To increase effectiveness at less cost, advertisers use several techniques:

- **Barrages.** Scheduling advertisements in intensive bursts called *flights* or *waves*.
- **Bunching.** Promoting a product in a limited period, like running advertisements for school supplies in late August and September.
- **Trailing.** Running condensed versions of advertisements after the original has been introduced, as AT&T did with its hostility advertisements on workplace tensions beginning in 1987. Powerful 60-second advertisements introduced the campaign, followed in a few weeks by 15-second versions. Automakers introduce new models with multipage magazine spreads, following with single-page placements.
- **Multimedia Trailing.** Using less expensive media to reinforce expensive advertisements. Relatively cheap drive-time radio in major markets is a favorite follow-through to expensive television advertisements created for major events like the Super Bowl.

RESEARCH AND PSYCHOLOGY

STUDY PREVIEW Freudian ideas about the human subconscious influenced advertising in the 1950s, and research tried to tap hidden motivations that could be exploited to sell products and services. The extreme in appealing to the subconscious, called *subliminal advertising*, worried many people, but it was an approach whose effectiveness was never demonstrated.

MOTIVATIONAL RESEARCH

Whatever naïveté Americans had about opinion shaping was dispelled by the mid-20th century. Sinister possibilities were evident in the work of *Joseph Goebbels*, the Nazi minister of propaganda and public enlightenment. In the Pacific, the Japanese beamed the infamous Tokyo Rose radio broadcasts to GIs to lower their morale. Then, during the Korean War, a macabre fascination developed with the so-called *brainwashing* techniques used on American prisoners of war. In this same period, the work of Austrian psychiatrist *Sigmund Freud*, which emphasized hidden motivations and repressed sexual impulses, was being popularized in countless books and articles.

TEACHING OBJECTIVE 12-6
Advertising uses psychology to tap audience interests.

KEY PERSON
Nazi Joseph Goebbels brought new awareness to potential of public-opinion shaping.

No wonder, considering this intellectual context, advertising people in the 1950s looked to the social sciences to find new ways to woo customers. Among the advertising pioneers of this period was *Ernest Dichter*, who accepted Freud's claim that people act on motivations that they are not even aware of. Depth interviewing, Dichter felt, could reveal these motivations, which could then be exploited in advertising messages.

Dichter used his interviewing, called *motivational research*, for automotive clients. Rightly or wrongly, Dichter determined that the American male was loyal to his wife but fantasized about a mistress. Men, he noted, usually were the decision makers in purchasing a car. Then, in what seemed a quantum leap, Dichter equated sedans, which were what most people drove, with wives. Sedans were familiar, reliable. Convertibles, impractical for many people and also beyond their reach financially, were equated with mistresses—romantic, daring, glamorous. With these conclusions in hand, Dichter devised advertisements for a new kind of sedan without a center door pillar. The *hardtop*, as it was called, gave a convertible effect when the windows were down. The advertising clearly reflected Dichter's thinking: "You'll find something new to love every time you drive it." Although they were not as solid as sedans and tended to leak air and water, hardtops were popular among automobile buyers for the next 25 years.

Dichter's motivational research led to numerous campaigns that exploited sexual images. For Ronson lighters, the flame, in phallic form, was reproduced in extraordinary proportions. A campaign for Ajax cleanser, hardly a glamour product, had a white knight charging through the street, ignoring law and regulation with a great phallic lance. Whether consumers were motivated by sexual imagery is hard to establish. Even so, many campaigns flowing from motivational research worked.

SUBLIMINAL ADVERTISING

The idea that advertising can be persuasive at subconscious levels was taken a step further by market researcher *Jim Vicary*, who coined the term *subliminal advertising*. Vicary claimed in 1957 that he had studied the effect of inserting messages like "Drink Coca-Cola" and "Eat popcorn" into movies. The messages, although flashed too fast to be recognized by the human eye, still registered in the brain and, said Vicary, prompted moviegoers to rush to the snack bar. In experiments at a New Jersey movie house, he said, Coke sales increased 18 percent and popcorn almost 60 percent. Vicary's report stirred great interest, and also alarm, but researchers who tried to replicate his study found no evidence to support his claim.

Despite Vicary's dubious claims, psychologists have identified a phenomenon they call *subception*, in which certain behavior sometimes seems to be triggered by messages perceived subliminally. Whether the effect works outside laboratory experiments and whether the effect is strong enough to prod a consumer to go out and buy is uncertain. Nevertheless, there remains a widespread belief among the general population that subliminal advertising works, and fortunes are being made by people who peddle various devices and systems with extravagant claims that they can control human behavior. Among these are the "hidden" messages in stores' sound systems that say shoplifting is not nice.

This idea that advertising is loaded with hidden messages has been taken to extremes by *Wilson Bryan Key*, who spins out books alleging that plugs are hidden in all kinds of places for devil worship, homosexuality and a variety of libertine activities. He has accused the Nabisco people of baking the word "sex" into Ritz

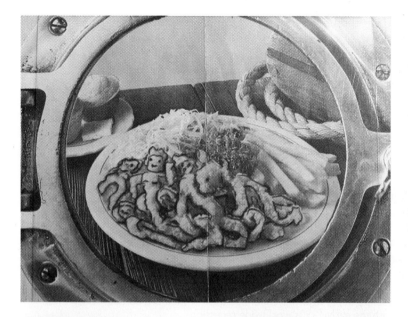

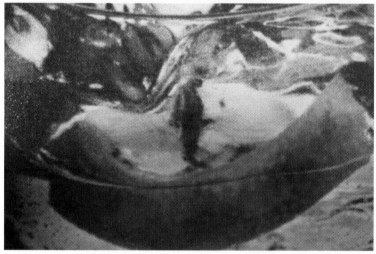

Sex in the Clams? Author Wilson Bryan Key is convinced that Madison Avenue hides sex in advertisements to attract attention and sell products. To demonstrate his point, he outlines the human figures that he saw in an orgy in a photograph of clam strips on restaurant menu. Can you see the hidden sex that Key claims was designed into the liquor ad photos? Most advertising people, who dismiss his claims, cannot see it either.

crackers. At Howard Johnson restaurants, he has charged, placemat pictures of plates heaped with clams portray orgies and bestiality. Though widely read, Key offers no evidence beyond his own observations and interpretations. In advertising circles, his views are dismissed as amusing but wacky. The view of Nabisco and Howard Johnson is less charitable.

In 1990 Wilson Bryan Key's views suffered a serious setback. He was a primary witness in a highly publicized Nevada trial on whether the Judas Priest heavy metal album "Stained Glass" had triggered the suicide of an 18-year-old youth and the attempted suicide of his 20-year-old friend. The families said that the pair had obsessed on a Judas Priest album that dealt with suicide and that one song was subliminally embedded with the words "Do it" over and over. The families' attorneys hired Key as an expert witness to help make their point. From Key's perspective, the case did not go well. Millions of television viewers who followed the trial strained to make out the supposed words "Do it," but even when isolated from the rest of the music, they were almost impossible to make out. It turned out the sounds were neither lyrics nor even vocal but rather instrumental effects. Members of Judas Priest testified that they had not equated the sound to any words at all and had inserted it for artistic effect, hardly to encourage suicide. The jury sided with Judas Priest, and Key left town with his wobbly ideas on subliminal messages having taken a serious blow under a jury's scrutiny.

David Ogilvy, founder of the Ogilvy & Mather agency, once made fun of claims like Key's, pointing out the absurdity of "millions of suggestible consumers getting up from their armchairs and rushing like zombies through the traffic on their way to buy the product at the nearest store." The danger of "Vote Bolshevik" being flashed during the "NBC Nightly News" is remote, and whether it would have any effect is dubious.

CONGLOMERATION AND GLOBALIZATION

STUDY PREVIEW   A tremendous consolidation in the advertising business occurred in the 1980s. Agencies bought agencies, and some of the resulting super agencies continued their acquisitions abroad. Today, these global agencies are beset with problems that came with the early 1990s worldwide recession.

ACQUISITION BINGE

TEACHING OBJECTIVE 12-7
Conglomeration, globalization of advertising has created opportunities, problems.

In the late 1970s under President Carter, the federal government backed off on antitrust actions and other regulatory controls, fueling a great number of mergers and consolidations in American business. Advertising was no exception, and many agencies swallowed up others. The Reagan and Bush administrations continued the hands-off-business approach into the 1980s and 1990s, and dominant big businesses, including major advertising agencies, became even more so.

One Billion Customers. By one count, 50 foreign advertising agencies are in China trying to carve a share out of a virtually untapped market of 1.2 billion people. The effect is tremendous. Steven Strasser, writing in *Newsweek*, said: "China cares about its athlete's foot problem—Johnson & Johnson's subsidiary made sure of that. When its recent J & J commercial revealed that a fungus causes the itch, sales of Daktarin fungicidal cream soared from Shanghai to Xian." Other major U.S. brands vying for China trade include Heinz, Procter & Gamble, Philip Morris and Coca-Cola.

MEDIA DATABANK

Largest Advertising Agencies

Here are the largest global advertising agencies ranked by their annual income. Many of these are international companies known in the United States by the name of subsidiaries, some of which are listed.

Agency	Headquarters	Annual Income
WWP Group	London	$2.8 billion
Ogilvy & Mather;		
Scali, McCabe, Sloves;		
J. Walter Thompson		
Interpublic	New York	2.0 billion
Fahlgren Martin;		
Lintas;		
Long Haymes & Carr;		
Lowe;		
McCann-Erickson		
Omnicom	New York	1.8 billion
BBDO;		
DDB Needham;		
Rainoldi, Kerzner & Radcliff;		
Rapp Collins		
Saatchi & Saatchi	London	1.7 billion
Backer Spielvogel Bates;		
CME KHBB;		
Conill;		
Saatchi & Saatchi		
Dentsu	Tokyo	1.4 billion
Dentsu America		
Young & Rubicam	New York	1.0 billion
Young & Rubicam;		
Sudler & Hennessey;		
Wunderman Cato Johnson		
Euro RSCG	Paris	1.0 billion
Robert Becker;		
Cohn & Wells, Comart;		
Tatham Euro		
Grey	New York	700 million
Beaumont-Bennett;		
Font & Vaamonde;		
Grey		
Foote, Cone & Belding	Chicago	700 million
Foote, Cone & Belding;		
IMPACT;		
Krupp Taylor,		
Vicom, Wahlstrom		
Hakuhodo	Tokyo	700 million
Hakuhodo America		

The demassification of the mass media was also a factor. Several big agencies, whose favored choice for most clients had been network television for 40 years, realized that the network audience was fragmenting, and they had to find a new way to do business. These agencies lacked in-house expertise at direct-mail advertising and other emerging advertising media, so they began buying smaller, specialized ad shops, successful regional agencies, and public relations companies to fill in the gaps.

While U.S. agencies were consolidating, there was also an international consolidation occurring that wiped out the traditional dominance of U.S. advertising agencies abroad. Not only did some foreign agencies like Dentsu of Japan become giant multinational organizations, but an upstart London agency, Saatchi & Saatchi, went on an acquisition binge that absorbed several U.S. agencies. The result is fewer but bigger agencies.

This globalization of the advertising business had detractors who were concerned that the new super agencies, all based in leading Western societies, would further diminish indigenous values in less developed countries under the steamroller they called "cultural imperialism." Many ad people saw the situation differently, arguing that people buy only what they want and that it would be the choice of Third World people whether to respond to advertising that originates with multinational advertising agencies. Also, noted advertising guru David Ogilvy, successful advertising always is adapted to local conditions: "The advertising campaigns for these brands will emanate from the headquarters of multinational agencies but will be adapted to respect differences in local culture." If local appeals and themes are necessary to sell a product, those are the ones that will be employed.

AGENCY CONSOLIDATION PROBLEMS

The agency consolidation of the 1980s was driven mostly by two factors. First, agencies that were turning huge profits had money to spend on acquisitions, and other profitable agencies were attractive acquisition targets. Second, banks and other lending institutions were willing to finance highly leveraged acquisitions. The pace of acquisitions came to a halt in the worldwide recession that developed in 1990, and some of the new super agencies began to unravel.

With the recession, many manufacturers, retailers and other advertisers cut back on spending. Agency revenue plummeted. As a result, the source of money for super agencies to repay loans disappeared. Some agencies shut down subsidiary agencies or consolidated them. There were massive layoffs, and businesses were scaled back. Some agencies bought time to get their finances back in order under the auspices of bankruptcy courts. Even still, the prospects for some of these troubled agencies remain unsure.

ADVERTISING REGULATION

STUDY PREVIEW   The "buyer beware" underpinning of much of 19th-century advertising has given way to "seller beware." Today, advertising is regulated on many fronts, by the media that carry advertisements, by the advertising industry itself and by governmental agencies.

GATEKEEPING REGULATION BY MEDIA

TEACHING OBJECTIVE 12-8
Advertisers have shifted to seller beware sensitivity.

A dramatic reversal in thinking about advertising has occurred in the 20th century. The earlier *caveat emptor* mindset, "buyer beware," tolerated extravagant claims. Anybody who believed that the same elixir could cure dandruff, halitosis and cancer deserved to be conned, or so went the thinking. Over the years, due partly to the growing consumer movement, the thinking changed to *caveat venditor*, "seller beware," placing the onus on the advertiser to avoid misleading claims and to demonstrate the truth of claims.

In advertising's early days, newspapers and magazines skirted the ethics question posed by false advertisements by saying their pages were open to all advertisers. Under growing pressure, publications sometimes criticized dubious advertisements editorially, but most did not ban them. *Edward Bok*, who made *Ladies' Home Journal* a runaway success in the 1890s, crusaded against dishonest advertising. In one exposé on Lydia E. Pinkham's remedies for "female maladies," Bok reported that Lydia, to whom women readers were invited in advertisements to write for advice, had been dead for 22 years. Yet the advertisements continued.

KEY PERSON
Edward Bok set media standards for advertising.

In 1929, NBC adopted a code of ethics to preclude false or exaggerated claims. Other networks followed. At the peak of the networks' concern about broadcast standards, it was estimated that half the commercials for products were turned away for violating network codes. Codes for broadcast advertising have come and gone over the years, all voluntary with stations that chose to subscribe.

The print media also have seen a variety of industry wide codes, all voluntary. Most publications spurn misleading advertisements. Typical is the Minot *Daily News* in North Dakota, which refuses advertisements for "clairvoyance, fortune telling, magnetic healing, doubtful medicines and fake sales." Many college newspapers refuse advertisements from term-paper services. Some metropolitan papers turn away advertisements for pornographic movies.

A case can be made that the media do not go far enough in exercising their prerogative to ban dubious advertisements. Critics argue that on nettling questions, such as the morality of printing ads for carcinogenic tobacco products, with major revenue at stake, many newspapers and magazines sidestep a moral judgment, run the advertisements and reap the revenue. The critics note, for example, that most commercial broadcasters ran cigarette advertisements until the federal government intervened. The media, so goes the argument, are too devoted to profits to do all the regulating they should.

INDUSTRY SELF-REGULATION

The advertising industry itself has numerous organizations that try, through ethics codes and moral suasion, to eradicate falsity and deception. Besides the explicit purposes of these self-policing mechanisms, their existence can be cited by advertising people to argue that their industry is able to deal with misdeeds itself with a minimum of government regulation.

LECTURE RESOURCE 12-F
Video: *The Advertising Industry: The Case for Self-Regulation.*

NATIONAL ADVERTISING REVIEW COUNCIL.   The *National Advertising Review Council* investigates complaints from anybody. When it finds a problem, the council asks the offending advertiser to correct the situation. If that does not work, the council turns its file over to whichever government agency it thinks is appropriate.

Although it is a creation of advertising trade associations, the National Advertising Review Council has earned a reputation as a dispassionate attempt at self-regulation. Its 50 members include 10 people appointed from the public—with no connection to the advertising business. Of the complaints the council investigates, two-thirds typically are found to be deceptive advertising. About half of those adver-

Miracle Cures. Potions and gizmos for curing just about whatever ails you led to government regulation of advertising. In 1914 the Federal Trade Commission was established to rid commerce of false claims. Later, the FTC became a firmer regulator, even ordering advertisers to run corrective advertisements. In one case, American Home Products was ordered to spend $24 million in ads to say "Anacin is not a tension reliever" to offset earlier advertising claims that could not be substantiated.

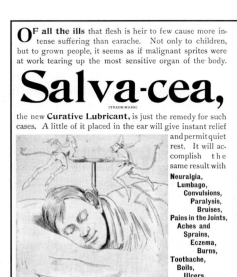

OF all the ills that flesh is heir to few cause more intense suffering than earache. Not only to children, but to grown people, it seems as if malignant sprites were at work tearing up the most sensitive organ of the body.

Salva-cea,
(TRADE-MARK)

the new **Curative Lubricant**, is just the remedy for such cases. A little of it placed in the ear will give instant relief and permit quiet rest. It will accomplish the same result with

Neuralgia,
Lumbago,
Convulsions,
Paralysis,
Bruises,
Pains in the Joints,
Aches and
Sprains,
Eczema,
Burns,
Toothache,
Boils,
Ulcers,
Stings,

and all kindred ills and complaints. It is in truth the most powerful healing agent ever discovered.

Only quite recently has this marvellous remedy been before the public. During this short time the marvellous cures that have been effected, and the numerous important testimonials that have been received, have been absolutely unprecedented in the history of the world. Salva-cea forms a medicine chest in itself, and is absolutely invaluable in every household.

Salva-cea should be in every Home, Workshop, Police-Station, Hospital, and Institution—and wherever a Pain-Relieving, Soothing, and Curative Lubricant is likely to be required. No discovery in the world of Healing Remedies has had such high testimony.

Salva-cea
(TRADE-MARK)

. . . Cures . . .

CHILBLAINS

For Chilblains, Chaps, Roughness, Red Noses, Coughs, and Colds in the Head, Salva=cea stands unrivalled as a universal and permanent cure and preventive. The first application always gives relief.

CNN **Anti-Smoking Push**
The mass media are a battleground in which opposing views are laid out. In news, the media decide what to report. In advertising, the special interests do it. This video segment, reported by CNN's Brian Jenkins, details how the American Medical Association is buying television time to promote a quit-smoking kit. The AMA, however, is spending only a fraction of the $400 million a year that tobacco companies put into advertising. This segment aired March 30, 1994.

tisements are discontinued or modified under council pressure. The council has no legal authority, but its willingness to go to federal agencies or to state attorneys general, in effect recommending prosecution, is a powerful tool for honesty in advertising.

CODES.   Typical of codes of advertising trade groups is that of the *American Association of Advertising Agencies*, which says member agencies are expected never to produce ads with:

- False, misleading statements or exaggerations, visual or verbal, including misleading price claims.
- Testimonials from unknowledgeable people.
- Unfair disparagement of competitive products.
- Distorted or insufficiently supported claims.
- Anything offending public decency.

Acceptance of the code is a kind of loose condition of membership—more a statement of the association's values than an enforcement tool.

LECTURE RESOURCE 12-G
Video: Ad Council: Finding Solutions.

PUBLIC INTEREST ADVERTISING.   The advertising industry has set up an organization, the *Ad Council*, which creates advertisements free for worthy causes. For 50 years the council's existence has helped offset criticism that the advertising business is an unscrupulous manipulator.

   The Ad Council has roots in World War II when the ad industry, major media organizations and advertisers created the *War Advertising Council* to create ads for the war effort. Advertisers funded the council, agencies created the advertisements gratis and media ran donated time and space for them. The first campaign, to recruit military nurses, stressed, "Nursing is a proud profession." Within weeks, 500,000 women applied for the Cadet Nurses Corps—almost eight times more than needed. After the war the Ad Council was formed to continue *pro bono* work on behalf of socially significant national issues.

Because the ads are well done, the media are pleased to run them as a contribution to the public good. Magazines, newspapers and broadcasters donate about $800 million a year in time and space to the Ad Council's ads.

In a typical year, 300 noncommercial organizations ask the Ad Council to take them on. The council chooses a dozen, which are turned over to agencies that rotate their services. The United Way has received continuing support from the council. Other campaigns have included restoring the Statue of Liberty, combating illiteracy, and improving American productivity. Campaigns that have left an imprint on the public mind have included:

- Forest fire prevention with the character Smokey Bear.
- Environmental protection with the memorable "Don't be fuelish" slogan.
- Fund-raising for the United Negro College Fund, with the line, "A mind is a terrible thing to waste."

CNN Smoking Ad Ban
The health and anti-smoking lobbies succeeded some years back in banning tobacco ads from television and radio. Now these lobbies want the government to eliminate the tax deduction that tobacco companies receive for what they spend on advertising. The tobacco industry says it would be unfairly singled out if it couldn't deduct the cost of advertising. In the meantime, advertising continues at a $400-million-a-year pace with campaigns, some controversial, like Joe Camel, who critics say is enticing kids to smoke, and some clever, sophisticated appeals to smokers as independent people. The report, by CNN's Irv Chapman, aired February 25, 1994.

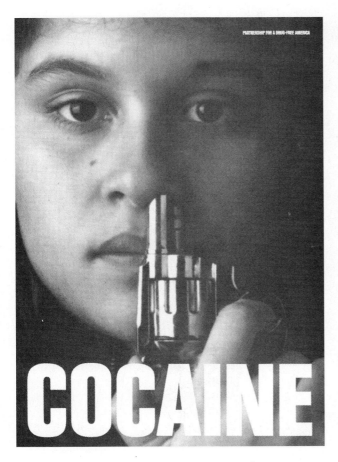

Public Service. The DDB Needham Worldwide agency created this 1987 advertisement free for the Partnership for a Drug-Free America, which distributed it to publications that ran it at no cost. Every year, major agencies and the media donate their services to the Partnership on behalf of the anti-drug organization.

UNRESOLVED PROBLEMS AND ISSUES

STUDY PREVIEW People are exposed to such a blur of ads that advertisers worry that their messages are being lost in the clutter. Some advertising people see more creativity as the answer so people will want to see and read ads, but there is evidence that creativity can work against an ad's effectiveness.

ADVERTISING CLUTTER

TEACHING OBJECTIVE 12-9
Advertising problems include ad clutter, creative excesses.

Leo Bogart of the Newspaper Advertising Bureau noted that the number of advertising messages doubled through the 1960s and 1970s, and except for the recession at the start of the 1990s, the trend continues. This proliferation of advertising creates a problem—too many ads. CBS squeezed so many ads into its coverage of the 1992 winter Olympics that some viewers felt the network regarded the games as a sideshow. Even in regular programming, the frequency of ads has led advertisers to fret that their individual ads are being lost in the clutter. The problem has been exacerbated by the shortening of ads from 60 seconds in the early days of television to today's widely used 15-second format.

At one time, the National Association of Broadcasters had a code limiting the quantity of commercials. The Federal Communications Commission let station owners know that it supported the NAB code, but in 1981, as part of the Reagan

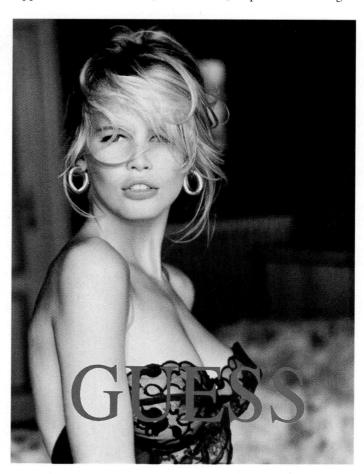

Favorite Print Advertisements. Video Storyboard Tests Inc. interviews more than 22,000 people for its annual list of the most memorable advertisements. Guess was among several print media winners announced in 1993.

administration's deregulation, the FCC backed away from any limitation. In 1983 a federal court threw out the NAB limitation as a monopolistic practice.

Ad clutter is less an issue in the print media. Many people buy magazines and newspapers to look at ads as part of the comparative shopping process. Even so, some advertisers, concerned that their ads are overlooked in massive editions, such as a seven-pound metro Sunday newspaper or a 700-page bridal magazine, are looking to alternative means to reach potential customers in a less cluttered environment.

The clutter that marks much of commercial television and radio today may be alleviated as the media fragment further. Not only will demassification create more specialized outlets, such as narrowly focused cable television services, but there will be new media. Videodiscs, for example, can be delivered by mail, and videotext can be called up on home computer screens. The result will be advertising aimed at narrower audiences.

EXCESSES IN CREATIVITY

Advertisers are reviewing whether creativity is as effective an approach as hard sell. *Harry McMahan* studied Clio Awards for creativity in advertising and discovered that 36 agencies that produced 81 winners of the prestigious awards for advertisements had either lost the winning account or gone out of business.

Predicts advertising commentator E. B. Weiss: "Extravagant license for creative people will be curtailed." The future may hold more heavy-handed pitches, perhaps with over-the-counter regimens not only promising fast-fast-fast relief but also spelling it out in all caps and boldface with exclamation marks: **F-A-S-T! F-A-S-T! F-A-S-T!!!**

AN OVERRATED MARKETING TOOL?

Long-held assumptions about the effectiveness of advertising itself are being questioned. *Gerald Tellis*, a University of Iowa researcher, put together a sophisticated statistical model that found that people are relatively unmoved by television advertisements in making brand choices, especially on mundane everyday products like toilet paper and laundry detergents.

Tellis's conclusions began with consumer purchasing studies in Eau Claire, Wisconsin. Not surprisingly, considering its self-interest, the advertising industry has challenged Tellis's studies. Meanwhile, Tellis and other scholars have continued the studies.

The jury is still out on whether Tellis is correct in his doubts about television advertising, on whether the style of advertising makes a difference, or on whether it is just ads for generic products, such as toilet paper and detergent, that are virtually identical and that fail to influence consumers when they are in the store picking products off the shelves.

CHAPTER WRAP-UP

The role of advertising in American mass media cannot be overstated. Without advertising, most media would go out of business. In fact, in the 1960s, when advertisers switched to television from the giant general-interest magazines like *Life* and *Look*, those magazines went under. Today, the rapid expansion of cable net-

---

CNN **Japan Heavy Smokers** CNN reporter Andrea Koppel discusses the success of U.S. cigarette brands in Japan, where the government profits from tobacco sales and has only a lackluster warning program. This video segment, which aired March 17, 1994, highlights the potential for U.S. tobacco companies to continue their growth abroad to offset declines in sales in the United States.

KEY PERSON Harry McMahan dubious about ad creativity.

LECTURE RESOURCE 12-H Audiotape and Video: *Clio Awards.*

LECTURE RESOURCE 12-I Video: *The More Creative the Ad, the Harder It Will Work.*

KEY PERSON Gerald Tellis dubious about effectiveness of TV ads.

LECTURE RESOURCE 12-J Slides: *Art in Advertising.*

works is possible only because advertisers are buying time on the new networks to reach potential customers. In one sense, advertisers subsidize readers, viewers and listeners who pay only a fraction of the cost of producing publications and broadcasts. The bulk of the cost is paid by advertisers, who are willing to do so to make their pitches to potential customers who, coincidentally, are media consumers.

Besides underwriting the mass media, advertising is vital for a prosperous, growing consumer economy. It triggers demand for goods and services, and it enables people to make wise choices by providing information on competing products. The result is efficiency in the marketplace, which frees more capital for expansion. This all speaks to an intimate interrelationship involving advertising in a democratic and capitalistic society.

Today, as democracy and capitalism are reintroduced in Central and Eastern Europe, advertising can be expected to have an essential role in fostering new consumer economies. American, European and Japanese advertising agencies will be called on for their expertise to develop campaigns for goods and services that will make for better lives and stronger economies. This process will provide a greater revenue base for the mass media in these countries, which will result in better journalistic and entertainment content.

QUESTIONS FOR REVIEW

1. Why is advertising essential in a capitalistic society?

2. Trace the development of advertising since the time of Johannes Gutenberg.

3. What is the role of advertising agencies?

4. Why do some advertisements appear in some media and not other media?

5. What are the major tactics used in advertising? Who devised each one?

6. How do advertising people use psychology and research to shape their messages?

7. What are the advantages and the problems of the globalization of the advertising industry?

8. Does advertising still follow the "buyer beware" dictum?

9. What are some problems and unanswered issues in advertising?

QUESTIONS FOR CRITICAL THINKING

1. How does the development of modern advertising relate to Johannes Gutenberg's technological innovation? To the Industrial Revolution? To long-distance mass transportation? To mass marketing?

2. Why does advertising flourish more in democratic than in autocratic societies? In a capitalistic more than in a controlled economy? In a prosperous society?

3. What were the contributions to advertising of Volney Palmer, Wayland Ayer, Rosser Reeves, Jack Trout, Ernest Dichter, Wilson Bryan Key and David Ogilvy?

4. What are the responsibilities of advertising account executives, copywriters, media buyers, researchers, brand managers, ad reps, brokers?

5. What are the advantages of the commission system for advertising agency revenue? Of the fee system? The disadvantages of both?

6. Describe these advertising tactics: brand-name promotion, unique selling proposition, lowest common denominator approach, positioning and redundancy.

7. Ad clutter is an emerging problem. How is it a problem? What can be done about it?

8. How has the Ad Council improved the image of companies that advertise, agencies that create advertisements, and media that carry advertisements? Give examples.

FOR FURTHER LEARNING

Mary Billard. "Heavy Metal Goes on Trial." *Rolling Stone* (July 12–26, 1990):582–583 double issue, 83–88, 132. Billard examines the events leading to a shotgun suicide of a Nevada youth whose family claimed that subliminal messages in a Judas Priest song led him to do it.

Stephen Fox. *The Mirror Makers: A History of American Advertising and Its Creators* (Morrow, 1984).

Wilson Bryan Key. *Subliminal Seduction: Ad Media's Manipulation of a Not So Innocent America* (New American Library, 1972). Sex appeal has a special dimension for Key, who argues that an advertisement for Gilbey's gin has the letters s-e-x carefully carved in ice cubes in an expensive *Time* magazine advertisement. Key offers no corroborating evidence in this and later books, *Media Sexploitation* (New American Library, 1976), *The Clam-Plate Orgy: And Other Subliminal Techniques for Manipulating Your Behavior* (New America, 1980) and *The Age of Manipulation* (Holt, 1989).

Otto Kleppner, Thomas Russell and Glenn Verrill. *Advertising Procedure*, 8th ed. (Prentice Hall, 1990).

Bob Levenson. *Bill Bernbach's Book: A History of the Advertising That Changed the History of Advertising* (Random House, 1987). Levenson focuses on the "creative revolution" typified in the Bernbach agency's "Think Small" Volkswagen advertisements of the 1950s and early 1960s.

Nancy Millman. *Emperors of Adland: Inside the Advertising Revolution* (Warner Books, 1988). This fast-paced book by a Chicago newspaper columnist traces the mergers of advertising agencies in the 1980s and questions whether mega-agencies are good for advertising.

David Ogilvy. *Confessions of an Advertising Man* (Atheneum, 1963). The man who created a leading agency explains his philosophy in this autobiography. In *Ogilvy on Advertising* (Vintage, 1985), Ogilvy offers lively advice about effective advertising.

Anthony Pratkanis and Elliot Aronson. *Age of Propaganda: The Everyday Use and Abuse of Persuasion* (W. H. Freeman, 1992). Pratkanis and Aronson, both scholars, provide a particularly good, lively status report on "subliminal sorcery."

Michael Schudson. *Advertising: The Uneasy Persuasion: Its Dubious Impact on American Society* (Basic Books, 1984). Schudson, a media theorist, challenges the effectiveness of advertising while exploring the ideological impact of advertisements.

FOR KEEPING UP TO DATE

Weekly trade journals are *Advertising Age* and *AdWeek.* Scholarly publications include *Journal of Marketing Research* and *Journal of Advertising.* The *New York Times* regularly reports on the industry.

THE BATTLE FOR MINDS AND LUNGS

Tobacco companies in the United States are under siege. Clinical evidence mounts that cigarettes can be devastating to health. The government wants to slap an additional 75-cents-a-pack tax on cigarettes. Anti-smoking zealots are targeting smokers and shaming them about their habit. Physician groups and the health lobby have mounted mighty campaigns against tobacco products.

For the tobacco industry, a tremendous amount is at stake. Although fewer Americans smoke today than in the past, cigarettes remain a tremendously profitable business. One British conglomerate bought American Tobacco Company for $1 billion in 1994. At the time, analysts were expecting huge profit growth in the industry, led by RJR Nabisco at 35.5 percent. The earnings of Philip Morris, RJR Nabisco and American Brands, which represent more than 80 percent of the domestic market, were expected to create excess cash flow of $3 billion.

Naturally, the tobacco industry is not taking these attacks lying down. Much of the battleground is the mass media, which traditionally are viewed as well suited as a forum for opposing views. On the cigarette issue, however, there is some thinking that there need to be restraints on the tobacco interests because, among other things, their advertising is so effective.

ADVERTISING. Some of the catchiest ads around are for tobacco products. Take Joe Camel. Studies say he's more recognized among kids than Mickey Mouse.

Some advertising is subtle in its appeal. Marlboro became a successful brand with ads featuring macho cowboys doing their work. The product was in a noble context of rugged masculinity, hard work and honest values. Over the years, Marlboro ads have shifted to dramatic Western vistas, placing the product in a natural, outdoor healthy context. The new implied message: Smoking is healthful.

Benson and Hedges is making a badge of honor out of the ostracism that smokers feel. Ads show smokers on the wings of airliners in flight and at desks hanging outside office skyscrapers.

All tolled, the U.S. cigarette industry spends about $400 million a year on advertising.

Meanwhile, the government runs media announcements about the dangers of smoking. In 1994, the American Medical Association launched a major television campaign for a quit-smoking kit.

The government also has narrowed the forums in which cigarette makers can advertise. Since 1971, cigarette ads have been banned from television and radio. In response, tobacco manufacturers beefed up print media and billboard advertising and shifted to sponsoring events that would promote their products through association. Marlboro, Camel and other brands have moved into the mail order business, offering brand-related products in exchange for proof-of-purchase bar codes. Marlboro, for example, offers Western boots, cowboy hats, belt buckles, denim shirts and leather jackets.

NEWS. Both sides in the tobacco war vie for news media attention. RJR Nabisco was delighted, for example, to go public rebutting criticism that Joe Camel glamorizes smoking among kids. The study, by the respected Roper Organization, confirmed that Joe Camel was widely recognized among young people, but that only 3 percent of 16- and 17-year-olds who recognized Joe had a positive attitude about smoking.

Meanwhile, with news conferences and briefings and news releases, the health lobby, often led by the U.S. surgeon general, feeds the negative message about smoking to the media. Articles on the horrors of smoking abound in newspapers and magazines and on television and radio.

TALK SHOWS. The battle for the public's mind is perhaps its most direct on talk shows, where articulate representatives of the tobacco industry make their freedom of choice defense. With patriotic fervor in their voices, they say government is going too far, being un-American even, to consider taking away the "right" of people to enjoy pleasures like a cigarette. This is an appeal that goes to the heart of what it is to be an American.

The tobacco spokespersons are always well equipped with data that challenge many of the health studies. And, correctly, they point to flaws in the sometimes-overstated and hysterical points made by anti-smoking zealots. On talk shows, this makes good drama.

PRODUCT LIABILITY. The greatest fear of tobacco companies is that someone, somewhere will prevail in a product liability suit. Many people have sued, blaming health problems on cigarettes, but no one has succeeded. The tobacco companies put major resources into defending against these actions, knowing that a loss could result in a cascade of suits that could wreck their industry, just as 20 years earlier product liability suits wrecked the U.S. asbestos industry.

The forum for product liability trials is the courtroom, and the tobacco companies know that the cases are widely reported. Their defense is part of the battle to win popular support for their cause. Admittedly, it's an uphill battle in the courtroom—rich tobacco companies with attorneys in three-piece suits versus terminally ill victims of lung cancer and heart disease. But, from the tobacco companies' perspective, it is better to make their case in the public courtroom than to lose one of these cases or let the sad stories of the ailing plaintiffs go unaddressed.

A theme in these cases is that the plaintiffs say the cigarette companies used advertising to entice them into a fatal addiction. The courtroom then becomes a forum for tobacco lawyers to point out that tobacco is not addictive. Their evidence? Forty million Americans have quit.

MEDIA ATTACKS. Traditionally, tobacco companies sparred with their opponents in the media. Now Philip Morris has changed its rules of engagement. In 1994 the company filed a $10 billion libel suit against ABC for a television report that the company had spiked cigarettes with extra nicotine to make them more addictive. ABC stood by its report.

Philip Morris may or may not prevail in the suit, but more important long term is that the mass media are now on notice not to take sources who criticize the tobacco industry at face value—or they may be faced with an expensive libel suit. Under American law, the media are responsible for the truth of what sources tell them. That means that one upshot of the Philip Morris vs. ABC is that news reporters may be more cautious in the future in reporting criticism of the tobacco industry.

SUE, SUE, SUE. In its new aggressiveness, Philip Morris is suing governments that adopt anti-smoking policies. The company has sued San Francisco to drop a strict smoking ban in the workplace. In another action, Philip Morris has sued the U.S. Environmental Protection Agency for a claim that secondary smoke can cause cancer.

EVENTS, STUNTS, GOOD DEEDS. The battle for people's minds includes events that attract media attention. Philip Morris, for example, helped organize a tobacco farmers' protest at the nation's capitol against a proposed cigarette tax. The protest underscores how important tobacco is to the economy of many states from Wisconsin into the Deep South.

The tobacco companies also curry public favor by associating themselves with good causes. They share their profits with dance companies, theaters, art museums and educational institutions. They contribute to causes like promoting racial equality. In this sense, the companies are good citizens.

GROWING FRONTIERS. Anti-smoking lobbyists accuse cigarette companies of targeting minors and teenagers, women and minorities in their advertising. The companies are quick to deny they are encouraging young people to smoke. The companies point to thousands of signs they provide retailers about customers needing to provide proof of age. With a straight face, RJR Nabisco says Joe Camel, and also his friend Josephine, are just lovable characters that kids like, noting too, that the adults the company seeks to reach also like the characters.

U.S. tobacco companies have learned that their brands have appeal abroad, where governments and health lobbies generally are less vigorous. The companies have been especially successful in Asia, and they have moved into the former communist bloc with major marketing and advertising programs in Czechoslovakia, Hungary, Kazakhstan, Lithuania and Russia.

The media battle for minds and for lungs continues—on a broader and more intense scale than ever.

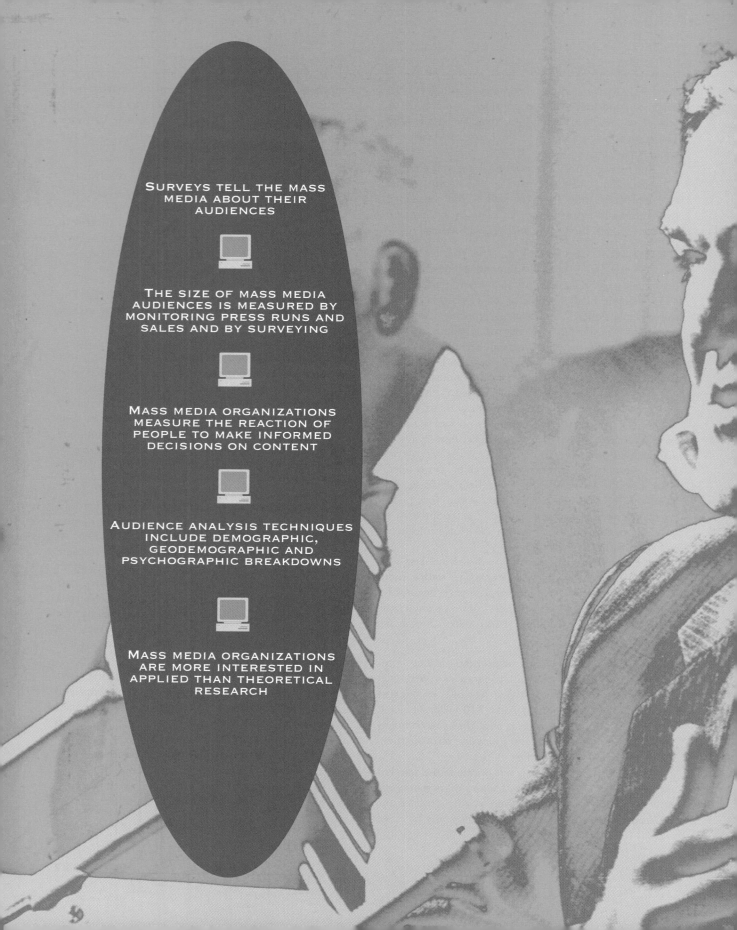

SURVEYS TELL THE MASS MEDIA ABOUT THEIR AUDIENCES

THE SIZE OF MASS MEDIA AUDIENCES IS MEASURED BY MONITORING PRESS RUNS AND SALES AND BY SURVEYING

MASS MEDIA ORGANIZATIONS MEASURE THE REACTION OF PEOPLE TO MAKE INFORMED DECISIONS ON CONTENT

AUDIENCE ANALYSIS TECHNIQUES INCLUDE DEMOGRAPHIC, GEODEMOGRAPHIC AND PSYCHOGRAPHIC BREAKDOWNS

MASS MEDIA ORGANIZATIONS ARE MORE INTERESTED IN APPLIED THAN THEORETICAL RESEARCH

chapter 13

MEDIA RESEARCH
THE QUEST FOR USEFUL DATA

George Gallup was excited. His mother-in-law, Ola Babcock Miller, had decided to run for secretary of state. If elected, she would become not only Iowa's first Democrat but also the first woman to hold the statewide office. Gallup's excitement, however, went beyond the novelty of his mother-in-law's candidacy. The campaign gave him an opportunity to pull together his three primary intellectual interests: survey research, public opinion and politics. In that 1932 campaign, George Gallup conducted the first serious poll in history for a political candidate. Gallup's surveying provided important barometers of public sentiment that helped Miller gear her campaign to the issues most on voters' minds. She won and was reelected twice by large margins.

Four years after that first 1932 election campaign, Gallup tried his polling techniques in the presidential race and correctly predicted that Franklin Roosevelt would beat Alf Landon. In 1936, he called another Roosevelt victory accurately, and then his Gallup Poll organization had clients knocking at his door.

Gallup devoted himself to accuracy. Even though he predicted Roosevelt's 1936 victory, Gallup was bothered that his reliability was not better. His method, *quota sampling*, could not call a two-way race within 4 percentage points. With quota sampling, a representative percentage of women and men was surveyed, as was a representative percentage of Democrats and Republicans, westerners and easterners, Christians and Jews, and other constituencies.

Despite their current ambivalence about Clinton's health care plan, Americans feel -- by more than a two-to-one margin -- that the Clinton administration has had a positive (62%) rather than negative (28%) influence on efforts to reform the health care system. Also by a substantial margin, Democrats in Congress are seen as having a positive (52%) rather than negative (28%) influence. On the other hand, Republicans in Congress are seen as having more of a negative (51%) than positive (29%) influence.

Clinton has criticized the insurance companies and lobbyists who have strongly opposed his health care plan, and most Americans have taken his side. By more than a three-to-one margin, these groups are viewed as having a negative rather than positive influence on health reform. Doctors and hospitals are also viewed as a negative (51%) rather than positive (33%) influence.

Methodology

The current results are based on telephone interviews with a randomly selected national sample of 1,019 adults, 18 years and older, conducted June 25-28, 1994. For results based on the whole sample, one can say with 95 percent confidence that the error attributable to sampling and other random effects could be plus or minus 3 percentage points. For results based on just half the sample, the margin of error is plus or minus 5 percentage points. In addition to sampling error, question wording and practical difficulties in conducting surveys can introduce error or bias into the findings of public opinion polls.

How well do you understand the details you have heard or read so far about the debate over health care reform in this country? Would you say you understand most of those details, many of them, a few of them, or none of them at all?

Most	29%
Many	26
A few	30
None	5
No opinion	1
	100%

Do you think Congress should pass a bill to reform the health care system, or should Congress leave the health care system as it is?

Should pass a bill	69%
Leave system as is	26
No opinion	5
	100%

Would you support or oppose a health care reform package that guarantees every American private health insurance that can never be taken away?

Guaranteed Insurance - Trend

	Jan 28-30	Jun 25-28
Support	79%	77%
Oppose	16	17
No opinion	5	6
	100%	100%

Suppose Congress passes a bill which would improve the country's health care system, but would not guarantee coverage for every American. Do you think President Clinton should veto the bill and send it back to Congress, or should he sign it?

Veto if No Guaranteed Coverage? - Trend

	Jan 28-30	Jun 25-28
Veto bill	73%	62%
Sign it	22	26
Depends (vol.)	3	4
No opinion	2	8
	100%	100%

Which of the following do you think is the more important change that needs to take place in health care -- Making sure that Americans cannot lose their health insurance, even if they lose their job or have a medical problem, or, providing health insurance for those who cannot now afford it?

Guaranteed coverage	54%
Providing insurance	31
Both equally (vol.)	12
No opinion	3
	100%

Which of the following do you think is the more important change that needs to take place in health care...

In general, how much of the costs of health insurance should be paid for by employers and how much by employees? Do you think -- Employers should pay all, employers should pay most, with employees paying some, employers and employees should share the costs equally, employees should pay most, with employers paying some, or employees should pay all?

Who Should Pay? - Trend

	Apr 16-18	Jun 25-28
Employers pay all	8%	8%
Employers pay most	46	44
Share the costs equally	35	37
Employees pay most	2	4
Employees pay all	4	3
No opinion	4	4
	100%	100%

Now I am going to read you five benefits which could be guaranteed to all Americans if Congress passes a health care reform bill this year. Which benefit among the five do you consider the most important benefit you would want guaranteed: Prescription drugs; mental health and substance abuse services; care for catastrophic, long-term illnesses; dental care; nursing home care. (RANDOM ORDER) Which do you consider the second most important benefit you would want guaranteed?

Most Important Benefit

(1st & 2nd choices combined)

Catastrophic illness	69%
Nursing home care	45
Prescription drugs	39
Mental health/substance abuse	23
Dental care	14
None (vol.)	

The GALLUP POLL
NEWS SERVICE

Volume 59, No. 9   Friday, July 1, 1994

Public Firm On Health Reform Goals

Although Unclear On Details of Clinton's Plan

By David W. Moore

PRINCETON, NJ -- Americans may not know the details of Clinton's health care reform plan, but - according to a new Gallup poll -- they do want Congress to pass a reform bill and they are quite firm about some of the provisions they want included. Only 29% say they know most of the details of Clinton's plan, and just 39% say they have enough information to judge whether that plan is acceptable or not. But, by a margin of 69% to 26%, Americans want Congress to reform the system rather than leave it as is.

When asked about certain provisions currently being debated, the public shows a strong consensus for several items:

♦ The most important provision should be guaranteed coverage for all Americans that can never be taken away: 77% support this provision, only 17% oppose it. If Congress passes a bill without the guaranteed coverage for every American, 62% want the President to veto the bill.

♦ Guaranteed coverage is more important than universal coverage: by 54% to 31%, Americans say it is more important to provide guaranteed coverage to those who have it now than to cover those who cannot afford insurance.

♦ Controlling costs is also more important than universal coverage: by 57% to 32%, Americans say it is more important to control costs so they don't rise so fast in the future than it is to cover those who cannot afford insurance.

♦ Most Americans feel that employers should pay most (44%) or all (8%) of the costs of insurance. Another third (37%) are willing to share the costs equally, but only a few Americans feel that workers should pay most (4%) or all (3%) of the costs.

♦ Apart from routine health care, Americans most desire coverage for catastrophic, long-term illnesses (69%). Nursing home care (45%) and prescription drugs (39%) are also seen as important elements in a new health care coverage, while mental health coverage (23%) and dental care (14%) are seen as less important among these five items.

♦ Finally, most Americans are opposed to government-financed abortions. If the government guarantees medical benefits as part of the health reform package, only one-third of Americans (34%) think abortion should be included among them, while 59% say it should not be included.

Political Impact of Health Care Reform Positive for Democrats

Americans remain split on Clinton's health care plan, with 49% opposed and 43% in favor, essentially unchanged for the past four months. Support has dropped, however, from the high point a year ago when Clinton introduced his plan, then favored by 59% of the public, and opposed by 33%.

George Gallup

The Whole Story. Reputable pollsters believe in full disclosure about how they go about doing their work. Note the detail on sample size, confidence level, margin of error and other specifics in this Gallup release to media clients.

Gallup, correct in 1948 that underdog Harry Truman would win the presidency over Thomas Dewey, was nonetheless off 5.3 percentage points, so he decided to switch to a tighter method, *probability sampling,* which theoretically gave everyone in the population being sampled an equal chance to be surveyed. With probability sampling, there was no need for quotas because, as Gallup explained in his folksy midwestern way, it was like a cook making soup. "When a housewife wants to test the quality of the soup: she is making, she tastes only a teaspoonful or two. She knows that if the soup is thoroughly stirred, one teaspoonful is enough to tell her whether she has the right mixture of ingredients." With the new method, Gallup narrowed his error rate to less than 2 percentage points.

Even with improvements pioneered by Gallup, public opinion surveying has detractors. Some critics say polls influence undecided voters toward the front-runner—a *bandwagon effect.* Other critics say polls make elected officials too responsive to the momentary whims of the electorate, discouraging courageous leadership. George Gallup, who died in 1984, tirelessly defended polling, arguing that good surveys give voice to the "inarticulate minority" that legislators otherwise might not hear. Gallup was convinced that public-opinion surveys help make democracy work.

PUBLIC-OPINION SURVEYING

STUDY PREVIEW Public-opinion polling is an important ancillary activity for the mass media. One polling technique, probability sampling, relies on statistical guidelines that can be incredibly accurate. Sad to say, less reliable survey techniques also are used, which sullies the reputation of serious sampling.

THE SURVEYING INDUSTRY

Public-opinion surveying is approaching a $1 billion-a-year business whose clients include major corporations, political candidates, and the mass media. Today, just as in 1935, the Institute of American Public Opinion, founded by *George Gallup*, cranks out regular columns for newspaper clients. Major news organizations hire survey companies to tap public sentiment regularly on specific issues.

About 300 companies are in the survey business in the United States, most performing advertising and product-related opinion research for private clients. During election campaigns, political candidates become major clients. There are dozens of other survey companies that do confidential research for and about the media. Their findings are important because they determine what kind of advertising will run and where, what programs will be developed and broadcast and which ones will be canceled. Some television stations even use such research to choose anchors for major newscasts.

PROBABILITY SAMPLING

Although polling has become a high-profile business, many people do not understand how questions to a few hundred individuals can tell the mood of 250 million Americans. In the *probability sampling* method pioneered by George Gallup in the 1940s, four factors figure into accurate surveying:

SAMPLE SIZE.   To learn how Layne College students feel about abortion on demand, you start by asking one student. Because you can hardly generalize from one student to the whole student body of 2,000, you ask a second student. If both agree, you start developing a tentative sense of how Layne students feel, but because you cannot have much confidence in such a tiny sample, you ask a third student, and a fourth and a fifth. At some point between interviewing just one and all 2,000 Layne students, you can draw a reasonable conclusion.

Statisticians have found that 384 is a magic number for many surveys. Put simply, no matter how large the population being sampled, if every member has an equal

TEACHING OBJECTIVE 13-1
Surveys tell mass media about audiences.

KEY PERSON
George Gallup.

CNN Poll Variables

Why do public-opinion surveys not all agree? CNN reporter Bill Dorman looks at polls during the 1992 Clinton-Bush presidential contest to explain variations in survey techniques. Generally, the variations among surveys are minor. This segment aired October 26, 1992.

opportunity to be polled, you need ask only 384 people to be 95 percent confident that you are within 5 percentage points of a precise reading. For a lot of surveys, that is close enough. Here is a breakdown, from Philip Meyer's *Precision Journalism*, a book for journalists on surveying, on necessary sample sizes for 95 percent confidence and being within 5 percentage points:

Population Size	Sample Size
Infinity	384
500,000	384
100,000	383
50,000	381
10,000	370
5,000	357
3,000	341
2,000	322
1,000	278

At Layne, with a total enrollment of 2,000, the sample size would need to be 322 students.

SAMPLE SELECTION.   Essential in probability sampling is giving every member of the population being sampled an equal chance to be interviewed. If, for example, you want to know how Kansans intend to vote, you cannot merely go to a Wichita street corner and survey the first 384 people who pass by. You would need to check a list of the state's 675,000 registered voters and then divide by the magic number, 384:

$$\frac{675,000}{384} = 1,758$$

You would need to talk with every 1,758th person on the list. At Layne College, 2,000 divided by 322 would mean an interval of 6.2. Every sixth person in the student body would need to be polled.

Besides the right sample size and proper interval selection, two other significant variables affect survey accuracy: margin of error and confidence level.

MARGIN OF ERROR.   For absolute precision, every person in the population must be interviewed, but such precision is hardly ever needed, and the process would be prohibitively expensive and impracticable. Pollsters, therefore, must decide what is an acceptable margin of error for every survey they conduct. This is a complex matter, but, in simple terms, you can have a fairly high level of confidence that a properly designed survey with 384 respondents can yield results within 5 percentage points, either way, of being correct. If the survey finds that two candidates for statewide office are running 51 to 49 percent, for example, the race is too close to call with a sample of 384. If, however, the survey says that the candidates are running 56 to 44 percent, you can be reasonably confident who is ahead in the race because, even if the survey is 5 points off on the high side for the leader, the candidate at the very least has 51 percent support (56 percent minus a maximum 5 percentage points for possible error). At best, the trailing candidate has 49 percent (44 percent plus a maximum 5 percentage points for possible error).

Increasing the sample size will reduce the margin of error. Meyer gives this breakdown:

Population Size	Sample Size	Margin of Error
Infinity	384	5 percentage points
Infinity	600	4 percentage points
Infinity	1,067	3 percentage points
Infinity	2,401	2 percentage points
Infinity	9,605	1 percentage point

Professional polling organizations that sample American voters typically use sample sizes between 1,500 and 3,000 to increase accuracy. Also, measuring subgroups within the population being sampled requires that each subgroup, such as men and women, Catholics and non-Catholics, or northerners and southerners, be presented by 384 properly selected people.

CONFIDENCE LEVEL.   With a sample of 384, pollsters can claim a relatively high 95 percent confidence level, that is, that they are within 5 percentage points of being on the mark. For many surveys, this is sufficient statistical validity. If the confidence level needs to be higher, or if the margin of error needs to be decreased, the number of people surveyed will need to be increased. In short, the level of confidence and margin of error are inversely related. A larger sample can improve confidence, just as it also can reduce the margin of error.

QUOTA SAMPLING

Besides probability sampling, pollsters survey cross-sections of the whole population. This quota sampling technique gave Gallup his historic 1936 conclusions about the Roosevelt-Landon presidential race. With quota sampling, a pollster checking an election campaign interviews a sample of people that includes a quota of men and women that corresponds to the number of male and female registered voters. The sample might also include an appropriate quota of democrats, republicans and independents; of poor, middle-income and wealthy people; of Catholics, Jews and Protestants; of southerners, midwesterners and New Englanders; of the employed and unemployed; and other breakdowns significant to the pollster.

Both quota and probability sampling are valid if done correctly, but Gallup abandoned quota sampling because he could not pinpoint public opinion closer than 4 percentage points on average. With probability sampling, he regularly came within 2 percentage points.

EVALUATING SURVEYS

Sidewalk interviews cannot be expected to reflect the views of the population. The people who respond to such polls are self-selected by virtue of being at a given place at a given time. Just as unreliable are call-in polls with 800 or 900 telephone numbers. These polls test the views only of people who are aware of the poll and who have sufficiently strong opinions to want to be heard.

Judging Surveys

A 1975 poll found that one in seven American adults had been polled at least once by some survey or another.

■ Have you ever played a part in a Gallup poll or any other survey? Has anyone in your family? Any of your friends?

■ Did you see the poll results to determine whether your views coincided with the majority's?

■ Do you think that the poll extrapolated accurately from the small sample? Did you know the sample size? How it was selected? The margin of error? The confidence level?

Journalists run the risk of being duped when special-interest groups suggest that news stories be written based on their privately conducted surveys. Some organizations selectively release self-serving conclusions.

Incompetence in designing a survey can mar results. Surveys by college research methodology classes are notorious. Results can be seriously skewed if even one student, perhaps under deadline pressure at the end of a semester, fakes data and is not caught.

In response to sloppy and dishonest surveying, the Associated Press insists on knowing methodology details before running poll stories. The AP tells reporters to ask:

■ **How Many Persons Were Interviewed and How Were They Selected?** Any survey of fewer than 384 persons selected randomly from the population group has a greater margin for error than usually is tolerated.

■ **When Was the Poll Taken?** Opinions shift over time. During election campaigns, shifts can be quick, even overnight.

■ **Who Paid for the Poll?** With privately commissioned polls, reporters should be skeptical, asking whether the results being released constitute everything learned in the survey. The timing of the release of political polls to be politically advantageous is not uncommon.

■ **What Was the Sampling Error for a Poll and for Subgroups?** Margins of error exist in all surveys unless everyone in the population is surveyed. If the margin of error exceeds the margin between candidates, the results are indicative only that the race is tight.

■ **How Was the Poll Conducted?** Whether a survey was conducted over the telephone or face to face in homes is important. Polls conducted on street corners or in shopping malls are not worth much statistically unless the question is what the people at a particular street corner or mall think. Mail surveys are also flawed unless surveyors follow up on people who do not answer the original questionnaires.

■ **How Were Questions Worded and in What Order Were They Asked?** Drafting questions is an art. Sloppily worded questions yield sloppy conclusions. Leading questions and loaded questions can skew results. So can question sequencing.

It is at great risk that a polling company's client misrepresents survey results. Most polling companies, concerned about protecting their reputations, include a clause in their contracts with clients that gives the pollster the right to approve the release of findings. The clause usually reads: "When misinterpretation appears, we shall publicly disclose what is required to correct it, notwithstanding our obligation for client confidentiality in all other respects."

LATTER-DAY STRAW POLLS

The ABC television network dabbled, some say irresponsibly, with phone-in polling on public issues in the mid-1980s. So did Cable News Network. The vehicle was the 900 telephone number, which listeners could dial at 50 cents a call to register yea or nay on a question. MTV, the rock music channel, did something similar that left the impression of being a legitimate public test of a recording's popularity.

To its credit, ABC sometimes ran scientific surveys the same evening that Ted Koppel was conducting a 900 phone-in and compared the results. Sometimes the results coincided. Other times, the latter-day straw polls were nowhere near close.

Also dubious are the candid camera features, popular in weekly newspapers, in which a question is put to citizens on the street. The photos of half a dozen individuals and their comments are then published, often on the editorial page. These features are circulation builders for small publications whose financial success depends on how many local names and mug shots can be crammed into an issue, but it is only coincidental when the views expressed are representative of the population as a whole.

These roving-photographer features are at their worst when people are not given time to formulate an intelligent response. The result too often is contributions to the public babble, not public understanding. The result is irresponsible pseudojournalism. A defensible variation on the "inquiring camera" feature is used by *USA Today* for its editorial page. The newspaper maintains a cross-section panel of several hundred people nationwide. Members of the panel are asked their thoughts on a specific question and given a few days to respond. Also, panel members are chosen in part for presumed articulateness. *USA Today*'s goal is a meaningful contribution to public dialogue—not off-the-cuff chatter.

- -

MEASURING AUDIENCE SIZE

STUDY PREVIEW   To attract advertisers, the mass media need to know the number and kinds of people they reach. This is done for the print media by audits and for the broadcast media by surveys. Although surveying is widely accepted for obtaining such data, some approaches are more reliable than others.

NEWSPAPER AND MAGAZINE AUDITS

The number of copies a newspaper or magazine puts out, called *circulation*, is fairly easy to calculate. It is simple arithmetic involving data like press runs, subscription sales and unsold copies returned from newsracks. Many publishers follow strict procedures, which are checked by independent audit organizations, such as the *Audit Bureau of Circulations*, to assure advertisers that the system is honest and circulation claims comparable.

TEACHING OBJECTIVE 13-2
Size of mass media audiences is measured by monitoring press runs and sales, by surveying.

KEY PERSON
Archibald Crossley.

The Audit Bureau of Circulations was formed in 1914 to remove the temptation for publishers to inflate their claims to attract advertisers and hike ad rates. Inflated claims, contagious in some cities, were working to the disadvantage of honest publishers. Today, most newspapers and magazines belong to ABC, which means that they follow the bureau's standards for reporting circulation and are subject to the bureau's audits.

Some fuzziness enters circulation data when newspapers and magazines try to count the number of people who see a single copy. The commonly used factors for this *pass-around circulation*, usually three to four readers per copy, underrate some publications and overrate others. The Audit Bureau of Circulation, however, endorses only its own firm rules for substantiating circulation claims for the print media.

BROADCAST RATINGS

Radio and television audiences are harder to measure, but advertisers have no less need for counts to help them decide where to place ads and to know what is a fair price. To keep track of broadcast audiences, a whole industry, now with about 200 companies, has developed. The *A. C. Nielsen Co.* tracks network television viewership. The American Research Bureau, usually called *Arbitron*, is the leader in measuring radio and local television audiences.

Radio ratings began in 1929 when advertisers asked pollster *Archibald Crossley* to determine how many people were listening to network programs. Crossley checked a small sample of households and then extrapolated the data into national ratings, the same process that radio and television audience tracking companies still use, although there have been refinements.

In the 1940s, Nielsen began telling advertisers which radio programs were especially popular among men, women and children. Nielsen also divided listenership into age brackets: 18–34, 35–49, and 50 plus. These were called *demographic breakdowns.* When Nielsen moved into television monitoring in 1950, it expanded audience data into more breakdowns, including income, education, religion, occupation, neighborhood, and even which products the viewers of certain programs use frequently.

While Archibald Crossley's early ratings were sponsored by advertisers, today networks and individual stations also commission ratings to be done. The television networks pass ratings data on to advertisers immediately. Local stations usually recast the raw data for brochures that display the data in ways that put the station in the most favorable light. These brochures are distributed by station sales representatives to advertisers. While advertisers receive ratings data from the stations and networks, major advertising agencies have contracts with Nielsen, Arbitron and other market research companies to gather audience data to meet their specifications.

AUDIENCE MEASUREMENT TECHNIQUES

The primary techniques, sometimes used in combination, for measuring broadcast audiences are:

INTERVIEWS.   In his pioneer 1929 listenership polling, Archibald Crossley placed telephone calls to randomly selected households. Today, many polling companies use telephone interviews exclusively. Some companies conduct face-to-face

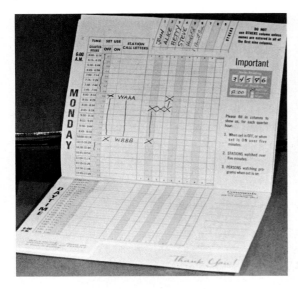

Measuring Broadcast Audiences. Many audience measurement companies ask selected households to keep diaries on their listening and viewing habits. Through statistical extrapolations, these companies claim they can discover the size of the total audience for particular programs and stations. This Nielsen diary asks participants to list who is watching, which allows broadcast executives and advertisers to learn demographic details about this audience. Under pressure for more accurate television ratings, Nielsen, Arbitron and other audience measurement companies are shifting from written diaries to electronic meters. With a meter, members of participating households punch in when they start watching. With more advanced meters, punching in is not even required. The meters sense who is watching by body mass, which is programmed into the meter for every member of the household when it is installed.

interviews, which can elicit fuller information, although it is more expensive and time-consuming.

DIARIES.   Many ratings companies give forms to selected households to record what stations were on at particular times. Some companies distribute diaries to every member of a household. Arbitron's diaries go to everybody over age 12 in selected households, which provide data on age and gender preferences for certain stations and programs. Participants mail these diaries back to Arbitron, which tabulates the results.

METERS.   For television ratings, Nielsen and Arbitron install meters to record when television sets are on and to which channels they are tuned. Early devices like Nielsen's Audimeter recorded data on film cartridges, which were mailed back every two weeks to Nielsen. Today, new devices transmit data daily by telephone to

Inside the Beltway. Political leaders, including President and Hillary Clinton, keep tabs on the public's pulse to guide their actions. There was some solace in the White House in 1994 when a sophisticated survey by the Times Mirror Center for People and Press found that fewer than 40 percent of Americans were aware of or interested in the White-water scandal that had been plaguing the Clintons. These surveys also help newspeople determine what subjects their audiences want covered.

Nielsen's central computer. With the new meters, Nielsen is able to generate next-day reports, called *overnights*, for the networks.

Ratings companies make ongoing adjustments to their sample sizes and methods. Nielsen once said that the 1,170 homes that had Audimeters provided a sound sample. Later, Nielsen added diaries to 2,000 more homes to widen the statistical base. With a larger base, audiences could be subdivided into categories to determine viewing preferences by age groups, regions and other breakdowns. Today, Nielsen has 4,000 selected households wired with meters, and Arbitron 5,000.

Though an improvement over interviews and diaries in several respects, the early meters recorded only whether a television set was turned on and to which channel it was turned—not whether anybody was watching. In many households, it came to be realized, people left the television on as background noise, which distorted the final data. To address this problem, Nielsen and Arbitron installed new push-button devices called *people meters* and asked people in the surveyed households to punch in personal codes to identify who was watching certain programs—mom, dad, oldsters, teenagers, little kids, or nobody at all.

Like diaries, the first people meters required participants to log their viewing dutifully. It was recognized that not everyone in every wired household could be expected to be equally conscientious about recording their "entries" and "exits." To address this problem, new *passive meters* can recognize household members automatically by body mass, which eliminates the hazard of some viewers' failing to record their watching.

CRITICISM OF RATINGS

However sophisticated the ratings services have become, they have critics. Many fans question the accuracy of ratings when their favorite television program is cancelled because the network finds the ratings inadequate. Something is wrong, they say, when the viewing preferences of a few thousand households determine network programming for the entire nation. Though it seems incredible to someone unknowledgeable about statistical probability, the sample base of major ratings services like Nielsen and Arbitron generally is considered sufficient to extrapolate reliably on viewership in the 87 million U.S. households.

It was not always so. Doubts peaked in the 1940s and 1950s when it was learned that some ratings services lied about sample size and were less than scientific in choosing samples. A congressional investigation in 1963 prompted the networks to create the *Broadcast Ratings Council* to accredit ratings companies and audit their reports.

Ratings have problems, some inherent in differing methodologies and some attributable to human error and fudging:

DISCREPANCIES.   When different ratings services come up with widely divergent findings in the same market, advertisers become suspicious. Minor discrepancies can be explained by different sampling methods, but significant discrepancies point to flawed methodology or execution. It was discrepancies of this sort that led to the creation of the Broadcast Ratings Council in 1963.

SLANTED RESULTS.   Sales reps of some local stations, eager to demonstrate to advertisers that their stations have large audiences, extract only the favorable data from survey results. It takes a sophisticated local advertiser to reconcile slanted and fudged claims.

SAMPLE SELECTION.   Some ratings services select their samples meticulously, giving every household in a market a statistically equal opportunity to be sampled. Some sample selections are seriously flawed: How reliable, for example, are the listenership claims of a rock 'n' roll station that puts a disc jockey's face on billboards all over town and then sends the disc jockey to a teenage dance palace to ask about listening preferences?

HYPING.   Ratings-hungry stations have learned how to build audiences during *sweeps weeks* in February, May and November when major local television ratings are done. Consider:

- It was no coincidence in 1989 that syndicated talk-show host Geraldo Rivera took his cameras to a nudist colony during the February sweeps. It helped the local stations that buy his program to attract extra viewers in a critical sweeps period.
- Radio give-aways often coincide with ratings periods.
- Many news departments promote sensationalistic series for the sweeps and then retreat to routine coverage when the ratings period is over. Just ahead of one 1988 Minneapolis sweeps, one station mailed out thousands of questionnaires, asking people to watch its programs and mail back the form. Accused of trickery to look good in the ratings, the station responded with a straight face that it merely was trying a new technique to strengthen viewership. The timing, it argued, was mere coincidence.
- To boost ratings during the May 1990 sweeps, Denver television station KCNC heavily promoted a four-part series, "Blood Sport," on illegal dogfights. The series, however, turned out not to be the scandal. Unable to find any real dogfights, reporter Wendy Bergin and photojournalists Scott Wright and Jim Stair

staged a gruesome dogfight. All three ended up indicted for dogfighting for "monetary gain or entertainment," a Colorado felony punishable by four years in prison. Bergin later explained to the newspaper *Westword* that she had been pushed by a "ratings frenzy" to outdo competing stations: "Everyone was in sort of an altered state. Everybody was saying, 'We've got to beat them at 10. We've got to beat them at 10.' Nobody understood they'd moved a few degrees out of reality."

■ Besides sweep weeks, there are *black weeks* when no ratings are conducted. In these periods, some stations run all kinds of odd and dull serve-the-public programs that they would never consider during a sweeps period.

RESPONDENT ACCURACY.   Respondents don't always answer truthfully. People have an opportunity to tell interviewers or diaries that they watched "Masterpiece Theater" on PBS instead of less classy fare. Shock radio and trash television may have more audience than the ratings show.

ZIPPING, ZAPPING AND FLUSHING.   Ratings services measure audiences for programs and for different times of day, but they do not measure whether commercials are watched. Advertisers are interested, of course, in whether the programs in which their ads are sandwiched are popular, but more important to them is whether people are watching the ads.

This vacuum in audience measurements was documented in the 1960s when somebody with a sense of humor correlated a major drop in Chicago water pressure with the Super Bowl halftime. Football fans were getting off the couch by the thousands at halftime to go to the bathroom. Advertisers were missing many people because viewers were watching the program but not the ads. This *flush factor* was also at work with all other programs. Television viewers find all kinds of things to do when the commercials come on—go to the refrigerator, let the dog in, chat with someone else watching the program. The same thing happens in radio. With a push-button car radio, drivers easily change stations whenever an ad comes up to find a station that is playing music or delivering news.

This problem has been exacerbated with the advent of hand-held television remote controls. Viewers can zip from station to station to avoid commercials, and when they record programs for later viewing they can zap out the commercials.

MEASURING AUDIENCE REACTION

STUDY PREVIEW   The television ratings business has moved beyond measuring audience size to measuring audience reaction. Today, Nielsen and Arbitron have systems to determine what it is about a program that stirs an audience, and also whether a particular advertisement is prompting people to buy the advertised product. Other methods to measure audience reaction include focus groups, galvanic skin checks, and prototypes.

CHECKING WHETHER ADS WORK

TEACHING OBJECTIVE 13-3
Mass media organizations measure audience reaction to decide content.

Today, Nielsen and Arbitron measure not only audience size and demographics for particular programs and parts of the day, but they also have devised methods to determine whether particular television advertisements are likely to prompt viewers to purchase a product.

In 1991 Nielsen launched a two-stage system, called *Comprehensive Advertising Tracking System,* which first checks the effectiveness of advertisements for competing products through pretesting. Test groups are asked their brand preferences, shown advance copies of competing television spots and then tested again on their preferences. In the second CATS stage, Nielsen tracks viewership of the competing ads when they run on the networks. With both pretest and viewership data, advertisers are better able to make informed judgments on how to place ads to counter the competition's ads and even whether to change their pitches.

Arbitron, meanwhile, has offered advertisers its *ScanAmerica* data, which tabulate both who in a household is watching a particular ad and whether the advertised product is purchased. To determine which advertised products are purchased, everyone in participating households is issued a *scanner wand* to run over the universal product code on the items they buy. If General Mills discovers that viewers who see its Wheaties ads are still buying Kellogg's Corn Flakes, General Mills knows it needs to make some changes in its advertising.

Both CATS and ScanAmerica have their detractors. CATS relies heavily on the reactions of small groups of people previewing ads, which is less precise statistically than larger samples. ScanAmerica's weakness is that it requires participants to remember to use their scanner wands. In an interview with the *Wall Street Journal*, Joel Segal, executive vice president of the McCann-Erickson agency, expressed his doubts this way: "Everytime you make a sophisticated demand of the consumer, you become less sure of the results."

FOCUS GROUPS

Television consulting companies measure audience reaction with *focus groups*. Typically an interview crew goes to a shopping center, chooses a dozen individuals by gender and age, and offers them cookies, soft drinks and $25 each to sit down and watch a taped local newscast. A moderator then asks their reactions, sometimes with loaded and leading questions to open them up. It is a tricky research method that depends highly on the skill of the moderator. In one court case, an anchor who lost her job as a result of responses to a focus group complained that the moderator contaminated the process with prejudicial assertions and questions:

- "This is your chance to get rid of the things you don't like to see on the news."
- "Come on, unload on those sons of bitches who make $100,000 a year."
- "This is your chance to do more than just yell at the TV. You can speak up and say I really hate that guy or I really like that broad."
- "Let's spend 30 seconds destroying this anchor. Is she a mutt? Be honest about this."

Even when conducted skillfully, focus groups have the disadvantage of reflecting the opinion of the loudest respondent.

GALVANIC SKIN CHECKS

Consulting companies hired by television stations run a great variety of studies to determine audience reaction. Local stations, which originate news programs and not much else, look to these consultants for advice on news sets, story selection, and even which anchors and reporters are most popular. Besides surveys, these consultants sometimes use *galvanic skin checks*. Wires are attached to individuals in a sample group of viewers to measure pulse and skin reactions, such as perspiration.

Advocates of these tests claim that they reveal how much interest a newscast evokes and whether it is positive or negative.

These tests were first used to check audience reaction to advertisements, but today some stations look to them in deciding whether to remodel a studio. A dubious use, from a journalistic perspective, is using galvanic skin checks to determine what kinds of stories to cover and whether to find new anchors and reporters. The skin checks reward short, photogenic stories like fires and accidents rather than significant stories, which tend to be longer and don't lend themselves to flashy video. The checks also favor good-looking, smooth anchors and reporters regardless of their journalistic competence. One wag was literally correct when he called this "a heart-throb approach to journalism."

PROTOTYPE RESEARCH

Before making major investments, media executives need as much information as they can obtain to determine how to enhance a project's chances for success or whether it has a chance at all. The *American Research Institute* of Los Angeles specializes in showing previews of television programs and even promotional ads to sample audiences. It is a method originated by movie studios, which invite people to advance showings and watch their reaction to decide how to advertise a new film most effectively, how to time the film's release, and even whether to re-edit the film.

When Gannett decided to establish a new newspaper, *USA Today*, it created prototypes, each designed differently, to test readers' reactions. Many new maga-

What the Audience Wants. The mass media reduce chances for flops by testing their products on live audiences. A Hollywood company, National Research Group, charges moviemakers $200,000 for information on actors and subjects that people are interested in at the moment. NRG also test-previews movies to help determine which scenes don't go over well, and even to figure out how to end the movie. It was NRG's advice that resulted in Anne Archer's killing Glenn Close in the finale of *Fatal Attraction*. That, said NRG, was what people wanted to have happen to the rabbit-boiling Close.

zines are preceded with at least one trial issue to sample marketplace reaction and to show to potential advertisers.

In network television, a prototype may even make it on the air in the form of a *pilot*. One or a few episodes are tested, usually in prime time with a lot of promotion, to see if the audience goes for the program concept. Some made-for-television movies actually are test runs to determine whether a series might be spun off from the movies.

AUDIENCE ANALYSIS

STUDY PREVIEW   Traditional demographic polling methods divided people by gender, age and other easily identifiable population characteristics. Today, media people use sophisticated life-style breakdowns such as geo-demographics and psychographics to match the content of their publications, broadcast programs and advertising to the audiences they seek.

DEMOGRAPHICS

Early in the development of public-opinion surveying, pollsters learned that broad breakdowns had limited usefulness. Archibald Crossley's pioneering radio surveys, for example, told the number of people who were listening to network programs, which was valuable to the networks and their advertisers, but Crossley's figures did not tell how many listeners were men or women, urban or rural, old or young. Such breakdowns of overall survey data, called *demographics*, were developed in the 1930s as Crossley, George Gallup and other early pollsters refined their work.

TEACHING OBJECTIVE 13-4
Audience analysis techniques: demographic, geodemographic, psychographic breakdowns.

Adrenalin Video. Television producers know from research what kinds of videos excite viewers. During the Persian Gulf war, combat footage was repeated again and again under voice-overs that told about war developments. This led some observers to say that war coverage had become video entertainment.

Today, if demographic data indicate a political candidate is weak in the midwest, campaign strategists can gear the candidate's message to midwestern concerns. Through demographics, advertisers keen on reaching young women can identify magazines that will carry their ads to that audience. If advertisers seek an elderly audience, they can use demographic data to determine where to place their television ads.

While demographics remains valuable today, newer methods can break the population into categories that have even greater usefulness. These newer methods, which include geodemography, provide life-style breakdowns.

GEODEMOGRAPHICS

KEY PERSON
Jonathan Robbin.

Computer whiz *Jonathan Robbin* provided the basis for more sophisticated breakdowns in 1974 when he began developing his *PRIZM* system for *geodemography*. From census data, Robbin grouped every zip code by ethnicity, family life cycle, housing style, mobility and social rank. Then he identified 34 factors that statistically distinguished neighborhoods from each other. All this information was cranked through a computer programmed by Robbin to plug every zip code into 1 of 40 clusters. Here are the most frequent clusters created through PRIZM, which stands for Potential Rating Index for Zip Markets, with the labels Robbin put on them:

- **Blue-Chip Blues.** These are the wealthiest blue-collar suburbs with a median household income of $32,000 and house value of $72,600. These Blue-Chip Blues, as Robbin calls them, comprise about 6 percent of U.S. households. About 13 percent of these people are college graduates.
- **Young Suburbia.** Child-rearing outlying suburbs, 5.3 percent of U.S. population; median income, $38,600; median house value, $93,300; college grads, 24 percent.
- **Golden Ponds.** Rustic mountain, seashore or lakeside cottage communities, 5.2 percent; income, $20,100; house, $51,500; college grads, 13 percent.
- **New Beginnings.** Fringe-city areas of singles apartment complexes, garden apartments and trim bungalows, 4.3 percent; income, $24,800; house, $75,400; college grads, 19 percent.
- **New Homesteaders.** Exurban boom towns of young midscale families, 4.2 percent; income, $25,900; house, $67,200; college grads, 19 percent.
- **Share Croppers.** Primarily southern hamlets devoted to farming and light industry, 4 percent; income, $16,900; house, $33,900; college grads, 7 percent.

The potential of Robbin's PRIZM system was clear at *Time, Newsweek* and *McCall's*, which re-sorted subscriber lists and created new zoned editions to allow advertisers to mix and match their messages with a great variety of subaudiences of potential customers. Cadillac could choose editions aimed at these PRIZM neighborhoods:

- **Blue-Blood Estates.** Wealthiest neighborhoods; income, $70,300; house, $200,000 plus; college grads, 51 percent.
- **Money and Brains.** Posh big-city enclaves of townhouses, condos and apartments; income, $45,800; house, $159,800; college grads, 46 percent.

Geodemographics. Many magazines can customize their advertising and editorial content to match the interests of readers through sophisticated geodemographic audience analysis. *Time* demonstrated the potential of its TargetSelect geodemographic program by printing the name of each subscriber as part of the cover art for the November 26, 1990, issue. The cover underscored the point of the lead article about the sort of TargetSelect sophistication also used by "junk mail" companies to match fliers sent through the mail with the likeliest customers for their products.

For its household products, Colgate-Palmolive might focus on:

■ **Blue-Collar Nursery.** Middle-class, child-rearing towns; income, $30,000; house, $67,300; college grads, 10 percent.

Geodemographic breakdowns are used not only for magazine advertising but also for editorial content. At Time Warner magazines, geodemographic analysis permits issues to be edited for special audiences. *Time*, for example, has a 600,000 circulation edition for company owners, directors, board chairs, presidents, other titled officers and department heads. Among others are editions for physicians and college students.

Theoretically, using PRIZM geodemographic breakdowns and other data, newsmagazines customize their agribusiness coverage for chicken farmers, offer expanded golf coverage for golf fans, and beef up articles on problems of the aged in the Gray Power and Golden Ponds PRIZM clusters. More book reviews might be added for Town and Gowns, the PRIZM cluster for college towns (income, $17,600; houses, $60,900; college grads, 28 percent).

In a 1990 stunt that demonstrated the potential for customizing magazines, *Time* printed the name of each subscriber in big print as part of the cover art, using the same computerized ink-jet printing that it uses for localizing advertisements.

PSYCHOGRAPHICS

A refined life-style breakdown introduced in the late 1970s, *psychographics*, divides the population into life-style segments. One leading psychographics approach, the *Values* and *Life-Styles* program, known as VALS for short, uses an 85-page survey that was used to identify broad categories of people:

- **Belongers.** Comprising about 38 percent of the U.S. population, these people are conformists who are satisfied with mainstream values and are reluctant to change brands once they're satisfied. Belongers are not very venturesome and fit the stereotype of Middle America. They tend to be churchgoers and television watchers.
- **Achievers.** Comprising about 20 percent of the population, these are prosperous people who fit into a broader category of inner-directed consumers. Achievers pride themselves on making their own decisions. They're an upscale audience to which a lot of advertising is directed. As a group, achievers aren't heavy television watchers.
- **Societally Conscious.** Comprising 11 percent of the population, these people are aware of social issues and tend to be politically active. The societally conscious also are upscale and inner-directed, and they tend to prefer reading to watching television.
- **Emulators.** Comprising 10 percent of the population, these people aspire to a better life but, not quite understanding how to do it, go for the trappings of prosperity. Emulators are status seekers, prone to suggestions on what makes the good life.
- **Experientials.** Comprising 5 percent of the population, these people are venturesome, willing to try new things in an attempt to experience life fully. They are a promising upscale audience for many advertisers.
- **I-Am-Me's.** Comprising 3 percent of the population, these people work hard to set themselves apart and are susceptible to advertising pitches that offer ways to differentiate themselves, which gives them a kind of subculture conformity. SRI International, which developed the VALS technique, characterized I-Am-Me's as "a guitar-playing punk rocker who goes around in shades and sports an earring." Rebellious youth, angry and maladjusted, fit this category.
- **Survivors.** This is a small downscale category that includes pensioners who worry about making ends meet.
- **Sustainers.** These people live from paycheck to paycheck. Although they indulge in an occasional extravagance, they have slight hope for improving their lot in life. Sustainers are a downscale category and aren't frequent advertising targets.
- **Integrateds.** Comprising only 2 percent of the population, integrateds are both creative and prosperous—willing to try different products and ways of doing things, and they have the wherewithal to do it.

Applying psychographics is not without hazard. The categories are in flux as society and life-styles change. SRI researchers charted growth in the percentage of I-Am-Me's, experientials and the societally conscious in the 1980s and projected

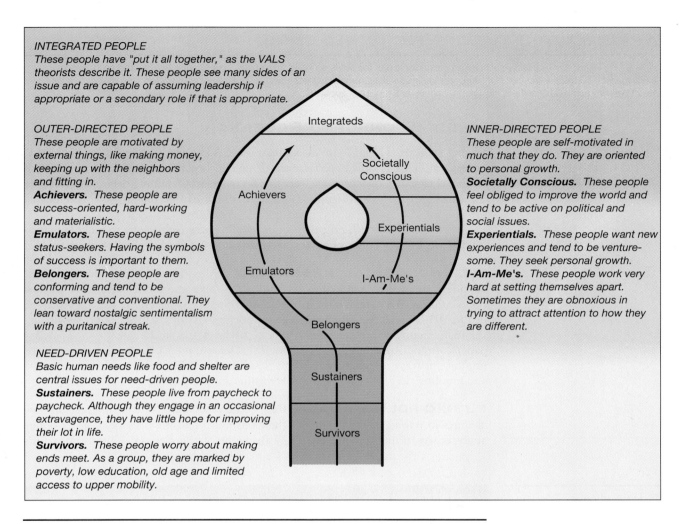

INTEGRATED PEOPLE
These people have "put it all together," as the VALS theorists describe it. These people see many sides of an issue and are capable of assuming leadership if appropriate or a secondary role if that is appropriate.

OUTER-DIRECTED PEOPLE
These people are motivated by external things, like making money, keeping up with the neighbors and fitting in.
Achievers. These people are success-oriented, hard-working and materialistic.
Emulators. These people are status-seekers. Having the symbols of success is important to them.
Belongers. These people are conforming and tend to be conservative and conventional. They lean toward nostalgic sentimentalism with a puritanical streak.

NEED-DRIVEN PEOPLE
Basic human needs like food and shelter are central issues for need-driven people.
Sustainers. These people live from paycheck to paycheck. Although they engage in an occasional extravagence, they have little hope for improving their lot in life.
Survivors. These people worry about making ends meet. As a group, they are marked by poverty, low education, old age and limited access to upper mobility.

INNER-DIRECTED PEOPLE
These people are self-motivated in much that they do. They are oriented to personal growth.
Societally Conscious. These people feel obliged to improve the world and tend to be active on political and social issues.
Experientials. These people want new experiences and tend to be venturesome. They seek personal growth.
I-Am-Me's. These people work very hard at setting themselves apart. Sometimes they are obnoxious in trying to attract attention to how they are different.

Labels in diagram: Integrateds, Societally Conscious, Achievers, Experientials, Emulators, I-Am-Me's, Belongers, Sustainers, Survivors

VALS Hierarchy. Developmental psychologists have long told us that people change their values as they mature. Today, advertisers rely on the Values and Life-Styles model, *VALS* for short, which was derived from developmental psychology, to identify potential consumers and to design effective messages. Relatively few advertising messages are aimed at survivors and sustainers, who have little discretionary income. However, belongers and people on the divergent outer-directed or inner-directed paths are lucrative advertising targets of many products and services.

that they would be one-third of the population within a few years. Belongers were declining.

Another complication is that no person fits absolutely the mold of any one category. Even for individuals who fit one category better than another, there is no single mass medium to reach them. VALS research may show that achievers constitute the biggest market for antihistamines, but belongers also head to the medicine cabinet when they're congested.

APPLIED AND THEORETICAL RESEARCH

STUDY PREVIEW   Media-sponsored research looks for ways to build audiences, to enhance profits and to program responsibly. In contrast, mass communication scholarship asks theoretical questions that can yield new understandings, regardless of whether there is a practical application.

MEDIA-SPONSORED RESEARCH

TEACHING OBJECTIVE 13-5
Mass media organizations interested mostly in applied research.

Studies sponsored by mass media companies seek knowledge that can be put to use, or applied. This is called *applied research*. When broadcasters underwrite research on media violence, they want answers to help make programming decisions. Audience measures and analysis are applied research, which can be put to work to enhance profits.

Mass media research ranges from developing new technology to seeking historical lessons from previous practices. Here are some fields of applied media research:

TECHNOLOGICAL RESEARCH.   Mass media companies and their suppliers finance research into technology to take economic advantage of new opportunities. Early television in the United States, for example, was spearheaded in the 1930s by RCA, which saw new opportunities for its NBC radio subsidiary. Ink manufacturers introduced nonsmudge soybean inks in the late 1980s for newspapers. Besides cutting-edge technological research, media companies also sponsor finding out ways to adapt innovations developed in other fields, such as computers and satellites, to reduce costs, improve profits and remain competitive.

PUBLIC POLICY ANALYSIS.   The media have intense interests in how changes in public policy will affect their business. The importance of good policy analysis was illustrated by the 1979 decision of the Federal Communications

Fickle Audience. Television executives look to survey research to find ways to reach more viewers. In 1994, CNN's ratings were down 25 percent from a year earlier. That prompted the network to scrap some soft-news programs, including "Living in the '90s," and to create new call-in sports and news programs, one with a live audience. CNN's problem is that it cannot sustain the huge audience it draws when everybody is intently interested in major news, like the O. J. Simpson case or Operation Desert Storm. The network typically draws only about 400,000 viewers. Although CNN's audience is educated, affluent and attractive to advertisers, more viewers would mean more revenue. CNN accounts for 70 percent of Turner Broadcasting System's operating earnings.

CNN Anchor
Bernard Shaw

Commission to allow people to install backyard satellite dishes to pick up television signals. Analysts anticipated correctly that the television networks would go to satellites to send programs to their affiliates, but they failed to anticipate that network affiliates would use their new downlink dishes to pick up programming from nonnetwork sources and accelerate the fragmentation of the television industry.

FINANCIAL STUDIES.   Whether Merrill Lynch recommends that investors be bullish on Gannett depends on how analysts interpret Gannett's periodic financial reports. Even privately held media companies are subject to analysis. Competitors make decisions based on their assessment of the marketplace and all the players.

OPINION SURVEYS.   When anchor Dan Rather began wearing a sweater on the "CBS Evening News," ratings improved. The network learned about the "sweater factor" from audience surveys. Survey research helps media executives make content decisions—whether to expand sports coverage, to hire a disc jockey away from the competition, or to ax a dubious sitcom. Advertisers and public relations practitioners also look to public-opinion surveys.

MASS COMMUNICATION SCHOLARSHIP

In contrast to applied research, *theoretical research* looks for truths regardless of practical application. Scholars consider most theoretical research on a higher level than applied research, partly because the force that drives it is the seeking of truths for their own sake rather than for any economic goal.

Profit motivated as they are, media organizations are not especially enthusiastic about funding theoretical research. There usually is no apparent or short-term economic return from theoretical scholarship. For this reason, most theoretical research occurs at major universities, whose institutional commitments include pushing back the frontiers of human knowledge, even if no economic reward is likely. Here are some of the kinds of studies and analyses that are the subject of theoretical research:

EFFECTS STUDIES.   The greatest ferment in mass communication scholarship has involved questions about effects. In the 1920s, as mass communication theory took form, scholars began exploring the effects of mass communication and of the mass media themselves on society and individuals. Conversely, scholars are also interested in how ongoing changes and adjustments in society influence the mass media and their content.

PROCESS STUDIES.   A continuing interest among scholars is the mystery of how the process of mass communication works. Just as human beings have developed theories to explain other great mysteries, such as thunder being caused by unhappy gods thrashing about in the heavens, mass communication scholars have developed a great many explanations to help us understand mass communication.

Examples of these theories include the diverse models that scholars have created of the mass communication process. You might recall the general, concentric circle and narrative models from Chapter 1. None of these models is as way out as the thrashing-gods explanation for thunder, but their diversity indicates that many questions still need to be asked and explored before we can ever develop the kind of understanding about mass communication that scientists now have about thunder.

GRATIFICATIONS STUDIES.   Beginning in the 1940s, studies about how and why individuals use the mass media attracted scholarly interest. These today are called *uses and gratifications* studies.

CONTENT ANALYSIS.   George Gerbner, a scholar of media violence, studied the 8 p.m. hour of network television for 19 years and found an average of 168 violent acts a week. Gerbner arrived at his disturbing statistic through *content analysis*, a research method involving the systematic counting of media content. Gerbner's tallying became a basic reference point for important further studies that correlated media-depicted violence with changes in incidents of violence in society at large.

It is also content analysis when a researcher tallies the column inches of sports in a newspaper to determine what percentage of available space goes to sports. While interesting for its own sake, such information can become a significant indicator of the changing role of sports in American life.

HISTORICAL STUDIES.   Some scholars specialize in deriving truths about the mass media and mass communication by examining evidence from the past.

CRITICAL STUDIES.   Scholars who are engaged in critical studies question underlying institutions and their economic, philosophical and political assumptions that shape the mass media. These scholars pose provocative questions from the frameworks of diverse disciplines, questioning things that most people take for granted, such as whether capitalism works for or against media responsibility.

CHAPTER WRAP-UP

The mass media are a rich field for study, partly because there are so many mysteries about how the process of mass communication works. Scholars have devised fascinating theories to explain the process, but their theories are widely divergent, and they squabble among themselves even about basic premises. Students aspiring to media careers have the special problem of trying to sort out these theories, which stem from scholarship and research on the same campuses where the work of journalism, advertising, broadcasting and public relations is taught.

Besides scholarship, often of an abstract sort, media research includes work that is distinctly practical. Publishers and broadcast executives need data on their circulations and reach in order to attract advertisers, and they are eager for research that can help them to reduce costs and tailor their product to larger or more profitable audiences. Both the media themselves and special research companies perform this kind of research.

Both theoretical research, which mostly is campus-based, and applied research, which the media eagerly fund, use many of the same tools. A unifying tool of these disparate research approaches is public-opinion sampling. It is used to track public opinion, which is essential in public relations work; to learn which television programs are the most watched, which is essential in programming and advertising decisions; and to determine the effects of media and how people use the media, which are scholarly endeavors.

QUESTIONS FOR REVIEW

1. What do surveys tell the mass media about their audiences?

2. How is the size of mass media audiences measured?

3. How is the reaction of people to the mass media measured?

4. What are techniques of audience analysis?

5. Why are mass media organizations more interested in applied than theoretical research?

QUESTIONS FOR CRITICAL THINKING

1. Street-corner polls are called *straw polls* because they are based on such weak methodology. Explain how quota sampling and probability sampling are improvements.

2. What is the basis for arguments that public-opinion surveys subvert democracy? What is the counter-argument?

3. The Audit Bureau of Circulations and television rating services like A. C. Nielsen and Arbitron are essential media services to advertisers. How are these services similar? How different?

4. How can local television and radio stations manipulate their ratings? Why can't the Broadcast Ratings Council do anything about it?

5. Explain how applied research and theoretical research differ.

FOR FURTHER LEARNING

James Atlas. "Beyond Demographics: How Madison Avenue Knows Who You Are and What You Want." *Atlantic* 254 (October 1984):4, 49–58. Atlas explores the uses and hazards of psychographics in shaping advertising campaigns.

Charles O. Bennett. *Facts Without Opinion: First Fifty Years of the Audit Bureau of Circulations* (Audit Bureau of Circulations, 1965).

George Gallup. *The Sophisticated Poll Watcher's Guide* (Princeton Opinion Press, 1972). Gallup, a pioneer pollster, answers critics who charge that polls pervert the democratic process. Gallup argues that polling oils the wheels of democracy by helping elected leaders determine the majority will.

Shearson A. Lowery and Melvin L. DeFleur. *Milestones in Mass Communication Research: Media Effects* (Longman, 1983). Beginners will find Lowery and DeFleur's chronicle an easily followed primer on developments in mass communication research.

Philip Meyer. *Precision Journalism*, 2nd ed. (Indiana University Press, 1979). Meyer, a reporter who became a professor, explains how scholarly research methods, including survey research, can be applied in journalistic truth seeking.

Alan Prendergast. "Wendy Bergin's Exclusive Hoax." *Washington Journalism Review* 13 (October 1991):8, 30–34. Prendergast, a newspaper reporter, offers a case study on how pressure to attract viewers during a ratings period led three Denver journalists to stage an illegal dogfight to illustrate a television newscast series.

William S. Rubens. "A Personal History of TV Ratings, 1929 to 1989 and Beyond." *Feedback* 30 (Fall 1989):4, 3–15. Rubens, a former NBC vice president for research, draws on his experience for this thumbnail history of measuring broadcast audience.

Michael J. Weiss. *The Clustering of America* (Harper & Row, 1988). Weiss, a clever writer, describes Jonathan Robbin's geodemographic research and then takes the reader on a tour to view America through PRIZM eyes.

Richard Saul Wurman. *Information Anxiety* (Doubleday, 1989). Wurman, an architect, advocates new ways of organizing words and graphics to help people understand a growing deluge of information.

FOR KEEPING UP TO DATE

Public Opinion Quarterly is a scholarly publication. *American Demographics* and *Public Opinion* have a lot of general-interest content for media observers.

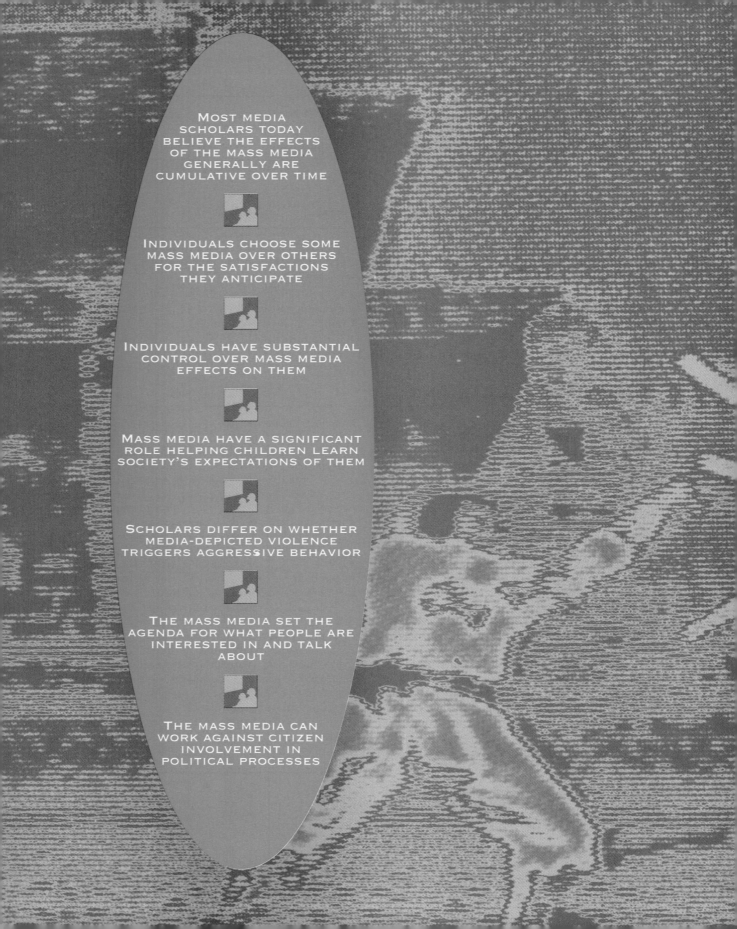

MOST MEDIA
SCHOLARS TODAY
BELIEVE THE EFFECTS
OF THE MASS MEDIA
GENERALLY ARE
CUMULATIVE OVER TIME

INDIVIDUALS CHOOSE SOME
MASS MEDIA OVER OTHERS
FOR THE SATISFACTIONS
THEY ANTICIPATE

INDIVIDUALS HAVE SUBSTANTIAL
CONTROL OVER MASS MEDIA
EFFECTS ON THEM

MASS MEDIA HAVE A SIGNIFICANT
ROLE HELPING CHILDREN LEARN
SOCIETY'S EXPECTATIONS OF THEM

SCHOLARS DIFFER ON WHETHER
MEDIA-DEPICTED VIOLENCE
TRIGGERS AGGRESSIVE BEHAVIOR

THE MASS MEDIA SET THE
AGENDA FOR WHAT PEOPLE ARE
INTERESTED IN AND TALK
ABOUT

THE MASS MEDIA CAN
WORK AGAINST CITIZEN
INVOLVEMENT IN
POLITICAL PROCESSES

chapter

The boy genius Orson Welles was on a roll. By 1938, at age 23, Welles's dramatic flair had landed him a network radio show, "Mercury Theater on the Air," at prime time on CBS on Sunday nights. The program featured adaptations of well-known literature. For their October 30 program, Welles and his colleagues decided on a scary 1898 British novel. Their enthusiasm faded five days before airtime when writer Howard Koch concluded that the novel did not lend itself to radio. Koch said that he in effect was required to create a one-hour original play and five days was not enough time, but neither was there time to switch to another play. The Thursday rehearsal was flat. Koch, frantic, scrambled to rewrite the script, but the Saturday rehearsal was disappointing too. Little did Welles expect that Koch's loose adaptation of H. G. Welles's "War of the Worlds" would become one of broadcasting's most memorable programs.

Orson Welles opened with the voice of a wizened chronicler from some future time, intoning eerily: "We know now that in the early years of the 20th century this world was being watched closely by intelligences greater than man's. . . ." Welles's unsettling monologue was followed by an innocuous weather forecast, then hotel dance music. To casual listeners, the monologue seemed a mistake dropped inadvertently into typical radio music. Then the music was interrupted by a news bulletin. An astronomer reported several explosions on Mars, propelling something at enormous velocity toward Earth. The bulletin over, listeners were transported back to the hotel orchestra. After applause, the orchestra started up again, only to be interrupted: Seismologists had picked up an earthquake-like shock in New Jersey. Then it was one bulletin after another. A huge cylinder had crashed into a New Jersey farm. On the scene, a reported asked what happened.

FARMER: A hissing sound. Like this: sssssssss . . . kinda like a fourt' of July rocket.
REPORTER: Then what?
FARMER: Turned my head out the window and would have swore I was to sleep and dreamin'.
REPORTER: Yes?
FARMER: I seen a kinda greenish streak and then zingo! Somethin' smacked the ground. Knocked me clear out of my chair!

Orson Welles. Young Orson Welles scared the living daylights out of several million radio listeners with the 1939 radio drama "War of the Worlds." Most of the fright was short-lived, though. All but the most naive listeners quickly realized that Martians really had not devastated the New Jersey militia as they marched toward the Hudson River to destroy Manhattan.

The story line accelerated. Giant Martians moved across the countryside spewing fatal gas. One at a time, reporters at remote sites vanished off the air. The Secretary of the Interior came on: "Citizens of the nation: I shall not try to conceal the gravity of the situation. . . . Placing our faith in God we must continue the performance of our duties, each and every one of us, so that we may confront this destructive adversary with a nation united, courageous, and consecrated to the preservation of human supremacy on this earth."

Meanwhile, the Martians decimated the Army and were wading across the Hudson River. Amid sirens and other sounds of emergency, a reporter on a Manhattan rooftop described the monsters advancing through the streets. He passed on bulletins that Martian cylinders were coming down in St. Louis, Chicago, near Buffalo, all over the country. From his vantage, he described the Martians felling people by the thousands and moving in on him, the gas crossing Sixth Avenue, then Fifth Avenue, then 100 yards away, then 50 feet. Then silence. A lonely ham radio voice somehow became patched into the network: 2X2L calling CQ . . . 2X2L calling CQ . . . 2X2L calling CQ, New York . . . Isn't there anyone on the air? . . . Isn't there anyone? . . . Anyone? . . ." Silence.

To the surprise of Orson Welles and his crew, the drama triggered widespread mayhem. Neighbors gathered in streets all over the country, wet towels to their faces to slow the gas. In Newark, New Jersey, people, many undressed, fled their apartments. Said a New York woman, "I never hugged my radio so closely. . . . I held a crucifix in my hand and prayed while looking out my open window to get a faint whiff of gas so that I would know when to close my window and hermetically seal my room with waterproof cement or anything else I could get a hold of. My plan was to stay in the room and hope that I would not suffocate before the gas blew away." A Midwest man told of his grandparents, uncles, aunts and children, on their knees, "God knows but we prayed. . . . My mother went out and looked for Mars. Dad was hard to convince or skeptical or sumpin', but he even got to believing it. Brother Joe, as usual, got more excited than he could show. Brother George wasn't home. Aunt Gracie, a good Catholic, began to pray with Uncle Henry. Lily got sick to her stomach. I prayed harder and more earnestly than ever before. Just as soon as we were convinced that this thing was real, how petty all things on earth seemed; how soon we put our trust in God."

In one Pacific Northwest village, a power outage reinforced the panic. Switchboards throughout the country were swamped by people trying to call relatives, fueling the hysteria. The telephone volume in northern New Jersey was up 39 percent. Most CBS stations reported a six-fold increase in calls. Many people jumped into their cars to drive to safety but did not know where to go and so just drove around, which put hysterical strangers in touch with each other.

Researchers estimate that one out of six people who heard the program, more than one million in all, suspended disbelief and braced for the worst.

The effects were especially amazing considering that:

- An announcer identified the program as fiction at four points.
- Almost 10 times as many people were tuned to a popular comedy show on another network.
- The program ran only one hour, an impossibly short time for the sequence that began with the blastoffs on Mars, included a major military battle in New Jersey, and ended with New York's destruction.

Unwittingly, Orson Welles and his Mercury Theater crew had created an evening of infamy and raised questions about media effects to new intensity. In this chapter, you will learn what scholars have found out about the effects of the mass media on individuals.

EFFECTS STUDIES

STUDY PREVIEW Early mass communication scholars assumed that the mass media were so powerful that ideas and even ballot-box instructions could be inserted as if by hypodermic needle into the body politic. Doubts arose in the 1940s about whether the media were really that powerful, and scholars began shaping their research questions on assumptions that media effects were more modest. Recent studies are asking about long-term, cumulative media effects.

POWERFUL EFFECTS THEORY

The first generation of mass communication scholars thought the mass media had a profound, direct effect on people. Their idea, called *effects theory*, drew heavily on social commentator *Walter Lippmann's* influential 1922 book, *Public Opinion*. Lippmann argued that we see the world not as it really is but as "pictures in our heads." The "pictures" of things we have not experienced personally, he said, are shaped by the mass media. The powerful impact that Lippmann ascribed to the media was a precursor of the effects theory that evolved among scholars over the next few years.

TEACHING OBJECTIVE 14-1
Scholars today favor the cumulative effect theory.

KEY PERSON
Walter Lippmann assumed powerful media effects in *Public Opinion*.

KEY PERSON
Harold Lasswell's mass communication model assumed powerful effects.

Yale psychologist *Harold Lasswell*, who studied World War II propaganda, embodied the effects theory in his famous model of mass communication: *Who, Says what, In which channel, To whom, With what effect*. At their extreme, effects theory devotees assumed that the media could inject information, ideas and even propaganda hypodermically into the public. The theory was explained in terms of a hypodermic needle model or bullet model. Early effects scholars would agree that newspaper coverage and endorsements of political candidates decided elections.

The early scholars did not see that the hypodermic metaphor was hopelessly simplistic. They assumed wrongly that individuals are passive and absorb uncritically and unconditionally whatever the media spew forth. The fact is that individuals read, hear and see the same things differently. Even if they did not, people are exposed to many, many media—hardly a single, monolithic voice. Also, there is a skepticism among media consumers that is manifested at its extreme in the saying, "You can't believe a thing you read in the paper." People are not mindless, uncritical blotters.

MINIMALIST EFFECTS THEORY

KEY PERSON
Paul Lazarsfeld found voters more influenced by other people than mass media.

Scholarly enthusiasm for the hypodermic needle model dwindled after two massive studies of voter behavior, one in Erie County, Ohio, in 1940 and the other in Elmira, New York, in 1948. The studies, led by sociologist *Paul Lazarsfeld* of Columbia University, were the first rigorous tests of media effects on an election. Lazarsfeld's researchers went back to 600 people several times to discover how they developed their campaign opinions. Rather than citing particular newspapers, magazines or radio stations, as had been expected, these people generally mentioned friends and acquaintances. The media had hardly any direct effect. Clearly, the hypodermic needle model was off base, and the effects theory needed rethinking. From that rethinking emerged the *minimalist effects theory*, which included:

TWO-STEP FLOW MODEL.   Minimalist scholars devised the two-step flow model to show that voters are motivated less by the mass media than by people they know personally and respect. These people, called *opinion leaders*, include many clergy, teachers and neighborhood merchants, although it is impossible to list categorically all those who comprise opinion leaders. Not all clergy, for example, are influential, and opinion leaders are not necessarily in an authority role. The minimalist scholars' point is that personal contact is more important than media contact. The two-step flow model, which replaced the hypodermic needle model, showed that whatever effect the media have with the majority of the population is through opinion leaders. Later, as mass communication research became more sophisticated, the two-step model was expanded into a *multistep flow model* to capture the complex web of social relationships that affects individuals.

KEY PEOPLE
Maxwell McCombs and Don Shaw articulated agenda-setting theory.

STATUS CONFERRAL.   Minimalist scholars acknowledge that the media create prominence for issues and people by giving them coverage. Conversely, neglect relegates issues and personalities to obscurity. Related to this *status conferral* phenomenon is *agenda setting*. Professors *Maxwell McCombs* and *Don Shaw*, describing the agenda-setting phenomenon in 1972, said the media do not tell people *what to think* but tell them *what to think about*. This is a profound distinction. In covering a political campaign, explain McCombs and Shaw, the media choose which issues or topics to emphasize, thereby setting the campaign's agenda. "This ability to affect cognitive change among individuals," say McCombs and Shaw, "is one of the most important aspects of the power of mass communication."

Opinion Leaders

Imagine the value of being able to identify opinion leaders if you were running a political campaign, handling an advertising account, or managing a public relations campaign. Since the introduction of the two-step flow model in mass communication theory, researchers have tried to identify who these influential people are. In 1971 scholars Everett Rogers and Floyd Shoemaker pulled together the research on the question and concluded that opinion leaders generally are distinguished from their followers because they:

■ Pay attention to the mass media more avidly and thoroughly.
■ Are especially accessible to their followers.
■ Hold higher social status.
■ Are more involved in community affairs, which gives them access to people in positions of responsibility and power who can effect changes.

■ Are more cosmopolitan, which can take the form of being widely knowledgeable, traveled and experienced.
■ Tend to be more innovative in crises or other situations necessitating change.

Identifying opinion leaders is elusive, as epitomized by a waitress quoted in a report on the Erie County, Ohio, studies of the 1940s. The waitress said she decided how to vote because she overheard a customer "who looked like he knew what he was talking about." She didn't even know the man.

Name as many opinion leaders as you can in your neighborhoods, schools, churches and other organizations in your community. How about state, national and even world opinion leaders? Be sure you have supporting rationales.

NARCOTICIZING DYSFUNCTION.   Some minimalists claim that the media rarely energize people into action, such as getting them to go out to vote for a candidate. Rather, they say, the media lull people into passivity. This effect, called *narcoticizing dysfunction*, is supported by studies that find that many people are so overwhelmed by the volume of news and information available to them that they tend to withdraw from involvement in public issues. Narcoticizing dysfunction occurs also when people pick up a great deal of information from the media on a particular subject—poverty, for example—and believe that they are doing something about a problem when they are really only smugly well-informed. Intellectual involvement becomes a substitute for active involvement.

CUMULATIVE EFFECTS THEORY

In recent years some mass communication scholars have parted from the minimalists and resurrected the powerful effects theory, although with a twist that avoids the simplistic hypodermic needle model. German scholar *Elisabeth Noelle-Neumann*, a leader of this school, conceded that the media do not have powerful immediate effects but argues that effects over time are profound. Her *cumulative effects theory* notes that nobody can escape either the media, which are ubiquitous, or the media's messages, which are driven home with redundancy. To support her point, Noelle-Neumann cites multimedia advertising campaigns that hammer away with the same message over and over. There's no missing the point. Even in news reports there is a redundancy, with the media all focusing on the same events.

LECTURE RESOURCE 14-A
Class exercise: Students reflect on recent purchase.

KEY PERSON
Elisabeth Noelle-Neumann is leading cumulative effects theorist.

Noelle-Neumann's cumulative effects theory has troubling implications. She says that the media, despite surface appearances, work against diverse, robust public consideration of issues. Noelle-Neumann bases her observation on human psychology, which she says encourages people who feel they hold majority viewpoints to speak out confidently. Those views gain credibility in their claim to be dominant when they are carried by the media, whether they are really dominant or not. Meanwhile, says Noelle-Neumann, people who perceive that they are in a minority are inclined to speak out less, perhaps not at all. The result is that dominant views can snowball through the media and become consensus views without being sufficiently challenged.

To demonstrate her intriguing theory, Noelle-Neumann has devised the ominously labeled *spiral of silence model*, in which minority views are intimidated into silence and obscurity. Noelle-Neumann's model raises doubts about the libertarian concept that the media provide a marketplace in which conflicting ideas fight it out fairly, each receiving a full hearing.

USES AND GRATIFICATIONS STUDIES

STUDY PREVIEW Beginning in the 1940s, many mass communication scholars shifted from studying the media to studying media audiences. These scholars assumed that individuals use the media to gratify needs. Their work, known as uses and gratifications studies, focused on how individuals use mass media—and why.

CHALLENGES TO AUDIENCE PASSIVITY

TEACHING OBJECTIVE 14-2
Individuals choose some mass media for satisfactions they anticipate.

As disillusionment with the powerful effects theory set in after the Lazarsfeld studies of the 1940s, scholars reevaluated many of their assumptions, including the idea that people are merely passive consumers of the mass media. From the reevaluation came research questions about why individuals tap into the mass media. This research, called *uses and gratifications studies*, explored how individuals choose certain media outlets. One vein of research said people seek certain media to gratify certain needs.

These scholars worked with social science theories about people being motivated to do certain things by human needs and wants, such as seeking water, food and shelter as necessities and wanting to be socially accepted and loved. These scholars identified dozens of reasons that people use the media, among them surveillance, socialization and diversion.

SURVEILLANCE FUNCTION

With their acute sense of smell and sound, deer scan their environment constantly for approaching danger. In modern human society, surveillance is provided for individuals by the mass media, which scan local and global environments for information that helps individuals make decisions to live better, even survive.

News coverage is the most evident form through which the mass media serve this *surveillance function*. From a weather report, people decide whether to wear a raincoat; from the Wall Street averages, whether to invest; from the news, whether the president will have their support. Although most people don't obsess about being on top of all that's happening in the world, there is a touch of the "news junkie" in everybody. All people need reliable information on their immediate environment. Are tornadoes expected? Is the bridge fixed? Are vegetable prices coming down? Most of us are curious about developments in politics, economics, science and other fields. The news media provide a surveillance function for their audiences, surveying the world for information that people want and need to know.

It is not only news that provides surveillance. From drama and literature, people learn about great human issues that give them a better feel for the human condition. Popular music and entertainment, conveyed by the mass media, give people a feel for the emotional reactions of other human beings, many very far away, and for things going on in their world.

SOCIALIZATION FUNCTION

Except for recluses, people are always seeking information that helps them fit in with other people. This *socialization function*, a lifelong process, is greatly assisted by the mass media. Without paying attention to the media, for example, it is hard to participate in conversations about how the Yankees did last night, or Tom Cruise's latest movie or the current Pentagon scandal. Jay Leno's monologues give late-night television watchers a common experience with their friends and associates the next day, as do the latest movie and the evening news.

Using the media can be a social activity, bringing people together. Gathering around the radio on Sunday night for the Mercury Theater in the 1930s was a family activity. Going to the movies with friends is a group activity.

The media also contribute to togetherness by creating commonality. Friends who subscribe to *Newsweek* have a shared experience in reading the weekly cover story, even though they do it separately. The magazine helps individuals maintain social relationships by giving them something in common. In this sense, the media are important in creating community, even nationhood and perhaps, with global communication, a fellowship of humankind.

Less positive as a social function of the mass media is *parasocial interaction*. When a television anchor looks directly into the camera, as if talking with individual viewers, it is not a true social relationship that is being created. The communication is one-way without audience feedback. However, because many people enjoy the sense of interaction, no matter how false it is, many local stations encourage on-camera members of the news team to chat among themselves, which furthers the impression of an ongoing conversation with an extended peer group that includes the individual viewer.

This same false sense of reciprocal dialogue exists also among individuals and their favorite political columnists, lovelorn and other advice writers, and humorists. Some people have the illusion that the friends David Letterman interviews on his program are their friends, and so are Jay Leno's and Larry King's. It is also illusory parasocial interaction when someone has the television set on for companionship.

LECTURE RESOURCE 14-B
Film: *Impact of Television.*

LECTURE RESOURCE 14-C
Guest speaker: Psychology professors on television and children.

DIVERSION FUNCTION

Through the mass media, people can escape everyday drudgery, immersing themselves in a soap opera, a murder mystery or pop music. The result can be stimulation, relaxation or emotional release.

STIMULATION.   Everybody is bored occasionally. When our senses—sight, hearing, smell, taste and touch—are without sufficient external stimuli, a sensory vacuum results. Following the physicist's law that a vacuum must be filled, we seek new stimuli to correct our sensory deprivation. In modern society the mass media are almost always handy as boredom-offsetting stimulants. It's not only in boring situations that the mass media can be a stimulant. To accelerate the pace of an already lively party, for example, someone can put on quicker music and turn up the volume.

RELAXATION.   When someone's sensory abilities are overloaded, the media can be relaxing. Slower, softer music sometimes can help. Relaxation, in fact, can come through any change of pace. In some situations, a high-tension movie or book can be as effective as a lullaby.

RELEASE.   People can use the mass media to blow off steam. Somehow a Friday night horror movie dissipates the frustration pent up all week. So can a good cry over a tear-jerking book.

Using the mass media as a stimulant, relaxant or release is quick, healthy escapism. Escapism, however, can go further, as when soap-opera fans so enmesh themselves in the programs that they perceive themselves as characters in the story line. Carried too far, escapism becomes withdrawal. When people build on media portrayals to the point that their existence revolves on living out the lives of, say, Elvis Presley or Marilyn Monroe, the withdrawal from reality has become a serious psychological disorder.

CONSISTENCY THEORY

Gratifications scholars learned that people generally are conservative in choosing media, looking for media that reinforce their personal views. Faced with messages consistent with their own views and ones that are radically different, people pay attention to the one they're comfortable with and have slight recall of contrary views. These phenomena—selective exposure, selective perception, selective retention and selective recall—came to be called *consistency theory.*

Consistency theory does a lot to explain media habits. People read, watch and listen to media with messages that don't jar them. The theory raised serious questions about how well the media can meet the democratic ideal that the media be a forum for the robust exchange of divergent ideas. The media can't fulfill their role as a forum if people hear only what they want to hear.

INDIVIDUAL SELECTIVITY

STUDY PREVIEW   Individuals choose to expose themselves to media whose perspective and approach reinforce their personal interests and values. These choices, called selective exposure, are consciously made. Similar selectivity phenomena are at work subconsciously in how individuals perceive and retain media content.

SELECTIVE EXPOSURE

TEACHING OBJECTIVE 14-3
Individuals have substantial control over mass media effects.

People make deliberate decisions in choosing media. For example, outdoors enthusiasts choose *Field & Stream* at the newsrack. Academics subscribe to the *Chronicle of Higher Education.* Young rock fans watch MTV. People expose themselves to media whose content relates to their interests. In this sense, individuals exercise control over the media's effects on them. Nobody forces these selections on any-body.

This process of choosing media, called *selective exposure*, continues once an individual is involved in a publication or a broadcast. A hunter who seldom fishes will gravitate to the hunting articles in *Field & Stream*, perhaps even skipping the fishing pieces entirely. On MTV, a hard-rock aficionado will be attentive to wild music but will take a break when the video jock announces that a mellow piece will follow the commercial.

SELECTIVE PERCEPTION

The selectivity that occurs in actually reading, watching and listening is less con-scious than in selective exposure. No matter how clear a message is, people see and hear egocentrically. This phenomenon, known as *selective* or *autistic perception*, was demonstrated in the 1950s by researcher Roy Carter, who found that physicians concerned about socialized medicine at the time would hear "social aspects of med-icine" as "socialized medicine." Rural folks in North Carolina, anxious for news about farming, thought they heard the words "farm news" on the radio when the announcer said "foreign news."

Scholars Eugene Webb and Jerry Salancik explain it this way: "Exposure to information is hedonistic." People pick up what they want to pick up. Webb and Salancik state that nonsmokers who read an article about smoking focus subcon-sciously on passages that link smoking with cancer, being secure and content, even joyful, in the information that reinforces the wisdom of their decision not to smoke. In contrast, smokers are more attentive to passages that hedge the smoking–cancer link. In using the mass media for information, people tend to perceive what they want. As social commentator Walter Lippmann put it, "For the most part we do not first see and then define, we define first and then see." Sometimes the human mind distorts facts to square with predispositions and preconceptions.

SELECTIVE RETENTION AND RECALL

Experts say that the brain records forever everything to which it is exposed. The problem is recall. While people remember many things that were extremely plea-surable or that coincided with their beliefs, they have a harder time calling up the memory's file on other things.

"Selective forgetting" happens to mothers when they tend to deemphasize or even forget the illnesses or disturbances of pregnancy and the pain of birth. This phenomenon works the opposite way when individuals encounter things that rein-force their beliefs.

Nostalgia also can affect recall. For example, many mothers grossly predate when undesirable behavior like thumb sucking was abandoned. Mothers tend also to suggest precocity about the age at which Suzy or José first walked or cut the first tooth. In the same way, people often use rose-colored lenses, not 20/20 vision, in recalling information and ideas from the media.

In summary, individuals have a large degree of control over how the mass media affect them. Not only do individuals make conscious choices in exposing themselves to particular media, but also their beliefs and values subconsciously

Selective Retention. The influence of the mass media is a function of both media and audience. The success of nostalgia magazines like *Memories*, which was introduced in 1989 and whose circulation soared to 650,000, is a result of the rose-colored lenses through which most people view the past. This is an example of *selective retention* at work.

shape how their minds pick up and store information and ideas. The phenomena of selective exposure, selective perception and selective retention and recall are over-looked by people who portray the mass media as omnipotent and individuals as helpless and manipulated pawns.

The 1938 "War of the Worlds" scare demonstrates this point. The immediate response was to heap blame on the media, particularly *Orson Welles* and CBS, but panic-stricken listeners bore responsibility too. A Princeton University team led by psychologist *Hadley Cantril*, which studied the panic, noted that radio listeners brought to their radio sets predispositions and preconceptions that contributed to what happened. Among their subconscious baggage:

KEY PERSON
Orson Welles's radio drama cast doubt on powerful effects theory.

KEY PERSON
Hadley Cantril concluded less media effect than had been thought.

- A preconception, almost a reverence, about radio, especially CBS, as a reliable medium for major, breaking news.
- A predisposition to expect bad news, created by a decade of disastrous global economic developments and another war imminent in Europe.
- Selective perception, which caused them to miss announcements that the pro-gram was a dramatization. While many listeners tuned in late and missed the initial announcement, others listened straight through the announcements without registering them.
- An awe about scientific discoveries, technological progress and new weapons, which contributed to gullibility.
- Memories from World War I about the horror of gas warfare.
- An inability to test the radio story with their own common sense. How, for example, could the Army mobilize for a battle against the Martians within 20 minutes of the invasion?

SOCIALIZATION

STUDY PREVIEW The mass media have a large role in initiating children into the society. This socialization process is essential to perpetuating cultural values, but some people worry that it can be negative if the media report and portray undesirable behavior and attitudes, such as violence and racism.

MEDIA'S INITIATING ROLE

Nobody is born knowing how to fit into society. This is learned through a process that begins at home. Children imitate their parents and brothers and sisters. From listening and observing, children learn values. Some behavior is applauded, some is scolded. Gradually this culturization and socialization process expands to include friends, neighbors, school and at some point the mass media.

In earlier times, the role of the mass media came late because books, magazines and newspapers required reading skills that were learned in school. The media were only a modest part of early childhood socialization. Today, however, television is omnipresent from the cradle. A young person turning 18 will have spent more time watching television than in any other activity except sleep. Television, which requires no special skills to use, has displaced much of the socializing influence that once came from parents. "Sesame Street" imparts more information on the value of nutrition than Mom's admonition to eat spinach.

By definition, socialization is *prosocial*. Children learn that motherhood, baseball and apple pie are valued, that buddies frown on tattling, that honesty is virtuous, and that hard work is rewarded. The stability of a society is assured through the transmission of such values to the next generation.

ROLE MODELS

The extent of media influence on individuals may never be sorted out with any precision, in part because every individual is a distinct person and because media exposure varies from person to person. Even so, some media influence is undeniable. Consider the effect of entertainment idols as they come across through the media. Many individuals, especially young people casting about for an identity all their own, groom themselves in conformity with the latest heartthrob. Consider the Mickey Mantle butch haircuts in the 1950s, Elvis Presley ducktails in the 1960s, Beatle mopheads in the 1970s, and punk spiking in the 1980s. Remember all the Madonna look-alikes in high schools a few years ago? This imitation, called *role modeling*, even includes speech mannerisms from whomever is hip at the moment— "Know what I mean?" "Grody to the max." "Isn't that special." "Not!"

No matter how quirky, fashion fads are not terribly consequential, but serious questions can be raised about whether role modeling extends to behavior. Many people who produce media messages recognize a responsibility for role modeling. Whenever Batman and Robin leaped into their Batmobile in the campy 1960s television series, the camera always managed to show them fastening their seat belts. Many newspapers have a policy to mention in accident stories whether seat belts were in use. In the 1980s, as concern about AIDS mounted, moviemakers went out of their way to show condoms as a precaution in social situations. For example, in the movie *Broadcast News*, the producer character slips a condom into her purse before leaving the house on the night of the awards dinner.

TEACHING OBJECTIVE 14-4
Mass media significant for children learning societal expectations.

If role modeling can work for good purposes, such as promoting safety consciousness and disease prevention, it would seem that it could also have a negative
effect. Such was the argument against the 1988 movie *Colors*, which was built
around Los Angeles gang violence. Said Curtis Sliwa, leader of the Guardian
Angels, which opposed the movie, "It doesn't take much creative analysis to know
that this could foment a problem. . . . It's almost like a how-to movie. It starts with
a drive-by shooting." When the movie opened, two teenagers at one movie house
were shot, one fatally, and police made 13 arrests at another theater. Experts were
divided, as might be expected, on whether or not the violence was inspired by
depictions on the screen.

STEREOTYPING

Close your eyes. Think "professor." What image forms in your mind? Before 1973
most people would have envisioned a harmless, absent-minded eccentric. Today,
the image is more likely to be the brilliant, sometimes brutal Professor Kingsfield
portrayed by John Houseman in the 1973 movie and subsequent television series
"The Paper Chase." Both the absent-minded pre-1973 professor and the steel-trap
post-1973 Kingsfield are images known as stereotypes. Both flow from the mass
media. While neither is an accurate generalization about professors, both have
long-term impact.

Stereotyping is a kind of shorthand that can facilitate communication. Putting
a cowboy in a black hat allows a movie director to sidestep complex character
explanation and move quickly into a story line, because moviegoers hold a generalization about cowboys in black hats. They are the bad guys—a stereotype. Newspaper
editors pack lots of information into headlines by drawing on stereotypes held by

the readers. Consider the extra meanings implicit in headlines that refer to the "Castro regime," or a "Southern belle," or a "college jock." Stereotypes paint broad strokes that help create impact in media messages, but they are also a problem. A generalization, no matter how useful, is inaccurate. Not all Scots are cheap, nor are all Wall Street brokers crooked, nor are all college jocks dumb—not even a majority.

By using stereotypes, the mass media perpetuate them. With benign stereotypes, there is no problem, but the media can perpetuate social injustice with stereotypes. In the late 1970s, the U.S. Civil Rights Commission found that blacks on network television were portrayed disproportionately in immature, demeaning or comic roles. By using a stereotype, television was not only perpetuating false generalizations but also being racist. Worse, network thoughtlessness was robbing black people of strong role models.

Feminists have leveled objections that women are both underrepresented and misrepresented in the media. One study by sociologist Eve Simson found that most female television parts were decorative, played by pretty California women in their 20s. Worse were the occupations represented by women, said Simson. Most frequent were prostitutes, at 16 percent. Traditional female occupations—secretaries, nurses, flight attendants and receptionists—represented 17 percent. Career women tended to be man-haters or domestic failures. Said Simson, "With nearly every family, regardless of socioeconomic class, having at least one TV set and the average set being turned on 6.3 hours per day, TV has emerged as an important source for promulgating attitudes, values and customs. For some viewers, it is the only major contact with outside 'reality,' including how to relate to women. Thus, not only is TV's sexism insulting, but it is also detrimental to the status of women."

Media critics like Simson call for the media to become activists to revise demeaning stereotypes. While often right-minded, such calls can interfere with accurate portrayals. In the 1970s, Italian-American activists, for example, lobbied successfully against Mafia characters being identified as Italian.

SOCIALIZATION VIA EAVESDROPPING

The mass media, especially television, have eroded the boundaries that people once respected between the generations, genders and other social institutions. Once adults whispered when they wanted to discuss certain subjects, like sex, when children were around. Today, children eavesdrop on all kinds of adult topics by seeing them depicted on television. Though meant as a joke, these lines ring true today to many squirming parents:

> **Father to a Friend:** My son and I had that father-and-son talk about the birds and the bees yesterday.
> **Friend:** Did you learn anything?

Joshua Meyrowitz, a communication scholar at the University of New Hampshire, brought the new socialization effects of intergenerational eavesdropping to wide attention with his 1985 book, *No Sense of Place*. In effect, the old socially recognized institution of childhood, which long had been protected from "big-people issues" like money, divorce and sex, was disappearing. From television sitcoms, kids today learn that adults fight and goof up and sometimes are just plain silly. These are things kids may always have been aware of in a vague sense, but now they have front row seats.

KEY PERSON
Joshua Meyrowitz said media have reduced generational, gender barriers.

Television also cracked other protected societal institutions, such as the "man's world." Through television, many women entered the man's world of the locker room, the fishing trip, and the workplace beyond the home. Older mass media, including books, had dealt with a diversity of topics and allowed people in on the "secrets" of other groups, but the ubiquity of television and the ease of access to it accelerated the breakdown of traditional institutional barriers.

MEDIA-DEPICTED VIOLENCE

STUDY PREVIEW   Some individuals mimic aggressive behavior they see in the media, but such incidents are exceptions. Some experts argue, in fact, that media-depicted violence actually reduces real-life aggressive behavior.

LEARNING ABOUT VIOLENCE

TEACHING OBJECTIVE 14-5
Scholars differ whether depicted violence triggers aggression.

LECTURE RESOURCE 14-D
Film: *The Question of Television Violence.*

LECTURE RESOURCE 14-E
Video: *Shock Waves: Television in America.*

The mass media help bring young people into society's mainstream by demonstrating dominant behaviors and norms. This prosocial process, called *observational learning*, turns dark, however, when children learn deviate behaviors from the media. In Manteca, California, two teenagers, one only 13, lay in wait for a friend's father in his own house and attacked him. They beat him with a fireplace poker, kicked him and stabbed him, and choked him to death with a dog chain. Then they poured salt in his wounds. Why the final act of violence, the salt in the wounds? The 13-year-old explained that he had seen it on television. While there is no question that people can learn about violent behavior from the media, a major issue of our time is whether the mass media are the cause of aberrant behavior.

Individuals on trial for criminal acts occasionally plead that "the media made me do it." That was the defense in a 1974 California case in which two young girls playing on a beach were raped with a beer bottle by four teenagers. The rapists told police they had picked up the idea from a television movie they had seen four days earlier. In the movie, a young woman was raped with a broom handle, and in court, the youths' attorneys blamed the movie. The judge, as is typical in such cases, threw out media-projected violence as an unacceptable scapegoating defense and held the young perpetrators responsible.

Although the courts have never accepted transfer of responsibility as a legal defense, it is clear that violent behavior can be imitated from the media. Some experts, however, say that the negative effect of media-depicted violence is too often overstated and that media violence actually has a positive side.

MEDIA VIOLENCE AS POSITIVE

KEY PERSON
Aristotle defended portrayals of violence.

People who downplay the effect of media portrayals of blood, guts and violence often refer to a *cathartic effect*. This theory, which dates to ancient Greece and the philosopher *Aristotle*, suggests that watching violence allows individuals vicariously to release pent-up everyday frustration that might otherwise explode dangerously. By seeing violence, so goes the theory, people let off steam. Most advocates of the cathartic effect claim that individuals who see violent activity are stimulated to fantasy violence, which drains off latent tendencies toward real-life violence.

KEY PERSON
Seymour Feshbach found evidence for media violence as a release.

In more recent times, scholar *Seymour Feshbach* has conducted studies that lend support to the cathartic effect theory. In one study, Feshbach lined up 625 junior high school boys at seven California boarding schools and showed half of them a

Aggressive Reaction

Has your stomach ever tightened at a scary moment during a movie? Your skin tingled? These are the responses that the moviemaker, an expert at effective storytelling, had intended. They work, however, only if the moviemaker has succeeded at sweeping you into the story line. This process of getting "into" the story requires *suspending disbelief.* It is not unique to movies. In all fiction, no matter what the medium, the storyteller needs to move the audience from knowing the story is fictitious, which is disbelief, to going along with it and being affected, which is the suspending of disbelief. In a movie, you have suspended disbelief if you grab the arm of the person next to you to survive a frightening turn of events on the screen, or if you scream, or gasp, or cry.

There is no question that the media affect people, but there is considerable question whether these effects are momentary or long term and whether these effects can prompt people into antisocial behavior. Some outspoken media critics charge that media-depicted male violence against women leads to rape on the streets and at home. There is wide concern that children are especially susceptible to violence on television and the movies and imitate media violence in their own lives. What are your own experiences with the effects of media depictions of antisocial behavior?

■ Have you ever been inspired to an antisocial act because you saw it on the screen?
■ Do you know anyone who has?
■ Do you worry that children might be affected by media depictions of violence in ways that you never were?
■ Does concern for your own safety increase after seeing violence depicted on the media?

---

steady diet of violent television programs for six weeks. The other half were shown nonviolent fare. Every day during the study, teachers and supervisors reported on each boy's behavior in and out of class. Feshbach found no difference in aggressive behavior between the two groups. Further, there was a decline in aggression among boys watching violence who were determined by personality tests to be more inclined toward aggressive behavior.

Opponents of the cathartic effect theory, who include both respected researchers as well as reflexive media bashers, were quick to point out flaws in Feshbach's research methods. Nonetheless, his conclusions carried a lot of influence because of the study's unprecedented massiveness—625 individuals. Also, the study was conducted in a real-life environment rather than in a laboratory, and there was a consistency in the findings.

PRODDING SOCIALLY POSITIVE ACTION

Besides the cathartic effects theory, an argument for portraying violence is that it prompts people to socially positive action. This happened after NBC aired "The Burning Bed," a television movie about an abused woman who could not take any more and set fire to her sleeping husband. The night the movie was shown, battered-spouse centers nationwide were overwhelmed with calls from women who had been putting off doing anything to extricate themselves from relationships with abusive mates.

Wow, Pow, Zap. The notion that media-depicted violence triggers real-life violence gained currency in the 1960s after researcher Albert Bandura wrote a *Look* magazine article about his Bobo doll research. Kids in a laboratory began really whacking Bobos after seeing people doing the same thing in a film. There is a continuing debate, however, about whether people were accurate in inferring that media violence directly causes real violence. Bandura himself has been dismayed at some of the simplistic conclusions that have been drawn from the *Look* article.

On the negative side, one man set his estranged wife afire and explained that he was inspired by "The Burning Bed." Another man who beat his wife senseless gave the same explanation.

MEDIA VIOLENCE AS NEGATIVE

The preponderance of evidence is that media-depicted violence has the potential to cue real-life violence, and most catharsis theorists concede this possibility. The *aggressive stimulation theory*, however, is often overstated to the point that it comes across smacking of the now generally discredited bullet, or hypodermic needle, theory of mass communication. The fact is that few people act out media violence in their own lives.

CNN **Television Influence**
CNN reporter Jamie McIntyre reports that powerful images on television can prompt viewers into action. This segment, which aired September 5, 1992, cites a correlation between TV news coverage and charitable giving. A numbing effect is acknowledged in the segment, at least in some cases. McIntyre used the term "compassion fatigue" from seeing too many distressing images.

An exaggerated reading of the aggressive stimulation theory became impressed in the public mind, indelibly it seems, after a 1963 *Look* magazine article by Stanford researcher *Albert Bandura*. In his research, Bandura had found that there was an increase in aggressive responses by children shown films of people aggressively punching and beating on large inflated clowns called Bobos. After the film, the children's toys were taken away except for a Bobo doll, which, Bandura reported, was given a beating—just like on the film. The inference was that the children modeled their behavior on the film violence. Bandura also conducted other experiments that all pointed in the same direction.

The *Bobo doll studies* gained wide attention, but, as with most research on the contentious media-triggered violence issue, other scholars eventually became critical of Bandura's research methodologies. One criticism is that he mistook child playfulness with the Bobo dolls for aggressiveness. Even so, everyone who has been stirred to excitement by a violent movie knows from personal experience that there is an effect, and the early publicity on the Bobo studies seemed to verify that growing societal violence was caused by the media.

Such cause-and-effect connections frequently are inferred from individual incidents that are widely played in the news media. Here is a sampler:

■ Fifteen-year-old Ronald Zamora of Miami, a fan of the television police shows "Kojak" and "Police Woman," murdered an 83-year-old neighbor woman, and then said he was the victim of "involuntary subliminal television intoxication."
■ Before going to the electric chair, serial killer Ted Bundy reported that media depictions inspired him to stalk women and kill them.

KEY PERSON
Albert Bandura found media violence stimulated aggression in children.

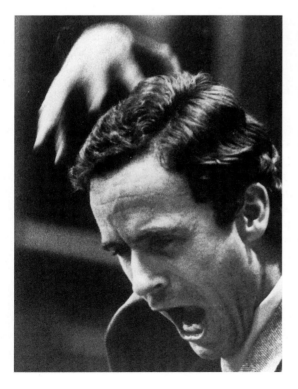

Scape Goating. On the eve of his execution, serial killer Ted Bundy claimed his violence was sparked by girlie magazines. Whatever the truth of Bundy's claim, scholars are divided about whether media depictions precipitate violent behavior. At one extreme is the view that media violence is a safety valve for people inclined to violence. At the other extreme is the aggressive stimulation theory that media violence causes real-life violence. Most thinking, to paraphrase a pioneer 1961 study on television and children, is that certain depictions under certain conditions may prompt violence in certain persons.

■ Twenty-nine people shot themselves playing Russian roulette in separate incidents across the nation after watching the movie "The Deer Hunter," which keeps cutting to a high-tension Russian roulette Saigon gambling scene.

Inferences from such anecdotal cases have contributed to the common notion that media-depicted violence leads directly to aggressive and violent behavior. This widely held notion was also supported by casual readings of numerous serious studies, among them:

■ In upstate New York, researcher Monroe Lefkowitz identified third graders who watched a lot of violent television, and then, 10 years later, found that these individuals were rated by their peers as "aggressive."
■ Psychologist Leonard Berkowitz of Wisconsin showed violent film scenes to children and college students and then moved them to a lab where they were given push buttons and told that they could administer electric shocks to an individual who, depending on the experiment, either had insulted them or resembled a violent character in the film, or who, they were told, had made a mistake on an exam and needed a reminder. Those who had seen the violence on film pushed their shock buttons more and longer than other subjects who had not seen the film.
■ The National Institute of Mental Health reported that serious fights in high schools were more common among students who watched violent television programs.

These studies, however, do not prove that media-depicted violence leads to real-life violence. There are other plausible explanations for a correlation between media-depicted and actual violence. One is that people whose feelings and general view of the world tend toward aggressiveness and violence gravitate to violent movies and television shows because of their predisposition. This leads us to the catalytic theory, which sees media-depicted violence as a bystander, not a trigger, to violent behavior.

CATALYTIC THEORY

Simplistic readings of both cathartic and aggressive stimulation effects research can yield extreme conclusions. A careful reading, however, points more to the media having a role in real-life violence but not necessarily triggering it and doing so only infrequently—and only if several non-media factors are also present. For example, evidence suggests that television and movie violence, even in cartoons, is arousing and can excite some children to violence, especially hyperactive and easily excitable children. These children, like unstable adults, become wrapped up psychologically with the portrayals and are stirred to the point of acting out. However, this happens only when a combination of other influences are also present. Among these other influences are:

■ Whether violence portrayed on the media is rewarded. In 1984 David Phillips of the University of California at San Diego found that the murder rate increases after publicized prizefights, in which the victor is rewarded, and decreases after publicized murder trials and executions, in which, of course, violence is punished.

- Whether media exposure is heavy. A lesson from Monroe Lefkowitz's upstate New York research and dozens of other studies is that aggressive behavioral tendencies are strongest among people who see a lot of media-depicted violence. This suggests a cumulative media effect rather than a single hypodermic injection leading to violence.
- Whether a violent person fits other profiles. Studies have found correlations between aggressive behavior and many variables besides violence viewing. These include income, education, intelligence and parental child-rearing practices. This is not to say that any of these third variables cause violent behavior. The suggestion, rather, is that violence is far too complex to be explained by a single factor.

Most researchers note too that screen-triggered violence is increased if the aggression:

- Is realistic and exciting, like a chase or suspense sequence that sends adrenalin levels surging.
- Succeeds in righting a wrong, like helping an abused or ridiculed character get even.
- Includes situations or characters similar to those in the viewer's own experience.

All these things would prompt a scientist to call media violence a *catalyst*. Just as the presence of a certain element will allow other elements to react explosively but itself not be part of the explosion, the presence of media violence can be a factor in real-life violence but not a cause by itself. This *catalytic theory* was articulated by scholars *Wilbur Schramm*, *Jack Lyle* and *Edwin Parker*, who investigated the effects of television on children and came up with this statement in their 1961 book, *Television in the Lives of Our Children*, which has become a classic on the effects of media-depicted violence on individuals: "For *some* children under *some* conditions, *some* television is harmful. For other children under the same conditions, or for the same children under *other* conditions, it may be beneficial. For *most* children, under *most* conditions, *most* television is probably neither particularly harmful nor particularly beneficial."

KEY PEOPLE
Wilbur Schramm and colleagues concluded minimal effects of television on children.

SOCIETALLY DEBILITATING EFFECTS

Media-depicted violence scares far more people than it inspires to violence, and this, according to *George Gerbner*, a leading researcher on screen violence, leads some people to believe the world is more dangerous than it really is. Gerbner calculates that 1 in 10 television characters is involved in violence in any given week. In real life, the chances are only about 1 in 100 per *year*. People who watch a lot of television, Gerbner found, see their own chances of being involved in violence nearer the distorted television level than their local crime statistics or even their own experience would suggest. It seems that television violence leads people to think they are in far greater real-life jeopardy than they really are.

The implications of Gerbner's findings go to the heart of a free and democratic society. With exaggerated fears about their safety, Gerbner says, people will demand greater police protection. They are also likelier, he says, to submit to established authority and even to accept police violence as a tradeoff for their own security.

KEY PERSON
George Gerbner speculates that democracy is endangered by media violence.

Desensitization. Critics of media violence saw slasher movies like *Halloween 5* were desensitizing people, especially teenagers, to the horrors of violence. That concern now has been transferred to video games. In one Mortal Kombat sequence, a crowd shouts encouragement for Kano to rip the heart out of Scorpion, his downed protagonist. Kano waves the dismembered heart to the crowd, which roars approvingly. Although scholars disagree about whether media violence begets real-life violence, most do agree that media violence leaves people more accepting of violence around them in their everyday lives.

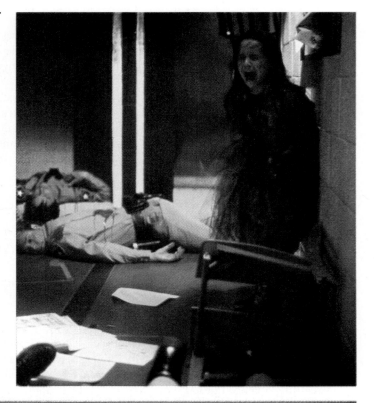

TOLERANCE OF VIOLENCE

An especially serious concern about media-depicted violence is that it has a numbing, callousing effect on people. This *desensitizing theory*, which is widely held, says not only that individuals are becoming hardened by media violence but also that society's tolerance for such antisocial behavior is increasing.

Media critics say the media are responsible for this desensitization, but many media people, particularly movie and television directors, respond that it is the desensitization that has forced them to make the violence in their shows even more graphic. They explain that they have run out of alternatives to get the point across when the story line requires that the audience be repulsed. Some movie critics, of course, find this explanation a little too convenient for gore-inclined moviemakers and television directors, but even directors not inclined to gratuitous violence feel their options for stirring the audience have become scarcer. The critics respond that this is a chicken-or-egg question and that the media are in no position to use the desensitization theory to excuse increasing violence in their products if they themselves contributed to the desensitization. And so the argument goes on about who is to blame.

Desensitization is apparent in news also. The absolute ban on showing the bodies of crime and accident victims in newspapers and on television newscasts, almost universal a few years ago, is becoming a thing of the past. No longer do newsroom practices forbid showing body bags or even bodies. During the 1991 Persian Gulf war, U.S. television had no reluctance about airing videos of allied troops picking up the bodies of hundreds of strafed Iraqi soldiers and hurling them, like sacks of flour, onto flatbed trucks for hauling to deep trenches, where the cameras recorded the heaped bodies being unceremoniously bulldozed over with sand.

In summary, we know far less about media violence than we need to. Various theories explain some phenomena, but the theories themselves do not dovetail. The desensitizing theory, for example, explains audience acceptance of more violence, but it hardly explains research findings that people who watch a lot of television actually have heightened anxiety about their personal safety. People fretting about their own safety hardly are desensitized.

MEDIA AGENDA-SETTING FOR INDIVIDUALS

STUDY PREVIEW   Media coverage helps define the things people think about and worry about. This is called agenda-setting. It occurs as the media create awareness of issues through their coverage, which lends importance to those issues. The media don't set agendas unilaterally, but they look to their audiences in deciding their priorities for coverage.

MEDIA SELECTION OF ISSUES

When the New York police wanted more subway patrols, their union public relations person, Morty Martz, asked officers to call him with every subway crime. Martz passed the accounts, all of them, on to newspapers and television and radio stations. Martz could not have been more pleased with his media blitz. News coverage of subway crime, he later boasted, increased several thousand percent, although there had been no appreciable change in the crime rate itself. Suddenly, for no reason

TEACHING OBJECTIVE 14-6
The mass media set the agenda for people

other than dramatically stepped-up coverage, people were alarmed. Their personal agendas of what to think about—and worry about—had changed. The sudden new concern, which made it easier for the union to argue for more subway patrols, was an example of media *agenda-setting* at work. Martz lured news media decision makers into putting subway crime higher on their lists of issues to be covered, and individuals moved it up on their lists of personal concerns.

The agenda-setting phenomenon has been recognized for a long time. Sociologist *Robert Park*, writing in the 1920s, articulated the theory in rejecting the once-popular notion that the media tell people what to think. As Park saw it, the media create awareness of issues more than they create knowledge or attitudes. Today, agenda-setting theorists put it this way: The media do not tell people *what to think* but *what to think about*. Agenda-setting occurs at several levels:

CREATING AWARENESS.   Only if individuals are aware of an issue can they be concerned about it. Concern about parents who kill their children becomes a major issue with media coverage of spectacular cases. In 1994 when Susan Smith, a South Carolina woman, attracted wide attention with her horrific report that her sons, ages 3 and 1, had been kidnapped. The story darkened later when the woman confessed to driving the family car into the lake and drowning the boys herself. Over several days of intense media attention, the nation learned not only the morbid details of what happened but also became better informed about a wide range of parental, family and legal issues that the coverage brought to the fore.

ESTABLISHING PRIORITIES.   People trust the news media to sort through the events of the day and make order of them. Lead-off stories on a newscast or on Page 1 are expected to be the most significant. Not only does how a story is played affect people's agendas, but so do the time and space afforded it. Lavish graphics can propel an item higher.

PERPETUATING ISSUES.   Continuing coverage lends importance to an issue. A single story on a bribed senator might soon be forgotten, but day-after-day follow-ups can fuel ethics reforms. Conversely, if gatekeepers are diverted to other stories, a hot issue can cool overnight—out of sight, out of mind.

INTRAMEDIA AGENDA-SETTING

Agenda-setting also is a phenomenon that affects media people, who constantly monitor one another. Reporters and editors many times are concerned more with how their peers are handling a story than with what their audience wants. Sometimes the media harp on one topic, making it seem more important than it really is, until it becomes tedious.

The media's agenda-setting role extends beyond news. Over time, life-styles and values portrayed in the media can influence not just what people think about but what they do. Hugh Hefner's *Playboy* magazine of the 1950s helped to usher in the sexual revolution. Advertising has created a redefinition of American values by whetting an appetite for possessions and glamorizing immediate gratification.

Even so, individuals exercise a high degree of control in their personal agendas. For decades, William Randolph Hearst campaigned with front-page editorials in all his newspapers against using animals in research, but animal rights did not become a pressing public issue. Even with the extensive media coverage of the Vietnam war, polls late in the 1960s found that many Americans still were unmoved. For the most part, these were people who chose to tune out the war coverage. The fact is that journalists and other creators of media messages cannot automatically impose their agendas on individuals. If people are not interested, an issue won't become part of their agendas. The individual values at work in the processes of selective exposure, perception and retention can thwart media leadership in agenda-setting.

Also, media agendas are not decided in a vacuum. Dependent as they are on having mass audiences, the media take cues for their coverage from their audiences. Penny press editors in the 1830s looked over the shoulders of newspaper readers on the street to see what stories attracted them and then shaped their coverage accordingly. Today, news organizations tap the public pulse through scientific sampling to deliver what people want. The mass media both exert leadership in agenda-setting and mirror the agendas of their audiences.

MEDIA-INDUCED ANXIETY AND APATHY

STUDY PREVIEW   The pervasiveness of the mass media is not necessarily a good thing, according to some theorists who say a plethora of information and access to ideas and entertainment can induce information anxiety. Another theory is that the news media even encourage passivity by leaving an impression that their reporting is so complete that there's nothing left to know or do.

INFORMATION ANXIETY

The New York *Times* had a landmark day on November 13, 1987. It published its largest edition ever—12 pounds, 1,612 pages and 12 million words. How could anyone, even on a quiet Sunday, manage all that information? One of the problems in contemporary life is the sheer quantity of information technology allows us as a society to gather and disseminate. Even a relatively slender weekday edition of the New York *Times* contains more information than the average person in the 17th century was likely to come across in a lifetime, according to Richard Saul Wurman in his book *Information Anxiety.*

TEACHING OBJECTIVE 14-7
The mass media can work against citizen involvement.

While educated people traditionally have thirsted for information, the quantity has become such that many people feel overwhelmed by what is called *information pollution.* We are awash in it and drowning, and the mass media are a factor in this. Consider college students at a major metropolitan campus:

- They pass newspaper vending machines and racks with a dozen different papers—dailies, weeklies, freebies—en route to class.
- On the radio, they have access to 40 stations.
- In their mailbox, they find a solicitation for discount subscriptions to 240 magazines.
- They turn on their television during a study break and need to choose among 50 channels.
- At lunch, they notice advertisements everywhere—on the placemat, on the milk carton, on table standups, on the butter pat, on the walls, on the radio coming over the public-address system, on the pen used to write a check.
- At the library, they have almost instant on-line access through computer systems to more information than any human being could possibly deal with.

Compounding the quantity of information available is the accelerating rate at which it is available. Trend analyst John Naisbitt has made the point with this example: When President Lincoln was shot in 1865, people in London learned about it five days later. When President Reagan was shot in 1981, journalist Henry Fairlie, in his office one block away, heard about the assassination attempt from his London editor who had seen it on television and phoned Fairlie to get him to go to the scene. Databases to which almost every college student today has access are updated day by day, hour by hour, even second by second.

It is no wonder that conscientious people who want good and current data to form their judgments and opinions, even to go about their jobs, feel overwhelmed. Wurman, who has written exclusively on this frustration, describes *information anxiety* as the result of "the ever-widening gap between what we understand and what we think we should understand."

The solution is knowing how to locate relevant information and tune out the rest, but even this is increasingly difficult. Naisbitt reported in *Megatrends* that scientists planning an experiment are spending more time figuring out whether someone somewhere already has done the experiment than conducting the experiment itself.

On some matters, many people do not even try to sort through all the information that they have available. Their solution to information anxiety is to give up. Other people have a false sense of being on top of things, especially public issues, because so much information is available.

MEDIA-INDUCED PASSIVITY

One effect of the mass media is embodied in the stereotypical couch potato, whose greatest physical and mental exercise is heading to the refrigerator during commercials. Studies indicate that the typical American spends four to six hours a day with the mass media, mostly with television. The experience is primarily passive, and it has been blamed, along with greater mobility and access to more leisure activities, for major changes in how people live their lives.

- **Worship Services.** In 1955 Gallup found that 49 percent of Americans attended worship services weekly. By 1986, it had declined to 40 percent.
- **Churches and Lodges.** The role of church auxiliaries and lodges, like the Masons, Odd Fellows and Knights of Pythias, once central in community social life with weekly activities, has diminished.
- **Neighborhood Taverns.** Taverns at busy neighborhood corners and rural crossroads once were the center of political discussion in many areas, but this is less true today.
- **Participatory Sports.** Despite the fitness and wellness craze, more people than ever are overweight and out of shape, which can be partly attributed to physical passivity induced by television and media-based homebound activities.

While these phenomena may be explained in part by people's increased use of the mass media and the attendant passivity, it would be a mistake not to recognize that social forces besides the media have contributed to them.

WELL-INFORMED FUTILITY

The news media take pride in purveying information to help people be active and involved in public matters, but, ironically, the media contribute insidiously to passivity by lulling people into accepting news reports as the last word on a subject. To attract and impress audiences, reporters use techniques to enhance their credibility, coming across as more authoritative than they really are and making their stories seem comprehensive and complete. Consider the well-groomed, clear-spoken television reporter on the Capitol steps whose 40-second report seems to address all inherent questions. The slickness in presentation works against the journalistic ideal of promoting intelligent citizen involvement in the political and social process by seeming to be so complete that nothing more can be said. The result is called the *syndrome of well-informed futility.* Readers, listeners and viewers feel satisfied that they're fully informed, which becomes an end in itself rather than actual involvement. This phenomenon works against democracy, which is predicated on citizen involvement, not apathy.

As agenda-setters, the mass media may also be working against the democratic ideal. The greater the role of the media in choosing the society's issues and fashions and even setting the values, the less the role of the people at a grassroots level.

CHAPTER WRAP-UP

The mass media influence us, but scholars are divided about how much. There is agreement that the media help initiate children into society by portraying social and cultural values. This is a serious responsibility because portrayals of aberrant behavior, like violence, have effects, although we are not sure about their extent. This is not to say that individuals are unwitting pawns of the mass media. People choose what they read and what they tune in to, and they generally filter the information and images to conform with their preconceived notions and personal values.

In other respects too, the mass media are a stabilizing influence. The media try to fit into the lives of their audiences. An example is children's television programs on weekend mornings when kids are home from school but still on an early-rising schedule. The media not only react to audience life-styles but also contribute to the patterns by which people live their lives, like going to bed after the late news. In short, the media have effects on individuals and on society, but it is a two-way street. Society is a shaper of media content, but individuals make the ultimate decisions about subscribing, listening and watching. The influence issue is a complex one that merits further research and thought.

QUESTIONS FOR REVIEW

1. Why have most media scholars abandoned the powerful and minimalist effect theories for the cumulative theory?

2. What is the uses and gratifications approach to mass media studies?

3. Do individuals have any control over mass media effects on them?

4. What role do the mass media have in socializing children?

5. How do scholars differ on whether media-depicted violence triggers aggressive behavior?

6. What is meant when someone says: "The mass media don't tell people what to think as much as tell them what to think about"?

7. Does being informed by mass media necessarily improve citizen involvement in political processes?

QUESTIONS FOR CRITICAL THINKING

1. Although generally discredited by scholars now, the powerful effects theory once had many adherents. How do you explain the lingering popularity of this thinking among many people?

2. Name at least three opinion leaders who influence you on issues that you do not follow closely in the media. On what issues are you yourself an opinion leader?

3. Give specific examples of each of the seven primary mass media contributing to the lifelong socialization process. For starters, consider a current nonfiction best-selling book.

4. Explain how selective exposure, selective perception and selective retention would work in the imaginary case of a devout Muslim who was studying English literature at Harvard University at the time Salman Rushdie's book, *The Satanic Verses*, was published. You may want to check newsmagazines in February and March 1989 for background.

5. Discuss the human needs that the mass media help satisfy in terms of the news and entertainment media.

6. Among the functions that the mass media serve for individuals are diversion and escape. Is this healthy?

7. Explain the prosocial potential of the mass media in culturization and socialization. What about the media as an antisocial force in observational learning?

8. Cite at least three contemporary role models who you can argue are positive. Explain how they might also be viewed as negative. Cite three role models who you can argue are negative.

9. What stereotype comes to your mind with the term "Uncle Remus"? Is your image of Uncle Remus one that would be held universally? Why or why not?

10. How can serious scholars of mass communication hold such diverse ideas as the cathartic, aggressive stimulation and catalytic theories? Which camp is right?

FOR FURTHER LEARNING

George Comstock. *Television in America* (Sage, 1980). Professor Comstock's Chapter 5, "Growing Up," offers a quick review of research on television and violence, the effects of television commercials, and socialization.

Cham Eyal, Jim Winter and Maxwell McCombs. "The Agenda-Setting Role in Mass Communication." In Michael Emery and Ted Curtis Smythe, *Reading in Mass Communication: Concepts and Issues in the Mass Media*, 6th ed. (Wm. C. Brown, 1986), 169–174. The authors, all scholars, trace the development of agenda-setting theory and identify the status of research.

Leo W. Jeffres. *Mass Media: Processes and Effects* (Waveland, 1986). Professor Jeffres discusses the variety of perspectives that attempt to understand the mysterious process of mass communication and then focuses on effects of the media on individuals and on society.

Robert M. Liebert, Joyce N. Spafkin and Emily S. Davidson. *The Early Window: Effects of Television on Chil-*

dren and Youth, 2nd ed. (Pergamon, 1985). This compendium covers the broad range of studies on television and children with special emphasis on research into media-depicted violence.

Joshua Meyrowitz. *No Sense of Place: The Impact of Electronic Media on Social Behavior* (Oxford, 1985). Professor Meyrowitz says television allows everybody, adult and child alike, to eavesdrop into other generations, which has eroded if not undone intergenerational distinctions that once were essential components of the social structure.

John Naisbitt. *Megatrends: Ten New Directions Transforming Our Lives* (Warner, 1982). Naisbitt identifies trends in society, particularly the shift from the industrial age to the information age.

Williard D. Rowland, Jr. *The Politics of TV Violence: Policy Uses of Communication Research* (Sage, 1983). Rowland argues that the mass media have used a heavy hand behind the scenes to dilute research findings that screen violence begets real-life violence. Rowland, a scholar, goes back to the Payne studies in the late 1920s.

Richard Saul Wurman. *Information Anxiety* (Double-day, 1989). Wurman discusses information overload as a modern problem for individuals and suggests ways to deal with it.

For Keeping Up to Date

Among numerous scholarly journals that publish research on media effects are the *Journal of Communication*, *Journalism Quarterly*, *Journal of Broadcasting & Electronic Media* and *Mass Communication Review*.

Also valuable is *Mass Communication Review Yearbook* published annually by Sage of Beverly Hills, Calif.

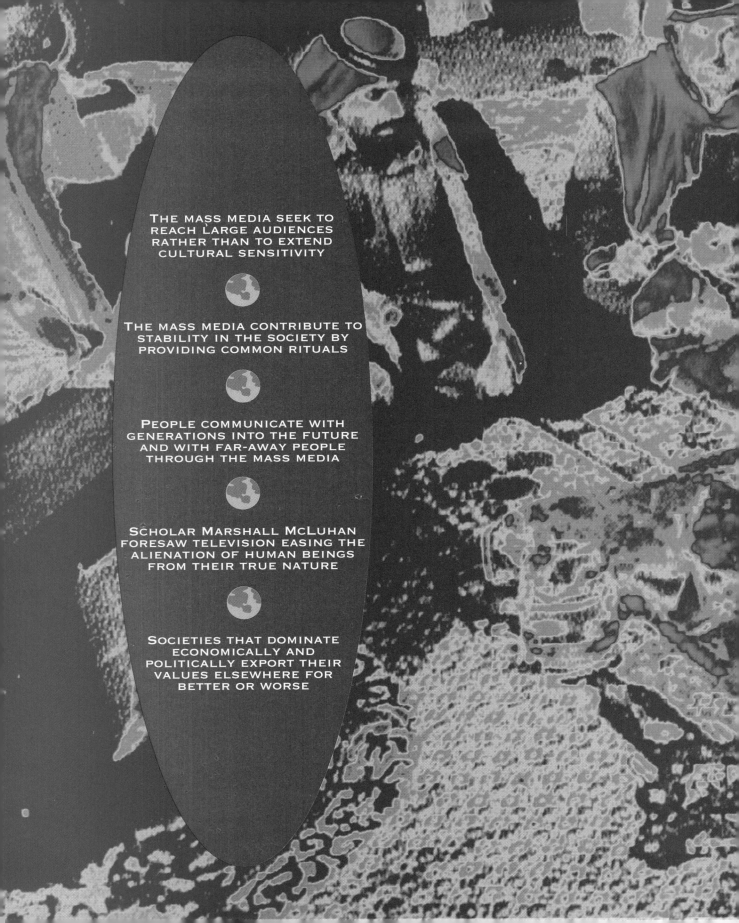

THE MASS MEDIA SEEK TO REACH LARGE AUDIENCES RATHER THAN TO EXTEND CULTURAL SENSITIVITY

THE MASS MEDIA CONTRIBUTE TO STABILITY IN THE SOCIETY BY PROVIDING COMMON RITUALS

PEOPLE COMMUNICATE WITH GENERATIONS INTO THE FUTURE AND WITH FAR-AWAY PEOPLE THROUGH THE MASS MEDIA

SCHOLAR MARSHALL MCLUHAN FORESAW TELEVISION EASING THE ALIENATION OF HUMAN BEINGS FROM THEIR TRUE NATURE

SOCIETIES THAT DOMINATE ECONOMICALLY AND POLITICALLY EXPORT THEIR VALUES ELSEWHERE FOR BETTER OR WORSE

chapter

MASS MEDIA
AND SOCIETY

15

It was love over the statistics, Robert and Linda Lichter met while working on a massive study of major media decision makers and married. Later they formed the Center for Media and Public Affairs in Washington, which today is a leading research organization on the mass media and social change. One of the most troubling findings of the Lichters and co-researcher Stanley Rothman is that the major U.S. media are out of touch with the American people. This conclusion comes out of massive studies of the people who run the entertainment media.

The Lichter–Rothman studies say that television executives and key creative people are overwhelmingly liberal on the great social issues of our time. More significantly, the studies have found that the programming these people produce reflects their political and social agenda. For example:

- Television scripts favor feminist positions in 71 percent of the shows, far more than public-opinion surveys find among the general population.
- Three percent of television murders are committed by blacks, compared to half in real life.
- Two out of three people are portrayed in positive occupations on television, but only one out of three businesspeople is depicted in a positive role.

These examples, according to the Lichters and Rothman, indicate a bias toward feminism and minority people and against businesspeople. The Lichter–Rothman work documents a dramatic turnaround in television entertainment fare. Two generations ago, leading programs, ranging from sitcoms like "Leave It to Beaver" and dramatic programs like "Wagon Train" extolled traditional values. In the 1970s came programs like "Mork and Mindy" and "All in the Family" that questioned some values. Today, network schedules make plenty of room for programs like "L.A. Law" and "Murphy Brown" that examine nontraditional views and exhibit a dramatically different social orientation than, say, "Leave It to Beaver."

Stanley Rothman

Linda and Robert Lichter

Media Elite. Researchers Linda and Robert Lichter and Stanley Roth-man say that the people who create most of television's entertainment programming have a liberal agenda that influences their shows. According to the Lichter-Rothman studies, this "media elite" is overwhelmingly urban, secular and antagonistic to business and other powerful institutions in society. As a group, these people have far more education and higher incomes than the general population. Because they move in relatively small social circles of like-minded and similarly situated people largely from Los Angeles and New York, these media leaders are insulated from what most Americans are thinking.

It is hazardous, of course, to paint too broad a picture of contemporary television, where a sitcom like "The Cosby Show" is much in the 1950s mode, but the Lichters and Rothman, by analyzing 620 shows over a 30-year period, argue persuasively that there has been a dramatic shift. They characterize the shift this way: "Television's America may once have looked like Los Angeles' Orange County writ large—Waspish, businesslike, religious, patriotic and middle class. Today it better resembles San Francisco's Marin County—trendy, self-expressive, culturally diverse and cosmopolitan."

The Lichter-Rothman studies indicate that this liberal, urban and secular "media elite," which creates television entertainment programming, is moving farther and farther away from traditional values. This might be just an interesting phenomenon, except that, to critics, this media elite is subverting American culture by glamorizing alternative life-styles and values. The Lichters and Rothman add fuel to this concern by noting that television's creative people not only deal with vexsome issues but, both subtly and overtly, slant the issues to their point of view.

This raises all kinds of serious questions about the mass media's effects on society. Can the media change bedrock social values? If values can be changed, are they really bedrock? While there is no doubt that the media affect society, how much? And how do these effects work? In this chapter you will learn what many leading researchers and scholars have concluded in their studies and reflections so far. You also will learn that much remains a mystery.

MASS MEDIA ROLE IN CULTURE

STUDY PREVIEW The mass media are inextricably linked with culture because it is through the media that creative people have their strongest sway. While the media have the potential to disseminate the best creative work of the human mind and soul, some critics say the media are obsessive about trendy, often silly subjects. These critics find serious fault with the media's concern for *pop culture,* claiming it squeezes out things of significance.

ELITIST VERSUS POPULIST VALUES

The mass media can enrich society by disseminating the best of human creativity, including great literature, music and art. The media also carry a lot of lesser things that reflect the culture and, for better or worse, contribute to it. Over time, a continuum has been devised that covers this vast range of artistic production. At one extreme is artistic material that requires sophisticated and cultivated tastes to appreciate. This is called *high art*. At the other extreme is *low art*, which requires little sophistication to enjoy.

One strain of traditional media criticism has been that the media underplay great works and concentrate on low art. This *elitist view* argues that the mass media do society a disservice by pandering to low tastes. To describe low art, elitists sometimes use the German word *kitsch*, which translates roughly as garish or trashy. The word captures their disdain. In contrast, the *populist view* is that there is nothing unbecoming in the mass media's catering to mass tastes in a democratic, capitalist society.

In a widely cited 1960 essay, "Masscult and Midcult," social commentator *Dwight Macdonald* made a virulent case that all popular art is kitsch. The mass media, which depend on finding large audiences for their economic base, can hardly ever come out at the higher reaches of Macdonald's spectrum.

This kind of elitist analysis was given a larger framework in 1976 when sociologist *Herbert Gans* categorized cultural work along socioeconomic and intellectual lines. Gans said that classical music, as an example, appealed by and large to people of academic and professional accomplishments and higher incomes. These were *high-culture* audiences, which enjoyed complexities and subtleties in their art and entertainment. Next came *middle-culture* audiences, which were less abstract in their interests and liked Norman Rockwell and prime-time television. *Low-culture* audiences were factory and service workers whose interests were more basic; whose educational accomplishments, incomes and social status were lower; and whose media tastes leaned toward kung fu movies, comic books and supermarket tabloids.

Gans was applying his contemporary observations to flesh out the distinctions that had been taking form in art criticism for centuries—the distinctions between high art and low art.

HIGH-BROW. The high art favored by elitists generally can be identified by its technical and thematic complexity and originality. High art often is highly individualistic because the creator, whether a novelist or a television producer, has explored issues in fresh ways and often with new and different methods. Even when a collaborative effort, a piece of high art is distinctive. High art requires a sophisticated audience to appreciate it fully. Often it has enduring value, surviving time's test as to its significance and worth.

The sophistication that permits an opera aficionado to appreciate the intricacies of a composer's score, the poetry of the lyricist and the excellence of the

TEACHING OBJECTIVE 15-1
Mass media seek large audiences rather than cultural sensitivity.

KEY PERSON
Dwight Macdonald argued anything popular is kitsch.

KEY PERSON
Herbert Gans equated cultural sophistication to demographics.

Identifying Kitsch

Although *quality* is an elusive term, students of the mass media need to come to grips with it to assess media performance. Are the media realizing their potential to enrich the culture? Are the media being responsible when they pander to the lowest common denominator in cultural sensitivity to attract the largest possible audiences?

Where do you fit on a scale of cultural appreciation? Where do you expect to fit in another year? Two years? Ten years?

To address these questions, the high-brow, middle-brow and low-brow breakdown is useful. For example: A gourmet works at developing a sophisticated taste for food. Such taste has not been acquired yet by a child who wolfs down two catsup-oozing hamburgers and cannot conceive of a better meal.

On a high-brow/low-brow scale of quality, where do these fit?

■ The Cleveland Orchestra's recorded performance of Beethoven's Symphony No. 3, *Eroica*.

■ An album of singer Barry Manilow's most romantic music.
■ A video of a Guns n' Roses concert.

Some media content is hard to fit into pigeonholes easily. Keep this difficulty in mind when you classify:

■ Robert Wise's 1961 movie of the Broadway musical *West Side Story*.
■ *Romeo and Juliet*, performed for video at the annual Stratford, Ontario, Shakespeare festival.
■ *Atlantic* magazine.
■ The *National Enquirer*.
■ The "MacNeil-Lehrer Report" on the Public Broadcasting System.
■ The "Oprah Winfrey" syndicated television talk show program.
■ The "Wheel of Fortune" television game show.
■ The Fox television series "The Simpsons."

Assessing Newspapers. The level of intellectual interest to enjoy and appreciate high-end news coverage, like that in the New York *Times*, is much more sophisticated than that to enjoy low-end tabloids. The audiences of such diverse publications correlate with educational background, professional accomplishment, income and social status.

performance sometimes is called *high-brow*. The label has grim origins in the idea that a person must have great intelligence to have refined tastes, and a high "brow" is necessary to accommodate such a big brain. Generally the term is used by people who disdain those who have not developed the sophistication to enjoy, for example, the abstractions of a Fellini film, a Matisse sculpture or a Picasso painting. High-brows generally are people who, as Gans noted, are interested in issues by which society is defining itself and look in literature and drama for stories on conflicts inherent in the human condition and between the individual and society.

MIDDLE-BROW. Middle-brow tastes recognize some artistic merit but without a high level of sophistication. There is more interest in action than abstractions, in Captain Kirk aboard the starship *Enterprise* than in the childhood struggles of Ingmar Bergman that shaped his films. In socioeconomic terms, middle-brow appeals to people who take comfort in media portrayals that support their status quo orientation and values.

LOW-BROW. Someone once made this often-repeated distinction: High-brows talk about ideas, middle-brows talk about things, and low-brows talk about people. Judging from the circulation success of the *National Enquirer* and other supermarket tabloids, there must be a lot of low-brows in contemporary America. Hardly any sophistication is needed to recognize the machismo of Rambo, the villainy of Simon Legree, the heroism of Superman, or the sexiness of Madonna.

THE CASE AGAINST POP ART

Pop art is of the moment, including things like mood rings, hula-hoops and grunge garb—and trendy media fare. Even elitists may have fun with pop, but they traditionally have drawn the line at anyone who mistakes it as having serious artistic merit. Pop art is low art that has immense although generally short-lived popularity.

Elitists see pop art as contrived and artificial. In their view, the people who create *popular art* are masters at identifying what will succeed in the marketplace and then providing it. Pop art, according to this view, succeeds by conning people into liking it. When Nehru jackets were the fashion rage in the late 1960s, it was not because they were superior in comfort or utility or aesthetics, but because promoters sensed profits could be made in touting them via the mass media as new and cashing in on easily manipulated mass tastes. It was the same with Cabbage Patch dolls, pet rocks, showy petticoats and countless other faddy products.

The mass media, according to the critics, are obsessed with pop art. Partly this is because the media are the carriers of the promotional campaigns that create popular followings but also because competition within the media creates pressure to be first, to be ahead, to be on top of things. The result, say elitists, is that junk takes precedence over quality.

Much is to be said for this criticism of pop art. The promotion by CBS of the screwball 1960s sitcom "Beverly Hillbillies," as an example, created an eager audience that otherwise might have been reading Steinbeck's critically respected *Grapes of Wrath*. An elitist might chortle, even laugh at the unbelievable antics and travails of the Beverly Hillbillies, who had their own charm and attractiveness, but an elitist would be concerned all the while that low art was displacing high art in the marketplace and that the society was the poorer for it.

POP ART REVISIONISM

Pop art has always had a few champions among intellectuals, although their voices were usually drowned out in the din of elitist pooh-poohing. In 1965, however, essayist *Susan Sontag* wrote an influential piece, "One Culture and the New Sensibility," which prompted many elitists to take a fresh look at pop art.

POP ART AS EVOCATIVE.   Sontag made the case that pop art could raise serious issues, just as could high art. She wrote: "The feeling given off by a Rauschenberg painting might be like that of a song by the Supremes." Sontag soon was being called the high priestess of *pop intellectualism*. More significantly, the Supremes were being taken more seriously, as were a great number of Sontag's avant-garde and obscure pop artist friends.

POPULARIZATION OF HIGH ART.   Sontag's argument noted that the mass appeal of pop artists meant that they could convey high art to the masses. A pop pianist like Liberace might omit the trills and other intricacies in performing a sonata, but he nonetheless gave a mass audience an access to Mozart that otherwise would never occur. Sontag saw a valuable service being performed by artists who both understood high art and could "translate" it for unsophisticated audiences, a process known as *popularization*.

As Sontag saw it, the mass media were at the fulcrum in a process that brings diverse kinds of cultural products and audiences together in exciting, enriching ways. The result of popularization, Sontag said, was an elevation of the cultural sensitivity of the whole society.

POP ART AS A SOCIETAL UNIFIER.   In effect, Sontag encouraged people not to look at art on the traditional divisive, class-conscious, elitist-populist continuum. Artistic value, she said, could be found almost anywhere. The word "camp" gained circulation among 1960s elitists who were influenced by Sontag. These high-brows began finding a perversely sophisticated appeal in pop art as diverse as Andy Warhol's banal soup cans and ABC's outrageous "Batman." The mass media, through which most people experienced Warhol and all people experienced "Batman," became recognized more broadly than ever as a societal unifier.

The Sontag-inspired revisionist look at pop art coincides with the view of many mass media historians that the media have helped bind the society rather than divide it. In the 1840s, these historians note, books and magazines with national distribution provided Americans of diverse backgrounds and regions with common reference points. Radio did the same even more effectively in the 1940s. Later, so did network television. In short, the mass media are purveyors of cultural production that contributes to social cohesion, whether it be high art or low art.

HIGH ART AS POPULAR.   While kitsch may be prominent in media programming, it hardly elbows out all substantive content. In 1991, for example, Ken Burns's public television documentary, *The Civil War*, outdrew low art prime-time programs on ABC, CBS and NBC five nights in a row. It was a glaring example that high art can appeal to people across almost the whole range of socioeconomic levels and is not necessarily driven out by low art. Burns's documentary was hardly a lone example. Another, also from 1991, was Franco Zeffirelli's movie *Hamlet*, starring pop movie star Mel Gibson, which was marketed to a mass audience and yet could hardly be dismissed by elitists as kitsch. In radio, public broadcasting stations, marked by high-brow programming, in some cities have become major players for ratings.

SOCIAL STABILITY

STUDY PREVIEW The mass media create rituals around which people structure their lives. This is one of many ways that the media contribute to social stability. The media foster socialization through adulthood, contributing to social cohesion by affirming beliefs and values and helping reconcile inconsistent values and discrepancies between private behavior and public morality.

MEDIA-INDUCED RITUAL

Northwest Airlines pilots, flying their Stratocruisers over the Dakotas in the 1950s, could tell when the late-night news ended on WCCO, the powerful Minneapolis radio station. They could see lights at ranches and towns all across the Dakotas going off as people, having heard the news, went to bed. The 10 o'clock WCCO news had become embedded as a ritual. Today, for people on the East and West coasts, where most television stations run their late news at 11 p.m., the commonest time to go to bed is 11:30, after the news. In the Midwest, where late newscasts are at 10 o'clock, people tend to go to bed an hour earlier and also to rise an hour earlier. Like other rituals that mark a society, media-induced rituals contribute order and structure to the lives of individuals.

The effect of media-induced rituals extends even further. Collectively, the lifestyles of individuals have broad social effect. Consider just these two effects of evening newspapers, an 1878 media innovation:

TEACHING OBJECTIVE 15-2
Mass media contribute to social stability with common rituals.

Demanding a Better Life.
Muscovites rioted against their government in 1993 when it became clear that the first wave, post-Communist reformers could not deliver the Western-style prosperity that the Russian people had learned about through the mass media. They were acting out a process called "diffusion of innovation." Through media coverage of Western consumer economies, the people knew there was a better way, and they wanted their leaders to adopt the innovations that would make them prosperous also.

EVENING NEWS.   E. W. Scripps changed people's habits with his evening newspapers, first in Cleveland in 1878, then elsewhere. Soon, p.m. papers outnumbered a.m. papers. The new habit, however, was not so much for *evening newspapers* as for *evening news*, as newspaper publishers discovered a hundred years later when television siphoned readers away with evening newscasts. The evening ritual persists, even though the medium is changing as p.m. newspapers go out of business or retreat to mornings.

COMPETITIVE SHOPPING.   In the era before refrigeration and packaged food, household shopping was a daily necessity. When evening newspapers appeared, housewives, who were the primary shoppers of the period, adjusted their routines to read the paper the evening before their morning trips to the market. The new ritual allowed time for more methodical bargain hunting, which sharpened retail competition.

Besides shaping routines, ritual contributes to the mass media's influence as a shaper of culture. At 8:15 a.m. every Sunday, half the television sets in Japan are tuned to "Serial Novel," a tear-jerking series that began in the 1950s. Because so many people watch, it is a common experience that is one element in the identification of contemporary Japanese society. In American society, a ritual that marked the society for years was "Dallas," Friday, 9 p.m. Eastern time, 8 p.m. Central time. Other rituals are going to Saturday movie matinees, reading a book at bedtime, and watching Monday night football.

THE MEDIA AND THE STATUS QUO

In their quest for profits through large audiences, the mass media need to tap into their audience's common knowledge and widely felt feelings. Writers for network sitcoms avoid obscure, arcane language. Heroes and villains reflect current morals. Catering this way to a mass audience, the media reinforce existing cultural beliefs and values. People take comfort in learning through the media that they fit into their community and society, which furthers social cohesion. This is socialization continued beyond the formative years. It also is socialization in reverse, with the media taking cues from the society and playing them back.

The media's role in social cohesion has a negative side. Critics say that the media pander to the lowest common denominator by dealing only with things that fit the status quo easily. The result, the critics note, is a thwarting of artistic exploration beyond the mainstream. Critics are especially disparaging of predictable, wooden characters in movies and television and of predictability in the subjects chosen for the news.

A related negative aspect of the media's role as a contributor to social cohesion is that dominant values too often go unchallenged, which means that some wrong values and practices persist. Dudley Clendinen, a newspaper editor who grew up in the South, faults journalists for, in effect, defending racism by not covering it: "The news columns of Southern papers weren't very curious or deep or original in the late 1940s and 1950s. They followed sports and politics actively enough, but the whole rational thrust of Southern culture from the time of John C. Calhoun on had been self-defensive and maintaining. It had to be, to justify the unjustifiable in a society dedicated first to slavery and then to segregation and subservience. Tradition was everything, and the news pages were simply not in the habit of examining the traditions of the South."

THE MEDIA AND COGNITIVE DISSONANCE

The media are not always complacent. Beginning in the late 1950s, after the period to which Clendinen was referring, media attention turned to racial segregation. News coverage, literary comment, and dramatic and comedy portrayals began to point up flaws in the status quo. Consider the effect, through the mass media, of these individuals on American racism:

- **John Howard Griffin.** In 1959 Griffin, a white journalist, dyed his skin black for a six-week odyssey through the South. His book, *Black Like Me*, was an inside look at being black in America. It had special credibility for the white majority because Griffin was white.
- **George Wallace.** The mass audience saw the issue of segregation personified in news coverage of Governor George Wallace physically blocking black students from attending the University of Alabama. The indelible impression was that segregation could be defended only by a clenched fist and not by reason.
- **Martin Luther King Jr.** News photographers captured the courage and conviction of Martin Luther King Jr. and other civil rights activists, black and white, taking great risks through civil disobedience to object to racist public policies.
- **Archie Bunker.** Archie Bunker, a television sitcom character, made a laughingstock of bigots.

To some people, the media coverage and portrayals seemed to exacerbate racial tensions. In the longer run, however, media attention contributed to a new consensus through a phenomenon that psychologists call *cognitive dissonance*. Imagine white racists as they saw George Wallace giving way to federal troops under orders

Cognitive Dissonance. Many white Americans from racist backgrounds found themselves challenging their own values when the federal government adopted proactive civil rights policies in the 1950s and 1960s. This dissonance escalated as these people followed news coverage of the long-overdue demands of blacks for fair treatment, as in this 1963 march. Some white racists resolved the discrepancy by abandoning racism. Many others simply retreated from discussion on the issue.

Influencing Mores. Safe sex campaigns, prompted by the AIDS crisis, have used the mass media to discourage promiscuity, unprotected intercourse and high-risk sexual practices. The messages work. One indicator is that the average age that young people become sexually active is going up. Another indicator is rising condom sales. Long-term government campaigns about the dangers of smoking have also been effective, as measured by dropping cigarette sales. The campaigns of organizations, such as Mothers Against Drunk Driving, commonly known as MADD, have seriously influenced excessive drinking as unfashionable.

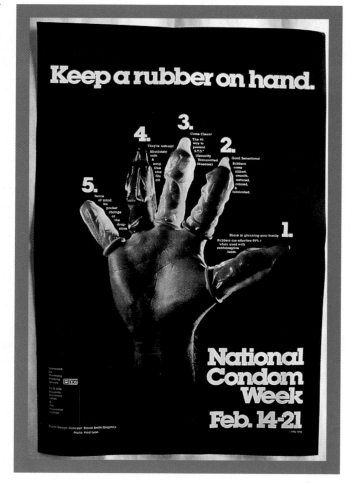

from the White House. The situation pitted against each other two values held by individual racists—segregation as a value and an ordered society as symbolized by the presidency. Suddenly aware that their personal values were in terrible disharmony, or *dissonance*, many of these racists avoided the issue. Instead of continuing to express racism among family and friends, many tended to be silent. They may have been as racist as ever, but they were quiet, or watched their words carefully. Gradually their untenable view is fading into social unacceptability. This is not to say that racism does not persist. It does, and continues to manifest itself in American life although, in many ways, in forms much muted since the media focused on the experiment of John Howard Griffin, the clenched fist of George Wallace, and the crusade of Martin Luther King Jr.

When the media go beyond pap and the predictable, they are examining the cutting edge issues by which the society defines its values. Newsmagazines, newspapers and television, utilizing new printing, photography and video technology in the late 1960s, put war graphically into American living rooms, pointing up all kinds of discrepancies between Pentagon claims and the Vietnam reality. Even the glamorized, heroic view of war, which had persisted through history, was countered by media depictions of the blood and death. Unable to resolve the discrepancies, some people withdrew into silence. Others reassessed their views and then, with changed positions or more confident in their original positions, they engaged in a dialogue from which a consensus emerged. And the United States, the mightiest power in history, began a militarily humiliating withdrawal. It was democracy at work, slowly and painfully, but at work.

AGENDA-SETTING AND STATUS CONFERRAL

Media attention lends a legitimacy to events, individuals and issues that does not extend to things that go uncovered. This conferring of status occurs through the media's role as agenda-setters. It puts everybody on the same wavelength, or at least a similar one, which contributes to social cohesion by focusing our collective attention on issues we can address together. Otherwise, each of us could be going in separate directions, which would make collective action difficult if not impossible.

MEDIA AND MORALITY

A small-town wag once noted that people read the local newspaper not to find out what is going on, which everybody already knows, but to find out who got caught. The observation was profound. The mass media, by reporting deviant behavior, help enforce society's moral order. When someone is arrested for burglary and sentenced, it reaffirms for everybody that human beings have property rights.

Beyond police blotter news, the mass media are agents for reconciling discrepancies between *private actions* and *public morality*. Individually, people tolerate minor infractions of public morality, like taking pencils home from work. Some people even let life-threatening behavior go unreported, like child abuse. When the deviant behavior is publicly exposed, however, toleration ceases and social processes come into action that reconcile the deviance with public morality. The reconciling process maintains public norms and values. Consider Douglas Ginsburg. In the 1970s, Ginsburg, a young law professor, smoked marijuana at a few parties. It was a

CNN Condom Flash
The biggest government-financed public service campaign in history, calling for precautions to prevent AIDS, is underway. No one expects the campaign to stop the spread of AIDS but rather to slow it. CNN reporter Gary Tuchman interviews an anti-AIDS activist who says the ads need person-to-person reinforcement. Some earlier massive public-service campaigns have discouraged cigarette smoking, the purchase of government bonds, and the worthiness some causes like, "A Mind Is a Terrible Thing to Waste." This segment aired January 5. 1994.

Nannygate. Friends and associates didn't take much notice when insurance executive Zoe Baird hired illegal aliens for household work—after all, "everybody did it." But when Baird was under scrutiny as President Clinton's appointee for attorney general in 1993, the revelations about her skirting the law in hiring domestic help became a classic collision between private actions and public morality. President Clinton withdrew the nomination. Mass media coverage of morality issues reminds society to keep re-evaluating its values.

misdemeanor, but Ginsburg's friends tolerated it, and not a word was said publicly. In 1988, however, when President Reagan nominated Ginsburg to the U.S. Supreme Court, reporter Nina Totenberg of National Public Radio reported Ginsburg's transgressions. Exposed, he withdrew his name. There was no choice. His private action, publicly exposed, could not be tolerated, and his withdrawal maintained public norms and values, without which a society cannot exist.

This same phenomenon occurred in the 1980s when homelessness became a national issue. For years, homeless people in every major city had slept in doorways and alleys and, during winter, at steam vents. The homeless were seen but invisible. When social policies and economic factors in the 1980s sent the numbers skyrocketing, homelessness became a media issue that could not be ignored, and the society had to do something. Under the glare of media attention, people brought their private behavior, which had been to overlook the problem, into conformity with the tenet of public morality that says we are all our brothers' keepers. Across the nation, reform policies to relieve homelessness began moving through legislative channels.

CULTURAL TRANSMISSION

STUDY PREVIEW The mass media transmit cultural values through history. Past generations talk to us through mass media, mostly books, just as we, often not realizing it, talk to future generations. The media also diffuse values and ideas contemporaneously.

HISTORICAL TRANSMISSION

TEACHING OBJECTIVE 15-3
People communicate over time and distance through mass media.

Human beings have a compulsion to leave the wisdom they have accumulated for future generations. There is a compulsion, too, to learn from the past. In olden times, people gathered around campfires and in temples to hear storytellers. It was a ritual through which people learned the values that governed their community.

Five thousand years ago, the oral tradition was augmented when Middle Eastern traders devised an alphabet to keep track of inventories, transactions and rates of exchange. When paper was invented, clay tablets gave way to scrolls and eventually books, which became the primary vehicle for storytelling. Religious values were passed on in holy books. Military chronicles laid out the lessons of war. Literature provided lessons by exploring the nooks and crannies of the human condition.

Books remain the primary repository of our culture. For several centuries, it has been between hard covers, in black ink on paper, that the experiences, lessons and wisdom of our forebears have been recorded for posterity. Other mass media today share in the preservation and transmission of our culture over time. Consider these archives:

- Museum of Broadcasting in New York, with 1,200 hours of television documentaries; great performances, productions, debuts and series; and a sample of top-rated shows.
- Library for Communication and Graphic Arts at Ohio State University, whose collection includes editorial cartoons.
- Vanderbilt Television News Archive in Nashville, Tennessee, with 7,000 hours of network nightly news programs and special coverage such as political conventions and space shots.

CONTEMPORARY TRANSMISSION

The mass media also transmit values among contemporary communities and societies, sometimes causing changes that otherwise would not occur. Anthropologists have documented that mass communication can change society. When Edmund Carpenter introduced movies in an isolated New Guinea village, the men adjusted their clothing toward the Western style and even remodeled their houses. This phenomenon, which scholars call *diffusion of innovations*, occurs when ideas move through the mass media. Consider the following:

- **American Revolution.** Colonists up and down the Atlantic seaboard took cues on what to think and how to act, from newspaper reports on radical activities, mostly in Boston, in the decade before the Declaration of Independence. These included inflammatory articles against the 1765 Stamp Act and accounts of the Boston Tea Party in 1773.
- **Music, Fashion and Pop Culture.** In modern-day pop culture, the cues come through the media, mostly from New York, Hollywood and Nashville.
- **Third World Innovation.** The United Nations creates instructional films and radio programs to promote agricultural reform in less developed parts of the world. Overpopulated areas have been targets of birth control campaigns.
- **Democracy in China.** As China opened itself to Western tourists, commerce and mass media in the 1980s, the people glimpsed Western democracy and prosperity, which precipitated pressure on the Communist government to westernize and resulted in the 1989 Tiananmen Square confrontation. A similar phenomenon was a factor in the *glasnost* relaxations in the Soviet Union in the late 1980s.
- **Demise of Main Street.** Small-town businesses are boarding up throughout the United States as rural people see advertisements from regional shopping malls, which are farther away but offer greater variety and lower prices than Main Street.

Scholars note that the mass media can be given too much credit for the diffusion of innovations. Diffusion almost always needs reinforcement through interpersonal communication. Also, the diffusion hardly ever is a one-shot hypodermic injection but a process that requires redundancy in messages over an extended period. The 1989 outburst for democracy in China did not happen because one Chinese person read Thomas Paine one afternoon, nor do rural people suddenly abandon their local Main Street for a Wal-Mart 40 miles away. The diffusion of innovations typically involves three initial steps in which the mass media can be pivotal:

- **Awareness.** Individuals and groups learn about alternatives, new options and possibilities.
- **Interest.** Once aware, people need to have their interest further whetted.
- **Evaluation.** By considering the experience of other people, as relayed by the mass media, individuals evaluate whether they wish to adopt an innovation.

The adoption process has two additional steps in which the media play a small role: the trial stage, in which an innovation is given a try, and the final stage, in which the innovation is either adopted or rejected.

MASS MEDIA AND FUNDAMENTAL CHANGE

STUDY PREVIEW   The detribalization theory says the written word changed tribal communities by deemphasizing interpersonal communication. Written communication engaged the mind, not the senses, and, according to the theory, a lonely, cerebral-based culture resulted. Now, as sense-intensive television displaces written communication, retribalization is creating a global village.

TEACHING OBJECTIVE 15-4
Marshall McLuhan foresaw television easing human alienation.

KEY PERSON
Marshall McLuhan saw retribalization occurring.

HUMAN ALIENATION

An intriguing, contrarian assessment of the media's effects on human society was laid out by Canadian theorist *Marshall McLuhan* in the 1960s. McLuhan argued that the print media had alienated human beings from their natural state. In pre–mass media times, McLuhan said, people acquired their awareness about their world through their own observation and experience and through their fellow human beings, whom they saw face to face and with whom they communicated orally. As McLuhan saw it, this was a pristine communal existence—rich in that it involved all the senses, sight, sound, smell, taste and touch. This communal, tribal state was eroded by the written word, which involved the insular, meditative act of reading. The printing press, he said, compounded this alienation from humankind's tribal roots. The written word, by engaging the mind, not the senses, begat *detribalization*, and the printing press accelerated it.

According to McLuhan, the printed word even changed human thought processes. In their tribal state, he said, human beings responded spontaneously to everything that was happening around them. The written word, in contrast, required people to concentrate on an author's relatively narrow, contrived set of data that led from Point A to Point B to Point C. Following the linear serial order of the written word was a lonely, cerebral activity, unlike participatory tribal communication, which had an undirected, helter-skelter spontaneity.

TELEVISION AND THE GLOBAL VILLAGE

McLuhan saw television bringing back tribalization. While books, magazines and newspapers engaged the mind, television engaged the senses. In fact, the television screen could be so loaded with data that it could approximate the high level of sensual stimuli that people found in their environments back in the tribal period of human history. Retribalization, he said, was at hand because of the new, intensely sensual communication that television could facilitate. Because television could far exceed the reach of any previous interpersonal communication, McLuhan called the new tribal village a *global village*.

With retribalization, McLuhan said, people will abandon the print media's linear intrusions on human nature. Was McLuhan right? His disciples claim that certain earmarks of written communication—complex story lines, logical progression and causality—are less important to today's young people, who grew up with sense-intensive television. They point to the music videos of the 1980s, which excited the senses but made no linear sense. Many teachers say children are having a harder time finding significance in the totality of a lesson. Instead, children fasten on to details.

As fascinating as McLuhan was, he left himself vulnerable to critics who point out that, in a true nonlinear spirit, he was selective with evidence and never put his ideas to rigorous scholarly examination. McLuhan died in 1980. Today the jury remains divided, agreeing only that he was a provocative thinker.

Television Everywhere. The influence of Western society has permeated cultures around the world, which critics say results in a superimposition of Western values and styles that erode worthy but fragile cultural values elsewhere. Here, cultural intrusion shows itself with latter-day Bedouins outside Ragga, Syria, and in a rural home in Hungary.

CULTURAL INTRUSION

STUDY PREVIEW   Some experts claim that the export of American and Western popular culture is latter-day imperialism, motivated by profit and without concern for its effect on other societies. This theory of cultural dominance claims too that Third World countries are pawns of the Western-based global entertainment media and news services. Other experts disagree, saying the charges of cultural imperialism are overblown and hysterical.

LATTER-DAY IMPERIALISM

TEACHING OBJECTIVE 15-5
Dominant societies export their values elsewhere for better or worse.

Some scholars claim that international communication has a dark side, which they call *cultural imperialism*. Their view is that the media are like the 19th-century European colonial powers, exporting Western values, often uninvited, to other cultures. At stake, these critics say, is the cultural sovereignty of non-Western nations. These critics note that the international communication media have their headquarters in the United States and also in the former European colonial powers. The communication flow, they claim, is one way, from the powerful nations to the weak ones. The result, as they see it, is that Western values are imposed in an impossible-to-resist way. A Third World television station, for example, can buy a recycled American television program for far less than it costs to produce an indigenous program.

KEY PERSON
Herbert Schiller sees Western values preempting other cultures.

Scholar *Herbert Schiller*, who wrote *Mass Communications and American Empire*, argued that the one-way communication flow is especially insidious because the Western productions, especially movies and television, are so slick that they easily outdraw locally produced programs. As a result, says Schiller, the Western-controlled international mass media preempt native culture, a situation he sees as robbery, just like the earlier colonial tapping of natural resources to enrich the home countries.

The presence of American popular culture in the Third World is easy to spot. American movies, television, pop music, books and magazines are everywhere, and so are their residues—life-styles, fashions, fads. Even in Japan, which might seem resistant to cultural invasions because of its economic might, Western cultural influence is omnipresent. Magazine House, a Tokyo publishing company, has brought out one successful magazine after another, blatantly imitating American pop culture even in titling its magazines. Among them: *Popeye*, for high school boys; *Olive*, for junior high school girls; *Tarzan*, on fitness and life-style; *Brutus*, for college men; *Gulliver*, a travel magazine; and *Croissant*, for middle-aged women. Throughout the world, in Japan and elsewhere, the American soap opera "Dallas" plays and replays.

American cultural hegemony has been blamed partly on the global dominance of American advertising agencies. Said British commentator Philip Kleinman: "All over the world, admen look to Madison Avenue as Moslems look to Mecca."

DEFENDING WESTERN HEGEMONY

Being leaders of pop culture abroad, says advertising executive David Ogilvy, does not necessarily mean that American values are being imposed abroad. Most Ogilvy & Mather employees abroad, he notes, are not American. When agencies use American campaigns, they modify them to fit the local culture. In addition, local subsidiaries of multinational agencies create many of their campaigns. Some of the outcry against American agencies abroad, according to Ogilvy, has little to do with

Americanizing the World

British traders introduced opium in China in the 1600s. The habit spread, and soon the British had a profitable trade importing opium to Chinese ports and exporting silver to pay for it. Resentful at British profits from the death and misery they had introduced, the Chinese government acted in 1839 against any further opium importation. In response, the British bombarded Canton, and the Opium War ensued.

Today, a similar struggle, dubbed the Second Opium war, is under way. Yielding to American trade pressure, Japan, South Korea and Taiwan lifted bans on foreign tobacco in 1987, and the Marlboro man instantly became a familiar poster figure. Propelled by huge advertising budgets and American-style promotion, United States tobacco sales increased 24-fold almost overnight in Taiwan, to 5.1 billion cigarettes a year.

Is this cultural imperialism at its worst? Massachusetts Congressman Chet Atkins called it "the ultimate ugly Americanism." Noting that the U.S. government had mounted an extensive domestic campaign against smoking, Atkins said, "We are sending a message through our trade negotiators that Asian lungs are more expendable than American lungs." In Taiwan, a leading antismoking activist, David Yen, said, "We want American friendship, machinery and food—but not your drugs."

Meanwhile, the Marlboro man, taller in the saddle than ever, rides on. Smoking in Japan, South Korea and Taiwan continues to grow to record levels.

Samurai Cowboy. For better or worse, American culture has permeated cultures almost everywhere on the globe. In Tokyo, a number of country and western bars have found legions of customers eager to don a Stetson, light a Marlboro, twang a guitar and sing Willie Nelson music. American beer is big too. Critics fret that American cultural icons and values are squeezing out indigenous cultural production and values. "Cultural imperialism," they call it.

any cultural invasion but is a cry for profits. Locally owned agencies, he says, "have a habit of wrapping themselves in their national flag and appealing to their governments for protection against foreign invaders. They accuse us of imposing an alien culture, particularly in countries that have little culture of their own."

Some people could accuse Ogilvy of insensitivity, but he also defines another way of viewing transcultural mass communication. The goal of advertising, Ogilvy reminds critics, is to sell goods—regardless of where advertisements originate. Just because a campaign was invented elsewhere does not make it an insult to anyone's self-respect.

In some ways, cultural imperialism is in the eyes of the beholder. Some Latin American countries, for example, scream "cultural imperialism" at the United

Cultural Intrusion. When Tokyo children grow up loving American pop culture characters like Minnie and Mickey Mouse, is native Japanese culture being lost? Scenes like this, at Disneyland in Tokyo, lead some scholars to question whether American cultures and values are displacing others around the globe. Some scholars call this phenomenon *cultural imperialism.*

States but don't object when Mexico exports soap operas to the rest of Latin America, as do Brazil and Argentina. Although they are exercising a form of cultural imperialism, nobody puts the label on them. Media observer Larry Lorenz, who has studied this phenomenon, explains it this way: "What is occurring is simply internationalism brought on by the ever more sophisticated media of mass communication."

The cultural imperialism theory has other doubters among scholars. The doubters note that the theory is a simplistic application of the now-discredited hypodermic needle model of mass communication. Media messages do not have immediate direct effects. In challenging the idea of cultural imperialism as a world-changing, sinister force, scholar Michael Tracey notes that the U.S. soap opera "Dallas" is available in many different countries but is not as popular as home-produced soaps, and is almost completely ignored in many countries even though, because it can be bought cheap, it is run and re-run. In 1982, Tracey noted, "Dallas" was 69th in the Brazilian television ratings and 109th in the Mexican—hardly a world-beater.

Also overstated are charges that news from Europe and the United States dominates coverage in other parts of the world. One study found that 60 to 75 percent of the foreign news in the Third World is about other Third World countries, mostly those nearby. While the giant Western news services, AP, Agence France-Presse, Reuters, UPI and to a lesser degree TASS, are the main purveyors of foreign news, the coverage that reaches Third World audiences is extremely parochial.

TRANSNATIONAL CULTURAL ENRICHMENT

Some scholars see transnational cultural flow in more benign terms than Herbert Schiller and his fellow cultural imperialism theorists. George Steiner has noted that European and American culture have been enriched, not corrupted, by the continuing presence of Greek mythology over 2,000 years. In a homely way, sociologist Michael Tracey makes a similar point:

"I was born in a working-class neighborhood called Oldham in the north of England. Before the First World War, Oldham produced most of the world's spun cotton. It is a place of mills and chimneys, and I was born and raised in one of the areas of housing—called St. Mary's—built to serve those mills. I recently heard a record by a local group of folk singers called the Oldham Tinkers, and one track was about Charlie Chaplin. This song was apparently very popular with local children in the years immediately after the First World War. Was that evidence of the cultural influences of Hollywood, a primeval moment of the imperialism of one culture, the subjugation of another? It seems almost boorish to think of it that way. Was the little man not a deep well of pleasure through laughter, a pleasure that was simply universal in appeal? Was it not Chaplin's real genius to strike some common chord, uniting the whole of humanity? Is that not, in fact, the real genius of American popular culture, to bind together, better than anything, common humanity?"

Despite the controversy alleging cultural imperialism and the arguments to debunk it, the issue is not settled. Many Third World countries, speaking through the United Nations, have demanded subsidies from Western nations to finance local cultural enterprises. They also have demanded a policy voice in the major Western-operated global news services.

CHAPTER WRAP-UP

The mass media have caused fundamental changes in human communication. When Gutenberg introduced movable type in the 15th century, people began shifting from largely intuitive interpersonal communication to reading, which, says communication theorist Marshall McLuhan, required a different kind of concentration. The result, according to McLuhan, was less spontaneous communication, an alienation among individuals and a fragmented society. With electronic, visual media like television, which engage numerous senses and require less cerebral participation than reading, McLuhan saw a return to communication more consistent with human nature. He called it *retribalization*. Not everyone accepts McLuhan's vision, but there is agreement that the mass media profoundly affect society.

The mass media do not operate in a vacuum. The people who decide media content are products of the society, and the necessity to turn a profit requires that the media be in touch with the society's values or lose audience. In one sense, this reality of capitalism works against the media venturing too far from mainstream values. Critics say the media pander too much to popular tastes and ignore culturally significant works that could enrich society. An alternate view, more charitable to the media, is that great works trickle down to mass audiences through media popularization.

The media contribute both to social stability and to change. A lot of media content gives comfort to audiences by reinforcing existing social values. At the same time, media attention to nonmainstream ideas, in both news and fiction forms, requires people to reassess their values and, over time, contributes to social change.

QUESTIONS FOR REVIEW

1. Why are mass media more interested in reaching large audiences rather than contributing to cultural sensitivity?

2. How do the mass media contribute to stability in the society?

3. What are historical and cultural transmission?

4. How did scholar Marshall McLuhan foresee that television would ease the human alienation that he said was created by the mass-produced written word?

5. Are there disadvantages when dominant societies export their values elsewhere?

QUESTIONS FOR CRITICAL THINKING

1. Why do the mass media find little room for great works that could elevate the cultural sensitivity of the society?

2. Explain essayist Susan Sontag's point that the mass media bring culturally significant works to mass audiences through the popularization process.

3. Give examples of how people shape their everyday lives around rituals created by the mass media. Also, give examples of how the mass media respond to social rituals in deciding what to present and how and when to do it.

4. Why would a radical social reformer object to most mass media content?

5. How has cognitive dissonance created through the mass media worked against racial separatism in American society since the 1950s?

6. How do the mass media help determine the issues that society sees as important?

7. How do the media contribute to social order and cohesion by reporting private acts that deviate from public morality? You might want to consider the 1992 presidential campaign of Bill Clinton, or any of the televangelism scandals.

8. Give examples of the mass media allowing cultural values to be communicated through history to future societies. Also, give examples of contemporary cultural transmission.

9. Explain scholar Marshall McLuhan's theory that the mass-produced written word has contributed to an alienation of human beings from their true nature. How did McLuhan think television could reverse this alienation?

10. Is *imperialism*, a word with strong negative implications, the best term to describe the transmission of cultural ideas and values from developed to less developed societies?

FOR FURTHER LEARNING

Howard Hampton. "Out of Our Heads." *Gannett Center Journal* 1:133–147. Hampton, an arts critic, reviews current thinking on the media and pop culture. This entire issue of the *Gannett Center Journal* is devoted to articles on the arts and the media.

S. Robert Lichter, Linda S. Lichter and Stanley Rothman. *Watching America: What Television Tells Us About Our Lives* (Prentice Hall, 1991).

Marshall McLuhan. *The Gutenberg Galaxy: The Making of Typographic Man* (University of Toronto Press, 1967). Most of the array of McLuhan's speculations about media effects can be found in this book and in his earlier *Understanding Media: The Extensions of Man* (McGraw-Hill, 1964).

Herbert Schiller. *Mass Communications and American Empire* (Kelley, 1969). Schiller sees "an imperial network" of American forces, including the media, building a cultural dominance in less developed parts of the world.

Susan Sontag. "One Culture and New Sensibility." *Against Interpretation* (Farrar Straus & Giroux, 1966). Sontag sees pop art as a vehicle for bringing cultural sensitivity to mass audiences.

Michael Tracey. "The Poisoned Chalice: International Television and the Idea of Dominance." *Daedalus* 114 (Fall 1985):4, 17–56. Tracey sees cultural imperialism as an overstated theory that is unsupported by evidence and hardly sinister.

For Keeping Up to Date

Recommended are *Journal of Popular Culture*, *Journal of American Culture* and *Journal of International Popular Culture*, all scholarly publications.

NATIONAL MEDIA SYSTEMS
CONFORM TO THE POLITICAL
SYSTEMS WITHIN WHICH
THEY OPERATE

MODERN AUTHORITARIAN MEDIA
SYSTEMS USE CENSORSHIP,
LICENSING, BRIBERY AND
REPRESSION TO CONTROL THE
MASS MEDIA

COMMUNIST MEDIA SYSTEMS
DIFFER FROM AUTHORITARIAN
SYSTEMS IN THEIR PREMISES
ABOUT THE NATURE OF TRUTH

LIBERTARIAN MEDIA SYSTEMS ARE
OPTIMISTIC ABOUT THE
CAPABILITIES OF HUMAN REASON

MODERN U.S. MEDIA
PRACTICES EMPHASIZE SOCIAL
RESPONSIBILITY MORE THAN
LIBERTARIANISM'S EMPHASIS
ON FREEDOM

chapter 16

MASS MEDIA IN A POLITICAL ENVIRONMENT

Of necessity, Oriana Fallaci grew up fast. A teenager in Mussolini's Italy, she figured out early whose side she was on. She delivered grenades inside cabbage heads for the antifascist resistance. She had a keen sense of who were the good guys and who the bad—and later, as a journalist, she devised interview techniques to smoke them out. Along the way, she figured out how the world and its political systems worked, which enabled her to become one of the foremost journalists of our time.

Both bright and hard-working, she learns a whole language to conduct interviews in her sources' native tongue. Sometimes she puts six months into preparing for one of her marathon interviews. She flouts danger. In fact, she was shot twice covering stories in Mexico. She adapts to whatever the situation to get a story. Although not Muslim, she agreed to wear a Muslim veil, a chador, to interview Iranian leader Ayatollah Khomeini. As an interviewer, she keeps her sights on finding revealing truths about important people through cleverness, disquieting and unexpected questions and persistence.

Those qualities showed in Fallaci's famous interview with Ayatollah Khomeini in his Teheran quarters. In deference, she wore the chador veil, which gave her an opportunity for a question that would so unsettle the ayatollah that she learned things no earlier interviewer had about his temper and his temperament. From her own account: "I was wearing the thing, all seven meters of it, pins everywhere, perspiring, and I began to ask him about the chador as a symbol of women's role in Iran." The question penetrated to the core of Khomeini's value system. Off guard, he instantly turned nasty, and in a revealing outburst shouted: "If you don't like the chador, don't wear it,

Caustic Interviewing. Italian journalist Oriana Fallaci is known for her no-holds-barred interview style. She brings out significant truths about the world leaders and celebrities she interviews through her carefully crafted questions and quick follow-ups. Fallaci prepares meticulously for her interviews, sometimes taking months and even learning a new language. She also knows the political and media systems within which her interviewees function.

because the chador is for young, proper women!" Insulted, she ripped the veil off: "This is what I do with your stupid medieval rag!" Shocked, the Ayatollah shot up and left, with Fallaci calling after him: "Where do you go? Do you go to make pee-pee?" Quick-witted Fallaci's pee-pee afterthought was calculated to elicit further personal revelations, but Khomeini didn't turn around. Fallaci's detractors see her caustic interview style as grand theater. Whatever the criticism, she gets at sources in ways that conventional approaches do not, which gives her readers fresh insights into their characters.

Once an interview is under way, Fallaci won't take no for an answer. When Khomeini stomped out, she sat waiting for him to return. Again and again, aides asked her to leave. "No," she said, "I have only half an interview." She sat immobile for three hours, knowing that Khomeini's aides, all devoted to his brand of Islam, would not physically remove a woman. "You are Iranian. Your religion says you cannot touch me," she told them. "I'm going to stay until he comes back."

Finally, Khomeini's son came pleading for her to leave. On his fifth time back, he said Khomeini would see her the next day if she left. Her response: "Ahmad, if you get him to swear on the Koran, I'll get up." By that point, she recalled later, she too needed to pee-pee. At the appointed hour the next day, Khomeini, faithful to his promise, arrived to continue the interview. And Fallaci, true to her goal, looked him in the eye: "Now, Imam, let's start where we left off yesterday. We were talking about my being an indecent woman."

Fallaci's interviews are mostly for an Italian magazine, but because of their significance they are reprinted all over the world. Imagine the insights that came from this accusatory Fallaci question to Portuguese communist leader Alvaro Cunhal: "Aren't you ashamed of what you are saying? For Christ's sake, don't you blush?" Interviewing Henry Kissinger when he was U.S. secretary of state, Fallaci asked: "To what extent does power fascinate you? Try to be sincere."

In this chapter you will read how fundamental issues about human nature shape our political and media systems. It is a knowledge of these issues and also a commitment to a basic set of fundamental values that enables Oriana Fallaci to move from one place to another on the globe, from one political environment to another, and to ask questions that beget important answers from people in high places.

POLITICAL-MEDIA SYSTEMS

STUDY PREVIEW Authoritarian governments, including modern-day dictatorships, regard the mass media as subservient: The government is beyond challenge. In libertarian systems like ours, the media decide their content independent of government control. Frequently they challenge government policy. Communist systems conceive of government and media as partners in the common task of moving the society to a perfected state.

AUTHORITARIAN

Through the history of the mass media, dating to Johannes Gutenberg, authoritarian political systems have been the most common. At that time it generally was the monarchy that had great power over the expression of ideas. England was an authoritarian state that permitted neither open inquiry nor free expression. In this century, Nazi Germany, Franco's Spain and Third World dictatorships have continued the authoritarian tradition. An assumption in authoritarian systems is that the government is infallible, which means its policies are beyond question. The media role in the society is subservience to government.

LIBERTARIAN

Later, when democracies developed, first in the United States and then in France and elsewhere in western Europe, the role of the mass media was substantially different. These were libertarian countries whose political systems encouraged free expression. In democratic countries, the mass media have great liberty as unbridled forums for the expression and exchange of ideas. Leading libertarian systems today include the United States, Japan, England and the other Western democracies. Libertarianism has great faith in the wisdom of the people, who utilize the mass media to arrive at decisions on public policy. Governments, which are elected to carry out the will of the people, are under the independent scrutiny of the mass media.

COMMUNIST

Political philosopher Karl Marx inspired the youngest political and media system, which came into existence after the 1917 Bolshevik revolution in Russia. Communist mass media are regarded as government's partners in moving the society toward a perfect state. This political-media system suffered a major setback after 1990 with the overthrow of communism in the Soviet Union and in most of the countries in central Europe. It still remains the system in China and in several smaller countries, including Albania and Cuba.

AUTHORITARIAN SYSTEMS

STUDY PREVIEW England in the 1500s and 1600s was the prototypical authoritarian state. The government asserted control over the press when it became apparent that the mass-produced written word could be used to encourage dissent and even revolution among the people. To control the mass media, authoritarian governments use censorship, licensing, repression and bribery. Defenders of authoritarian systems argue that their regimes are infallible. Others argue that bridled media are necessary for political and social stability.

ENGLAND UNDER HENRY VIII

When Johannes Gutenberg invented movable type in the 1400s, making mass production of the written word possible, authorities were enthusiastic. Early printers produced Bibles and religious tracts, which were consistent with the values of the intertwined institutions of state and church. It did not occur to anybody that the new invention might be used for heretical or traitorous purposes. Later, occasional tracts appeared that challenged the authorities, but their threat was easily dismissed because, even in the early 1500s, printing still was mostly in Latin, which could be read only by the ruling elite. Most common people were unable to read even their native language, let alone Latin. The printed word seemed an unlikely vehicle for the foment of popular revolution.

Within two generations, however, the comfortable relationship between the authorities and the fast-growing printing industry changed, and the authorities clamped down. What happened in England was typical. In 1529, after Dutch tracts that challenged royal authority began showing up in England, *King Henry VIII* outlawed imported publications. He also decreed that every English printer must be licensed. Printers caught producing anything objectionable to the crown lost their licenses, in effect being put out of business. Remaining in the government's

TEACHING OBJECTIVE 16-2
Discuss rationale for authoritarian media control.

KEY PERSON
King Henry VIII was prototypical authoritarian.

Authoritarian Execution.
Authoritarian governments prevent mass media criticism of their policies with numerous methods, including execution. In authoritarian England, the Crown made public spectacles of executions, as in the case of John of Barneveld in 1619, above, which had a chilling effect on other people who might have challenged the Crown.

LECTURE RESOURCE 16-A
Guest Speaker: Foreign-born faculty member.

LECTURE RESOURCE 16-B
Guest Speaker: Foreign-born student.

good graces brought favors. A license was a guaranteed local monopoly and a lock on government and church printing jobs.

Henry VIII's clampdown, a turnabout in official attitudes toward the press, was triggered by major social and political changes that were occurring in England:

■ Literacy was increasing. More common people were learning to read. It became apparent that wider literacy increased the possible effect of seditious and heretical ideas on the general population.

■ A mercantile class was emerging. Merchants and tradespeople were accumulating modest wealth, which permitted discretionary time in their lives and the lives of their families. This mercantile class, not needing to work from dawn to dusk to survive, had sufficient time to contemplate matters of state, religion and things in general. These were people who read, and a sense was developing among them that their interests as a group did not always coincide with the Crown's.

■ Parliament was developing as an expression of popular will. Mercantilists found Parliament could be a powerful forum for challenging the Crown's policies, and they began using it to those ends.

■ Printers were becoming bolder. The growing volume of material produced by the young printing industry included more political books and tracts, some disturbing to the Crown. The Crown perceived the threat as being all the worse because printed words were more frequently in English, not Latin, which dramatically increased their potential to stir up the masses.

Frederick Siebert, a scholar on the authoritarian English press, describes the main function of the mass media in an authoritarian system this way: "to support and advance the policies of government as determined by the political machinery then in operation." Siebert's phrase "then in operation" points out how fickle an authoritarian system can be. In 1530, when England under Henry VIII was still a

Catholic state, a man was executed for selling a book by a Protestant author. Only 50 years later, after the government had rejected Catholicism, a printer was executed for printing a Catholic pamphlet. In an authoritarian system, the media are subservient to government and adjust their coverage to coincide with changes in government policy.

METHODS OF AUTHORITARIAN CONTROL

Censorship usually comes to mind as an authoritarian method to control the mass media, but censorship is labor intensive and inefficient. Other methods include licensing, bribery and repression.

CENSORSHIP.   Authoritarian regimes have found numerous ways, both blatant and subtle, to control the mass media. Censorship is one. The most thorough censoring requires that manuscripts be read by governmental agents before being printed or aired. To work, prepublication censorship requires a governmental agent in every newsroom and everywhere else that mass media messages are produced. This is hardly practicable, although governments sometimes establish elaborate censorship bureaucracies during wartime to protect sensitive military information and to ban information that runs counter to their propaganda. Even democracies like the United States and Israel have required reporters to run battlefield stories past censors.

MEDIA: PEOPLE

John Twyn

John Twyn died a particularly gruesome death. In 1663 Twyn, a printer, published a book that held that the monarch should be accountable to the people. While hardly a radical concept today, the idea was heretical in 17th-century England, where kings considered themselves divinely appointed. Twyn, who had not even written the book but merely printed it, was arrested and convicted of seditious libel. His sentence: "You shall be hanged by the neck, and being alive, shall be cut down and your privy members shall be cut off, your entrails shall be taken from your body, and you living, the same to be burnt before your eyes."

The political climate in England and the other modern Western democracies has changed dramatically since John Twyn's time. But mass communicators are still profoundly affected by the political systems within which they operate. The Committee to Protect Journalists, which tracks repression against the press, reports that dozens of reporters are jailed every year. In 1989 there were 65 journalists in 16 countries in prison or held hostage. A 66th was confined by the state to a psychiatric ward.

Even in the United States, a democracy with a constitution guaranteeing free expression and a free press, journalists are sentenced to jail from time to time, usually for refusing to identify their confidential sources when asked to do so by a judge. There are even stories of reporters' lives being threatened. Washington *Post* reporters Carl Bernstein and Bob Woodward said they learned their lives were in danger as they dug into 1972 Nixon re-election campaign scandals. In that same period, columnist Jack Anderson reported that a government plot had been hatched in the Justice Department to assassinate him for his Watergate reporting.

LICENSING.   Authoritarian governments generally favor less obtrusive methods of control than censorship. Henry VIII introduced a licensing system that limited the printing trade to people who held royal patents. The mechanism for bestowing these licenses rested with the Stationers Company, a trade association. Royal patents were available only to association members, and membership was tightly controlled. To stay in the Crown's favor, the Stationers Company expelled members who produced forbidden materials, in effect putting them out of business.

Four hundred years later, Nazi Germany used a more complex system. Under the guise of improving the quality of news, entertainment and culture, *Joseph Goebbels*, the minister of propaganda and public enlightenment, established guilds to which "cultural workers" had to belong. There were "chambers," as these guilds were called, for advertising, film, literature, music, the press, radio and theater. The chambers could deny membership to cultural workers whose work did not qualify. As Nazi anti-Semitism became frenzied, however, the chambers shifted their membership criteria to exclude Jews. Membership in the press chamber, for example, was limited to third-generation so-called Aryans.

The Spanish dictator *Francisco Franco*, who came to power in 1936, employed rigid licensing. News organizations could hire only people listed on an official register of journalists. To be on the list required graduation from one of Franco's three-year journalism schools, which wove political indoctrination into the curriculum. The success of the schools, from Franco's perspective, was further assured because admission was limited to students who were sympathetic to the generalissimo.

BRIBERY.   Germany's "Iron Chancellor," Otto von Bismarck, maintained an immense fund for bribing editors, which kept much of the German press of the 1860s on his side. The practice is institutionalized in much of the impoverished Third World today, where journalists, earning barely subsistence salaries, accept gratuities on the side for putting certain stories in the paper and on the air.

Bribery also can occur when a government controls supplies that are necessary for the media to function. Franco cut newsprint deliveries to a Spanish newspaper in the early 1960s after several pro-monarchist articles appeared. In Mexico, a country with no newsprint manufacturing plants, PIPSA, a quasi-government agency, allocates imported newsprint. The goal, purportedly, is to assure an even stream of paper to newspapers and magazines. In practice, however, a correlation exists between articles unfavorable to the regime and either interruptions in paper delivery or the delivery of inferior paper. The publisher of a slick magazine gets the message quickly when PIPSA will supply only very rough pulp. This is subtle bribery: Publications that play ball with the regime receive a payoff in supplies essential for doing business.

REPRESSION.   Authoritarian rulers are at their most obvious when they arrest journalists who challenge their authority. Execution is the ultimate sanction. While such extreme action usually comes only after, not before, an article critical of the regime appears, it still has a chilling effect on other journalists. To learn that a fellow journalist was dragged away in the middle of the night for writing a critical article is mighty intimidating to other journalists considering similar pieces.

KEY PERSON
Joseph Goebbels was mastermind for Nazi authoritarian media.

KEY PERSON
Francisco Franco created authoritarian media system.

Irrepressible. Author Salman Rushdie was the target of a death contract issued by Iran's religious-political leader, Ayatollah Ruhollah Khomeini, who found blasphemy in Rushdie's book *Satanic Verses*. Rushdie was forced into hiding, but the Ayatollah's attempt to suppress the book backfired. Instead, it whetted public interest in the book, which became a best-seller, and fueled readership for follow-up Rushdie books.

EFFECTIVENESS OF CONTROLS

Authoritarian controls have short-term effectiveness, but the truth is impossible to suppress for very long. In Franco's Spain, which was allied with Germany in World War II, the news media were mum for years about Nazi atrocities against Jews. Despite the media blackout, the Spanish people were aware of the Holocaust. People do not receive all their information from the mass media, and if they tend to doubt the accuracy or thoroughness of an authoritarian medium, they pay special attention to alternative sources of information, such as talking to travelers, reading contraband publications and listening secretly to transborder newscasts.

Not even prepublication censorship can stop truth. If censors purge parts of a foreign correspondent's story, editors indicate in notes inserted in the truncated story that it was subject to censorship. When reporters are denied access to censor-controlled satellite uplinks, telephones and other ways to transmit their stories, they hitch a ride elsewhere to file their stories, albeit later. Even when an authoritarian government expels journalists, stories get out. During the apartheid violence in South Africa in the late 1980s, the government monitored foreign publications and newscasts for stories it did not like and then ousted the foreign correspondents who produced them. The result was that news gathering in South Africa was more difficult, but it hardly stopped the reporting of government abuses. Journalists instead relied on travelers to get information out of South Africa about what was happening.

In some authoritarian countries, the mass media are so compliant with the regime that the government seldom needs to crack down. In Mexico, for example, President Miguel de la Madrid Hurtado suggested in 1983 that publishers pay reporters more so that they would be less susceptible to bribes for writing favorable stories. Respectfully but forcefully, the publishers said that they would not. In 1989, de la Madrid's successor, President Carlos Salinas de Gortar, proposed that PIPSA be done away with, but the publishers objected strenuously, and PIPSA

Authoritarianism in the Video Age

Thwarting alien ideas, always the goal of authoritarian regimes, is becoming more and more difficult, thanks to technology. Even in Henry VIII's time, when there were relatively few presses, it was impossible to track down all the sources of printed dissent. In the 20th century, ditto machines, photocopiers and fax machines compounded the frustration.

Then, in the 1980s, came low-cost videotape cameras, which anybody could operate, and videocassette recorders, which allowed people to watch forbidden things privately. Journalist Richard Zoglin, writing in *Time* magazine, said, "No matter how firm a clamp is placed on a nation's media, it can be thwarted by a determined opposition armed with video cameras." Videotape was both subverting authoritarian governments and spurring profound cultural changes:

- Strongly anti-Soviet videos, such as *Rambo,* were being bootlegged behind the Iron Curtain, where their entertainment value kept them in high demand.
- Amazon Indians were toting camcorders to meetings with Brazilian officials to, as one leader put it, "catch their lies and make them hold true to their promises."
- Palestinians were taping brutally wounded hospital patients as evidence of Israeli excesses in suppressing the revolutionary Intifada movement.
- Muslim theocracies were finding it impossible to intercept underground copies of video porn like *Debbie Does Dallas* and *Nude Jell-O Wrestling.*
- The government's pretense of democracy was exposed in Mexico, Panama and other countries by people with camcorders who recorded election fraud on videotapes that were inexpensively duplicated and put into wide circulation.

Camcorders in the Amazon. Video technology gives oppressed people a low-cost weapon to document promises by governments they don't trust. In the Amazon, the Kayapo tribe videotaped negotiations with Brazilian officials about a proposed dam.

- Distrust between Pakistanis and Indians was being undermined as Hindi music videos made their way north across the border to eager viewers and as Pakistani soap operas made their way south.

remained. In another example of media commitment to authoritarianism, the operator of the private Mexican television network has proclaimed himself "a soldier of the PRI." The PRI has long been Mexico's controlling political party, and the network executive was saying that he would do nothing to disrupt the status quo. With that sort of attitude expressed at the top, the troops in the newsroom are not even threatened by external censorship. In short, in some countries, control of the media by government is a joint operation of the media and the government. Media owners willingly, even eagerly acquiesce.

NATURE OF TRUTH

Authoritarian media systems make sense to anyone who accepts the premise that the government, whether embodied in a king or a dictator, is right in all that it says and does. Such a premise is anathema to most Americans, but a mere 400 years ago it was mainstream Western thought. King James VII of Scotland, who later became *King James I* of England, made an eloquent argument for the *divine right of kings* in 1598. He claimed that legitimate kings were anointed by the Almighty and thereby were better able to express righteousness and truth than anyone else. By definition, therefore, anybody who differed with the king was embracing falsity and probably heresy.

    The authoritarian line of reasoning justifies suppression on numerous grounds:

- Truth is a monopoly of the regime. Commoners can come to know it only through the ruler, who, in King James's thinking, has an exclusive pipeline to the Almighty. Advocates of authoritarianism have little confidence in individuals.
- Challenges to the government are based on falsity. It could not be otherwise, considering the premise that government is infallible.
- Without strong government, the stability necessary for society to function may be disrupted. Because challenges to government tend to undermine stability and because the challenges are presumed to be false to begin with, they must be suppressed.

KEY PERSON
King James I saw monarchy as divinely connected.

Divine Right. King James I, who fancied himself a scholar, wrote a treatise in 1598 that claimed monarchies were legitimate because of a pipeline to God. His theory, called the divine right of kings, is a classic defense for authoritarian political and media systems.

To the authoritarian mind, journalists who support the government are purveying truth and should be rewarded. The unfaithful, who criticize, are spreading
falsity and should be banished. It all makes sense if King James was right with his
divine right theory. It was no wonder that sedition was a high crime.

An inherent contradiction in authoritarianism is the premise that the ruler is
uniquely equipped to know truth. Experience over the centuries makes it clear that
monarchs and dictators come in many stripes. Regimes have been known to change
in midstream, as in Henry VIII's change of heart on Roman Catholicism. A fair
question to put to authoritarian advocates is whether Henry was right when he was
a Catholic, or later when he was an Anglican.

COMMUNIST SYSTEMS

STUDY PREVIEW   Many people equate authoritarian and communist media systems, but there are fundamental
differences. The concepts of truth and how human beings can come to know truth, for example,
are widely divergent.

MARXIST UNDERPINNINGS

TEACHING OBJECTIVE 16-3
Distinguish communist from
authoritarian media systems.

KEY PERSON
Karl Marx provided philosophical
inspiration for Soviet media system.

LECTURE RESOURCE 16-C
Class Exercise: Students tape
shortwave broadcasts from foreign
countries.

The German philosopher *Karl Marx*, who wrote in the mid-1800s, had the idea
that humankind was evolving toward a perfect state. As Marx saw it, people eventually would be living in such perfect social harmony that they would not even need
government to maintain social order. The process, he said, might take a long time,
centuries perhaps, but the evolution was inevitable.

In the interim before "perfection," Marx called for governments to recognize
the inevitability of history and adopt policies to hasten the evolution toward the
perfect state. The mass media, he said, should be government's partners in facilitat-
ing these undeniable historical processes.

In 1917, after Bolshevik revolutionaries replaced the authoritarian Russian
czars, Marxists established a different kind of government, and it became the prototypical communist state until the collapse of the Soviet Union in 1991. Although
the Soviet Union's successor states have moved away from the communist model,
the media system of the former Soviet Union remains the best way to understand
how the media are designed to work in China and other remaining communist
states such as Cuba.

MARXIST NOTION OF TRUTH

The Bolshevik-created Soviet government had many earmarks of brutal authoritarianism, but its philosophical underpinnings were different. The Marxist notion of
truth, for example, was radically different.

The pre-communist Russian czars, like Henry VIII and most other monarchs,
had claimed an inherited superiority in developing a perfect understanding. Coming to know truth was a matter of tapping into revelation, a kind of communion
with God. Only by heeding their divinely anointed ruler could common people
approach such perfect understanding.

The Marxists, in contrast, said that coming to know truth was simply to recognize the inevitability of history: Historical process was truth, and truth was historical process. In short, people need not look beyond ideology for truth. Marxism's
implications for the mass media were profound.

***Pravda* in Translation.** Minnesota businessman Charles Cox began publishing an English translation of the leading Soviet daily, *Pravda,* something the Russians do not do. In 1985, Cox was faithful in text, layout and graphics to the original. Early subscribers were primarily government agencies (both U.S. and foreign) and colleges and universities. The paper was distributed to 21 nations around the world. But at $630 a year there were not enough subscribers to keep Cox's enterprise going.

Communist Mastermind. Vladimir Lenin, who created the Soviet Union out of the 1917 Bolshevik revolution, conceived of the mass media as government's partner in moving society toward perfection. Under this concept, leaders of the government and the Communist Party held key posts in the media. After the collapse of the Soviet Union in the early 1990s, the people who ran the country's newspapers and magazines and broadcast media found it difficult to switch to the new reality of democracy in a Western vein.

Marxist *Vladimir Lenin,* who founded the Soviet state as well as the Communist party newspaper *Pravda,* called for the media to be "collective propagandists, agitators and organizers." The 1925 Soviet constitution was clear: The fundamental purpose of the press was "to strengthen Communist social order."

KEY PERSON
Vladimir Lenin put Soviet media concept into operation.

MEDIA UNIFIED WITH GOVERNMENT

Authoritarian and communist media are structured differently. Most authoritarian systems are rooted in capitalism. The mass media are owned by people whose business is to make money, and the profit motive is a major factor in deciding what goes to print and what is put on the air. In general, authoritarian governments interfere only on issues directly affecting the government's ability to stay in power and maintain social order. Most of the time, the media in authoritarian states operate independent of government.

In communist countries, the economic structure is socialist. Unconcerned about profit, communist media people choose to provide coverage that furthers the government's ideological goals. In fact, media decision makers usually are government officials chosen because they are in tune with Marx's central idea on the inevitability of historical processes. When the Soviet Union was in full flower as a communist state, for example, the editors of the leading publications all were high officials in the Communist Party. One media scholar called it akin to having the vice president of the United States editing the Washington *Post.*

In practice, communist governments and media often fall short of their ideological mandate and appear authoritarian. Still, Marxist roots show through. A Polish journalist who defected to the United States when Poland was still a communist state gave this account of a gang rape he covered: "The story did not appear in its original form. The details of the incident were heavily toned down, as they would have marred the image of happy and idealistic youngsters building socialism." In an authoritarian system, in contrast, ideology would not be a factor in deciding how to report such a story.

Also unlike authoritarian systems, communist media criticize government. Throughout the history of the Soviet Union, the media were loaded with stories on official bungling and inefficiency, although usually at a low level, such as a factory commissar who was looking the other way at warehouse thievery. Typical was "Bring the Parasites to Account," a *Pravda* story on chronic production shortages blamed on bad managers. Soviet newspapers and magazines invited readers to be whistle-blowers. The accusations were investigated, and the resulting stories were intended to discourage practices that were retarding the arrival of a perfect state.

Off-limits in the communist media, however, is criticism of Marxist ideology, which is accorded the sacred respect that ultimate truth deserves.

Journalism Colombia-Style

Journalistic War Zone. Reporting the news takes special courage in Colombia, where drug lords take terrorist initiatives when they are unhappy with coverage. In September 1989, the newspaper *El Espectador* in Bogota was bombed. One person died and 70 were injured. Damage totaled $2.5 million, including the loss of 1,200 tons of newsprint.

Journalists in some countries do their work in fear of authoritarian governments. In Colombia the dangers are from the cocaine cartels, which object to being covered in the news media. From 1985 to 1989, at least 33 Colombian journalists were killed. Dozens more have fled the country after receiving death threats.

The leading newspaper, *El Espectador,* has been a particular target. Gunmen on motorcycles shot the editor and the newspaper's lawyer on a street in 1986. In 1989 two other *El Espectador* employees were similarly cut down on the street. More than 70 people were injured when a bomb planted in a pickup truck blew up at the newspaper's plant.

Here is a look at the working news media in Colombia:

- Security guards hold machine guns on visitors at the entrance to the Caricol radio station in Bogota.
- Fifteen-foot concrete walls topped by razor-wire lines surround *El Colombiano's* newspaper plant in Medellin.
- A photographer for Colombian Television tucks a .38-calibre revolver in his battery-pack belt.
- Armed guards and bullet-proof cars protect television reporters as they make their rounds.

LIBERTARIAN SYSTEMS

STUDY PREVIEW Libertarian thinkers have faith in the ability of human beings to come to know great truths by applying reason. Libertarians feel that a robust, open exchange of ideas will eliminate flawed notions and reinforce good ones. This process, however, may take time because people individually and collectively make short-term mistakes.

OPTIMISM ABOUT THE HUMAN MIND

Physicists love telling young science pupils the story of an English lad, Isaac Newton, who, sitting in an orchard one late-summer day, was struck on the head by a falling apple. Voilà! At that moment the law of gravity was instantly clear to Isaac Newton. It is a good story, though not a true one. Deriving the law of gravitation was a much more sophisticated matter for Newton, the leading 17th-century physicist, but the orchard story lives on. It is a story also told to pupils in their first world history class to illustrate a period in intellectual history called the *Enlightenment.* In this version, young Newton not only discovered gravity at the very instant that he was bumped on the head, but he also realized that he could come to know great truths like the law of gravity by using his own mind. He did not need to rely on a priest or a monarch or anyone else claiming a special relationship with God. He could do it on his own. This revelation, say the history teachers, was a profound challenge to authoritarian premises and ushered in the era of rationalist thinking that marks the modern age. Individually and together, people were capable of learning the great truths, called the *natural law*, unassisted by governing authorities. The insight of the Enlightenment was that human beings are rational beings. It marked the beginning of quantum progress in the sciences. The insight also contributed to the development of *libertarianism*, which held the intellectual roots of modern democracy.

TEACHING OBJECTIVE 16-4
Explain intellectual foundations of libertarian media systems.

MARKETPLACE OF IDEAS

An English writer, *John Milton*, was the pioneer libertarian. In his 1644 pamphlet *Areopagitica*, Milton made a case for free expression based on the idea that individual human beings were capable of discovering truth if given the opportunity. Milton called for a *marketplace of ideas* in which people could choose from the range of human ideas and values, just as shoppers pinch a lot of fruits and vegetables at the produce market until they find the best. Milton's marketplace of ideas was not a place but a concept. It existed whenever people exchanged ideas, whether in conversation or letters or the printed word.

KEY PERSON
John Milton argued that falsity should not be censored.

Milton was eloquent in his call for free expression. He saw no reason to fear any ideas, no matter how subversive, because human beings inevitably would choose the best ideas and values. "Let [Truth] and Falsehood grapple: whoever knew Truth put to the worse in a free and open encounter?" he wrote. Milton reasoned that people would gain confidence in their own ideas and values if they tested them continually against alternative views. It was an argument against censorship. People need to have the fullest possible selection in the marketplace if they are going to go home with the best product, whether vegetables or ideas. Also, bad ideas should be present in the marketplace because, no matter how obnoxious, they might contain a grain of truth worth considering.

Milton acknowledged that people sometimes err in sorting out alternatives, but these mistakes are corrected as people continually reassess their values against

Marketplace of Ideas. John Milton gave the world the marketplace of ideas concept in his 1644 pamphlet *Areopagitica*, which paved the way for libertarianism. Milton said that everyone should be free to express ideas, no matter how traitorous, blasphemous, deleterious or just plain silly, for the consideration of other people. It was a strong argument against restrictions on free expression.

competing values in the marketplace. Milton saw this truth seeking as a never-ending, lifelong human pursuit, which meant that people would shed flawed ideas and values for better ones over time. Milton called this a *self-righting process.*

First Amendment

Libertarian ideas took strong root in England's North American colonies in the 1700s. Pamphleteer *Thomas Paine* stirred people against British authoritarianism and incited them to revolution. The rhetoric of the Enlightenment was clear in the Declaration of Independence, which was drafted by the libertarian philosopher Thomas Jefferson. His document declared that people possessed *natural rights* and were capable of deciding their own destiny. No king was needed. There was an emphasis on liberty and individual rights. Libertarianism spread rapidly as colonists rallied against Britain in the Revolutionary War. Not everyone who favored independence was a firm libertarian, however, and when it came time to write a constitution for the new republic, there was a struggle between libertarian and authoritarian principles. The libertarians had the greater influence, but sitting there prominently were Alexander Hamilton and a coterie of individuals who would have severely restricted the liberties of the common people. The Constitution that resulted was a compromise. Throughout it an implicit trust of the people vies with an implicit distrust. Even so, the government that emerged was the first so influenced by libertarian principles, and "the great experiment in democracy," as it has been called, began.

In 1791 the Constitution was expanded to include the *First Amendment*, which barred governmental interference in the exchange of ideas. The First Amendment declares that "Congress shall make no law . . . abridging the freedom of speech, or of the press. . . ." In practice, there have been limits on both free speech and free expression since the beginning of the republic. Legal scholars debate where to draw the line when the First Amendment comes into conflict with other rights, such as the right not to be slandered and the right to privacy. Even so, for 200 years the First Amendment has embodied the ideals of the Enlightenment. The United States clearly is in the libertarian tradition, as are the other Western-style democracies that followed.

LIBERTARIANS AND RELIGION

Early libertarian headiness over the potential of the human mind created conflicts with religious authorities. The traditional clerics were authoritarian, with an essentially negative view of human nature. According to some theologians, people were incapable of fulfilling their human nature on their own. Libertarians, on the other hand, were intoxicated with the belief that human beings could fulfill their nature and come to know ultimate truths by applying reason alone. Implicit in libertarianism, it seemed, was that traditional religion was an extraneous vestige of less-enlightened times.

The conflict has not been entirely resolved, but many modern libertarians note that the natural law, which they claim can be learned through human analytical processes, coincides with the ultimate truths to which churches in an authoritarian period sought to bring the faithful. The reconciliation equates the libertarians' notion of natural law with the religious notion of God's will. The American thinker *Carl Becker* addressed the conflict in 1945 when he updated John Milton with this summation of libertarianism: "If men were free to inquire about all things, to form opinions on the basis of knowledge and evidence, and to utter their opinions freely, the competition of knowledge and opinion in the marketplace of rational discourse would ultimately banish ignorance and superstition and enable men to shape their conduct and their institutions in conformity with the fundamental and *invariable laws of nature* and the *will of God*."

KEY PERSON
Carl Becker updated libertarianism for 20th century.

FREEDOM AND RESPONSIBILITY

STUDY PREVIEW An uneasiness developed in the 20th century over the validity of the libertarian assumptions necessary for the marketplace of ideas to work. In 1947 a private panel, the Hutchins Commission, gave voice to this uneasiness in identifying abuses of press freedom and recommending a change in emphasis from a *free* to a *responsible* press. This new emphasis came to be called the *social responsibility* concept, and it gradually was adopted by the media as a modification of traditional libertarian thinking.

TEACHING OBJECTIVE 16-5
Discuss shift in emphasis from freedom to social responsibility.

FLAWED LIBERTARIAN ASSUMPTIONS

The novelist and muckraker *Upton Sinclair* raised questions about the integrity of newspapers in his novel *The Brass Check*, published in 1919. Sinclair offered a look inside an imaginary newsroom in which powerful interests could bribe their way into print. He outlined how newspapers could abuse their freedom. The doubts that Sinclair planted about the news media grew. Many people were bothered about one-sidedness in newspapers, especially as consolidations reduced the number of competing newspapers. Orson Welles's 1941 movie *Citizen Kane*, based on newspaper publisher William Randolph Hearst, undermined public confidence in the people who ran newspapers. So did the quirkiness of other prominent publishers, such as *Robert McCormick*, who turned the Chicago *Tribune* into a campaign vehicle for simplified spellings like "thru" for "through," "frate" for "freight" and "buro" for "bureau." McCormick was always quick to defend his eccentricities, as well as

KEY PERSON
Upton Sinclair exposed newsroom abuses. See Index.

KEY PERSON
Robert McCormick.

Impetus to Social Responsibility.
The blue-ribbon Hutchins Commission
called in 1947 for the media to be more
socially responsible, but not until the
1950s did news people begin a serious
self-assessment of their practices. One
trigger of the self-assessment was the
damage that resulted from news coverage
of false charges by Wisconsin Senator
Joseph McCarthy that communists had
infiltrated federal agencies. The reporting
that McCarthy made the allegations was
literally accurate, but it failed to raise
essential questions about McCarthy's
credibility. When the news media realized
they had been duped by McCarthy, and
that the American people had been duped
through them, there developed an emphasis
on reporting to put events "in a context
that makes them meaningful," as the
Hutchins Commission had recommended
in 1947.

Electronic Town Hall. Ross Perot took
his bid for the presidency directly to the
people with live televised speeches and
appearances on talk shows. This bypassed
the usual processes that the news media
use in boiling down, summarizing and
packaging the news. Bypassing media gatekeepers allowed Perot to maintain more
control over his messages. Other candidates also are using new technology to
communicate directly with voters.

the *Tribune's* blatantly right-wing news coverage, in the name of a free press. Americans, imbued with libertarian idealism, were hesitant to challenge McCormick and
other media barons but there were growing doubts by the late 1940s about whether
modern society provided a proper environment for the marketplace of ideas. These
doubts concerned basic libertarian assumptions:

PEOPLE ARE CAPABLE OF DISTINGUISHING TRUTH.   In
their enthusiasm about human nature, libertarians assumed that people are
involved in a life-long quest for knowledge, truth and wisdom. There was evidence
aplenty, however, that many people could not care less about the great questions of
human existence. People might be capable of sorting truth from falsity in the marketplace of ideas, but many do not work at it.

MEDIA ARE DIVERSE.   Libertarians imagined a world of so many diverse publications that there would be room for every outlook. In the 20th century, however, some people saw a reduction in media diversity. Cities with several newspapers lost papers one by one to the point that in the 1940s few cities had more than two newspapers. Only three broadcast networks dominated radio coverage of national and international affairs.

MEDIA INDEPENDENCE.   Libertarianism assumes that truth-seeking individuals exchange ideas in an unstructured, free-wheeling marketplace. As governments picked up public relations skills, however, the media have experienced varying degrees of manipulation, which has detracted from their role as the vehicles of the marketplace. Also, the reliance of American media on advertising means that media whose coverage is not attractive to advertisers are squeezed out of existence.

EASY ACCESS TO MEDIA.   The libertarian notion of all citizens engaging in great dialogues through the media seemed naïve to some people. Few newspapers published more than a half a dozen reader letters a day, and the reduction in the number of cities with multiple newspapers had further devalued newspapers as a vehicle for citizen exchange.

HUTCHINS COMMISSION

Doubts about some libertarian assumptions took firm shape in 1947 when magazine tycoon *Henry Luce* gave a grant of $200,000 to an old college friend, *Robert Maynard Hutchins*, to study the American press. Hutchins, chancellor of the University of Chicago, assembled a group of scholars. The *Hutchins Commission*, as it was called, issued a bombshell report that expressed concern that the news media were becoming too powerful. The commission cited the growth of newspaper chains. To Luce's dismay, the commission also seemed concerned about the power of magazine groups like his own *Time*, *Life* and *Fortune*. The commission said the news media needed to be more responsible and specifically called on the press to provide:

- A truthful, comprehensive and intelligent account of the day's events in a context that makes them meaningful.
- A forum for exchange of comment and criticism, including contrary ideas.
- A representative picture of society's constituent groups, including blacks and other minorities.
- Coverage that challenges society's goals and values and helps clarify them.

Luce was livid. He had established the commission hoping to blunt criticism that his own magazines were one-sided and too powerful. It backfired. The commission raised serious questions about news media practices that Luce and other media barons had defended in the name of freedom of the press. *Robert McCormick*, publisher of the *Chicago Tribune*, mounted a tirade and commissioned a book to rip the commission's report apart. Newspaper trade associations went on record that the republic was best served when nobody was looking over journalists' shoulders. Freedom of the press, they argued, was at stake when government or anybody else, including a private group of eggheads under Robert Hutchins's direction, tried to prescribe what the press should do.

KEY PERSON
Henry Luce financed Hutchins Commission on freedom of the press.

KEY PERSON
Robert Maynard Hutchins headed commission that encouraged social responsibility.

KEY PERSON
Robert McCormick railed against Hutchins's emphasis on responsibility. See Index.

Despite the negative initial reception, the Hutchins Commission's recommendations have shaped how the most respected news organizations go about their work today. Following are some examples:

LOCAL AUTONOMY.   One Hutchins Commission concern was that consolidated ownership resulted in one-minded coverage and commentary. At the time, Hearst's newspapers everywhere carried mandatory editorials from the chain headquarters, including Hearst's own quirky editorials that were transmitted with the order "must run front page." Newspaper chains today, with rare exceptions, do not issue directives on content to their individual newspapers, and it is the same with most other media organizations. Chain ideology seldom extends beyond a commitment to exploiting opportunities for profit.

BALANCED COVERAGE AND COMMENTARY.   At the time of the Hutchins report, many newspapers blatantly used their whole editorial page, and sometimes their news columns, to advance one point of view to the exclusion of others. Front-page political coverage in McCormick's *Chicago Tribune* might as well have been written by the Republican National Committee. Today almost all newspapers, magazines and radio and television stations label opinion articles clearly. Most newspapers carry a greater variety of views on their editorial pages. Many solicit contrary views. Larger newspapers have added a page opposite the editorial page to accommodate more views. These *op-ed pages* also provide room for more letters from readers. The increased space for commentary and the greater diversity would please the Hutchins Commission.

MEDIA CRITICS.   Today, news media face more external pressure to be responsible than before the Hutchins report. Leading media monitors include the Pulitzer School of Journalism's *Columbia Journalism Review*, the Society of Professional Journalists' *Quill* magazine, and the University of Maryland's *American Journalism Review*.

Since the 1947 Hutchins Commission's recommendations, several *news councils*, comprising disinterested persons who review complaints against news media performance and issue verdicts, have come and gone. The news councils don't have any legal authority, but their reports, which usually are reported widely, encourage accuracy, fairness and balance through moral suasion.

In the almost half century since the Hutchins Commission, numerous media critics and advocates have established media watchdog organizations whose diversity spans the ideological spectrum. Among them are Accuracy in Media, Fairness and Accuracy in Media, Media Watch, and Project Censored. These groups issue newsletters, write letters of protest and testify at public hearings.

KEY PERSON
Norman Isaacs first newspaper ombudsman.

READER ADVOCATES.   In the 1960s *Norman Isaacs*, executive editor of the *Louisville Courier-Journal* and *Louisville Times*, created a new position, called *ombudsman*, to solicit reader reaction to coverage, to confer with newspaper decision makers on problems and to write corrections and commentaries on newsroom practices as an independent voice. Establishing such autonomous in-house critics was unthinkable before the Hutchins report. Today ombudsmen are not uncommon at major newspapers whose newsroom budgets can accommodate freeing a seasoned journalist to represent reader interests. About two dozen newspapers have full-time ombudsmen.

RESPONSIBILITY VERSUS PROFITABILITY

The U.S. mass media's concern for social responsibility is sometimes at odds with the imperative placed on media managers to turn profits, which is reasonable in a capitalistic system. However, profitability can be damaged by the kind of socially responsible journalism that the Hutchins Commission had in mind. For example:

- The Hutchins Commission called for comprehensive news coverage, but newspapers can keep costs down with fewer pages and more ads than news.
- A major grocery chain threatens to discontinue advertising if a television station proceeds with a story about unsanitary practices in the grocery store's delicatessens.
- The Hutchins Commission called for coverage for all of society's constituent groups, including minorities and the poor, but most advertisers buy space and time in media geared for upscale audiences with buying power.
- A reporter proposes a significant investigative project that is journalistically promising, but the time and expenses, and possible legal costs, would undercut the station's profitability.

The fact is that the mass media today, particularly the news media, are pursuing divergent policies. Doing what is right journalistically does not always coincide with doing what will enhance profits, and doing what is profitable can work against good journalism.

The New York *Times*, whose journalistic reputation is among the most solid in the nation, has pursued significant stories despite advertiser and even political pressure. In the long term, the newspaper's priorities have created great reader respect and secured the *Times* as a profitable enterprise.

Murphy Brown and Baby. When television character Murphy Brown found herself pregnant and unwed, then Vice-President Dan Quayle made a political issue out of it. It was a bad example, he said. Quayle was assuming that Brown somehow was undermining family values among the millions of people who watched the program regularly. Whether Quayle was overly concerned is open to debate: Some experts say the media mirror social values, including those that are in flux; other experts say that the media are in the vanguard of ushering in change and setting the direction for evolving values; others say the media both follow and lead. Whatever the case, mother and baby are doing fine.

Distinguishing Media Systems

Scholars Fred Siebert, Theodore Peterson and Wilbur Schramm created models for looking at national media systems in a pioneering work, *Four Theories of the Press.* Their book, published in 1956, helped many later scholars make sense of the roles that mass media play in vastly different political systems.

Siebert, Peterson and Schramm identified authoritarian, communist and libertarian models, and also a latter-day adaptation of libertarianism that they called *social responsibility.* There is quibbling about whether social responsibility should be a separate model, but the point really is how these models offer a systematic picture of the mass media in different nations.

Review the characteristics of media in different systems in the following table, and then see where a national media system that you or your classmates know about fits in. A good starting point would be England in the latter years of Henry VIII's reign. How about the United States? Classmates who have lived abroad or studied foreign political systems can help with other countries.

Remember, a model is never perfect, and no national media system fits into a Siebert, Peterson and Schramm pigeonhole exactly. Some developed, relatively stable countries, like the United States, are better fits than countries in the developing world that are still working out their political systems. A special challenge is where to plug in Mexico: The country has privately owned media, but criticism of government, while allowed, can bring indirect sanctions from the government.

	Authoritarian	Communist	Libertarian	Social Responsibility
Who Owns the Mass Media?	Privately owned.	State owned.	Privately owned.	Privately owned.
Is Criticism of Government Allowed?	No.	Yes, but ideology is off-limits.	Yes, even encouraged.	Yes, as long as it is responsible.
Who Decides What the Media Will Say?	The media.	The state.	The media.	Experts.
Who Decides What the Media Will Not Say?	The state.	The state.	The media.	Experts.
Who Enforces Decisions on Media Content?	The state.	The state.	Nobody.	Ideally the media, perhaps the state.

Not all newspapers, however, can take such a long view, especially if shareholders are pressuring for higher returns on their investments every quarter. In a not untypical situation, Newell Grant, publisher of the Wahpeton, North Dakota, *Daily Herald,* thought it was important for his readers to know the salaries of faculty at the local state-funded technical college, so he published them. By law, the salaries were public information available to any citizen. Incredible as it may seem, the faculty objected and then pressured local merchants to withdraw their advertising unless Grant ceased publishing the salaries. Grant knew an advertiser boycott could hurt the *Herald*'s profitability, perhaps even put the newspaper out of business. Also, he was mindful of his responsibility to turn a profit for the Wick chain, which owned the paper. Grant gave up publishing the salaries, despite the journalistic rationale for doing so.

In short, good journalism and good profits are not always easy partners. Financially strong newspapers like the New York *Times* are in better positions to resist forces that can work against good journalism, but there are some news organizations that have built their financial strength by bowing to powerful influences and diluting their journalistic aggressiveness.

EXCEPTIONS TO SOCIAL RESPONSIBILITY

Despite the evidence that the news media operate in a more socially responsible framework today than before the Hutchins Commission, there are exceptions. Some media companies, particularly absentee chain owners of many smaller papers, begrudge newsroom expenditures and do not even run editorials regularly. Some newspapers find it cheaper to print news-service stories from remote parts of the globe than to send a reporter to the courthouse every day.

A notorious throwback to the period before social responsibility was the late *William Loeb*, publisher of the Manchester, New Hampshire, *Union Leader*. In 1972 Loeb decided that Los Angeles Mayor Sam Yorty should be the next president of the United States. Yorty was an obscure candidate, yet during the important New Hampshire primary, Loeb published 53 stories and 17 photos on Yorty, to 40 stories and 4 photographs on George McGovern, who eventually won the national Democratic nomination. Adding to the lopsided coverage were anonymous letters to the editor, smearing another leading candidate. Many suspect that Loeb himself wrote the letters. He reduced one stumping candidate to tears with a false front page attack on the man's wife. Loeb defended his irresponsibility by saying that the First Amendment guaranteed him freedom to print what he wanted. There are other media owners, though not many, who hold the same view today. Few, however, interject themselves so flamboyantly and recklessly into national politics. The *Union Leader*, as the only statewide newspaper, was in a position to influence the presidential selection process significantly because the early New Hampshire primary was so closely watched.

KEY PERSON
William Loeb was among last practicing press libertarians.

Campaigning with a Sax.
Political candidates have learned to take their campaigns live directly to the people via radio and television. Bill Clinton did it with entertainment program appearances during the 1992 elections, including the "Arsenio Hall Show" where he played the saxophone. This form of campaigning through electronic media bypasses journalists who once were an intermediary between candidates and voters.

CHAPTER WRAP-UP

A nation's political and media systems mirror each other. Democracies have libertarian media systems in which government functions under the watchful eye of the independent news media. The media, in fact, are called "watchdogs" because they are expected to identify misdeeds by government and bring them to public attention.

The United States was the pioneer democracy with a libertarian media system, and others followed. Today, most developed Western nations are in the libertarian tradition. The development of these governing and media systems was a reaction to authoritarian systems in which the government operated dictatorially and controlled the media through a variety of means, including censorship, licensing, bribery and repression.

Authoritarian and libertarian systems spring from philosophically distinct premises. Authoritarianism, which operates today in much of the world, is doubtful about the ability of people to govern themselves. Trust is placed in a dictator, monarch or other ruler, sometimes assumed to be divinely appointed. In authoritarian systems, the media follow the leadership of the infallible governing authority. Libertarianism, on the other hand, has confidence in the ability of human beings, individually and collectively, to conduct their affairs on their own.

In the 20th century, Soviet communism emerged as a third and distinct government and media system. On a philosophical plane, communism respects neither a single leader nor the people. Instead, it trusts great historical movements to bring about, eventually, a perfect society. The government and the media are interim entities expected to facilitate and hasten the inevitable arrival of utopia. The Soviet Union, which led the way with communism, began a dramatic shift to libertarianism in the late 1980s after 60 years of frustration at making its style of communism work, but communist media systems remain in China and some tertiary communist countries.

QUESTIONS FOR REVIEW

1. Name the major national political and media systems in the world today.

2. How would someone defend authoritarian media systems?

3. How do communist media systems differ from authoritarian systems regarding the nature of truth?

4. How do libertarians regard human reason, and how does this figure into libertarian media systems?

5. Why have U.S. media practices shifted away from an emphasis on freedom to an emphasis on social responsibility?

QUESTIONS FOR CRITICAL THINKING

1. Why is it impossible for a libertarian country to have an authoritarian or communist media system? Can an authoritarian country have a libertarian or communist media system? Can a communist country have a libertarian or authoritarian system?

2. How did 16th-century England embody the thinking that still is at the heart of authoritarian media systems?

3. Describe how modern dictatorships, as well as the fascist Nazi and Mussolini regimes of the 1930s and

1940s, used the same methods of authoritarian control as Henry VIII.

4. Why are government attempts at suppressing information usually futile in the long term?

5. In the authoritarian scheme of thinking, how do people come to know truth? In a libertarian scheme? In a communist scheme?

6. How do authoritarians view the potential of human reason? Libertarians? Communists?

7. How did Enlightenment thinking lead to libertarian media systems? Discuss this in terms of specific libertarian philosophers.

8. How did Upton Sinclair, Orson Welles and Robert Hutchins contribute to 20th-century changes in the libertarian media concept?

9. In what periods of history did the authoritarian media concept thrive? Libertarian? Communist?

10. Name as many countries as you can with a libertarian media system. Name those with an authoritarian system. Name those with a communist system.

FOR FURTHER LEARNING

Carl L. Becker. *Freedom and Responsibility in the American Way of Life* (Vintage, 1945). Becker, a historian, updates classic libertarianism in terms of mid-20th-century American life.

Isaiah Berlin. *Karl Marx: His Life and Environment* (Oxford University Press, 1939). This enduring biography of Marx and his ideas was written by a British scholar and diplomat.

Kevin Cash. *Who the Hell Is William Loeb?* (Amoskeog Press, 1975). A former Manchester *Union Leader* staff member writes unflatteringly about how Loeb ran New Hampshire's dominant newspaper.

Commission of Freedom of the Press. *A Free and Responsible Press* (University of Chicago, 1947). This is the Hutchins Commission report from which have sprung the social responsibility modifications of libertarian thinking about the press.

Frank Hughes. *Prejudice and the Press* (Devin-Adair, 1950). Commissioned by Robert McCormick, publisher of the Chicago *Tribune*, this is an attempt to refute the 1947 Hutchins Commission report that said the U.S. mass media were so obsessed with freedom of the press that they overlooked an obligation to be responsible.

John C. Merrill. *An Imperative of Freedom: A Philoso-*
phy of Journalistic Autonomy (Hastings House, 1974). Merrill, a media scholar, offers a totalitarian-anarchy continuum model of major media systems.

Fred Siebert, Theodore Peterson and Wilbur Schramm. *Four Theories of the Press* (University of Illinois Press, 1956). Siebert, Peterson and Schramm root national political and media systems in philosophical premises about the nature of knowledge, humankind and society. *Four Theories* remains the seminal work for later treatments of the subject.

Robert Scheer. "Oriana Fallaci." In G. Barry Golson, *Playboy Interview, II* (Perigree, 1983). A veteran interviewer for *Playboy* magazine's question-answer pieces turns the tables on Fallaci to explore her interview techniques. For examples of Fallaci's work, check indexes to the *New Republic*, the *New York Times Magazine* and *Redbook*.

Joseph Robson Tanner. *English Constitutional Conflicts of the Seventeenth Century, 1603-1689* (Cambridge University Press, 1928). Tanner explains the intellectual foundation of James I's argument for the divine right of kings and explores how the doctrine was debated through the 1600s. Tanner's frequent citations of 17th-century documents, with their cumbersome verbiage, makes for heavy reading.

FOR KEEPING UP TO DATE

Index on Censorship, published in London, provides monthly country-by-country status reports.

Scholarly journals that carry articles on foreign media systems, international communication and media responsibility include the *Journal of Broadcasting & Electronic Media*, the *Journal of Communication* and *Journalism Quarterly*.

Professional journals that carry articles on foreign media systems and on media responsibility include *Columbia Journalism Review*, *Quill* and *American Journalism Review*.

Ongoing discussion on media responsibility also appears in the *Journal of Mass Media Ethics*.

MASS MEDIA ETHICS
CODES CANNOT ANTICIPATE
ALL MORAL QUESTIONS

MASS MEDIA PEOPLE DRAW ON
NUMEROUS MORAL PRINCIPLES,
NOT ALL OF THEM CONSISTENT, TO
DEAL WITH ETHICAL QUESTIONS

MASS MEDIA PEOPLE DISAGREE ON
ETHICS DEPENDING ON WHETHER
THEY FAVOR PROCESS-BASED OR
OUTCOME-BASED APPROACHES

SOME MASS MEDIA PEOPLE
CONFUSE ETHICS WITH OBEYING
THE LAW, BEING PRUDENT, OR
ADHERING TO ACCEPTED
PRACTICES

DUBIOUS MASS MEDIA
PRACTICES CONFOUND
EFFORTS TO ESTABLISH
CLEAR STANDARDS THAT
WOULD BE UNIVERSALLY
ACCEPTED

chapter

ETHICS
AND THE MASS MEDIA

Tennis champion Arthur Ashe was glad but then leery to hear his old high school chum Doug Smith on the phone. Smith, tennis reporter for *USA Today*, wanted to see him for an interview. It was not unusual for reporters to call on Ashe. He was the first world-class American black male tennis player, and after his athletic prime he had campaigned vigorously against apartheid. But by 1992, he worried with every interview that the question of whether he had AIDS would surface.

Ashe, in fact, had AIDS. He had contracted the virus apparently in 1983 during surgery. Five years later when doctors found the infection, Ashe began therapy for the debilitating and inevitably fatal disease. He decided against going public that he had the disease, and his family and friends went along with what Ashe called "a silent and generous conspiracy to assist me in maintaining my privacy."

When Doug Smith showed up for the interview, he asked the dreaded question: "Do you have AIDS?" Although Ashe realized that some reporter some day would ask the question, it nonetheless caught him off guard. "Could be," he quipped. Then he recognized how much more revealing his words were than he intended. The secret was out.

The next afternoon, before Smith's article could appear, Ashe called a news conference to announce that he suffered from AIDS. Although he was gentle on *USA Today,* Ashe criticized the mass media for intruding into the private lives of people. In the news conference, carried live by CNN, Ashe said: "I am sorry that I have been forced to make this revelation at this time. After all, I am not running for some office of public trust, nor do I have stockholders to account to. It is only that I fall in the dubious umbrella of, quote, public figure, end of quote."

Ironically, *USA Today* had decided against going with the story, but Ashe's news conference nonetheless epitomized one of the great media ethics questions of our time: Who prevails when the mass media are at the intersection of the public's interest in knowing certain information and an individual's interest in preserving personal privacy? Like all vexsome ethics questions, people on both sides feel strongly and mount powerful arguments for their positions. Journalists themselves are hardly of one mind.

Here are arguments supporting *USA Today*'s initiative:

- Gerry Callahan of the Boston *Herald* said the violation of Ashe's privacy was committed by whoever in his circle of friends tipped the newspaper anonymously. The newspaper, he said, merely was performing its function to check out tips.
- *USA Today* editor Peter Prichard told the trade journal *Editor & Publisher* that it would have been news too if someone had tipped the paper that Ashe was suffering terminal cancer. Said Prichard: "I do not see any public service in sweeping this under the rug."
- The Atlanta *Constitution* equated "public interest" in Ashe to "the deep affection people hold for him" and noted that he could not reasonably have expected to preserve his privacy much longer. "The gentle circle of conspirators that had kept his secret for three years simply had grown too large, and the evidence of his physical decline had become too marked not to be noticed," the newspaper said.

Not everyone saw it that way. *USA Today* received almost 1,100 calls, with 60 people canceling their subscriptions. Among journalists, there were negative reactions too:

■ Mona Charen, a syndicated columnist, wrote that the fact that Ashe was a great athlete who established a milestone for blacks was "no reason to treat his personal
struggle as a peep show."

■ DeWayne Wickham, whose column appears in *USA Today,* equated AIDS victims with
rape victims. "Like them he too should not be twice victimized by being made to suffer from the harsh glare of the public spotlight."

As with most ethics issues, many people, including mass communicators, see
both sides:

■ Burl Osborne, publisher of the Dallas *Morning News,* said, "One should think about it
a long time and make absolutely certain what you are doing, but I really can't fault the
publication of the story in this case."

■ Gregory Favre, executive editor of the Sacramento, California, *Bee,* called it "one of
those tough questions." On whether to print it, however, Favre's paper did so.

■ The Milwaukee *Journal* said it "took seriously the public's right to know about its leaders and heroes" and then added: "But the media must balance that right against the
harm that can come in certain cases from the publication of damaging information."
The *Journal* noted the hesitancy that some people have about disclosing AIDS as
opposed to other ailments and concluded its editorial by saying: "The wise editor will,
perhaps with rare exception, forgo the scoop and encourage the person to go public
as a way of better controlling what is disclosed and emboldening others to reveal
their own secrets about AIDS."

Much of the criticism of *USA Today*'s initiative centered on "cheap scoops." Jeff
Cohen, who heads the FAIR media watchdog group, said: "In recent years, mass
media have been sliding down the slippery slope in pursuit of private lives of celebrities. These stories sell newspapers and pump up TV ratings, but they do little for
public discourse."

Paul McMasters, executive director of the Freedom Forum, cast the incident as a
no-win situation all around, as is the case with many ethics issues. Said McMasters:
"The fact that Arthur Ashe is stricken with AIDS is a tragedy. The fact that he lost a
measure of his privacy is a tragedy."

In this chapter, you will learn about the great principles that leading thinkers have
devised over the centuries to sort through dilemmas that are part of the human condition, and how they can be applied to media issues.

- -

THE DIFFICULTY OF ETHICS

STUDY PREVIEW Mass media organizations have put together codes of ethics that prescribe how practitioners should
go about their work. While useful in many ways, these codes neither sort through the bedeviling problems that result from conflicting prescriptions nor help much when the only open options are negative.

PRESCRIPTIVE ETHICS CODES

The mass media abound with codes of ethics. One of the earliest was adopted in
1923, the Canons of Journalism of the American Society of Newspaper Editors.
Advertising, broadcast and public relations practitioners also have codes. Many
newcomers to the mass media make an erroneous assumption that the answers to

TEACHING OBJECTIVE 17-1
Ethics codes fail to anticipate all
moral questions.

LECTURE RESOURCE 17-A
Class Exercise: Review a media
code of ethics.

all the moral choices in their work exist in the prescriptions of these codes. While the codes can be helpful, ethics is not so easy.

The difficulty of ethics becomes clear when a news reporter is confronted with a conflict between moral responsibilities to different concepts. Consider:

RESPECT FOR PRIVACY.   The code of the Society of Professional Journalists prescribes that reporters will show respect for the dignity, privacy, rights and well-being of people "at all times." The SPJ prescription sounds excellent, but moral priorities such as dignity and privacy sometimes seem less important than other priorities, as many people would argue in the case of Arthur Ashe. The public interest also overrode privacy in 1988 when the Miami *Herald* staked out presidential candidate Gary Hart overnight when he had a woman friend in his Washington townhouse.

COMMITMENT TO TIMELINESS.   The code of the Radio-Television News Directors Association prescribes that reporters be "timely and accurate." In practice, however, the virtue of accuracy is jeopardized when reporters rush to the air with stories. It takes time to confirm details and be accurate—and that delays stories.

BEING FAIR.   The code of the Public Relations Society of America prescribes dealing fairly with both clients and the general public. However, a persuasive message prepared on behalf of a client is not always the same message that would be prepared on behalf of the general public. Persuasive communication is not necessarily dishonest, but how information is marshaled to create the message depends on whom the PR person is serving.

A Politician's Political Demise. The Miami *Herald,* tipped that presidential hopeful Gary Hart was about to have a weekend fling while his wife was away, posted reporters outside his Washington townhouse. As the tipster predicted, a woman came and spent the night. With the *Herald*'s story, the Hart candidacy was over. The issue, it turned out, was not only Hart's ethics but the *Herald*'s. Should there be a limit on how closely a newspaper trails a candidate? Do people in the news deserve at least some privacy? At which side of the bedroom door, figuratively, should the reporting stop?

CONFLICT IN DUTIES

Media ethics codes are well-intended, usually helpful guides, but they are simplistic when it comes to knotty moral questions. When media ethicians Clifford Christians, Mark Fackler and Kim Rotzoll compiled a list of five duties of mass media practitioners, some of these inherent problems became obvious.

DUTY TO SELF.   Self-preservation is a basic human instinct, but is a photojournalist shirking a duty to subscribers by avoiding a dangerous combat zone?

Self-aggrandizement can be an issue too. Many college newspaper editors are invited, all expenses paid, to Hollywood movie premieres. The duty-to-self principle favors going: The trip would be fun. In addition, it is a good story opportunity, and, as a free favor, it would not cost the newspaper anything. However, what of an editor's responsibility to readers? Readers have a right to expect writers to provide honest accounts that are not colored by favoritism. Can a reporter write straight after being wined and dined and flown across the continent by movie producers who want a gung ho story? Even if reporters rise above being affected and are true to conscience, there are the duty-to-employer and the duty-to-profession principles to consider. The newspaper and the profession itself can be tarnished by suspicions, no matter whether they are unfounded, that a reporter has been bought off.

DUTY TO AUDIENCE.   Television programs that reenact violence are popular with audiences, but are they a disservice because they frighten many viewers into also inferring that the streets are more dangerous than they really are?

Tom Wicker of the New York *Times* tells a story about his early days as a reporter in Aberdeen, North Carolina. He was covering a divorce case involving one spouse's chasing the other with an ax. Nobody was hurt physically, and everyone who heard the story in the courtroom, except the divorcing couple, had a good laugh. "It was human comedy at its most ribald, and the courtroom rocked with laughter," Wicker recalled years later. In writing his story, Wicker captured the darkly comedic details so skillfully that his editor put the story on Page 1. Wicker was proud of the piece until the next day when the woman in the case called on him. Worn out, haggard, hurt and angry, she asked, "Mr. Wicker, why did you think you had a right to make fun of me in your paper?"

The lesson stayed with Wicker for the rest of his career. He had unthinkingly hurt a fellow human being for no better reason than evoking a chuckle, or perhaps a belly laugh, from his readers. To Wicker, the duty-to-audience principle never again would transcend his moral duty to the dignity of the subjects of his stories. Similar ethics questions involve whether to cite AIDS as a contributor to death in an obituary, to identify victims in rape stories, and to name juveniles charged with crimes.

DUTY TO EMPLOYER.   Does loyalty to an employer transcend the ideal of pursuing and telling the truth when a news reporter discovers dubious business deals involving the parent corporation? This is a growing issue as the mass media become consolidated into fewer gigantic companies owned by conglomerates. In 1989, for example, investigative reporter Peter Karl of Chicago television station WMAQ broke a story that General Electric had manufactured jet engines with untested and sometimes defective bolts. Although WMAQ is owned by NBC which in turn is owned by General Electric, Karl's exclusive, documented and accurate

Naming Rape Victims

The editor of the Des Moines *Register*, Geneva Overholser, faced the question of how to deal with rape in a journalistically serious way in 1990. A woman who had been assaulted and raped, Nancy Ziegenmeyer, was willing to discuss the crime in graphic detail and to describe her emotions about testifying when the assailant went on trial. Overholser decided to go ahead, and a five-part series was published.

How would you sort through these considerations in such a decision?

- Nancy Ziegenmeyer's courage could inspire other rape victims to report this largely unreported crime.
- Many people might be offended and cancel subscriptions and advertisements.
- The series could improve social awareness about rape and reduce its incidence.
- If Nancy Ziegenmeyer's name is printed, then the names of all rape victims should be published.
- Printing the name adds to the rape victim's obloquy, which can delay psychological recovery.
- Facts are facts, and they should be printed. It is not the job of the news media to keep secrets.

Can you identify other positions on this ethics question?

Overholser decided to go with the Ziegenmeyer series, including a graphic account of the assault. Critical of mainstream news media practice, Overholser argued that the media participate in the stigma of rape when

Shielding Victims. When Patricia Bowman charged that a Kennedy scion had raped her, the media divided on whether to name her in news coverage. It was an ethics question. Eventually Bowman went public, granting numerous interviews, including this one with television network reporter Diane Sawyer. The issue has many facets. One is that the American system of open justice requires someone making a serious charge to do so publicly. A counterargument is that publicity cruelly and needlessly increases the victim's suffering.

they treat rape victims differently from the victims of other crimes. Also, she said, refusing to talk openly about rape weakens society's ability to deal with it.

story aired. However, when the story was passed on to the network itself, Marty Ryan, executive producer of the "Today" show, ordered that the references to General Electric be edited out.

DUTY TO THE PROFESSION.   At what point does an ethically motivated advertising-agency person blow the whistle on misleading claims by other advertising people?

DUTY TO SOCIETY.   Does duty to society ever transcend duty to self? To audience? To employer? To colleagues? Does ideology affect a media worker's sense of duty to society? Consider how Joseph Stalin, Adolf Hitler and Franklin Roosevelt would be covered by highly motivated communist, fascist and libertarian journalists.

Are there occasions when the duty-to-society and the duty-to-audience principles are incompatible? Nobody enjoys seeing the horrors of war, for example, but journalists may feel that their duty to society demands that they go after the most grisly photographs of combat to show how horrible war is and, thereby, in a small way, contribute to public pressure toward a cessation of hostilities and eventual peace.

MORAL PRINCIPLES

STUDY PREVIEW Concern about doing the right thing is part of human nature, and leading thinkers have developed a great number of enduring moral principles over the centuries. The mass media, like other institutions and also like individuals, draw on these principles, but this does not always make moral decisions easy. The principles are not entirely consistent, especially in sorting through dilemmas.

THE GOLDEN MEAN

The Greek philosopher *Aristotle*, writing almost 2,400 years ago, devised the *golden mean* as a basis for moral decision making. The golden mean sounds simple and straightforward: Avoid extremes and seek moderation. Modern journalistic balance and fairness are founded on this principle.

The golden mean's dictate, however, is not as simple as it sounds. As with all moral principles, application of the golden mean can present difficulties. Consider the federal law that requires over-the-air broadcasters to give "equal opportunity" to candidates for public office. If one candidate buys 30 seconds at 7 p.m. for $120, a station is obligated to allow other candidates for the same office to buy 30 seconds at the same time for the same rate. On the surface, this application of the

TEACHING OBJECTIVE 17-2
Different moral principles lead media to different decisions.

LECTURE RESOURCE 17-B
Video: *Eyeball to Eyeball: Dilemma in the Newsroom.*

KEY PERSON
Aristotle chose middle ground between extremes.

Golden Mean. The Greek thinker Aristotle told his students almost 2,400 years ago that right courses of action avoid extremes. His recommendation: moderation.

golden mean, embodied in federal law, might seem to be reasonable, fair and morally right, but the issue is far more complex. The equality requirement, for example, gives an advantage to candidates who hold simplistic positions that can be expressed compactly. Good and able candidates whose positions require more time to explain are disadvantaged, and the society is damaged when inferior candidates win public office.

While minute-for-minute equality in broadcasting can be a flawed application of the golden mean, Aristotle's principle is valuable to media people when making moral decisions, as long as they do not abdicate their power of reason to embrace formulaic tit-for-tat measurable equality. It takes the human mind, not a formula, to determine fairness. And therein lies the complexity of the golden mean. No two human beings think exactly alike, which means that applying the golden mean involves individuals making judgment calls that are not necessarily the same. This element of judgment in moral decisions can make ethics intellectually exciting. It takes a sharp mind to sort through issues of balance and fairness.

"DO UNTO OTHERS"

The Judeo-Christian principle of "Do unto others as you would have them do unto you" appeals to most Americans. Not even the do-unto-others prescription, however, is without problems. Consider the photojournalist who sees virtue in serving a mass audience with a truthful account of the human condition. This might manifest itself in portrayals of great emotions, like grief. But would the photojournalist appreciate being photographed herself in a grieving moment after learning that her own infant son had died in an accident? If not, her pursuit of truth through photography for a mass audience would be contrary to the "do-unto-others" dictum.

CATEGORICAL IMPERATIVES

KEY PERSON
Immanuel Kant opted for universals.

About 200 years ago, German philosopher *Immanuel Kant* wrote that moral decisions should flow from thoroughly considered principles. As he put it, "Act on the maxim that you would want to become universal law." He called his maxim the *categorical imperative*. A categorical imperative, well thought out, is a principle that the individual who devised it would be willing to apply in all moral questions of a similar sort.

Kant's categorical imperative does not dictate specifically what actions are morally right or wrong. Moral choices, says Kant, go deeper than the context of the immediate issue. He encourages a philosophical approach to moral questions, with people using their intellect to identify principles that they, as individuals, would find acceptable if applied universally.

Kant does not encourage the kind of standardized approach to ethics represented by professional codes. His emphasis, rather, is on hard thinking. Says philosopher Patricia Smith, of the University of Kentucky, writing in the *Journal of Mass Media Ethics:* "A philosophical approach to ethics embodies a commitment to consistency, clarity, the principled evaluation of arguments, and unrelenting persistence to get to the bottom of things."

UTILITARIAN ETHICS

KEY PERSON
John Stuart Mill said favored good for most people.

In the mid-1800s, British thinker *John Stuart Mill* declared that morally right decisions are those that result in "happiness for the greatest number." Mill called his idea the *principle of utility*. It sounds good to many of us because it parallels the

Universal Law. Immanuel Kant, an 18th-century German philosopher, urged people to find principles that they would be comfortable having applied in all situations. He called these principles *categorical imperatives.*

Utilitarianism. American journalists tend to like 19th-century British thinker John Stuart Mill's utilitarianism, which favors actions that result in the greatest good for the greatest number of people. This approach to ethics dovetails well with majority rule and modern democracy.

democratic principle of majority rule, with its emphasis on the greatest good for the greatest number of people.

By and large, journalists embrace Mill's utilitarianism today, as evinced in notions like *the people's right to know,* a concept originally meant to support journalistic pursuit of information about government, putting the public's interests ahead of government's interests, but which has come to be almost reflexively invoked to defend pursuing very personal information about individuals, no matter what the human toll.

PRAGMATIC ETHICS

John Dewey, an American thinker who wrote in the late 1800s and early 1900s, argued that the virtue of moral decisions had to be judged by their results. A difficulty in Dewey's *pragmatic ethics* is that people do not have perfect crystal balls to tell them for sure whether their moral actions will have good consequences.

KEY PERSON
John Dewey looked for favorable outcomes.

EGALITARIAN ETHICS

In this century, philosopher *John Rawls* introduced the *veil of ignorance* as an element in ethics decisions. Choosing a right course of action, said Rawls, requires blindness to social position or other discriminating factors. An ethical decision requires that all people be given an equal hearing and the same fair consideration.

KEY PERSON
John Rawls avoided wrongful discrimination.

To Rawls, a brutal slaying in an upscale suburb deserves the same journalistic attention as a slaying in a poor urban neighborhood. All other things being equal, a $20,000 bank burglary is no more newsworthy than a $20,000 embezzlement.

SOCIAL RESPONSIBILITY ETHICS

KEY PERSON
Robert Hutchins advised social responsibility.

The Hutchins Commission, a learned group that studied the American mass media in the 1940s, recommended that journalists and other media people make decisions that serve the society responsibly. For all its virtues, the *social responsibility system*, like all ethics systems, has difficulties. For one thing, decision makers can only imperfectly foresee the effects of their decisions. It is not possible to predict with 100 percent confidence whether every decision will turn out to be socially responsible. Also, well-meaning people may differ honestly about how society is most responsibly served.

PROCESS VERSUS OUTCOME

STUDY PREVIEW The various approaches to ethics fall into two broad categories: deontological ethics and teleological ethics. Deontologists say people need to follow good rules. Teleologists judge morality not by the rules but by the consequences of decisions.

DEONTOLOGICAL ETHICS

TEACHING OBJECTIVE 17-3
Different moral decisions come from process-based and outcome-based ethics.

The Greek word "deon," which means "duty," is the heart of *deontological ethics*, which holds that people act morally when they follow good rules. Deontologists feel that people are duty bound to identify these rules.

Deontologists include people who believe that Scripture holds all the answers for right living. Their equivalent among media practitioners are those who rely entirely on codes of ethics drafted by organizations they trust. Following rules is a prescriptive form of ethics. At first consideration, ethics might seem as easy as following the rules, but not all questions are clear-cut. In complicated situations, the rules sometimes contradict each other. Some cases are dilemmas with no right option—only a choice among less-than-desirable options.

Deontological ethics becomes complicated, and also more intellectually interesting, when individuals, unsatisfied with other people's rules, try to work out their own universally applicable moral principles.

Here are some major deontological approaches:

- **Theory of divine command.** This theory holds that proper moral decisions come from obeying the commands of God, with blind trust that the consequences will be good.
- **Theory of divine right of kings.** This theory sees virtue in allegiance to a divinely anointed monarch, such as in England at the time of Henry VIII.
- **Theory of secular command.** This theory is a nonreligious variation that stresses allegiance to a dictator or other political leader from whom the people take cues when making moral decisions.
- **Libertarian theory.** This theory stresses a laissez-faire approach to ethics: Give free rein to the human ability to think through problems, and people almost always will make morally right decisions.
- **Categorical imperative theory.** This theory holds that virtue results when people identify and apply universal principles.

TELEOLOGICAL ETHICS

Unlike deontological ethics, which is concerned with the right actions, teleological ethics is concerned with the consequences of actions. The word "teleological" comes from the Greek word "teleos," which means "result" or "consequence."

Teleologists see flaws in the formal, legalistic duty to rules of deontologists, noting that great harm sometimes flows from blind allegiance to rules.

Here are some major teleological approaches:

- **Pragmatic theory.** This theory encourages people to look at human experience to determine the probable consequences of an action and then decide its desirability.
- **Utilitarian theory.** This theory favors ethics actions that benefit more people than they damage—the greatest good for the greatest number.
- **Social-responsibility theory.** This theory judges actions by the good effect they have on society.

SITUATIONAL ETHICS

Firm deontologists see two primary flaws in teleological ethics:

- Imperfect foresight.
- Lack of guiding principles.

Despite these flaws, many media practitioners apply teleological approaches, sometimes labeled *situational ethics*, to arrive at moral decisions. They gather as much information as they can about a situation and then decide, not on the basis of principle but on the facts of the situation. Critics of situational ethics worry about decisions governed by situations. Much better, they argue, would be decisions flowing from principles of enduring value. With situational ethics, the same person might do one thing one day and on another day go another direction in a similar situation.

Consider a case at the *Rocky Mountain News* in Denver. Editors learned that the president of a major suburban newspaper chain had killed his parents and sister in another state when he was 18. After seven years in a mental hospital, the man completed college, moved to Colorado, lived a model life and became a successful newspaper executive. The *Rocky Mountain News* decided not to make a story of it. Said a *News* official: "The only reason for dredging up [his] past would be to titillate morbid curiosity or to shoot down, maliciously, a successful citizen."

However, when another newspaper revealed the man's past, the *Rocky Mountain News* reversed itself and published a lengthy piece of its own. Why? The newspaper that broke the story had suggested that *News* editors knew about the man's past and decided to protect him as a fellow member of the journalistic fraternity. *News* editors denied that their motivation was to protect the man. To prove it, they reversed their decision and published a story on him. The *News* explained its change of mind by saying that the situation had changed. *News* editors, concerned that their newspaper's credibility had been challenged, felt that printing a story would set that straight. Of less concern, suddenly, was that the story would titillate morbid curiosity or contribute to the destruction of a successful citizen. It was a classic case of situational ethics.

Flip-flops on moral issues, such as happened at the *Rocky Mountain News*, bother critics of situational ethics. The critics say decisions should be based on deeply rooted moral principles—not immediate, transient facts or changing peripheral contexts.

ETHICS AND OTHER ISSUES

STUDY PREVIEW   Right and wrong are issues in both ethics and law, but they are different issues. Obedience to law, or even to professional codes of ethics, will not always lead to moral action. There are also times when practical issues can enter moral decisions.

DIFFERENTIATING ETHICS AND LAW

TEACHING OBJECTIVE 17-4
Ethics not same as law, prudence or accepted practices.

Ethics is an individual matter that relates closely to conscience. Because conscience is unique to each individual, no two people have exactly the same moral framework. There are, however, issues about which there is consensus. No right-minded person condones murder, for example. When there is a universal feeling, ethics becomes codified in law, but laws do not address all moral questions. It is the issues of right and wrong that do not have a consensus that make ethics difficult. Was it morally right for *USA Today* to initiate coverage of Arthur Ashe's AIDS?

Ethics and law are related but separate. The law will allow a mass media practitioner to do many things that the practitioner would refuse to do. Since the 1964 *New York Times* v. *Sullivan* case, the U.S. Supreme Court has allowed the news media to cause tremendous damage to public officials, even with false information. However, rare is the journalist who would intentionally push the Sullivan latitudes to their limits to pillory a public official.

Images of Grief. After a Vietnamese husband and wife, parents of five children, were shot in a gangland slaying, photographer Eric Luse of the San Francisco *Chronicle* was assigned to the funeral. As the couple's oldest daughter came out of the services clutching her mother's photograph, Luse took this picture. Because the funeral procession was on a public street, there was no legal issue, but intrusions into private moments can also be an ethics issue. Typical of how views are divided on many ethics issues, media people saw this photo two ways. The *Chronicle* decided against running the picture on grounds that it was "very intrusive," but judges in the World Press Photo contest gave it first place. In the Picture of the Year contest, it placed third.

The ethics decisions of an individual mass media practitioner usually are more limiting than the law. There are times, though, when a journalist may choose to break the law on the grounds of ethics. Applying John Stuart Mill's principle of "the greatest good," a radio reporter might choose to break the speed limit to reach a chemical plant where an accident is threatening to send a deadly cloud toward where her listeners live. Breaking a speed limit may seem petty, but it demonstrates that obeying the law and obeying one's conscience do not always coincide.

ACCEPTED PRACTICES

Just as there is not a reliable correlation between law and ethics, neither is there one between accepted media practices and ethics. What is acceptable at one advertising agency to make a product look good in photographs might be unacceptable at another. Even universally accepted practices should not go unexamined, for unless accepted practices are examined and reconsidered on a continuing basis, media practitioners can come to rely more on habit than on principles in their work.

PRUDENCE AND ETHICS

Prudence is the application of wisdom in a practical situation. It can be a leveling factor in moral questions. Consider the case of Irvin Lieberman, who had built his *Main Line Chronicle* and several other weeklies in the Philadelphia suburbs into aggressive, journalistically excellent newspapers. After being hit with nine libel suits, all costly to defend, Lieberman abandoned the editorial thrust of his newspapers. "I decided not to do any investigative work," he said. "It was a matter of either feeding my family or spending my whole life in court." Out of prudence, Lieberman decided to abandon his commitment to hard-hitting, effective journalism.

Courageous pursuit of morally lofty ends can, as a practical matter, be foolish. Whether Irvin Leiberman was exhibiting a moral weakness by bending to the chilling factor of libel suits, which are costly to fight, or being prudent is an issue that could be debated forever. The point, however, is that prudence cannot be ignored as a factor in moral decisions.

- -

UNSETTLED, UNSETTLING ISSUES

STUDY PREVIEW   When mass media people discuss ethics, they talk about right and wrong behavior, but creating policies on ethics issues is not easy. Many standard media practices press the line between right and wrong, which muddies clear-cut standards that are universally applicable and recognized. There is further muddiness because many ethics codes confuse unethical behavior and behavior that may appear unethical but that is not necessarily so.

PLAGIARISM

In 1988, Chicago *Tribune* editors became concerned after running a story from their Jerusalem correspondent and then discovering that some passages were incredibly similar to a story that was printed in the Jerusalem *Post* a few days earlier.

TEACHING OBJECTIVE 17-5
Some media practices inconsistent with moral principles.

Compare these passages:

The injured can be found in many homes, as well—men, women and children bearing bruises, fractures and bandaged limbs, the victims of Israeli gunfire, beatings, rubber bullets, and tear gas inhalation.

—Chicago *Tribune*

The injured can be seen in many homes: young and older men and even children with bruises and fractures, women with black and blue marks and bandaged arms—victims of beatings, rubber bullets, tear gas inhalation and sometimes gunfire.

—Jerusalem *Post*

The *Tribune's* Jerusalem correspondent resigned. Some newspapers fire writers who pass off other people's work as their own. Commoner, though, is simply reassigning an offending writer to a low-visibility job on the copy desk or doing nothing at all. Although many journalists talk firmly about plagiarism as unethical, the issue is not simple. The fact is that standard journalistic practices encourage a lot of "borrowing," which complicates drawing clear lines. Among factors that make journalists uncomfortable when pressed hard on plagiary questions are:

- Institutionalized exchanging of stories.
- The role of public relations in generating news stories.
- Monitoring the competition.
- Subliminal memory and innocent recall.

SWAPPING STORIES.   Some creative work, like scholarship, requires that information and ideas be attributed to their sources. Journalists are not so strict, as shown by story swapping through the Associated Press. The AP picks up stories from its members and distributes them to other members, generally without any reference to the source. Some AP publications and broadcasters do not even acknowledge AP as the intermediary.

Conditioned by 150 years of the AP's being a journalistic model and under pressure to gather information quickly, many journalists have a high tolerance for "borrowing." When the Chicago *Tribune* was apologizing for its cribbed Jerusalem story, for example, one of the writer's colleagues defended the story: "Everybody rewrites the Jerusalem *Post.* That's how foreign correspondents work."

Incredible as it seems, journalistic tolerance for plagiarism even allows radio stations to pirate the local newspaper for newscasts. Sometimes you can hear the announcer turning the pages. A sad joke that acknowledges this practice is that some stations buy their news at 50 cents a copy, which is cheaper than hiring reporters to cover the community. So pervasive is the journalistic tolerance for "borrowing" that few newspapers even mildly protest when their stories are pirated.

NEWS RELEASES.   In many newsrooms, the plagiarism question is clouded further by the practice of using news releases from public relations people word for word without citing the source. Even in newsrooms that rewrite releases to avoid the embarrassment of running a story that is exactly the same as the competition's, it is standard practice not to cite the source. Public relations people, who are paid for writing favorable stories on their clients, have no objections to being plagiarized, and news organizations find it an easy, inexpensive way to fill space. Despite the mutual convenience, the arrangement raises serious questions of ethics to which many in the media have not responded. The practice leaves the false impression that stories originating with news releases actually originated with the news organization. More serious is that the uncredited stories are a disservice to democracy. Marie Dunn White, in the *Journal of Mass Media Ethics*, wrote: "In order for the reader to evaluate the information he or she is receiving correctly and completely, he or she must know which information came from a press release and, therefore, may be biased."

MONITORING COMPETITION.　Competitive pressure also contributes to fuzziness on the plagiarism issue. To avoid being skunked on stories, reporters monitor each other closely to pick up tips and ideas. Generally, reporters are not particular about where they pick up information as long as they are confident that it is accurate. For background, reporters tap newsroom libraries, databases, journals, books and other sources, and, in the interest of not cluttering their stories, they do not use footnotes.

SUBLIMINAL MEMORY.　Covering breaking events has its own pressure that puts journalists at special risk. Almost every journalist who writes under the pressure of a deadline has had the experience of writing a story and later discovering that phrases that came easily at the keyboard were actually somebody else's. In their voracious pursuit of information, reporters store phrases and perhaps whole passages subliminally in their memories. This happened to a drama critic at the St. Paul, Minnesota, *Pioneer Press Dispatch*, who was horrified when a reader pointed out the similarity between his review of a play and an earlier review of the same play in the New York *Times*. Once aware of what he had done unwittingly, the critic offered his resignation. His editors instead moved him to the copy desk.

The muddiness on the issue of journalistic plagiarism is encapsulated in the fact that the Society of Professional Journalists' ethics code makes a flat statement that plagiarism is "dishonest and unacceptable," but then sidesteps the knotty part of the issue by declining to define "plagiarism."

MISREPRESENTATION

Janet Cooke's meteoric rise at the Washington *Post* unraveled quickly the day after she received a Pulitzer Prize. Her editors had been so impressed with her story, "Jimmy's World," about a child who was addicted to heroin, that they nominated it for a Pulitzer Prize. The gripping tale began: "Jimmy is 8 years old and a third-generation heroin addict, a precocious little boy with sandy hair, velvety brown eyes and needle marks freckling the baby-smooth skin of his thin brown arms." Janet Cooke claimed that she had won the confidence of Jimmy's mother and her live-in man friend, a drug dealer, to do the story. Cooke said she had promised not to reveal their identities as a condition for her access to Jimmy.

The story, played on the front page, so shocked Washington that people demanded that Jimmy be taken away from his mother and placed in a foster home. The *Post* declined to help authorities, citing Cooke's promise of confidentiality to her sources. The mayor ordered the police to find Jimmy with or without the newspaper's help, and millions of dollars in police resources went into a door-to-door search. After 17 days, the police gave up knocking on doors for tips on Jimmy. Some doubts emerged at the *Post* about the story, but the newspaper stood behind its reporter.

KEY PERSON
Janet Cooke a classic misrepresentation case.

Manipulating Data. These June 27, 1994, magazine covers were based on the same Los Angeles police mug shot, but O. J. Simpson's facial tones were manipulated at *Time* to appear flatter and darker. *Time* artist Matt Mahurin also enclosed Simpson in a grayish box. Critics said this was prejudicial. *Time*'s defenders said Mahurin did what he did to tell the story better. They said the photo illustration stripped away Simpson's aura, as did the new murder charges against him. Since the beginning of photography, artists have adjusted light and other variables, both on-site and in the darkroom, to create the effect they wish. Today, new electronic tools make manipulation easier, and the question has become: How far should the news media go in adjusting photographs to capture the mood and ambiance of a story?

Janet Cooke, 25 when she was hired by the *Post*, had extraordinary credentials. Her résumé showed a baccalaureate degree, magna cum laude, from Vassar; study at the Sorbonne in Paris; a master's degree from the University of Toledo; abilities in several languages; and two years of journalistic experience with the Toledo *Blade*. Said Ben Bradlee, editor of the *Post*, "She had it all. She was bright. She was well-spoken. She was pretty. She wrote well." She was black, which made her especially attractive to the *Post*, which was working to bring the percentage of black staff reporters nearer to the percentage of blacks in its circulation area.

"Jimmy's World" was published in September 1980. Six months later, the Pulitzer committee announced its decision and issued a biographical sheet on Janet Cooke. The Associated Press, trying to flesh out the biographical information, spotted discrepancies right away. Janet Cooke, it turned out, had attended

Vassar one year but had not been graduated with the honors she claimed. The University of Toledo had no record of awarding her a master's. Suddenly, doubts that had surfaced in the days immediately after "Jimmy's World" was published took on a new intensity. The editors sat Cooke down and grilled her on the claims on which she was hired. No, she admitted, she was not multilingual. The Sorbonne claim was fuzzy. More importantly, they grilled her on whether there was really a Jimmy. The interrogation continued into the night, and finally Janet Cooke confessed all: There were no confidential sources, and there was no Jimmy. She had fabricated the story. She resigned, and the *Post*, terribly embarrassed, returned the Pulitzer.

In cases of outright fabrication, as in "Jimmy's World," it is easy to identify the lapses in ethics. When Janet Cooke emerged briefly from seclusion to explain herself, she said that she was responding to pressures in the *Post* newsroom to produce flashy, sensational copy. Most people found the explanation unsatisfying, considering the pattern of deception that went back to her falsified résumé.

There are misrepresentations, however, that are not as clearly unacceptable. Much debated are:

STAGING NEWS.   To attract favorable attention to their clients, public relations people organize *media events*. These are designed to be irresistible to journalists. Rallies and demonstrations on topical issues, for example, find their way onto front pages, magazine covers and evening newscasts because their photogenic qualities give them an edge over less visual although sometimes more significant

Rigged Explosion. To illustrate a story on vehicle safety, NBC "Dateline" showed a General Motors pickup truck exploding in a collision. Not told to viewers was that the explosion had been rigged for the cameras. The misrepresentation came to light when GM filed a suit, claiming it had been wrongly damaged. For most media people, the issue was one of ethics more than law. The misrepresentation in the re-creation violated the trust that the network had cultivated for its news. After an internal investigation, changes were ordered in the "Dateline" staff, and NBC News Vice President Michael Gartner soon found himself out of a job. Also, besides apologizing to GM, which then withdrew its suit, NBC apologized to its viewers.

Appearances and Ethics

Would you consider working for a mass media organization with policies like these?

The Milwaukee *Journal* insists that staff members avoid financial investments that "could conflict with the *Journal*'s ability to report the news or that create the impression of such a conflict." Is the *Journal*, in order to protect its credibility, reasonable in barring employees from investing their own money in companies being covered in the news? Is the policy a sign of distrust in the judgment of the newspaper's employees? Is the *Journal* intruding in the private affairs of its employees?

The New York *Times* declined to participate in the National News Council, which was established to review public complaints about news coverage and to issue statements after reviewing the facts. The council's goal was to encourage responsible reporting. The *Times* said it would not be a party to a constituted entity, like the news council, that set itself up as a jury, because that would erode the newspaper's journalistic autonomy.

The Manhattan, Kansas, *Mercury* prohibits staff members from holding public office or accepting a paid political appointment, saying, "We must not give any person reason to suspect that our handling of a story, editorial or picture is related in any way to political activity by a staff member." Is this a justified restriction on a citizen's right to participate in civic activities? If so, what is the justification? Is it wrongful action or merely the possible appearance thereof? Is there another side to the issue?

The Philadelphia *Inquirer* has a ban on "business-connected gifts or gratuities," yet makes an exception for gifts of token value, such as a calendar, pencil or key chain. The *Inquirer* explains the exceptions to its policy by saying that many gifts of insignificant value would be awkward to send back. Do the exceptions undermine principles that the *Inquirer* is trying to uphold? Are they reasonable exceptions? Why do you imagine that the *Inquirer* insists that bottles of liquor and wine are specifically excluded as token gifts?

---

events. The ethics question is less important for publicists, who generally are upfront about what they are doing. The ethics question is more serious for journalists, who claim that their job is to present an accurate, balanced account of a day's events but who regularly overplay staged events that are designed by publicists to be photogenic and easy to cover.

RE-CREATIONS.   A wave of *reality programs* on television that began in the late 1980s featured reenactments that were not always labeled as such. Philip Weiss, writing in *Columbia Journalism Review*, offered this litany: shadows on the wall of a woman taking a hammer to her husband, a faceless actor grabbing a tin of kerosene to blow up his son, a corpse in a wheelbarrow with a hand dangling, a detective opening the trunk of a car and reeling from the smell of a decomposing body. While mixing re-creations with strictly news footage rankles many critics, others argue that it helps people understand the situation. The same question arises with *docudramas*, which mix actual events and dramatic re-creations.

SELECTIVE EDITING.   The editing process, by its nature, requires journalists to make decisions on what is most worth emphasizing and what is least worth even including. In this sense, all editing is selective, but the term "selective editing" refers to making decisions with the goal of distorting. Selective editing can occur in drama too, when writers, editors and other media people take literary license too far and intentionally misrepresent.

FICTIONAL METHODS.   In the late 1960s, many experiments in media portrayals of people and issues came to be called the *New Journalism*. The term was hard to define because it included so many approaches. Among the most controversial were applications of fiction-writing methods on topical issues, an approach widely accepted in book publishing but suddenly controversial when it appeared in the news media. Character development became more important than before, including presumed insights into the thinking of people being covered. The view of the writer became an essential element in much of this reporting. The defense for these approaches was that traditional, facts-only reporting could not approach complex truths that merited journalistic explorations. The profound ethics questions that these approaches posed were usually mitigated by clear statements about what the writer was attempting. Nonetheless, it was a controversial approach to the issues of the day. There was no defense when the fictional approach was complete fabrication passing itself off as reality, as in "Jimmy's World."

GIFTS, JUNKETS AND MEALS

In his 1919 book *The Brass Check*, a pioneer examination of newsroom ethics, *Upton Sinclair* told how news people took bribes to put stories in the paper. Today, media ethics codes universally condemn gifts and certainly bribes, but there still are many people who curry favor with the mass media through gifts, such as a college sports information director who gives a fifth of whisky at Christmas to a sports writer as a gesture of goodwill. Favors can take many forms: media-appreciation luncheons, free trips abroad for the experience necessary to do a travel article, season passes to cover the opera, discounts at certain stores.

Despite the consistent exhortation of the ethics codes against gifts, favors, free travel and special treatment and privileges, there is nothing inherently wrong in taking them if they do not influence coverage and if the journalist's benefactor understands that. The problem with favors is more a practical one than one of ethics. Taking a favor *may or may not be bad*, but it *looks bad*. Many ethics codes do not make this important distinction. One that does is the code of the Associated Press Managing Editors, which states: "Journalists must avoid impropriety and *the appearance of impropriety* as well as any conflict of interest or *the appearance of conflict.*

They should neither accept anything nor pursue any activity that might compromise or *seem to compromise* their integrity." The APME admonitions at least recognize the distinction between the inherent wrongness of impropriety, which is an ethics question, and the perception that something may be wrong, which is an unwise perception to encourage but which is not necessarily unethical.

While ethics codes are uniform against *freebies*, as gifts and favors are called, many news organizations accept free movie, drama, concert and other tickets, as well as recordings, books and other materials for review. The justification usually is that their budgets allow them to review only materials that arrive free and that their audiences would be denied reviews if the materials had to be purchased. A counterargument is that a news organization that cannot afford to do business right should not be in business. Many news organizations, however, insist on buying tickets for their reporters to beauty pageants, sports events and other things to which there is an admission fee. A frequent exception occurs when a press box or special media facility is available. With recordings, books and free samples, some media organizations return them or pass them on to charity to avoid any appearance that they have been bought off.

When junkets are proposed, some organizations send reporters only if they can pay the fare and other expenses. The Louisville *Courier-Journal* is firm: "Even on chartered trips, such as accompanying a sports team, or hitchhiking on a State Police plane, we insist on being billed for our pro-rata share of the expense." An exception is made by some news organizations for trips that they could not possibly arrange on their own, such as covering a two-week naval exercise aboard a ship.

Some media organizations address the issue of impropriety by acknowledging favors. Many quiz shows say that "promotional consideration" has been provided to companies that give them travel, lodging and prizes. Just as forthright are publications that state that reviews are made possible through season passes or free samples. Acknowledging favors does not remove the questions but at least it is up-front.

CHAPTER WRAP-UP

Mass media people need to be concerned about ethics because they can have powerful effects. But answers do not come easily. Personal information can embarrass a person inexcusably. However, it can be argued that privacy is less important, for example, with candidates for high office.

Philosophers have devised numerous systems to help individuals address moral issues. Influential is John Stuart Mill's utilitarianism, which favors choices that lead to the greatest good for the most people. Mill's reasoning was implicit when some media people defended their coverage of Gary Hart by saying that choosing a president of high moral character overrode the discomfort that intense coverage caused an individual. Other moral principles favor more respect for individual privacy.

Moral decision making is rooted in conscience, which makes it highly individual. Attempts to bring order to moral issues in journalism and the mass media have included codes of ethics. These codes identify behaviors that are recognized as ethically troublesome, but because they are generalized statements, the codes cannot anticipate all situations. There is no substitute for human reason and common sense.

QUESTIONS FOR REVIEW

1. Why cannot ethics codes anticipate all moral questions? And does this limit the value of codes for mass media people?

2. List and explain moral principles that mass media people can use to sort through ethics questions.

3. How can mass media people come to different conclusions depending on whether they use process-based or outcome-based ethics?

4. Is ethics the same as law? As prudence? As accepted practices?

5. Discuss dubious mass media practices that are inconsistent with many moral principles.

QUESTIONS FOR CRITICAL THINKING

1. The Manchester, New Hampshire, *Union Leader* has been criticized for giving more space to some candidates than to others in presidential primaries. Is this disparity necessarily a sign of unfair coverage?

2. How are traditional libertarians deontological in their approach to ethics? How is the social responsibility approach teleological?

3. As someone who reads newspapers and watches newscasts, would you favor deontological or teleological ethics? Which is easier? Which system do you think most journalists prefer?

4. Can you identify the ethics principle or system most associated with Aristotle? Immanuel Kant? John Stuart Mill? John Dewey? John Rawls? Robert Maynard Hutchins?

5. How can codes of ethics help mass media people make the right decisions? Do codes always work? Why or why not?

6. A candidate for mayor tells a news reporter that the incumbent mayor is in cahoots with organized crime. What should the reporter do before going on the air with this bombshell accusation? Why?

7. Can media people ever defend breaking the law as ethical?

8. Is there a difference between ethics and accepted practices?

FOR FURTHER LEARNING

Clifford G. Christians, Kim B. Rotzoll and Mark Fackler. *Media Ethics*, 2nd ed. (Longman, 1987). These scholars are especially good at describing Kant's categorical imperative and other philosophical systems on which media ethics can be based.

Roy Peter Clark. "The Original Sin: How Plagiarism Poisons the Press," *Washington Journalism Review* (March 1983), 43–47.

Carl Hausman. *The Decision-Making Process in Journalism* (Nelson-Hall, 1990). Hausman, a journalism professor, provides a checklist to help sort the way through ethics problems.

Walter B. Jaehnig. "Harrison Cochran—The Publisher with a Past," *Journal of Mass Media Ethics* 2 (Fall/Winter 1986–87):1, 80–88. This is a case study examination of the *Rocky Mountain News* situational ethics case. Every issue of this journal contains a media ethics problem with commentary from professional and scholarly observers.

Janet Malcolm. *The Journalist and the Murderer* (Knopf, 1990). Malcolm argues that journalists exploit their sources of information, using the relationship of author Joe McGinniss and a convicted murderer for the book *Fatal Vision*.

John C. Merrill. *The Dialectic in Journalism: Toward a Responsible Use of Press Freedom* (Louisiana State University Press, 1990). Professor Merrill, who has written several books on journalism ethics, favors philosophical frameworks for solving ethics questions rather than codes of ethics.

Phillip Weiss. "Bad Rap for TV Tabs," *Columbia Journalism Review* 28 (May/June 1989):1, 39–42. Weiss deals with ethics questions raised by tabloid television programs, including dramatized re-creations.

Marie Dunn White. "Plagiarism and the News Media," *Journal of Mass Media Ethics* 4 (1989):2, 265–280. White examines the hazards when journalists read their competitors for story ideas and information.

FOR KEEPING UP TO DATE

Ethicists sort through moral dilemmas involving mass communication in the scholarly *Journal of Mass Media Ethics*.

Many trade and professional journals also deal with media ethics, including *Quill, Columbia Journalism Review* and *American Journalism Review*.

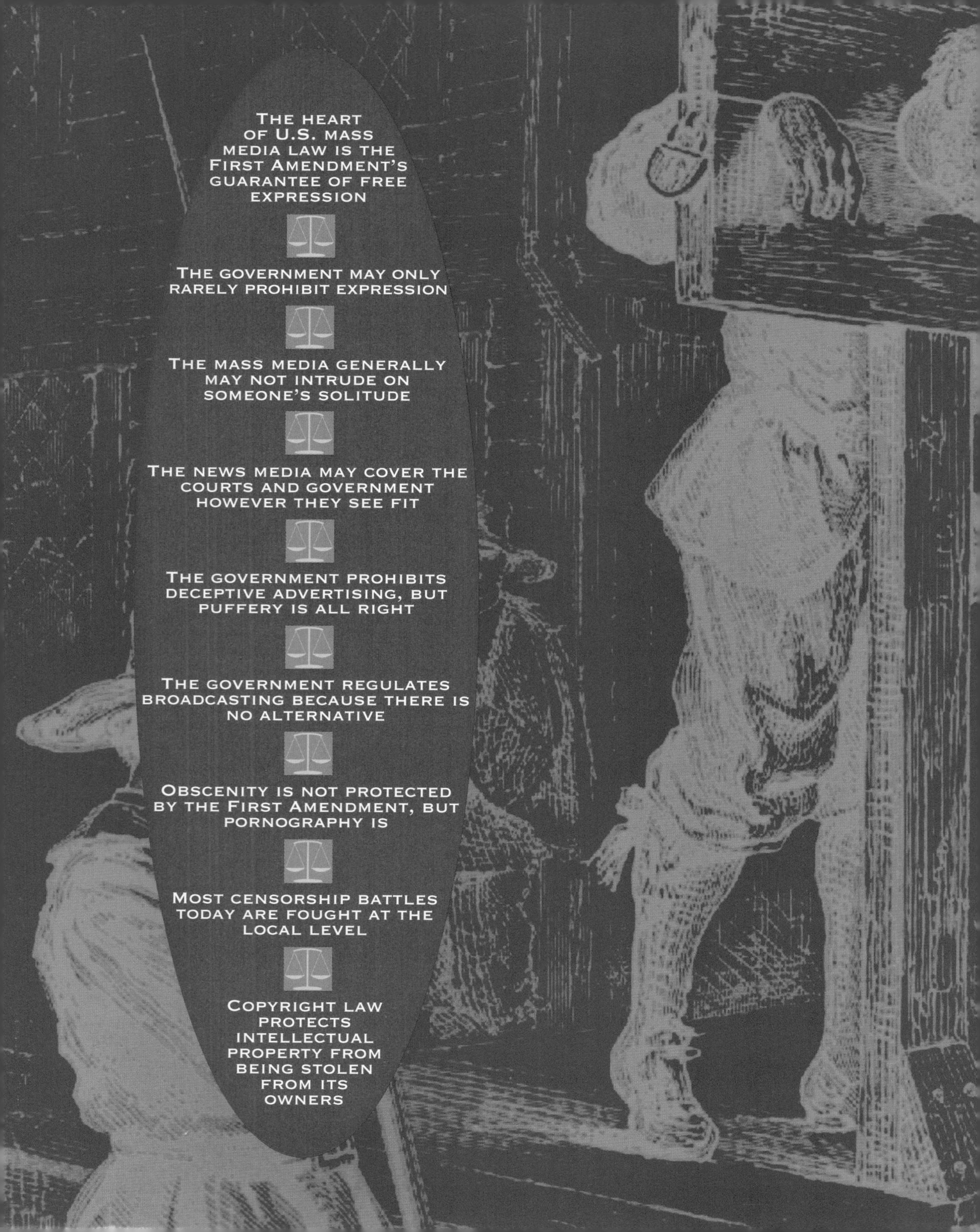

THE HEART
OF U.S. MASS
MEDIA LAW IS THE
FIRST AMENDMENT'S
GUARANTEE OF FREE
EXPRESSION

THE GOVERNMENT MAY ONLY
RARELY PROHIBIT EXPRESSION

THE MASS MEDIA GENERALLY
MAY NOT INTRUDE ON
SOMEONE'S SOLITUDE

THE NEWS MEDIA MAY COVER THE
COURTS AND GOVERNMENT
HOWEVER THEY SEE FIT

THE GOVERNMENT PROHIBITS
DECEPTIVE ADVERTISING, BUT
PUFFERY IS ALL RIGHT

THE GOVERNMENT REGULATES
BROADCASTING BECAUSE THERE IS
NO ALTERNATIVE

OBSCENITY IS NOT PROTECTED
BY THE FIRST AMENDMENT, BUT
PORNOGRAPHY IS

MOST CENSORSHIP BATTLES
TODAY ARE FOUGHT AT THE
LOCAL LEVEL

COPYRIGHT LAW
PROTECTS
INTELLECTUAL
PROPERTY FROM
BEING STOLEN
FROM ITS
OWNERS

chapter 18

MASS MEDIA LAW

Everybody in Cleveland was talking about the brutal slaying of Marilyn Sheppard. The wife of a prominent Cleveland osteopath, pregnant at the time, had been bludgeoned to death in their upscale home. Her husband told police he had struggled with an intruder, who knocked him out. When he regained consciousness, his wife was dead.

Then it was discovered that Sheppard was involved with a younger woman. The headlines were provocative: "Love Secrets Barred." Then came Page One editorials. Under one headline, "Quit Stalling and Bring Him In," the Cleveland *Press* accused investigators of being soft on Sheppard because of his social standing.

Every day the case became more of a media circus. The inquest was held in a gymnasium to accommodate the oversize crowd. It was broadcast live. Radio stations carried debates on Sheppard's guilt. Newspapers speculated that Marilyn Sheppard lived in fear of her husband. When Sheppard was arrested, hundreds of excited people were there to witness him being brought in.

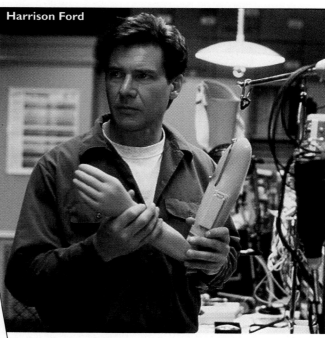

David Jansson

Harrison Ford

Fair Trial? Hyped news coverage that led to the murder conviction of Cleveland osteopath Sam Sheppard resulted in an important 1966 U.S. Supreme Court ruling on fair trials. The Supreme Court said it is the job of judges, not the media, to ensure a fair trial. In a second trial, Sheppard was exonerated. The injustice of the case inspired the long-running television series "The Fugitive" starring David Janssen and later the movie starring Harrison Ford.

Newspapers printed the names of potential jurors, who then were inundated with calls from people who had formed opinions on the case. During the trial, jurors had access to stories about Sheppard's "fiery temper" and a detective's claim that Sheppard was a "bare-faced liar." Two jurors heard a radio story that a woman in New York claimed that Sheppard fathered her child.

The case was a classic constitutional conflict: The First Amendment assures a free press, which would seem to allow even excessive coverage, and the Sixth Amendment assures a fair trial. Considering the media-stirred hysteria, could jurors be found who could block out what they knew from the media and consider the evidence dispassionately?

Sam Sheppard was convicted and sentenced to life. He appealed, and the U.S. Supreme Court ordered a new trial. In this second trial, Sheppard was acquitted. While critical of the media at the original trial, the Supreme Court said the coverage was protected by the First Amendment. The responsibility for a fair trial, the Court said, fell to the courts—not the news media. The decision was a victory for the First

Amendment, settling a fundamental issue in the free press vs. fair trial controversy. Judicial supervision, said the court, could have precluded a "carnival atmosphere."

The Sheppard case, on which the television series "The Fugitive" was modeled, as was the 1993 movie of the same name, illustrates just one fascinating issue in mass media law. In this chapter you will read about other First Amendment and media law issues as well.

THE U.S. CONSTITUTION

STUDY PREVIEW The First Amendment to the Constitution guarantees freedom of expression, including expression in the mass media, or so it seems. However, for the first 134 years of the amendment's existence, it appeared that the states could ignore the federal constitution and put their own restrictions on free expression because it did not apply to them.

FIRST AMENDMENT

The legal foundation for free expression in the United States is the *First Amendment* to the Constitution. The amendment, penned by *James Madison*, boiled down the eloquence of Benjamin Franklin, Thomas Jefferson and earlier libertarian thinkers during the American colonial experience to a mere 45 words: "Congress shall make no law respecting an establishment of religion, or prohibiting the free exercise thereof; or *abridging the freedom of speech, or of the press;* or of the right of the people peaceably to assemble, and to petition the Government for a redress of grievances."

The amendment, which became part of the Constitution in 1791, seemed a definitive statement that set the United States apart from all other nations at the time in guaranteeing free expression. It turned out, however, that the First Amendment did not settle all the questions that could be raised about free expression. This chapter looks at many of these unsettled issues and attempts to clarify them.

TEACHING OBJECTIVE 18-1
Free expression is central in U.S. media law.

KEY PERSON
James Madison.

SCOPE OF FIRST AMENDMENT

The First Amendment explicitly prohibited only Congress from limiting free expression, but there was never a serious legal question that it applied also to the executive branch of the national government. There was a question, however, about whether the First Amendment prohibited the states from squelching free expression.

From the early days of the republic, many states had laws that limited free expression, and nobody seemed to mind much. In fact, all the way through the 1800s the First Amendment seemed largely ignored. Not until 1925, when the U.S. Supreme Court considered the case of *Benjamin Gitlow*, was the First Amendment applied to the states. In this case, Gitlow, a small-time New York agitator, rankled authorities by publishing his "Left Wing Manifesto" and distributing a socialist paper. He was arrested and convicted of violating a state law that forbade advocating "criminal anarchy." Gitlow appealed that the First Amendment to the U.S. Constitution should override any state law that contravenes it, and the U.S. Supreme Court agreed. Gitlow, by the way, lost his appeal on other grounds. Even so, his case was a significant clarification of the scope of the First Amendment.

KEY PERSON
Benjamin Gitlow.

PRIOR RESTRAINT

STUDY PREVIEW   When the government heads off an utterance before it is made, it is engaging in *prior restraint*. In the 20th century, the U.S. Supreme Court has consistently found that prior restraint violates the First Amendment. At the same time, the Court says there may be circumstances, although rare, in which the public good would justify such censorship.

PUBLIC NUISANCES

TEACHING OBJECTIVE 18-2
First Amendment bars government generally from infringing free expression.

KEY PEOPLE
Jay Near and Howard Guilford.

KEY PERSON
Robert McCormick.

KEY PERSON
Charles Evans Hughes.

The U.S. Supreme Court was still finding its voice on First Amendment issues when a Minnesota case came to its attention. The Minnesota Legislature had created a "public nuisance" law that allowed authorities to shut down "obnoxious" newspapers. The legislature's rationale was that government has the right to remove things that work against the common good: Just as a community can remove obnoxious weeds, so can it remove obnoxious "rags." In 1927 in Minneapolis, authorities used the law to padlock the *Saturday Press*, a feisty weekly owned by *Jay Near* and *Howard Guilford*.

Most right-minded people would agree that the *Saturday Press* was obnoxious, especially its racist hate-mongering. Other people, however, including publisher *Robert McCormick* of the Chicago *Tribune* and the fledgling American Civil Liberties Union, saw another issue. To their thinking, the First Amendment protected all expression, regardless of how obnoxious it was. They also were bothered that government, in this case the county prosecutor, was the determiner of what was obnoxious.

Three and one-half years after the *Saturday Press* was silenced, the U.S. Supreme Court, in a 5-4 decision, threw out the Minnesota law. The Court ruled that *prior restraint*, prohibiting expression before it is made, was disallowed under the U.S. Constitution. Said Chief Justice *Charles Evans Hughes:* "The fact that the liberty of the press may be abused by miscreant purveyors of scandal does not make any less the immunity of the press from previous restraint in dealing with official misconduct."

The decision was a landmark limitation on governmental censorship, although the Court noted, as it always does in such cases, that protection for the press "is not absolutely unlimited." The Court has always noted that it can conceive of circumstances, such as a national emergency, when prior restraint might be justified.

NATIONAL SECURITY

LECTURE RESOURCE 18-A
Slides: *Pentagon Papers.*

KEY PERSON
Daniel Ellsberg.

The U.S. Supreme Court, which is the ultimate interpreter on constitutional questions, has been consistent that government has a censorship right when national security is at stake. This position was underscored in the Pentagon Papers case. A government contract researcher, *Daniel Ellsberg,* spent several years with a team preparing an internal Pentagon study on U.S. policy in Vietnam. In 1971, at the height of the war, Ellsberg decided that the public should have an inside look at Pentagon decision making. He secretly photocopied the whole 47-volume study, even though it was stamped "top secret," and handed it over to the New York *Times.* After several weeks, the *Times* began a front-page series drawn from the Pentagon Papers. Saying that the study could hurt national security, but also knowing that it could embarrass the government, the Nixon administration ordered the *Times* to stop the series.

NEW YORK, SUNDAY, JUNE 13, 1971
75¢ beyond 50-mile zone from New York City, except Long Island. Higher in air delivery cities.

Vietnam Archive: Pentagon Study Traces 3 Decades of Growing U. S. Involvement

By NEIL SHEEHAN

A massive study of how the United States went to war in Indochina, conducted by the Pentagon three years ago, demonstrates that four administrations progressively developed a sense of commitment to a non-Communist Vietnam, a readiness to fight the North to protect the South, and an ultimate frustration with this effort—to a much greater extent than their public statements acknowledged at the time.

The 3,000-page analysis, to which 4,000 pages of official documents are appended, was commissioned by Secretary of Defense Robert S. McNamara and covers the American involvement in Southeast Asia from World War II to mid-1968—the start of the peace talks in Paris after President Lyndon B. Johnson had set a limit on further military commitments and revealed his intention to retire. Most of the study and many of the appended documents have been obtained by The New York Times and will be described and presented in a series of articles beginning today.

> Three pages of documentary material from the Pentagon study begin on Page 35.

Though far from a complete history, even at 2.5 million words, the study forms a great archive of government decision-making on Indochina over three decades. The study led its 30 to 40 authors and researchers to many broad conclusions and specific findings, including the following:

¶That the Truman Administration's decision to give military aid to France in her colonial war against the Communist-led Vietminh "directly involved" the United States in Vietnam and "set" the course of American policy.

¶That the Eisenhower Administration's decision to rescue a fledgling South Vietnam from a Communist takeover and attempt to undermine the new Communist regime of North Vietnam gave the Administration a "direct role in the ultimate breakdown of the Geneva settlement" for Indochina in 1954.

¶That the Kennedy Administration, though ultimately spared from major escalation decisions by the death of its leader, transformed a policy of "limited-risk gamble," which it inherited, into a "broad commitment" that left President Johnson with a choice between more war and withdrawal.

¶That the Johnson Administration, though the President was reluctant and hesitant to take the final decisions, intensified the covert warfare against North Vietnam and began planning in the spring of 1964 to wage overt war, a full year before it publicly revealed the depth of its involvement and its fear of defeat.

¶That this campaign of growing clandestine military pressure through 1964 and the expanding program of bombing North Vietnam in 1965 were begun despite the judgment of the Government's intelligence community that the measures would not cause Hanoi to cease its support of the Vietcong insurgency in the South, and that the bombing was

Continued on Page 38, Col. 1

The *Times* objected that the government was attempting prior restraint but agreed to suspend the series while it appealed the government order. Meanwhile, the Washington *Post* somehow obtained a second copy of the Pentagon Papers and began its own series, to which the government also objected. Before the U.S. Supreme Court, the government argument that national security was at stake proved weak, and the *Times* and the *Post* resumed their series. So did dozens of other newspapers, and the Pentagon Papers eventually were published in their entirety and sold at bookstores throughout the land.

Despite the journalistic victory in the Pentagon Papers case, the court said that it could conceive of circumstances in which the national security could override the First Amendment guarantees against prior restraint. In earlier cases, justices had said that the government would be on solid ground to restrain reports on troop movements and other military activities in wartime if the reports constituted "a clear and present danger."

MILITARY OPERATIONS

At times the United States has employed battlefield censorship, requiring correspondents to submit their copy for review before transmission. This practice was discarded by the time of the Vietnam War, but it appeared in a variant form in 1983 when the Reagan administration ordered troops to the Caribbean island of Grenada. The Pentagon, which controlled all transportation to the battle area, refused to take reporters along. A few print reporters rented yachts and airplanes

MEDIA: PEOPLE

Jay Near

Jay Near and Howard Guilford, who started a scandal sheet in Minneapolis in 1927, did not have far to look for stories on corruption. Prohibition was in effect, and Minneapolis, because of geography, was a key American distribution point for bootleg Canadian whiskey going south to Chicago, St. Louis and other cities. A former county prosecutor was knee-deep in the illicit whiskey trade. Mose Barnett, the leading local gangster, never needed an appointment with the police chief. He could walk into the chief's office any time. The mayor was on the take. A standard joke was that city hall had been moved to McCormick's Cafe, notorious for its payoff activity. Gambling, prostitution and booze palaces flourished in blatant violation of the law. Mobsters extorted protection payments from local merchants. Contract murder went for $500, on slow days $200.

Hearing about the kind of newspaper that Near and Guilford had in mind, the crooked police chief, aware of his own vulnerability, told his men to yank every copy off the newsstands as soon as they appeared. *The Saturday Press* thus became the first American newspaper banned even before a single issue had been published.

The confrontation between the corrupt Minneapolis establishment and the Near-Guilford scandal-mongering team worsened. One afternoon a few days after the first issue, gunmen pulled up beside Guilford's car at an intersection and fired four bullets at him, one into his abdomen. Not even that silenced *The Saturday Press*. While Guilford lay critically wounded in the hospital, Near stepped up their crusade, pointing out that mob kingpin Mose Barnett had threatened Guilford before the attack. Near also went after Barnett for ordering thugs to terrorize an immigrant launderer who had bought his own dry cleaning equipment rather than send his customers' laundry to a mob-controlled plant.

Near's other targets included the mayor, the police chief, the head of the law enforcement league, the grand jury and the county prosecutor.

Two months after the first issue of *The Saturday Press*, Floyd Olson, the prosecutor, was fed up, and he went to court and obtained an order to ban Near and Guilford from producing any more issues. Olson based his case on a 1925 Minnesota gag law that declared that "a malicious, scandalous and defamatory newspaper" could be banned as a public nuisance.

Despite their crusading for good causes, Near and Guilford's brand of journalism was hard to like. Both were bigots, who peppered their writing with references to "niggers," "yids," "bohunks" and "spades." From his hospital bed after he was shot, Guilford not only blamed gangster Mose Barnett, who was Jewish, but wrote a gratuitously racist account for *The Saturday Press* on what happened: "I headed into the city on September 26, ran across three Jews in a Chevrolet; stopped a lot of lead and won a bed for myself in St. Barnabas Hospital for six weeks. Wherefore, I have withdrawn all allegiance to anything with a hook nose that eats herring." Criticizing other newspapers as soft on crime, Near wrote: "I'd rather be a louse in the cotton shirt of a nigger than be a journalistic prostitute." Near and Guilford not only were anti-Semitic and antiblack but also anti-Catholic, anti–labor union and even anti–Salvation Army.

Could they get away with saying such things in print?

The Minnesota constitution seemed clear that they could: "The liberty of the press shall forever remain inviolate, and all persons may freely speak, write and publish their sentiments on all subjects." Although the Minnesota constitution was consistent with the First Amendment to the U.S. Constitution, which protected the communication of almost any idea, no matter how obnoxious,

and made it through a naval barricade, but photographers and television crews, their equipment giving away their identity as journalists, were turned back.

Journalists objected strenuously to the Grenada news blackout. As a result, the Pentagon agreed to include a few "pool reporters" in future military actions. These reporters' stories then would be made available to other news organizations. The pool system was used in the 1989 invasion of Panama, but the military manipulated the arrangement. Reporters were confined to a windowless briefing room at a U.S. Army post and given history lessons on U.S.-Panama relations, not current infor-

The Saturday Press

Vol 1, No. 1   Minneapolis, Minn., Sept. 21, 1927   Price 5 Cents

CONTENTS

Following a Custom
Page 2

A Friendly Tip
Page 4

Home Town Gambling
Page 11

Tom and Jake
Page 8

Gil's Chatterbox
Page 9

CHAFF!
Page 13

Just Kidding
Page 3

Two Toms Beat One Tom's Tom-Tom
Page 6

Jay Near

1927 Scandal Sheet. Page One of Jay Near and Howard Guilford's inaugural issue looked bland enough, but inside were stories that infuriated officials. The officials eventually declared *The Saturday Press* a public nuisance and shut it down to head off further incriminating coverage of local corruption. In the landmark court case that resulted, *Near* v. *Minnesota*, the U.S. Supreme Court ruled that such "prior restraint" was unconstitutional.

state judges were more moved by the argument of the local prosecutor that *The Saturday Press,* like a noxious weed, should be eradicated for the public good.

Guilford gave up the court fight after a few months, but not Near. Reviving the paper obsessed him. In a roundabout way, the wealthy publisher of the Chicago *Tribune,* Robert McCormick, learned of the case, put his own lawyers on it and vowed to bankroll the case to the U.S. Supreme Court. McCormick too was obsessed, not with reviving *The Saturday Press* but with proving the unconstitutionality of the 1925 Minnesota Public Nuisance Act under which the *Saturday Press* was silenced. McCormick saw the law as a dangerous model for politicians anywhere who, upset with news coverage, might enact public nuisance legislation to silence the offending newspapers.

The U.S. Supreme Court concurred in a landmark decision known as *Near* v. *Minnesota.* The court said that no government at any level has the right to suppress a publication because of what it might say in its next issue. Except in highly exceptional circumstances, such as life-and-death issues in war time, legal action against a publication can come only after something has been published.

After the ruling, Near resumed *The Saturday Press* and Guilford rejoined the enterprise. The paper floundered commercially, however, and Guilford quit. In 1934 Guilford announced for mayor and promised to campaign against the underworld. Before campaigning got started, gangsters crowded Guilford's car to the curb and fired a shotgun into his head.

Two years later, Near, age 62, died of natural causes. The local obituary didn't even mention *Near* v. *Minnesota* despite its being one of the most important court decisions in American media history.

mation on what was happening. Overall, the pool arrangement was to the liking of the military, not the media.

Most journalists were skeptical of the military's argument that it needed to control reporters to keep information on its activities from the enemy. Journalists said the true motive was to prevent honest and truthful reporting that might undermine public support at home for the military intervention. This skepticism proved well-founded in 1991 when the Pentagon went to extraordinary lengths to shape field reporting from the Persian Gulf war. These were the main Pentagon

War Coverage. Whatever the political system, the rules of government–media relations can be lost in combat. Reporters covering the Persian Gulf war found strict rules imposed on their movements by the military. In the Croatian war in 1991, reporters had other problems. In one situation, reporters fled into a cornfield when they found their car being fired on, and then a Croatian soldier moved in and used the car for cover. This was all despite the large and universally recognized "TV" taped on the windshield.

tactics, none involving explicit censorship but being nonetheless effective in shaping news coverage:

- The military arranged reporter pools for some coverage, which facilitated showing reporters what the military wanted seen.
- The military placed vast areas off limits to reporters with a variety of explanations, including sensitivity to the policies of "host nations" such as Saudi Arabia.
- Pentagon public relations people overwhelmed reporters with carefully structured news briefings and news conferences with top brass, and provided so much data, including spectacular video, that reporters had scant time left for pursuing alternate perspectives.

"FIRE!" IN A CROWDED THEATER

Prior restraint may be justified in situations other than national security. Supreme Court Justice *Oliver Wendell Holmes* wrote for the court in a 1919 case: "The most stringent protection of free speech would not protect a man in falsely shouting 'fire' in a theater and causing panic." First Amendment scholars point out, however, that prosecution for such an abuse of free expression cannot be anticipated easily. When the government is tempted to restrain expression before an act, it carries a heavy burden to demonstrate that the expression would cause so severe an effect that it should be banned ahead of time. Justice Holmes called this the *clear and present danger test*.

It is a judgment call whether an anticipated negative effect warrants suppression, but the Court has rendered decisions that give some sense of when prior restraint is justified. In one case, the Supreme Court upheld the conviction of Philadelphia socialist *Charles Schenck*, who published 15,000 leaflets during World War I that described that war as a Wall Street scheme and encouraged young men to defy their draft orders. Although Schenck's case did not involve prior restraint, the Court's line of reasoning included a guideline on when restraint may be permissible. The Court declined to say that Schenck's leaflets constituted a clear and present danger, but it ruled that they were unacceptable in a time of war. This was called the *bad tendency test*, which could be applied in times of domestic unrest and riot.

The bad tendency and the clear and present danger tests are closely related, but there is a distinction. It is harder for the government to make a convincing case that an article or utterance represents a clear and present danger than it is to argue

KEY PERSON
Oliver Wendell Holmes.

KEY PERSON
Charles Schenck.

Press Law in Britain

When a professional soccer player in Aberdeen, Scotland, was charged with indecent exposure, the Scottish *Daily Record* ran his picture the next morning. Under British law, it was a mistake. The British mass media are prohibited from publishing anything that might prejudice a criminal defendant's right to trial by an impartial jury. For running the picture, the court held the *Record* in contempt of court and said somebody should go to jail, but because the supervising editor was at home sick when the decision was made, there was only a $21,000 fine against the paper and a $1,400 fine against the assistant editor.

Such government action against the mass media would be unthinkable in the United States, but it demonstrates how another country, with many of the

same traditions, has developed a vastly different approach to media law. Consider the following aspects of British restrictions on news reporting:

- Crimes may be reported, but the names of suspected persons, even when they have been charged, may be used only if the police request or authorize the use of the name.
- If the government learns that a story defaming the royal family is in the works, it may enjoin the publication or broadcast organization from going ahead.
- The government may seek an injunction to stop stories it suspects will damage national security—even before they are published or aired.

that there is merely a bad tendency. Over the years since the Schenck case, the courts generally have insisted that the government be held to the stiffer clear and present danger test, and the bad tendency rationale is hardly ever considered in prior-restraint cases any more. The tougher standard was evident, for example, in the Supreme Court's 1989 decision that burning the American flag was a permissible form of expression. Today, the right to speak is almost absolute.

SLANDER AND MASS MEDIA

STUDY PREVIEW   When the mass media carry disparaging descriptions and comments, they risk being sued for libel. The media have a strong defense if the libel was accurate. If not, there can be big trouble. Libel is a serious matter. Not only are reputations at stake when defamation occurs, but also losing a suit can be so costly that it can put a publication or broadcast organization out of business.

CONCEPT OF LIBEL LAW

TEACHING OBJECTIVE 18-3
Anyone falsely slandered may sue for libel.

LECTURE RESOURCE 18-D
Video: *Anatomy of a Libel Case: Business Versus the Media.*

LECTURE RESOURCE 18-E
Class Exercise: Students assess articles that put people in negative light

If someone punches you in the face for no good reason, knocking out several teeth, breaking your nose and causing permanent disfigurement, most courts would rule that your attacker should pay your medical bills. If your disfigurement or psychological upset causes you to lose your job, to be ridiculed or shunned by friends and family, or perhaps to retreat from social interaction, the court probably would order your attacker to pay additional amounts. Like fists, words can also cause damage. If someone says or writes false, damaging things about you, you can sue for *libel*. Freedom of speech and the press is not a license to say absolutely anything about anybody.

If a libeling statement is false, the utterer may be liable for millions of dollars in damages. This is serious for the mass media. When the *Saturday Evening Post* reported that Alabama football coach Bear Bryant and Georgia athletic director Wally Butts fixed a game, Butts sued. The magazine lost the case, and it was ordered to pay $6 million in damages. Although the amount was eventually reduced, the judgment contributed to the demise of the magazine. When a former Miss Wyoming felt embarrassed by a fictitious article in *Penthouse* magazine, she was awarded $26.5 million even though she was not even named in the article. The verdict was set aside on appeal, but there was concern for a time about the magazine's well-being. A $9.2 million judgment against the Alton, Illinois, *Telegraph* forced the newspaper to file for bankruptcy protection.

SULLIVAN CASE

Elected officials have a hard time winning libel suits today. Noting that democracy is best served by robust, unbridled discussion of public issues and that public officials are inseparable from public policy, the U.S. Supreme Court has ruled that public figures can win libel suits only in extreme circumstances. The Court also has said that people who foist themselves into the limelight forfeit some of the protection available to other citizens. The key court decision in developing current U.S. libel standards originated in an advertisement carried by the New York *Times* in 1960.

A civil rights coalition, the Committee to Defend Martin Luther King and the Struggle for Freedom in the South, escalated its antisegregationist cause by placing a full-page advertisement in the *Times*. The advertisement accused public officials in the south of violence and illegal tactics against the civil rights struggle. While the advertisement was by and large truthful, it was marred by minor factual errors. Police Commissioner *L. B. Sullivan* of Montgomery, Alabama, filed a libel action saying that the errors damaged him, and he won $500,000 in an Alabama trial. On appeal to the U.S. Supreme Court, the case, *New York Times* v. *Sullivan*, became a landmark in libel law. The Supreme Court said that the importance of "free debate" in a democratic society generally was more important than factual errors that might upset and damage public officials. To win a libel suit, the Court said, public officials needed to prove that damaging statements were uttered or printed with the knowledge that they were false. The question in the Sullivan case became whether the *Times* was guilty of "reckless disregard of the truth." The Supreme Court said it was not, and the newspaper won.

KEY PERSON
L. B. Sullivan.

Questions lingered after the Sullivan decision about exactly who was and who was not a *public official*. The courts struggled for definition, and the Supreme Court eventually changed the term to *public figure*. In later years, as the Court refined its view on issues raised in the Sullivan case through several decisions, it remained consistent in giving the mass media a lot of room for error, even damaging error, in discussing government officials, political candidates and publicity hounds.

GOVERNMENT OFFICIALS. All elected government officials and appointed officials with high-level policy responsibilities are "public figures" as far as their performance in office is concerned. A member of a state governor's cabinet fits this category. A cafeteria worker in the state capitol does not.

POLITICAL CANDIDATES. Anyone seeking public office is subject to intense public review, during which the courts are willing to excuse false statements as part of robust, wide open discussion.

PUBLICITY HOUNDS. Court decisions have gone both ways, but generally people who seek publicity or intentionally draw attention to themselves must prove "reckless disregard of the truth" if they sue for libel.

How far can the media go in making disparaging comments? It was all right, said a Vermont court, when the Barre, Vermont, *Times Argus* ran an editorial that said a political candidate was "a horse's ass, a jerk, an idiot and a paranoid." The court said open discussion on public issues excused even such insulting, abusive and unpleasant verbiage. Courts have generally been more tolerant of excessive language in opinion pieces, such as the Barre editorial, than in fact-based articles.

FAIR COMMENT AND CRITICISM

People flocked to see the Cherry Sisters' act. Effie, Addie, Jessie, Lizzie and Ella toured the country with a song and dance act that drew big crowds. They were just awful. They could neither sing nor dance, but people turned out because the sisters were so funny. Sad to say, the Cherry Sisters took themselves seriously. In 1901, desperate for respect, they decided to sue the next newspaper reviewer who gave them a bad notice. The reviewer, it turned out, was Billy Hamilton, who included a

KEY PEOPLE
Cherry Sisters.

Fair Comment and Criticism. Upset with what an Iowa reviewer said about their show, the Cherry Sisters sued. The important 1901 court decision that resulted said that journalists, critics and anybody else can say whatever they want about a public performance. The rationale was that someone who puts on a performance for public acceptance has to take a risk also of public rejection.

lot of equine metaphors in his piece for the Des Moines *Leader:* "Effie is an old jade of 50 summers, Jessie a frisky filly of 40, and Addie, the flower of the family, a capering monstrosity of 35. Their long skinny arms, equipped with talons at the extremities, swung mechanically, and anon waved frantically at the suffering audience. The mouths of their rancid features opened like caverns, and sounds like the wailings of damned souls issued therefrom. They pranced around the stage with a motion that suggested a cross between the *danse du ventre* and the fox trot—strange creatures with painted faces and hideous mien. Effie is spavined, Addie is stringhalt, and Jessie, the only one who showed her stockings, has legs with calves as classic in their outlines as the curves of a broom handle."

The outcome of the suit was another setback for the Cherrys. They lost in a case that established that actors or others who perform for the public must be willing to accept both positive and negative comments about their performance. This right of *fair comment and criticism*, however, does not make it open season on performers in aspects of their lives that do not relate to public performance. The *National Enquirer* could not defend itself when entertainer Carol Burnett sued for a story that described her as obnoxiously drunk at a restaurant. Not only was the description false (Carol Burnett abstains from alcohol), but Burnett was in no public or performing role at the restaurant. This distinction between an individual's public and private life also has been recognized in cases involving public officials and candidates.

PRIVACY LAW

STUDY PREVIEW   The idea that people have a right to limit intrusions on their privacy has been taking form in American law through much of this century. In general, permission is not required in news coverage, although the courts have been consistent in saying that there are limits on how far news reporters can go with their cameras and in writing about personal information.

INTRUDING ON SOLITUDE

The courts have recognized a person's right to solitude and punished overzealous news reporters who tap telephone lines, plant hidden microphones, use telephoto lenses, and break into homes and offices for stories. In general, reporters are free to pursue stories in public places and, when invited, in private places. Sometimes the courts have had to draw the line between public and private places. Here are some examples:

TEACHING OBJECTIVE 18-4
Privacy is emerging area of law.

LECTURE RESOURCE 18-F
Video: *Eye on the Media: Private Lives, Public Press.*

- **A hospital room.** *Dorothy Barber* entered a Kansas City hospital with a metabolic disorder. No matter how much she ate, she lost weight. One day, two newspaper reporters, one with a camera, paid Barber a visit for a story and took a picture without permission. United Press International published the photograph, showing Dorothy Barber in her hospital bed, and *Time* magazine ran the picture. The caption read: "The starving glutton." Barber sued *Time* and won. The court said that reporters have a right to pursue people in public places, but the right of privacy protects a person in bed for treatment and recuperation.

KEY PERSON
Dorothy Barber.

- **Inside a private business.** A Seattle television photographer wanted to tape a pharmacist charged with Medicaid fraud, but the man would not cooperate. The photographer then set himself on the sidewalk outside the pharmacy and filmed the pharmacist through a front window. The pharmacist sued, charging the television station with photographic eavesdropping, but the court dismissed the suit, ruling that the photographer recorded only what any passerby was free to see. The outcome would have been different had the photographer gone into the shop, a private place, and taped the same scene without permission.
- **Expectation of privacy.** Some intrusion cases have hinged on whether the person being reported upon had "a reasonable expectation of privacy." Someone lounging nude at a fenced-in backyard pool would have a strong case against a photographer who climbed a steep, seldom-scaled cliff with a telephoto lens for a picture. A similar case can be made against hidden cameras and microphones.

HARASSMENT

By being in a public place, a person surrenders most privacy protections, but this does not mean that journalists have a right to hound people mercilessly. *Ron Galella*, a free-lance celebrity photographer, learned this lesson, or should have, in two lawsuits filed by *Jacqueline Kennedy Onassis*. Galella stalked the former First Lady, darting and jumping and grunting at her to catch off-guard facial expressions that would make interesting photographs that he could sell to magazines and photo archives. Mrs. Onassis became Galella's specialty, but he also was building a photo file on the Kennedy children. Galella broke Mrs. Onassis's patience in 1973 when he frightened a horse ridden by young John Kennedy, and the horse bolted. John

KEY PEOPLE
Jacqueline Kennedy Onassis and Ron Galella.

Kennedy escaped serious injury, but Mrs. Onassis asked her Secret Service protection detail to intervene to prevent Galella from endangering her children. Not long thereafter, the guards and Galella got into a tussle. Galella filed a $1.3 million suit, claiming he had been roughed up and that the guards were interfering with his right to earn a livelihood. He also claimed that his First Amendment rights were being violated. Mrs. Onassis responded with a $1.5 million suit, asking for an injunction to halt Galella.

A federal judge acknowledged that Galella could photograph whomever he wanted in public places and write stories about them, but that the First Amendment could not justify incessant pursuits that "went far beyond the reasonable bounds of news gathering." The judge said that harassment was impermissible, and he ordered Galella to stay 300 feet from the Onassis and Kennedy homes and the schools of the Kennedy children, 225 feet from the children in public places, and 150 feet from Mrs. Onassis. Further, Galella was ordered to stop his surveillance of the family and to attempt no communication with them. Galella appealed, but the principle articulated in the lower court was upheld, although the restrictions were reduced to 30 feet from the children and 25 feet from Mrs. Onassis.

Nine years later, Mrs. Onassis returned to court to object to Galella's overzealous journalistic techniques. He was found in contempt of court for violating the 1973 order on 12 separate occasions. The Onassis-Galella issue was a further recognition that a *right to be left alone* exists among other constitutional rights, including the right of a free press.

Aggressive Photojournalism. Photographer Ron Galella made a living by shadowing former First Lady Jacqueline Kennedy Onassis and selling the pictures. Although not pleased, Mrs. Onassis tolerated the paparazzi photographer until he began scaring her and the Kennedy children in an effort to get fresh shots. She asked a judge for an order to keep Galella away, and it was granted.

JOURNALISM LAW

STUDY PREVIEW The Constitution gives journalists great liberty in covering trials, seeking access to information held by the government, and even in withholding confidential information from the government.

COURT COVERAGE

News media have great liberty under the First Amendment to cover events as they see fit. Such was the case with *Sam Sheppard*, the Cleveland osteopath you read about at the beginning of this chapter. He was convicted of murder in a media circus. Even when he was acquitted after 12 years in prison, it was too late for him. He was unable to reestablish his medical practice. He died, a ruined man, a few years later.

A free press does not come without cost, and some people, like Sheppard, end up paying dearly. It is from such cases, however, that we learn the implications of the First Amendment and how to sidestep some of the problems it creates. When the U.S. Supreme Court ordered a new trial for Sheppard in 1966, it declared that it is the responsibility of the courts to assure citizens a fair trial regardless of media irresponsibility. The justices were specific about what the judge presiding at Sheppard's trial could have done. Among options:

- Seat only jurors who had not formed prejudicial conclusions.
- Move the trial to another city not so contaminated by news coverage.
- Delay trial until publicity subsided.
- Put jurors under 24-hour supervision so they would not have access to newspapers and newscasts during the trial.
- Insist that reporters respect appropriate courtroom decorum.
- Order attorneys, litigants and witnesses not to talk with reporters.
- Issue gag orders against the media but only in "extraordinary circumstances."

In other cases, the U.S. Supreme Court has allowed actions against the media to preclude unfavorable, prejudicial coverage of hearings, but those involve unusual circumstances. In the main, the news media have First Amendment-guaranteed access to the courts and the freedom to cover court stories regardless of whether the courts are pleased with the coverage. The same applies to news coverage of government in general.

SUNSHINE LAWS

Implicit in any democracy is that public policy is developed in open sessions where the people can follow their elected and appointed leaders as they discuss issues. Every state has an *open meeting law* that specifically declares that legislative units, including state boards and commissions, city councils, school boards and county governing bodies, be open to the public, including journalists. The idea is for public policy to be created and executed in the bright sunshine, not in the secrecy of back rooms.

Open meeting laws vary. Some insist that almost every session be open, while others are not nearly as strict with the state legislatures that created them as they are with city, county and school units and with state executive agencies. Some of these laws proclaim the virtues of openness but lack teeth to enforce openness. In

TEACHING OBJECTIVE 18-5
News media have great freedom to cover courts and government.

KEY PERSON
Sam Sheppard.

LECTURE RESOURCE 18-G
Speaker: Media lawyer.

contrast, some states specify heavy fines and jail terms for public officials who shut the doors. Here are provisions of strong open meeting laws:

- Legislative units are required to meet at regular times and places and to announce their agendas ahead of time.
- Citizens can insist on quick judicial review if a meeting is closed.
- Closed sessions are allowed for only a few reasons, which are specifically identified, such as discussion on sensitive personnel matters, collective bargaining strategy, and deciding security arrangements.
- Any vote in a closed session must be announced immediately afterward.
- Decisions made at a closed meeting are nullified if the meeting is later declared to have been closed illegally.
- Penalties are specified for any official who illegally authorizes a closed meeting.

Besides open meeting laws, the federal and state governments have *open record laws* to assure public access to government documents. These laws are important to journalists in tracking policy decisions and actions that they could not cover personally. Journalists especially value documents because, unlike human sources, they do not change their stories.

The federal *Freedom of Information Act* was passed in 1966, specifying how people could request documents. Since 1974 federal agencies have been required to list all their documents to help people identify what documents they are seeking and help the agencies locate them quickly. Despite penalties for noncompliance, some agencies sometimes drag their feet and stretch the FOI Act's provisions in order to keep sensitive documents off-limits. Even so, the law was a landmark of legislative commitment to governmental openness that allowed only a few exceptions. Among those exceptions are:

- Documents classified to protect national security.
- Trade secrets and internal corporate information obtained on a confidential basis by the government.
- Preliminary drafts of agency documents and working papers.
- Medical and personnel files for which confidentiality is necessary to protect individual privacy.
- Police files which, if disclosed, might jeopardize an investigation by tipping off guilty people or, worse, falsely incriminating innocent people.

CONFIDENTIAL SOURCES

One unresolved conflict between government and the news media involves confidential sources. There are important stories, although not many, that would never be written if reporters were required to divulge their sources. In 1969, at a time of racial unrest in the United States, *Earl Caldwell* of the New York *Times* spent 14 months cultivating sources within the Black Panthers organization and produced a series of insightful stories on black activism. A federal grand jury in San Francisco, where Caldwell was assigned, was investigating bombings and other violence blamed on the Black Panthers, and Caldwell's stories caught the jury's attention, especially quotations attributed to unnamed Black Panther leaders, such as "We advocate the direct overthrow of the government by ways of force and violence."

Defying a Subpoena. New York *Times* reporter Earl Caldwell faced jail for defying court orders to reveal the sources of his 1970 articles about urban terrorism. Caldwell argued that he had obtained his information on a confidential basis and that he would not break the covenant he had made with his sources. Others argued that journalists, like all citizens, have an obligation to tell all they know to officials who are investigating criminal activity.

The grand jury asked to see Caldwell's notebooks, tapes and anything else that could help its investigation. Caldwell defied the subpoena, saying his appearance before the grand jury would interfere with his relationship with his sources. Furthermore, he had promised these sources that he would not identify them. Journalists watching the showdown were mindful of the historical responsibility of the press as an independent watchdog on government. If Caldwell testified, he in effect would become part of the investigative arm of the government. Tension mounted when a federal judge supported the grand jury, noting that all citizens are required to cooperate with criminal investigations and that journalists are no different.

A federal appeals judge ruled, however, that "the public's First Amendment right to be informed would be jeopardized by requiring a journalist to submit to secret grand jury interrogation." The government, said the judge, could command a journalist to testify only if it demonstrated "a compelling need." Meanwhile, journalists were running the risk of going to jail for contempt of court for refusing to respond to government subpoenas for their testimony, notes and films. In 1972 the U.S. Supreme Court considered the issue and ruled that journalists "are not exempt from the normal duty of all citizens."

After that Supreme Court decision, several states adopted *shield laws*, which reorganized reporter-source confidentiality. A problem with shield laws is that they require government to define who is a journalist. This raises the specter of the government's deciding who is and who is not a journalist, which smacks of authoritarian press control. The Ohio shield law protects "bona fide journalists," who are defined as people employed by or connected to newspapers, radio stations, television stations and news services. Not only is it disturbing when government defines who is a journalist in a free society, but such attempts are destined to fail. The Ohio definition, for example, fails to protect free-lance journalists and writers who do their work on their own in the hope that they might eventually sell it.

ADVERTISING LAW

STUDY PREVIEW The government prohibits false, deceptive advertising but allows puffery. What's the difference? When there is a dispute whether an advertisement goes too far, the Federal Trade Commission or the courts decide. There also are limits against using people unwillingly to promote products.

GOVERNMENT REGULATION

TEACHING OBJECTIVE 18-6
Deceptive advertising is forbidden, but not puffery.

The federal government began regulating advertisements in 1914 when Congress created the Federal Trade Commission. The commission was charged with protecting honest companies that were being disadvantaged by competitors that made false claims. Today, nine federal agencies besides the FTC are involved heavily in regulating advertising. These include the Food and Drug Administration, the Postal Service, the Federal Communications Commission and the Securities and Exchange Commission. In addition, most states have laws against advertising fraud.

In its early days, the Federal Trade Commission went about its work meekly, but fueled by the consumer movement in the 1960s it became aggressive. Although the agency never had the authority to review advertisements ahead of their publication or airing, the FTC let it be known that it would crack down on violations of *truth-in-packaging* and *truth-in-lending* requirements. The FTC also began insisting on clarity so that even someone with low intelligence would not be confused. The FTC took particular aim at the overused word "free." To be advertised as "free," an offer had to be without conditions. The FTC moved further to protect the gullible. It was unacceptable, said the FTC, to leave the impression that actors in white coats speaking authoritatively about over-the-counter drugs and toothpastes were physicians or dentists. When Ocean Spray claimed that its cranberry juice offered "food energy," the FTC insisted that the language be changed to "calories." The FTC clamped down on a claim that Profile bread helped people lose weight, noting that the only difference from regular bread was thinner slices. The FTC pressed the Kroger grocery chain on its claim that it carried 150 everyday items cheaper than the competition, found that the claim was misleading and told Kroger to drop it.

Even with its crackdown, the FTC never ventured into regulating taste. Advertisements in poor taste were allowed, as long as they were not deceptive or unfair. *Puffery* was allowed, as long as there was no misstatement of fact. In borderline cases about what constituted puffery, an advertiser could always appeal to the courts.

The FTC became less aggressive in regulating advertising during the Reagan and Bush administrations, which deemphasized government regulation. Consumer activists, however, continue to complain to the FTC and other federal and state agencies and to bring pressure on the media not to run certain advertisements. Most of the concerns today are to protect impressionable children.

COMMERCIAL EXPLOITATION

The bosses at the Franklin Mills flour company were attracted right away to the pretty, demure girl in a picture that had come their way, and they wanted her as a mascot. They printed 25,000 lithographs, putting the words "Flour of the Family" above the child's head. They printed the company name underneath. Soon the smiling picture of *Abigail Roberson* of Rochester, New York, was all over town. The picture was a favorable likeness, and the Franklin flour people, presuming that young Abigail and her family would be flattered, did not think to ask permission. Little did they expect to be sued.

In court, Abigail Roberson's parents said that their daughter had been scoffed at and jeered at because of the posters. She retreated to bed with "nervous shock" and was put under a physician's care. Her parents demanded that the flour company take down the posters, and they asked for $15,000 for the "young, innocent girl of breeding with whose tender sensibilities gross liberties were taken." At issue in this pioneer 1902 case was a new legal concept: *expropriation.* The court decided against the Robersons, but their case attracted wide sympathy, and in 1903 the New York Legislature responded with the nation's first law to bar anyone from expropriating someone else's likeness, even a person's name, for commercial purposes without permission.

Today, the expropriation concept is widely recognized in law. In general, photographers may take whatever pictures they want in public places for news purposes, though not for commercial purposes.

RIGHT OF PUBLICITY

Over the years, the courts have come to recognize that individuals should be able to control publicity about themselves for commercial purposes. This legal concept, called the *right of publicity*, was strengthened by television comedian Johnny Carson, who objected when a Michigan portable toilet manufacturer called itself "Here's Johnny" and promoted its product as "the world's foremost commodian."

KEY PERSON
Abigail Roberson.

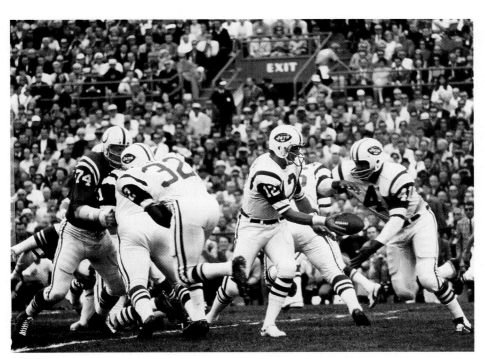

Joe Namath's Newsworthiness. The 1969 Super Bowl led to a new fine-line distinction in expropriation law. *Sports Illustrated* used a news photo from the game to solicit subscriptions, and player Joe Namath objected that the magazine was exploiting his likeness without permission. Generally, the courts have found against unauthorized use of someone's likeness for commercial purposes, but this time the court said that "incidental use" of once-newsworthy photos was all right. Namath lost.

Carson argued that Ed McMahon's "Here's Johnny" line introducing him on the "Tonight Show" was a signature item that the toilet people had expropriated without permission. He won.

The concept of the right of publicity is being expanded to protect celebrities from having their most identifiable traits exploited commercially by impersonators. In 1988 singer Bette Midler sued Ford Motor Company for hiring a former backup singer from Midler's band to sing her popular 1960s hit "Do You Want to Dance?" for a Mercury commercial. The backup singer was told to "sound as much as possible like the Bette Midler record." The court ruled that impersonating Midler's voice was "to pirate her identity."

BROADCAST REGULATION

STUDY PREVIEW   Complex regulations govern American broadcasting today. These regulations govern station engineering and ownership. The Federal Communications Commission also regulates content in a limited way.

TRUSTEESHIP RATIONALE

After World War I, commercial radio stations with powerful signals boomed their way onto the airwaves. There were not enough frequencies, and the airwaves became a deafening cacophony. A station finding itself drowned out might boost power to keep listeners, thereby able to drown out weaker signals in a kind of king-of-the-mountain competition. An alternative was jumping to a less cluttered frequency and asking listeners to follow. It was chaos.

Failing to solve the problem among themselves, radio station owners finally called on the federal government for a solution. In 1927 Congress borrowed language from 19th-century railroad regulatory legislation and established the *Federal Radio Commission*. The commission was given broad licensing authority. The authorizing legislation, the *Federal Radio Act*, said licenses would be for limited terms. The FRC could specify frequency, power and hours of operation.

The new commission's immediate problem was that it inherited 732 stations that had been licensed by the Commerce and Labor Department, but the technology of the time allowed room for only 568. In the end, the commission allowed 649 to remain on the air with strict limits on transmission to prevent signal overlaps. Even so, some stations were silenced, solid evidence that government was in the business of broadcast regulation.

As might be expected in a nation of libertarian traditions, there was uneasiness about licensing a medium that not only purveyed information and ideas but that also was a forum for artistic creativity. What about the First Amendment? As a practical matter, the broadcast spectrum had a real and absolute capacity. Someone had to be the arbiter of the airwaves, or a scarce resource would be rendered unusable. The *trusteeship concept* developed. It held that the airwaves are public property and should be subject to regulation for the public good, just as are public roads. The test of who should be granted licenses, and who denied, would be service to the "*public interest, convenience and necessity*," a phrase from the 1927 Federal Radio Act that remains a cornerstone of American broadcasting.

With the Federal Communications Act of 1934, Congress replaced the FRC with the Federal Communications Commission. Television, under development at the time, was incorporated into the FCC's charge. Otherwise, the FCC largely continued the FRC's regulatory responsibility.

MEDIA: PEOPLE

John Brinkley

John Brinkley and his bride arrived in Milford, Kansas, population 200, in 1917 and rented the old drug store for $8 a month. Mrs. Brinkley sold patent medicines out front, while Brinkley talked to patients in a back room. One day an elderly gentleman called on "Dr. Brinkley" to do something about his failing manhood. As the story goes, the conversation turned to Brinkley's experience with goats in the medical office of the Swift meatpacking company, a job he had held for barely three weeks. Said Brinkley, "You wouldn't have any trouble if you had a pair of those buck glands in you." The operation was performed in the back room, and word spread. Soon the *goat gland surgeon* was charging $750 for the service, then $1,000, then $1,500. In 1918 Brinkley, whose only credentials were two mail-order medical degrees, opened the Brinkley Hospital. Five years later he set up a radio station, KFKB, to spread the word about his cures.

Six nights a week, Brinkley extolled the virtues of his hospital over the air. "Don't let your doctor two-dollar you to death," he said. "Come to Dr. Brinkley." If a trip to Milford was not possible, listeners were encouraged to send for Brinkley compounds. Soon the mail-order demand was so great that Brinkley reported he was buying goats from Arkansas by the boxcar.

"Dr. Brinkley" became a household word. *Radio Digest* awarded Brinkley's KFKB (for Kansas First, Kansas Best) its Golden Microphone Award as the most popular radio station in the country. The station had received 356,827 votes in the magazine's write-in poll. Brinkley was a 1930 write-in candidate for governor. Harry Woodring won with 217,171 votes to Brinkley's 183,278, but Brinkley would have won it had it not been for misspellings that disqualified thousands of write-in ballots.

Also in 1930 the KFKB broadcast license came up for renewal by the Federal Radio Commission, which had been set up to regulate broadcasting.

The American Medical Association wanted the license to be revoked. The medical profession had been outraged by Brinkley but had not found a way to derail his thriving quackery. In fact, Brinkley played to the hearts of thousands of Middle America's listeners when he attacked the AMA as "the meat-cutter's union." At the license hearing, Brinkley argued that the First Amendment guaranteed him freedom to speak his views on medicine, goat glands and anything else he wanted. He noted that Congress had specifically forbidden the FRC to censor. It would be a censorious affront to the First Amendment, he said, to take away KFKB's license for what the station put on the air. Despite Brinkley's arguments, the FRC denied renewal.

Brinkley challenged the denial in federal court, and the case became a landmark on the relationship between the First Amendment and American broadcasting. The appeals court sided with the FRC, declaring that broadcast licenses should be awarded for serving "the public interest, convenience and necessity." It was appropriate, said the court, for the commission to review a station's programming to decide on renewal. Brinkley appealed to the U.S. Supreme Court, which declined to hear the case. The goat gland surgeon was off the air, but not for long. In 1932 Dr. Brinkley, proving himself unsinkable, bought a powerful station in Villa Acuna, Mexico, just across the Rio Grande from Del Rio, Texas, to continue peddling his potions. By telephone linkup from his home in Milford, Brinkley continued to reach much of the United States until 1942, when the Mexican government nationalized foreign-owned property.

Goat Gland Surgeon. Eager for publicity, John Brinkley obliges a photographer by placing a healing hand on a supposedly insane patient he is about to cure. Broadcasting such claims from his Kansas radio station, Brinkley developed a wide market for his potions. Because of his quackery, he lost the station in a significant First Amendment case.

ENGINEERING REGULATIONS.   Over the years, the FCC has used its regulatory authority to find room in the radio spectrum for more and more stations. Almost 5,000 AM stations are broadcasting today, compared to 649 when the FRC was set up, and there are more than 5,000 FM stations.

By limiting the power of station signals, the FCC squeezes many stations onto a single frequency. For example, WBAL in Baltimore, Maryland, and KAAY in Little Rock, Arkansas, both broadcast at 1090 on the dial, but restrictions on their signal strengths prevent overlapping. Dozens of stations, scattered around the nation, are sandwiched at some frequencies. At night, when the atmosphere extends the range of AM transmissions, many stations are required to reduce their power; go off the air; or transmit directionally, like north-south, to avoid overlap. The FCC, with its licensing authority, insists that stations comply strictly with engineering restrictions to avoid the pre-1927 chaos.

OWNERSHIP REGULATIONS.   The FCC regulates station ownership. To encourage diverse programming, the FCC limits how many stations a single individual or company may own. Whether diverse ownership creates diverse programming is debatable, but the FCC has prevented local broadcast monopolies.

The FCC insists that licensees be of good character, follow sound business practices, and operate within the letter and spirit of the law and FCC regulations. No nonsense is tolerated. Consider these cases, all of which sent strong signals to station owners:

- Being in bad corporate company can jeopardize a station's license. In 1980 the commission yanked RKO's licenses for WOR, New York; WNAC, Boston; and KHJ, Los Angeles. The FCC was upset with shady deals by RKO's parent corporation, General Tire & Rubber, even though the stations were not involved in any misconduct.
- Concealing information from the FCC is hazardous. WOKO in Albany, New York, secretly gave away stock in the company to win a CBS network affiliation. To conceal the bribe, the station doctored its required periodic reports to the FCC. Twelve years after the bribery, in 1946, the commission discovered the irregularities and took away the license.
- The FCC insists on appropriate hiring practices. WLBT-TV in Jackson, Mississippi, made no attempt to bring blacks onto its staff even though Jackson was largely a black community. Also, the station carried virtually no black-oriented programming. The FCC hesitated to refuse license renewal in this case, but the license was revoked in 1969 by a court order.

CONTENT REGULATIONS.   The 1934 Federal Communications Act specifically forbids censorship, and the government has never had anyone sitting at any radio stations to keep things off the air. Yet the FCC has a powerful influence over what is aired because broadcasters are accountable for what they have aired when license renewal time comes up. Radio licenses are granted for seven years, television for five.

The government has provided clues aplenty to broadcasters on what it, as trustee for the public, does not want on the air. Although FCC policy today has shifted somewhat, many broadcasters, not wanting to risk their licenses, still regard the lessons from these cases as indelible:

- **Unanswered personal attacks.** In 1962 a station in Pennsylvania aired an attack by a right wing Oklahoma evangelist on author Fred Cook. Cook was called a liar, and it was implied that he championed communist causes. Cook asked for time to respond, but the station refused. The FCC sided with Cook, and eventually so did the U.S. Supreme Court in a decision called *Red Lion* after the name of the company that owned the station.
- **Realistic, alarming spoofs.** The FCC fined a St. Louis station, KSHE, $25,000 in 1991 after disc jockey John Ulett broadcast a mock nuclear attack on the United States. The FCC was not amused. The case harkened back to 1938 when CBS aired a drama on a Martian invasion in New Jersey, which many listeners feared was really happening. The suffering that CBS endured in the aftermath, including a variety of congressional threats, served to warn broadcasters, except apparently John Ulett, to be careful with scary spoofs.
- **Exclusive forum for licensee.** A Methodist preacher used his church-owned station, KGEF in Los Angeles, as an extension of the pulpit to attack Catholics, Jews, lawyers, judges, labor unions and other groups. The FRC denied renewal in 1930. On appeal, the courts said a licensee has no unlimited right to spread hatred.
- **Dirty words.** WBAI-FM in New York, a noncommercial station, included a George Carlin comedy cut in a 1975 program examining social attitudes toward language. The Carlin monologue included "dirty words," which the FCC ruled indecent at times of day when children might be listening. The U.S. Supreme Court agreed.
- **Off-color jokes.** WDKD in Kingstree, South Carolina, lost its license in 1962 because of legendary country-western disc jockey Charley Walker's bucolic humor, which the FCC called "coarse, vulgar and susceptible to indecent double meaning." In 1989 WLLZ-FM in Detroit was fined $2,000 for playing the Singing Erudites' "Walk with an Erection," a parody of the Bangles' pop hit "Walk Like an Egyptian."

While stations are subject to discipline, the FCC provides only general guidance on what it does want aired. It encourages local origination over network programming, and it also encourages public affairs and community-oriented programming, but the FCC assiduously avoids dictating what goes on the air, even when under pressure to do so. Pressure shows up inevitably when a classical music station switches to another format. To classical music lovers who ask the FCC to intervene, the commission has said again and again that it considers formats a function of the marketplace. If a station cannot find enough listeners with one format to attract advertisers, then it should be free to try another.

REGULATING NETWORKS

The networks deliver programming to local stations, and local stations pass network programming on to listeners. Because networks do not themselves broadcast on the public airwaves, they have never been subject to FCC licensing as stations are. Even so, the government can put a lot of pressure on the networks. Consider:

AFFILIATE PRESSURE. As licensed entities, affiliate stations are answerable to the FCC, which means that network programming must conform to FCC standards. The networks have entire departments to review programs to ensure that they comply with acceptable guidelines.

ANTITRUST.   The size of the major networks leaves them vulnerable to antitrust action. It was after the FCC's rumblings that NBC was too powerful that the network sold one branch to candy manufacturer Edward Nobel in 1943 rather than risk an FCC recommendation to the Justice Department to dismantle the company.

NETWORKS AS LICENSEES.   The networks themselves own radio and television stations, which are subject to licensing. The stations, all in major cities, are significant profit sources for the networks, which do not want to risk losing the FCC licenses to operate them.

BROADCAST DEREGULATION

In the spirit of the presidential administration of *Ronald Reagan*'s hands-off policy toward business, the FCC relaxed controls on broadcasting in the 1980s. The period between license renewals was extended from three years to five years for television and to seven years for radio. In 1981 the FCC dropped its renewal requirement that stations conduct *ascertainment studies* of community needs to help develop community-oriented programming. The studies, which broadcasters considered onerous, had required demographic profiles of service station areas, interviews with as many as 220 community leaders, and a general public survey. In dropping the ascertainment requirement, the FCC said it would be satisfied to let the marketplace decide whether a station was in tune with its community. It was a laissez-faire concept: Good stations will attract listeners and advertisers and survive, and bad ones will not.

For all practical purposes, the *fairness doctrine*, which required broadcasters to air all sides of controversial public issues, was also dropped. *Mark Fowler*, the FCC chairman who championed deregulation in the 1980s, regarded the doctrine as censorship—a dramatic departure from the long-standing commission position, upheld in the courts, that regulation was consistent with the First Amendment. The FCC under Fowler felt that a government agency should not tell broadcasters how to use airtime, just as newspapers are not told how to fill their pages. Even so, one element of the fairness doctrine remained in place: Stations still were required to broadcast a response from anyone who was attacked personally on the air.

Dropping the fairness doctrine, although welcomed by broadcasters, was controversial. A strong movement developed in Congress to restore the fairness doctrine by making it law. The doctrine had been an FCC-created regulation, not a law, and Congress had the authority to impose it on the FCC. In that spirit, Congress was unwilling to consider revoking the *equal time law*, which requires stations to give equal advertising opportunities at low rates to political candidates. Mark Fowler opposed the equal time law on the same grounds he opposed the fairness doctrine, but equal time was in the law, Section 315 of the Federal Communications Act of 1934, and could not be dropped by the FCC without congressional approval.

Also eliminated in the deregulation movement of the 1980s were requirements that:

- Station owners keep their stations at least three years.
- News and public affairs constitute 8 percent of AM and 6 percent of FM programming.
- Commercials be limited to 18 minutes per hour.
- Minute-by-minute program logs be kept.

CRITICISM OF DEREGULATION

With fewer regulations, broadcasters have trimmed costs and improved profits. There are concerns, however, that deregulation might be working against "the public interest, convenience and necessity." Many stations, for example, cut down public affairs programs and reduced high-cost news staffs.

Another negative effect of deregulation involved the elimination of the FCC's *antitrafficking provision*. The provision had required license holders to hold stations for three years. Without it, stations became hot takeover items on Wall Street, and corporations with no broadcast experience scrambled to buy stations for short-term profits or to resell to the next highest bidder. The trade journal *Broadcasting* quoted a Washington broadcast lawyer: "Broadcast properties have become like pork bellies, without much concern as to whether the viewers are getting a better grade of service." Congressman John Dingell, who favored the public trusteeship concept rather than Fowler's marketplace concept, was worried: "In this climate, takeover pressures and other financial concerns are leading broadcasters with a history of public service to re-examine their commitment to public interest programming."

OBSCENITY AND PORNOGRAPHY

STUDY PREVIEW Despite the First Amendment's guarantee of free expression, the U.S. government has tried numerous ways during this century to regulate obscenity and pornography.

IMPORT RESTRICTIONS

A 1930 tariff law was used as an import restriction to intercept James Joyce's *Ulysses* at the docks because of four-letter words and explicit sexual references. The importer, Random House, went to court, and the judge ruled that the government was out of line. The judge, *John Woolsey*, acknowledged "unusual frankness" in *Ulysses*, but said he could not "detect anywhere the leer of the sensualist." The judge, who was not without humor, made a strong case for freedom in literary expression: "The words which are criticized as dirty are old Saxon words known to almost all men, and, I venture, to many women, and are such words as would be naturally and habitually used, I believe, by the types of folks whose life, physical and mental, Joyce is seeking to describe. In respect to the recurrent emergence of the theme of sex in the minds of the characters, it must always be remembered that his locale was Celtic and his season Spring."

Woolsey was upheld on appeal, and *Ulysses*, still critically acclaimed as a pioneer in stream-of-consciousness writing, remains in print today.

POSTAL RESTRICTIONS

Postal restrictions were used against a 1928 English novel, *Lady Chatterly's Lover*, by *D. H. Lawrence*. The book was sold in the United States in expurgated editions for years, but in 1959, Grove Press issued the complete version. Postal officials denied mailing privileges. Grove sued and won.

In some respects, the Grove case was *Ulysses* all over again. Grove argued that Lawrence, a major author, had produced a work of literary merit. Grove said the explicit, rugged love scenes between Lady Chatterly and Mellors the gamekeeper

TEACHING OBJECTIVE 18-8
First Amendment protects pornography, not obscenity.

KEY PERSON
James Joyce.

KEY PERSON
John Woolsey.

KEY PERSON
D. H. Lawrence.

were essential in establishing their violent yet loving relationship, the heart of the story. The distinction between the *Ulysses* and *Lady Chatterly* cases was that one ruling was against the customs service and the other against the postmaster general.

PORNOGRAPHY VERSUS OBSCENITY

Since the *Ulysses* and *Lady Chatterly* cases, much more has happened to discourage federal censorship. The U.S. Supreme Court has ruled that pornography, material aimed at sexual arousal, cannot be stopped. Import and postal restrictions, however, still can be employed against obscene materials, which the court has defined as going beyond pornography. Obscenity restrictions apply, said the court, if the answer is yes to *all* of the following questions:

- Would a typical person applying local standards see the material as appealing mainly for its sexually arousing effect?
- Is the material devoid of serious literary, artistic, political or scientific value?
- Is sexual activity depicted offensively, in a way that violates state law that explicitly defines offensiveness?

CENSORSHIP TODAY

STUDY PREVIEW   Local governments have tried numerous ways to restrict distribution of sexually explicit material. Local libraries and schools also sometimes act to ban materials, but these attempts at censorship are not restricted to obscenity and pornography. Anything to which a majority of a local board objects can be fair game.

LOCAL CENSORSHIP

TEACHING OBJECTIVE 18-9
Censorship mostly local issue.

LECTURE RESOURCE 18-H
Video: *Censorship or Selection: Choosing Books for Public Schools.*

Municipalities and counties have tried heavy-handed restrictions against sexually explicit publications and video material, generally without lasting success. Outright bans fail if they are challenged in the courts, unless the material is legally obscene. The U.S. Supreme Court spoke on this issue after Mount Ephraim, New Jersey, revised zoning laws to ban all live entertainment from commercial areas. The Court said the rezoning was a blatant attempt to ban lawful activities, and the decision was widely interpreted to apply to porn shops and other businesses that are often targets of local censorship campaigns. A federal court applied the same reasoning when it threw out a Keego Harbor, Michigan, zoning ordinance that forbade an adult theater within 500 feet of a school, church or bar. In Keego Harbor, there was no site not within 500 feet of a school, church or bar.

Some local governments have been innovative in acting against sexually explicit materials. One successful approach has been through zoning laws to rid neighborhoods of porn shops by forcing them into so-called war zones. Owners of adult-oriented businesses generally have been pleased to go along. By complying, they face less heat from police and other official harassment. The courts have found that war zone ordinances are legitimate applications of the principle underlying zoning laws in general, which is to preserve and protect the character of neighborhoods. So just as local governments can create single-residence, apartment, retail and other zones, they also can create zones for adult bookstores and theaters.

An opposite zoning approach, to disperse these kinds of businesses instead of concentrating them, has also been upheld in court. In Detroit, an ordinance insists that a 1,000-foot space separate "problem businesses," which include porn shops, adults-only theaters, pool halls and cabarets. This is all right, say the courts, as long as it does not exclude such businesses entirely.

Unlike the publishers in the landmark *Ulysses* and *Lady Chatterly* cases, in recent years book publishers have not taken the initiative against local restrictions aimed at pornography distributors and porn shops. Litigation is expensive, and major publishing houses do not produce porn-shop merchandise. Magazine publishers, notably *Playboy* and *Penthouse*, have fought some battles, but the issue has become fragmented since the Supreme Court's insistence that local standards be a measure of acceptability. Because what is obscene to people in one town may not be to people in another, it is impossible for the producers of nationally distributed books and magazines to go after all the restrictive local actions.

LIBRARY AND SCHOOL BOARDS

Local libraries sometimes decide to keep certain books off the shelves, usually because of content that offends the sensitivities of a majority of the library board. This kind of censorship survives challenges only when legal obscenity is the issue, which is seldom. Also, the wide availability of banned books renders library bans merely symbolic.

Some school boards still attempt censorship, although there is little support in the courts unless the issue is legal obscenity, which is rare. Whatever latitude school boards once had was strictly limited in 1982 when the U.S. Supreme Court decided against the Island Trees, New York, school board after several members had gone into the high school library and removed 60 books. Among them were *The Fixer* by Bernard Malamud and *Laughing Boy* by Oliver Lafarge, both of which had won Pulitzer Prizes. School board members argued that the 60 books were anti-American, anti-Semitic, anti-Christian, and "just plain filthy." The Court did not accept that. School boards, said the Court, "may not remove books from library shelves simply because they dislike the ideas in those books and seek their removal to prescribe what shall be orthodox in politics, nationalism, religion or other matters of opinion."

MEESE PORNOGRAPHY COMMISSION

A presidential commission concluded in 1970 that pornography had hardly any ill effects and recommended the repeal of most obscenity laws. The commission's report did not sit well with President Richard Nixon, who denounced it. When Ronald Reagan became president, he told Attorney General Edwin Meese to appoint a new commission to reassess the effects of pornography, except this time the commission was set up to develop the kinds of conclusions that the White House could endorse.

The new commission was packed with prominent members of the antipornography movement. Notably absent were civil libertarians. The Meese commission staff ignored scientific research on pornographic effects. For testimony, the staff lined up antiporn witnesses with personal stories and anecdotes but no hard evidence that pornography causes crime and other antisocial behavior.

Smut Battler. Edwin Meese, former U.S. attorney general for President Reagan, was the namesake of a commission that examined pornography. The commission came up with the politically acceptable conclusion that pornography was a serious threat to society and that government should take a tough stance against it. The problem, however, was that the commission ignored scientific evidence on the issue, which is far from conclusive.

COPYRIGHT

STUDY PREVIEW   Mass media people are vulnerable to thievery. Because it is so easy for someone to copy someone else's creative work, copyright laws prohibit the unauthorized re-creation of intellectual property, including books, music, movies and other creative production.

HOW COPYRIGHT WORKS

TEACHING OBJECTIVE 18-10
Intellectual property has legal protection.

Congress has had a copyright law on the books since 1790. The law protects authors and other creators of intellectual property from having someone profit by reproducing their works without permission. Permission is usually granted for a fee.

Almost all books have copyright protection the moment they are created in a tangible form. So do most movies, television programs, newspaper and magazine articles, songs and records, and advertisements. It used to be that a creative work needed to be registered with the Library of Congress for a $10 fee. Formal registration is no longer required, but many people still do it for the fullest legal protection against someone pirating their work.

Protecting a Name. A company that develops a unique name for a product can register the name with the federal government as a trademark. This prevents competitors from using the name. Even so, popular use can erode the protection of a trademark, as Xerox points out in this advertisement aimed at news reporters. Xerox wants to prevent any photocopiers from being called *xeroxes*, with a lowercase *x*, and the process from being called *xeroxing*, also with a lowercase *x*.

The current copyright law protects a creative work for the lifetime of the author plus 50 years. After the 50 years, a work enters what is called the *public domain*, and anyone may reproduce it without permission.

The creator of an original work may sell the copyright, and many do. Authors, for example, typically give their copyright to a publisher in exchange for a percentage of income from the book's profits.

MUSIC LICENSING

Songwriters have a complex system to make money from their copyrighted works through music licensing organizations every time their music is played. These organizations collect fees from broadcast stations and other places that play recorded music, even restaurants and bowling alleys. The licensing organizations pass the fees on to their members. The largest licensing organizations are known in the trade by their abbreviations, the American Society of Composers, Authors and Performers, known as ASCAP, and Broadcast Music Inc., known in the field as BMI:

ASCAP.   For a commercial radio station to play ASCAP-licensed music, there is a charge of 2 percent of the station's gross receipts. ASCAP tapes six-hour segments from selected radio stations to determine whose music is being played. From the analysis, a complex formula is derived to divvy the license income among songwriters, music publishers and other members of ASCAP who own the music.

BMI.   The organization known as BMI, which licenses most country, western and soul music, checks radio station playlists every 12 to 14 months to create a formula for distributing license income.

CNN Video Piracy

The perennial U.S. movie industry problem of bootleg video copies may not be as insoluble as once thought. Detective Dick O'Neill went to South Korea and generated information that allowed the government to crack down. Now, says CNN's Jean Apostol, virtually no pirated tapes remain on store shelves in South Korea. Even so, the problem remains a major drain on movie industry profits in other countries. This report aired March 27, 1993.

CNN Music Pirates

Black-market music recordings have been a strain in relations between the United States and countries where pirate recordings are manufactured and sold openly. In Thailand, however, there has been a crackdown. In this February 24, 1993, report, CNN reporter Tom Mintier covers a major Bangkok raid. The video provides students with a good feel for how this illegal copying industry operates.

CHAPTER WRAP-UP

The American mass media enjoy great freedom under the First Amendment, which forbids the government from impinging on expression. Even so, the freedom has limits. When the First Amendment guarantee of a free press runs against the constitutional guarantee of a free trial, there is a conflict of values that must be resolved. This is also true when the mass media violate someone's right to be left alone, which, although not an explicit constitutional guarantee, has come to be recognized as a basic human right. An understanding of mass media law and regulation involves studying how the American judicial system, headed by the U.S. Supreme Court, has reconciled conflicting interests. In short, the First Amendment is not inviolate.

Major restrictions on the mass media involve prior restraint, censorship, commercial exploitation, invasion of privacy, libel, fair trials and obscenity. The courts have struggled to square these restrictions with the absolutist language of the First Amendment, finding a balance between the guarantee of free expression with other interests, such as national security, and other rights, such as personal privacy.

QUESTIONS FOR REVIEW

1. Why is the First Amendment important to mass media in the United States?

2. In what situations may the government exercise prior restraint to silence someone?

3. Who can sue the mass media for libel?

4. Do the mass media face limits on intruding on an individual's privacy?

5. Do the mass media face limits in covering government meetings or the courts? Or digging into government documents?

6. Are advertisements free of government regulation?

7. Discuss the trusteeship model as a justification for government regulation of broadcasting.

8. How is obscenity different from pornography?

9. How did a U.S. Supreme Court decision pretty much end federal concern about pornography?

10. How does copyright law protect intellectual property from being stolen from its owners?

QUESTIONS FOR CRITICAL THINKING

1. How can any restriction on free expression by the mass media or by individuals be consistent with the absolutist language of the First Amendment?

2. Define censorship. In a strict sense, who is a censor?

3. What lessons about prior restraint are contained in *Near v. Minnesota* (1931) and *New York Times Co. v. United States* (1971)?

4. Explain the significant change in the U.S. Supreme Court's thinking about the First Amendment and "commercial speech."

5. How could Judge Blythin, who presided at the 1954 murder trial of Cleveland osteopath Sam Sheppard, have headed off the news media orgy that led to an appeal to the U.S. Supreme Court and an acquittal?

6. How do authors and creators of other intellectual property copyright their works, and why do they do it?

7. What kinds of meetings by public agencies can be closed to the public and the news media under the terms of open meeting laws? Are the public and the press barred from seeking any government documents under the U.S. Freedom of Information Act and sunshine laws?

8. Discuss the role of book publishers in the struggle for free expression through the *Ulysses* and Grove Press cases. Why have book publishers moved out of the forefront of the free expression struggle on today's most pressing issue—municipal pornography bans?

9. What is the trend with local censorship by library boards and school boards?

FOR FURTHER LEARNING

Morris L. Ernst and Alan U. Schwartz. *Censorship: The Search for the Obscene* (Macmillan, 1964). Ernst and Schwartz put the complexities of censorship in highly readable form.

Fred W. Friendly. *Minnesota Rag: The Dramatic Story of the Landmark Supreme Court Case That Gave New Meaning to Freedom of the Press* (Random House, 1981). Friendly, a pioneer television journalist, colorfully traces the *Near* v. *Minnesota* prior-restraint case.

Michael Gartner. "Fair Comment," *American Heritage* 33 (October–November 1982):6, 28–31. Gartner, a newspaper and television executive, delights in digging up the details of the colorful Cherry Sisters case that decided that almost anything could be said by reviewers of public performances.

Richard T. Kaplar, ed. *Beyond the Courtroom: Alternatives for Resolving Press Disputes* (Media Institute, 1991). This collection of articles explores ways besides litigation to settle libel and other media legal problems.

Clark R. Mollenhoff. "25 Years of *Times* v. *Sullivan*," *Quill* 77 (March 1989):3, 27–31. A veteran investigative reporter argues that journalists have abused the landmark *Sullivan* decision and have been irresponsibly hard on public figures.

Philip Nobile and Eric Nadler. *United States of America vs. Sex: How the Meese Commission Lied About Pornography* (Minotaur, 1986). Nobile and Nadler, editors of the *Penthouse* magazine spinoff *Forum*, discredit the 1986 attorney general's report on pornography, which called for stricter laws against adult material. They argue that the commission ignored and distorted scientific evidence on the effects of pornography.

Vaughan Scully. "Shield Laws: Unequal Protection," *NewsInc.* 2 (April 1990):4, 23–24. Scully has compiled information on what kind of protection is provided for news sources and reporter notes in the 26 states that have shield laws.

Thomas L. Tedford. *Freedom of Speech in the United States* (Random House, 1985). Professor Tedford offers an easily understood history and an examination of perennial and current First Amendment issues.

Sanford J. Ungar. *The Papers & the Papers: An Account of the Legal and Political Battle Over the Pentagon Papers* (Dutton, 1975). Ungar, a news reporter, provides a comprehensive chronology of our era's major prior-restraint case.

Robert J. Wagman. *The First Amendment Book* (Pharos, 1991). This lively history of the First Amendment is endorsed by leading journalists as a primer on the subject.

John J. Watkins. *The Mass Media and the Law* (Prentice Hall, 1990). This is a comprehensive upper-division textbook for mass communication students.

FOR KEEPING UP TO DATE

Censorship News is published by the National Coalition Against Censorship.

Media Law Bulletin tracks developments in media law.

News Media and the Law is published by the Reporters' Committee for Freedom of the Press.

Media Law Reporter is an annual collection of major court cases.

Student Press Law Reports, from the Student Press Law Center, follows events in the high school and college press and broadcast media.

The *Wall Street Journal* has a daily law section that includes media cases.

NAME INDEX

Note: The letter "f" or "b" following a page number indicates that the name is cited in a figure or box, respectively.

SUBJECT INDEX

Note: The letter "f" or "b" following a page number indicates that the topic is cited in a figure or box, respectively.

PHOTO CREDITS

This page constitutes a continuation of the copyright page.